Connect™ Accounting

Instructors...

Q Want to **streamline** lesson planning, student progress reporting, and assignment grading? (Less time planning means more time teaching...)

Need to **collect data and generate reports** required by accreditation organizations, such as AACSB and AICPA? (Say goodbye to manually tracking student learning outcomes...)

Want an **instant view** of student or class performance relative to learning objectives? (No more wondering if students understand...)

A With **McGraw-Hill Connect™ Accounting,**

INSTRUCTORS GET

- The ability to **post assignments** and other communication between students and instructors.
- Simple **assignment management**, allowing you to spend more time teaching.
- **Auto-graded homework.**
- **Customized course gradebook** where grades are automatically posted.
- **Online testing capability**.
- A **progress-tracking** function that allows you to easily assign materials that conform to AACSB and AICPA standards.

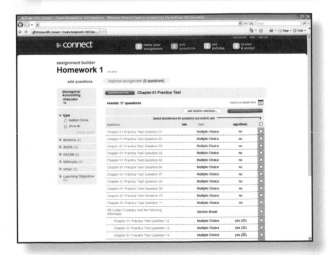

Q Want an online, **searchable version** of your textbook?

Wish your textbook could be available online while you're doing your homework?

A *Connect*™ **Plus Accounting eBook**

If your instructor has chosen to use *Connect*™ *Plus Accounting*, you have an affordable and searchable online version of your book integrated with your other online homework tools.

Connect™ **Plus Accounting eBook offers features like:**

- topic search
- adjustable text size
- jump to page number
- print by section

Q Want to get more **value** from your textbook purchase?

Think learning accounting should be a little bit more **interesting**?

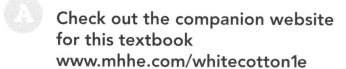

A **Check out the companion website for this textbook www.mhhe.com/whitecotton1e**

We put it there for you. Go online for test tips and practice problems whenever you study. The companion website for this book includes **quizzes, PowerPoints, and Internet activities** to help you study. Get more from your textbook—use the Online Learning Center.

Managerial
ACCOUNTING

www.mhhe.com/whitecotton1e

STACEY WHITECOTTON
Arizona State University

ROBERT LIBBY
Cornell University

FRED PHILLIPS
University of Saskatchewan

McGraw-Hill
Irwin

MANAGERIAL ACCOUNTING

Published by McGraw-Hill/Irwin, a business unit of The McGraw-Hill Companies, Inc., 1221 Avenue of the Americas, New York, NY, 10020. Copyright © 2011 by The McGraw-Hill Companies, Inc. All rights reserved. No part of this publication may be reproduced or distributed in any form or by any means, or stored in a database or retrieval system, without the prior written consent of The McGraw-Hill Companies, Inc., including, but not limited to, in any network or other electronic storage or transmission, or broadcast for distance learning.

Some ancillaries, including electronic and print components, may not be available to customers outside the United States.

This book is printed on acid-free paper.

1 2 3 4 5 6 7 8 9 0 DOW/DOW 1 0 9 8 7 6 5 4 3 2 1 0

ISBN   978-0-07-811077-1
MHID   0-07-811077-7

Vice president and editor-in-chief: *Brent Gordon*
Editorial director: *Stewart Mattson*
Publisher: *Tim Vertovec*
Director of development: *Ann Torbert*
Sponsoring editor: *Donna Dillon*
Senior development editor: *Kimberly D. Hooker*
Vice president and director of marketing: *Robin J. Zwettler*
Marketing manager: *Kathleen Klehr*
Vice president of editing, design and production: *Sesha Bolisetty*
Lead project manager: *Christine A. Vaughan*
Lead production supervisor: *Michael R. McCormick*
Designer: *Matt Diamond*
Senior photo research coordinator: *Jeremy Cheshareck*
Photo researcher: *Editorial Image, LLC*
Lead media project manager: *Kerry Bowler*
Cover images: *Toyota, Starbucks, and Lowe's,* © Corbis; *Toll Brothers house,* © Getty; *Under Armour, courtesy Under Armour; Cold Stone Creamery, courtesy Cold Stone Creamery*
Typeface: *10.5/12 Goudy*
Compositor: *Laserwords Private Limited*
Printer: *R. R. Donnelley*

Library of Congress Cataloging-in-Publication Data

Whitecotton, Stacey.
    Managerial accounting / Stacey Whitecotton, Robert Libby, Fred Phillips.
        p. cm.
    Includes index.
    ISBN-13: 978-0-07-811077-1 (alk. paper)
    ISBN-10: 0-07-811077-7 (alk. paper)
    1. Managerial accounting. I. Libby, Robert. II. Phillips, Fred. III. Title.
HF5657.4 .W495 2011
658.15/11—dc22

                                                                    2009042924

www.mhhe.com

Dedication

To Mark, Riley, and Carley and to my sisters Betty, Debbie, and Alice!
Thanks for your inspiration.
STACEY WHITECOTTON

Herman and Doris Hargenrater, Laura Libby, Oscar and Selma Libby
ROBERT LIBBY

I dedicate this book to the best teachers I've ever had:
my Mom and Dad, Barb, Harrison, and Daniel
FRED PHILLIPS

A Letter to Instructors

As accounting instructors, we all face the challenge of getting our students to realize that accounting is both interesting and important. Whether you're teaching an accounting major, marketing major, or theater major, you know that motivation is the key to student success, and so do we. Now, more than ever, students need to be engaged, even entertained, to learn accounting.

We wrote *Managerial Accounting* with the goal of engaging and motivating students to learn managerial accounting. We strive to help students understand how the decisions they make in their daily lives relate to the decisions made in businesses every day. We believe that accounting is best learned in context. If the business context is familiar, the accounting content will be less challenging and more easily understood. *Managerial Accounting* uses three distinct features to accomplish these objectives:

- **An integrated focus company approach.** Each chapter is written around a real-world business that students are familiar with, such as Starbucks Coffee, Mattel Toys, and Toyota Motor Company. The entire chapter and its examples revolve around the focus company, so that it reads like an integrated business story rather than a series of disjointed definitions and examples.

- **A focus on products and services that students can easily visualize and understand.** Most accounting students have never been inside a factory and will not work for a traditional manufacturing company. Yet many managerial accounting topics require students to understand how products are made. We use products and services that students encounter every day, such as Tombstone pizza, Cold Stone Creamery, and Blockbuster video. This balance of service, retail, and manufacturing firms allows students to see that managerial accounting applies to all types of organizations.

- **An emphasis on decision making.** Solid decision-making skills make good sense no matter what path your life takes and *Managerial Accounting* helps students understand how accounting is used to make business decisions. We know most students will not go on to be accountants, but whether they end up in business environments, serving the public, or simply managing their own money, *Managerial Accounting* will provide the introduction students need to stimulate their interests and foster their decision-making skills.

As an author team, our teaching and research interests are at the intersection of accounting, education, and decision making. *Managerial Accounting* brings Stacey Whitecotton's conversational writing style and modern approach to teaching managerial accounting and couples it with the proven pedagogical approach that Bob Libby and Fred Phillips have perfected in their *Financial Accounting* texts. This makes *Managerial Accounting* the perfect accounting text for today's students.

Stacey Whitecotton   Robert Libby   Fred Phillips

Meet the Authors

Stacey Whitecotton

Stacey Whitecotton is an associate professor in the School of Accountancy at Arizona State University. She received her Ph.D. and Masters of Accounting from The University of Oklahoma and her B.B.A. from Texas Tech University.

Stacey teaches managerial accounting topics and has received numerous awards for outstanding teaching at the undergraduate and graduate level. She also serves as the faculty director for the W.P. Carey online MBA program.

Stacey's research interests center around the use of decision aids to improve the decision-making behavior of financial analysts, managers, and auditors. Her research has been published in *The Accounting Review*, *Organizational Behavior and Human Decision Processes*, *Behavioral Research in Accounting*, *Auditing: A Journal of Practice and Theory*, and *The Journal of Behavioral Decision Making*.

Stacey and her husband Mark enjoy traveling and the many outdoor activities Arizona has to offer with their two children, Riley and Carley.

Robert Libby

Robert Libby is the David A. Thomas Professor of Accounting at Cornell University where he teaches the Financial Accounting course. He previously taught at the University of Illinois, Pennsylvania State University, the University of Texas at Austin, the University of Chicago, and the University of Michigan. He received his B.S. from Pennsylvania State University and his M.A.S. and Ph.D. from the University of Illinois; he is also a CPA.

Bob is a widely published author and researcher specializing in behavioral accounting. He was selected as the AAA Outstanding Educator in 2000, received the AAA Outstanding Service Award in 2006, and received the AAA Notable Contributions to the Literature Award in 1985 and 1996. He is the only person to have received all three of the Association's highest awards for teaching, service, and research. He has published numerous articles in journals such as *The Accounting Review, Journal of Accounting Research, and Accounting, Organizations, and Society.* He has held a variety of offices including vice president in the American Accounting Association. He is a member of the American Institute of CPAs and serves on the editorial boards of *The Accounting Review; Accounting, Organizations, and Society; Journal of Accounting Literature;* and *Journal of Behavioral Decision Making.*

Fred Phillips

Fred Phillips is a professor and the George C. Baxter Scholar at the University of Saskatchewan where he teaches introductory Principles of Accounting. He also has taught introductory accounting at the University of Texas at Austin and the University of Manitoba. Fred has an undergraduate accounting degree, a professional accounting designation, and a Ph.D. from the University of Texas at Austin. He previously worked as an audit manager at KPMG.

Fred's main interest is accounting education. He has won 11 teaching awards, including three national case-writing competitions. Recently, Fred won the 2007 Alpha Kappa Psi Outstanding Professor award at The University of Texas at Austin; and in 2006, he was awarded the title Master Teacher at the University of Saskatchewan. He has published instructional cases and numerous articles in journals such as *Issues in Accounting Education, Journal of Accounting Research,* and *Organizational Behavior and Human Decision Processes.* He received the American Accounting Association's Outstanding Research in Accounting Education Award in 2006 and 2007 for his articles. Fred is a past associate editor of *Issues in Accounting Education* and a current member of the Teaching & Curriculum and Two-Year College sections of the American Accounting Association. In his spare time, he likes to work out, play video games, and drink iced cappuccinos.

What Today's Students Are **Craving**:

Chapters 9 & 10 Focus Company:
Cold Stone Creamery

Chapter 1 Focus Company:
Tombstone Pizza

Chapters 5 & 6 Focus Company:
Starbucks Coffee

A textbook that is **MODERN**, **MOTIVATING**, and **ENGAGING!**

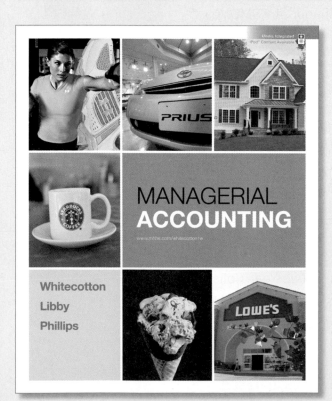

From the award-winning, market-leading Libby author team comes a modern, relevant, and engaging textbook for today's managerial accounting student. Whitecotton/Libby/Phillips *Managerial Accounting* brings lively and engaging coverage of managerial accounting topics and decision-making focus to the managerial accounting course.

> *This text is awesome. It uses a **student-centered approach** and is easy for readers to follow with its **clear framework**.*
>
> —Chuo-Hsuan (Jason) Lee,
> State University of New York at Plattsburg

Managerial Accounting
by Whitecotton/Libby/Phillips

Unique to this text's approach are three key components that motivate and guide students through managerial accounting:

1 Managerial accounting in the context of real business

The greatest challenges instructors have are to engage students in the managerial accounting course, keep them motivated throughout the course, and teach them accounting in a way that connects conceptual understanding to the real world. **Managerial Accounting engages and motivates students by presenting accounting in the context of recognizable companies such as Starbucks, Mattel, Cold Stone Creamery, and Tombstone Pizza,** and then integrates those companies throughout the chapter discussions.

2 Managerial accounting with a focus on decision making

Most students taking managerial accounting will not become accounting majors and accountants; instead, they will use accounting information in their professional lives to *make business decisions*. **Managerial Accounting allows students to see real accounting information being used to make real business decisions In companies that are part of their everyday lives, which helps them connect their learning to the real world.** This approach helps students develop the analytical and critical thinking skills they will need to succeed in their future careers.

3 Managerial accounting with the aid of technology

Today's students have diverse learning styles and numerous commitments. They want technology supplements that help them study more efficiently and effectively. **McGraw-Hill's *Connect Accounting, Personal Learning Plan, LearnSmart,* and a repository of additional resources tied directly to Whitecotton/Libby/Phillips *Managerial Accounting*** will improve students' engagement in and out of class and help them maximize their study time to make their learning experiences more enjoyable.

> *This is a text with innovative features and highly motivating examples and writing. The students will benefit tremendously from the text while the instructors will have very good materials to work with. Highly recommended.*
>
> —Chiaho Chang, Montclair State University

> *The text includes a comprehensive set of managerial accounting tools with very useful examples and exhibits that students can relate to and understand.*
>
> —Jeanette Maier-Lytle, University of Southern Indiana

Engaging Features and Relevant Pedagogy

> *A fresh approach to an old topic, this book uses real company examples that students can easily relate to.*
>
> –Debora Constable,
> Georgia Perimeter College

> *This text has attention-grabbing effective chapter openers and is well written and provides appropriate depth of coverage for an introductory accounting text.*
>
> –Darlene Coarts,
> University of Northern Iowa

Chapters 7 & 8 Focus Company:
Mattel Toys

Chapter 11 Focus Company:
Blockbuster

Managerial Accounting has a variety of features that complement the way you teach and the way today's students learn. From study tips and advice to guide students through difficult topics to clear and relevant examples, each chapter offers students the tools they need to succeed.

Chapter Openers—Focus Companies

Each chapter of *Managerial Accounting* opens with an engaging scenario or story using a familiar company. The same focus company is used throughout the entire chapter so that students can see how the concepts and calculations apply to a real-world company they are already familiar with.

Bring Managerial Accounting Content **to Life**

Self-Study Practice

Research shows that students learn best when they are actively engaged in the learning process. These quizzes ask students to pause at critical points throughout each chapter to ensure they understand the material presented before moving ahead.

Coach's Tips

Students might not always grasp the concepts without some needed encouragement. Coach's Tips appear throughout the text offering tips, advice, and suggestions about how to learn the key concepts of managerial accounting.

Self-Study Practice

1. Which of the following statements best describes the difference between financial accounting and managerial accounting?
   a. Managerial accounting is targeted at external stakeholders while financial accounting is targeted at individuals within the company.
   b. Financial accounting relies more on subjective, future-oriented information than managerial accounting does.
   c. The major focus of managerial accounting is the preparation of the income statement, balance sheet, and statement of cash flows.
   d. Managerial accounting tends to focus on relevant, subjective, and future-oriented information while financial accounting relies primarily on objective, reliable, and historical information.

2. Which of the following statement(s) regarding the key management functions is (are) false? (You may select more than one answer.)
   a. Planning involves setting both long-term objectives and the short-term tactics necessary to achieve those objectives.
   b. Directing/leading involves comparing actual results to planned objectives and making any adjustments as necessary.
   c. Each of the management functions (planning, organizing, leading/directing, and control) is completely independent of the others.
   d. All of the above.

After you have finished, check your answers with the solutions in the margin.

COACH'S TIP

The best way to know whether you are reading the chapter carefully enough is to see how well you do on a short exercise. Therefore, at important points throughout each chapter, you will find an exercise that will reinforce the concepts you have just learned and provide feedback on how well you learned them. We urge you not to skip these practices.

Solution to Self-Study Practice
1. d
2. b and c (Item b describes control, not leading/directing; Item c is false because the management functions are interdependent.)

Spotlight On DECISION MAKING

Buying a home is one of the most important investment decisions most people make during their lives. For this investment, the time value of money is reflected in home mortgage rates. The following graph below shows the fluctuation in average mortgage rates from 1963–2008.

(Copyright © 2008 Mortgage-X.com)

National Average Contract Mortgage Rate

Copy right © 1998-2009 Mortgage-X.com

Mortgage rates were at a historic high in the early 1980s, approaching an average of 15 percent.

By 2009, mortgage rates had dropped below 5 percent. Unfortunately, when housing prices fell, many people realized they could not afford their home in spite of extremely low interest rates.

Spotlight on Decision Making

Good decision making is essential in business whether you are preparing, using, or analyzing accounting information. This feature helps students develop good decision-making skills by using examples to illustrate the relevance of accounting in real-world decision making.

Spotlight on Ethics

Recent events in the accounting profession have made ethics more crucial than ever. This feature conveys the importance of acting responsibly in business practice.

Spotlight On ETHICS

Accounting Scandals

Accounting scandals are driven by the fear of personal failure and greed. Initially, some people may appear to benefit from fraudulent reporting. In the long run, however, fraud harms most individuals and organizations. When it is uncovered, the corporation's stock price drops dramatically. In the case involving MicroStrategy, the stock price dropped 65 percent from $243 to $86 per share in a single day of trading. Creditors are also harmed by fraud. WorldCom's creditors recovered only 42 percent of what they were owed. They lost $36 billion. Innocent employees also are harmed by fraud. At Enron, 5,600 employees lost their jobs, and many lost all of their retirement savings.

Review and Practice Material Build a

Each chapter of **Managerial Accounting** is followed by an extensive variety of end-of-chapter material that examines and integrates concepts presented in the chapter.

> *This is a very readable and thorough text with a wealth of high-quality end-of-chapter materials. The examples will help maintain student interest and engagement, and the Coach's Tips help students focus and understand the information.*
>
> –Dana Carpenter, Madison Area Technical College

Chapter Summary by Learning Objectives

Each chapter concludes with an end-of-chapter summary that revisits the learning objectives from the beginning of the chapter.

which was undercosted?

6. Explain why ABC provided different information than the current cost system.

See pages 154–155 for solution.

CHAPTER SUMMARY

Assign indirect cost to products or services using a single volume-based allocation measure. p. 135   LO1

- A traditional cost system assigns indirect (overhead) costs to products or services using a volume-based measure such as the number of direct labor hours, machine hours, or units produced. These systems, while simple, assume that all indirect costs are driven by volume and ignore other factors such as the complexity of the production process and other non-volume drivers of cost.
- Unlike traditional cost systems that rely strictly on volume-based allocation measures, ABC systems include measures that capture something other than the sheer volume of units produced or customers served.

Classify activities as unit, batch, product, customer, or facility level. p. 138   LO2

- Activity based costing systems capture the following types of activities:
  - Unit-level activities are performed for each individual unit.
  - Batch-level activities are performed for a group of units all at once.
  - Product-level activities are performed to support a general product line, not specific units or batches.
  - Customer-level activities are performed for a specific customer.
  - Facility-level or companywide activities are performed for the company overall and do not relate to specific products, customers, batches, or units.

Assign indirect costs to activity cost pools (Stage 1) and select a driver for each pool. p. 140   LO3

- The first stage of ABC is to assign indirect costs to activity cost pools. The goal is to create as few activity cost pools as possible while capturing the major activities performed.
- The next step is to identify an activity cost driver for each of the activity cost pools. The goal is to identify a driver that has a cause-and-effect relationship with the underlying activity that occurs in each activity cost pool.

Assign activity costs to products or services (Stage 2) using activity rates. p. 142   LO4

KEY TERMS

Contribution Margin (p. 187)	High-Low Method (p. 179)	Scattergraph (p. 179)
Contribution Margin Income Statement (p. 186)	Independent Variable (p. 179)	Step Costs (p. 177)
Contribution Margin Ratio (p. 188)	Least-Squares Regression (p. 179)	Step-Fixed Cost (p. 177)
Cost Behavior (p. 175)	Linearity Assumption (p. 178)	Step-Variable Cost (p. 177)
Cost Driver (p. 175)	Mixed Costs (p. 177)	Unit Contribution Margin (p. 187)
Dependent Variable (p. 179)	Relevant Range (p. 175)	Variable Costing (p. 189)
Full Absorption Costing (p. 174)	R Square (p. 184)	Visual Fit Method (p. 179)

See complete definitions in glossary at back of text.

Key Terms

Includes key terms, definitions, and page references. Full definitions for all key terms are found in the back of the text.

Strong Foundation for Future Success

QUESTIONS

1. Identify and briefly describe the assumptions of CVP.
2. Why should managers create a CVP graph?
3. When considering a CVP graph, how is the break-even point shown?
4. Your supervisor has requested that you prepare a CVP graph for your company's product but does not understand its meaning or how changes would affect the graph. Explain to your supervisor how your graph would be affected by:
   a. an increase in the selling price.
   b. a decrease in variable cost per unit.
   c. an increase in fixed costs.
5. Why is it important for a company to know its break-even point? What happens to the break-even point if variable cost per unit decreases? If total fixed cost increases?
6. Explain the difference between unit contribution margin and contribution margin ratio.
7. A company's cost structure can have a high proportion of fixed costs or a high proportion of variable costs. Which cost structure is more vulnerable to decreases in demand? Why?
8. Explain the difference in calculating the break-even point in units and in dollars. How can one be used to double-check the other?
9. Apple Company and Baker Company are competitors in the same industry, producing the same product. They have similar variable costs per unit and selling prices, but Baker has more fixed costs. Explain the impact of this on each company's break-even point.
10. Bert Company and Ernie Company are competitors in the same industry. The companies produce the same product

and have the same amount of fixed costs and the same selling price per unit. However, Bert has higher variable cost per unit. Compare the break-even point of each company.

11. Explain the difference between break-even analysis and target profit analysis.
12. Explain margin of safety. Why is it important for managers to know their margin of safety?
13. Give an example of a company to which margin of safety is particularly important and explain why.
14. Explain how a decision to automate a manufacturing facility would likely impact a company's cost structure and its break-even point.
15. Explain degree of operating leverage and how it relates to fixed cost.
16. How does degree of operating leverage help managers predict changes in profit? In general, would you prefer a higher or lower degree of operating leverage?
17. Why is sales mix important to multiproduct CVP analysis? Explain how sales mix is factored into CVP analysis.
18. How is weighted average contribution margin calculated?
19. What will happen to a company's break-even point if the sales mix shifts to favor a product with a lower contribution margin per unit?
20. How do you use the weighted average contribution margin ratio in cost-volume-profit analysis?
21. Why is the weighted average contribution margin ratio approach commonly used in practice?
22. What is the difference between the product mix and the sales mix?

MULTIPLE CHOICE

1. Which of the following is **not** an assumption of CVP analysis?

   Quiz 6
   www.mhhe.com/whitecotton1e

   a. A straight line can be used to approximate the relationship between cost and revenue within the relevant range.
   b. Production and sales are equal.
   c. Sales mix remains constant for any company selling more than one product.

   c. (Fixed Cost − Variable Cost)/Sales.
   d. Variable Cost/Sales.

3. When total contribution margin equals total fixed cost, a company has
   a. A net loss.
   b. Net income.
   c. Zero profit.
   d. Higher variable cost and fixed cost.

Questions

Each chapter includes 10–20 questions that ask students to explain and discuss terms and concepts from the chapter.

Multiple-Choice Questions

Each chapter includes 10 multiple-choice questions that let students practice basic concepts. Solutions for all questions are provided in the back of the text.

---

c. The common fixed costs allocated to that product line.
d. All of the above will be completely eliminated.

| Answers to Multiple-Choice Questions located in back of the text. |

MINI EXERCISES

connect | ACCOUNTING

M7-1 Matching Key Terms and Concepts to Definitions   LO1, 2, 3, 4, 5, 6

A number of terms and concepts from this chapter and a list of descriptions, definitions, and explanations follow. For each term listed on the left, choose at least one corresponding item from the right. Note that a single term may have more than one description and a single description may be used more than once or not at all.

_____ 1. Excess capacity.
_____ 2. Identify the decision problem.
_____ 3. Constrained resource.
_____ 4. Special-order decision.
_____ 5. Differential costs.
_____ 6. Evaluate the costs and benefits of alternatives.
_____ 7. Make-or-buy decision.
_____ 8. Sunk costs.
_____ 9. Opportunity costs.
_____ 10. Keep or drop decision.
_____ 11. Full capacity.
_____ 12. Avoidable costs.

(a) Short-term management decision made using differential analysis.
(b) Management decision in which lost revenue is compared to the reduction of costs to determine the overall effect on profit.
(c) Exists when a company has not yet reached the limit on its resources.
(d) Costs that have already been incurred.
(e) Management decision in which fixed manufacturing overhead is ignored as long as there is enough excess capacity to meet the order.
(f) Costs that can be avoided by choosing one option over another.
(g) Step 5 of the management decision-making process.
(h) Management decision in which relevant costs of making a product internally are compared to the cost of purchasing that product.
(i) Cost that is relevant to short-term decision making.
(j) Resource that is insufficient to meet the demands placed on it.
(k) First step of the management decision-making process.
(l) Costs that are always irrelevant to management decisions.
(m) Exists when a company has met its limit on one or more resources.

Mini Exercises

Assignments that illustrate and apply a single learning objective from the chapter.

Exercises

Additional assignments that illustrate and apply single and multiple learning objectives from the chapter.

> *The Whitecotton/Libby/Phillips Managerial Accounting textbook utilizes a writing style that is straightforward and to the point. The writing is at the perfect reading level for our students . . .*
>
> –John Gabelman, Columbus State Community College

> *Very visual. Superb graphics. Well-integrated real-life examples*
>
> –Angela Sandberg, Jacksonville State University

Problems (Set A and B)

Each chapter includes two problem sets to help students develop decision-making skills.

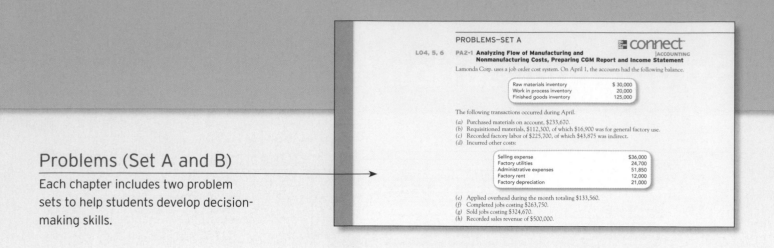

Skills Development Cases

Each chapter offers cases designed to help students develop critical thinking skills. These cases allow for group discussions and projects.

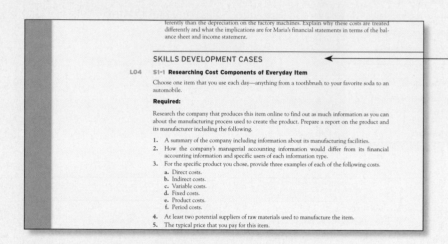

The following icons appear throughout the chapters and end-of-chapter materials. Please refer to the text Web site, www.mhhe.com/Whitecotton1e to download content and access Excel templates. All iPod content can be downloaded to your **iPod, Zune,** or **MP3 devices** (audio and visual depending on your device).

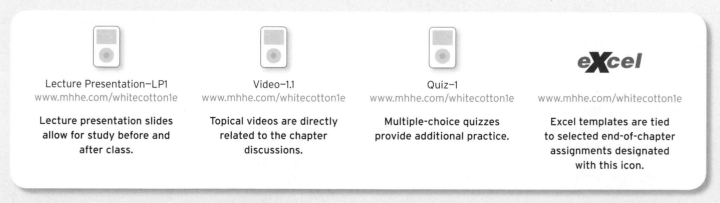

Lecture Presentation–LP1	Video–1.1	Quiz–1	eXcel
www.mhhe.com/whitecotton1e	www.mhhe.com/whitecotton1e	www.mhhe.com/whitecotton1e	www.mhhe.com/whitecotton1e
Lecture presentation slides allow for study before and after class.	Topical videos are directly related to the chapter discussions.	Multiple-choice quizzes provide additional practice.	Excel templates are tied to selected end-of-chapter assignments designated with this icon.

Technology That Supports Success and Moves Learning Forward

McGraw-Hill Connect Accounting

Less Managing. More Teaching. Greater Learning.

Chapter 4 Focus Company: Toyota

☑ **McGraw-Hill *Connect Accounting*** is an online assignment and assessment solution that connects students with the tools and resources they'll need to achieve success.

☑ **McGraw-Hill *Connect Accounting*** helps prepare students for their future by enabling faster learning, more efficient studying, and higher retention of knowledge.

McGraw-Hill *Connect Accounting* Features

Connect Accounting offers a number of powerful tools and features to make managing assignments easier so faculty can spend more time teaching. With *Connect Accounting,* students can engage with their coursework anytime and anywhere, making the learning process more accessible and efficient. *Connect Accounting* offers you the following features.

Simple Assignment Management

With *Connect Accounting* creating assignments is easier than ever, so you can spend more time teaching and less time managing. The assignment management function enables you to:

- Create and deliver assignments easily with selectable end-of-chapter questions and test bank items.
- Streamline lesson planning, student progress reporting, and assignment grading to make classroom management more efficient than ever.
- Go paperless with the eBook and online submission and grading of student assignments.

Smart Grading

When it comes to studying, time is precious. *Connect Accounting* helps students learn more efficiently by providing feedback and practice material when they need it, where they need it. When it comes to teaching, your time also is precious. The grading function enables you to:

- Have assignments scored automatically, giving students immediate feedback on their work and side-by-side comparisons with correct answers.
- Access and review each response; manually change grades or leave comments for students to review.
- Reinforce classroom concepts with practice tests and instant quizzes.

Instructor library

The *Connect Accounting* Instructor Library is your repository for additional resources to improve student engagement in and out of class. You can select and use any asset that enhances your lecture. The *Connect Accounting* Instructor Library includes:

- eBook
- PowerPoint slides
- Videos

Student Study Center

The *Connect Accounting* Student Study Center is the place for students to access additional resources. The Student Study Center:

- Offers students quick access to lectures, practice materials, eBooks, and more.
- Provides instant practice material and study questions, easily accessible on the go.
- Gives students access to the Personal Learning Plan described next.

Personal Learning Plan

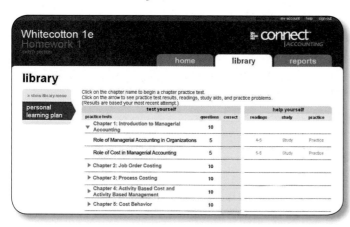

The Personal Learning Plan (PLP) connects each student to the learning resources needed for success in the course. For each chapter, students:

- Take a practice test to initiate the Personal Learning Plan.
- Immediately upon completing the practice test, see how their performance compares to chapter learning objectives or content by sections within chapters.
- Receive a Personal Learning Plan that recommends specific readings from the text, supplemental study material, and practice work that will improve their understanding and mastery of each learning objective.

Diagnostic and adaptive learning of concepts: LearnSmart

Students want to make the best use of their study time. The LearnSmart adaptive self-study technology within *Connect Accounting* provides students with a seamless combination of practice, assessment, and remediation for every concept in the textbook. LearnSmart's intelligent software adapts to every student response and automatically delivers concepts that advance the student's understanding while reducing time devoted to the concepts already mastered. The result for every student is the fastest path to mastery of the chapter concepts.

LearnSmart

- Applies an intelligent concept engine to identify the relationships between concepts and to serve new concepts to each student only when he or she is ready.
- Adapts automatically to each student, so students spend less time on the topics they understand and practice more those they have yet to master.
- Provides continual reinforcement and remediation, but gives only as much guidance as students need.
- Integrates diagnostics as part of the learning experience.
- Enables you to assess which concepts students have efficiently learned on their own, thus freeing class time for more applications and discussion.

Student Progress Tracking

Connect Accounting keeps instructors informed about how each student, section, and class is performing, allowing for more productive use of lecture and office hours. The progress-tracking function enables you to:

- View scored work immediately and track individual or group performance with assignment and grade reports.
- Access an instant view of student or class performance relative to learning objectives.
- Collect data and generate reports required by many accreditation organizations, such as AACSB and AICPA.

Lecture Capture

Increase the attention paid to lecture discussion by decreasing the attention paid to note taking. For an additional charge, Lecture Capture offers new ways for students to focus on the in-class discussion, knowing they can revisit important topics later. For more information on Lecture Capture capabilities in *Connect*, see the discussion of Tegrity on this page.

Tegrity Campus: Lectures 24/7

 Tegrity Campus is a service that makes class time available 24/7 by automatically capturing every lecture. With a simple one-click start-and-stop process, you capture all computer screens and corresponding audio in a format that is easily searchable, frame by frame. Students can replay any part of any class with easy-to-use browser-based viewing on a PC or Mac, an iPod or other mobile device.

Educators know that the more students can see, hear, and experience class resources, the better they learn. In fact, studies prove it. Tegrity Campus's unique search feature helps students efficiently find what they need, when they need it, across an entire semester of class recordings. Help turn your students' study time into learning moments immediately supported by your lecture. With Tegrity Campus, you also increase intent listening and class participation by easing students' concerns about note-taking. Lecture Capture will make it more likely you will see students' faces, not the tops of their heads.

To learn more about Tegrity, watch a 2-minute Flash demo at http://tegritycampus.mhhe.com.

McGraw-Hill Connect Plus Accounting

 McGraw-Hill reinvents the textbook learning experience for the modern student with *Connect Plus Accounting*.

A seamless integration of an eBook and *Connect Accounting*, *Connect Accounting Plus Accounting* provides all of the *Connect Accounting* features plus the following:

- An integrated eBook, allowing for anytime, anywhere access to the textbook.
- Dynamic links between the problems or questions you assign to your students and the location in the eBook where that problem or question is covered.
- A powerful search function to pinpoint and connect key concepts in a snap.

In short, *Connect Accounting* offers you and your students powerful tools and features that optimize your time and energies, enabling you to focus on course content, teaching, and student learning. *Connect Accounting* also offers a wealth of content resources for both instructors and students. This state-of-the-art, thoroughly tested system supports you in preparing students for the world that awaits.

For more information about *Connect,* go to www.mcgrawhillconnect.com, or contact your local McGraw-Hill sales representative.

CourseSmart

Learn Smart. Choose Smart.

 CourseSmart is a new way for faculty to find and review eTextbooks. It's also a great option for students who are interested in accessing their course materials digitally and saving money.

CourseSmart offers thousands of the most commonly adopted textbooks across hundreds of courses from a wide variety of higher education publishers. It is the only place for faculty to review and compare the full text of a textbook online, providing immediate access without the environmental impact of requesting a print exam copy.

With the CourseSmart eTextbook, students can save up to 45 percent off the cost of a print book, reduce their impact on the environment, and access powerful Web tools for learning. CourseSmart is an online eTextbook, which means users access and view their textbook online when connected to the Internet. Students can also print sections of the book for maximum portability. CourseSmart eTextbooks are available in one standard online reader with full text search, notes and highlighting, and e-mail tools for sharing-notes between classmates. http://www.coursemart.com

Instructor Support Tools

☑ Instructor CD-ROM

ISBN 007-7269055

We have put access to the instructor's key text ancillary materials at your fingertips. You can find all of the instructor ancillaries available on one convenient CD-ROM: PowerPoint slides, Solutions Manual, Instructor's Resource Manual, Test Bank and Computerized Test Bank, Solutions to Excel templates, text exhibits, and more.

☑ Solutions Manual

Prepared by Stacey Whitecotton. Provides solutions to end-of-chapter questions, mini exercises, exercises, problems, and cases. Available on the Instructor CD-ROM and text Web site, www.mhhe.com/whitecotton1e.

☑ Test Bank

Prepared by Christine Denison, Iowa State University. Available on the Instructor CD-ROM and password-protected text Web site, this comprehensive Test Bank includes more than 1,500 true/false, multiple-choice questions, problems, essay, and matching questions.

☑ Presentation Slides

Prepared by Susan Galbreath at David Lipscomb University and Jon Booker and Charles Caldwell at Tennessee Technological University. Completely customized PowerPoint presentations for use in your classroom. Available on the Instructor CD-ROM and text Web site.

☑ Instructor's Resource Manual

Prepared by Chuo-Hsuan (Jason) Lee, State University of New York (SUNY) at Plattsburgh. Includes topical references to the *Managerial Accounting* Videos, PowerPoint presentations, and Study Guide. Designed to help instructors direct students to specific ancillaries to reinforce key concepts. Available on the Instructor CD-ROM and text Web site.

☑ Instructor Excel Templates

Solutions to the student Excel Templates used to solve selected end-of-chapter exercises and problems. These assignments are designated by the EXCEL icon. Available on the Instuctor CD-ROM and text Web site.

☑ EZ Test

ISBN 007 7269047

McGraw-Hill's EZ Test is a flexible and easy-to-use electronic testing program that allows instructors to create tests from book-specific items. EZ Test accommodates a wide range of question types and allows instructors to add their own questions. Multiple versions of the test can be created, and any test can be exported for use with course management systems such as BlackBoard/WebCT. EZ Test Online is a new service that gives instructors a place to easily administer EZ Test–created exams and quizzes online. The program is available for Windows and Macintosh environments.

☑ ASSURANCE OF LEARNING READY

Many educational institutions today are focused on the notion of *assurance of learning*, an important element of some accreditation standards. *Managerial Accounting* is designed specifically to support your assurance of learning initiatives with a simple yet powerful solution.

Each test bank question for *Managerial Accounting* maps to a specific chapter learning outcome/objective listed in the text. You can use our test bank software, EZ Test and EZ Test Online, or *Connect Accounting* to easily query for learning outcomes/objectives that directly relate to the learning objectives for your course. You can then use the reporting features of EZ Test or *Connect Accounting* to aggregate student results in similar fashion, making the collection and presentation of assurance of learning data simple and easy.

☑ AACSB STATEMENT

The McGraw-Hill Companies is a proud corporate member of AACSB International. Understanding the importance and value of AACSB accreditation, *Managerial Accounting* recognizes the curricula  guidelines detailed in the AACSB standards for business accreditation by connecting selected questions in the test bank to the six general knowledge and skill guidelines in the AACSB standards.

The statements contained in *Managerial Accounting* are provided only as a guide for the users of this textbook. The AACSB leaves content coverage and assessment within the purview of individual schools, the mission of the school, and the faculty. While *Managerial Accounting* and the teaching package make no claim of any specific AACSB qualification or evaluation, we have within the Test Bank to accompany *Managerial Accounting* labeled selected questions according to the six general knowledge and skills areas.

☑ MCGRAW-HILL CUSTOMER CARE CONTACT INFORMATION

At McGraw-Hill, we understand that getting the most from new technology can be challenging. That's why our services don't stop after you purchase our products. You can e-mail our Product Specialists 24 hours a day to get product training online. Or you can search our knowledge bank of Frequently Asked Questions on our support Web site. For Customer Support, call 800-331-5094, e-mail hmsupport@mcgraw-hill.com, or visit www.mhhe.com/support. One of our Technical Support Analysts will be able to assist you in a timely fashion.

Student Learning Tools

☑ Online Learning Center

www.mhhe.com/whitecotton1e

The online learning center includes multiple-choice quizzes, Excel templates, PowerPoint presentations, and iPod downloadable content.

☑ Presentation Slides

Selected presentation slides reproduced in student version. Presentation slides are located on the text's Online Learning Center.

☑ Check Figures

Prepared by Stacey Whitecotton. Provide answers to select Problems-Set A. Check Figures are located in the back of the text.

☑ Study Guide

ISBN: 0077269071

Prepared by Jeannie Folk at College of DuPage. An outstanding learning tool, this guide gives students a deeper understanding of the course material and reinforces, step by step, what they are learning in the main text.

☑ Excel Templates

Available on the text's Online Learning Center, these templates are tied to selected end-of-chapter problems. These assignments are designated by the EXCEL icon.

☑ Managerial Accounting Video Library

Created to stimulate classroom discussion and illustrate key concepts in managerial accounting. These videos are available on the text Web site, **www.mhhe.com/whitecotton1e**

☑ Personal Learning Plan

See page xvi.

☑ LearnSmart

See page xvi.

☑ iPod Downloadable Content

Managerial Accounting is a media-integrated textbook that provides students with portable educational contents—just right for those students who want to study when and where it's most convenient for them. Students have the option to download content for review and study to their Apple ® iPods and most other MP3 and MP4 devices. IPod icons appear throughout the text pointing students to chapter-specific audio lecture presentations slides, course-related videos, and practice multiple-choice questions.

Photo Courtesy of Apple.®

Acknowledgements

Many dedicated instructors have devoted their time and effort to help us develop this text. We would like to acknowledge and thank all of our colleagues who helped guide our decisions. This text would not be what it is without the help of our dedicated contributors:

Editorial Review Panel

Dawn Addington, *Central New Mexico Community College*
Gilda Agacer, *Monmouth University*
Markus Ahrens, *Saint Louis Community College*
Jane Austin, *Oklahoma City University*
Vidya Awasthi, *Seattle University*
Bala Balachandran, *New York University*
Amy Bentley, *Tallahassee Community College*
Phillip Blanchard, *University of Arizona*
Patrick Borja, *Citrus College*
Esther Bunn, *Stephen F. Austin State University*
Laurie Burney, *Mississippi State University*
Dana Carpenter, *Madison Area Technical College*
Karin Caruso, *Southern New Hampshire University*
Nancy Cassidy, *University of Nebraska-Lincoln*
Chiaho Chang, *Montclair State University*
Chak-Tong Chau, *University of Houston-Downtown*
Darlene Coarts, *University of Northern Iowa*
Debora Constable, *Georgia Perimeter College–Dunwoody*
Robert Conway, *University of Wisconsin at Platteville*
Debra Cosgrove, *University of Nebraska*
Nancy Coulmas, *Bloomsburg University of Pennsylvania*
Cheryl Crespi, *Central Connecticut State University*
Kathy Crusto-Way, *Tarrant County College*
David Deeds, *University of Northern Iowa*
Edward Douthett, *George Mason University*
Jan Duffy, *Iowa State University*
Dennis Elam, *Texas A&M–San Antonio*
Emmanuel Emenyonu, *Southern Connecticut State University*
Diane Eure, *Texas State University–San Marcos*
Xiujun (Sue June) Farrier, *Tarrant County College*
Christos Fatouros, *Curry College*
Jerry Ferry, *University of Northern Alabama*
John Gabelman, *Columbus State Community College*
Mohamed Gaber, *State University of New York at Plattsburgh*
Deborah Garvin, *University of Florida at Gainesville*
Olen Greer, *Missouri State University*
Cindy Gruber, *Marquette University*
Margaret Hicks, *Howard University*
Rob Hochschild, *Ivy Tech Community College*
Maggie Houston, *Wright State University*
Peggy Hughes, *Montclair State University*
John Illig, *State College of Florida*

Pamela Jackson, *Augusta State University*
Iris Jenkel, *Saint Norbert College*
Celina Jozsi, *University of South Florida*
Cindi Khanlarian, *University of North Carolina at Greensboro*
Mehmet Kocakulah, *University of Southern Indiana*
Cynthia Krom, *Marist College*
Scott Lane, *Quinnipiac University*
Chuo-Hsuan (Jason) Lee, *State University of New York at Plattsburgh*
Joan Luft, *Michigan State University*
Catherine Lumbattis, *Southern Illinois University at Carbondale*
Jeanette Maier-Lytle, *University of Southern Indiana*
Linda Marquis, *Northern Kentucky University*
Scott Martens, *University of Minnesota*
Angie Martin, *Tarrant County College*
Josephine Mathias, *Mercer County Community College*
Suzanne McCaffrey, *University of Mississippi*
Florence McGovern, *Bergen Community College*
Brian McGuire, *University of Southern Indiana*
Pam Meyer, *University of Louisiana at Lafayette*
Arabian Morgan, *Orange Coast College*
Michael Newman, *University of Houston*
Jo Ann Pinto, *Montclair State University*
Jessica Rakow, *Louisiana State University*
Ronald Reed, *University Northern Colorado*
Luther Ross, *Central Piedmont Community College*
Angela Sandberg, *Jacksonville State University*
Michael Schusler, *Portland State University*
Patrick Stegman, *College of Lake County*
Scott Stroher, *Glendale Community College*
Holly Sudano, *Florida State University*
Ellen Sweatt, *Georgia Perimeter College*
Diane Tanner, *University of North Florida*
Kiran Verma, *University Massachusetts–Boston*
Sharon Walters, *Morehead State University*
Mary Ann Welden, *Wayne State University*
Anne Wessely, *Saint Louis Community College*
Jane Wiese, *Valencia Community College*
George Williams, *Bergen Community College*
Jeffrey Wong, *University of Nevada at Reno*
Pete Woodlock, *Youngstown State University*
Janet Woods, *Macon State College*
John Woodward, *Polk State College*
Christian Wurst, *Temple University*
Jeffrey Yost, *College of Charleston*
Ronald Zhao, *Monmouth University*

We are grateful to the following individuals who helped develop, critique, and shape the extensive ancillary package: Jill Hooper; Christine Denison, Iowa State University; Jeannie Folk, College of DuPage; Susan Galbreath, David Lipscomb University; Jon Booker, Tennessee Technological University; Charles Caldwell, Tennessee Technological University; Jeff Wong, University of Nevada-Reno; LuAnn Bean, Florida Institute of Technology; Chuo-Hsuan (Jason) Lee, State University of New York (SUNY) at Plattsburgh; George Williams, Bergen Community College; Beth Woods, Accuracy Counts; Jay Holman, University of Wisconsin–EauClaire; and Jack Terry, ComSource Associates, Inc.

Last, we thank the extraordinary efforts of a talented group of individuals at McGraw-Hill/Irwin who made all of this come together. We would especially like to thank our editorial director, Stewart Mattson; Tim Vertovec, our publisher; Donna Dillon, our sponsoring editor; Kimberly Hooker, our developmental editor; Kathleen Klehr, our marketing manager; Christine Vaughan, our project manager; Matt Diamond, our designer; Michael McCormick, our production supervisor; Kerry Bowler, our media producer; Jeremy Cheshareck, our photo research coordinator; David Tietz, our photo researcher; and Marcy Lunetta, our permission researcher.

Stacey Whitecotton
Robert Libby
Fred Philips

Assurance of Accuracy

Dear Colleagues,

Accuracy is always a top priority in producing a textbook, particularly for a first edition text. We have taken every effort to ensure the accuracy of *Managerial Accounting*. With the help of professional accuracy checkers, copy editors, proofreaders, and contributing authors, we have performed the following activities to ensure the quality and accuracy of this text:

- **Three drafts of manuscript:** The entire manuscript was written and rewritten to ensure appropriate topical coverage and to ensure vocabulary and pedagogy were consistent throughout.

- **125 reviews:** Detailed reviews of every chapter from managerial accounting instructors around the country were compiled, synthesized, studied, and acted upon during each draft of our manuscript.

- **Three rounds of accuracy checking:** Three professional accuracy checkers reviewed and tested every problem at three different stages of the production.

- **Faculty focus groups** 18 participants at McGraw-Hill's Managerial Accounting Focus Group, held in New York, NY and Burr Ridge, IL, helped guide the decisions we made on the organization of the text and coverage.

All of our editorial advisors, reviewers, and attendees are listed on pages xxi–xxii.

You and your students can be assured that our dedication and commitment to producing an error-free text have gone into every page of *Managerial Accounting*.

Stacey Whitecotton   Robert Libby   Fred Phillips

BRIEF CONTENTS

CONTENTS

CHAPTER 13

Managerial
ACCOUNTING

www.mhhe.com/whitecotton1e

CHAPTER 1

Introduction to Managerial Accounting

At the beginning of each chapter, you'll see a list of learning objectives that identify the key topics you need to master. You can also use the list as an outline for taking notes as you read through the chapter.

YOUR LEARNING OBJECTIVES

After completing this chapter, you should be able to:

LO1   Describe the key differences between financial accounting and managerial accounting.

LO2   Describe how managerial accounting is used in different types of organizations to support the key functions of management.

LO3   Explain the role of ethics in managerial decision making and the effects of the Sarbanes-Oxley Act.

LO4   Define and give examples of different types of cost:

        Out-of-pocket or opportunity costs
        Direct or indirect costs
        Variable or fixed costs
        Relevant or irrelevant costs
        Manufacturing or nonmanufacturing costs
        Product or period costs

Lecture Presentation-LP1
www.mhhe.com/whitecotton1e

FOCUS COMPANY: Tombstone Pizza

"What Do You Want On Your Tombstone?"

www.kraft.com/brands

A s you start what is probably your second accounting course, you may be wondering why you are taking yet another accounting class. Wasn't one course enough? Which of the following reasons for taking managerial accounting best describes your motivation?

Top 10 Reasons to Take a Managerial Accounting Course

10. Accounting is truly interesting and exciting.
9. I didn't learn enough in my first accounting course.
8. My academic advisor said to take it.
7. My parents said to take it.
6. Accountants get jobs, even in the most troubled economy.
5. Enron and other Wall Street scandals proved that accounting matters.
4. I want to get rich and stay that way.
3. I want to start my own business and need to create a business plan.
2. Accounting will fulfill my foreign language requirement. (It's Greek to me.)
1. I'm enrolled in an accounting course???

Whatever your reason for taking this course, it will come in handy at some point in your future. This is true regardless of your intended career path, whether it is to start your own business, work for a large corporation, go into politics, work in health care, become a fashion designer, teach high school, work on a farm, or start a charitable foundation. Accounting is the language of business, and understanding it will help you to make better business and personal decisions.

Even if you are not yet convinced that accounting is interesting and important, you will see that managerial accounting differs from what most people think of as accounting. In your prior accounting course, you probably learned about debits and credits and how to

3

prepare financial reports such as the income statement and balance sheet. In this course, we rarely use the terms *debit* or *credit* and almost never prepare formal financial statements. Instead, our focus is on understanding how to use accounting information to make personal and business decisions. Throughout, we use companies that you are already familiar with and show you how to apply the concepts to your personal life and to business scenarios. Let's get started by talking about a topic everyone knows something about: pizza.

Tombstone Pizza began in 1960 with two brothers working in a small Wisconsin pub across the street from a local cemetery. Ron Simek poured beer while "Pep" experimented with pizza recipes to serve along with it. Eventually, customers started coming to the pub more for the pizza than the beer. As the buzz about the deliciously spicy pizza spread, the Simeks transformed the back of the pub into a pizza factory and began selling pizzas to other local businesses. By 1966, the Simek brothers bought the first in what would eventually become a fleet of refrigerated trucks to deliver Tombstone Pizzas to small businesses and grocery stores across the country. In 1986, Kraft Foods made the Simek brothers an offer they couldn't refuse, and Tombstone Pizza became a subsidiary—or freestanding operating unit—of Kraft.

Throughout this chapter, we will use Tombstone Pizza to illustrate some basic managerial accounting terms and concepts. As you read the chapter, try putting yourself in the shoes of one of the following managers at Tombstone Pizza:

- Regional sales manager responsible for sales and distribution to grocery stores in California, Nevada, Utah, and Arizona.
- Marketing manager responsible for the pricing and promotion of existing products.
- New product development manager responsible for the development and introduction of a new whole wheat pizza.
- Production manager responsible for the rising-crust production line.
- Human resource manager responsible for hiring, training, and evaluating Tombstone employees.

Think about the activities you would need to perform and the types of decisions you would have to make in your chosen role and, most of all, the information you would need as a manager. Chances are that much of that information would come from the company's managerial accounting system.

ORGANIZATION OF THE CHAPTER

Role of managerial accounting in organizations

- Decision-making orientation
- Comparison of financial and managerial accounting
- Types of organizations
- Functions of management
- Ethics and internal reporting

Role of cost in managerial accounting

- Definition of cost
- Out-of-pocket versus opportunity costs
- Direct versus indirect costs
- Variable versus fixed costs
- Relevant versus irrelevant costs
- Manufacturing versus nonmanufacturing costs
- Product versus period costs

Role of Managerial Accounting in Organizations

DECISION-MAKING ORIENTATION

The primary goal of accounting is to provide information for decision making. A company's accounting system must serve the information needs of two types of decision makers, as shown in Exhibit 1.1.

As you can see, the major difference between financial accounting and managerial accounting is the intended user of the information. **Financial accounting** information is used by external parties, such as investors, creditors, and regulators; **managerial accounting** information is used by internal business owners and managers. Of course, these different types of users have different information needs. This user perspective results in several other differences between financial and managerial accounting.

COMPARISON OF FINANCIAL AND MANAGERIAL ACCOUNTING

External financial statements are prepared according to generally accepted accounting principles (GAAP), which provide external users certain advantages in terms of their comparability and objectivity. However, internal managers often need more detailed information that is not restricted by GAAP—information that is not captured in the financial reports prepared for external parties. More often than not, the information managers seek is relevant, future oriented, and subjective.

Throughout this text, we will provide you with tips to highlight explanations of selected topics. Please read them carefully.

Video 1-1
www.mhhe.com/whitecotton1e

> **Learning Objective 1**
> Describe the key differences between financial accounting and managerial accounting.

> ✎ **COACH'S TIP**
>
> Financial accounting is sometimes referred to as **external** reporting while managerial accounting is referred to as **internal** reporting. The difference is whether the intended users are inside or outside the company.

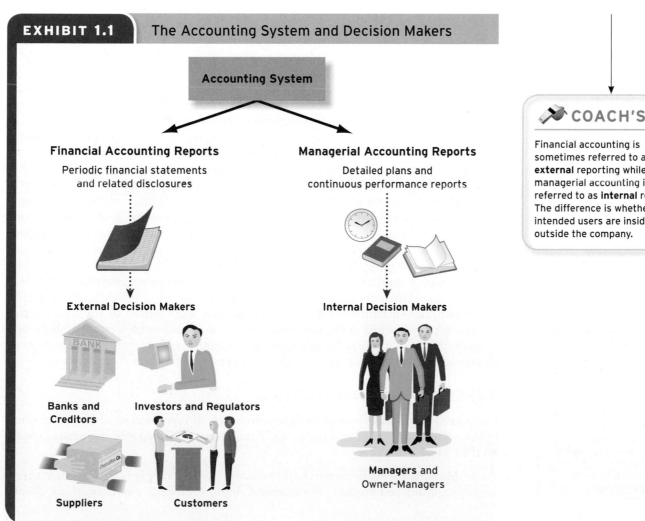

EXHIBIT 1.1   The Accounting System and Decision Makers

Accounting System

Financial Accounting Reports
Periodic financial statements and related disclosures

Managerial Accounting Reports
Detailed plans and continuous performance reports

External Decision Makers

Banks and Creditors

Investors and Regulators

Suppliers

Customers

Internal Decision Makers

Managers and Owner-Managers

EXHIBIT 1.2	Differences between Financial and Managerial Accounting	

	Financial Accounting	**Managerial Accounting**
User perspective	Used by external parties, such as investors, creditors, and regulators	Used by internal parties, such as managers and employees
Types of reports	Classified financial statements prepared according to GAAP	Various non-GAAP reports, such as budgets, performance evaluations, and cost reports
Nature of information	Objective, reliable, historical	Subjective, relevant, future oriented
Frequency of reporting	Prepared periodically (monthly, quarterly, annually)	Prepared as needed, perhaps day-to-day or even in real time
Level of detail	Information reported for the company as a whole	Information reported at the decision-making level (by product, region, customer, or other business segment)

See Exhibit 1.2 for a comparison of the key differences between financial accounting and managerial accounting.

To illustrate these differences, let's return to Tombstone Pizza. For external financial reporting, Kraft Foods combines the Tombstone Pizza subsidiary with other well-known brands, such as DiGiorno pizza, Kraft macaroni and cheese, and Oscar Mayer hot dogs. At the end of the fiscal year, accountants at Kraft Foods prepare the company's annual report, including a consolidated income statement, balance sheet, and statement of cash flows, along with other relevant information and disclosures. These financial statements are audited by an independent public accounting firm, such as PricewaterhouseCoopers LLC. They are publicly available to anyone with an interest in Kraft Foods, including government regulators, financial analysts, and investors who are considering buying or selling stock in the company.

Although financial statements are an extremely important source of information to external decision makers, they probably are not that useful to individual managers responsible for making decisions in Kraft's Tombstone Pizza division. In particular, financial reports tend to be too focused on the past and too general for managerial decision making. Managers often need more detailed information related to their specific responsibilities—information that focuses on what will happen in the future rather than on what happened in the past. For example, a manager who is responsible for new product development must be able to predict, identify, and interpret consumers' ever-changing tastes to develop products that will appeal to consumer preferences.

TYPES OF ORGANIZATIONS

Managerial accounting is used by organizations of all types and sizes: large and small, public and private, profit and nonprofit. Another way to categorize businesses is based on the type of goods or services offered:

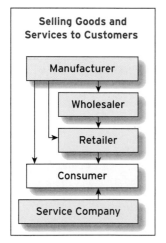

Selling Goods and Services to Customers

- Manufacturer
- Wholesaler
- Retailer
- Consumer
- Service Company

- **Manufacturing firms** purchase raw materials from suppliers and use them to create a finished product. For example, Tombstone Pizza purchases flour, cheese, meat, and other ingredients and uses them to manufacture frozen pizzas. Other well-known manufacturers include Dell computers, Harley Davidson motorcycles, Levi Strauss jeans, and Ford cars and trucks.

- **Merchandising companies** sell the goods that manufacturers produce. Merchandisers that sell exclusively to other businesses are called wholesalers. Merchandisers that sell to the general public are called retailers. For example, Sam's Club initially started out as a wholesaler but eventually became more of a retailer. Other well known retailers include Wal-Mart, Macy's, Bed Bath & Beyond, and Safeway.

- **Service companies** provide a service to customers or clients. Hilton Hotels provides lodging services. Southwest Airlines provides air transportation services. Restaurants such as Outback and Subway provide food services. Other service providers include hair salons, accounting firms, lawyers, architects, and health care providers.

Historically, managerial accounting focused heavily on manufacturing firms. Managerial accounting reports were prepared to keep track of the costs of raw materials, labor, and other costs incurred to produce a physical product.

In today's economy, nonmanufacturing firms are becoming increasingly important. According to recent data from the U.S. Bureau of the Census (2007), the service sector accounts for 55 percent of the U.S. economy. Manufacturers and merchandisers are estimated to account for the remaining 30 percent and 15 percent, respectively. Given these trends, managerial accounting systems must meet the needs of both manufacturing and nonmanufacturing firms.

The first few chapters of this textbook illustrate how to use managerial accounting to determine the cost of manufacturing physical products such as frozen pizza, a custom home, or an automobile. Later chapters illustrate how managers in nonmanufacturing firms such as Starbucks Coffee, Lowe's, Coldstone Creamery, and Blockbuster Inc. use managerial accounting for decision making, planning, control, and performance evaluation.

Managerial accounting information is also vital to nonprofit organizations such as hospitals, universities, and charitable organizations. Although these organizations do not exist to earn a profit, their managers still need managerial accounting information to prepare budgets, manage resources, and make strategic and operational decisions.

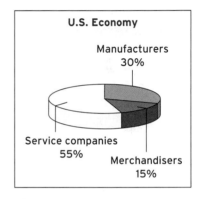

Learning Objective 2
Describe how managerial accounting is used in different types of organizations to support the key functions of management.

FUNCTIONS OF MANAGEMENT

Regardless of the type and size of the organization they manage, all managers perform the same basic functions, which revolve around the functions of planning, organizing, leading/directing, and control. Refer to Exhibit 1.3 for an illustration of this managerial process.

- **Planning** is the future-oriented aspect of the managerial process. It involves setting long-term goals and objectives along with the short-term tactics necessary to achieve them.

- **Organizing** involves arranging for the necessary resources needed to achieve the goals and objectives.

- **Directing/leading** involves putting the plan into action and motivating others to work to make the plan a success.

- **Control** involves comparing actual results to planned results to determine whether the objectives set in the planning stage are being met. If not, managers must take corrective action to adjust the objectives and/or their implementation of the plan.

EXHIBIT 1.3 | Functions of Management

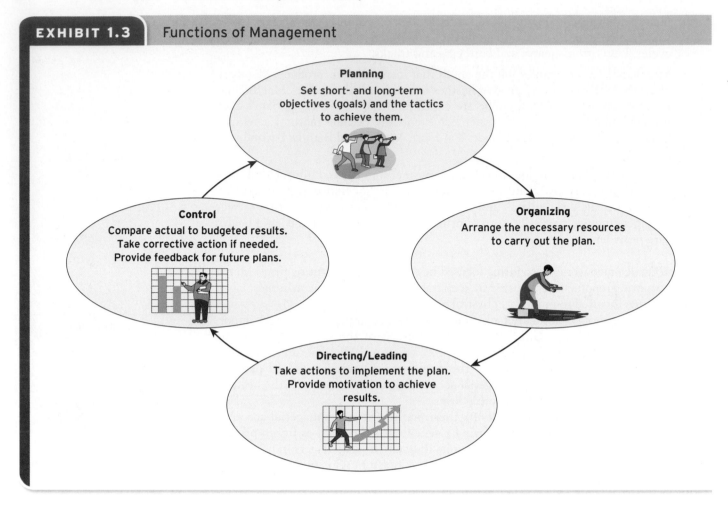

Planning
Set short- and long-term objectives (goals) and the tactics to achieve them.

Organizing
Arrange the necessary resources to carry out the plan.

Directing/Leading
Take actions to implement the plan. Provide motivation to achieve results.

Control
Compare actual to budgeted results. Take corrective action if needed. Provide feedback for future plans.

COACH'S TIP

To grasp the management functions, think about taking a road trip across the country.

Planning involves deciding what route to take and where to stop along the way.

Organizing is making sure you have everything ready for the trip—gas in the car and money in your wallet.

Leading/Directing involves driving the car or instructing someone else where to drive.

Control involves making adjustments for unexpected events along the way, such as detours, road construction, and the like.

To illustrate these functions, assume that managers at Tombstone Pizza want to introduce a new low-calorie pizza with a whole wheat crust to appeal to health-conscious consumers.

The **planning** process lays out what managers hope to achieve by introducing the new product. Managers should state the plan in terms of specific and measurable objectives such as sales volume, market share, or profitability over the product's life cycle. Once these objectives have been set, managers must identify the tactics they plan to use to achieve those objectives, including the details of how to develop, test, produce, market, distribute, and sell the new product.

The **organizing** process involves making sure the company has the necessary resources to achieve the plan. A key part of the organizing process is the development of a **budget** that details how much time and money the company will spend on the various phases of the product development cycle, including research and development, testing, production, marketing, and distribution. Managers might also offer bonuses for meeting project deadlines and staying within budget in each phase of the new product's development and introduction.

Leading/directing occurs when managers actually begin to implement the plan. Here managers must make all of the detailed actions to implement the plan, including buying raw materials, hiring workers, purchasing new equipment, and the like. They might also provide incentives to motivate the sales force to sell the new whole wheat pizza as well as negotiate with retailers for shelf space for the product.

Control involves measuring and monitoring actual results to see whether the objectives set in the planning stage are being met. For example, if managers determined that sales of Tombstone's whole wheat pizza are falling short of expectations, they might decide to spend more money on marketing to advertise the new product's health benefits.

As you can see, the managerial functions of planning, organizing, directing, and control are interconnected. One function feeds into another, and feedback from the process is used to improve future decision making. Throughout, managers must make a variety of decisions, and they need relevant, up-to-date information including cost estimates, competitor pricing, market demand, and consumer preferences. Much of the information managers need to make these decisions comes from the managerial accounting system. You can think of managerial accounting as the provider of information to aid management decisions.

Before we move on, take the following Self-Study Practice to make sure you understand the key differences between financial and managerial accounting as well as the key functions of management.

 Self-Study Practice

1. Which of the following statements best describes the difference between financial accounting and managerial accounting?
   a. Managerial accounting is targeted at external stakeholders while financial accounting is targeted at individuals within the company.
   b. Financial accounting relies more on subjective, future-oriented information than managerial accounting does.
   c. The major focus of managerial accounting is the preparation of the income statement, balance sheet, and statement of cash flows.
   d. Managerial accounting tends to focus on relevant, subjective, and future-oriented information while financial accounting relies primarily on objective, reliable, and historical information.

2. Which of the following statement(s) regarding the key management functions is (are) false? (You may select more than one answer.)
   a. Planning involves setting both long-term objectives and the short-term tactics necessary to achieve those objectives.
   b. Directing/leading involves comparing actual results to planned objectives and making any adjustments as necessary.
   c. Each of the management functions (planning, organizing, leading/directing, and control) is completely independent of the others.
   d. All of the above.

After you have finished, check your answers with the solutions in the margin.

COACH'S TIP

The best way to know whether you are reading the chapter carefully enough is to see how well you do on a short exercise. Therefore, at important points throughout each chapter, you will find an exercise that will reinforce the concepts you have just learned and provide feedback on how well you learned them. We urge you not to skip these practices.

Solution to Self-Study Practice
1. d
2. b and c. (Item b describes control, not leading/directing. Item c is false because the management functions are interdependent.)

ETHICS AND INTERNAL REPORTING

In addition to the managerial functions described in the previous section, managers are increasingly being held responsible for creating and maintaining an ethical work environment, including the reporting of accounting information. **Ethics** refers to the standards of conduct for judging right from wrong, honest from dishonest, and fair from unfair. Although some accounting and business issues have clear answers that are either right or wrong, many situations require accountants and managers to weigh the pros and cons of alternatives before making final decisions.

Spotlight On ETHICS

Accounting Scandals

Accounting scandals are driven by the fear of personal failure and greed. Initially, some people may appear to benefit from fraudulent reporting. In the long run, however, fraud harms most individuals and organizations. When it is uncovered, the corporation's stock price drops dramatically. In the case involving MicroStrategy, the stock price dropped 65 percent from $243 to $86 per share in a single day of trading. Creditors are also harmed by fraud. WorldCom's creditors recovered only 42 percent of what they were owed. They lost $36 billion. Innocent employees also are harmed by fraud. At Enron, 5,600 employees lost their jobs, and many lost all of their retirement savings.

Learning Objective 3
Explain the role of ethics in managerial decision making and the effects of the Sarbanes-Oxley Act.

COACH'S TIP

Internal controls are designed to protect assets from loss and ensure the accuracy of the accounting records. Controls you have seen include the security tags on clothing and the use of a bank to keep cash safe.

Unfortunately, the reputation of business managers and accountants has been tarnished in recent years due to high-profile scandals such as those at Enron and WorldCom. In response to these scandals, Congress enacted the **Sarbanes-Oxley (SOX) Act of 2002**. Although SOX was primarily aimed at renewing investor confidence in the external financial reporting system, it has many implications for managers.

The Sarbanes-Oxley Act focuses on three factors that affect the accounting reporting environment: O (opportunity), I (incentives), and C (character), as shown in Exhibit 1.4

Opportunities for Error and Fraud

SOX attempts to reduce the opportunity (O) for error and fraud. A new requirement under SOX is that management must conduct a review of the company's internal control system and issue a report that indicates whether the controls are effective at preventing errors and fraud. This requirement places more responsibility on all managers (not just accountants) for the accuracy of the reporting system. For example, marketing managers are now responsible for making sure their staff members submit accurate sales and expense reports. SOX also places additional responsibilities on the boards of directors and external auditors to reduce the opportunity for errors and fraud.

Incentives for Committing Fraud

SOX attempts to counteract the incentive (I) to commit fraud by providing much stiffer penalties in terms of monetary fines and jail time. For example, violators must repay any money obtained via fraud and can be assessed additional fines of up to $5 million. Executives cannot avoid these penalties by declaring personal bankruptcy, which explains why

---

EXHIBIT 1.4	**Significant Changes Introduced by the Sarbanes-Oxley Act of 2002**

Reduce opportunity (O) for error and fraud
- Internal control report from management
- Stronger oversight by directors
- Internal control audit by external auditors

Encourage good character (C)
- Anonymous tip lines
- Whistle-blower protection
- Code of ethics

Counteract incentives (I) for fraud
- Stiffer fines and prison terms

a former sales director at Computer Associates will be giving 15 percent of every paycheck he earns for the rest of his life to a fraud restitution fund. SOX also increased the maximum jail sentence for fraudulent reporting to 20 years. The jail time can add up because federal sentencing guidelines allow judges to declare consecutive jail terms for each violation.

Character of Managers and Employees

Finally, SOX emphasizes the importance of the character (C) of managers and employees. Admittedly, it is difficult for a law to make people act appropriately, but SOX introduces new rules that should help employees of good character make the right decision when confronted with ethical dilemmas. For example, audit committees are now required to create tip lines that allow employees to secretly submit concerns they may have about suspicious accounting or auditing practices. SOX also gives federal employee "whistle-blowers" protection from retaliation by those charged with fraud.

Finally, to reinforce good character, public companies must adopt a code of ethics for senior financial officers. Unfortunately, simply adopting a code of ethics does not ensure that managers will act ethically. Most experts agree that ethics must be embedded in the organizational culture and that top managers who "lead by example" will drive the ethical behavior in the organization.

According to a recent Statement on Management Accounting (SMA) released by the Institute of Management Accountants (IMA), companies with strong ethical cultures are rewarded with higher productivity, improved team dynamics, lower risks of fraud, streamlined processes, improved product quality, and higher customer satisfaction. But to achieve these rewards, companies must move beyond simply complying with laws such as SOX to create a culture in which ethics is embedded throughout the organization.

In the next section, we discuss the role of cost information in managerial decision making. But first take a moment to complete the following Self-Study Practice to make sure you can identify factors that influence ethical behavior.

 Self-Study Practice

Identify whether each of the following actions is most likely to increase (+) or decrease (−) the risk of error or fraud arising from opportunities (O), incentives (I), or an individual's character (C).

	+/ −	I/O/C
1. Enron implemented a "rank-and-yank" practice that involved ranking the financial performance of each business unit and then firing managers in the lowest 20 percent.	_____	_____
2. Microsoft Corporation invites anonymous or confidential submission of questionable accounting or auditing matters to msft.buscond@alertline.com.	_____	_____
3. The H. J. Heinz Company's board of directors is one of the strongest boards in the United States, according to Institutional Shareholder Services.	_____	_____

After you have finished, check your answers with the solutions in the margin.

Role of Cost in Managerial Accounting

Video 1-2
www.mhhe.com/whitecotton1e

As described earlier in this chapter, the goal of managerial accounting is to help managers make decisions as they perform the functions of planning, organizing, leading/directing, and control. As shown in Exhibit 1.5, three areas of managerial accounting support this overarching objective and provide a road map or structure of the remaining chapters in this book.

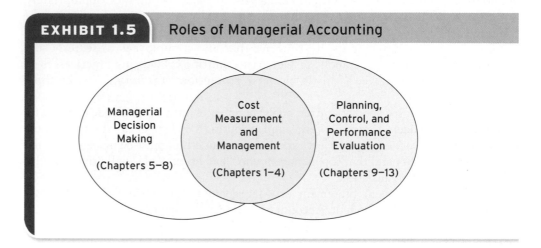

EXHIBIT 1.5	Roles of Managerial Accounting

Managerial Decision Making (Chapters 5–8)

Cost Measurement and Management (Chapters 1–4)

Planning, Control, and Performance Evaluation (Chapters 9–13)

We start in the center of the diagram with cost measurement and management. Cost accounting is a small but important part of managerial accounting. Managers need cost information to make many decisions. For example, a marketing manager at Tombstone Pizza might need to know how much it costs to make the pizza to determine the appropriate price. A production manager might need to know the cost of a specific component such as dough or sauce in order to decide whether to make it in-house or buy it from a supplier. Managers also need cost information to prepare budgets, which are an important part of the planning and control cycle.

The first four chapters of this book focus on alternative ways to measure the cost of various products, services, and customers. But measuring cost is only the first step. The ultimate goal is to provide information to help managers **manage** or control costs, make decisions, and plan for the future.

Chapters 5–8 illustrate how managers can use cost and other information to make decisions. The cost data often provide a starting point for evaluating the decision alternatives, but managers need to bring many other factors into their decision process, including strategic considerations, quality issues, environmental concerns, ethical and legal concerns, and the like.

The final chapters of the book introduce the use of accounting information for planning, control, and performance evaluation. Again, although cost information provides much of the foundation for these functions, it is only one piece of the puzzle. Increasingly, managers are being evaluated and rewarded based on nonfinancial measures of performance, such as employee productivity, product quality, customer satisfaction, innovation, learning, and growth.

Even so, cost control remains a critical concern for most organizations. As such, the next section defines cost and discusses alternative ways to categorize or classify cost based on different objectives or purposes.

DEFINITION OF COST

Learning Objective 4
Define and give examples of different types of cost.

When you incur a cost, you give up one thing, such as money or time, in exchange for something else. **Cost** is the value given up during this exchange. Determining what something costs is fairly straightforward if you are paying cash or credit for an item. It is a lot trickier when you are giving up something of less obvious value, such as your time, your services, or your expertise. In this section, we classify and define various types of costs including those that are stated routinely in dollars and cents and those that are not.

OUT-OF-POCKET VERSUS OPPORTUNITY COSTS

Out-of-pocket costs involve an actual outlay of cash. In your personal life, these are costs you pay "out of your pocket" for things such as food, clothing, and entertainment. For Tombstone Pizza, it would include payments for items such as rent, wages, utilities, advertising, and insurance.

Unlike an out-of-pocket cost that involves an outlay of cash, an **opportunity cost** is the cost of **not** doing something. In other words, it is the forgone benefit (or lost opportunity) of the path not taken. Anytime you choose to do one thing instead of another because of a limit on your time or money, you incur an opportunity cost. For example, if you are going to school full-time, you are giving up the opportunity to earn money by working full-time. The potential earnings you give up to go to school are an opportunity cost of pursuing your education.

Similarly, business managers incur opportunity costs any time they are forced to choose one alternative over another because of limited resources, such as cash, equipment, or space. If Tombstone Pizza has a limited number of ovens in which to bake its various pizza products, managers may need to reduce production of an existing pizza product in order to produce the new whole wheat pizza. If so, the value of the lost sales from the existing product should be treated as an opportunity cost of introducing the new whole wheat pizza.

Spotlight On DECISION MAKING

Should You Continue Your Education?

You have obviously made the decision to further your education by taking this class. At some point in the future, you may even think of getting an advanced degree, such as an MBA, law degree, or medical degree.

The decision to pursue a degree is a very important one that should consider both the costs and benefits. As you know, the costs of education, including tuition, fees, and books, are very high. You also incur opportunity costs when you forgo working to go to school. These costs must be offset by the future career opportunities (and higher salary) the degree will bring.

If you ever consider getting an MBA, Forbes has an online decision tool that can help you weigh the costs and benefits of the advanced degree.* This tool estimates the five-year gain from getting an MBA as the difference between the salary and bonuses you would expect to earn in the five years after graduation minus the tuition and potential earnings you would give up while getting your MBA. Because these costs and benefits occur across a number of years, the online tool factors in the time value of money, or the opportunity cost of giving up cash today to earn cash at some point in the future.

This same approach can be applied to almost any decision so long as you can estimate the future costs and benefits of the particular decision you are trying to make.

———
*http://www.forbes.com/2005/08/16/cz_05mba_business_schools_gain_calulator.html

DIRECT VERSUS INDIRECT COSTS

When managers use cost information, they typically need to know the cost of something specific, whether it is a specific unit of product (such as a 16-inch pizza), a particular component of the product (such as the pizza dough), or an area or division in the company (such as the baking department). The item for which managers are trying to determine cost is the **cost object**.

Costs that can be traced directly to a specific cost object are **direct costs**. Costs that cannot be traced to a specific cost object, or that are not worth the effort of tracing, are **indirect costs**. Assume, for example, you want to know the cost of taking a specific course, such as this accounting course. Some costs, such as those for tuition

 **COACH'S TIP**

Whether a cost is treated as direct or indirect depends on whether tracing it is both **possible** and **feasible**. Some minor costs, such as the cost of glue or other supplies, may not be worth the effort needed to trace to individual products. These costs are classified as **indirect costs**.

EXHIBIT 1.6   Real-World Examples of Direct versus Indirect Costs

Company	Cost Object	Direct Costs	Indirect Costs
Supercuts Hair Salons	Individual haircut and style	Stylist's time	Styling products, receptionist's service, depreciation on salon equipment
Federal Express	Package delivered	Packaging materials (envelopes, etc.)	Planes, delivery personnel
GAP	Pair of blue jeans	Cost of the jeans, commissions paid to salesperson	Store supervision, rent, and inventory control
Dell Computer	Personal computer	Cost of the components, wages of workers who assembled the computer, and delivery costs	Production supervision, factory space, and quality control

and books, can be traced directly to the course, so they would be considered direct costs. If you are taking multiple courses, some costs may not be directly traceable to a single course. Examples would be the cost of traveling to and from campus, the cost of your personal computer, and the supplies you use in class. These costs would be considered indirect costs.

For Tombstone Pizza, direct costs would include the costs of materials and labor that can be traced directly to each pizza produced. Indirect costs would include items such as depreciation on the ovens used to bake the pizzas as well as the costs of utilities, advertising, and plant supervision. See Exhibit 1.6 for examples of direct and indirect costs at other real-world companies.

VARIABLE VERSUS FIXED COSTS

For internal decision making, managers are often interested in how costs will change with a change in activity level, such as the number of units produced or sold. **Variable costs** are those that change, in total, in direct proportion to changes in activity levels. For example, if Tombstone Pizza were to increase production of pizzas by 20 percent, certain costs, such as direct materials and the power required to run the ovens, would increase proportionally.

COACH'S TIP

In deciding whether a cost is variable or fixed, be sure to think about whether the **total cost** will change. Looking at average or unit cost will reveal an entirely different pattern, which we examine more closely in Chapter 5.

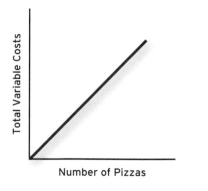

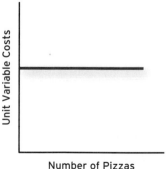

Although **total** variable costs vary in direct proportion to changes in activity, **unit** variable costs remain the same. For example, the cost of dough used to make one pizza should be the same regardless of the number of pizzas produced. This ignores other factors that drive down unit variable costs such as discounts for buying ingredients in bulk.

Fixed costs are those that stay the same, in total, regardless of activity level, at least within some range of activity. Examples of fixed costs for Tombstone Pizza include rent on the factory, depreciation of equipment, factory supervision, and insurance. These costs remain the same, in total, regardless of the number of units produced.

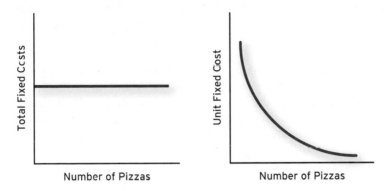

Although **total** fixed costs remain the same, **unit** fixed costs vary inversely with the number of units produced. This is simply due to the fact that the same amount of fixed cost is being spread over more units, which drives down the cost per unit.

In the real world, many costs have both fixed and variable properties. These more complex costs will be covered in Chapter 5.

Spotlight On DECISION MAKING

The Need to Understand Fixed and Variable Costs

Assume you are the treasurer of a student club at your university and you are on the planning committee for the end-of-year social event. The committee is in charge of finding a location, renting tables and chairs, and hiring a DJ, photographer, and caterer for the event. Your responsibility as treasurer is to set the budget for the event and make sure the committee stays within that budget. One of the first questions you ask is how many people are likely to attend the event.

Which costs would you expect to vary with the number of people attending? Which costs will be the same regardless of how many people attend the event? Why is it important for you to know the answers to these questions? Check the Coach's Tip for answers to these questions.

Managers must answer similar questions when making business decisions. They need to understand which costs will vary with the number of units produced or the number of customers served and which will be incurred regardless of these factors.

RELEVANT VERSUS IRRELEVANT COSTS

Often managers are interested only in those costs that are relevant to a particular decision. A **relevant cost** is one that has the potential to influence a decision; an **irrelevant cost** is one that will not influence a decision. For a cost to be relevant, it must meet both of the following criteria:

- It must differ between the decision alternatives.
- It must be incurred in the future rather than in the past.

The first criterion means that the cost must change depending on the choice the manager makes. Costs that differ between decision alternatives are also called **differential costs**. The second criterion, that the cost must be incurred in the future, eliminates costs that have already been incurred or **sunk costs**. Because those costs have already been paid for (that is, they are sunk), they will not change depending on the manager's decision. Therefore, they are not relevant to future decisions.

COACH'S TIP

When planning a social event, the cost of the venue, DJ, and photographer will be incurred regardless of how many people attend the event.

The cost of catering (food and drinks), tables, and chairs will vary with the number of people who are expected to attend.

You need to understand these relationships to prepare a budget for the event because the total cost will depend on the number of guests.

Assume, for example, you are thinking of selling your old car and buying a new one. Is the amount you paid for your old car a relevant cost? The answer is no; it is a sunk cost that will not change regardless of what you do in the future. However, the amount of money you can get for your old car now (its current value) and the cost of the new car are relevant to your decision. Any difference in fuel costs and insurance for the old and the new cars are also relevant. What about the parking fee you pay each semester: Is that a relevant cost? The answer is no because you will have to pay for parking no matter which car you drive.

Now assume that you are thinking of getting rid of your car altogether and either riding a bike or relying on public transportation. Is the cost of on-campus parking relevant to that decision? In this case, the cost is relevant because it will change depending on whether or not you own a car. In Chapter 7, we rely heavily on this concept of relevant versus irrelevant costs to analyze a variety of managerial decisions.

MANUFACTURING VERSUS NONMANUFACTURING COSTS

Another important distinction is whether costs are related to manufacturing or nonmanufacturing activities. This distinction is important only in companies that make a physical product, such as Apple (iPods), Toyota (cars and trucks), Harley Davidson (motorcycles), and Maytag (appliances). Service companies and merchandisers do not make this distinction.

Manufacturing costs include all costs incurred to produce a physical product. They are generally classified into one of three categories:

> Prime Cost =
>
> Direct Materials
> +
> Direct Labor

> Conversion Cost =
>
> Direct Labor
> +
> Manufacturing Overhead

- **Direct materials** are the major material inputs that can be physically and conveniently traced to the product. For Tombstone Pizza, direct materials would include the major ingredients (dough, sauce, cheese, and meat), as well as packaging materials (plastic and cardboard). This category would not include minor materials that cannot be conveniently traced to individual units (such as seasoning and glue).

- **Direct labor** is the cost of labor that can be conveniently traced to the physical product. This category includes all **hands-on labor** associated with making the physical product. It would not include the labor of those who do not touch the physical product, such as supervisors, maintenance workers, and engineers.

- **Manufacturing overhead** includes all manufacturing costs **other than direct materials and direct labor** that must be incurred to manufacture a physical product. For Tombstone Pizza, examples would include rent, insurance, utilities, and supervision at the manufacturing facility. Costs that are not related to manufacturing (such as distribution or marketing costs) are not included in manufacturing overhead.

Taken together, direct materials and direct labor are referred to as **prime costs** because they represent the primary costs that can be traced to the end product. Direct labor and manufacturing overhead are referred to as **conversion cost**, or the total cost required to convert direct materials into a finished product.

Nonmanufacturing costs are the costs associated with running the business and selling the product as opposed to manufacturing the product. They are generally classified into two groups:

- **Marketing or Selling expenses** are incurred to get the final product to the customer. For Tombstone Pizza, examples include the depreciation on trucks that deliver the pizzas to supermarkets, sales managers' salaries, and advertising costs.

- **General and Administrative expenses** are associated with running the overall organization. They include general management salaries, rent and utilities for corporate headquarters, and corporate service functions such as the accounting, payroll, and legal departments.

PRODUCT VERSUS PERIOD COSTS

The distinction between product and period costs is closely tied to the distinction between manufacturing and nonmanufacturing costs. This terminology has to do with **when** the cost will be matched up against revenue on the income statement (for external financial reporting).

For external reporting, GAAP requires that all manufacturing costs be treated as **product costs**, or costs that are attached to the product as it is being produced. Product costs are sometimes called **inventoriable costs** because they are initially counted as part of the cost of inventory and are not expensed until the inventory is sold. In contrast, **period costs** are never counted as inventory but are expensed during the period they are incurred. Refer to Exhibit 1.7 for an illustration of the different treatment of product and period costs under GAAP.

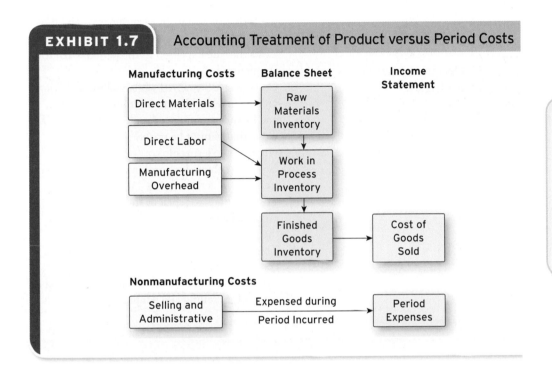

EXHIBIT 1.7 | Accounting Treatment of Product versus Period Costs

COACH'S TIP

The distinction between period and product costs is a matter of **when** the cost is matched against revenue on the income statement. Period costs are expensed as soon as they are incurred. Product costs are recorded initially as inventory and do not appear on the income statement until the product is sold.

Product costs follow the flow of the physical product as it moves through the manufacturing process. As the product is being manufactured, the manufacturing costs are recorded as Raw Materials Inventory or Work in Process Inventory. Once the product is completed (but not sold), the manufacturing costs are transferred out of Work in Process Inventory and into Finished Goods Inventory. All product costs remain on the balance sheet until the product is sold, at which point they are reported as Cost of Goods Sold and matched up against sales on the income statement.

Nonmanufacturing costs do not relate specifically to the product that is being manufactured, and so they are expensed during the period incurred. Note that these rules apply only to external financial reporting (GAAP). For internal purposes, we can use other rules for deciding which costs to trace to specific products and services.

The next chapter provides a detailed description of how the manufacturing costs are recorded and flow through the various inventory accounts and eventually into Cost of Goods Sold and the income statement. For now, you just need to understand the basic cost terminology and definitions.

Before continuing, take the following Self-Study Practice to see how well you understand this terminology.

Self-Study Practice

Match the appropriate description on the right to the terms on the left.

_____ 1. Cost
_____ 2. Product costs
_____ 3. Period costs
_____ 4. Manufacturing costs
_____ 5. Nonmanufacturing costs
_____ 6. Variable costs
_____ 7. Fixed costs
_____ 8. Direct costs
_____ 9. Indirect costs
_____ 10. Out-of-pocket costs
_____ 11. Opportunity cost
_____ 12. Sunk costs

A. Costs that remain the same in total regardless of activity level

B. Costs that involve an outlay of cash for items such as rent, utilities, and salaries

C. The benefit that you forgo when you select one alternative over another

D. Costs that can be traced conveniently and physically to a specific cost object

E. Costs that have already been incurred and thus are not relevant to future decisions

F. Costs that are expensed in the period when they are incurred

G. Costs that are incurred while making a physical product, such as direct materials, direct labor, and manufacturing overhead

H. Costs that cannot be traced conveniently or physically to a specific cost object

I. Costs that change in total in direct proportion to a change in activity level

J. Costs that are attached to the product being produced and are included in inventory until the product is sold

K. The value that is given up in an exchange of goods or services

L. Costs that are not related to producing a product, such as selling and administrative costs

After you have finished, check your answers with the solutions in the margin.

Solution to Self-Study Practice

1. K
2. J
3. F
4. G
5. L
6. I
7. A
8. D
9. H
10. B
11. C
12. E

DEMONSTRATION CASE

Barnaby's Bicycle Company manufactures high-quality mountain bikes. The company's managerial accountant has come to you for help. She needs to classify and identify each of the following costs before she can calculate the cost to produce each mountain bike.

Classify each of the costs listed on the following chart into three categories based on the following questions.

1. Can this cost be directly and conveniently traced to each bicycle that is manufactured, or is doing so either not possible or not worth the effort?

2. Is this cost related to manufacturing the bicycles? If so, what type of cost is it? Or is it a non-manufacturing or period expense?

3. Will the total cost vary with the number of bicycles manufactured or sold, or will it remain the same regardless of how many bikes are produced and sold?

The first item in the chart is completed as an example.

| | QUESTION 1 | | QUESTION 2 | | | | QUESTION 3 | |
| | | | PRODUCT COSTS | | | PERIOD COSTS | COST BEHAVIOR | |
	Direct Cost	Indirect Cost	Direct Materials	Direct Labor	Mfg. Overhead	Nonmfg. Expenses	Variable Cost	Fixed Cost
Alloy tubing used to make the bicycle frames	X		X				X	
Hourly wages paid to employees who cut and weld the alloy tubing								
Factory rent								
Bicycle wheels and tires								
Miscellaneous bicycle components								
Insurance on the factory								
Insurance on the president's company car								

See page 21 for solution.

CHAPTER SUMMARY

Describe the key differences between financial accounting and managerial accounting. p. 5   LO1

- Financial accounting is used by external stakeholders, such as investors, creditors, and bankers.

- Managerial accounting is used by managers inside the organization.

- Other differences:
  - Financial accounting information tends to be reliable, objective, and historical in nature.
  - Managerial accounting information tends to be relevant, timely, and future oriented.
  - Financial accounting is reported through the income statement, balance sheet, and cash flow statement.
  - Managerial accounting relies on a variety of reports targeted at specific decisions, including budgets, cost reports, and performance evaluations.
  - Financial accounting reports are prepared on a monthly, quarterly, or annual basis.
  - Managerial accounting reports are prepared as needed.
  - Financial accounting reports are prepared at the company level.
  - Managerial accounting reports are prepared at the divisional or departmental level appropriate to the decision being made.

Describe how managerial accounting is used in different types of organizations to support the key functions of management, p. 7   LO2

- Managerial accounting is used in all types of organizations, including manufacturing, merchandising, and service firms.

- Although managerial accounting often focuses on manufacturing firms, it is becoming increasingly important for service companies and merchandisers, which are gaining importance in today's economy. It is also useful for nonprofit organizations such as universities, charities, and hospitals.

- Regardless of the type of organization, all managers perform the same basic functions:
  - Planning, or the process of setting long-term objectives along with the short-term tactics needed to achieve those objectives.
  - Organizing, or gathering the necessary resources to carry out the plan.
  - Directing/Leading, or putting the plan into action.
  - Control, or monitoring actual results against the plan and making any necessary adjustments.

LO3   Explain the role of ethics in managerial decision making and the effects of the Sarbanes-Oxley Act. p. 10

- Ethics refers to the standards for judging right from wrong, honest from dishonest, and fair from unfair. Managers confront ethical dilemmas that do not have clear-cut answers. Managers must apply their own personal judgment and values to weigh the pros and cons of alternative courses of action.

- The Sarbanes-Oxley (SOX) Act of 2002 increases managers' responsibility for creating and maintaining an ethical business and reporting environment. It attempts to reduce fraudulent reporting in three key ways:
  - **Opportunity.** SOX requires managers to issue a report that indicates whether the company's internal controls are effective in preventing fraud and inaccurate reporting. The act also places increased responsibility on the Board of Directors, audit committee, and external auditor.
  - **Incentives.** SOX imposes stiffer penalties, including jail time and monetary fines, for those who commit fraud.
  - **Character.** SOX emphasizes the importance of individual character in preventing fraudulent reporting and requires public companies to implement anonymous tip lines, whistle-blower protection, and codes of ethics.

- Creating an ethical business environment requires more than compliance with SOX and the creation of a corporate code of ethics. To be truly effective, ethics and values must be embedded throughout the organizational culture from top management on down.

LO4   Define and give examples of different types of costs. p. 12

- When you incur a cost, you give up something of value in exchange for something else.

- Costs can be classified in a variety of ways:
  - Out-of-pocket costs require a cash outlay.
  - Opportunity costs are the benefits you give up when you choose one alternative over another.
  - Direct costs can be traced directly to a specific cost object.
  - Indirect costs either cannot be traced to a specific cost object or are not worth the effort to do so.
  - Variable costs change in direct proportion to changes in the level of activity.
  - Fixed costs remain the same in total regardless of the level of activity.
  - Relevant costs are those that differ between alternatives.
  - Irrelevant costs are those that remain the same regardless of the alternatives and thus will not affect the decision.
  - Manufacturing costs are associated with making a physical product.
  - Nonmanufacturing costs are associated with selling a product or service or running the overall business.
  - GAAP requires manufacturing costs to be treated as product costs and nonmanufacturing costs to be expensed as period costs.
  - Product costs are assigned to a product as it is being produced; they accumulate in inventory accounts until the product is sold.
  - Period costs are reported as expenses as they are incurred.

SOLUTION TO DEMONSTRATION CASE

| | QUESTION 1 | | QUESTION 2 | | | | QUESTION 3 | |
| | | | PRODUCT COSTS | | | PERIOD COSTS | COST BEHAVIOR | |
	Direct Cost	Indirect Cost	Direct Materials	Direct Labor	Mfg. Overhead	Nonmfg. Expenses	Variable Cost	Fixed Cost
Alloy tubing used to make the bicycle frames	X		X				X	
Wages paid to employees who cut and weld the alloy tubing	X			X			X	
Factory rent		X			X			X
Bicycle wheels and tires	X		X				X	
Miscellaneous bicycle components		X			X		X	
Insurance on the factory		X			X			X
Insurance on the president's company car		X				X		X

KEY TERMS

Budget (p. 8)
Control (p. 7)
Conversion Cost (p. 16)
Cost (p. 12)
Cost Object (p. 13)
Differential Cost (p. 15)
Direct Costs (p. 13)
Directing/Leading (p. 7)
Direct Labor (p. 16)
Direct Materials (p. 16)
Ethics (p. 9)
Financial Accounting (p. 5)
Fixed Costs (p. 15)

General and Administrative Expenses (p. 16)
Indirect Costs (p. 13)
Inventoriable Cost (p. 17)
Irrelevant Cost (p. 15)
Managerial Accounting (p. 5)
Manufacturing Costs (p. 16)
Manufacturing Firm (p. 6)
Manufacturing Overhead (p. 16)
Marketing or Selling Expenses (p. 16)
Merchandising Company (p. 7)
Nonmanufacturing Costs (p. 16)

Opportunity Cost (p. 13)
Organizing (p. 7)
Out-of-Pocket Cost (p. 13)
Period Cost (p. 17)
Planning (p. 7)
Prime Cost (p. 16)
Product Cost (p. 17)
Relevant Cost (p. 15)
Sarbanes-Oxley (SOX) Act of 2002 (p. 10)
Service Company (p. 7)
Sunk Cost (p. 15)
Variable Cost (p. 14)

See complete definitions in glossary at back of text.

QUESTIONS

1. What is the primary difference between financial accounting and managerial accounting?

2. Explain how the primary difference between financial and managerial accounting results in other differences between the two.

3. Why are traditional, GAAP-based financial statements not necessarily useful to managers and other internal parties?

4. Explain the difference between service companies, merchandising companies, and manufacturing companies.

5. Consider the area within a 3-mile radius of your campus. What service companies, merchandising companies, and manufacturing firms are located within that area?

6. What are the four basic functions of management?

7. How are the four basic management functions interrelated?

8. What are ethics and why is ethical behavior important to managers?

9. What events or factors led to the creation and enactment of the Sarbanes-Oxley Act of 2002?

10. How did the Sarbanes-Oxley Act affect managers' responsibility for creating and maintaining an ethical business and reporting environment?

11. How did the Sarbanes-Oxley Act attempt to reduce fraudulent reporting by addressing opportunity, incentives, and character?

12. According to a recent Statement on Management Accounting (SMA), what are some of the potential benefits of a strong ethical business climate?

13. Think about your activities over the last week. Identify two exchanges or transactions for which the cost incurred would be measured in dollars and two that would were nonmonetary.

14. Think about all of the choices you make on a day-to-day basis: everything from driving versus riding a bike to school or deciding where to have lunch. Pick three decisions you have made today. Identify an out-of-pocket and opportunity cost for each decision.

15. Why is it important for managers to be able to determine the cost of a particular item? Name one decision that a company might make using cost information.

16. Explain the difference between a direct cost and an indirect cost. Look at the pen or pencil you are using to do your homework. Give an example of a direct cost that went into making that pen or pencil and an indirect cost of making it.

17. Explain the difference between fixed and variable costs. Give an example of a cost that varies with the number of miles you drive your car each week and an example of a cost that is fixed regardless of how many miles you drive your car each week.

18. Explain the difference between relevant and irrelevant costs. What are the two criteria used to determine whether a cost is relevant?

19. Suppose you and your friends are planning a trip for spring break. You have narrowed the destination choices to Panama City, Florida, and Galveston Bay, Texas. List three relevant costs for this decision. List two costs that are irrelevant to this decision.

20. What are prime costs? How are they different than other manufacturing costs?

21. What types of costs are included in manufacturing overhead? Other than direct materials and direct labor, what costs would *not* be included in manufacturing overhead?

22. Why can't prime cost and conversion cost be added together to arrive at total manufacturing cost?

23. What is the difference between product and period costs in terms of how and when they are treated in the financial statements (balance sheet and income statement)?

24. Explain why product costs are also called *inventoriable costs* and how those costs move through a company's financial statements.

25. What triggers the movement of product costs from an asset on the balance sheet to an expense on the income statement?

26. If you wanted to know the total amount of period costs for a company, which financial statement(s) would you consult?

27. Suppose a company accountant incorrectly classified advertising costs as a product cost. What impact would this have on the company's financial statements?

MULTIPLE CHOICE

1. The **primary** difference between financial accounting and managerial accounting is that

   Quiz 1
   www.mhhe.com/whitecotton1e

   a. Financial accounting is used by internal parties while managerial accounting is used by external parties.
   b. Financial accounting is future oriented while managerial accounting is historical in nature.
   c. Financial accounting is used by external parties while managerial accounting is used by internal parties.
   d. Financial accounting is prepared as needed (perhaps even daily), but managerial accounting is prepared periodically (monthly, quarterly, annually).

2. Which of the following companies is most likely to be considered a manufacturing company:

   a. Burger King.   c. Supercuts.
   b. Abercrombie and Fitch.   d. Maytag.

3. Which of the four functions of management involves monitoring actual results to see whether the objectives set in the planning stage are being met and, if necessary, taking corrective action to adjust the objectives or implementation of the plan?

   a. Directing.   c. Planning.
   b. Control.   d. Organizing.

4. Suppose you have decided that you would like to purchase a new home in five years. To do this, you will need a down payment of approximately $20,000, which means that you need to save $350 each month for the next five years. This is an example of

   a. Directing.   c. Planning.
   b. Control.   d. Organizing.

5. If the number of units produced increases,

   a. Unit variable costs will increase.
   b. Unit fixed costs will decrease.
   c. Total variable costs will remain the same.
   d. Total fixed costs will increase.

Use the following information regarding Garcia Company for questions 6–8.

Factory rent	$5,000
Direct labor	8,000
Indirect materials	1,000
Direct materials used	3,500
Sales commissions	2,500
Factory manager's salary	4,000
Advertising	1,500

6. What is Garcia's total manufacturing cost?

   a. $25,500.   c. $21,500.
   b. $24,000.   d. $10,000.

7. What is Garcia's prime cost?

   a. $11,500.   c. $15,500.
   b. $12,500.   d. $21,000.

8. What is Garcia's manufacturing overhead?

   a. $24,000.   c. $14,000.
   b. $12,500.   d. $10,000.

9. Suppose you are trying to decide whether to sell your accounting book at the end of the semester or keep it for a reference book in future courses. If you decide to keep the book, the money you would have received from selling it is a(n)

   a. Sunk cost.
   b. Opportunity cost.
   c. Out-of-pocket cost.
   d. Indirect cost.

10. Which of the following would *not* be treated as a product cost under GAAP?

   a. Direct materials.
   b. Manufacturing supervisor's salary.
   c. Sales commissions.
   d. All of the above are product costs.

> Answers to Multiple-Choice Questions located in back of the text.

MINI EXERCISES

M1-1 Comparing Financial and Managerial Accounting   **L01**

Match each of the following characteristics that describe **financial** accounting, **managerial** accounting, **both** financial and managerial accounting, or **neither** financial nor managerial accounting.

_____ 1. Is future oriented.

_____ 2. Is used primarily by external parties.

_____ 3. Is relied on for making decisions.

_____ 4. Is historical in nature.

_____ 5. Reports can be obtained through the company Web site or requested from the company CFO for publicly traded companies.

_____ 6. Is reported in aggregate for the company as a whole.

_____ 7. Reports may be reported daily or even in real time.

_____ 8. Is used mostly by managers within the company.

_____ 9. Must be accurate to help decision makers.

_____ 10. Is always available on the Internet to any interested party.

A. Financial accounting

B. Managerial accounting

C. Both financial and managerial accounting

D. Neither financial nor managerial accounting

M1-2 Identifying Management Functions   **L02**

You were recently hired as a production manager for Medallion Company. You just received a memo regarding a company meeting being held this week. The memo stated that one topic of discussion will be the basic management functions as they relate to the Production Department. You are expected to lead this discussion. To prepare for the discussion, briefly list the four basic functions of management and how those functions might relate to your position as production manager.

LO3   **M1-3 Classifying Sarbanes-Oxley (SOX) Objectives and Requirements**

Match each of the following SOX requirements to the corresponding objective by entering the appropriate letter in the space provided.

_____ 1. Establish a tip line for employees to report questionable acts.

_____ 2. Increase maximum fines to $5 million.

_____ 3. Require management to report on effectiveness of internal controls.

_____ 4. Legislate whistle-blower protections.

_____ 5. Require external auditors' report on internal control effectiveness.

A. Counteract incentives for fraud.

B. Reduce opportunities for error and fraud.

C. Encourage good character.

LO3   **M1-4 Identifying Ethical Dilemmas**

The following is a short list of scenarios. Write a brief statement about whether you believe the scenario is an ethical dilemma and, if so, who will be harmed by the unethical behavior.

1. You are a tax accounting professional and a client informs you that some of the receipts used in preparing the tax return have been falsified.

2. A friend gives you his accounting homework assignment. You change his name to yours on the top of the paper and turn in the assignment as your work.

3. You are an employee at a local clothing store. Your manager asks you to sell her a few expensive items priced at $1,200 but charge her only $100.

LO4   **M1-5 Classifying Costs**

Top Shelf Company builds oak bookcases. Determine whether each of the following is a direct material (DM), direct labor (DL), manufacturing overhead (MOH), or a period cost (P) for Top Shelf.

_____ 1. Depreciation on factory equipment.

_____ 2. Depreciation on delivery trucks.

_____ 3. Wood used to build a bookcase.

_____ 4. Production supervisor's salary.

_____ 5. Glue and screws used in the bookcases.

_____ 6. Wages of persons who assemble the bookcases.

_____ 7. Cost to run an ad on local radio stations.

_____ 8. Rent for the factory.

_____ 9. CEO's salary.

_____ 10. Wages of person who sands the wood after it is cut.

LO4   **M1-6 Classifying and Calculating Cost**

Refer to M1-5. Assume that you have the following information about Top Shelf's costs for the most recent month.

Depreciation on factory equipment	$2,000
Depreciation on delivery trucks	900
Wood used to build bookcases	1,300
Production supervisor's salary	3,000
Glue and screws used in the bookcases	250
Wages of persons who assemble the bookcases	2,800
Cost to run an ad on local radio stations	1,200
Rent for the factory	4,000
CEO's salary	1,500
Wages of person who sands the wood after it is cut	1,600

Determine each of the following costs for Top Shelf.

1. Direct materials used.
2. Direct labor.
3. Manufacturing overhead.
4. Prime cost.
5. Conversion cost.
6. Total manufacturing cost.
7. Total nonmanufacturing (period) cost.

M1-7 **Classifying Costs**   LO4

You are considering the possibility of pursuing a master's degree after completing your undergraduate degree.

1. List three costs (or benefits) that would be relevant to this decision including at least one opportunity cost.
2. List two costs that would be irrelevant to this decision.

M1-8 **Classifying Costs**   LO4

Lighten Up Lamps, Inc., manufactures table lamps and other lighting products. For each of the following costs, use an X to indicate the category of product cost and whether it is a prime cost, conversion cost, or both.

	PRODUCT COSTS			Prime Cost	Conversion Cost
	Direct Materials	Direct Labor	Mfg. Overhead		
Production supervisor salary					
Cost of lamp shades					
Wages of person who assembles lamps					
Factory rent					
Wages of person who paints lamps					
Factory utilities					
Screws used to assemble lamps					

M1-9 **Calculating Missing Amounts**   LO4

For each of the following independent cases A–D, compute the missing values in the table below.

Case	Direct Materials	Direct Labor	Manufacturing Overhead	Prime Cost	Conversion Cost
A	$800	$1,400	$2,100	$?	$?
B	400	?	1,325	2,550	?
C	?	675	1,500	2,880	?
D	?	750	?	1,500	2,000

M1-10 **Classifying Type of Company**   LO3

Indicate whether each of the following businesses would most likely be classified as a service company (S), merchandising company (Mer), or manufacturing company (Man).

_____ 1. Merry Maids.

_____ 2. Dell Computer.

_____ 3. Brinks Security.

_____ 4. Kmart.

_____ 5. PetSmart.

_____ 6. Ford Motor Company.

_____ 7. Bank One.

_____ 8. Ralph Lauren.

_____ 9. Dillard's.

_____ 10. Sam's Club.

LO4   M1-11

Refer to M1-10. Choose one of the companies you classified as a service company. For that company, identify two direct costs and two indirect costs. What is the cost object?

LO4   M1-12

Refer to M1-10. Choose one of the companies you classified as a merchandising company. For that company, identify two direct costs and two indirect costs. What is the cost object?

EXERCISES

LO1   E1-1 Making Decisions Using Managerial Accounting

Suppose you are a sales manager for Books on Wheels, Inc., which makes rolling book carts often used by libraries. The company is considering adding a new product aimed at university students. The new product will be a small, collapsible, wheeled tote designed specifically to aid students in transporting textbooks across campus.

Required:

1. List five questions you and the company would need to answer before proceeding with the development and marketing of this new product.
2. For each question identified in requirement 1, identify the information you would need to answer the question as well as the expected source of that information.
3. Identify three serious consequences of either not obtaining the information you need or obtaining inaccurate information.

LO2   E1-2 Identifying Management Functions

Refer to E1-1. Suppose that after a thorough investigation, Books on Wheels decided to go forward with the new product aimed at university students. The product, The Campus Cart, has gone into production, and the first units have already been delivered to campuses across the country.

Required:

Match each of the following steps that took place as Books on Wheels moved through the decision making, production, marketing, and sale of The Campus Cart with the correct phase of the management process: planning (setting long- and short-term objectives), organizing (organizing the necessary resources to implement the plan), directing/leading (taking action to implement the plan), and control (making adjustments to the plan based on actual results).

_____ 1. Identifying five college campuses to serve as test markets.   A. Planning

_____ 2. Setting the goal of $1 million in annual sales by the year 2015.   B. Organizing

_____ 3. Hiring workers for the manufacturing facility.   C. Directing/Leading

_____ 4. Overseeing the production and shipment of The Campus   D. Control
Cart.

_____ 5. Preparing one-, three-, and five-year budgets that detail the
necessary resources and costs that will be incurred to meet
the projected sales forecasts.

_____ 6. Deciding which new markets to expand into based on the
first year's sales results.

_____ 7. Implementing a bonus system to reward employees for meeting sales and production goals.

_____ 8. Deciding to spend more advertising dollars in regions where
sales were slower than expected.

E1-3 **Classifying Costs** · LO4

Suppose you have just finished your third year of college and expect to graduate with a bachelor's degree in accounting after completing two more semesters of coursework. The salary for entry-level positions with an accounting degree is approximately $48,000 in your area. Shelton Industries has just offered you a position in its northwest regional office. The position has an annual salary of $40,000 and would not require you to complete your undergraduate degree. If you accept the position, you would have to move to Seattle.

Required:

Identify with an X whether each of the following costs/benefits would be relevant to the decision to accept the offer from Shelton or stay in school. You may have more than one X for each item.

	Relevant Cost or Benefit	Irrelevant Cost or Benefit	Sunk Cost	Opportunity Cost
$40,000 salary from Shelton				
Anticipated $48,000 salary with an accounting degree				
Tuition and books for years 1–3 of college				
Cost to relocate to Seattle				
Tuition and books for remaining two semesters				
$19,000 from your part-time job, which you plan to keep until you graduate				
Cost to rent an apartment in Seattle (assume you are currently living at home with your parents)				
Food and entertainment expenses, which are expected to be the same in Seattle as where you currently live				
Increased promotional opportunities that will come from having a college degree				

E1-4 **Classifying Costs** · LO4

Seth's Skateboard Company has provided the following information about its company.

Required:

For each of the following costs, use an X to indicate the category of product cost (or period cost) and whether it is a prime cost, conversion cost, both, or neither.

	PRODUCT COSTS					
	Direct Materials	Direct Labor	Mfg. Overhead	Period Cost	Prime Cost	Conversion Cost
Production supervisor salary						
Cost of fiberglass						
Wages of assembly person						
Sales commission						
Cost of high-grade wheels						
Screws						
Factory rent						
Wages of skateboard painter						
Factory utilities						
Utilities for corporate office						

LO4   **E1-5 Calculating Costs**

Cotton White, Inc., makes specialty clothing for chefs. The company reported the following costs for 2010.

Factory rent	$36,000
Company advertising	24,000
Wages paid to seamstresses	75,000
Depreciation on salespersons' vehicles	30,000
Thread	1,000
Utilities for factory	23,000
Cutting room supervisor's salary	30,000
President's salary	75,000
Premium quality cotton material	40,000
Buttons	750
Factory insurance	18,000
Depreciation on sewing machines	6,000
Wages paid to cutters	50,000

Required:

Compute the following for Cotton White:
1. Direct materials.
2. Direct labor.
3. Manufacturing overhead.
4. Total manufacturing cost.
5. Prime cost.
6. Conversion cost.
7. Total period cost.

LO4   **E1-6 Calculating Missing Amounts**

Required:

For each of the following independent cases (A–E), compute the missing values in the table:

Case	Prime Cost	Conversion Cost	Direct Materials	Direct Labor	Manufacturing Overhead	Total Manufacturing Cost
A	$?	$?	$2,000	$1,000	$3,500	$?
B	6,800	11,500	2,300	?	7,000	?
C	?	7,850	1,400	3,250	?	9,250
D	?	?	?	2,100	3,100	5,800
E	11,500	20,500	3,500	?	?	?

LO4   **E1-7 Classifying and Calculating Costs**

The following information is available for Wonderway, Inc., for 2010.

Factory rent	$28,000
Company advertising	19,000
Wages paid to laborers	83,500
Depreciation for president's vehicle	8,000
Indirect production labor	1,800
Utilities for factory	30,000
Production supervisor salary	30,000
President's salary	60,000
Direct materials used	34,500
Sales commissions	7,500
Factory insurance	12,000
Depreciation on factory equipment	26,000

Required:

Calculate each of the following costs for Wonderway:
1. Direct labor.
2. Manufacturing overhead.
3. Prime cost.
4. Conversion cost.
5. Total manufacturing costs.
6. Period expenses.

E1-8 Classifying Costs   LO4

Blockett Company makes automobile sunshades and has provided the following information about its company.

Required:

For each cost listed below, use an X to indicate the category of product cost and whether it is a prime cost, conversion cost, or both.

	Period Cost	Direct Materials	Direct Labour	Manufacturing Overhead	Prime Cost	Conversion Cost
		PRODUCT COSTS				
Company president salary						
Factory rent						
Cost of reflective material						
Wages of material cutter						
Wages of office receptionist						
Thread and glue						
Depreciation for salesperson car						
Salary of factory supervisor						
Factory utilities						
Factory insurance						

E1-9 Classifying and Calculating Cost   LO4

Noteworthy, Inc., produces and sells small electronic keyboards. Assume that you have the following information about Noteworthy's costs for the most recent month.

Depreciation on factory equipment	$ 800
Depreciation on CEO's company car	100
Speakers used in the keyboard	1,100
Production supervisor's salary	2,200
Glue and screws used in the keyboards	370
Wages of persons who install the speakers	2,800
Cost to run an ad on local radio stations	600
Utilities for the factory	1,200
Personnel manager's salary	2,500
Wages of person who attaches legs to keyboards	1,950

Required:

Determine each of the following for Noteworthy.
1. Total product cost
2. Prime cost
3. Conversion cost
4. Manufacturing overhead
5. Direct labor
6. Total variable cost (with # units produced as the activity)
7. Total fixed cost (with # units produced as the activity)

LO4   **E1-10 Identifying Relevant and Irrelevant Costs**

Suppose that your brother, Raymond, recently bought a new laptop computer for $800 to use in his land surveying business. After purchasing several add-on components for $400, he realized that they are not compatible with the laptop and, therefore, he cannot use the computer for its intended purpose of mapping land coordinates using GPS satellites. He has also purchased a one-year service agreement and warranty for the add-on components for $75. The computer cannot be returned, but Raymond has found a new laptop costing $1,200 that will work with his GPS mapping components. Raymond is trying to decide what to do now and has asked your advice.

Required:

1. Identify the costs that are relevant to Raymond's decision.
2. Are there any costs that are irrelevant?
3. Suppose that Raymond made the following statement: "I can't get a new computer now. I have to get my money's worth from the old one." Is Raymond's logic correct?

LO4   **E1-11 Calculating Missing Amounts**

Complete the table of partial information shown below for Belgatto Company.

Case	Prime Cost	Conversion Cost	Direct Materials	Direct Labor	Manufacturing Overhead	Total Manufacturing Cost
A	$ 9,400	$ 16,300	$ 4,100	$?	$11,000	$?
B	?	?	10,000	7,300	24,500	41,800
C	55,300	109,500	43,200	?	?	?
D	?	47,350	21,400	13,250	?	68,750
E	?	?	?	14,900	23,100	55,700

LO4   **E1-12 Explaining Manufacturing Cost Categories**

Manufacturing costs can be classified into three categories—direct materials, direct labor, and manufacturing overhead. Over the years, manufacturing companies have changed significantly with advances in technology and the automation of many manufacturing processes.

Required:

Explain how the relative proportion of materials, labor, and overhead is likely to have changed over the last 100 years. Be specific in your discussion of which types of costs have increased and which have decreased.

LO4   **E1-13 Explaining Effects of Cost Misclassification**

Donna is a cost accountant for Northwind Corp. She is very efficient and hard-working; however, she occasionally transposes numbers when recording transactions. While working late recently, Donna accidentally recorded $19,000 of advertising cost instead of the correct $91,000. The transaction was correctly recorded in all other respects.

Required:

Explain how Donna's error will affect the following:
Manufacturing Costs
Inventory
Cost of Goods Sold
Period Expenses
Net Income

PROBLEMS—SET A

LO1   **PA1-1 Comparing Financial and Managerial Accounting**

You have been asked to take part in an upcoming Young Professionals meeting in your area. The program planned for the evening will cover many aspects of today's business world. Specifically, you have been asked to explain why there are two types of accounting—financial and managerial—and why they are both relevant to a company's employees. The program director would like for you to cover differences between the two types of accounting as well as how each type plays a role within today's competitive environment.

You will have 15 minutes for your presentation plus a 15-minute question-and-answer period at the end. Your audience is comprised primarily of entry-level managers from all fields (marketing, human resources, production, etc.). Assume that they all have some familiarity with accounting, but few are practicing accountants.

Required:

1. Prepare a detailed outline identifying your topic of discussion.
2. List at least five questions you may be asked during the question-and-answer period. Briefly discuss your answers to these questions.

PA1-2 Identifying Management Functions

LO2

Your friend, Suzie Whitson, has designed a new type of outdoor toy that helps children learn basic concepts such as colors, numbers, and shapes. Suzie's product will be targeted for two groups: day care centers in warm climates and home school programs for which few activity-intensive programs aim at toddlers' developmental processes. Suzie has come to you for help in getting her idea off the ground. She has never managed a business before and is not sure what functions she will need to perform to make her venture successful.

Required:

Briefly explain to Suzie the four major functions of management. For each function, give three examples of questions that Suzie will need to answer to make her business venture a success.

PA1-3 Identifying and Resolving Ethical Dilemmas

LO3

You are one of three partners who own and operate Mary's Maid Service. The company has been operating for seven years. One of the other partners has always prepared the company's annual financial statements. Recently, you proposed that the statements be audited each year because it would benefit the partners and prevent possible disagreements about the division of profits. The partner who prepares the statements proposed that his Uncle Ray, who has a lot of financial experience, do the job and at little cost. Your other partner remained silent.

Required:

1. What position would you take on the proposal? Justify your response.
2. What would you strongly recommend? Give the basis for your recommendation.

PA1-4 Classifying Costs; Calculating Total Costs; Identifying Impact of Misclassification

LO4

www.mhhe.com/whitecotton1e

Assume that Suzie Whitson (PA1-2) has decided to begin production of her outdoor children's toy. Her company is Jiffy Jet and costs for last month follow.

Factory rent	$ 3,000
Company advertising	1,000
Wages paid to assembly workers	30,000
Depreciation for salespersons' vehicles	2,000
Screws	500
Utilities for factory	800
Assembly supervisor's salary	3,500
Sandpaper	150
President's salary	5,000
Plastic tubing	4,000
Paint	250
Sales commissions	1,200
Factory insurance	1,000
Depreciation on cutting machines	2,000
Wages paid to painters	7,500

Required:

1. Identify each of the preceding costs as either a product or a period cost. If the cost is a product cost, decide whether it is for direct materials (DM), direct labor (DL), or manufacturing overhead (MOH).

2. Determine the total cost for each of the following.
   a. Direct material.
   b. Direct labor.
   c. Manufacturing overhead.
   d. Prime cost.
   e. Conversion cost.
   f. Total product cost.

3. Suppose all period costs were incorrectly identified as product costs. What impact could that have on Jiffy Jet's financial statements? Be specific.

PROBLEMS–SET B

LO4   **PB1-1 Comparing Product and Period Costs**

You have been asked to take part in an upcoming Young Professionals meeting in your area. The program planned for the evening focuses on today's manufacturing environment. Specifically, you have been asked to explain how manufacturing firms determine how much it costs to make their product and why some costs are initially recorded as inventory while other costs are expensed immediately. The program director would like for you to (1) discuss the rules for determining whether a cost should be treated as a product cost or period cost and (2) explain the types of costs that would be included in each category, how each flows through the accounting system, and the implications of the distinction between product costs and period costs for financial reporting (income statement versus balance sheet).

You will have 15 minutes for your presentation plus a 15-minute question-and-answer period at the end. Your audience is comprised primarily of entry-level production personnel although people from other fields (marketing, human resources, production, etc.) will be attending. Assume that they all have some familiarity with accounting but few are practicing accountants.

Required:

1. Prepare a detailed outline identifying your topic of discussion.
2. List at least five questions you may be asked during the question-and-answer period. Briefly discuss your answers to these questions.

LO2   **PB1-2 Identifying Management Functions**

Your friend, Maria Cottonwood, has designed a new type of fire extinguisher that is very small and easy to use. It will be targeted for two groups of people: elderly or people with disabilities who often have trouble operating the heavy traditional extinguishers and people who need to store it in small spaces such as a vehicle or storage room where the size of traditional extinguishers makes them cumbersome. Maria has come to you for help in getting her idea off the ground. She has never managed a business before and she is not sure what functions she will need to perform to make her venture successful.

Required:

Briefly explain to Maria the four major functions of management. For each function, give three examples of questions that Maria will need to answer to make her business venture a success.

LO3   **PB1-3 Identifying and Resolving Ethical Dilemmas**

When some people think about inventory theft, they imagine a shoplifter running out of a store with goods stuffed inside a jacket or bag. But that's not what the managers at the Famous Footwear store on Chicago's Madison Street thought. No, they suspected their own employees were the main cause of their unusually high shrinkage. One scam involved dishonest cashiers who would let their friends take a pair of Skechers without paying for them. To make it look like the shoes had been bought, cashiers would ring up a sale, but instead of charging $50 for shoes, they would charge only $2 for a bottle of shoe polish. When the company's managers saw a drop in gross profit, they decided to put the accounting system to work. In just two years, the company cut its Madison Street inventory losses in half. Here's how a newspaper described the store's improvements:

Retailers Crack Down on Employee Theft
SouthCoast Today, September 10, 2000, Chicago
By Calmetta Coleman, *Wall Street Journal* Staff Writer

. . . Famous Footwear installed a chainwide register-monitoring system to sniff out suspicious transactions, such as unusually large numbers of refunds or voids, or repeated sales of cheap goods.

. . . [B]efore an employee can issue a cash refund, a second worker must be present to see the customer and inspect the merchandise.

. . . [T]he chain has set up a toll-free hotline for employees to use to report suspicions about co-workers.

These improvements in inventory control came as welcome news for investors and creditors of Brown Shoe Company, the company that owns Famous Footwear. Although these improvements helped the Chicago store, the company has been forced to shut down operations in other cities.

Brown Shoe Company

Required:

1. Explain how the register-monitoring system would allow Famous Footwear to cut down on employee theft.
2. Think of and describe at least four different parties that are harmed by the type of inventory theft described in this case.

PB1-4 Classifying Costs, Calculating Total Costs, and Identifying Impact of Classifications

LO4

Assume that Maria Cottonwood (PB1-2) has decided to begin production of her fire extinguisher. Her company is Blaze Be Gone, whose costs for last month follow.

Factory rent	$ 2,000
Company advertising	500
Wages paid to assembly workers	25,000
Depreciation for salespersons' vehicles	1,000
Screws	250
Utilities for factory	1,200
Production supervisor's salary	4,500
Sandpaper	150
President's salary	6,000
Sheet metal	8,000
Paint	750
Sales commissions	1,700
Factory insurance	3,000
Depreciation on factory machinery	5,000
Wages paid to painters	5,500

Required:

1. Identify each of the preceding costs as either a product or a period cost. If the cost is a product cost, decide whether it is direct materials (DM), direct labor (DL), or manufacturing overhead (MOH).
2. Determine the total amount for each of the following.
   a. Direct materials.
   b. Direct labor.
   c. Manufacturing overhead.

        d. Prime cost.

        e. Conversion cost.

        f. Total product cost.

3. Maria wants you to explain why the depreciation on the salespersons' vehicles is treated differently than the depreciation on the factory machines. Explain why these costs are treated differently and what the implications are for Maria's financial statements in terms of the balance sheet and income statement.

SKILLS DEVELOPMENT CASES

LO4   **S1-1 Researching Cost Components of Everyday Item**

Choose one item that you use each day—anything from a toothbrush to your favorite soda to an automobile.

Required:

Research the company that produces this item online to find out as much information as you can about the manufacturing process used to create the product. Prepare a report on the product and its manufacturer including the following.

1. A summary of the company including information about its manufacturing facilities.
2. How the company's managerial accounting information would differ from its financial accounting information and specific users of each information type.
3. For the specific product you chose, provide three examples of each of the following costs.
   - **a.** Direct costs.
   - **b.** Indirect costs.
   - **c.** Variable costs.
   - **d.** Fixed costs.
   - **e.** Product costs.
   - **f.** Period costs.
4. At least two potential suppliers of raw materials used to manufacture the item.
5. The typical price that you pay for this item.

LO4   **S1-2 Identifying Changes in Manufacturing Process and Costs Due to Automation**

In recent years, many companies have converted from a labor-intensive manufacturing process to an automated one. As an example, think of a car wash company that used to wash cars by hand but has now invested in an automatic washing and drying system.

Required:

Think of another company that might upgrade to an automated system and answer the following questions.

1. What physical changes would the conversion to automation cause in the manufacturing process?
2. What impact, both positive and negative, might automation have on employee morale?
3. What impact might automation have on the skill level of the company's workforce?
4. How might automation affect the quality of the product manufactured and the efficiency of the manufacturing process?
5. How would you expect automation to affect direct material, direct labor, and manufacturing overhead costs? Would you expect any of these costs to increase or decrease?
6. How would you expect automation to affect variable costs and fixed costs? Would you expect either of these costs to increase or decrease?
7. How might this change in the manufacturing process affect the price consumers pay for the product?
8. How might this change in the manufacturing process affect the company's bottom line both immediately and several years in the future?

S1-3 **Finding Future-Oriented Information in Financial Statements**   **LO1**

Consider the following statement about the use of forward-looking information on Kraft's Web site.

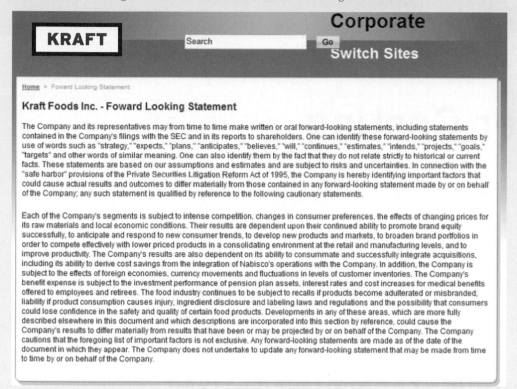

Required:

1. What was the safe harbor provision of the Private Securities Litigation Reform Act of 1995? What was its intended purpose?

2. Does Kraft have to make similar statements about reports prepared for internal (managerial) use? Would you expect to see more or less forward-looking information in internal reports than external reports?

3. Can you think of other words that accountants might use to describe what they expect to happen in the future other than "strategy," "expects," "plans," "anticipates," "believes," "will," "continues," "estimates," "intends," "projects," "goals," or "targets"? (*Hint:* See the title to Chapter 10.)

4. Go to the Web site of another public company and find a similar statement about the use of forward-looking information. Alternatively, you can search for "forward-looking information" and "safe harbor" using a search engine such as Google. What factors does the company list as potential reasons that actual results may differ from the "forward-looking" information? Why does the company list these factors?

S1-4 **Identifying Service, Merchandising, and Manufacturing Firms:**   **LO2**
Internet Research

As discussed in the chapter, companies can be classified into one of three categories: service, merchandising, and manufacturing.

Required:

1. Choose one publicly traded company from each category and explore that company's Web site. On the Web site, find a brief company description as well as the most recent published financial statements. Based on the company description, support your categorization of the company as service, merchandising, or manufacturing. If the company falls into more than one of these categories, describe how.

2. Look at the income statement and balance sheet for the company and list any factors that would support your categorization of the company as a service, merchandising, or manufacturing organization.

CHAPTER 2

Job Order Costing

YOUR LEARNING OBJECTIVES

After completing this chapter, you should be able to:

LO1 Describe the key differences between job order costing and process costing.

LO2 Describe the source documents used to track direct materials and direct labor costs to the job cost sheet.

LO3 Calculate a predetermined overhead rate and use it to apply manufacturing overhead cost to jobs.

LO4 Describe how costs flow through the accounting system in job order costing.

LO5 Calculate and dispose of overapplied or underapplied manufacturing overhead.

LO6 Calculate the cost of goods manufactured and cost of goods sold.

Lecture Presentation-LP2
www.mhhe.com/whitecotton1e

FOCUS COMPANY: Toll Brothers Inc.

"America's Luxury Home Builder"

www.tollbrothers.com

Toll Brothers
America's Luxury Home Builder®

Have you ever found yourself in the following situation? You go out to a trendy new restaurant with a group of friends. You are on a limited budget, so you order the cheapest dish on the menu and a glass of ice water. Meanwhile, your friends indulge in a full-course meal with drinks, appetizers, entrees, and dessert. When it is time to pay the bill, would you prefer to split the check or get a separate tab for each person at the table?

This common scenario illustrates the basic difference between the two costing systems discussed in the next two chapters. Process costing is similar to splitting the check, or spreading the total cost over the number of units produced (or in the case of a restaurant meal, the number of customers at the table). This simple method works well as long as each unit (or customer) consumes about the same amount of cost (or food). Process costing is discussed in the next chapter.

With job order costing, a separate cost record is kept for each individual product or customer, similar to getting separate checks at a restaurant. This method makes sense when products or customers consume vastly different resources and thus have different costs. Job order costing systems are used for companies that provide customized products or services, such as a custom home builder.

Imagine that you have just landed a great new job and are building your dream home with a luxury home builder such as Toll Brothers Inc. Founded by Bruce and Robert Toll in 1967, Toll Brothers has grown from a small family-owned business to become the nation's leading luxury home builder with operations in all of the major regions throughout the United States. Toll Brothers prides itself on "building communities in picturesque settings where luxury meets convenience, and where neighbors become lifelong friends."

In this chapter, we track the cost of building a custom home using a job order costing system. Of course, we simplify many of the details, and the numbers we use are fictional. Nevertheless, this extended example should give you a good idea of how an actual job order costing system works, and how your dream home will be accounted for should you be fortunate enough to build one someday.

Job order versus process costing	**Assigning manufacturing costs to jobs**	**Recording the flow of costs in job order costing**	**Overapplied or underapplied manufacturing overhead**
• Process costing • Job order costing	• Manufacturing cost categories • Materials requisition form • Direct labor time tickets • Job cost sheet • Predetermined overhead rates	• Recording the purchase and issue of materials • Recording labor costs • Recording actual manufacturing overhead • Recording applied manufacturing overhead • Transferring costs to finished goods inventory and cost of goods sold • Recording nonmanufacturing costs	• Calculating overapplied and underapplied manufacturing overhead • Disposing of overapplied or underapplied manufacturing overhead • Preparing the cost of goods manufactured report

Job Order versus Process Costing

The key difference between job order costing and process costing is whether the company's products or services are heterogeneous (different) or homogeneous (similar). See Exhibit 2.1 for a summary of other differences between job order and process costing.

PROCESS COSTING

Learning Objective 1
Describe the key differences between job order costing and process costing.

Process costing is used by companies that make **standardized** or **homogeneous** products or services, such as:

- Coca-Cola beverages.
- Kraft macaroni and cheese.
- Charmin toilet tissue.
- Exxon petroleum products.

These and many other common products are produced in a continuous manufacturing process in which raw materials are put through a standardized production process so that each unit of the final product comes out identical to the next. Because each unit is the same, there is no need to track the cost of each unit individually. Instead, process costing

Video 2-1
www.mhhe.com/whitecotton1e

	Job Order Costing	Process Costing
EXHIBIT 2.1	**Job Order Costing versus Process Costing**	
Type of product	Unique products and services, such as a custom-built ship	Homogeneous products and services, such as cans of soft drinks.
Manufacturing approach	Customized to the needs of the customer or client	Mass-produced using a series of standardized processes
Cost accumulation	Costs accumulated by job or customer	Costs accumulated by process
Major cost report	Job cost sheet for each unique unit, customer, or job	Production report for each major production process

breaks the production process down into its basic steps, or processes, and then averages the total cost of the process over the number of units produced. The basic process cost-ing formula is:

$$\frac{\text{Average Unit Cost}} = \frac{\text{Total Manufacturing Cost}}{\text{Total Units Produced}}$$

Although this formula makes process costing sound simple, a few questions com-plicate its use in the real world. For example, how much cost should Coca-Cola assign to soft drinks that are still in process at the end of the month—that is, when all of the ingredients have been added but the bottling process is not yet complete? These issues will be discussed in more detail in the next chapter, which focuses specifically on process costing.

JOB ORDER COSTING

Job order costing is used in companies that offer **customized** or **unique** products or services. Unlike process costing, in which each unit is identical to the next, job order costing is used for situations in which each unit or customer tends to be very different from the next. Examples include:

- A custom home built by Toll Brothers.
- A skyscraper built by Trump Industries.
- A nuclear submarine built for the U.S. Department of Defense.
- A one-of-a-kind wedding gown designed by Vera Wang.

Job order costing is also common in service industries that serve clients or customers with unique needs. For example, the accounting firm Ernst and Young, LLP tracks the billable hours spent on each individual client's account. Law firms, architectural firms, and consulting firms also track the costs of serving individual clients.

Video 2-2
www.mhhe.com/whitecotton1e

COACH'S TIP

In job order costing, each unique product or customer order is called a **job.** The cost of each unique job is recorded on a document called a **job cost sheet.**

In the next section, we illustrate the basics of job order costing using the example of a custom home built by Toll Brothers. First, to make sure you understand the difference between job order costing and process costing, take a moment to complete the following Self-Study Practice.

Self-Study Practice

Indicate which of the following statements are true (T) and which are false (F).

___ 1. Job order costing systems are appropriate for companies that produce many units of an identical product.

___ 2. Job order costing is often used in service industries in which each client or customer has unique requirements.

___ 3. A builder of custom pools is more likely to use process costing than job order costing.

___ 4. A company such as Coca-Cola is more likely to use a process costing system than a job order costing system.

___ 5. In process costing, costs are averaged to determine the unit cost of homogeneous goods and services.

After you have finished, check your answers with the solutions in the margin.

Assigning Manufacturing Costs to Jobs

In this section, we illustrate how to assign manufacturing costs to unique products, called **jobs**, using job order costing. Although job order cost systems are commonly used by service firms, accounting for manufacturing costs is more complicated because a physical product can be stored as inventory, while services cannot. GAAP requires that all manufacturing costs be traced to the product, which means that manufacturing costs should be counted as inventory (an asset) until the product is sold.

MANUFACTURING COST CATEGORIES

As you learned in Chapter 1, manufacturing costs are divided into three categories:

- **Direct materials** are the primary material inputs that can be directly and conveniently traced to each job. Examples of direct materials used in building a home include concrete, piping, lumber, drywall, fixtures, and appliances.
- **Direct labor** is the hands-on work that goes into producing a product or service. Examples of direct labor used in building a home include the work of pouring the foundation, framing the home, and installing the plumbing.
- **Manufacturing overhead** includes all other costs of producing a product that cannot be directly or conveniently traced to a specific job. Examples of the manufacturing overhead required to build (not sell) a home include the costs of site supervision, construction insurance, depreciation on construction equipment, and indirect materials (nails, screws, and so on).

In a job order cost system, all of these manufacturing costs are recorded on a document called the **job cost sheet**, which provides a detailed record of the cost incurred to complete a specific job. Refer to Exhibit 2.2 for an illustration of how the three types of manufacturing costs are assigned in a job order cost system.

COACH'S TIP

If you have ever done your own home improvement project, think of the direct materials as the materials you purchased at The Home Depot and the direct labor as the number of hours you put into the job. Unlike do-it-yourself enthusiasts, large construction companies also have many **indirect costs** including equipment, supervision, and insurance. These costs are called **manufacturing overhead**.

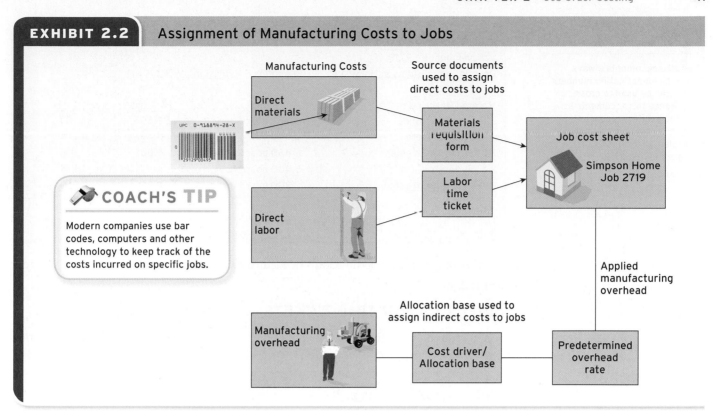

EXHIBIT 2.2   Assignment of Manufacturing Costs to Jobs

COACH'S TIP

Modern companies use bar codes, computers and other technology to keep track of the costs incurred on specific jobs.

The most important thing to notice in Exhibit 2.2 is that direct materials and direct labor costs are assigned to jobs differently than manufacturing overhead costs. For direct costs, all that is needed to keep track of the costs of specific jobs is a set of records called **source documents.** In a manual (paper-based) accounting system, a source document is a hard copy document similar to the receipt you get when you buy something at a store. But more companies are moving to paperless systems that record all of the information electronically and track it using technology such as bar codes, computer scanning devices, and other technologies. For simplicity, we illustrate the "old-fashioned" method using paper documents to trace direct materials and direct labor costs to specific jobs.

In contrast to direct materials and direct labor, which can be traced directly to jobs using source documents, manufacturing overhead is made up of costs that **cannot** be directly or conveniently traced to specific jobs. To assign these indirect costs to jobs, accountants must use a predetermined overhead rate that is based on some secondary allocation measure, or cost driver.

Let's start by assigning the direct cost to specific jobs using materials requisition forms and direct labor time tickets.

MATERIALS REQUISITION FORM

Before materials can be used on a job, a **materials requisition form**—a form that lists the quantity and cost of the direct materials used on a specific job—must be filled out. This form is used to control the physical flow of materials out of inventory and into production. It also provides the information needed to record the cost of raw materials in the accounting system.

As an example, assume that Toll Brothers is getting ready to frame the interior and exterior walls of the Simpson family's new 2,500-square-foot custom home. The Simpson home has been numbered Job 2719. Before the lumber can be delivered to the job site, a materials requisition form like the one that follows must be completed.

Learning Objective 2
Describe the source documents used to track direct material and direct labor costs to the job cost sheet.

Materials Requisition Number:	MR 5236		Date: 8/11/2010	

Job Number   2719

Description: Simpson Home, Lot 79, Cambridge Subdivision

Material Description	Quantity	Unit Cost	Total Cost
2 X 6 Exterior studs	6,362 board ft.	$0.50	$3,181
2 X 6 Double plate	2,600 board ft.	0.49	1,274
2 X 6 Pressure treated	450 board ft.	0.68	306
2 X 4 Interior studs	5,400 board ft.	0.21	1,134
2 X 4 Pressure treated	300 board ft.	0.35	105
Total cost			$6,000

Authorized Signature _____

This document provides the details needed to record direct material costs in a job order cost system.

DIRECT LABOR TIME TICKETS

A **direct labor time ticket** is a source document that shows how much time a worker spent on various jobs each week, as in the following illustration:

Direct Labor Time Ticket   Dates: Monday 8/11 – Friday 8/15, 2010

Ticket Number: TT 335

Employee   Bill Robertson

Date	Time Started	Time Ended	Total Hours	Hourly Rate	Total Amount	Job Number
8/11/2010	7:00 AM	3:00 PM	8 hours	$25	$ 200	2719
8/12/2010	7:00 AM	3:00 PM	8 hours	25	200	2719
8/13/2010	7:00 AM	3:00 PM	8 hours	25	200	2719
8/14/2010	7:00 AM	11:00 AM	4 hours	25	100	2719
8/14/2010	12:00 PM	4:00 PM	4 hours	25	100	3335
8/15/2010	7:00 AM	3:00 PM	8 hours	25	200	3335
		Weekly totals	40 hours		1,000	

Authorized Signature _____

Like the materials requisition form, a direct labor time ticket is used to record direct labor costs in a job order cost system.

JOB COST SHEET

The **job cost sheet** is a document that summarizes all of the costs incurred on a specific job. For example, the costs from the preceding materials requisition form and labor time ticket would be posted to the job cost sheet for the Simpson home (Job 2719) as follows:

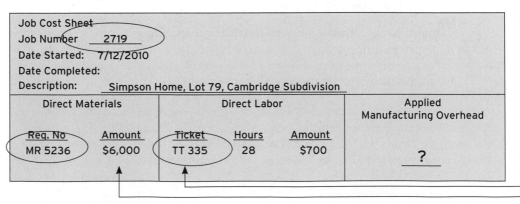

Job Cost Sheet

Job Number   2719

Date Started: 7/12/2010

Date Completed:

Description: Simpson Home, Lot 79, Cambridge Subdivision

Direct Materials		Direct Labor			Applied Manufacturing Overhead
Req. No	Amount	Ticket	Hours	Amount	
MR 5236	$6,000	TT 335	28	$700	?

Notice that this job cost sheet shows the actual amount of direct materials and direct labor incurred on Job 2719. But we have not yet recorded the manufacturing overhead or indirect costs of building the home. The method for assigning indirect costs to jobs is described next.

PREDETERMINED OVERHEAD RATES

The third type of cost that must be recorded is **manufacturing overhead.** Unlike direct materials and direct labor costs, which can be traced to individual jobs using source documents, manufacturing overhead costs cannot be directly traced to specific jobs. The production supervisor's salary, for example, and depreciation on construction equipment are common costs that relate to multiple jobs. Theoretically, some indirect costs such as indirect materials (screws, nails, and so on) could be traced to individual jobs, but doing so is probably not worth the effort.

As a simple example, think about the last time you had your car repaired. The cost of the repair probably included parts and labor plus some additional amount to cover the indirect costs of operating the garage, such as oil, lubricants, and machines. How does the owner or manager of the garage decide how much to charge for those indirect costs? They probably add some percentage to the direct labor cost, which assumes that more time spent on a repair will result in more indirect costs as well. This rate or percentage must be calculated in advance so that the shop can provide a bid or estimate for customers who bring their car in for repair.

In our home-building example, indirect manufacturing overhead costs must be **assigned** to specific jobs using a secondary measure called an **allocation base**. Ideally, the allocation base should explain why the cost is incurred. An allocation base that is causally related to cost incurrence is sometimes called a **cost driver.** For example, some manufacturing overhead costs, such as employee taxes and site supervision, are driven by the number of direct labor hours worked. Other costs such as machine maintenance and fuel are driven by the amount of time that construction equipment is used. The cost of indirect materials such as glue, sandpaper, and insulation is driven by the square footage of the home under construction.

For simplicity, we use a single allocation base to assign manufacturing overhead costs to jobs. Because home building is a labor-intensive business, we assume that Toll Brothers uses direct labor hours as the allocation base for assigning manufacturing overhead costs to jobs. In Chapter 4, we describe more sophisticated methods for assigning indirect costs using multiple activity drivers.

Before we can assign manufacturing overhead costs to jobs, we must first calculate a predetermined overhead rate using our chosen allocation base. The **predetermined overhead rate** is calculated as follows:

$$\text{Predetermined Overhead Rate} = \frac{\text{Estimated Total Manufacturing Overhead Cost}}{\text{Estimated Units in the Allocation Base}}$$

This overhead rate is calculated for an entire accounting period (typically a year) and is based on **estimated** rather than actual values. We often do not know the actual manufacturing overhead cost until after the month, quarter, or year has ended. Thus, accountants must use their best estimate of the coming period's manufacturing overhead based on past experience and any expectations they have about how the costs might change in the future.

Assume Toll Brothers estimates the total manufacturing overhead cost for the upcoming year to be $750,000 and total direct labor hours to be 10,000. Based on these estimates, the predetermined overhead rate is calculated as follows:

$$\frac{\text{Estimated Total Manufacturing Overhead Cost}}{\text{Estimated Direct Labor Hours}} = \frac{\$750,000}{10,000} = \text{Predetermined Overhead Rate } (\$75 \text{ per direct labor hour})$$

This rate suggests that the company needs to assign $75 in manufacturing overhead cost for each direct labor hour worked. This is not the cost of the direct labor itself, but rather all of the **indirect costs** of building a home such as indirect materials, depreciation on construction equipment, supervisors' salaries, and insurance.

Once the predetermined overhead rate is established, managers can use it to determine how much overhead should be added to each job. They calculate the **applied manufacturing overhead** by multiplying the predetermined overhead rate by the actual value of the allocation base used on the job, as follows:

Assume that during the first week of construction, the Simpson home (Job 2719) required a total of 300 direct labor hours. Because the predetermined overhead rate is $75 per direct labor hour, the manufacturing overhead applied to the job is $22,500, calculated as follows:

Predetermined Overhead Rate $75	×	Actual Direct Labor Hours for job 2719 300	=	Overhead Applied to Job 2719 $22,500

Accountants can apply manufacturing overhead costs as they record direct labor hours (based on the actual number of hours worked during a given week), or they can wait until the job is completed and apply all of the manufacturing overhead at once (based on the total direct labor hours worked on the job). If some jobs are still in process at the end of an accounting period, however, accountants must make sure that all cost records are up to date by applying overhead to all jobs in process at the end of the period. Assume the job cost sheet for the Simpson home at the end of the first week is as follows:

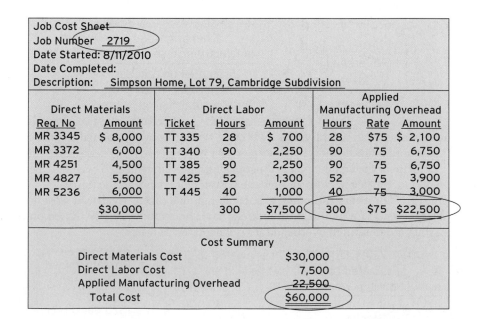

Job Cost Sheet
Job Number   2719
Date Started: 8/11/2010
Date Completed:
Description: Simpson Home, Lot 79, Cambridge Subdivision

Direct Materials		Direct Labor			Applied Manufacturing Overhead		
Req. No	Amount	Ticket	Hours	Amount	Hours	Rate	Amount
MR 3345	$ 8,000	TT 335	28	$ 700	28	$75	$ 2,100
MR 3372	6,000	TT 340	90	2,250	90	75	6,750
MR 4251	4,500	TT 385	90	2,250	90	75	6,750
MR 4827	5,500	TT 425	52	1,300	52	75	3,900
MR 5236	6,000	TT 445	40	1,000	40	75	3,000
	$30,000		300	$7,500	300	$75	$22,500

Cost Summary	
Direct Materials Cost	$30,000
Direct Labor Cost	7,500
Applied Manufacturing Overhead	22,500
Total Cost	$60,000

Notice that manufacturing overhead was applied to the job cost sheet based on the predetermined (estimated) overhead rate of $75 per direct labor hour. Because this rate was based on estimated data, applied manufacturing overhead is unlikely to be exactly the same as the actual manufacturing overhead cost incurred. You will see how to record actual manufacturing overhead costs and how to account for any difference between actual and applied manufacturing overhead later in this chapter. First, complete the following Self-Study Practice to make sure you know how to calculate the predetermined overhead rate and apply manufacturing overhead costs to jobs.

 Self-Study Practice

Carlton Brothers Construction Company applies manufacturing overhead to jobs on the basis of direct labor hours. The following estimated and actual information is available.

	Estimated	Actual
Total manufacturing overhead	$96,000	$90,000
Total direct labor hours	12,000	11,000

Based on these data, calculate the following:

1. Predetermined overhead rate.
2. Applied manufacturing overhead.

After you have finished, check your answers with the solutions in the margin.

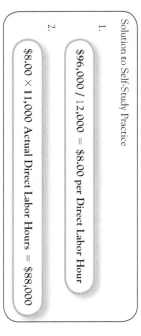

Solution to Self-Study Practice

1. $96,000 / 12,000 = $8.00 per Direct Labor Hour

2. $8.00 × 11,000 Actual Direct Labor Hours = $88,000

Recording the Flow of Costs in Job Order Costing

This section describes how manufacturing costs are recorded in a job order cost system. Although we do not show the detailed journal entries, we use T-accounts to show how the manufacturing costs flow through the various inventory accounts before eventually being recognized as Cost of Goods Sold.

The three inventory accounts that are used to record manufacturing costs follow:

- **Raw Materials Inventory** represents the cost of materials purchased from suppliers but not yet used in production. This account includes all raw materials, including the direct materials that will be traced to specific jobs (lumber, piping) and the **indirect materials** that cannot be traced to specific jobs (screws, nails, and so on).

- **Work in Process Inventory** represents the total cost of jobs that are in process. Any cost that is added to the Work in Process Inventory account must also be recorded on the individual job cost sheet. Thus, the total cost of all jobs in process should equal the balance in Work in Process Inventory.

- **Finished Goods Inventory** represents the cost of jobs that have been completed but not yet sold. The cost of a completed job remains in the Finished Goods Inventory account until it is sold.

> **Learning Objective 4**
> Describe how costs flow through the accounting system in job order costing.

When a job is sold, its total cost is transferred out of Finished Goods Inventory and into **Cost of Goods Sold**. See Exhibit 2.3 for an illustration of the flow of manufacturing costs through these inventory accounts before being recognized as Cost of Goods Sold.

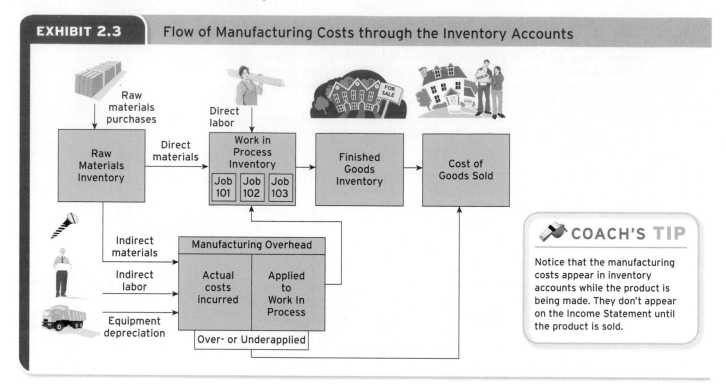

EXHIBIT 2.3 Flow of Manufacturing Costs through the Inventory Accounts

COACH'S TIP

Notice that the manufacturing costs appear in inventory accounts while the product is being made. They don't appear on the Income Statement until the product is sold.

COACH'S TIP

For simplicity, we ignore many other accounts (such as Cash, Accounts Payables, etc.) that would be needed to record a complete transaction.

Although we focus only on recording inventory and costs, remember that every transaction has two sides (a debit and a credit).

When materials are purchased, the cost is initially recorded in Raw Materials Inventory. As materials are used, the cost is transferred to either Work in Process Inventory (for direct materials) or to Manufacturing Overhead (for indirect materials).

All costs added to the Work in Process Inventory account must be assigned to a specific job (and recorded on the individual job cost sheet). Notice that only direct materials and direct labor costs are recorded directly in the Work in Process Inventory account. All indirect or manufacturing overhead costs flow through the Manufacturing Overhead account.

The Manufacturing Overhead account is a temporary holding account used to record actual and applied manufacturing overhead costs. Actual manufacturing overhead costs are accumulated on the debit (left-hand) side of the Manufacturing Overhead account. The credit (right-hand) side of the account shows the manufacturing overhead that is applied to specific jobs based on the predetermined overhead rate described in the previous section.

As jobs are in process, the Work in Process Inventory account accumulates the **actual** direct materials, **actual** direct labor, and **applied** manufacturing overhead cost of each job. When a job is completed, its total manufacturing cost is transferred out of Work in Process Inventory and into the Finished Goods Inventory account. When the job is sold, these costs are transferred to the Cost of Goods Sold account where they will be matched against Sales Revenue on the income statement.

At the end of the reporting period, any difference between actual and applied manufacturing overhead (represented by the balance in the Manufacturing Overhead account) must be accounted for. Companies can either adjust Cost of Goods Sold directly, as shown in Exhibit 2.3, or adjust Work in Process Inventory, Finished Goods Inventory, and Cost of Goods Sold. Later in the chapter, we illustrate the simpler of these two methods.

The next section provides an example to illustrate the flow of manufacturing costs in job order costing. The detailed journal entries for each transaction are shown in the Supplement to this chapter. For simplicity, we assume that none of the accounts had a beginning balance and that the company worked on only two jobs during the period.

RECORDING THE PURCHASE AND ISSUE OF MATERIALS

When materials are purchased, they are initially recorded in Raw Materials Inventory. This account shows the cost of all materials purchased but not yet issued into production, and includes both direct and indirect material purchases.

Before materials can be issued out of Raw Materials Inventory, managers must fill out a materials requisition form that indicates which job or jobs the material will be used for. The direct materials are recorded on the specific job cost sheet and in Work in Process Inventory. Indirect materials, or materials that cannot be traced to a specific job, are not recorded directly to the job cost sheet or Work in Process Inventory. Rather, these indirect costs are accumulated in the Manufacturing Overhead account and will be applied to the product using the predetermined overhead rate.

As an example, assume that $150,000 worth of materials is withdrawn from Raw Materials Inventory for the following uses:

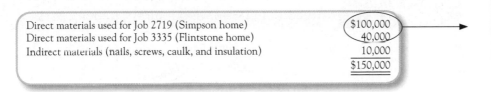

Direct materials used for Job 2719 (Simpson home)	$100,000
Direct materials used for Job 3335 (Flintstone home)	40,000
Indirect materials (nails, screws, caulk, and insulation)	10,000
	$150,000

Exhibit 2.4 shows how these direct and indirect materials would be recorded in the Raw Materials Inventory, Work in Process Inventory, and Manufacturing Overhead accounts.

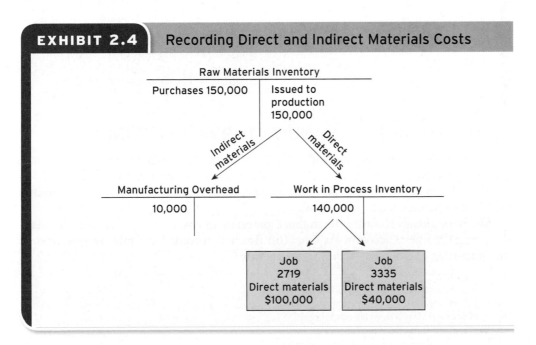

EXHIBIT 2.4 | **Recording Direct and Indirect Materials Costs**

Notice that $140,000 in direct materials is added directly to Work in Process Inventory with $100,000 being recorded on Job 2719 and $40,000 recorded on Job 3335. These job cost sheets serve as a subsidiary ledger to the overall Work in Process Inventory account. Thus, the total cost of all jobs in process should equal the overall balance in the Work in Process Inventory account.

The $10,000 cost of indirect materials (nails, screws, caulk, and insulation) is not traced to the individual jobs but is accumulated on the debit (left) side of the Manufacturing Overhead account.

RECORDING LABOR COSTS

Labor costs are recorded in much the same way as direct materials: based on the direct labor time tickets that show how much time was spent on each job. If the labor can be traced to a specific job, the cost is added to the job cost sheet and the Work in Process Inventory account. If it is not traceable to a specific job, the cost is considered indirect labor and is debited to the Manufacturing Overhead account.

Assume Toll Brothers recorded the following labor costs:

Direct labor on Job 2719 (Simpson home)	$30,000
Direct labor on Job 3335 (Flintstone home)	20,000
Indirect labor (such as maintenance and inspection work)	5,000
	$55,000

See Exhibit 2.5 for a summary of how these costs would appear in the Manufacturing Overhead and Work in Process Inventory accounts.

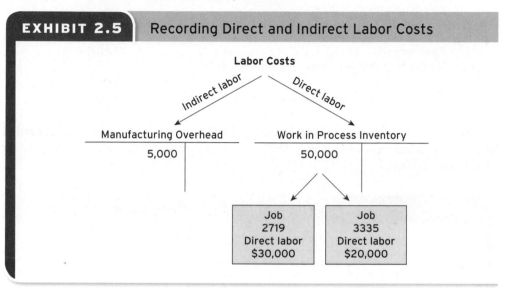

EXHIBIT 2.5 | Recording Direct and Indirect Labor Costs

RECORDING ACTUAL MANUFACTURING OVERHEAD

Actual manufacturing costs include all of the indirect manufacturing costs, or those that cannot be traced to specific units or jobs. These costs are not recorded directly in the Work in Process Inventory account. Instead, these indirect costs are accumulated in the Manufacturing Overhead account.

We have already recorded the indirect materials and indirect labor costs in the Manufacturing Overhead account. Assume Toll Brothers recorded the following additional manufacturing overhead costs during the month:

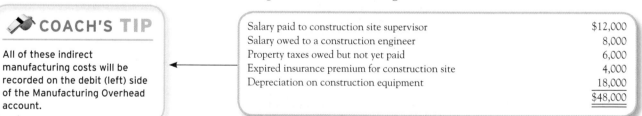

Salary paid to construction site supervisor	$12,000
Salary owed to a construction engineer	8,000
Property taxes owed but not yet paid	6,000
Expired insurance premium for construction site	4,000
Depreciation on construction equipment	18,000
	$48,000

> **🔨 COACH'S TIP**
>
> All of these indirect manufacturing costs will be recorded on the debit (left) side of the Manufacturing Overhead account.

These actual manufacturing overhead costs are added to the Manufacturing Overhead account (see Exhibit 2.6). Actual manufacturing overhead costs are always shown on the left-hand (debit) side of the Manufacturing Overhead account. Next we show how these indirect costs are applied to the Work in Process Inventory account using the predetermined overhead rate.

RECORDING APPLIED MANUFACTURING OVERHEAD

Remember that manufacturing overhead costs are **applied** to jobs based on the predetermined overhead rate that was estimated at the beginning of the accounting period. As jobs are worked on during the period, we determine the amount of manufacturing overhead cost to apply to specific jobs by multiplying the predetermined overhead rate by the actual number of direct labor hours worked.

In our home-building example, we estimated the manufacturing overhead rate to be $75 per direct labor hour. This rate is not the cost of the direct labor itself, but rather the amount of manufacturing overhead cost that needs to be added for each direct labor hour worked to cover the indirect costs of building the home (equipment depreciation, insurance, supervision, etc.).

Assume Toll Brothers' labor time tickets for the month revealed the following:

	Job Number	Direct Labor Hours
Simpson home	2719	600
Flintstone home	3335	200
Total direct labor hours		800

Because the overhead rate is $75 per direct labor hour, we need to apply a total of $60,000 (800 hours × $75 per direct labor hour) in manufacturing overhead costs to the Work in Process Inventory account. This amount is taken **out** of the Manufacturing Overhead account (with a credit) and added to the Work in Process Inventory account (with a debit), as shown in Exhibit 2.6.

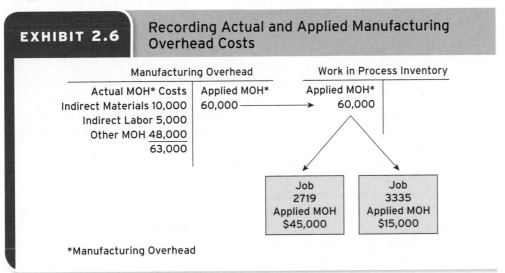

EXHIBIT 2.6   Recording Actual and Applied Manufacturing Overhead Costs

Anytime that we add cost to the Work in Process Inventory account, we must also update the individual job cost sheets. For the Simpson home, we would apply $45,000 (600 hours × $75 per hour) to Job 2719. For the Flintstone home, we would apply $15,000 (200 hours × $75) to Job 3335.

Notice that the $60,000 applied to Work in Process Inventory is not equal to the actual manufacturing overhead cost incurred of $63,000 ($10,000 + $5,000 + $48,000). We discuss how to handle the difference between actual and applied manufacturing overhead costs later in this chapter.

TRANSFERRING COSTS TO FINISHED GOODS INVENTORY AND COST OF GOODS SOLD

When a job is finally completed, the job cost sheet must be updated to reflect all direct materials, direct labor, and applied overhead costs that should be charged to the job. Once all manufacturing costs for the Simpson home have been updated, the summary section of the final job cost sheet appears as follows:

Job Cost Sheet
Job Number   2719
Date Started: 7/12/2010
Date Completed:
Description: Simpson Home, Lot 79, Cambridge Subdivision

Cost Summary	
Direct materials cost	$100,000
Direct labor cost	30,000
Applied manufacturing overhead	45,000
Total cost	$175,000

The total cost to complete the job is referred to as the **cost of goods manufactured** or **cost of goods completed**. This is the total cost that must be transferred from the Work in Process Inventory account to the Finished Goods Inventory account.

Because this home was built for a specific customer, the new owners should take ownership shortly after construction is complete (and it passes the owners' inspection). Once the sale is final, accountants will move the total cost of the job from the Finished Goods Inventory account to Cost of Goods Sold, as shown in Exhibit 2.7.

EXHIBIT 2.7	Recording Finished Good Inventory and Cost of Goods Sold

Work in Process Inventory				Finished Goods Inventory			Cost of Goods Sold
Direct Materials	140,000	When job is		Cost of goods	When job		
Direct Labor	50,000	completed		completed	is sold	Job 2719	
Applied MOH*	60,000	175,000 — Job 2719 →		175,000	175,000 — →	175,000	
Balance	75,000						
* Manufacturing overhead							

Cost of Goods Sold of $175,000 includes all manufacturing costs of building the Simpson home, including **actual** direct materials, **actual** direct labor, and **applied** manufacturing overhead. This amount will be matched against sales revenue on the income statement. For example, if the Simpsons agreed to pay $275,000 for their home, the company would report $275,000 in Sales Revenue and $175,000 in Cost of Goods Sold, for $100,000 in gross profit. However, we still need to account for two factors.

First, the $175,000 in Cost of Goods Sold includes only the **manufacturing** costs. We still need to account for the nonmanufacturing costs. Recall that nonmanufacturing costs are always expensed as they are incurred. Period expenses do not flow through the Work in Process, Finished Goods Inventory, and Cost of Goods Sold accounts, but rather are subtracted after gross profit on the income statement.

Second, we need to adjust for any difference in actual and applied manufacturing overhead. This is typically done at the end of the fiscal year, because any difference in actual or applied often balances out over time.

RECORDING NONMANUFACTURING COSTS

In addition to the manufacturing costs just described, companies incur many other **nonmanufacturing costs** to market the products and run the businesses. Nonmanufacturing costs are treated differently than manufacturing costs. Instead of being treated as part of the product cost (included in inventory and eventually cost of goods sold), nonmanufacturing costs are expensed during the period in which they are incurred.

Assume Toll Brothers incurred the following nonmanufacturing expenses last month:

COACH'S TIP

Notice that depreciation on office equipment is treated as a period expense while depreciation on construction equipment was treated as manufacturing overhead (a product cost). The difference has to do with whether the asset being depreciated is used for manufacturing or nonmanufacturing activities.

Commissions to sales agents	$20,000
Advertising expense	5,000
Depreciation on office equipment	6,000
Other selling and administrative expenses	4,000
Total	$35,000

These nonmanufacturing costs would be recorded in individual expense accounts, including Commissions Expense, Advertising Expense, Depreciation Expense, and Miscellaneous Expenses. The total selling and administrative expense of $35,000 would be subtracted from gross margin on the income statement.

Overapplied or Underapplied Manufacturing Overhead

CALCULATING OVERAPPLIED AND UNDERAPPLIED MANUFACTURING OVERHEAD

Because **applied** manufacturing overhead is based on a predetermined overhead rate that is estimated before the accounting period begins, it will probably differ from the **actual** manufacturing overhead cost incurred during the period. The difference between actual and applied overhead is called **overapplied** or **underapplied overhead**. Overhead cost is overapplied if the amount applied is more than the actual overhead cost. It is underapplied if the amount applied is less than the actual cost.

After recording the actual and applied manufacturing overhead in our home-building example, the Manufacturing Overhead account would appear as follows:

Manufacturing Overhead			
Actual Mfg. Overhead		**Applied Mfg. Overhead**	
Indirect Materials	10,000		
Indirect Labor	5,000		
Supervisor Salaries	12,000		
Engineering Salaries	8,000		
Property Taxes	6,000	60,000	Applied Overhead
Plant Insurance	4,000		
Factory Depreciation	18,000		
Balance	3,000		

(63,000 total Actual Mfg. Overhead)

Notice that actual overhead cost was $63,000, but applied overhead was only $60,000, resulting in $3,000 of **underapplied overhead.** We discuss how to dispose of this overhead balance next.

DISPOSING OF OVERAPPLIED OR UNDERAPPLIED MANUFACTURING OVERHEAD

The most common method for disposing of the balance in Manufacturing Overhead is to make a direct adjustment to Cost of Goods Sold. Doing so makes sense as long as most of the jobs worked on during the period were completed and sold. However, if a significant amount of cost remains in Work in Process Inventory or Finished Goods Inventory, then part of the over- or underapplied manufacturing overhead technically should be adjusted to those accounts.

In this example, the company worked on only two jobs. One was completed and sold, but the other is still in process at the end of the accounting period. In reality, most companies complete and sell more than two jobs during the accounting period. Thus, we demonstrate the simplest and most common method of transferring the balance in the Manufacturing Overhead account directly to Cost of Goods Sold. (The more complicated approach of adjusting multiple accounts is covered in advanced cost accounting textbooks.)

To eliminate the $3,000 debit balance in the Manufacturing Overhead account, we need to credit the Manufacturing Overhead account and debit the Cost of Goods Sold account. Debiting Cost of Goods Sold increases it by $3,000. Increasing Cost of Goods Sold makes sense in this case because manufacturing overhead was underapplied. In other words, we did not apply enough cost to the jobs that were completed and eventually sold.

If Manufacturing Overhead had been overapplied (with a credit balance), we would have debited the Manufacturing Overhead account (to remove the credit balance) and credited Cost of Goods Sold. Crediting Cost of Goods Sold decreases it to reflect the fact that actual manufacturing overhead was less than applied overhead—that is, overhead

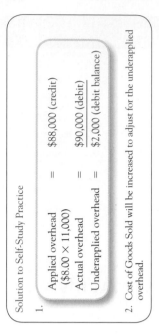

Solution to Self-Study Practice

1.

Applied overhead ($8.00 × 11,000)	=	$88,000 (credit)
Actual overhead	=	$90,000 (debit)
Underapplied overhead	=	$2,000 (debit balance)

2. Cost of Goods Sold will be increased to adjust for the underapplied overhead.

was overapplied. The effect of disposing of the Manufacturing Overhead balance to the Cost of Goods Sold account is as follows:

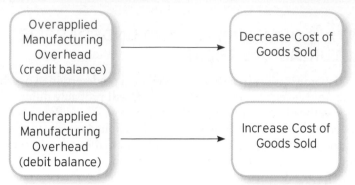

Take a moment to make sure you understand how to calculate over- and under-applied manufacturing overhead by completing this Self-Study Practice.

Self-Study Practice

Carlton Brothers Construction Company applies manufacturing overhead to jobs at a rate of $8.00 per direct labor hour. The following estimated and actual information is available.

	Estimated	Actual
Total manufacturing overhead	$96,000	$90,000
Total direct labor hours	12,000	11,000

1. Calculate the over- or underapplied overhead.
2. Will the adjustment for over- or underapplied overhead increase or decrease Cost of Good Sold?

After you have finished, check your answers with the solutions in the margin.

Learning Objective 6
Calculate the cost of goods manufactured and cost of goods sold.

PREPARING THE COST OF GOODS MANUFACTURED REPORT

The total cost that is transferred out of Work in Process Inventory and into Finished Goods Inventory is called the **cost of goods manufactured** or **cost of goods completed**. It represents the total cost of all jobs completed during the period.

The **cost of goods manufactured report** summarizes the flow of manufacturing costs through Raw Materials Inventory, Work in Process Inventory, and into Finished Goods Inventory. In addition to documenting the amount of direct materials, direct labor, and manufacturing overhead costs applied to Work in Process Inventory, it makes adjustments for the beginning and ending values of the inventory accounts. See Exhibit 2.8 for the final balance in each of the accounts after all of the previous transactions have been posted.

Recall that the company worked on only two jobs during the period. Because only one job (3335) is still in process at the end of the accounting period, the balance in the Work in Process Inventory account equals the total cost recorded on that job ($75,000). The ending balance in Finished Goods Inventory is zero because the only job completed during the period was also sold. The ending balance in Cost of Goods Sold represents the cost of Job 2719 ($175,000) plus the adjustment for underapplied manufacturing overhead ($3,000).

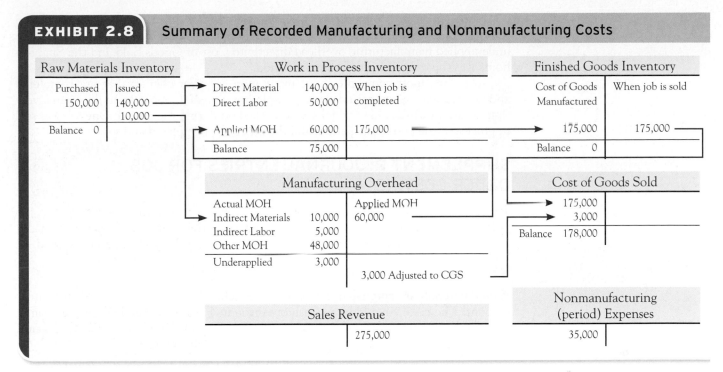

EXHIBIT 2.8 Summary of Recorded Manufacturing and Nonmanufacturing Costs

Using the T-accounts shown in Exhibit 2.8, we can prepare a cost of goods manufactured report as follows.

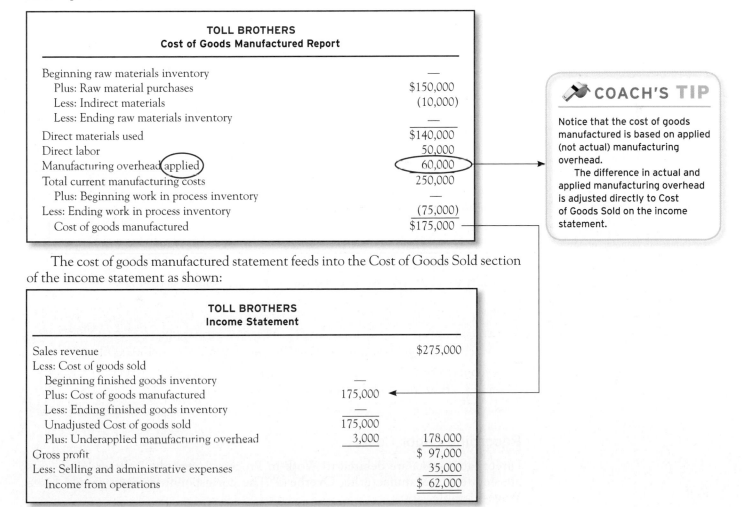

TOLL BROTHERS
Cost of Goods Manufactured Report

Beginning raw materials inventory	—
Plus: Raw material purchases	$150,000
Less: Indirect materials	(10,000)
Less: Ending raw materials inventory	—
Direct materials used	$140,000
Direct labor	50,000
Manufacturing overhead applied	60,000
Total current manufacturing costs	250,000
Plus: Beginning work in process inventory	—
Less: Ending work in process inventory	(75,000)
Cost of goods manufactured	$175,000

> **COACH'S TIP**
>
> Notice that the cost of goods manufactured is based on applied (not actual) manufacturing overhead.
>
> The difference in actual and applied manufacturing overhead is adjusted directly to Cost of Goods Sold on the income statement.

The cost of goods manufactured statement feeds into the Cost of Goods Sold section of the income statement as shown:

TOLL BROTHERS
Income Statement

Sales revenue		$275,000
Less: Cost of goods sold		
Beginning finished goods inventory	—	
Plus: Cost of goods manufactured	175,000	
Less: Ending finished goods inventory	—	
Unadjusted Cost of goods sold	175,000	
Plus: Underapplied manufacturing overhead	3,000	178,000
Gross profit		$ 97,000
Less: Selling and administrative expenses		35,000
Income from operations		$ 62,000

Notice that gross profit is $97,000, which is $3,000 less than the gross profit we initially computed for the sale of the Simpson home. The reason is that we adjusted the underapplied manufacturing overhead directly to Cost of Goods Sold and the Simpson home was the only job sold during the period.

In reality, most companies have many more jobs (or clients) that are completed and sold during a given period. This example was designed, however, to illustrate a very simple case in which only two jobs were worked on during the period. One job was still in process at the end of the period, and the other was completed and sold.

SUPPLEMENT 2: JOURNAL ENTRIES FOR JOB ORDER COSTING

This supplement illustrates the journal entries used to record the flow of costs in job order costing. For the sake of simplicity, we assume that none of the accounts had a beginning balance and that the company worked on only two jobs during the period.

Recording the Purchase and Issue of Materials

When materials are purchased, the total cost is debited to the Raw Materials Inventory account. The credit should be to Cash or Accounts Payable, depending on the form of payment. Assume that Toll Brothers purchased $150,000 in raw materials on account. The journal entry to record the purchase of raw materials follows:

	Debit	Credit
Raw Materials Inventory	150,000	
Accounts Payable		150,000

When materials are placed into production, the cost is debited to either Work in Process Inventory (for direct materials) or Manufacturing Overhead (for indirect materials). The credit entry should be to Raw Materials Inventory.

Assume that $150,000 worth of materials is withdrawn from inventory for the following uses:

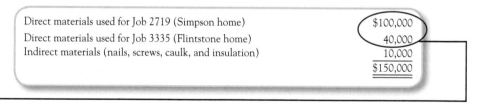

Direct materials used for Job 2719 (Simpson home)	$100,000
Direct materials used for Job 3335 (Flintstone home)	40,000
Indirect materials (nails, screws, caulk, and insulation)	10,000
	$150,000

> **COACH'S TIP**
>
> Only **direct** materials are debited to Work in Process Inventory. **Indirect** materials are debited to Manufacturing Overhead because they cannot be traced to specific jobs.

The entry to record the issuance of direct and indirect materials follows:

	Debit	Credit
Work in Process Inventory ($100,000 + $40,000)	140,000	
Manufacturing Overhead..	10,000	
Raw Materials Inventory		150,000

Recording Labor Costs

Direct labor costs are debited to Work in Process Inventory. Indirect labor costs are debited to Manufacturing Overhead. The corresponding credit should be to Wages Payable.

Assume Toll Brothers recorded the following information:

Direct labor on Job 2719 (Simpson home)	$30,000
Direct labor on Job 3335 (Flintstone home)	20,000
Indirect labor (such as maintenance and inspection work)	5,000
	$55,000

The journal entry to record the direct and indirect labor follows:

	Debit	Credit
Work in Process Inventory ($30,000 + $20,000).............	50,000	
Manufacturing Overhead	5,000	
Wages Payable		55,000

Recording Actual Manufacturing Overhead

Actual manufacturing overhead costs are debited to the Manufacturing Overhead account. The credit is to Cash, Accounts Payable, Prepaid Assets, and/or Accumulated Depreciation, depending on the nature of the transaction.

Assume Toll Brothers recorded the following actual manufacturing overhead costs during the month:

Salary paid to construction site supervisor	$12,000
Salary owed to a construction engineer	8,000
Property taxes owed but not yet paid	6,000
Expired insurance premium for construction site	4,000
Depreciation on construction equipment	18,000
	$48,000

The combined journal entry to record these actual manufacturing overhead costs is:

	Debit	Credit
Manufacturing Overhead	48,000	
Cash...		12,000
Salaries Payable		8,000
Taxes Payable...		6,000
Prepaid Insurance		4,000
Accumulated Depreciation		18,000

Recording Applied Manufacturing Overhead

Manufacturing overhead costs are **applied** to jobs by debiting the Work in Process Inventory account and crediting the Manufacturing Overhead account. Previously, we estimated the manufacturing overhead rate to be $75 per direct labor hour. Assume Toll Brothers' labor time tickets for the month revealed the following:

	Job Number	Direct Labor Hours Spent
Simpson home	2719	600
Flintstone home	3335	200
Total direct labor hours		800

Because the overhead rate is $75 per direct labor hour, we need to apply a total of $60,000 (800 hours × $75 per direct labor hour) in manufacturing overhead costs to the Work in Process Inventory account. A corresponding credit should be made to the Manufacturing Overhead account, as shown in the following entry:

	Debit	Credit
Work in Process Inventory	60,000	
Manufacturing Overhead		60,000

Transferring Costs to Finished Goods Inventory and Cost of Goods Sold

When a job is completed, the total cost of the job must be transferred from the Work in Process Inventory account to the Finished Goods Inventory account. For example, when Toll Brothers completes the Simpsons' home at a total cost of $175,000, the following journal entry would be made:

	Debit	Credit
Finished Goods Inventory	175,000	
Work in Process Inventory		175,000

When the job is sold, the total cost is transferred from Finished Goods Inventory to Cost of Goods Sold. A journal entry is also made to record sales revenue. For example, if the Simpsons agreed to pay $275,000 for their home, accountants would make the following journal entries to record the sales revenue and cost of the home.

COACH'S TIP

Remember that the difference between sales revenue and cost of goods sold is **gross profit,** or the profit before nonmanufacturing expenses have been deducted. In this case, the gross profit on the Simpson home is $100,000 ($275,000 − $175,000).

	Debit	Credit
Cash or Accounts Receivable	275,000	
Sales Revenue		275,000
Cost of Goods Sold	175,000	
Finished Goods Inventory		175,000

Recording Nonmanufacturing Costs

Unlike manufacturing costs, which are recorded in inventory until the product is sold, nonmanufacturing costs are expensed during the period in which they are incurred.

Assume Toll Brothers incurred the following nonmanufacturing expenses last month:

Commissions to sales agents	$20,000
Advertising expense	5,000
Depreciation on office equipment	6,000
Other selling and administrative expenses	4,000
Total	$35,000

The journal entries to record these nonmanufacturing costs would be:

	Debit	Credit
Commissions Expense..	20,000	
Cash or Commissions Payable.............................		20,000
Advertising Expense	5,000	
Cash, Prepaid Advertising, or Payables................		5,000
Depreciation Expense	6,000	
Accumulated Depreciation		6,000
Selling and Administrative Expenses................................	4,000	
Cash, Prepaids, or Payables		4,000

Overapplied or Underapplied Manufacturing Overhead

After recording the actual and applied manufacturing overhead in our home-building example, the Manufacturing Overhead account appears as follows:

Manufacturing Overhead				
Actual Mfg. Overhead		Applied Mfg. Overhead		
Indirect Materials	10,000			
Indirect Labor	5,000			
Supervisor Salaries	12,000			
63,000 Engineering Salaries	8,000			
Property Taxes	6,000	60,000	Applied Overhead	
Plant Insurance	4,000			
Factory Depreciation	18,000			
Balance	3,000			

> **COACH'S TIP**
>
> The debit balance in Manufacturing Overhead means that actual overhead cost was $3,000 more than the applied overhead cost. That is, overhead was **underapplied.** A credit balance will appear when actual overhead is less than applied overhead—that is, when overhead is **overapplied.**

To eliminate the $3,000 debit balance in the Manufacturing Overhead account, we need to credit the Manufacturing Overhead account and debit the Cost of Goods Sold account. The journal entry to dispose of the underapplied overhead is:

	Debit	Credit
Cost of Goods Sold	3,000	
Manufacturing Overhead		3,000

The effect of this entry is to increase the Cost of Goods Sold account by $3,000. If Manufacturing Overhead had been overapplied (with a credit balance), we would have debited the Manufacturing Overhead account to eliminate the balance and credited (decreased) the Cost of Goods Sold account.

After these transactions are posted to the general ledger, the accounts would appear as shown in Exhibit 2.8 on page 53.

DEMONSTRATION CASE

Pacific Pool Company (PPC) builds custom swimming pools for homeowners in California, Arizona, and Nevada. PPC uses material requisition forms and direct labor time tickets to trace direct materials and direct labor costs to specific jobs. Manufacturing overhead is applied to jobs at a rate of $100 per direct labor hour. During the first month of operations, the company recorded the following transactions:

(a) Purchased $200,000 in raw materials.
(b) Issued the following materials to production:
   • $130,000 was directly traceable to specific jobs.
   • $20,000 was not directly traceable to specific jobs.

(c) Recorded the following labor costs (paid in cash):
  • Direct labor $50,000
  • Construction supervision   30,000
(d) Recorded the following actual manufacturing overhead costs:
  • Construction insurance $ 5,000
  • Construction equipment depreciation   25,000
  • Pool permits and inspections   5,000
(e) Recorded the following nonmanufacturing costs:
  • Office equipment depreciation $ 3,000
  • Rent and insurance on owner's company car   2,000
  • Advertising costs   10,000
(f) Applied manufacturing overhead to jobs in process based on 900 actual direct labor hours.
(g) Completed 15 pools at a total cost of $195,000.
(h) Finalized the sale of 13 pools that cost $176,000. The other 2 pools are completed and awaiting inspection by the customer before the sale is finalized.
(i) Recorded sales revenue of $325,000 on the 13 pools that were sold.
(j) Closed the Manufacturing Overhead account balance to Cost of Goods Sold.

Required:

1. Show how all of these costs would flow through the following accounts:

2. Assuming there were no beginning balances in any of the accounts, calculate the ending balance in the following accounts:
   a. Work in Process Inventory.
   b. Finished Goods Inventory.
   c. Manufacturing Overhead (over/underapplied).
   d. Cost of Goods Sold (after the overhead adjustment).
3. Prepare a cost of goods manufactured report for PPC.
4. Prepare an income statement showing the adjustment to Cost of Goods Sold.

See page 60 for Solution.

CHAPTER SUMMARY

LO1   Describe the key differences between job order costing and process costing. p. 38

• Process costing is used in companies that make homogeneous products using a continuous production process.

• Job order costing is used in companies that make unique products or provide specialized services.

LO2   Describe the source documents used to track direct materials and direct labor costs to the job cost sheet. p. 41

• Direct materials are issued to production by using a materials requisition form showing the costs and quantities of all materials requested and the job they were used for.

• Direct labor costs are recorded using labor time tickets showing the amount of time workers spent on each specific job.

• The costs incurred for each job are recorded on a separate job cost sheet.

LO3   Calculate a predetermined overhead rate and use it to apply manufacturing overhead cost to jobs. p. 43

• Because manufacturing overhead costs cannot be traced directly to individual jobs, we use an allocation base or cost driver to apply manufacturing overhead cost to specific jobs.

- The predetermined overhead rate is calculated by dividing the estimated total manufacturing overhead cost by the estimated value of the allocation base.
- Manufacturing overhead is applied to specific jobs by multiplying the predetermined overhead rate by the actual amount of the allocation base used on the job.

Describe how costs flow through the accounting system in job order costing. p. 45   LO4

- Initially, raw material purchases are recorded in the Raw Materials Inventory account.
- When materials are placed into production, direct materials are recorded in the Work in Process Inventory account; indirect materials are recorded in the Manufacturing Overhead account.
- When labor costs are incurred, direct labor is recorded in the Work in Process Inventory account; indirect labor is recorded in the Manufacturing Overhead account.
- Actual manufacturing overhead costs are recorded on the debit side of the Manufacturing Overhead account.
- When manufacturing overhead is applied to specific jobs, the Work in Process Inventory account is debited and the Manufacturing Overhead account is credited.
- When a job is completed, the total cost of goods completed is transferred from the Work in Process Inventory account to the Finished Goods Inventory account.
- When the job is delivered to the customer, the total cost is transferred from Finished Goods Inventory to Cost of Goods Sold.
- Nonmanufacturing costs are recorded as period expenses rather than as part of the manufacturing cost flow.

Calculate and dispose of overapplied or underapplied manufacturing overhead. p. 51   LO5

- Actual overhead costs are recorded on the debit side of the Manufacturing Overhead account; applied manufacturing overhead costs are recorded on the credit side. Thus, the balance in the Manufacturing Overhead account represents the amount of overapplied or underapplied overhead.
- If the overhead account has a debit balance, actual overhead costs were higher than applied overhead costs; that is, overhead was underapplied.
- If the overhead account has a credit balance, applied overhead costs were higher than actual overhead costs; that is, overhead was overapplied.
- At the end of the year, the remaining overhead balance is typically transferred to the Cost of Goods Sold account. Overapplied overhead decreases (credits) the Cost of Goods Sold account; underapplied overhead increases (debits) the Cost of Goods Sold account.

Calculate the cost of goods manufactured and cost of goods sold. p. 52   LO6

- The total manufacturing cost that flows out of Work in Process Inventory and into Finished Goods Inventory is called cost of good manufactured. When the product is sold, the cost is transferred to the Cost of Goods Sold account.
- Initially, the cost of goods manufactured and the cost of goods sold are based on actual direct materials, actual direct labor, and applied manufacturing overhead costs.
- The Cost of Goods Sold account is updated to reflect actual manufacturing overhead costs through an adjustment for overapplied or underapplied manufacturing overhead.

Key Formulas	
To Calculate	**Formula**
Predetermined overhead rate	$\dfrac{\text{Estimated Total Manufacturing Overhead Cost}}{\text{Estimated Units of the Allocation Base}}$
Applied overhead	Predetermined Overhead Rate $\times$ Actual Units of the Allocation Base
Overapplied or underapplied overhead	Applied Overhead $-$ Actual Overhead
	A positive value indicates that overhead cost was overapplied.
	A negative value indicates that overhead cost was underapplied.

SOLUTION TO DEMONSTRATION CASE

1. and 2.

Raw Materials Inventory	
(a) 200,000	(b) 150,000
Bal. 50,000	

Work in Process Inventory	
(b) 130,000	(g) 195,000
(c) 50,000	
(f) 90,000	
Bal. 75,000	

Finished Goods Inventory	
(g) 195,000	(h) 176,000
Bal. 19,000	

Manufacturing Overhead	
(b) 20,000	(f) 900 × $100 = $90,000
(c) 30,000	
(d) 35,000	
	5,000 Overapplied
(j) 5,000 Adjustment	

Cost of Goods Sold	
(h) 176,000	(j) 5,000
Bal. 171,000	

Sales Revenue	
	(i) 325,000

Nonmanufacturing Expenses	
(e) 15,000	

3.

PACIFIC POOL COMPANY
Cost of Goods Manufactured Report

Beginning raw materials inventory	—
Plus: Raw material purchases	$200,000
Less: Indirect materials	(20,000)
Less: Ending raw materials inventory	(50,000)
Direct materials used	$130,000
Direct labor	50,000
Manufacturing overhead applied	90,000
Total current manufacturing costs	$270,000
Plus: Beginning work in process inventory	—
Less: Ending work in process inventory	(75,000)
Cost of goods manufactured	$195,000

4.

PACIFIC POOL COMPANY
Income Statement

Sales revenue		$325,000
Less: Cost of goods sold		
Beginning finished goods inventory	—	
Plus: Cost of goods manufactured	195,000	
Less: Ending finished goods inventory	19,000	
Unadjusted Cost of goods sold	176,000	
Less: Overapplied manufacturing overhead	5,000	171,000
Gross profit		$154,000
Less: Selling and administrative expenses		15,000
Income from operations		$139,000

KEY TERMS

Actual Manufacturing Costs (p. 48)

Allocation Base (p. 43)

Cost of Goods Completed (p. 50)

Cost of Goods Manufactured (p. 50)

Cost of Goods Sold (p. 45)

Direct Labor Time Ticket (p. 42)

Finished Goods Inventory (p. 45)

Indirect Materials (p. 45)

Job Cost Sheet (p. 40)

Job Order Costing (p. 39)

Materials Requisition Form (p. 41)

Overapplied Overhead (p. 51)

Predetermined Overhead Rate (p. 43)

Process Costing (p. 38)

Raw Materials Inventory (p. 45)

Underapplied Overhead (p. 51)

Work in Process Inventory (p. 45)

See complete definitions in glossary at back of text.

QUESTIONS

1. What is the difference between job order and process costing?

2. What types of companies are likely to use job order costing? Give three examples.

3. What types of companies are likely to use process costing? Give three examples.

4. Many service industries use job order costing to keep track of the cost of serving clients. Can you think of a service industry that provides fairly homogeneous services? Describe the industry and explain why it might use process costing rather than job order costing.

5. Many companies use a modified costing system that blends certain elements of process costing and job order costing. Can you think of a company that makes products or provides services that have certain similarities (similar to process costing) but also allows a certain degree of customization (similar to job order costing)? Give an example.

6. What are the three major types of manufacturing costs that are accounted for in a job order cost system? Describe and give an example of each type of cost for an auto repair shop that uses job order costing.

7. What is the purpose of a job cost sheet? What information should it contain?

8. The job cost sheet serves as a subsidiary ledger to the Work in Process Inventory account. Explain what this means and how you would verify this.

9. What is the purpose of a materials requisition form? What information should it contain?

10. Explain how the cost of direct and indirect materials flows through the Raw Materials, Work in Process, and Manufacturing Overhead accounts.

11. What is the primary source document used to trace the cost of direct labor to specific jobs? What information should it contain?

12. Some would argue that costs would be more accurate if overhead costs were assigned to jobs using an overhead rate based on actual overhead costs and actual value of the allocation base. Do you agree or disagree with this view? Explain.

13. Why is manufacturing overhead assigned to Work in Process Inventory in a different manner than direct materials and direct labor? Explain how it is different.

14. Explain how and why depreciation on office equipment is treated differently than depreciation on manufacturing equipment.

15. How is a predetermined overhead rate calculated? How does a company decide on an allocation base to use to calculate the rate?

16. How do you apply manufacturing overhead to the Work in Process Inventory account? Is it based on estimated or actual data?

17. Will the amount of manufacturing overhead that is applied to Work in Process Inventory be equal to the actual amount of manufacturing overhead costs incurred? Why or why not?

18. How do you know when manufacturing overhead is overapplied? What type of balance would you expect to see in the Manufacturing Overhead account?

19. How do you know when manufacturing overhead is underapplied? What type of balance would you expect to see in the Manufacturing Overhead account?

20. Explain the most common method of eliminating any balance in the Manufacturing Overhead account at year-end. What account(s) is (are) adjusted? What happens to the account(s) when manufacturing overhead is overapplied? Underapplied?

MULTIPLE CHOICE

Quiz 2
www.mhhe.com/whitecotton1e

1. Why would a company use process costing rather than job order costing to compute product cost?

   a. The company produces units to customer specifications.

   b. The company manufactures a product using a series of continuous processes that results in units that are virtually identical from one to the next.

   c. The company wants to track the cost of material, labor, and overhead to specific customers.

   d. The company wants to allocate manufacturing overhead using an overhead application rate based on direct labor hours.

   e. All of the above.

2. The source document used to specify the quantity and unit costs of raw materials issued into production is called a:

   a. Production order form.

   b. Materials requisition form.

   c. Direct labor time ticket.

   d. Predetermined overhead rate.

   e. Job order cost sheet.

3. Which of the following source documents serves as a subsidiary ledger for the Work in Process Inventory account?

    a. Production order form.
    b. Materials requisition form.
    c. Direct labor time ticket.
    d. Predetermined overhead rate.
    e. Job order cost sheet.

4. Comstock Company uses a predetermined overhead rate based on machine hours to apply manufacturing overhead to jobs. Estimated and actual total manufacturing overhead costs and machine hours follow:

	Estimated	Actual
Total overhead cost	$100,000	$110,250
Machine hours	20,000	21,000

    What is the predetermined overhead rate per machine hour?

    a. $4.75.
    b. $5.00.
    c. $5.25.
    d. $5.51.

5. Refer to the information in question 4. How much is over- or underapplied overhead?

    a. $10,250 overapplied.
    b. $10,250 underapplied.
    c. $ 5,250 overapplied.
    d. $ 5,250 underapplied.
    e. None of the above.

6. Which of the following cost(s) is (are) recorded directly into the Work in Process Inventory account?

    a. Direct materials.
    b. Indirect materials.
    c. Direct labor.
    d. Both a and c.
    e. All of the above.

7. Actual manufacturing overhead costs are recorded:

    a. On the left (debit) side of the Work in Process Inventory account.
    b. On the right (credit) side of the Work in Process Inventory account.
    c. On the left (debit) of the Manufacturing Overhead account.

    d. On the right (credit) side of the Manufacturing Overhead account.
    e. Both b and c.

8. Applied manufacturing overhead costs are recorded:

    a. On the left (debit) of the Work in Process Inventory account.
    b. On the right (credit) side of the Work in Process Inventory account.
    c. On the left (debit) of the Manufacturing Overhead account.
    d. On the right (credit) side of the Manufacturing Overhead account.
    e. Both a and d.

9. The Manufacturing Overhead account has a $10,000 debit balance that is closed directly to Cost of Goods Sold. Which of the following statements is true?

    a. Actual manufacturing overhead was less than applied manufacturing overhead.
    b. Actual manufacturing overhead was more than applied manufacturing overhead.
    c. The entry to eliminate the balance in Manufacturing Overhead will decrease Cost of Goods Sold.
    d. The entry to eliminate the balance in Manufacturing Overhead will increase Cost of Goods Sold.
    e. Both a and c.
    f. Both b and d.

10. Before disposing of its year-end manufacturing overhead balance, Delphi Corporation had the following amounts in Manufacturing Overhead and Cost of Goods Sold:

Applied manufacturing overhead	$100,000
Actual manufacturing overhead	90,000
Unadjusted cost of goods sold	800,000

    If Delphi closes the balance of its Manufacturing Overhead account directly to Cost of Goods Sold, how much is adjusted cost of goods sold?

    a. $790,000.
    b. $810,000.
    c. $890,000.
    d. $900,000.
    e. None of the above.

> Answers to Multiple-Choice Questions located in back of the text.

MINI EXERCISES

L01   **M2-1 Identifying Companies That Use Job Order versus Process Costing**

Indicate whether each of the following companies is likely to use job order (J) or process costing (P).

____ 1. Golf ball manufacturer.

____ 2. Landscaping business.

____ 3. Tile manufacturer.

____ 4. Auto repair shop.

____ 5. Pet food manufacturer.

——— 6. Light bulb manufacturer.

——— 7. Water bottling company.

——— 8. Appliance repair business.

——— 9. DVD manufacturer.

——— 10. Music video production company.

M2-2 Identifying Source Document Information   LO2

For each of the following items, indicate whether it would appear on a materials requisition form (MRF), a direct labor time ticket (DLTT), and/or a job cost sheet (JCS). Note: An item may appear on more than one document.

——— 1. Employee name.

——— 2. Quantity of direct material used.

——— 3. Total dollar value of direct materials.

——— 4. Applied manufacturing overhead.

——— 5. Hours worked by an employee.

——— 6. Hours a specific employee worked on a particular job.

——— 7. Job start date.

——— 8. Time an employee clocked in or out.

——— 9. Different jobs that a specific employee worked on.

M2-3 Calculating Predetermined Overhead Rates   LO3

Willard Company applies manufacturing overhead costs to products as a percentage of direct labor dollars. Estimated and actual values of manufacturing overhead and direct labor costs are summarized here:

	Estimated	Actual
Direct labor cost	$400,000	$350,000
Manufacturing overhead	800,000	725,000

1. Compute the predetermined overhead rate.
2. Interpret this rate and explain how it will be used to apply manufacturing overhead to jobs.
3. Explain whether you used estimated or actual values to compute the rate, and why.

M2-4 Calculating Applied Manufacturing Overhead   LO3

Refer to M2-3 for Willard Company.

1. Determine how much overhead to apply to production.
2. Explain whether applied overhead was based on actual values, estimated values, or both.

M2-5 Calculating Over- or Underapplied Manufacturing Overhead   LO4

Refer to M2-3 for Willard Company.

1. Compute over- or underapplied overhead.
2. Explain how you would handle the over- or underapplied overhead at the end of the accounting period. Which accounts will be affected? Will the accounts be increased or decreased?

M2-6 Determining Missing Amounts   LO5

Determine missing amounts to complete the following table:

Actual Mfg. Overhead	Applied Mfg. Overhead	Over-/Underapplied	Amount
$110,000	$105,000	?	$ 5,000
79,000	?	Overapplied	4,500
?	261,300	Underapplied	10,800
141,000	153,800	?	?

LO2, 4 **M2-7 Recording the Purchase and Issue of Raw Materials**

Kelly Company's raw materials inventory transactions for the most recent month are summarized here.

Beginning raw materials	$ 10,000	
Purchases of raw materials	100,000	
Raw materials issued		
Materials requisition 1445	50,000	For Job 101
Materials requisition 1446	40,000	For Job 102
Materials requisition 1447	15,000	Used on multiple jobs

1. How much of the raw materials cost would be added to the Work in Process Inventory account during the period?
2. How much of the raw materials costs would be added to the Manufacturing Overhead account?
3. Compute the ending balance in the Raw Materials Inventory account.

Supplement **M2-8**

Refer to the information in M2-7.

1. Prepare the journal entry to record the purchase of raw materials.
2. Prepare the journal entry to record the issuance of raw materials to production.

LO2, 4 **M2-9 Recording Direct and Indirect Labor Costs**

Kelly Company's payroll costs for the most recent month are summarized here:

Item	Description		Total Cost
Hourly labor wages	750 hours @ $25 per hour		
	200 hours for Job 101 =	$5,000	
	300 hours for Job 102 =	7,500	
	250 hours for Job 103 =	6,250	$18,750
Factory supervision			4,250
Production engineer			6,000
Factory janitorial work			2,000
General and administrative salaries			8,000
Total payroll costs			$39,000

1. Calculate how much of the labor costs would be added to the following accounts:

   Work in Process Inventory

   Manufacturing Overhead

   Selling and Administrative Expenses

2. Explain why some labor costs are recorded as work in process, some as manufacturing overhead, and some as period costs.

Supplement **M2-10 Preparing Journal Entries**

Refer to M2-9.

1. Prepare the journal entry to record Kelly Company's payroll costs.
2. The company applies manufacturing overhead to products at a predetermined rate of $50 per direct labor hour. Prepare the journal entry to apply manufacturing overhead to production.

LO3, 4, 5 **M2-11 Calculating Over- or Underapplied Overhead Costs**

Refer to M2-10 for Kelly Company. Its actual manufacturing costs for the most recent period are summarized here:

Item	Description		Total Cost
Direct materials	Used on Jobs 101 and 102		$90,000
Indirect materials	Used on multiple jobs		15,000
Hourly labor wages	750 hours @ $25 per hour		
	200 hours for Job 101 =	$5,000	
	300 hours for Job 102 =	7,500	
	250 hours for Job 103 =	6,250	18,750
Factory supervision			4,250
Production engineer			6,000
Factory janitorial work			2,000
General and administrative salaries			8,000
Other manufacturing overhead costs (factory rent, insurance, depreciation, etc.)			7,000
Other general and administrative costs (office rent, insurance, depreciation, etc.)			5,000

1. Post the preceding information to Kelly Company's Manufacturing Overhead T-account.
2. Compute over- or underapplied manufacturing overhead.

M2-12 Preparing Journal Entries

Supplement

Refer to M2-11 for Kelly Company.

1. Prepare the journal entry to close the Manufacturing Overhead account balance to Cost of Goods Sold.
2. Explain whether the entry in requirement 1 will increase or decrease Cost of Goods Sold and why.

M2-13 Calculating Total Current Manufacturing Cost

LO6

The following information is available for Carefree Industries:

Beginning work in process inventory	$ 75,000
Ending work in process inventory	90,000
Cost of goods manufactured	300,000

Compute total current manufacturing costs.

M2-14 Calculating Cost of Goods Sold

LO6

The following information is available for Carefree Industries.

Cost of goods manufactured	$300,000
Beginning finished goods inventory	140,000
Ending finished goods inventory	120,000

Compute the cost of goods sold.

M2-15 Calculating Direct Materials Used in Production

LO6

The following information is available for Carefree Industries.

Direct labor	$100,000
Total current manufacturing costs	370,000

Manufacturing overhead is applied to production at 150 percent of direct labor cost. Determine the amount of direct materials used in production.

M2-16 Calculating Missing Amounts and Cost of Goods Manufactured

LO6

For each of the following independent cases A–D, compute the missing values:

Case	Total Current Manufacturing Costs	Beginning Work in Process Inventory	Ending Work in Process Inventory	Cost of Goods Manufactured
A	$4,800	$1,400	$1,100	$?
B	2,200	?	1,325	2,550
C	?	675	1,500	6,880
D	7,900	750	?	6,875

M2-17 Calculating Missing Amounts and Cost of Goods Sold

LO6

For each of the following independent cases A–D, compute the missing values:

Case	Cost of Goods Manufactured	Beginning Finished Goods Inventory	Ending Finished Goods Inventory	Cost of Goods Sold
A	$3,100	$ 400	$ 100	$?
B	4,250	?	1,325	4,550
C	?	950	500	4,375
D	10,900	2,200	?	9,750

EXERCISES

LO2, 3, 4   **E2-1 Posting Direct Materials, Direct Labor, and Applied Overhead to T-Accounts, Calculating Ending Balances**

Stone Creek Furniture Factory (SCFF), a custom furniture manufacturer, uses job order costing to track the cost of each customer order. On March 1, SCFF had two jobs in process with the following costs:

Work in Process	Balance on 3/1
Job 33	$5,000
Job 34	4,000
	$9,000

Source documents revealed the following during March:

	Materials Requisitions Forms	Labor Time Tickets	Status of Job at Month-End
Job 33	$ 3,000	$ 5,000	Completed and sold
Job 34	3,000	4,000	Completed, but not sold
Job 35	4,000	3,000	In process
Indirect	1,000	2,000	
	$11,000	$14,000	

The company applies overhead to products at a rate of 75 percent of direct labor cost.

Required:

1. Compute the cost of Jobs 33, 34, and 35 at the end of the month.
2. Calculate the balance in the Work in Process Inventory, Finished Goods Inventory, and Cost of Goods Sold accounts at month-end.

Supplement   **E2-2 Preparing Journal Entries**

Refer to the information in E2-1 for Stone Creek Furniture Factory.

Required:

Prepare journal entries to record the materials requisitions, labor costs, and applied overhead.

LO2, 4   **E2-3 Analyzing Labor Time Tickets and Recording Labor Costs**

A weekly time ticket for Jim Bolton follows:

Direct Labor Time Ticket			Dates:	Monday 8/12 - Friday 8/16, 2010
Ticket Number:	TT338			
Employee:	Jim Bolton			
Date	Time Started	Time Ended	Total Hours	Job Number
8/12/2010	7:00 AM	3:00 PM	8 hours	Job 271
8/13/2010	7:00 AM	3:00 PM	8 hours	Job 271
8/14/2010	7:00 AM	3:00 PM	8 hours	Job 272
8/15/2010	7:00 AM	11:00 AM	4 hours	Job 272
8/15/2010	12:00 PM	4:00 PM	4 hours	Maintenance
8/16/2010	7:00 AM	3:00 PM	8 hours	Job 273
		Weekly Total	40 hours	
		Hourly Labor Rate	$25	
		Total Wages Earned	$1,000	

Required:

1. Determine how much of the $1,000 that Jim earned during this week would be charged to Job 271, Job 272, and Job 273.
2. Explain how the time spent doing maintenance work would be treated.

E2-4 **Preparing Journal Entries**   Supplement

Refer to the information presented in E2-3 for Jim Bolton.

Required:

Prepare a journal entry to record Jim's wages or assuming they have not yet been paid.

E2-5 **Calculating Predetermined Overhead Rate and Applied Overhead**   LO3

Spokesman Bike Company manufactures custom racing bicycles. The company uses a job order cost system to determine the cost of each bike. Estimated costs and expenses for the coming year follow:

Bike parts	$347,800
Factory machinery depreciation	52,500
Factory supervisor salaries	134,000
Factory direct labor	218,400
Factory supplies	36,900
Factory property tax	24,750
Advertising cost	18,000
Administrative salaries	46,000
Administrative-related depreciation	17,700
Total expected costs	$896,050

Required:

1. Determine the predetermined overhead rate per direct labor hour if the average direct labor rate is $12 per hour.
2. Determine the amount of applied overhead if 18,500 hours are worked in the upcoming year.

E2-6 **Finding Unknown Values in the Cost of Goods Manufactured**   LO3, 6
and Sold Report

Mulligan Manufacturing Company uses a job order cost system with overhead applied to products at a rate of 200 percent of direct labor cost. Selected manufacturing data follow:

	Case 1	Case 2	Case 3*
Direct materials used	$ 10,000	f.	$15,000
Direct labor	15,000	e.	i.
Manufacturing overhead applied	a.	16,000	j.
Total current manufacturing costs	b.	35,000	27,000
Beginning work in process inventory	8,000	g.	7,000
Ending work in process inventory	6,000	8,000	k.
Cost of goods manufactured	c.	40,000	30,000
Beginning finished goods inventory	5,000	10,000	l.
Ending finished goods inventory	7,000	h.	5,000
Cost of goods sold	d.	42,000	33,000

Hint: For Case 3 (parts i. and j.), first solve for conversion costs and then determine how much of that is direct labor and how much is manufacturing overhead.

Required:

Treating each case independently, find the missing amounts for letters a–l. You should do them in the order listed.

LO3, 4, 5   **E2-7 Calculating Overhead Rates, Actual and Applied Manufacturing Overhead, and Analyzing Over- or Underapplied Manufacturing Overhead**

Cayman Custom Manufacturing Company applies manufacturing overhead on the basis of machine hours. At the beginning of the year, the company estimated its total overhead cost to be $300,000 and machine hours to be 15,000. Actual manufacturing overhead and machine hours were $340,000 and 16,000, respectively.

Required:

1. Compute the predetermined overhead rate.
2. Compute applied manufacturing overhead.
3. Compute over- or underapplied manufacturing overhead.

Supplement   **E2-8 Preparing Journal Entries**

Refer to the information presented in E2-7 for Cayman Company.

Required:

1. Prepare the journal entries to record actual and applied manufacturing overhead.
2. Prepare the journal entry to transfer the overhead balance to Cost of Goods Sold.

LO3, 4   **E2-9 Calculating Cost of Finished and Unfinished Jobs**

Following is partial information for Delamunte Industries for the month of August:

	Work In Process
Balance, August 1	$132,000
Direct materials	114,800
Direct labor	167,000
Applied overhead	143,000

Jobs finished during August are summarized here:

Job #	Cost of Jobs Completed
234	$65,950
237	32,800
231	54,000
246	17,500

Required:

1. Determine the predetermined overhead rate if Delamunte applies overhead on the basis of direct labor dollars.
2. Determine the cost of unfinished jobs at August 31.

Supplement   **E2-10 Preparing Journal Entries**

Refer to the information presented in E2-9 for Delamunte Industries.

Required:

Prepare the journal entries to record the cost of jobs completed.

LO3, 4, 6   **E2-11 Calculating and Posting the Total Cost to Complete a Job and Sales Revenue to T-Accounts**

Aquazona Pool Company is a custom pool builder. It recently completed a pool for the Drayna family (Job 1324) as summarized on the following incomplete job cost sheet.

Job Cost Sheet
Job Number   1324
Date Started: 7/12/2010
Date Completed:
Description: Drayna Pool

Direct Materials		Direct Labor			Applied Manufacturing Overhead		
Req. No	Amount	Ticket	Hours	Amount	Hours	Rate	Amount
MR 3345	$1,500	TT 335	31	$ 600			
MR 3372	1,000	TT 340	39	800			
MR 4251	1,250	TT 385	31	600			
MR 4263	1,750	TT 425	34	700			
MR 5236	2,000	TT 445	23	500			
	$7,500		158	$3,200	?	?	?

Cost Summary	
Direct Materials Cost	$7,500
Direct Labor Cost	3,200
Applied Manufacturing Overhead	?
Total Cost	

The company applies overhead to jobs at a rate of $10 per direct labor hour.

Required:

1. Calculate how much overhead would be applied to Job 1324.
2. Compute the total cost of Job 1324.
3. Assume the company bids its pools at total manufacturing cost plus 30 percent. If actual costs were the same as estimated, determine how much revenue the company would report on the sale of Job 1324.
4. Calculate how much gross profit Aquazona made on the sale of the Drayna pool.

E2-12 Preparing Journal Entries

Supplement

Refer to the information presented in E2-11 for Aquazona Pool Company.

Required:

Prepare journal entries to show the completion of Job 1324 and to recognize the sales revenue for that job. Assume the total cost of Job 1324 is currently in the Finished Goods Inventory Account and that the Draynas paid for the pool with cash.

E2-13 Identifying Manufacturing Cost Flow through T-Accounts

LO4

The flow of costs through a company's cost accounting system is summarized in the following T-accounts:

Raw Materials Inventory		Manufacturing Overhead	
(a)	(b)	(b)	(d)
		(c)	
		(e)	

Work in Process Inventory		Finished Goods Inventory	
(b)	(g)	(g)	(h)
(c)			
(d)			

Sales Revenue		Cost of Goods Sold	
	(i)	(h)	

Selling and Administrative Expenses		Other Assets or Liabilities	
(c)		(i)	(a)
(f)			(c)
			(e)
			(f)

Required:

Describe the transactions represented by letters (a)–(i). When more than one debit appears in a single transaction, explain why the costs are recorded in multiple accounts.

LO3, 4, 5, 6   **E2-14 Calculating Actual and Applied Manufacturing Overhead Costs and Over- or Underapplied Overhead Costs**

Verizox Company uses a job order costing system with manufacturing overhead applied to products based on direct labor hours. At the beginning of the most recent year, the company estimated its manufacturing overhead cost at $200,000. Estimated direct labor cost was $500,000 for 20,000 hours (average of $25 per hour).

Actual costs for the most recent month are summarized here:

Item Description	Total Cost
Direct labor (2,000 hours @ $26 per hour)	$52,000
Indirect costs	
Indirect labor	2,400
Indirect materials	3,300
Factory rent	3,200
Factory supervision	4,700
Factory depreciation	5,600
Factory janitorial work	1,100
Factory insurance	1,700
General and administrative salaries	4,100
Selling expenses	5,300

Required:

1. Calculate the predetermined overhead rate.
2. Calculate the amount of applied manufacturing overhead.
3. Calculate actual manufacturing overhead costs. Explain which costs you excluded and why.
4. Compute over- or underapplied overhead.
5. Suppose that the over- or underapplied manufacturing overhead was not properly transferred to Cost of Goods Sold at the end of the period. Explain the impact that oversight would have on Verizox's cost of goods sold and net income for the period.

Supplement   **E2-15 Preparing Journal Entries**

Refer to the information presented in E2-14 for Verizox Company.

Required:

1. Prepare the journal entry to apply manufacturing overhead to Work in Process Inventory.
2. Prepare the journal entry to record actual manufacturing overhead costs. The credit can be to a generic account titled Cash, Payables, and so on.
3. Prepare the journal entry to transfer the Manufacturing Overhead account balance to Cost of Goods Sold. Does this increase or decrease Cost of Goods Sold? Why?

E2-16 Recording Manufacturing and Nonmanufacturing Costs   **LO3, 4**

Reyes Manufacturing Company uses a job order costing system. At the beginning of January, the company had one job in process (Job 201) and one job completed but not yet sold (Job 200). Other select account balances follow (ignore any accounts that are not listed).

Raw Materials Inventory	Work in Process Inventory	Finished Goods Inventory
1/1 32,000	1/1 15,500	1/1 20,000

Cost of Goods Sold	Manufacturing Overhead	Sales Revenue

During January, the company had the following transactions:

(a) Purchased $60,000 worth of materials on account.
(b) Recorded materials issued to production as follows:

Job Number	Total Cost
201	$ 10,000
202	20,000
Indirect materials	5,000
	$ 35,000

(c) Recorded factory payroll costs from direct labor time tickets that revealed the following:

Job Number	Hours	Total Cost
201	120	$ 3,000
202	400	10,000
Factory supervision		4,000
		$ 17,000

(d) Applied overhead to production at a rate of $30 per direct labor hour for 520 actual direct labor hours.
(e) Recorded the following actual manufacturing overhead costs:

Item	Total Cost	Description
Factory rent	$ 2,000	Paid in cash
Depreciation	3,000	Factory equipment
Factory utilities	2,500	Incurred but not paid
Factory insurance	1,500	Prepaid policy
	$ 9,000	

(f) Job 201 was completed and transferred to Finished Goods Inventory.
(g) Sold Job 200 for $50,000.

Job 202 was still in process at the end of January.

Required:

1. Complete the following job cost summary to calculate the total cost of the jobs that were worked on during the period.

Job Number	Beg. Balance (given)	Direct Material Cost	Direct Labor Cost	MOH* Applied @ $30 per DL† hour	Total Cost of Job
200	$20,000	$ 0	$ 0	$ 0	$20,000
201	15,500				
202	0				

* Manufacturing overhead
† Direct labor

2. Post the preceding transactions to T-accounts. Create an additional account called Miscellaneous Accounts to capture the offsetting debits and credits to other accounts such as Cash, Payables, Accumulated Depreciation, and so on.
3. Compute the ending balance in the following accounts:
   Raw Materials Inventory
   Work in Process Inventory
   Finished Goods Inventory
   Cost of Goods Sold (unadjusted)
   Manufacturing Overhead
4. Explain which jobs would appear in Work in Process Inventory, Finished Goods Inventory, and Cost of Goods Sold. Confirm that the total cost of each job is equal to the ending balance in its respective control accounts.

L06   **E2-17 Calculating Missing Amounts and Cost of Goods Manufactured and Sold**

Required:

For each of the following independent cases (1–4), compute the missing values. Note: Complete the missing items in alphabetical order.

	Case 1	Case 2	Case 3	Case 4
Beginning raw materials	$ 5,000	e.	$ 20,000	$110,000
Raw material purchases	45,000	12,250	41,640	o.
Indirect materials issued	1,000	1,000	1,500	2,000
Ending raw materials	2,000	2,250	i.	93,500
Direct materials used	a.	13,500	33,720	n.
Direct labor	29,000	f.	j.	123,250
Manufacturing overhead applied	52,000	40,350	31,080	541,730
Total current manufacturing costs	b.	75,600	92,900	m.
Beginning work in process	41,000	32,600	k.	102,520
Ending work in process	c.	g.	41,250	236,100
Cost of goods manufactured	139,000	79,800	89,225	825,900
Beginning finished goods	72,000	h.	51,900	p.
Ending finished goods	80,000	30,100	l.	397,200
Cost of goods sold	d.	71,000	113,375	839,400

L06   **E2-18 Calculating Cost of Goods Manufactured and Sold and Preparing an Income Statement**

StorSmart Company makes plastic organizing bins. The company has the following inventory balances at the beginning and end of March:

	Beginning Inventory	Ending Inventory
Raw materials	$30,000	$25,000
Work in process	23,000	45,000
Finished goods	80,000	68,000

Additional information for the month of March follows:

Raw materials purchases	$ 42,000
Indirect materials used	1,000
Direct labor	64,000
Manufacturing overhead applied	37,000
Selling and administrative expenses	25,000
Sales revenue	236,000

Required:

Based on this information, prepare the following for StorSmart:

1. A cost of goods manufactured report.
2. An income statement for the month of March.

E2-19 Recording Materials Based on Materials Requisitions

LO2, Supplement

A recent materials requisition form for Christopher Creek Furniture Manufacturers follows:

Requisition Number	Job Number	Item Description	Total Cost
MR 234	25	¼" maple planks	$400
MR 235	26	¼" cherry planks	500
MR 236	27	½" birch planks	450
MR 237	Indirect	Wood screws, etc.	100

Required:

Prepare the journal entry to record the issuance of materials.

E2-20 Preparing Entries for Manufacturing Costs

LO3, Supplement

Roy's Appliance Repair Shop uses a job order costing system to track the cost of each repair. Roy's applies its "garage or shop" overhead at a rate of $25 per direct labor hour spent on each repair. Roy's uses the following accounts to track the cost of all repairs:

Raw Materials (parts and supplies)	Repair Jobs in Process	Cost of Repairs Completed and Sold	Garage/Shop* Overhead Costs

* Because an auto shop does not manufacture a product, the overhead cost would include all of the indirect costs that are incurred in the "garage or shop" that cannot be traced to a specific repair job.

The following transactions occurred during the most recent month:

(a) Purchased raw materials (parts and supplies) on account $21,000.
(b) Used $16,000 in raw materials (parts and supplies). Of this, $14,000 was for major parts that were traceable to individual repair jobs, and the remainder was for incidental supplies such as lubricants, rags, fuel, and so on.
(c) Recorded a total of $8,000 in direct labor cost (for 400 hours) that are owed but not yet paid.
(d) Applied overhead to repair jobs at a rate of $25 per direct labor hour.
(e) Recorded the following actual overhead costs:

Rent on garage (pre-paid in the prior month)	14,000
Depreciation on repair equipment	2,000
Garage supervisor's salary (owed but not yet paid)	3,000

(f) Completed repair jobs costing $45,000 and charged customers at cost plus 30 percent. (**Note:** You can bypass the Finished Goods Inventory account, which is not appropriate in this context.)

Required:

Prepare journal entries for transactions (a)–(f) using the account names shown and other appropriate accounts such as Cash, Payables, Accumulated Depreciation, Prepaids, and Sales Revenue.

PROBLEMS—SET A

LO4, 5, 6   **PA2-1 Analyzing Flow of Manufacturing and Nonmanufacturing Costs, Preparing CGM Report and Income Statement**

Lamonda Corp. uses a job order cost system. On April 1, the accounts had the following balance.

Raw materials inventory	$ 30,000
Work in process inventory	20,000
Finished goods inventory	125,000

The following transactions occurred during April.

(a) Purchased materials on account, $233,670.
(b) Requisitioned materials, $112,300, of which $16,900 was for general factory use.
(c) Recorded factory labor of $225,700, of which $43,875 was indirect.
(d) Incurred other costs:

Selling expense	$36,000
Factory utilities	24,700
Administrative expenses	51,850
Factory rent	12,000
Factory depreciation	21,000

(e) Applied overhead during the month totaling $133,560.
(f) Completed jobs costing $263,750.
(g) Sold jobs costing $324,670.
(h) Recorded sales revenue of $500,000.

Required:

1. Post the April transaction to the following T-accounts. (**Note:** Some transactions will affect other accounts not shown; e.g., Cash, Accounts Payable, Accumulated Depreciation.) You do not need to show the offsetting debit or credit to those accounts.

Raw Materials Inventory	Work in Process Inventory	Finished Goods Inventory
Bal. 30,000	Bal. 20,000	Bal. 125,000

Manufacturing Overhead	Cost of Goods Sold

Sales Revenue	Nonmanufacturing Expenses

2. Compute the balance in the accounts at the end of April.

3. Compute over- or underapplied manufacturing overhead. If the balance in the Manufacturing Overhead account is closed directly to Cost of Goods Sold, will it increase or decrease?

4. Prepare Lamonda's cost of goods manufactured report for April.

5. Prepare Lamonda's April income statement. Include any adjustment to Cost of Goods Sold needed to dispose of over- or underapplied manufacturing overhead.

PA2-2 Preparing Journal Entries to Record Manufacturing and Nonmanufacturing Costs

Supplement

Refer to the information presented in PA2-1 for Lamonda Corp.

Required:

Prepare all of Lamonda's necessary journal entries for the month of April.

PA2-3 Calculating Predetermined Overhead Rates, Recording Manufacturing Cost Flows, and Analyzing Overhead

LO3, 4, 5

Tyler Tooling Company uses a job order costing system with overhead applied to products on the basis of machine hours. For the upcoming year, the company estimated its total manufacturing overhead cost at $250,000 and total machine hours at 62,500. During the first month of operations, the company worked on three jobs and recorded the following actual direct materials cost, direct labor cost, and machine hours for each job:

	Job 101	Job 102	Job 103	Total
Direct materials cost	$12,000	$9,000	$6,000	$27,000
Direct labor cost	$18,000	$7,000	$6,000	$31,000
Machine hours	2,000 hours	3,000 hours	1,000 hours	6,000 hours

Job 101 was completed and sold for $50,000.

Job 102 was completed but not sold.

Job 103 is still in process.

Actual overhead costs recorded during the first month of operations totaled $25,000.

Required:

1. Calculate the predetermined overhead rate.
2. Compute the total manufacturing overhead applied to the Work in Process Inventory account during the first month of operations.
3. Compute the balance in the Work in Process Inventory account at the end of the first month.
4. How much gross profit would the company report during the first month of operations before making an adjustment for over- or underapplied manufacturing overhead?
5. Determine the balance in the Manufacturing Overhead account at the end of the first month. Is it over- or underapplied?

PA2-4 Preparing Journal Entries to Record Manufacturing and Nonmanufacturing Costs

Supplement

Refer to the information in PA2-3 for Tyler Tooling Company.

Required:

1. Prepare a journal entry showing the transfer of Job 102 into Finished Goods Inventory upon its completion.
2. Prepare the journal entries to recognize the sales revenue and cost of goods sold for Job 101.
3. Prepare the journal entry to transfer the balance of the Manufacturing Overhead account to Cost of Goods Sold.

LO4, 5 **PA2-5** **Recording Manufacturing Costs and Analyzing Manufacturing Overhead**

Christopher's Custom Cabinet Company uses a job order costing system with overhead applied as a percentage of direct labor costs. Inventory balances at the beginning of 2009 follow:

Raw materials inventory	$15,000
Work in process inventory	5,000
Finished goods inventory	20,000

The following transactions occurred during January:

(a) Purchased materials on account for $26,000.
(b) Issued materials to production totaling $22,000, 90 percent of which was traced to specific jobs and the remainder treated as indirect materials.
(c) Payroll costs totaling $15,500 were recorded as follows:

$10,000 for assembly workers
3,000 for factory supervision
1,000 for administrative personnel
1,500 for sales commissions

(d) Recorded depreciation: $6,000 for machines, $1,000 for office copier.
(e) Had $2,000 in insurance expire, allocated equally between manufacturing and administrative expenses.
(f) Paid $6,500 in other factory costs in cash.
(g) Applied manufacturing overhead at a rate of 200 percent of direct labor cost.
(h) Completed all jobs but one; the job cost sheet for this job shows $2,100 for direct materials, $2,000 for direct labor, and $4,000 for applied overhead.
(i) Sold jobs costing $50,000; the company uses cost-plus pricing with a markup of 30 percent.

Required:

1. Set up T-accounts, record the beginning balances, post the January transactions, and compute the final balance for the following accounts:

   Raw Materials Inventory
   Work in Process Inventory
   Finished Goods Inventory
   Cost of Goods Sold
   Manufacturing Overhead
   Selling and Administrative Expenses
   Sales Revenue
   Other accounts (Cash, Payables, etc.)

2. Determine how much gross profit the company would report during the month of January **before** any adjustment is made for the overhead balance.

3. Determine the amount of over- or underapplied overhead.

4. Compute adjusted gross profit assuming that any over- or underapplied overhead balance is adjusted directly to Cost of Goods Sold.

LO4, 5 **PA2-6** **Finding Unknowns in the Cost of Goods Manufacturing and Sold Report and Analyzing Manufacturing Overhead**

The following information was obtained from the records of Appleton Corporation during 2009.

- Manufacturing Overhead was applied at a rate of 80 percent of direct labor dollars.
- Beginning value of inventory follows:
  - Beginning Work in Process Inventory, $10,000.
  - Beginning Finished Goods Inventory, $20,000.
- During the period, Work in Process Inventory increased by 20 percent, and Finished Goods Inventory decreased by 25 percent.
- Actual manufacturing overhead costs were $85,000.
- Sales were $400,000.
- Adjusted Cost of Goods Sold was $300,000.

Required:

Use the preceding information to find the missing values in the following table:

Item	Amount
Direct materials used in production	$?
Direct labor	?
Manufacturing overhead applied	80,000
Total current manufacturing costs	?
Plus: Beginning work in process inventory	10,000
Less: Ending work in process inventory	?
Cost of goods manufactured	?
Plus: Beginning finished goods inventory	20,000
Less: Ending finished goods inventory	?
Unadjusted cost of goods sold	?
Overhead adjustment	?
Adjusted cost of goods sold	300,000

PA2-7 Selecting Allocation Base and Analyzing Manufacturing Overhead

Amberjack Company is trying to decide on an allocation base to use to assign manufacturing overhead to jobs. In the past, the company has always used direct labor hours to assign manufacturing overhead to products, but it is trying to decide whether it should use a different allocation base such as direct labor dollars or machine hours.

Actual and estimated data for manufacturing overhead, direct labor cost, direct labor hours, and machine hours for the most recent fiscal year are summarized here:

LO3, 5

www.mhhe.com/whitecotton1e

	Estimated Value	Actual Value
Manufacturing overhead cost	$700,000	$655,000
Direct labor cost	$350,000	$360,000
Direct labor hours	17,500 hours	16,000 hours
Machine hours	14,000 hours	13,000 hours

Required:

1. Based on the company's current allocation base (direct labor hours), compute the following:
   a. Predetermined overhead rate.
   b. Applied manufacturing overhead.
   c. Over- or underapplied manufacturing overhead.

2. If the company had used direct labor dollars (instead of direct labor hours) as its allocation base, compute the following:
   a. Predetermined overhead rate.
   b. Applied manufacturing overhead.
   c. Over- or underapplied manufacturing overhead.

3. If the company had used machine hours (instead of direct labor hours) as its allocation base, compute the following:
   a. Predetermined overhead rate.
   b. Applied manufacturing overhead.
   c. Over- or underapplied manufacturing overhead.

4. Based on last year's data alone, which allocation base would have provided the most accurate measure for applying manufacturing overhead costs to production?

5. How does a company decide on an allocation base to use in applying manufacturing overhead? What factors should be considered?

LO3, 4, 5, 6   **PA2-8 Recording Manufacturing Costs, Preparing a Cost of Goods Manufactured and Sold Report, and Calculating Income from Operations**

Dobson Manufacturing Company uses a job order costing system with manufacturing overhead applied to products on the basis of direct labor dollars. At the beginning of the most recent period, the company estimated its total direct labor cost to be $50,000 and its total manufacturing overhead cost to be $75,000.

Several incomplete general ledger accounts showing the transactions that occurred during the most recent accounting period follow:

Raw Materials Inventory		
Beginning Balance	15,000	?
Purchases	95,000	
Ending Balance	30,000	

Work in Process Inventory		
Beginning Balance	30,000	?
Direct Materials	70,000	
Direct Labor	40,000	
Applied Overhead	?	
Ending Balance	20,000	

Finished Goods Inventory		
Beginning Balance	40,000	?
Cost of Goods Completed	?	
Ending Balance	50,000	

Cost of Goods Sold		
Unadjusted Cost of Goods Sold	?	
Adjusted Cost of Goods Sold	?	

Manufacturing Overhead			
Indirect Materials	10,000	?	Applied Overhead
Indirect Labor	15,000		
Factory Depreciation	13,000		
Factory Rent	7,000		
Factory Utilities	3,000		
Other Factory Costs	10,000		
Actual Overhead	58,000		

Sales Revenue		
	300,000	Sales Revenue

Selling and Administrative Expenses		
Adm. Salaries	28,000	
Office Depreciation	20,000	
Advertising	15,000	
Ending balance	63,000	

Required:

1. Calculate the predetermined overhead rate.
2. Fill in the missing values in the T-accounts.
3. Compute over- or underapplied overhead.
4. Prepare a statement of cost of goods manufactured and sold including the adjustment for over- or underapplied overhead.
5. Prepare a brief income statement for the company.

PROBLEMS–SET B

LO4, 5, 6   **PB2-1 Analyzing Flow of Manufacturing and Nonmanufacturing Costs and Preparing Cost of Goods Manufactured Report and Income Statement**

Coda Industries uses a job order cost system. On November 1, the company had the following balance in the accounts:

Raw materials inventory	$ 30,000
Work in process inventory	120,000
Finished goods inventory	145,000

The following transactions occurred during November.

(a) Purchased materials on account, $450,500.
(b) Requisitioned materials, $289,300, of which $44,600 was for general factory use.
(c) Recorded factory labor of $326,700 of which $93,200 was indirect.
(d) Incurred other costs:

Selling expense	$44,000
Factory utilities	59,200
Administrative expenses	79,500
Factory rent	25,000
Factory depreciation	94,200

(e) Applied overhead during the month totaling $290,000.
(f) Completed jobs costing $607,250.
(g) Sold jobs costing $557,700.
(h) Recorded sales revenue of $850,000.

Required:

1. Post the November transactions to the following T-accounts. (**Note:** Some transactions will affect other accounts not shown; e.g., Cash, Accounts Payable, Accumulated Depreciation.) You do not need to show the offsetting debit or credit to those accounts.

Raw Materials Inventory	Work in Process Inventory	Finished Goods Inventory
Bal. 30,000	Bal. 120,000	Bal. 145,000

Manufacturing Overhead	Cost of Goods Sold

Sales Revenue	Nonmanufacturing Expenses

2. Compute the balance in the accounts at the end of November.
3. Compute over- or underapplied manufacturing overhead. If the balance is closed directly to Cost of Goods Sold, will it increase or decrease?
4. Prepare Coda's cost of goods manufactured report for November.
5. Prepare Coda's November income statement. Include any adjustment to Cost of Goods Sold needed to dispose of over- or underapplied manufacturing overhead.

PB2-2 Preparing Journal Entries to Record Manufacturing   Supplement
and Nonmanufacturing Costs

Refer to the information presented in PB2-1 for Coda Corp.

Required:

Prepare all of Coda's necessary journal entries for the month of November.

LO3, 4, 5   **PB2-3 Calculating Predetermined Overhead Rates, Recording Manufacturing and Cost Flows, and Analyzing Overhead**

Babson Company uses a job order costing system with overhead applied to products on the basis of machine hours. For the upcoming year, Babson estimated its total manufacturing overhead cost at $360,000 and its total machine hours at 125,000. During the first month of operation, the company worked on three jobs and recorded the following actual direct materials cost, direct labor cost, and machine hours for each job:

	Job 101	Job 102	Job 103	Total
Direct materials cost	$15,000	$10,000	$5,000	$30,000
Direct labor cost	$ 7,000	$ 5,000	$8,000	$20,000
Machine hours	5,000 hours	4,000 hours	1,000 hours	10,000 hours

Job 101 was completed and sold for $50,000.

Job 102 was completed but not sold.

Job 103 is still in process.

Actual overhead costs recorded during the first month of operations were $28,000.

Required:

1. Calculate the predetermined overhead rate.
2. Compute the total overhead applied to the Work in Process Inventory account during the first month of operations.
3. Compute the balance in the Work in Process Inventory account at the end of the first month.
4. How much gross profit would the company report during the first month of operations before making an adjustment for over- or underapplied manufacturing overhead?
5. Determine the balance in the Manufacturing Overhead account at the end of the first month. Is it over- or underapplied?

Supplement   **PB2-4 Preparing Journal Entries to Record Manufacturing and Nonmanufacturing Costs**

Refer to the information in PB2-3 for Babson Company.

Required:

1. Prepare a journal entry showing the transfer of Job 102 into Finished Goods Inventory upon its completion.
2. Prepare the journal entries to recognize the sales revenue and cost of goods sold for Job 101.
3. Prepare the journal entry to transfer the balance of the Manufacturing Overhead account to Cost of Goods Sold.

LO4, 5   **PB2-5 Recording Manufacturing Costs and Analyzing Manufacturing Overhead**

Carrington Custom Cabinet Company uses a job order costing system with overhead applied based on direct labor cost. Inventory balances at the beginning of 2009 follow:

Raw materials inventory	$25,000
Work in process inventory	30,000
Finished goods inventory	40,000

The following transactions occurred during January:

(a) Purchased materials on account for $40,000.
(b) Issued materials to production totaling $30,000, 80 percent of which was traced to specific jobs and the remainder treated as indirect materials.
(c) Payroll costs totaling $25,500 were recorded as follows:
$15,000 for assembly workers

6,000 for factory supervision

2,000 for administrative personnel

2,500 for sales commissions

(d) Recorded depreciation: $5,000 for machines, $2,000 for office copier.

(e) Had $4,000 in insurance expire; allocated equally between manufacturing and administrative expenses.
(f) Paid $8,500 in other factory costs in cash.
(g) Applied manufacturing overhead at a rate of 150 percent of direct labor cost.
(h) Completed all jobs but one; the job cost sheet for this job shows $7,000 for direct materials, $6,000 for direct labor, and $9,000 for applied overhead.
(i) Sold jobs costing $60,000 during the period; the company uses cost-plus pricing with a markup of 35 percent.

Required:

1. Set up T-accounts, record the beginning balances, post the January transactions, and compute the final balance for the following accounts:

   Raw Materials Inventory

   Work in Process Inventory

   Finished Goods Inventory

   Cost of Goods Sold

   Manufacturing Overhead

   Selling and Administrative Expenses

   Sales Revenue

   Other accounts (Cash, Payables, etc.)

2. Determine how much gross profit the company would report during the month of January **before** any adjustment is made for the overhead balance.

3. Determine the amount of over- or underapplied overhead.

4. Compute adjusted gross profit assuming that any over- or underapplied overhead is adjusted directly to Cost of Goods Sold.

PB2-6 Finding Unknowns in the Cost of Goods Manufacturing and Sold Report and Analyzing Manufacturing Overhead　　　　LO5, 6

The following information was obtained from the records of Carrington Corporation during 2009.

1. Manufacturing overhead was applied at a rate of 150 percent of direct labor dollars.
2. Beginning value of inventory follows:

   a. Beginning Work in Process Inventory, $20,000.
   b. Beginning Finished Goods Inventory, $10,000.

3. During the period, Work in Process Inventory decreased by 20 percent, and Finished Goods Inventory increased by 25 percent.

4. Actual manufacturing overhead costs were $85,000.

5. Sales were $500,000.

6. Adjusted Cost of Goods Sold was $350,000.

Required:

Use the preceding information to find the missing values in the following table:

Item	Amount
Direct materials used in production	$?
Direct labor	?
Manufacturing overhead applied	90,000
Current manufacturing costs	?
Plus: Beginning work in process inventory	20,000
Less: Ending work in process inventory	?
Cost of goods manufactured	?
Plus: Beginning finished goods inventory	10,000
Less: Ending finished goods inventory	?
Unadjusted cost of goods sold	?
Overhead adjustment	?
Adjusted cost of goods sold	350,000

LO3, 5   **PB2-7 Selecting Allocation Base and Analyzing Manufacturing Overhead**

Timberland Company is trying to decide on an allocation base to use to assign manufacturing overhead to jobs. In the past, the company has always used direct labor hours to assign manufacturing overhead to products, but it is trying to decide whether it should use a different allocation base such as direct labor dollars or machine hours.

Actual and estimated results for manufacturing overhead, direct labor cost, direct labor hours, and machine hours for the most recent fiscal year are summarized here:

	Estimated Value	Actual Value
Manufacturing overhead cost	$900,000	$890,000
Direct labor cost	$450,000	$464,000
Direct labor hours	30,000 hours	29,000 hours
Machine hours	15,000 hours	15,000 hours

Required:

1. Based on the company's current allocation base (direct labor hours), compute the following:
   a. Predetermined overhead rate.
   b. Applied manufacturing overhead.
   c. Over- or underapplied manufacturing overhead.

2. If the company had used direct labor dollars (instead of direct labor hours) as its allocation base, compute the following:
   a. Predetermined overhead rate.
   b. Applied manufacturing overhead.
   c. Over- or underapplied manufacturing overhead.

3. If the company had used machine hours (instead of direct labor hours) as its allocation base, compute the following:
   a. Predetermined overhead rate.
   b. Applied manufacturing overhead.
   c. Over- or underapplied manufacturing overhead

4. Based on last year's data alone, which allocation base would have provided the most accurate measure for applying manufacturing overhead costs to production?

5. How does a company decide on an allocation base to use in applying manufacturing overhead? What factors should be considered?

LO3, 4, 5, 6   **PB2-8 Recording Manufacturing Costs, Preparing a Cost of Goods Manufactured and Sold Report, and Calculating Income from Operations**

Carlton Manufacturing Company uses a job order costing system with manufacturing overhead applied to products on the basis of direct labor dollars. At the beginning of the most recent period, the company estimated its total direct labor cost to be $30,000 and its total manufacturing overhead cost to be $60,000.

Several incomplete general ledger accounts showing the transactions that occurred during the most recent accounting period follow.

Raw Materials Inventory		
Beginning Balance	10,000	?
Purchases	85,000	
Ending Balance	20,000	

Work in Process Inventory		
Beginning Balance	30,000	?
Direct Materials	?	
Direct Labor	35,000	
Applied Overhead	?	
Ending Balance	20,000	

Finished Goods Inventory		
Beginning Balance	60,000	?
Cost of Goods Completed	?	
Ending Balance	40,000	

Cost of Goods Sold		
Unadjusted Cost of Goods Sold	?	
Adjusted Cost of Goods Sold	?	

Manufacturing Overhead			
Indirect Materials	10,000	?	Applied Overhead
Indirect Labor	20,000		
Factory Depreciation	13,000		
Factory Rent	12,000		
Factory Utilities	5,000		
Other Factory Costs	14,000		
Actual Overhead	74,000		

Sales Revenue		
	280,000	Sales Revenue

Selling and Administrative Expenses		
Adm. Salaries	30,000	
Office Depreciation	20,000	
Advertising	19,000	
Ending balance	69,000	

Required:

1. Calculate the predetermined overhead rate.
2. Fill in the missing values in the T-accounts.
3. Compute over- or underapplied overhead.
4. Prepare a statement of cost of goods manufactured and sold including the adjustment for over- or underapplied overhead
5. Prepare a brief income statement for the company.

SKILLS DEVELOPMENT CASES

S2-1 Multiple Allocation Bases and Ethical Dilemmas   LO3

Assume you recently accepted a job with a company that designs and builds helicopters for commercial and military use. The company has numerous contracts with the U.S. military that require the use of cost-plus pricing. In other words, the contracted price for each helicopter is calculated at a certain percentage (about 130 percent) of the total cost to produce it. Unlike the cost-plus pricing approach used for military contracts, the prices for civilian helicopters are based on the amount that individuals and corporations are willing to pay for a state-of-the-art helicopter.

As your first assignment, the company controller has asked you to reevaluate the costing system currently used to determine the cost of producing helicopters. The company assigns manufacturing overhead based on the number of units produced. The result is that every helicopter is assigned the same amount of overhead regardless of whether it is for military or civilian use.

As part of your assignment, you collected the following information about two other potential allocation bases (direct labor hours and machine hours) and how they differ for the two types of customers the company serves:

	Military Contracts		Civilian Contracts		
	Units in Allocation Base	Percent of Total	Units in Allocation Base	Percent of Total	Total
Units produced	1,000	50%	1,000	50%	2,000
Labor hours	800,000	40	1,200,000	60	2,000,000
Machine hours	700,000	70	300,000	30	1,000,000

These data show that while the company produces an equal number of military and civilian helicopters (1,000 of each), they require a different amount of direct labor and machine hours. In particular, civilian helicopters require relatively more direct labor hours (60 percent of the total), perhaps because of the labor required to install all of the "bells and whistles" that wealthy consumers expect on a luxury helicopter. However, military helicopters require more machine time (70 percent of the total) due to the precise machining and intensive instrument testing required to comply with the military contracts. Further analysis revealed that some of the manufacturing overhead items are logically related to labor hours (such as supervision and use of indirect materials) while other overhead items (such as machine depreciation and power) are more highly related to machine hours.

When you presented these data to the controller, you recommended that the company move to an allocation system whereby part of the overhead would be allocated based on direct labor hours and part of it based on machine hours. He responded that he wanted you to choose the system that would assign the highest percentage of the total overhead cost to the military contracts. His reasoning was that the cost-plus agreement with the U.S. government would result in a higher contract price for military helicopters without affecting the price of civilian helicopters, which are set by the market.

Required:

1. Explain how changing the allocation base can impact the profitability of the two types of products.
2. Which allocation base(s) do you think the company should use to apply manufacturing overhead to the two types of products?
3. Identify the ethical issues involved in this scenario. What are your potential courses of action for responding to the controller's request? What are the potential personal, professional, and legal implications of the alternative courses of action you considered? How would you ultimately respond to this situation?

LO1, 2, 3   **S2-2 Applying Job Order Costing to an Entrepreneurial Business**

Assume you are going to become an entrepreneur and start your own business. Think about your talents and interests and come up with an idea for a small business venture that provides a unique product or service to local customers. You can select any business venture you want, but if you are struggling to come up with an idea, here are some examples:

> Catering
> Wedding-planning consulting
> Video production company
> Pool building company
> Personal shopping service
> Interior design business
> Flower shop
> Rock-climbing guide service
> River-rafting company
> Web design company

Required:

For whatever business venture you select, answer the following questions:

1. What would the major costs of your business be? Try to classify the costs into the areas of direct materials, direct labor, manufacturing overhead, general and administrative costs, and selling costs. (**Hint:** Not all businesses will have all of these cost classifications.)
2. Why would you need to determine the cost of providing your product or service to individual customers? In other words, what types of decisions would you expect to make based on job order cost information?
3. In general, would you expect your company's indirect (overhead) costs to be less or more than the direct costs (direct labor and materials)? What allocation base do you think you would use to charge overhead costs to individual customers? How much do you think the overhead rate would need to be?
4. Create a job cost sheet for a hypothetical "average" customer that includes estimates of the major costs of serving that customer. How much do you think you would need to charge to cover all of the costs plus provide a reasonable profit for yourself?

LO3, 4, 5, 6   **S2-3 Comprehensive Job Order Costing Case**

Supplement

Sampson Company uses a job order cost system with overhead applied to products based on direct labor hours. Based on previous history, the company estimated its total overhead for the coming year (2009) to be $240,000 and its total direct labor hours to be 6,000.

On January 1, 2010, the general ledger of Sampson Company revealed that it had one job in process (Job 102) for which it had incurred a total cost of $15,000. Job 101 had been finished the previous month for a total cost of $30,000 but was not yet sold. The company had a contract for Job 103 but had not started working on it yet. Other balances in Raw Materials Inventory and other assets, liabilities, and owner's equity accounts are summarized here:

SAMPSON COMPANY
General Ledger Accounts

Raw Materials Inventory

| 1/1 Balance | 10,000 | |

Manufacturing Overhead

Work in Process Inventory (WIP)

| 1/1 Balance | 15,000 | |

Finished Goods Inventory

| 1/1 Balance | 30,000 | |

Individual Job Cost Sheets (subsidiary ledgers to WIP)

	Job 102	Job 103
Beg. Balance	15,000	—
+ Direct Materials		
+ Direct Labor		
+ Applied OH		
Total Mfg. Cost		

Cost of Goods Sold

Sales Revenue

Selling and Administrative Expenses

Cash and Other Assets

| 1/1 Balance | 100,000 | |

Payables and Other Liabilities

| | 85,000 | 1/1 Balance |

Stockholder's Equity

| | 70,000 | 1/1 Balance |

During January, the company had the following transactions:

(a) Purchased $10,000 worth of raw materials on account.
(b) Issued the following materials into production:

Item	Cost	Explanation
Direct materials	$7,000	Job 102, $2,000; Job 103, $5,000
Indirect materials	2,000	Used on both jobs
Total materials issued	$9,000	

(c) Recorded salaries and wages payable as follows:

Item	Cost	Explanation
Direct labor	$10,000	Job 102, $6,000; Job 103, $4,000
Indirect labor	4,000	For factory supervision
Salaries	5,000	For administrative staff
Total payroll cost	$19,000	

(d) Applied overhead to jobs based on the number of direct labor hours required:

Job Number	Direct Labor Hours
Job 102	300 hours
Job 103	200 hours
Total	500 hours

(e) Recorded the following actual manufacturing costs:

Item	Cost	Explanation
Rent	$ 6,000	Paid factory rent in cash
Depreciation	5,000	Factory equipment
Insurance	3,000	Had one month of factory insurance policy expire
Utilities	2,000	Received factory utility bill but did not pay it
Total cost	$ 16,000	

(f) Recorded the following general and administrative costs:

Item	Cost	Explanation
Advertising	$ 2,000	Advertising paid in cash
Depreciation	3,000	Office equipment
Other expenses	1,000	Micellaneous expenses incurred but not paid
Total cost	$ 6,000	

(g) Sold Job 101, which is recorded in Finished Goods Inventory at a cost of $30,000, for $55,000.
(h) Completed Job 102 but did not sell it; Job 103 is still in process at year-end.

Required:

1. Compute and interpret the predetermined overhead rate.
2. How much overhead would be applied to jobs during the period?

3. Compute the total cost of Jobs 102 and 103 at the end of the period. Where would the cost of each of these jobs appear on the year-end balance sheet?

4. Prepare journal entries to record the January transactions and post the entries to the general ledger T-accounts given earlier in the problem.

5. Calculate the amount of over- or underapplied overhead.

6. Prepare the journal entry to dispose of the overhead balance assuming that it had been a year-end balance instead of a month-end balance. Post the effect to the general ledger T-accounts.

7. Prepare a statement of cost of goods manufactured and sold report including the adjustment for over- or underapplied overhead.

8. Prepare a brief income statement for Sampson Company.

CHAPTER 3

Process Costing

YOUR LEARNING OBJECTIVES

After completing this chapter, you should be able to:

LO1 Describe the key features of a process costing system.

LO2 Reconcile the number of physical units using the weighted average method.

LO3 Calculate the number of equivalent units using the weighted average method.

LO4 Prepare a process costing production report using the weighted average method.

Lecture Presentation–LP3
www.mhhe.com/whitecotton1e

FOCUS COMPANY: CK Mondavi Family Vineyards

"Trust in a Family Name"

www.ckmondavi.com

State agencies often allocate funding to public universities based on the number of full-time students, or part-time equivalent. A full-time student is defined as someone who is enrolled in at least 12 credit hours per semester; a part-time-equivalent is based on the number of credit hours the student is taking. If your university has 10,000 full-time students and 8,000 part-time students enrolled in an average of 6 credit hours, what is the total number of full-time or part-time-equivalent students?

If you answered 14,000, (10,000 full-time) + (50% × 8,000 part-time), you have already mastered one of the most important topics in this chapter, the calculation of an equivalent unit. An equivalent unit is the mechanism that we use to convert partially completed units (similar to part-time students) into the equivalent of a full unit. In this example, a part-time student enrolled in 6 credit hours was equivalent to half of a full-time student.

In accounting, we must make a similar calculation for units that are partially complete at the end of an accounting period. Doing so provides information to managers about the cost of units still in process and meets GAAP's requirement that manufacturing costs be assigned to the product and counted as inventory until it is sold.

To illustrate how process costing works, we visit CK Mondavi, one of the oldest wineries in Napa Valley, California. Even if you are not old enough to drink wine, or prefer not to, you've probably heard the Mondavi name.[1] The Mondavi family history is part America success story, part soap opera.[2] In 1943, Italian immigrants Cesare and Rosa Mondavi purchased the Charles Krug (CK) winery, which had fallen on hard times during the Great Depression. Sons Robert and Peter helped their parents turn the troubled winery into a successful business. But brotherly rivalry turned bitter after Cesare died in 1959 and Peter took control of the family vineyards. Robert left the family business in 1966 to build his own wine dynasty in

---

[1] www.ckmondavi.com/family; www.charleskrug.com/familyhistory.
[2] Julia Flynn Siler, *The House of Mondavi: The Rise and Fall of an American Wine Dynasty*. New York: Gotham Books, 2007.

nearby Oakville. Robert Mondavi built a huge corporation that turned the Mondavi name into a household brand, but eventually lost control of his company when he was forced to sell to Constellation Brands Inc. Meanwhile, Peter Mondavi and his heirs continue to run the original family vinyard (CK Mondavi) with an emphasis on quality and innovation.

Throughout this chapter, we use the CK Mondavi winery as an example to show the cost of converting grapes into wine. Although we simplify things and the numbers we use in our examples are fictional, the accounting methods we show are actually used by wineries to determine the cost of making wine.

ORGANIZATION OF THE CHAPTER

Basic concepts in process costing	Preparation of the production report (weighted average method)
• Job order versus process costing • Flow of costs in process costing • Process costing production report • Weighted average versus FIFO costing	• Step 1: Reconcile the number of physical units • Step 2: Translate physical units into equivalent units • Step 3: Calculate the cost per equivalent unit • Step 4: Reconcile the total costs of work in process inventory • Step 5: Prepare a production report • Additional factors in process costing

Basic Concepts in Process Costing

In the last chapter, you learned about job order costing systems. This chapter describes another type of costing system, process costing.

JOB ORDER VERSUS PROCESS COSTING

Learning Objective 1
Describe the key features of a process costing system.

Remember that job order costing is used by companies that offer **customized** products or services, such as a custom-built home, highway construction project, or legal defense. Because each individual product or customer is unique, a job cost sheet is used to keep track of the cost of each individual unit, or job, in a job order costing system.

Process costing is used by companies that produce **homogeneous** products or services using a series of standardized processes. Canned and bottled goods, frozen foods, paper products, and petroleum products are examples of homogeneous products that result from a standardized process. Although process costing is most often identified with manufacturing companies, it can also be used by companies that offer homogeneous or standardized services, such as Jiffy Lube oil changes, standard medical tests such as X-rays or blood work, and haircuts at Supercuts.

Video 3-1
www.mhhe.com/whitecotton1e

Because each product or service that results from the standardized process is virtually the same, keeping a separate cost record for each unit produced or customer served is not necessary. Instead, process costing keeps track of the total cost of each major process and then spreads (averages) the total cost over the number of units produced or customers served.

Although this description makes process costing sound simple, a few questions complicate its use in the real world. For example, how much cost should CK Mondavi assign to wine that is still "in process" at the end of an accounting period—that is, when all of the ingredients (grapes) have been added, but the fermenting and aging process is not yet complete? Determining how much cost to assign to partially complete units is the focus of much of this chapter. But first, let's consider how costs flow through the accounting system in process costing.

FLOW OF COSTS IN PROCESS COSTING

Although different types of companies use job order costing and process costing, the two methods are very similar in terms of how manufacturing costs are recorded in the various inventory accounts. As a review, recall the three types of manufacturing costs that must be traced to the product and recorded as inventory until the product is sold:

- **Direct materials** are the major material inputs that can be directly traced to the product. For a winery, this category would include the cost of grapes and any other major material inputs such as the bottles, corks, and boxes used in the packaging process.

- **Direct labor** is the "hands-on" labor that can be directly and conveniently traced to the end product. Because today's wineries tend to be highly automated, direct labor is often a very small portion of the total manufacturing cost. Thus, wineries and other process-oriented industries may combine direct labor and manufacturing overhead costs together in a single category called **conversion cost**.

- **Manufacturing overhead** includes all manufacturing costs other than direct materials and direct labor that are incurred to make the product. For a winery, this category would include rent or mortgage payments, equipment depreciation, and supervision, utilities, and insurance for the winery.

> Conversion Cost =
> Direct Labor
> +
> Manufacturing
> Overhead

These manufacturing costs are recorded in one of the following inventory accounts until the product is sold:

- **Raw Materials Inventory** represents the cost of materials purchased from suppliers but not yet put into production.
- **Work in Process Inventory** represents the cost of units that are in process but not yet complete. In process costing, there is a separate Work in Process Inventory account for each of the major processes the product must go through as it is being manufactured.
- **Finished Goods Inventory** represents the cost of units finished but not yet sold.

When the product is sold, the manufacturing costs are transferred to **Cost of Goods Sold** where they are matched against sales revenue on the income statement. As you learned in previous chapters, **nonmanufacturing costs** are expensed as they are

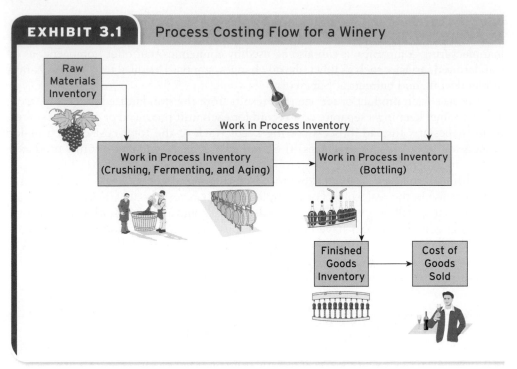

EXHIBIT 3.1 | Process Costing Flow for a Winery

incurred rather than being counted as part of the cost of the product. See Exhibit 3.1 for an illustration of how a winery's manufacturing costs flow through the inventory accounts and eventually into Cost of Goods Sold.

Wine making is an example of a **sequential process**. In other words, the grapes must be crushed before they can be fermented and then aged, which must occur before the wine can be bottled. Other companies use a **parallel processing** approach in which multiple processes occur simultaneously. For example, Toyota Motor Company could have two different assembly processes running at the same time, one that produces engines and another that produces transmissions.

Throughout the remainder of this chapter, we use process costing to determine the cost of crushing, fermenting, and aging wine at CK Mondavi. To simplify our example, we use a single Work in Process Inventory account to accumulate the total cost of these processes, which we refer to as the CFA process. When the CFA process is complete, the manufacturing costs are transferred to the Bottling department, which will incur additional costs to bottle and package the wine. When the bottling process is complete, the total manufacturing costs are transferred to Finished Goods Inventory. When the wine is sold, the total manufacturing cost is reported as Cost of Goods Sold on the Income Statement.

PROCESS COSTING PRODUCTION REPORT

The foundation of a process costing system is the **production report**. This report provides information about the number of units and manufacturing costs that flow through a production process during an accounting period. It is used to determine how much manufacturing cost to transfer out of Work in Process Inventory and into the next processing department (or Finished Goods Inventory if it is the last production process) and to value any units that are in process at the end of the accounting period. A separate production report is prepared for each major production process on either a monthly or a quarterly basis.

Throughout the remainder of this chapter, we illustrate how to prepare and interpret a production report for the crushing, fermenting, and aging (CFA) process at CK Mondavi. For this process, we define a *unit* as one barrel of wine. About 740 pounds of crushed grapes are required to fill a standard barrel of wine. After the crushed grapes have been fermented and the wine aged for an appropriate amount of time, the barrels are transferred to the Bottling process, where each barrel will yield about 300 bottles (25 cases) of wine.

See Exhibit 3.2 for a hypothetical production report for CK Mondavi's CFA process. We show how to calculate the numbers for this report later in the chapter. For now, just focus on the general structure and information contained in the report.

EXHIBIT 3.2	**Production Cost Report**

CK MONDAVI
Process Costing Production Report
Crushing, Fermenting, and Aging (CFA) Process

	Physical Units	Equivalent Units	
		Direct Materials	Conversion
Beginning inventory	200		
Started this period	1,800		
Total	2,000		
Completed	1,600	1,600	1,600
Ending inventory	400	400	240
Total	2,000	2,000	1,840

	Costs		
	Direct Materials	Conversion	Total Cost
Beginning inventory	$ 84,000	$ 81,120	$ 165,120
Current period costs	810,000	918,000	1,728,000
Total cost	894,000	999,120	$1,893,120
Equivalent units	÷ 2,000	÷ 1,840	
Cost per equivalent unit	$ 447	$ 543	
Cost of units completed	$715,200	$868,800	$1,584,000
Ending inventory	178,800	130,320	309,120
Total cost	$894,000	$999,120	$1,893,120

 **COACH'S TIP**

The first part of the report tells managers about the total number of units worked on and where they are in the process. Equivalent units are used to convert partially complete units into the equivalent of full units.

COACH'S TIP

The second part shows the total manufacturing costs incurred during the period. Here, the total cost of the CFA process was $1,893,120. This total cost is either transferred out with the units completed or kept in the department as the cost of units in ending inventory.

The production report serves two purposes. First, it is a tool that managers can use to monitor and control production costs. It tells managers how many units were completed during the period, how many are still in process, and how much it costs to produce each unit. This information is useful for many managerial decisions, including product pricing and cost control.

Second, the production report provides accountants the information needed to record manufacturing costs in the accounting system. Because this book focuses on the use of accounting information by managers rather than accountants, we do not show all of the journal entries needed to record manufacturing costs in process costing. These journal entries are illustrated in Supplement 3B.

WEIGHTED AVERAGE VERSUS FIFO PROCESS COSTING

In the remainder of this chapter, we illustrate how to prepare a production report for the CFA process at CK Mondavi. But first, we must make an assumption about how the units and costs flow through the department's Work in Process Inventory account.

We can use two different methods to prepare a process costing production report: the weighted average method or the first in, first out (FIFO) method. The key difference between the two methods is how they deal with any units and costs that are in Beginning Work in Process Inventory.

The weighted average method combines (averages) the cost of any units in beginning inventory with the cost of units that were started during the current period. This method ignores the fact that the units in beginning inventory were started in a prior period and assumes that all of the work (and cost) of those units occurred during the current period.

The FIFO method assumes that any units in beginning inventory are completed first, before any new units are started in the process. As a result, the units in beginning inventory are accounted for separately from the units that are started during the current period.

See Exhibit 3.3 for a summary of the key differences between the weighted average and FIFO methods of process costing.

EXHIBIT 3.3   Comparison of Weighted Average and FIFO Methods

	Weighted Average	FIFO
Cost flow assumption	Averages the cost of units in beginning inventory with the cost of units that were started during the period	Assumes that the units in beginning inventory were completed before any new units were started
Units	Combines the units in beginning inventory with the units that were started during the period	Separates the units in beginning inventory from those that were started during the current period
Cost	Combines the cost of beginning inventory with the costs that were incurred during the current period	Separates the costs of beginning inventory from the costs that were incurred during the current period
Advantages	Is simpler than FIFO and more frequently used in the real world	More closely matches the actual flow of costs in many process industries and therefore may be more accurate than weighted average

---

Either method is acceptable for external reporting (GAAP), but there are trade-offs in terms of simplicity and accuracy of reporting. The weighted average method is simpler and more commonly used in the real world, but the FIFO method gives more precise attention to the physical flow of units and manufacturing costs and thus may be more accurate. The two methods will provide approximately the same result for companies that maintain minimal Work in Process Inventory or have stable production patterns. For companies that use just-in-time inventory to minimize inventory levels, the weighted average method is preferred because it is simpler, less costly to prepare, and provides similar information for managerial decision making. Just-in-time inventory methods are discussed in Chapter 4.

The next section illustrates how to prepare a production report using the weighted average method. The FIFO method is covered in Supplement 3A.

Before continuing, take a moment to complete the following Self-Study Practice to make certain you understand the basic concepts in process costing.

Self-Study Practice

1. Which of the following statements about process costing is false?
   a. Process costing is used in companies that produce very homogeneous products or services.
   b. Process costing uses the same inventory accounts as job order costing to record the flow of manufacturing costs.
   c. Process costing typically has more Work in Process accounts than job order costing.
   d. Process costing keeps a separate record, or cost sheet, for each unit produced.

2. Process costing is most likely to be used to calculate cost for which of the following products?
   a. Golf balls.
   b. Custom-made golf clubs.
   c. A newly designed golf course.
   d. All of the above.

3. A production report contains information about all of the following except:
   a. The number units completed during a period.
   b. The number of units in process at the end of a period.
   c. The cost of a specific job that was completed during the period.
   d. All of the above.

After you have finished, check your answers with the solutions in the margin.

Solution to Self-Study Practice
1. d
2. a
3. c

Preparation of the Production Report (Weighted Average Method)

Five steps are involved in preparing a production report:

1. Reconcile the number of physical units worked on during the period.
2. Translate physical units into equivalent units.
3. Calculate the cost per equivalent unit.
4. Reconcile the total cost of Work in Process Inventory.
5. Prepare a production report.

Each of these steps is described in detail in the following sections.

STEP 1: RECONCILE THE NUMBER OF PHYSICAL UNITS

The first step in preparing a production report is to reconcile the number of physical units that were worked on during the period. To do so, we first add the number of units that were on hand at the beginning of the period to the units that were started during the current period. Then we determine whether those units were completed during the period or were still being worked on at the end of the period. The formula to reconcile the number of physical units is shown on the next page.

> **Learning Objective 2**
> Reconcile the number of physical units using the weighted average method.

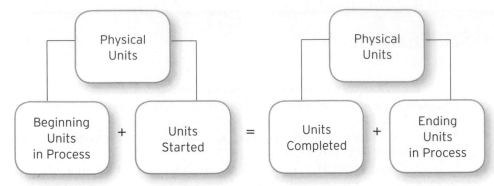

As an example, assume CK Mondavi had 200 barrels of wine in the CFA process at the start of a new accounting period. During the period, workers started another 1,800 barrels into the CFA process. At the end of the period, 400 barrels of wine were still in the CFA process. Based on this information, how many barrels of wine were completed and transferred out of the CFA process and into Bottling during the current period?

To answer this question, we can prepare a reconciliation of physical units as follows:

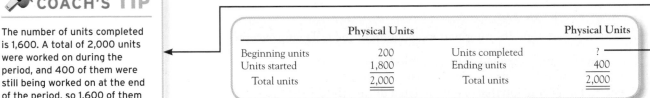

	Physical Units		Physical Units
Beginning units	200	Units completed	?
Units started	1,800	Ending units	400
Total units	2,000	Total units	2,000

We must account for a total of 2,000 units, 200 that were on hand at the beginning of the period plus 1,800 that were started this period. If we have only 400 on hand at the end of the period, we must have completed 1,600 units.

STEP 2: TRANSLATE PHYSICAL UNITS INTO EQUIVALENT UNITS

The next step in preparing the production report is to calculate the number of equivalent units. An **equivalent unit** is a measure used to convert partially completed units into the equivalent of a full unit.

Why must we calculate equivalent units? Companies often have units in process at the beginning and end of an accounting period. This is particularly true for products that take a long time to manufacture, such as wine that must be aged for months or even years before it is ready for sale. Even though the units are incomplete, their cost must be recorded on the balance sheet as Work in Process Inventory. Remember that GAAP requires all manufacturing costs to be counted as part of the cost of the product and reported as inventory (an asset) until the product is sold. By converting partially completed units into equivalent units, we can assign an appropriate value to those units for financial statement reporting.

Under the weighted average method, the only partially completed units we need to deal with are the units in ending inventory. The weighted average method ignores any units that were in process at the beginning of the period and assumes that all of the work (and cost) of those units occurred during the current period.

To illustrate the calculation of equivalent units using weighted average, we assume the following additional details about the CFA process:

- Direct materials (grapes) are added at the beginning of the process. Thus, once a unit has been started in the CFA process, it has 100 percent of the direct materials.
- Conversion costs (direct labor and manufacturing overhead) are incurred uniformly throughout the process.
- 1,600 units were completed and transferred to the Bottling department.
- The remaining 400 units in ending inventory were 60 percent through the CFA conversion process. These units have all required direct materials (crushed grapes) but are only 60 percent of the way through the fermenting and aging process.

See Exhibit 3.4 for a visual representation of these details.

EXHIBIT 3.4 Diagram of the Crushing, Fermenting, and Aging Process

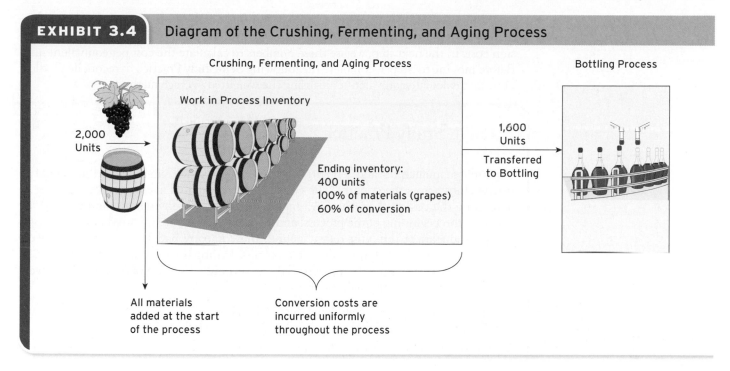

Crushing, Fermenting, and Aging Process

Bottling Process

Work in Process Inventory

2,000 Units

Ending inventory:
400 units
100% of materials (grapes)
60% of conversion

1,600 Units Transferred to Bottling

All materials added at the start of the process

Conversion costs are incurred uniformly throughout the process

To calculate equivalent units, we must convert the partially complete units in ending inventory into the equivalent of a full unit. This is analogous to the way we converted a part-time student into the equivalent of a full-time student in the introduction to this chapter. To calculate equivalent units, we multiply the number of physical units by their percentage of completion. Because all of the materials are added at the beginning of the process, the units in ending inventory are 100 percent complete with respect to direct materials but only 60 percent complete with respect to conversion cost. See the following table for the calculation of equivalent units.

	Physical Units	EQUIVALENT UNITS	
		Direct Materials	Conversion Cost
Completed and transferred	1,600	1,600	1,600
Ending inventory	400	400 (100% × 400)	240 (60% × 400)
Total	2,000	2,000	1,840

For the 1,600 units that were completed, equivalent units are the same as physical units. For the ending inventory, the equivalent units for direct materials are the same as the number of physical units. For conversion cost, the number of equivalent units would be 60 percent of the 400 units in inventory, or 240.

When we add the number of equivalent units for the units completed and ending inventory, we get total equivalent units of 2,000 for direct materials and 1,840 for conversion cost. In the next step, we use these numbers to calculate the cost per equivalent unit. Before moving to Step 3, complete the following Self-Study Practice to reconcile physical units and calculate equivalent units using the weighted average method.

💡 Self-Study Practice

Aqua-Fit manufactures and sells fitness drinks (with added vitamins and minerals) to fitness clubs across the country. The company uses weighted average process costing to determine the cost of the drinks. All materials (water, juice, vitamins, and bottles) are added at the beginning of the process, and conversion costs are incurred uniformly.

At the start of the most recent period, the company had 1,000 bottles that were about 40 percent through the conversion process. During the period, an additional 9,000 bottles were started into the process. The period ended with 3,000 bottles that were 20 percent of the way through the process.

1. How many units were **completed** during the period?
   a. 6,000   b. 7,000   c. 8,000   d. 9,000

2. For the ending inventory, the number of equivalent units for direct materials and conversion would be:

	Direct Materials Equivalent Units	Conversion Cost Equivalent Units
a.	3,000	2,400
b.	3,000	600
c.	600	2,400
d.	600	600

After you have finished, check your answers with the solutions in the margin.

Solution to Self-Study Practice

1. b
2. b

STEP 3: CALCULATE THE COST PER EQUIVALENT UNIT

To calculate the cost per equivalent unit, we divide total manufacturing cost by the total number of equivalent units that we calculated in Step 2. The total manufacturing cost includes the cost of the units in beginning inventory plus the costs that were incurred during the current period.

$$\text{Cost per Equivalent Unit} = \frac{\text{Beginning Inventory} + \text{Current Costs}}{\text{Equivalent Units}}$$

As this formula shows, the weighted average method combines (averages) the beginning inventory costs with the costs that were incurred during the current period. Because the number of equivalent units is different for direct materials and conversion costs, we must make a separate calculation for each category.

The cost per equivalent unit for the CFA process is calculated as follows:

	Direct Materials	Conversion Cost
Beginning inventory costs	$ 84,000	$ 81,120
Current manufacturing costs	810,000	918,000
Total manufacturing costs	$894,000	$999,120
Equivalent units (from Step 2)	2,000	1,840
Cost per equivalent unit	$ 447	$ 543

This table shows that the cost per equivalent unit is $447 for direct materials and $543 for conversion cost. Recall that a unit was defined as a standard barrel of wine. This suggests that it costs about $990 ($447 + $543) to process a barrel of wine in the CFA process. This is the total manufacturing cost **before** the barrels are sent to the Bottling department, where additional manufacturing cost will be incurred. The next step is to determine how much cost to transfer out of the CFA process (and into Bottling) and how much to attach to the units that are still in the CFA Work in Process Inventory at the end of the accounting period.

STEP 4: RECONCILE THE TOTAL COST OF WORK IN PROCESS INVENTORY

The fourth step in the preparation of the production report is to reconcile the total cost recorded in the Work in Process Inventory account. The following T-accounts shows the costs for our winery example:

Work in Process Inventory (CFA)				Work in Process Inventory (Bottling)
Beginning costs		Cost of goods		
Direct materials	84,000	completed		
Conversion costs	81,120	?	Transferred to Bottling → ?	
Current period costs				
Direct materials	810,000			
Conversion costs	918,000			
Total cost	1,893,120			
Ending Balance	?			

This T-account shows that the total cost incurred in the CFA process is $1,893,120. Some of this cost will be transferred out of the Work in Process Inventory account with the 1,600 units completed and transferred to Bottling, and some will remain in Work in Process Inventory. The 1,600 units transferred cost $990 each ($447 direct materials plus $534 conversion) for a total of $1,584,000. Because the units in ending inventory are not fully complete, we multiply the number of equivalent units by the cost per equivalent unit, as follows:

COST ASSIGNED TO UNITS COMPLETED AND ENDING INVENTORY

	Direct Materials	Conversion Cost	Total Cost
Units completed	1600 × $447 = $715,200	1600 × $543 = $868,800	$1,584,000
Ending inventory	400 × $447 = $178,800	240 × $543 = $130,320	309,120
Total cost			$1,893,120

After we transfer $1,584,000 out of the Work in Process account to reflect the cost of units completed and transferred to Bottling, the T-accounts appear as follows:

Work in Process Inventory (CFA)				Work in Process Inventory (Bottling)
Beginning costs		Cost of goods		
Direct materials	84,000	completed		
Conversion costs	81,120	1,584,000	Transferred to Bottling → 1,584,000	
Current period costs				
Direct materials	810,000			
Conversion costs	918,000			
Total cost	1,893,120			
Ending Balance	309,120			

STEP 5: PREPARE A PRODUCTION REPORT

The final step in process costing is to summarize the results of Steps 1–4 into a **production report**. This report provides a summary of what occurred in the production process during the accounting period. It includes information about the number of physical units (Step 1), number of equivalent units (Step 2), cost per equivalent unit (Step 3), and a reconciliation of the cost of Work in Process Inventory (Step 4).

Learning Objective 4
Prepare a process costing production report using the weighted average method.

EXHIBIT 3.5 | Production Report (Weighted Average Method)

CK MONDAVI WINERY

Process Costing Production Report (Weighted Average Method)

Crushing, Fermenting, and Aging (CFA) Department

For the Quarter Ended March 31, 2010

	Step 1			
NUMBER OF UNITS	**Reconcile**			
1 Number of units to be accounted for	**Physical Units**			
2 Beginning work in process	200			
3 Started into production	1,800			
4 Total number of units	2,000	**Step 2**		
5		**Calculate the Number of Equivalent Units**		
6 Number of units to be accounted for		Direct Materials	Conversion	
7 Completed and transferred	1,600	1,600	1,600	
8 Ending work in process	400	400	240	
9 Total number of units	2,000	2,000	1,840	
10				
11 **COSTS**		**Step 3**		
12		**Calculate Cost per Equivalent Unit**		
13		Direct Materials	Conversion	Total Cost
14 Cost of beginning inventory		$84,000	$81,120	$165,120
15 Current period costs		810,000	918,000	1,728,000
16 Total cost of units in process		$894,000	$999,120	$1,893,120
17 Number of equivalent units (from Step 2)		2,000	1,840	
18 Cost per equivalent unit		$447	$543	$990
19		**Step 4**		
20		**Reconcile the Total Cost of Work in Process**		
21 Cost to be accounted for		Direct Materials	Conversion	Total Cost
22 Beginning work in process		$84,000	$81,120	$165,120
23 Current period costs		810,000	918,000	1,728,000
24 Total costs		$894,000	$999,120	$1,893,120
25				
26 Cost to be accounted for				
27 Units completed and transferred (Row 7 × Row 18)		$715,200	$868,800	$1,584,000
28 Ending inventory (Row 8 × Row 18)		178,800	130,320	309,120
29		$894,000	$999,120	$1,893,120

The production report for the CFA process is based on the weighted average method (see Exhibit 3.5). This is the same report that was presented earlier in the chapter to provide a summary of the activity that occurred in the CFA process.

ADDITIONAL FACTORS IN PROCESS COSTING

The previous example illustrates the basic concepts in process costing. However, you should be aware of two issues that were not included in the example. First, as was mentioned earlier, some companies use an alternative method, FIFO process costing. Supplement 3A illustrates the FIFO method using the same data we used in the weighted average example. Your instructor may want you to learn the weighted average method, the FIFO method, or both. The steps for preparing the production report are the same. The only difference is how you treat the units and costs of the beginning inventory.

The second issue we did not consider is how to account for subsequent departments in process costing. We showed the first process in the production chain (CFA), but we did not extend the example to show how costs flow through the next process (Bottling).

The cost of the wine transferred out of the CFA process ($1,584,000) would enter the Bottling department's Work in Process Inventory account in the same way that the cost of direct materials (grapes) was added to the Work in Process Inventory (CFA) account. We would then prepare a production report to keep track of additional direct materials and conversion costs added in the Bottling department.

SUPPLEMENT 3A: FIFO METHOD

This supplement describes how to prepare a production report using the FIFO method of process costing. The primary difference between weighted average and FIFO has to do with the treatment of units in beginning inventory. FIFO assumes that the units in beginning inventory are completed before any new units are started in the process. Thus, FIFO gives more precise and detailed treatment of the costs and units in beginning inventory than the weighted average method.

The same five steps are required to prepare a production report using the FIFO method as the weighted average method:

1. Reconcile the number of physical units worked on during the period.
2. Translate physical units into equivalent units.
3. Calculate the cost per equivalent unit.
4. Reconcile the total cost of Work in Process Inventory.
5. Prepare a production report.

Step 1: Reconcile the Number of Physical Units

The first step in preparing a production report is to reconcile the number of physical units that were worked on during the period. To do so, we first add the number of units that were on hand at the beginning of the period to the number of units that were started during the current period. Then we determine whether those units were completed during the period or are still being worked on at the end of the period. The formula to reconcile the number of physical units is as follows:

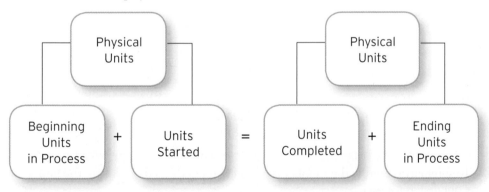

COACH'S TIP

This formula ignores any units lost due to spoilage or waste. Accounting for lost or spoiled units is covered in more advanced accounting texts.

As an example, assume CK Mondavi had 200 barrels of wine in the CFA process at the start of a new accounting period. During the period, workers started another 1,800 barrels into the CFA process. At the end of the period, 400 barrels of wine were still in the CFA process. Based on this information, how many barrels of wine were transferred out of the CFA process and into bottling during the current period?

To answer this question, we can prepare a reconciliation of physical units as follows:

	Physical Units		Physical Units
Beginning units	200	Units completed	?
Units started	1,800	Ending units	400
Total units	2,000	Total units	2,000

COACH'S TIP

The number of units completed is 1,600. A total of 2,000 units were worked on during the period, and 400 of them were still being worked on at the end of the period, so 1,600 of them must have been completed.

We must account for a total of 2,000 units, 200 that were on hand at the beginning of the period plus 1,800 that were started this period. If we have only 400 on hand at the end of the period, we must have completed 1,600 units.

Under the FIFO method, we must also determine how many units were both started **and** completed during the current period. Those units would have made it all the way through the CFA process during the current period, so they would not be part of either beginning or ending inventory, as the following formula shows:

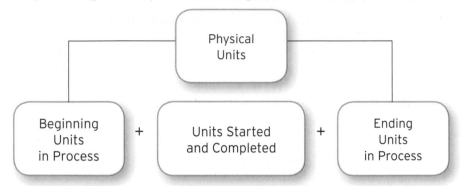

Remember that FIFO assumes that the units in beginning inventory were completed first. Thus, not all units that were completed during the current period were started during the current period; the units that were in the beginning inventory were started during the last period. Likewise, some of the units that were started during the period were not completed; they remain in the ending inventory.

In our example, we had a total of 2,000 physical units to account for: 200 from the beginning inventory plus 1,800 that were started during the period. During the period, 1,600 units were completed; 400 were still in process at the end of the period. How many units were both started **and** completed during the current period? The answer is 1,400 units, as shown in the following formulas:

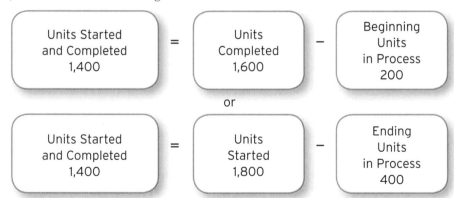

To summarize Step 1, the number of physical units worked on during the period can be reconciled as follows:

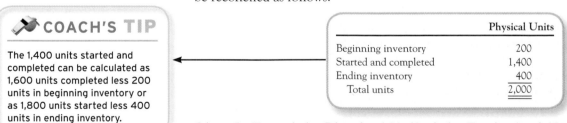

	Physical Units
Beginning inventory	200
Started and completed	1,400
Ending inventory	400
Total units	2,000

Step 2: Translate Physical Units into Equivalent Units

The next step in preparing the production report is to calculate the number of equivalent units. An **equivalent unit** is a measure used to convert partially completed units into the equivalent of a full unit.

Why must we calculate equivalent units? Companies often have units in process at the beginning and end of an accounting period. This is particularly true for products that take a long time to manufacture, such as wine that must be aged for months or even years before it is ready for sale. Even though the units are incomplete, their cost must be recorded on the balance sheet as Work in Process Inventory. Remember that GAAP requires all manufacturing costs to be counted as part of the cost of the product and reported as inventory (an asset) until the product is sold. By converting partially completed units into equivalent units, we can assign an appropriate value to those units for financial statement reporting.

To illustrate the calculation of equivalent units using FIFO, we assume the following additional details about the CFA process at CK Mondavi:

- Direct materials (grapes) are added at the beginning of the process. Thus, once a unit has started the CFA process, it will have 100 percent of the required direct materials.

- Conversion costs (direct labor and manufacturing overhead) are incurred uniformly throughout the process.

- The 200 units in beginning inventory were 70 percent through the CFA process.

- Only 1,400 of the units that were started during the current period were completed during the current period. Thus, those units made it all the way through the CFA process without getting "stuck" in beginning or ending inventory.

- The 400 units in ending inventory were 60 percent through the CFA conversion process. Thus, these units have all required direct materials (crushed grapes) but only 60 percent of the conversion effort (fermenting and aging).

These details are presented in the form of a diagram of the production process in Exhibit 3A.1.

To calculate equivalent units, we need to consider how much work was done during the **current** period to complete the 200 units in beginning inventory, to produce 1,400 units from start to finish, and to get the 400 units in ending inventory 60 percent complete with respect to conversion cost. This calculation must be made separately for direct materials and conversion costs because those costs are added at different points in the production process. See Exhibit 3A.2 for a summary of the calculation of equivalent units.

Because direct materials are added at the beginning of the process, we did not need to add any direct materials to the units in beginning inventory during the current

COACH'S TIP

To calculate the number of equivalent units, ask yourself the following questions: What did we do during the **current** period to get the beginning inventory units from 70 percent complete to fully complete? What did we do during the **current** period to start the ending inventory units and get them 60 percent complete?

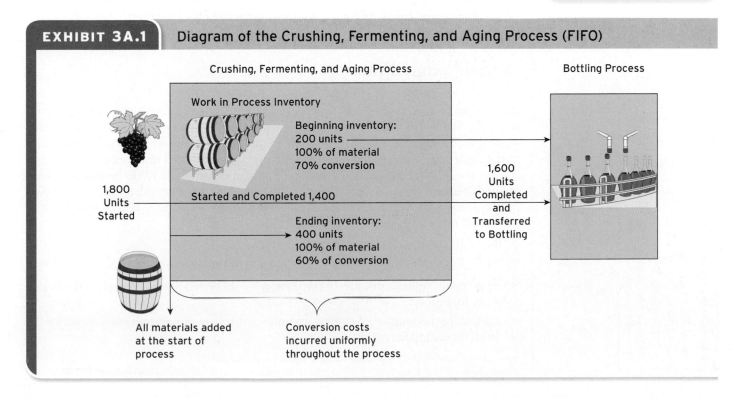

EXHIBIT 3A.1 | Diagram of the Crushing, Fermenting, and Aging Process (FIFO)

Crushing, Fermenting, and Aging Process

Bottling Process

Work in Process Inventory

Beginning inventory:
200 units
100% of material
70% conversion

Started and Completed 1,400

Ending inventory:
400 units
100% of material
60% of conversion

1,800 Units Started

1,600 Units Completed and Transferred to Bottling

All materials added at the start of process

Conversion costs incurred uniformly throughout the process

EXHIBIT 3A.2	Calculation of Equivalent Units, FIFO Method

| | Physical Units | EQUIVALENT UNITS | |
		Direct Materials	Conversion Cost
Beginning inventory	200	0 [200 × (100% − 100%)]	60 [200 × (100% − 70%)]
Started and completed	1,400	1,400	1,400
Ending inventory	400	400 (400 × 100%)	240 (400 × 60%)
Total	2,000	1,800	1,700

period. The beginning inventory required zero equivalent units of direct materials in the current period. Because those units were already 70 percent of the way through the conversion process, they required only 30 percent conversion effort during the current period. So, we multiply the 200 physical units by 30 percent to arrive at 60 equivalent units of conversion cost for the beginning inventory units.

The 1,400 units that were started **and** completed went all the way through the CFA process during the current period. Because all work on those units happened during the current period, the number of equivalent units is the same as the number of physical units.

The 400 units in ending inventory were started during the current period and received the entire amount of direct materials at the beginning of the process. Thus, the number of equivalent units for direct materials is the same as the 400 physical units in ending inventory. Those units went only 60 percent of the way through the conversion process during the current period, however. Therefore, the number of equivalent units for conversion would be 60 percent of the 400 units in ending inventory, or 240.

Finally, we calculate total equivalent units by adding the number of equivalent units for beginning inventory, units started **and** completed, and ending inventory. This calculation gives us 1,800 equivalent units of direct materials and 1,700 equivalent units of conversion cost. In the next step, we use these numbers to calculate the cost per equivalent unit.

Before moving to Step 3, complete the following Self-Study Practice to reconcile physical units and calculate equivalent units using the FIFO method:

 Self-Study Practice

Aqua-Fit manufactures and sells fitness drinks (with added vitamins and minerals) to fitness clubs across the country. The company uses a FIFO process costing system to determine the cost of the drinks. All materials (water, juice, vitamins, and bottles) are added at the beginning of the process, and conversion costs are added uniformly.

At the start of the most recent period, the company had 1,000 bottles that were about 40 percent through the conversion process. During the period, an additional 9,000 bottles were started in the process. The period ended with 3,000 bottles that were 20 percent of the way through the process.

1. How many units were **completed** during the period?
2. How many units were **started and completed** during the period?
3. How many equivalent units of conversion would be required to **complete** the beginning inventory?
4. Calculate the number of equivalent units of direct materials and conversion for the units in ending inventory.

After you have finished, check your answers with the solutions in the margin.

Solution to Self-Study Practice

1. 7,000(1,000 + 9,000 − 3,000)
2. 6,000(7,000 − 1,000) or (9,000 − 3,000)
3. 600[1,000 × (100% − 40%)]
4. 3,000 equivalent units of direct materials, 600 equivalent units of conversion (3,000 × 20%)

Step 3: Calculate the Cost per Equivalent Unit

To calculate the cost per equivalent unit under FIFO, we divide the current period's costs by the total number of equivalent units calculated in Step 2, as follows:

$$\text{Cost per Equivalent Unit} = \frac{\text{Current Period Costs}}{\text{Equivalent Units}}$$

The FIFO method includes only current period costs in the numerator because **equivalent units relate only to work that was performed during the current period.** We do not include the cost of beginning inventory because those costs were incurred in a prior period. Because the number of equivalent units differs for direct materials and conversion cost, we must calculate each category separately.

Exhibit 3A.3 shows the cost per equivalent unit calculations for our winery example. The cost per equivalent unit is $450 for direct materials and $540 for conversion cost. In the next step, we use these numbers to determine the cost of the units completed and transferred to Bottling, as well as the cost of the units that are still in process at the end the period.

| EXHIBIT 3A.3 | Calculation of the Cost per Equivalent Unit, FIFO Method |

	Direct Materials	Conversion Cost
Current period cost (given)	$810,000	$918,000
Equivalent units (from Exhibit 3A.2)	÷ 1,800	÷ 1,700
Cost per equivalent unit	$ 450	$ 540

Step 4: Reconcile the Total Cost of Work in Process Inventory

The fourth step in preparing the production report is to reconcile the total cost recorded in the Work in Process Inventory account. Its total cost includes the cost that was already in the account at the beginning of the period plus the direct materials and conversion costs that were added to the process during the period. See the following T-accounts for the costs for our winery example.

Work in Process Inventory (CFA)				Work in Process Inventory (Bottling)	
Beginning costs		Transferred		84,000	
Direct materials	84,000	to Bottling		81,120	
Conversion costs	81,120				
Current period costs					
Direct materials	810,000	?		?	
Conversion costs	918,000				
Total cost	1,893,120				
Ending Balance	?				

As you can see, we need to account for a total cost of $1,893,120 for the CFA process. Notice that part of this cost ($84,000 + $81,120) relates to the units that were already in process at the beginning of the period. Because FIFO assumes that these units are completed first, the cost of the beginning inventory is automatically transferred out of the Work in Process Inventory account with the units that were completed and transferred.

The current period costs of $810,000 and $918,000 were included in the calculation of cost per equivalent unit in Step 3. To determine how much of this cost should be transferred out and how much should remain in ending inventory, we must multiply the cost per equivalent unit (from Exhibit 3A.3) by the number of equivalent units (calculated in Exhibit 3A.2). See Exhibit 3A.4 for the calculations.

EXHIBIT 3A.4   Calculation of the Cost of Goods Completed and Ending Inventory Costs, FIFO Method

CURRENT PERIOD COSTS
(EQUIVALENT UNITS 3 COST PER EQUIVALENT UNITS)

	Direct Materials	Conversion Cost	Total Cost
Beginning inventory costs	$ 84,000	$ 81,120	$ 165,120
Cost to complete beginning inventory	—	60 × $540 = $ 32,400	32,400
Units started and completed	1,400 × $450 = $630,000	1,400 × $540 = $756,000	1,386,000
Ending inventory	400 × $450 = $180,000	240 × $540 = $129,600	309,600
Total cost to account for			$1,893,120

- The 200 units in beginning inventory carried a cost of $165,120 ($84,000 + $81,120) from the prior period. During the current period, the company incurred an additional 60 equivalent units of conversion to complete the beginning inventory at a total cost of $32,400 (60 × $540). Thus, the total cost of the units in beginning inventory is $197,520 ($165,120 + $32,400). Because FIFO assumes that the units in beginning inventory are completed first, this cost will be transferred out of the CFA Work in Process accounting and into the Bottling department.

- The 1,400 units that were started **and** completed during the current period made it all the way through the process during the current period. These units cost $450 for direct materials and $540 for conversion, for a total cost of $1,386,000 [1,400 × ($450 + $540)]. This cost will be transferred out of the CFA Work in Process account and into the Bottling department.

- The 400 units that remain in ending inventory are valued at $450 per equivalent unit for direct materials or $180,000 (400 × $450). The conversion cost attached to these units would be $129,600 (240 equivalent units × $540 per equivalent unit), for a total ending inventory cost of $309,600 ($180,000 + $129,600).

The following T-accounts show how these costs would appear in the Work in Process Inventory (CFA) account at the end of the accounting period:

Work in Process Inventory (CFA)				Work in Process Inventory (Bottling)
Beginning costs				
Direct materials	84,000	84,000	1,583,520	
Conversion costs	81,120	81,120		
Current period costs		60 × 540 = 32,400		
Direct materials	810,000	1,400 × 450 = 630,000		
Conversion costs	918,000	1,400 × 540 = 756,000	Cost of goods completed and	
Total cost	1,893,120	1,583,520	transferred to Bottling	
Ending Balance	309,600			

The total cost of goods completed is $1,583,520. This cost is transferred out of the CFA Work in Process Inventory account and into the Bottling department. The $309,600 that remains in the CFA Work in Process account represents the cost of the units that are still in process at the end of the accounting period. This will become the beginning Work in Process Inventory in the next accounting period.

Step 5: Prepare a Production Report

The final step in process costing is to summarize the results of Steps 1–4 into a production report. This report provides a summary of what occurred in the production process during the accounting period. It includes information about the number of physical units

(Step 1), equivalent units (Step 2), cost per equivalent unit (Step 3), and a reconciliation of the cost of work in process (Step 4). See Exhibit 3A.5 for a production report for the CFA process based on the FIFO method.

EXHIBIT 3A.5	Production Report (FIFO Method)

CK MONDAVI WINERY
Process Costing Production Report (FIFO Method)
Crushing, Fermenting, and Aging (CFA) Department
For the Quarter Ended March 31, 2010

		Step 1			
	NUMBER OF UNITS	**Reconcile**			
1	Number of units to be accounted for	**Physical Units**			
2	Beginning work in process	200			
3	Started into production	1,800			
4	Total number of units	2,000	**Step 2**		
5			**Calculate the Number of Equivalent Units**		
6	Number of units to be accounted for		Direct Materials	Conversion	
7	Beginning work in process	200		60	
8	Started and completed	1,400	1,400	1,400	
9	Ending work in process	400	400	240	
10	Total number of units	2,000	1,800	1,700	
11					
12	**COSTS**		**Step 3**		
13			**Calculate Cost per Equivalent Unit**		
14			Direct Materials	Conversion	Total Cost
15	Current period cost		$810,000	$918,000	$1,728,000
16	Number of equivalent units (Row 10)		1,800	1,700	
17	Cost per equivalent unit		$450	$540	$990
18			**Step 4**		
19			**Reconcile the Total Cost of Work in Process**		
20	Cost to be accounted for		Direct Materials	Conversion	Total Cost
21	Beginning work in process		$84,000	$81,120	$165,120
22	Current period costs		810,000	918,000	1,728,000
23	Total costs		$894,000	$999,120	$1,893,120
24					
25	Cost to be accounted for				
26	Beginning inventory balance (transferred out)		$84,000	$81,120	$165,120
27	Cost to complete beginning inventory (Row 7 × Row 17)		0	32,400	32,400
28	Started and completed (Row 8 × Row 17)		630,000	756,000	1,386,000
29	Ending inventory (Row 9 × Row 17)		180,000	129,600	309,600
30	Total costs		$894,000	$999,120	$1,893,120

If you compare this FIFO process costing report to the weighted average report from Exhibit 3.5, you will see that the reports are structured very similarly. The FIFO report is slightly more detailed and gives more attention to the units that were on hand at the beginning of the period. In this particular example, the end result is very similar. The cost of units completed during the period was $1,584,000 for the weighted average method compared to $1,583,520 for the FIFO method, a difference of only $480. You get the same $480 difference if you compare the value of ending Work in Process Inventory of $309,120 under weighted average to $309,600 for FIFO. The two methods may not always provide such similar results, particularly if production or manufacturing costs fluctuate from period to period and the company maintains significant levels of Work in Process Inventory. As a manager you need to understand when the methods will produce different results and whether the extra calculations required by FIFO are worth the effort.

SUPPLEMENT 3B: JOURNAL ENTRIES FOR PROCESS COSTING

This supplement describes the journal entries that record the flow of manufacturing costs in a process costing system. For the sake of simplicity, we begin our example on the first day of operations. Thus, there are no beginning balances in any of the accounts.

Purchase of Raw Materials

Raw materials purchased are recorded in the Raw Materials Inventory account. Assume, for example, that CK Mondavi purchased $35,000 of direct materials (grapes, bottles, and corks) on account from various suppliers. The journal entry to record the purchase of raw materials is:

	Debit	Credit
Raw Materials Inventory	35,000	
Accounts Payable		35,000

Issue of Raw Materials into Production

When raw materials are taken out of storage and placed into production, the cost is debited to the Work in Process Inventory account for the first production process. Assume, for example, that $20,000 worth of grapes is added to the CFA process. The journal entry to record the issue of direct materials into production is:

	Debit	Credit
Work in Process Inventory (CFA)	20,000	
Raw Materials Inventory		20,000

The Recording of Actual and Applied Conversion Costs

Remember that conversion costs include direct labor and manufacturing overhead. Most accounting systems maintain a separate general ledger account for each of these costs. However, direct labor is likely to be a very small percentage of the total conversion cost in a winery and many other process-oriented industries. For this reason, we combine direct labor and manufacturing overhead in a single account, Conversion Cost. This account is almost identical to the Manufacturing Overhead account we used in Chapter 2 except that it now includes a small amount of direct labor cost. We use this account to record actual and applied conversion cost just as we recorded actual and applied manufacturing overhead in Chapter 2. Actual costs are debited to the Conversion Cost account and applied costs are credited to the Conversion Cost account. Any difference between actual and applied conversion cost is adjusted directly to Cost of Goods Sold at the end of the accounting period.

To illustrate this process, assume that CK Mondavi incurred the following actual conversion costs:

Direct labor and supervision paid	$16,000
Winery utilities owed but not yet paid	5,000
Depreciation on winery equipment	15,250
Total conversion cost	$36,250

These actual conversion costs are debited to the Conversion Cost account. Depending on the nature of the transaction, the credit is to Cash, Payables, Prepaid

Assets, or Accumulated Depreciation. The journal entry to record the actual conversion costs follows:

	Debit	Credit
Conversion Cost	36,250	
Cash		16,000
Utilities Payable		5,000
Accumulated Depreciation		15,250

> **COACH'S TIP**
>
> The treatment of conversion cost is similar to the treatment of manufacturing overhead in the last chapter. The only difference is that conversion cost also includes a small amount of direct labor. These costs were directly traced to jobs in the last chapter but are treated as indirect costs in this chapter.

Conversion costs are then applied to Work in Process Inventory using a predetermined allocation base. For example, a winery might apply conversion cost based on the number of barrels, the number of fermentation tanks, or the cost of the grapes that are processed. Direct labor hours and machine hours are also common allocation bases. Assume CK Mondavi applies conversion cost in the CFA process at a rate equal to 125 percent of direct materials cost. In other words, for every $1.00 of direct materials cost, an additional $1.25 must be applied to cover the direct labor and manufacturing overhead costs. In a preceding transaction, we issued $20,000 worth of direct materials into the Work in Process Inventory (CFA) account. Now we need to apply $25,000 ($20,000 × 125%) of conversion cost to Work in Process Inventory. The journal entry to apply the conversion cost to the Work in Process Inventory account follows:

	Debit	Credit
Work in Process Inventory (CFA)	25,000	
Conversion Cost		25,000

At the end of the accounting period, we would account for any difference in actual and applied conversion cost. We do this after we have recorded all transactions for this example.

Transfer of Cost from One Work in Process Inventory Account to the Next

When the wine is through the CFA process, its total manufacturing cost must be transferred to the Bottling process. See Exhibit 3B.1 for a summary of the costs that have been recorded to this point.

EXHIBIT 3B.1   Summary of Recorded Transactions

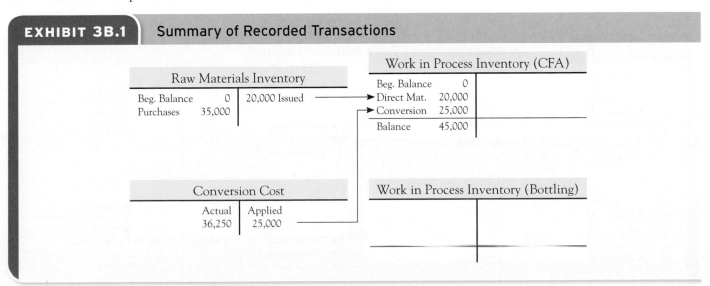

Note that a total of $45,000 has been recorded in the Work in Process Inventory (CFA) account. This cost needs to be transferred out of Work in Process Inventory (CFA) and into the next process (Bottling), which will have its own Work in Process Inventory account. The journal entry to transfer the total manufacturing costs from one process to the other follows:

	Debit	Credit
Work in Process Inventory (Bottling)	45,000	
Work in Process Inventory (CFA)		45,000

In the bottling process, the company will incur more direct material costs for items such as bottles, corks, and boxes. Assume that CK Mondavi issues $10,000 worth of direct materials into the Bottling process. The journal entry to record the issue of these direct materials into production is:

	Debit	Credit
Work in Process Inventory (Bottling)	10,000	
Raw Materials Inventory		10,000

Next, we need to apply conversion cost to the Bottling department's Work in Process Inventory account. Let's assume that the rate for applying conversion cost to the Bottling process is 87.5 percent of direct materials cost. Because we just recorded $10,000 in direct materials cost, we need to apply an additional $8,750 ($10,000 × 87.5%) in conversion cost. The journal entry to apply conversion cost to the Work in Process Inventory (Bottling) account is:

	Debit	Credit
Work in Process Inventory (Bottling)	8,750	
Conversion Cost		8,750

Exhibit 3B.2 shows the updated T-accounts.

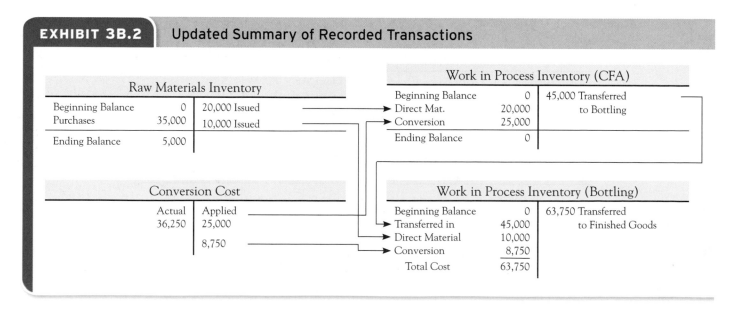

EXHIBIT 3B.2   **Updated Summary of Recorded Transactions**

Raw Materials Inventory

Beginning Balance	0	20,000 Issued
Purchases	35,000	10,000 Issued
Ending Balance	5,000	

Work in Process Inventory (CFA)

Beginning Balance	0	45,000 Transferred
Direct Mat.	20,000	to Bottling
Conversion	25,000	
Ending Balance	0	

Conversion Cost

Actual	Applied
36,250	25,000
	8,750

Work in Process Inventory (Bottling)

Beginning Balance	0	63,750 Transferred
Transferred in	45,000	to Finished Goods
Direct Material	10,000	
Conversion	8,750	
Total Cost	63,750	

So far, we have recorded a total of $63,750 in the Work in Process Inventory (Bottling) account. When the wine has finished the bottling process, this amount will be transferred to Finished Goods Inventory. The journal entry to transfer cost from the last Work in Process Inventory (Bottling) account to Finished Goods Inventory is:

	Debit	Credit
Finished Goods Inventory	63,750	
Work in Process Inventory (Bottling)...................		63,750

Assuming that the $63,750 transferred to the Finished Goods Inventory account represents the cost of processing 15,000 bottles (or 1,250 cases) of wine, the costs per case and per bottle are calculated as follows:

Total manufacturing cost	$63,750
Total number of cases	1,250
Total number of bottles	15,000
Cost per case ($63,750/1,250)	$ 51.00
Cost per bottle ($63,750/15,000)	$ 4.25

If CK Mondavi sold 12,000 bottles (1,000 cases) of this wine in the winery gift shop at a retail price of $8 per bottle, we would make additional journal entries to record cost of goods sold and sales revenue. The journal entry to record the cost of goods sold for 12,000 bottles at a cost of $4.25 per bottle is:

	Debit	Credit
Cost of Goods Sold (12,000 × $4.25)................................	51,000	
Finished Goods Inventory.......................................		51,000

The journal entry to record the sale of 12,000 bottles at a price of $8 per bottle is:

	Debit	Credit
Cash (12,000 × $8.00)...	96,000	
Sales Revenue..		96,000

Notice that the $4.25 cost per bottle was based on the amount of conversion cost **applied** to the Work in Process Inventory accounts and then transferred to Finished Goods Inventory and Cost of Goods Sold. But what if **actual** conversion costs were more or less than **applied** conversion cost? The Conversion Cost account for our example is summarized as follows:

Conversion Cost	
Actual	Applied
36,250	25,000
	8,750 } 33,750
2,500	
Underapplied	

> **COACH'S TIP**
>
> A debit balance indicates that actual conversion cost was more than applied conversion cost; that is, conversion cost was underapplied. Overapplied conversion cost would be reflected by a credit balance (because the applied cost was more than the actual cost).

This account shows that actual conversion cost was $36,250, but only $33,750 was applied. In short, conversion cost was **underapplied** by $2,500.

Because most of the applied conversion cost is now in the Cost of Goods Sold account, the easiest way to handle the $2,500 in underapplied conversion cost is to increase Cost of Goods Sold. The journal entry to adjust for $2,500 in underapplied conversion cost is:

	Debit	Credit
Cost of Goods Sold..	2,500	
Conversion Cost..		2,500

If the conversion cost had been **overapplied,** we would have **decreased** Cost of Goods Sold. Thus, the journal entry just given would be reversed (that is, Conversion Cost would be debited and Cost of Goods Sold would be credited). See Exhibit 3B.3 for the Cost of Goods Sold and Finished Goods Inventory accounts after these entries have been made.

COACH'S TIP

For simplicity, we will close the entire amount of underapplied conversion cost to the Cost of Goods Sold account. A more precise approach would have been to adjust the Work in Process Inventory, Finished Goods Inventory, and Cost of Goods Sold accounts based on the amount of conversion cost in each (if any). This more complicated method is covered in more advanced accounting books.

EXHIBIT 3B.3   **Final Summary of Recorded Transactions**

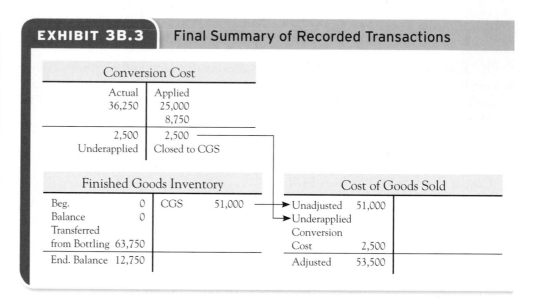

DEMONSTRATION CASE A (WEIGHTED AVERAGE METHOD)

Bellagio Olive Oil Company manufactures extra virgin olive oil using a series of processes to convert olives into olive oil. These steps include cleaning the olives, grinding them into a paste, mixing to increase olive oil yield, separating the olive oil from the fruit, extracting the olive oil, storing, and bottling.

In the Mixing department, direct materials (olives) are added at the beginning of the process, and conversion costs are incurred uniformly throughout the process. At the beginning of the most recent accounting period, Bellagio had 20,000 units in the mixing process that were 30 percent complete. It started an additional 150,000 units into the process and ended the period with 40,000 units in process, 40 percent complete. The Mixing department's partially completed production report follows:

Required:

1. Complete steps 1–4 by filling in the question marks in Bellagio's production report below.

		Step 1			
	NUMBER OF UNITS	**Reconcile**			
1	Number of units to be accounted for	**Physical Units**			
2	Beginning work in process	20,000			
3	Started into production	150,000			
4	Total number of units	170,000	**Step 2**		
5			**Calculate the Number of Equivalent Units**		
6	Number of units to be accounted for		Direct Materials	Conversion	
7	Completed	?	?	?	
8	Ending work in process	40,000	?	?	
9	Total number of units	170,000	?	?	
10					
11	**COSTS**		**Step 3**		
12			**Calculate Cost per Equivalent Unit**		
13			Direct Materials	Conversion	Total Cost
14	Beginning work in process		$145,000	$153,200	$298,200
15	Current period costs		450,000	679,000	1,129,000
16	Total manufacturing cost		$595,000	$832,200	$1,427,200
17	Number of equivalent units (from Step 2)		?	?	
18	Cost per equivalent unit		?	?	
19			**Step 4**		
20			**Reconcile the Total Cost of Work in Process**		
21	Cost to be accounted for		Direct Materials	Conversion	Total Cost
22	Beginning work in process		$145,000	$153,200	$298,200
23	Current period costs		450,000	679,000	1,129,000
24	Total costs		$595,000	$832,200	$1,427,200
25					
26	Cost to be accounted for				
27	Units completed and transferred (Row 7 × Row 18)		?	?	?
28	Ending inventory (Row 8 × Row 18)		?	?	?
29	Total costs		?	?	?

2. What is the total cost of the units completed and transferred during the quarter?
3. What is the balance in Work in Process Inventory (Mixing) at the end of the quarter?

See page 116 for solution.

DEMONSTRATION CASE B (FIFO METHOD)

Bellagio Olive Oil Company manufactures extra virgin olive oil using a series of processes to convert olives into olive oil. These steps include cleaning the olives, grinding them into a paste, mixing to increase olive oil yield, separating the olive oil from the fruit, extracting the olive oil, storing, and bottling.

In the Mixing department, direct materials (olives) are added at the beginning of the process, and conversion costs are incurred uniformly throughout the process. At the beginning of the most recent accounting period, Bellagio had 20,000 units in the mixing process that were 30 percent complete. It started an additional 150,000 units into the process and ended the period with 40,000 units in process, 40 percent complete. The mixing department's partially completed production report follows:

Required:

1. Complete Steps 1–4 by filling in the question marks in Bellagio's production report below.

		BELLAGIO OLIVE OIL			
		Process Costing Production Report (FIFO Method)			
		Mixing Department			
		For the Quarter Ended December 31, 2010			
		Step 1			
	NUMBER OF UNITS	Reconcile			
1	Number of units to be accounted for	Physical Units			
2	Beginning work in process	20,000			
3	Started into production	150,000			
4	Total number of units	170,000	Step 2		
5			Calculate the Number of Equivalent Units		
6	Number of units to be accounted for		Direct Materials	Conversion	
7	Beginning work in process	20,000	?	?	
8	Started and completed	?	?	?	
9	Ending work in process	40,000	?	?	
10	Total number of units	?	?	?	
11					
12	COSTS		Step 3		
13			Calculate Cost per Equivalent Unit		
14			Direct Materials	Conversion	
15	Current period costs		$450,000	$679,000	
16	Number of equivalent units (from Step 2)		?	?	
17	Cost per equivalent unit		$?	$?	
18			Step 4		
19			Reconcile the Total Cost of Work in Process		
20	Cost to be accounted for		Direct Materials	Conversion	Total
21	Beginning work in process		$145,000	$153,200	$298,200
22	Current period costs		450,000	679,000	1,129,000
23	Total costs		$595,000	$832,200	$1,427,200
24					
25	Cost to be accounted for				
26	Beginning inventory balance (transferred out)		$145,000	$153,200	$298,200
27	Cost to complete beginning inventory (Row 7 × Row 17)		?	?	?
28	Started and completed (Row 8 × Row 17)		?	?	?
29	Ending inventory (Row 9 × Row 17)		?	?	?
30	Total costs		$?	$?	$?

2. What is the total cost of the units completed and transferred during the quarter?
3. What is the balance in Work in Process Inventory (Mixing) at the end of the quarter?

See page 117 for solution.

CHAPTER SUMMARY

Describe the key features of a process costing system. (p. 90)   **LO1**

- Process costing is used by companies that produce homogeneous (similar) goods or services in a series of standardized processes.

- Manufacturing costs are recorded as Raw Materials Inventory, Work in Process Inventory, and Finished Goods Inventory accounts until the product is sold at which point they become part of Cost of Goods Sold.

- Process costing systems maintain a separate Work in Process Inventory account for each major production process. A production report is prepared for each production department to summarize the flow of units and costs through the process during an accounting period.

- Two methods can be used to prepare a process costing production report: the weighted average method and the FIFO method. The primary difference between the two methods is the treatment of the units and costs in beginning inventory. The weighted average method is simpler and preferred for companies that maintain stable or minimal inventory levels. The FIFO method may be more accurate when costs and inventory levels fluctuate from period to period.

Reconcile the number of physical units using the weighted average method. (p. 95)   **LO2**

- The total number of units that were worked on during the period can be reconciled with the following formulas:

  Total Units = Units in Beginning Inventory + Units Started

  Total Units = Units Completed + Units in Ending Inventory

Calculate the number of equivalent units using the weighted average method. (p. 96)   **LO3**

- An equivalent unit is an adjustment that is made to convert partially complete units into the equivalent of a full unit.

- The weighted average method calculates only equivalent units for the ending inventory.

- Equivalent Units = Physical Units × % of Completion

Prepare a process costing production report using the weighted average method. (p. 99)   **LO4**

- The production report summarizes the costs and units that flow into and out of the production process during a given period. It will summarize the following steps:

  Step 1: Reconcile the number of physical units.

  Step 2: Translate physical units into equivalent units.

  Step 3: Calculate the cost per equivalent unit.

  Step 4: Reconcile the total cost of work in process by multiplying the number of equivalent units by the cost per equivalent unit.

  Step 5: Prepare a production report by summarizing Steps 1–4.

SOLUTION TO DEMONSTRATION CASE A (WEIGHTED AVERAGE METHOD)

1.

	BELLAGIO OLIVE OIL			
	Process Costing Production Report (Weighted Average Method)			
	Mixing Department			
	For the Quarter Ended December 31, 2010			
	Step 1			
NUMBER OF UNITS	**Reconcile**			
1 Number of units to be accounted for	**Physical Units**			
2 Beginning work in process	20,000			
3 Started into production	150,000			
4 Total number of units	170,000	**Step 2**		
5		**Calculate the Number of Equivalent Units**		
6 Number of units to be accounted for		Direct Materials	Conversion	
7 Completed	130,000	130,000	130,000	
8 Ending work in process	40,000	40,000	16,000	
9 Total number of units	170,000	170,000	146,000	
10				
11 **COSTS**			**Step 3**	
12			**Calculate Cost per Equivalent Unit**	
13		Direct Materials	Conversion	Total Cost
14 Beginning work in process		$145,000	$153,200	$298,200
15 Current period costs		450,000	679,000	1,129,000
16 Total manufacturing cost		$595,000	$832,200	$1,427,200
17 Number of equivalent units (from Step 2)		170,000	146,000	
18 Cost per equivalent unit		3.50	5.70	
19			**Step 4**	
20			**Reconcile the Total Cost of Work in Process**	
21 Cost to be accounted for		Direct Materials	Conversion	Total Cost
22 Beginning work in process		$145,000	$153,200	$298,200
23 Current period costs		450,000	679,000	1,129,000
24 Total costs		$595,000	$832,200	$1,427,200
25				
26 Cost to be accounted for				
27 Units completed and transferred (Row 7 × Row 18)		$455,000	$741,000	$1,196,000
28 Ending inventory (Row 8 × Row 18)		140,000	91,200	231,200
29 Total costs		$595,000	$832,200	$1,427,200

2. $1,196,000
3. $231,200

SOLUTION TO DEMONSTRATION CASE B (FIFO METHOD)

1.

		BELLAGIO OLIVE OIL			
		Process Costing Production Report (FIFO Method)			
		Mixing Department			
		For the Quarter Ended December 31, 2010			
		Step 1			
	NUMBER OF UNITS	Reconcile			
1	Number of units to be accounted for	**Physical Units**			
2	Beginning work in process	20,000			
3	Started into production	150,000			
4	Total number of units	170,000	Step 2		
5			Calculate the Number of Equivalent Units		
6	Number of units to be accounted for		Direct Materials	Conversion	
7	Beginning work in process	20,000		14,000	
8	Started and completed	110,000	110,000	110,000	
9	Ending work in process	40,000	40,000	16,000	
10	Total number of units	170,000	150,000	140,000	
11					
12	**COSTS**		Step 3		
13			Calculate Cost per Equivalent Unit		
14			Direct Materials	Conversion	
15	Current period costs		$450,000	$679,000	
16	Number of equivalent units (from Step 2)		150,000	140,000	
17	Cost per equivalent unit		$3.00	4.85	
18				Step 4	
19			Reconcile the Total Cost of Work in Process		
20	Cost to be accounted for		Direct Materials	Conversion	Total Cost
21	Beginning work in process		$145,000	$153,200	$298,200
22	Current period costs		450,000	679,000	1,129,000
23	Total costs		$595,000	$832,200	$1,427,200
24					
25	Cost to be accounted for				
26	Beginning inventory balance (transferred out)		$145,000	$153,200	$298,200
27	Cost to complete beginning inventory (Row 7 × Row 17)		?	67,900	67,900
28	Started and completed (Row 8 × Row 17)		330,000	533,500	863,500
29	Ending inventory (Row 9 × Row 17)		120,000	77,600	197,600
30	Total costs		$595,000	$832,200	$1,427,200

2. $298,200 + $67,900 + $863,500 = $1,229,600$
3. $197,600

KEY TERMS

Equivalent Unit (p. 96)   Production Report (p. 92)

Parallel Processing (p. 92)   Sequential Process (p. 92)

See complete definitions in glossary at back of text.

QUESTIONS

1. Briefly describe the differences between job order and process costing. Give an example of a type of company that would use each one.

2. Briefly explain the underlying logic of a process costing system and its assignment of costs to products.

3. Explain the differences between Raw Materials Inventory, Work in Process Inventory, and Finished Goods Inventory accounts.

4. Explain the flow of costs in a manufacturing company including the type of accounts used and the respective financial statement on which the cost appears.

5. What is the difference between a sequential process and a parallel processing approach to manufacturing? Give an example of each.

6. What are the five steps in preparing a weighted average production report?

7. Why is a production report important to a company?

8. What is the difference between conversion cost and manufacturing overhead? Why would a company use a conversion cost account instead of a manufacturing overhead account?

9. What two methods can be used to prepare a process costing production report? What is the key difference between them?

10. How is the number of physical units reconciled in a production report?

11. Why must a company calculate equivalent units when using process costing?

12. How can a unit be 100 percent complete with respect to materials but only partially complete in terms of conversion effort?

13. How do the weighted average and the FIFO methods treat beginning inventory?

14. Is the weighted average method or FIFO method usually more accurate? Why?

15. What are the steps in preparing a FIFO production report? Is this different than the steps used for a weighted average production report?

16. When are the weighted average and FIFO methods likely to arrive at different estimates of product cost?

17. What does a credit to the Work in Process Inventory account represent?

18. What triggers the cost of manufacturing to be transferred from the balance sheet to the income statement?

MULTIPLE CHOICE

1. Which of the following is most likely to use a process costing system? **Quiz 3**

   a. A company that builds   www.mhhe.com/whitecotton1e
      and installs custom cabinetry.
   b. A company that makes one style of office chair.
   c. A janitorial service.
   d. A paving company.

2. Work in process includes

   a. Direct materials.
   b. Direct labor.
   c. Manufacturing overhead.
   d. All of the above.

3. Suppose Shadow Company has 250 units in beginning inventory, 400 units started in production, and 175 units in ending inventory. How many units did Shadow complete?

   a. 25.   c. 475.
   b. 325.   d. Number cannot be determined.

4. If Wilson Corp. has 450 units that are estimated to be 60 percent complete, how many equivalent units are there?

   a. 270.   c. 100.
   b. 210.   d. 450.

5. Masterson Company has calculated a cost per unit of $4.00 for materials and $8.50 for conversion to manufacture a specific product. Ending work in process has 1,000 units that are fully complete for materials and 70 percent complete for conversion. What amount will Masterson have in its ending Work in Process Inventory?

   a. $12,500.   c. $5,950.
   b. $8,750.   d. $9,950.

6. Testa Company has no beginning work in process; 12,000 units were transferred out and 6,000 units in ending work in process are 100% complete for materials and 40% complete for conversion. If total materials cost is $90,000, the direct materials cost per unit is:

   a. $4.   c. $6.
   b. $5.   d. None of the above.

7. Anderson, Inc., has 1,000 units of ending work in process that are 100% complete for materials and 60% complete for conversion. If the cost per equivalent unit is $3 for materials and $6 for conversion, what is the total value of Work in Process Inventory?

   a. $6,000.   c. $8,000.
   b. $9,000.   d. $6,600.

8. The primary difference between FIFO and weighted average methods of process costing has to do with the treatment of

   a. Beginning inventory.
   b. Ending inventory.
   c. Number of units started.
   d. Direct materials.

9. When calculating product cost using the weighted average method, which of the following amounts are combined?

   a. Ending finished goods and cost of goods sold.
   b. Beginning finished goods and cost of goods sold.

   c. Beginning work in process and beginning finished goods.
   d. Beginning work in process and current period costs.

10. The journal entry to record the issuance of direct materials into production includes

    a. A credit to cash.
    b. A debit to work in process.
    c. A credit to finished goods.
    d. A debit to cost of goods sold.

   > Answers to Multiple-Choice Questions located in back of the text.

MINI EXERCISES   Available with McGraw-Hill's Connect

 |ACCOUNTING   **LO1**

M3-1 Identifying Companies That Use Process Costing

Identify three manufacturing and three nonmanufacturing firms in which process costing is likely used. For each, explain the characteristics of that company that make it appropriate to use a process costing system.

M3-2 Calculating Physical Units   **LO2**

Roundtree Company had 575 units in work in process on January 1. During the month, Roundtree completed 2,400 units and had 1,000 units in process on January 31. Determine how many units Roundtree started during January.

M3-3 Calculating Physical Units   **LO2**

For each of the following independent cases (A–D), compute the missing value in the table.

Case	Beginning Units	Units Started	Units Completed	Ending Units
A	400	2,300	1,650	?
B	1,200	800	?	1,600
C	?	750	1,230	2,560
D	345	?	900	680

M3-4 Calculating Physical Units and Equivalent Units (Weighted Average)   **LO2, 3**

Bedford Company produces carrying cases for CDs. It has compiled the following information for the month of June:

	Physical Units	Percent Complete for Conversion
Beginning work in process	35,000	55%
Ending work in process	46,000	70

Bedford adds all materials at the beginning of its manufacturing process. During the month, it started 90,000 units.

Using the weighted average method, reconcile the number of physical units and calculate the number of equivalent units.

M3-5 Calculating Cost per Equivalent Unit (Weighted Average)   **LO2, 3**

Incontro Company manufactures file cabinets. The following cost information is available for the month of December.

Beginning work in process	
Direct materials	$ 34,000
Conversion cost	62,000
December costs	
Direct materials	68,000
Conversion cost	105,000

Incontro had 8,500 equivalent units of direct materials and 6,000 equivalent units of conversion activity during the month. Using the weighted average method, calculate Incontro's cost per equivalent unit for materials and conversion during December.

LO3, 4   **M3-6** **Assigning Costs to Units**

Randolph Company has the following production information for October: 30,000 units transferred out and 10,000 units in ending work in process that are 100 percent complete for materials and 60 percent complete for conversion costs. Materials cost is $6 per unit and conversion cost is $8 per unit. Determine the cost assigned to the units transferred out and the units in ending work in process.

LO3, 4   **M3-7** **Assigning Costs to Units**

London Corp. had the following production information for August:

Beginning work in process	0
Units started and completed	20,000
Ending work in process	4,000

London's ending work in process is 100 percent complete for materials and 30 percent complete for conversion. London uses the weighted average costing method and has computed direct materials cost per unit of $5 and conversion cost per unit of $12. Determine the cost assigned to units transferred out and to ending work in process.

Supplement 3B   **M3-8** **Preparing a Partial Production Report**

Refer to the information for London Corp. in M3-7. Prepare the journal entry to transfer the cost of completed units to Finished Goods Inventory.

Supplement 3A   **M3-9** **Calculating the Number of Physical Units and Equivalent Units (FIFO)**

Refer to M3-4 for information regarding Bedford Company. Using the FIFO method, reconcile the number of physical units and calculate the number of equivalent units.

Supplement 3A   **M3-10** **Calculating Cost per Equivalent Unit (FIFO)**

Refer to M3-5 for information regarding Incontro Company. Using the FIFO method, calculate Incontro's cost per equivalent unit for materials and conversion during December.

LO3   **M3-11** **Calculating Equivalent Units (Weighted Average)**

The Cutting department of Malcom's Textiles has the following information about production and costs for the month of July.

Beginning work in process, 4,600 units that are 100 percent complete as to materials and 35 percent complete as to conversion costs.

7,500 units transferred out.

Ending work in process, 3,100 units 100 percent complete as to materials and 65 percent complete for conversion.

Required:

Using the weighted average method, compute the number of equivalent units of production for materials and conversion for the month of July.

Supplement 3A   **M3-12** **Calculating Equivalent Units (FIFO)**

The Cutting department of Malcom's Textiles has the following information about production and costs for the month of July.

Beginning work in process, 4,600 units that are 100 percent complete as to materials and 35 percent complete as to conversion costs.

7,500 units transferred out.

Ending work in process, 3,100 units 100 percent complete as to materials and 65 percent complete for conversion.

Using the FIFO method, compute the equivalent units of production for materials and conversion for the month of July.

M3-13 Preparing Journal Entries for Process Costing System

Supplement 3B

During its first month of operation, Dutton Company purchased $45,000 of materials on account and requisitioned $32,000 of materials. The company also applied $50,000 of conversion process during the month. Prepare Dutton's journal entries to record these events.

EXERCISES

E3-1 Understanding Process Costing

LO1

Suppose your sister Sandra and her three best friends start a small business making beaded brace-lets. They plan to purchase the materials, assemble the jewelry themselves, and sell the finished pieces to friends at school. Other than minor color and design differences, the bracelets will be virtually alike. Your sister realizes that they must cover their costs before they can expect any profit and is trying to determine the cost per bracelet. Sandra thinks that she should include the cost of each individual bead used in a bracelet and is becoming frustrated with the process of trac-ing each bead.

Required:

Explain to Sandra why she should be using a process costing system to determine the cost of the bracelets. Include a description of process costing as well as reasons that it is appropriate for her business.

E3-2 Calculating Physical Units and Equivalent Units of Production

LO2, 3

Hunter Company adds all materials at the beginning of its manufacturing process. Production information for selected months of the year follows:

Month	Beginning Work in Process Units	Beginning Work in Process Conversion Complete (percent)	Units Started	Units Transferred Out	Ending Work in Process Units	Ending Work in Process Conversion Complete (percent)
February	1,500	50	?	19,000	6,500	30
June	4,200	75	23,300	?	4,000	45
September	?	20	26,400	25,000	2,300	60
December	2,900	30	22,000	21,400	?	70

Required:

1. Reconcile the number of physical units worked on during the period.
2. Calculate the number of equivalent units for both materials and conversion for each month.

E3-3 Calculating Physical Units and Equivalent Units of Production

LO2,3

Neechi Company adds all materials at the beginning of its manufacturing process. Production information for the third quarter of the year follows:

Month	Beginning Work in Process Units	Beginning Work in Process Conversion Complete (percent)	Units Transferred Out	Ending Work in Process Units	Ending Work in Process Conversion Complete (percent)
July	0	-	68,000	26,400	70
August	?	?	102,500	19,000	55
September	?	?	73,500	22,200	20

Required:

1. Reconcile the number of physical units worked on during the period.
2. Calculate the number of equivalent units for both materials and conversion for each month.

LO2,3   **E3-4 Calculating Equivalent Units Cost per Equivalent Unit, Reconciling the Cost of Work in Process (Weighted Average)**

GoFly Company manufactures kites and has the following information available for the month of April:

Work in process, April 1	
(100% complete for materials, 40% for conversion)	26,000 units
Direct materials	$ 40,000
Conversion cost	$ 55,000
Number of units started	79,000
April costs	
Direct materials	$ 113,000
Conversion cost	$ 168,000
Work in process, April 30	
(100% complete for materials, 20% for conversion)	40,000 units

Required:

Using the weighted average method, complete each of the following steps:

1. Reconcile the number of physical units worked on during the period.
2. Calculate the number of equivalent units.
3. Calculate the cost per equivalent unit rounded to five decimal places.
4. Reconcile the total cost of work in process.

Supplement 3A   **E3-5 Calculating Equivalent Units, Cost per Equivalent Unit, Reconciling the Cost of Work in Process (FIFO)**

Refer to E3-4 for information regarding GoFly Company.

Required:

Complete all requirements for E3-4 using the FIFO method.

LO2,3   **E3-6 Calculating Equivalent Units, Cost per Equivalent Unit, Reconciling the Cost of Work in Process (Weighted Average)**

Tien Company manufactures plastic storage crates and has the following information available for the month of April:

Work in process, April 1	15,600 units
(100% complete for materials, 40% for conversion)	
Direct materials	$ 24,000
Conversion	$ 33,000
Number of units started	47,400 units
April costs	
Direct materials	$ 67,800
Conversion	$ 100,800
Work in process, April 30	24,000 units
(100% complete for materials, 20% for conversion)	

Required:

Using the weighted average method of process costing, complete each of the following steps:

1. Reconcile the number of physical units worked on during the period.
2. Calculate the number of equivalent units.

3. Calculate the cost per equivalent unit rounded to five decimal places.

4. Reconcile the total cost of work in process.

E3-7 Calculating Equivalent Units, Cost per Equivalent Unit, Reconciling the Cost   Supplement 3A
of Work in Process (FIFO)

Refer to E3-6 for information regarding Tien Company.

Required:

Complete all requirements for E3-6 using the FIFO method.

E3-8 Calculating Equivalent Units, Cost per Equivalent Unit, Reconciling the Cost   LO2,3
of Work in Process (Weighted Average)

Raindrop Company manufactures umbrellas and has the following information available for the month of May:

Work in process, May 1	
(100% complete for materials, 90% for conversion)	72,000 units
Direct materials	$129,000
Conversion cost	$175,000
Number of units started	181,000
May costs	
Direct materials	$206,000
Conversion cost	$379,000
Work in process, May 31	
(100% complete for materials, 20% for conversion)	67,000 units

Required:

Using the weighted average method of process costing, complete each of the following steps:

1. Reconcile the number of physical units worked on during the period.

2. Calculate the number of equivalent units.

3. Calculate the cost per equivalent unit rounded to five decimal places.

4. Reconcile the total cost of work in process.

E3-9 Calculating Equivalent Units, Cost per Equivalent Unit, Reconciling the Cost   Supplement 3A
of Work in Process (FIFO)

Refer to E3-8 for information regarding Raindrop Company.

Required:

Complete all requirements for E3-8 using the FIFO method.

E3-10 Calculating Equivalent Units, Cost per Equivalent Unit, Reconciling the Cost   LO2,3
of Work in Process (Weighted Average)

Smith Company manufactures pencils and has the following information available for the month of July:

Work in process, July 1	
(100% complete for materials, 60% for conversion)	150,000 units
Direct materials	$10,000
Conversion	$35,000
Number of units started	200,000 units
July costs	
Direct materials	$13,000
Conversion	$48,000
Work in process, July 31	140,000 units
(100% complete for materials, 10% for conversion)	

Required:

Using the weighted average method of process costing, complete each of the following steps:

1. Reconcile the number of physical units worked on during the period.
2. Calculate the number of equivalent units.
3. Calculate the number of cost per equivalent unit.
4. Reconcile the total cost of work in process.

Supplement 3A **E3-11 Calculating Equivalent Units, Cost per Equivalent Unit, Reconciling the Cost of Work in Process (FIFO)**

Refer to E3-10 for information regarding Smith Company.

Required:

Complete all requirements for E3-10 using the FIFO method of process costing.

LO2,3 **E3-12 Calculating Equivalent Units, Cost per Equivalent Unit, Reconciling the Cost of Work in Process (Weighted Average)**

Hanson Company manufactures handheld calculators and has the following information available for the month of July.

Work in process, July 1	63,000 units
(100% complete for materials, 25% for conversion)	
Direct materials	$120,000
Conversion	$197,000
Number of units started	110,000 units
July costs	
Direct materials	$213,000
Conversion	$242,000
Work in process, July 31	72,000 units
(100% complete for materials, 10% for conversion)	

Required:

Using the weighted average method of process costing, complete each of the following steps:

1. Reconcile the number of physical units worked on during the period.
2. Calculate the number of equivalent units.
3. Calculate cost per equivalent unit, rounded to five decimal places.
4. Reconcile the total cost of work in process.

Supplement 3A **E3-13 Calculating Equivalent Units, Cost per Equivalent Unit, Reconciling the Cost of Work in Process (FIFO)**

Refer to E3-12 for information regarding Hanson Company.

Required:

Complete all requirements for E3-12 using the FIFO method of process costing.

LO3 **E3-14 Calculating Equivalent Units, Unit Costs, and Cost Assigned Using the Weighted Average Method**

Crandall's Ceramic Company has the following production information for the month of March. All materials are added at the beginning of the manufacturing process.

Production

    Beginning inventory of 3,000 units that are 100 percent complete for materials and 25 percent complete for conversion.

    14,000 units were started during the period and ending inventory of 4,500 units 20 percent complete for conversion.

Manufacturing Costs

    Beginning inventory was $20,000 ($9,700 materials and $10,300 conversion costs).

    Costs added during the month were $29,400 for materials and $56,900 conversion cost ($27,500 labor and $29,400 applied overhead).

Required:

1. Calculate the number of equivalent units of production for materials and conversion for March.
2. Calculate the unit costs for materials and conversion for March.
3. Determine the costs to be assigned to the units transferred out and the units in process.

E3-15 Calculating Cost per Equivalent Unit (Weighted Average Method)   LO4

Brockton Company's Assembly department has the following production and manufacturing information for February:

Units:

14,000 in beginning inventory that are 100 percent complete for material and 20 percent for conversion.

22,300 units finished and transferred out.

8,750 units in ending inventory that are 100 percent complete for materials and 45 percent complete for conversion.

Costs:

	Materials	Conversion
Beginning	$ 6,750	$23,600
Current	15,000	55,700

Required:

Calculate cost per equivalent unit using the weighted average method.

E3-16 Recording Manufacturing Costs in Process Costing   Supplement 3B

Forrest Co. makes wooden tables.

Required:

Prepare the journal entries to record each of the following transactions:

(a) Purchased $20,000 of raw materials on credit.
(b) Issued $18,000 of direct materials into production.
(c) Applied $47,500 of conversion cost.
(d) Paid in full the raw materials purchased on credit.
(e) Completed tables costing $52,750.
(f) Recorded actual conversion costs of $42,000.
(g) Sold tables for $93,000 that cost $50,000 to produce.
(h) Disposed of any over- or underapplied conversion cost.

E3-17 Recording Manufacturing Cost in Process Costing   Supplement 3B

Rock-On Company produces wooden rocking chairs. The company has two sequential production departments, Cutting and Assembly. The wood is cut and sanded in Cutting and then transferred to Assembly to be assembled and painted. From Assembly, the chairs are transferred to Finished Goods Inventory and then are sold.

Rock-On has compiled the following information for the month of February.

	Cutting Department	Assembly Department
Direct materials	$ 75,000	$ 12,000
Direct labor	65,000	99,000
Applied manufacturing overhead	150,000	167,000
Cost of goods completed and transferred out	234,000	253,000

Required:

Prepare the following journal entries for Rock-On:

1. Amount of direct materials, direct labor, and manufacturing overhead incurred for the Cutting department.
2. Transfer of products from Cutting to Assembly.
3. Amount of direct materials, direct labor, and manufacturing overhead incurred by the Assembly department.
4. Transfer of chairs from Assembly to Finished Goods.

Supplement 3B   **E3-18 Recording Manufacturing Costs in Process Costing**

Chico Company makes piñatas for children's birthday parties. Information for Chico's last six months of operation follows:

Required:

Prepare the journal entries to record each of the following transactions.

(a) Purchased $7,800 of raw materials on credit.
(b) Issued $4,600 of direct materials into production.
(c) Applied $16,500 of conversion cost.
(d) Paid in full for the raw materials purchased on credit.
(e) Completed costing $19,750 piñatas.
(f) Recorded actual conversion costs of $18,000.
(g) Sold piñatas for $33,000 that cost $22,000 to produce.
(h) Disposed of any over- or underapplied conversion cost.

Supplement 3B   **E3-19 Recording Manufacturing Costs in Process Costing**

Jambo Company produces homemade jam. The company has two sequential production departments, Cooking and Canning. The fruit is washed and cooked in the Cooking department and then transferred to Canning to be packaged in glass jars. From Canning, the jars are transferred to Finished Goods Inventory and then are sold.

Jambo has compiled the following information for the month of May:

	Cooking	Canning
Beginning work in process	$ 0	$ 8,350
Materials	3,500	2,000
Labor	4,000	3,100
Overhead	9,300	7,900
Costs transferred out	14,900	21,250

Required:

Prepare the following journal entries for Jambo:

1. Amount of direct materials, direct labor, and manufacturing overhead incurred for the Cooking department.
2. Transfer of products from Cooking to Canning.
3. Amount of direct materials, direct labor, and manufacturing overhead incurred by the Canning department.
4. Transfer of jam from Canning to Finished Goods.

PROBLEMS—SET A

Mc Graw Hill **connect**™
|ACCOUNTING

LO 2,3,4   **PA3-1 Preparing a Process Costing Production Report (Weighted Average)**

Boxer Corporation manufactures metal toolboxes. It adds all materials at the beginning of the manufacturing process. The company has provided the following information:

Beginning work in process (30% complete)	40,000 units
Direct materials	$ 40,000
Conversion cost	95,000
Total cost of beginning work in process	$135,000
Number of units started	76,000
Number of units completed and transferred to finished goods	82,000
Ending work in process (50% complete)	
Direct materials cost incurred	$ 90,000
Conversion cost applied	157,000
Total cost added	$247,000

Required:

1. Using the weighted average method of process costing, complete each of the following steps:

    a. Reconcile the number of physical units worked on during the period.
    b. Calculate the number of equivalent units.
    c. Calculate the cost per equivalent unit rounded to five decimal points.
    d. Reconcile the total cost of work in process.

2. Summarize the preceding steps in a production report for Boxer Corporation

PA3-2 Preparing a Process Costing Production Report (FIFO)

Supplement 3A

Refer to the information for Boxer Corporation in PA3-1.

Required:

Complete all requirements for PA3-1 using the FIFO method.

PA3-3 Preparing a Process Costing Production Report (Weighted Average)

LO 2,3,4

www.mhhe.com/whitecotton1e

Seemore Company makes camping lanterns using a single production process. All direct materials are added at the beginning of the manufacturing process. Information for the month of March follows:

Beginning work in process (30% complete)	58,900 units
Direct materials	$ 96,000
Conversion cost	172,000
Total cost of beginning work in process	$268,000
Number of units started	121,500
Number of units completed and transferred to finished goods	167,400
Ending work in process (65% complete)	
Direct materials cost incurred	$253,700
Conversion cost applied	324,000
Total cost added	$577,700

Required:

1. Using the weighted average method of process costing, complete each of the following steps:

    a. Reconcile the number of physical units worked on during the period.
    b. Calculate the number of equivalent units.
    c. Calculate the cost per equivalent unit rounded to five decimal places.
    d. Reconcile the total cost of work in process.

2. Summarize the preceding steps in a March production report for Seemore Company.

PA3-4 Preparing Journal Entries for Weighted Average Process Costing System

Supplement 3B

Refer to the information in PA3-3 for Seemore Company.

www.mhhe.com/whitecotton1e

Required:

Prepare Seemore's journal entries to record each of the following transactions.

(a) Added direct materials to production during March.
(b) Applied conversion cost during March.
(c) Transferred costs of completed units to Finished Goods Inventory.
(d) Sold units costing $650,000 for $1,000,000.
(e) Recorded $329,000 of actual conversion cost.
(f) Disposed of the ending balance in the Conversion Cost account.

PA3-5 Preparing a Process Costing Production Report (FIFO)

Supplement 3A

Refer to the information in PA3-3 for Seemore Company.

Required:

Complete all requirements for PA3-3 using the FIFO method.

LO 2,3,4   **PA3-6 Preparing a Process Costing Production Report (Weighted Average)**

Gotcha Co. makes one model of radar gun used by law enforcement officers. All direct materials are added at the beginning of the manufacturing process. Information for the month of September follows:

Beginning work in process (40% complete)	10,125 units
Direct materials	$ 668,250
Conversion	312,900
Total cost of beginning work in process	$ 981,150
Number of units started	18,200 units
Number of units completed and transferred to finished goods	17,400 units
Ending work in process (75% complete)	
Direct materials cost incurred	$1,201,200
Conversion cost applied	633,250
Total cost added	$1,834,450

Required:

1. Using the weighted average method of process costing, complete each of the following steps:
   a. Reconcile the number of physical units worked on during the period.
   b. Calculate the number of equivalent units.
   c. Calculate the cost per equivalent unit rounded to five decimal places.
   d. Reconcile the total cost of work in process.

2. Summarize the preceding steps in a September production report for Gotcha Company.

Supplement 3A   **PA3-7 Recording Manufacturing Costs and Preparing a Process Costing Production Report (FIFO)**

Refer to the information in PA3-6 for Gotcha Company.

Required:

Complete all requirements for PA3-6 using the FIFO method.

PROBLEMS—SET B

LO 2,3,4   **PB3-1 Preparing a Process Costing Production Report (Weighted Average)**

Zoinks Inc. produces a popular brand of energy drink. It adds all materials at the beginning of the manufacturing process. The company has provided the following information:

Beginning work in process (30% complete)	20,000 units
Direct materials	$ 10,000
Conversion cost	46,000
Total cost of beginning work in process	$ 56,000
Number of units started	52,000
Number of units completed and transferred to finished goods	49,000
Ending work in process (70% complete)	
Direct materials cost incurred	$ 31,000
Conversion cost applied	82,000
Total cost added	$113,000

Required:

1. Using the weighted average method of process costing, complete each of the following steps:

   a. Reconcile the number of physical units worked on during the period.
   b. Calculate the number of equivalent units.
   c. Calculate the cost per equivalent unit rounded to five decimal places.
   d. Reconcile the total cost of work in process.

2. Summarize the preceding steps in a production report for Zoinks Inc.

PB3-2 Preparing a Process Costing Production Report (FIFO)   Supplement

Refer to the information about Zoinks Inc. in PB3-1.

Required:

Complete all requirements for PB3-1 using the FIFO method.

PB3-3   Preparing a Process Costing Production Report (Weighted Average)   LO 2,3,4

Firelight Company makes camping tents in a single production department. All direct materials are added at the beginning of the manufacturing process. Information for the month of July follows:

Beginning work in process (30% complete)	23,100 units
Direct materials	$121,000
Conversion cost	184,000
Total cost of beginning work in process	$305,000
Number of units started	62,500
Number of units completed and transferred to finished goods	77,400
Ending work in process (35% complete)	
Direct materials cost incurred	$281,700
Conversion cost applied	386,200
Total cost added	$667,900

Required:

1. Using the weighted average method of process costing, complete each of the following steps:

   a. Reconcile the number of physical units worked on during the period.
   b. Calculate the number of equivalent units.
   c. Calculate the cost per equivalent unit rounded to five decimal places.
   d. Reconcile the total cost of work in process.

2. Summarize the preceding steps in a July production report for Firelight Company.

PB3-4 Preparing Journal Entries for Weighted Average Process Costing System   Supplement 3B

Refer to the information in PB3-3 for Firelight Company

Required:

Prepare Firelight's journal entries to record each of the following transactions.

(a) Added direct materials to production during July.
(b) Applied conversion cost during July.
(c) Transferred costs of completed units to Finished Goods Inventory.
(d) Sold units costing $450,000 for $800,000.
(e) Recorded $367,000 of actual conversion cost.
(f) Disposed of ending the balance in the Conversion Cost account.

Supplement 3A   PB3-5 Preparing a Process Costing Production Report (FIFO)

Refer to the information in PB3-3 for Firelight Company.

Required:

Complete all requirements for PB3-3 using the FIFO method.

LO 2,3,4, Supplement   PB3-6 Preparing a Process Costing Production Report (Weighted Average)

Bright Line Inc. makes one model of lighted baby toy. All direct materials are added at the beginning of the manufacturing process. Information for the month of September follows:

Beginning work in process (20% complete)	60,400 units
Direct materials	$ 75,500
Conversion	76,104
Total cost of beginning work in process	$151,604
Number of units started	128,700 units
Number of units completed and transferred to finished goods	147,400 units
Ending work in process (85% complete)	
Direct materials cost incurred	$160,875
Conversion cost applied	241,026
Total cost added	$401,901

Required:

1. Using the weighted average method of process costing, complete each of the following steps:
   a. Reconcile the number of physical units worked on during the period.
   b. Calculate the number of equivalent units.
   c. Calculate the cost per equivalent unit rounded to five decimal places.
   d. Reconcile the total cost of work in process.
2. Summarize the preceding steps in a September production report for Bright Line Inc.

Supplement 3A   PB3-7 Preparing a Process Costing Production Report (FIFO)

Refer to the information in PB3-6 for Bright Line Inc.

Required:

Complete all requirements for PB3-6 using the FIFO method.

SKILLS DEVELOPMENT CASES

LO1   S3-1 Researching Companies That Use Process Costing

Consider the many different manufactured products a person might use or consume in a typical day from toothpaste to a custom-made Harley Davidson motorcycle.

Required:

Choose three items that you use regularly and whose manufacturer you believe is likely to use process costing. Investigate the manufacturing company of each item and its Web site for information to support or contradict your belief.

LO1   S3-2 Evaluating the Implications of Process Costing in a Service Industry

Overnight package delivery is a multimillion dollar industry that has grown steadily since it began. The four largest package carriers are the US Postal Service (USPS), Federal Express (FedEx), United Parcel Service (UPS), and DHL. Suppose you have a document that must be delivered to each of the following cities by the close of business tomorrow. Using each company's Web site, determine the price to ship your letter and record the information in the following table.

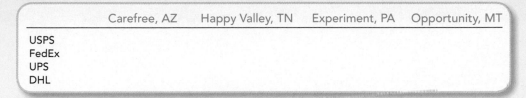

	Carefree, AZ	Happy Valley, TN	Experiment, PA	Opportunity, MT
USPS				
FedEx				
UPS				
DHL				

To answer the following questions, assume that the prices charged by the companies are directly related to the cost of delivery.

Required:

1. Based on their pricing, which of the delivery companies appear(s) to use process costing?
2. For each company that does not appear to use process costing, what factors are likely to impact the cost (and thus pricing) of the overnight delivery service?
3. In this industry, what are the potential advantages and disadvantages of process costing?

CHAPTER 4

Activity Based Cost Management

YOUR LEARNING OBJECTIVES

After completing this chapter, you should be able to:

L01   Assign indirect cost to products or services using a single volume-based allocation measure.

L02   Classify activities as unit, batch, product, customer, or facility level activities.

L03   Assign indirect costs to activity cost pools (Stage 1) and select a driver for each pool.

L04   Assign activity costs to products or services (Stage 2) using activity rates.

L05   Assign activity cost to products or services (Stage 2) using activity proportions.

L06   Compare the results of a volume-based cost system to activity based costing.

L07   Describe how managers use the results of activity based costing for activity based management.

Lecture Presentation–LP4
www.mhhe.com/whitecotton1e

FOCUS COMPANY: Toyota Motor Company

The Toyota Camry—"Made in America by Americans"

www.toyota.com

Every year, millions of Americans make a New Year's resolution to lose weight and keep it off, only to give up within a week or two. The reason so many diets fail is that they focus on short-term success (measured by changes in the scale) that are difficult to sustain in the long run.

Business managers face similar pressure to "trim the waste" (not waist), and consultants promising to deliver "lean" results are as plentiful as diet programs promising to help you lose weight. A lean enterprise is one that delivers high value at the lowest possible cost, with very little waste or inefficiency. This chapter illustrates the use of activity based costing as a tool to help managers achieve their cost reduction goals.

You can think of the cost system as a measurement tool, much like your bathroom scale tells you how much you weigh. The scale may provide some motivation to change, but if it is inaccurate, it can have detrimental effects. It also doesn't really tell you how to lose weight. Other measurement systems such as pedometers and calorie monitoring devices focus on the factors that drive weight loss. Similarly, contemporary costing methods such as activity based costing can provide valuable information that managers can use to pursue cost reduction and process improvement. But an accounting system in and of itself cannot make an organization lean any more than a more accurate scale can make you lose weight. It is simply a tool to help managers gauge their progress and identify potential opportunities for improvement.

Few companies have been as successful at adopting a truly lean philosophy as Toyota Motor Company. Toyota's success is due to its ability to build lean thinking into everything it does.[1] Lean thinking doesn't stop at the plant floor but permeates all business functions including corporate strategy and marketing.

---

[1]John Teresko, "Learning from Toyota—Again," *Industry Week*, February 1, 2006.

Take an online tour of Toyota's Kentucky plant at http://www.toyota.com/about/our_business/operations/manufacturing/index.html.

To illustrate the topics in this chapter, we will visit Toyota's manufacturing plant in Georgetown, Kentucky. This is where Toyota first combined its manufacturing know-how with an American workforce to produce a car "Made in America by Americans." Kentucky is also home to Toyota's North American engineering and manufacturing group (TEMA), which has responsibility for engineering design, research and development, and manufacturing activities throughout the United States, Canada, and Mexico. By 2010, Toyota will have the capacity to produce nearly 2.2 million vehicles in its North American facilities.

Toyota Motor Manufacturing Kentucky (TMMK) is Toyota's largest manufacturing facility outside Japan. This $6 billion facility has the capacity to produce 500,000 vehicles and engines per year, employs almost 7,000 workers, and is responsible for the creation of 20,000 local jobs. The Kentucky plant produces the Toyota Avalon, Camry sedan, Camry hybrid, Camry Solara coupe, and Camry Solara convertible as well as 4-cylinder and V6 engines and powertrain parts.

In this chapter, we limit our examples to three Toyota models: the Avalon, Camry, and Camry hybrid. The numbers used in the examples are hypothetical and not intended to represent the true price, cost, or production information for the various models. That information is proprietary and not publicly available to consumers or Toyota's competitors.

ORGANIZATION OF THE CHAPTER

Traditional volume-based cost systems

- Volume-based cost system
- Assignment of indirect cost to individual products or services
- Calculation of total manufacturing cost and profitability

Activity based costing (ABC)

- Stage 1: Assign indirect cost to activities
- Stage 2: Assign activity costs to individual products or services
- Comparison of volume-based and activity based cost systems
- Calculation of total manufacturing cost and gross margin

Activity based management (ABM)

- Life cycle cost management
- Total quality management (TQM)
- Target costing
- Just-in-time (JIT)
- Summary of ABC and ABM

Traditional Volume-Based Cost Systems

As you learned in previous chapters, the purpose of any cost system is to determine the cost of a company's products, services, or customers. Managers need cost information for a variety of reasons including pricing, resource allocation, and cost control. Some costs, such as direct materials and direct labor, are directly traceable to specific units, products, or customers and are therefore relatively easy to account for. The challenge comes in assigning indirect costs, or those that are not directly traceable to individual units, products, or customers. Indirect costs are also referred to as **overhead costs.** The focus of this chapter is on assigning indirect **manufacturing** costs, but the same principles apply to nonmanufacturing costs such as corporate overhead or selling and administrative expenses.

Because indirect costs cannot be directly traced to specific products or services, they must be assigned or allocated based on some observable measure called an **allocation base** or **cost driver:**

The cost driver or allocation base can be a simple measure such as the number of units produced or direct labor hours, or can include multiple measures that capture the cause-and-effect relationship between activities and costs. We start with the most simplistic system, which uses a single volume-based allocation measure to assign indirect costs to products.

VOLUME-BASED COST SYSTEM

In the previous chapters, we used the number of units produced or direct labor hours to assign indirect manufacturing overhead costs to specific products. The number of units produced and direct labor hours are examples of a **volume-based allocation measure,** which is directly related to the number of units produced or the number of customers served. Other volume-based allocation measures include the number of machine hours and direct materials cost, which also vary proportionally with the number of units produced or customers served.

To illustrate how a volume-based cost system works, assume TMMK produces three types of automobiles, with the following cost and production information:

> **Learning Objective 1**
> Assign indirect costs to products or services using a single volume-based allocation measure.

	PER UNIT COST INFORMATION		
	Avalon	Camry	Camry Hybrid
Direct materials	$8,000	$7,000	$6,500
Direct labor	2,800	2,400	2,400
Manufacturing overhead	?	?	?

	ANNUAL PRODUCTION INFORMATION			
	Avalon	Camry	Camry Hybrid	Total
Units produced (in thousands)	100	350	50	500
Direct labor hours per unit	35	30	30	
Total direct labor hours (in thousands)	3,500	10,500	1,500	15,500

Notice that the direct materials and direct labor cost of each product have already been determined. These costs are directly traceable to the specific models. What we do not know is the manufacturing overhead cost of each model. The purpose of the cost allocation method is to assign the indirect or manufacturing overhead costs to each product.

Assume that the total manufacturing overhead cost for the Kentucky plant is estimated at $3,720,000 (in thousands) per year. In the traditional cost system, this cost is assigned to the three products on the basis of direct labor hours.

The first step is to calculate the predetermined overhead rate. Recall from Chapter 2 that a predetermined overhead rate is computed as follows:

$$\frac{\text{Estimated Total Manufacturing Overhead Cost}}{\text{Estimated Units in the Allocation Base}} = \text{Predetermined Overhead Rate}$$

Because the allocation base is the number of direct labor hours, we need to divide the total manufacturing overhead cost by the total number of direct labor hours as follows:

$$\text{Predetermined Overhead Rate} = \frac{\$3,720,000}{15,500} = \$240 \text{ per direct labor}$$

For every hour of direct labor, we need to apply $240 in manufacturing overhead cost. This is not the cost of the direct labor itself, but rather all of the indirect manufacturing costs, such as depreciation on the facility and machines (robots), plant supervision, quality control, engineering, maintenance, insurance, utilities, and the like. The traditional (volume-based) cost system assigns these indirect costs at a rate of $240 per direct labor hour, regardless of whether these costs truly vary with the number of direct labor hours.

ASSIGNMENT OF INDIRECT COST TO INDIVIDUAL PRODUCTS OR SERVICES

To assign manufacturing overhead costs to the individual products, we multiply the $240 overhead rate by the number of direct labor hours required for each product:

COACH'S TIP

The Camry receives the most total manufacturing overhead cost because it is the highest volume product and thus requires the most direct labor hours. The Avalon is the second highest volume product and receives the second highest total manufacturing overhead. The Camry hybrid receives the smallest amount of total overhead because it is the product with the lowest volume. But is it really the least costly to produce?

		ANNUAL PRODUCTION INFORMATION		
	Avalon	Camry	Camry Hybrid	Total
Number of units produced (in thousands)	100	350	50	500
Number of direct labor hours per unit	35	30	30	
× Predetermined overhead rate	× $ 240	× $ 240	× $ 240	
Manufacturing overhead cost per unit	$ 8,400	$ 7,200	$ 7,200	
× Number of units produced	× 100	× 350	× 50	
Total manufacturing overhead	$840,000	$2,520,000	$360,000	$3,720,000

CALCULATION OF TOTAL MANUFACTURING COST AND PROFITABILITY

To compute **total manufacturing cost,** we need to add the **manufacturing overhead** cost to the **direct materials** and **direct labor** costs, which were provided earlier on a per unit basis.

PER UNIT COST INFORMATION			
	Avalon	Camry	Camry Hybrid
Direct materials	$ 8,000	$ 7,000	$ 6,500
Direct labor	2,800	2,400	2,400
Manufacturing overhead	8,400	7,200	7,200
Total manufacturing cost per unit	$19,200	$16,600	$16,100

This analysis shows that the Avalon is the most costly of the three models on a per unit basis. The Camry is the next most costly model followed by the Camry hybrid.

If we subtract the total manufacturing cost per unit from the unit sales price, we get the gross margin for each product. Remember that gross margin takes into account only the **manufacturing** costs of the product, before nonmanufacturing costs such as distribution fees, advertising, dealer costs and profit, and corporate administration charges have been deducted.

Assume the following hypothetical prices for the three models:

	Avalon	Camry	Camry Hybrid
Unit selling price	$20,000	$18,000	$35,000
Less: Manufacturing cost per unit	19,200	16,600	16,100
Gross profit per unit	$ 8,800	$ 1,400	$18,900
Gross profit margin (% of sales)	31.4%	7.8%	54.0%

The gross margin analysis suggests that the Camry hybrid is the most profitable product with a 54 percent gross margin, compared to 31 percent for the Avalon and 8 percent for the Camry. But do these profitability numbers represent the true cost of producing each model?

In the next section, we compute the cost of each product using an alternative costing system, activity based costing. But first complete the following Self-Study Practice to make sure you can calculate total manufacturing cost using a traditional volume-based cost system.

Self-Study Practice

KeepSafe Company makes floor and wall safes for storing valuables. The company applies manufacturing overhead to products on the basis of direct labor hours. Cost and production information on the two products follows:

UNIT COST INFORMATION		
	Floor Safe	Wall Safe
Direct materials	$20	$15
Direct labor	$10	$15
Manufacturing overhead	?	?
PRODUCTION INFORMATION		
Units produced	35,000	10,000
Direct labor hours per unit	1	1.5
Total direct labor hours	35,000	15,000

Total manufacturing overhead is $600,000.

1. Compute the predetermined overhead rate per direct labor hour.
2. How much of the total manufacturing overhead would be allocated to each product?
3. Compute the total manufacturing cost per unit for each product.

After you have finished, check your answers with the solutions in the margin.

Solution to Self-Study Practice

1. Predetermined overhead rate = $600,000/
(35,000 + 15,000) = $12 per direct labor hour.

2.

	Floor Safe	Wall Safe
Total direct labor hours	35,000	15,000
× Manufacturing overhead rate	× $12	× $12
Total manufacturing overhead	$420,000	$180,000

3.

Unit Cost	Floor Safe	Wall Safe
Direct materials	$20	$15
Direct labor	10	15
Manufacturing overhead (per unit)	($12 × 1) = 12	($12 × 1.5) = 18
Total manufacturing cost (per unit)	$42	$48

Activity Based Costing (ABC)

Activity based costing (ABC) is a method of assigning indirect costs to products and services based on the activities they require. ABC uses a two-stage process in which indirect costs are first assigned to activities and then to individual products and services based on their activities requirements. See Exhibit 4.1 for a diagram of this two-stage process.

Video 4-1
www.mhhe.com/whitecotton1e

EXHIBIT 4.1   Two-Stage Allocation Process Using ABC

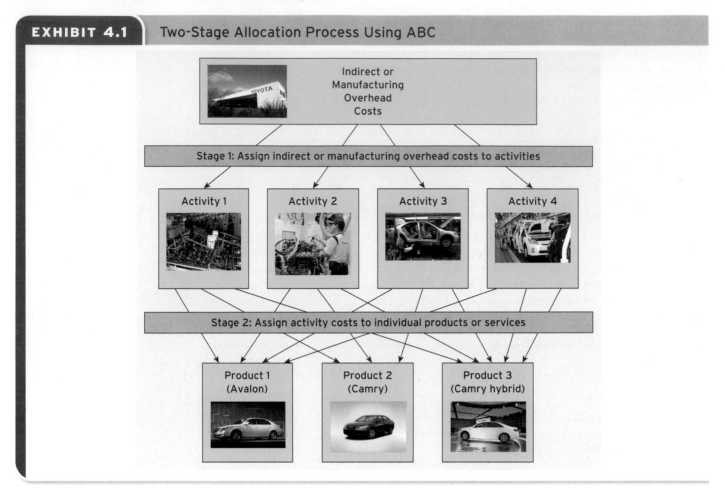

The next section describes Stage 1 of this process, which is to assign indirect costs to activities.

STAGE 1: ASSIGN INDIRECT COSTS TO ACTIVITIES

Identify and Classify Activities

The first step in an ABC system is to identify the activities required to make the product or provide the service. Activities can be classified into the categories or levels shown in Exhibit 4.2.

Facility or companywide activities are shown at the top because they are the most general category and are performed to benefit the organization as a whole, as opposed to specific products, customers, units, or batches. Examples include facility supervision, plant maintenance, janitorial services, and corporate support functions such as accounting, payroll, and legal services. The term "facility" applies primarily to manufacturing costs, but all company-level activities including selling activities, technical support, and general and administrative activities fall within this category. Although generally accepted accounting principles (GAAP) do not allow the costs of nonmanufacturing activities to be included in Cost of Goods Sold or Inventory for external reporting purposes, managers may find it useful to assign these costs to individual products and customers for internal decision making.

Product-level activities are performed to support a specific product line, but do not relate to specific customers or specific batches or units of the product. Examples include engineering and designing the product, creating and testing prototype models, and creating metal dies and casts that will be used to make the product. Once these activities are performed, the company can make numerous units and batches of the product without repeating these activities.

Customer-level activities are similar to product-level activities but are performed for a specific customer rather than a general product line. An example at Toyota would

Learning Objective 2
Classify activities as unit, batch, product, customer, or facility level activities.

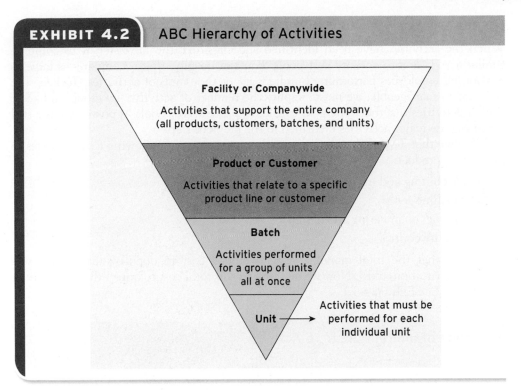

EXHIBIT 4.2   ABC Hierarchy of Activities

Facility or Companywide
Activities that support the entire company
(all products, customers, batches, and units)

Product or Customer
Activities that relate to a specific
product line or customer

Batch
Activities performed
for a group of units
all at once

Unit → Activities that must be
performed for each
individual unit

> **COACH'S TIP**
>
> Activity based costing recognizes that not all activities relate strictly to the volume of units produced and sold.
>
> An activity based cost system should capture these higher level activities (product, customer, or batch level activities), as well as unit-level activities.
>
> A traditional (volume-based) cost system captures only unit-level activities.

be the production of a customized version of the Camry for a rental car agency such as Hertz. All activities required to develop and deliver the customer-specific version of the product would be classified as a customer-level activity.

Batch-level activities are performed for a group or batch of units all at once. These activities vary with the number of batches produced but are independent of the number of units in each batch. An example is the "setup" activities that occur to produce a batch of units. Examples at Toyota would include reprogramming robotics, performing quality control for each batch (but not each unit), and ordering and receiving raw materials. These activities must be performed each time a batch of units is produced, regardless of the number of units in the batch.

Unit-level activities are performed for each individual unit or customer. These activities vary in direct proportion to the number of units produced or the number of customers served. Examples of unit-level activities for Toyota include the installation of automobile components such as the frame, body, engine, and tires. These activities also include any quality testing performed on each individual unit as it passes through the assembly process.

To make sure you understand how to classify activities into the ABC hierarchy, take the following Self-Study Practice.

> **COACH'S TIP**
>
> ABC can be applied to service firms, too. Consider the following activities performed in a restaurant:
>
> **Facility:** All general activities involved with running the restaurant.
>
> **Product:** Creating and testing a new menu item.
>
> **Customer:** Catering an event for a special customer.
>
> **Batch:** Creating a batch of food such as pasta or sauce; serving customers "family style."
>
> **Unit:** Preparing a plate and serving each customer (unit) individually.

 Self-Study Practice

1. Which of the following would be classified as a unit-level activity by an ice cream manufacturer such as Ben & Jerry's?
   a. Purchasing the ingredients to make a batch of cookie dough ice cream.
   b. Performing quality checks on each batch produced to make sure the flavor is right.
   c. Conducting research and development on a new flavor of ice cream.
   d. Maintaining the equipment used to produce various flavors of ice cream.
   e. Pouring the ice cream into containers before freezing it.

2. Which of the activities in question 1 (a–e) would be classified as a product-level activity by an ice cream manufacturer such as Ben & Jerry's?

After you have finished, check your answers with the solutions in the margin.

Solution to Self-Study Practice
1. e
2. c

Form Activity Cost Pools and Assign Indirect Costs to Each Activity

When the activities have been identified and classified, the next step is to combine similar activities into activity cost pools. You can imagine that a company as large as Toyota has employees performing hundreds if not thousands of activities. To keep the cost system manageable, we must simplify the number of activities by grouping like or similar activities together. The goal is to create as few cost pools as possible while still capturing the major activities identified in the previous step.

Assume that TMMK has determined that it requires the following four activities to produce its product:

- Machining and installation
- Machine setup
- Product engineering and design
- Quality control

> **Learning Objective 3**
> Assign indirect costs to activity cost pools (Stage 1) and select a driver for each pool.

Recall that the total manufacturing overhead cost in our Toyota example was $3,720,000 (in thousands). Now we must assign this total cost to one of the four activity cost pools. (See Exhibit 4.3.)

EXHIBIT 4.3   **Stage 1 Allocation of Indirect Costs to Activity Cost Pools**

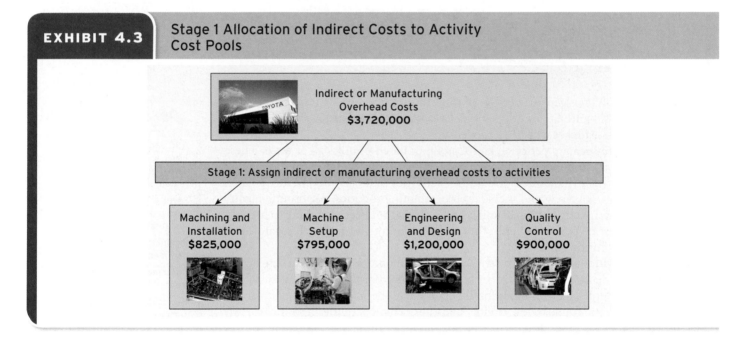

Notice that $825,000 of the $3,720,000 is assigned to the machining and installation activity cost pool. This activity pool includes all indirect costs related to machining and installing components such as the depreciation on the robots that produce the automobiles. The machine setup pool ($795,000) includes all indirect costs related to setting up for production such as the salaries of workers who perform setup activities and indirect materials used during the setup process. The engineering and design activity cost pool ($1,200,000) includes the salaries of product development and design engineers and the cost of developing prototype models. The quality control activity pool ($900,000) includes the salaries of quality control engineers and depreciation on testing equipment.

While some indirect costs are relatively easy to assign to specific activities, others need to be allocated among the various activity cost pools. For example, a general production manager at the TMMK plant oversees all manufacturing-related activities, including machining and installing components, machine setups, engineering, and quality control. In this case, the supervisor needs to keep track of the amount of time spent on each of these activities. These time records would then be used to estimate the amount of cost that should be assigned to each activity.

As an example, assume the production manager makes $120,000 per year and has kept track of the time spent on each of the four major activities. The allocation of the manager's salary across the four activity cost pools appears as follows:

	Supervision Hours	Allocation Percentage	Supervisor's Salary	Salary Allocation
Machining and installation	800	800/2,000 = 40%	× $120,000 =	$ 48,000
Machine setup	600	600/2,000 = 30%	× $120,000 =	36,000
Engineering and product design	200	200/2,000 = 10%	× $120,000 =	12,000
Quality control	400	400/2,000 = 20%	× $120,000 =	24,000
	2,000			$120,000

Because the supervisor spends 40 percent of the time overseeing machining and installation activities, $48,000 (40% × $120,000) should be assigned to that activity cost pool. The allocation to the remaining cost pools is determined by multiplying the allocation percentage (based on the percentage of total hours) by the total cost that needs to be allocated.

Similar Stage 1 allocations would be made for all indirect manufacturing overhead costs that relate to multiple activities such as rent on the manufacturing facility, utilities, janitorial services, insurance, and support functions such as payroll and legal services. A Stage 1 allocation driver must be selected for each of these costs. For example, facility costs such as rent, utilities, and janitorial services might be allocated based on the number of square feet, while payroll costs would be allocated based on the number of employees.

After all of the Stage 1 allocations have been completed, we are ready to begin Stage 2, in which the indirect costs of each activity are assigned to products and services.

STAGE 2: ASSIGN ACTIVITY COSTS TO INDIVIDUAL PRODUCTS OR SERVICES

Select an Activity Cost Driver for Each Cost Pool

The next step is to select an activity cost driver for each of the activity cost pools. An **activity cost driver** is a measure of the underlying activity that occurs in each activity cost pool. The goal is to identify a driver that has a cause-and-effect relationship with the underlying activity.

Unlike traditional cost systems, which rely strictly on volume-based allocation measures, ABC systems include measures that capture something other than the sheer volume of units produced or customers served. These measures are called **nonvolume-based cost drivers**. Some common examples of volume-based and nonvolume-based measures are:

Volume-Based Allocation Measures (used in traditional cost systems)	Nonvolume-Based Cost Drivers (used in activity based costing)
Number of units produced	Number of batches or setup time
Number of direct labor hours	Processing time per unit
Number of machine hours	Number of quality inspections
Direct materials cost	Number of design changes

COACH'S TIP

A traditional (non-ABC) costing system includes only volume-based measures such as those in the left column. An ABC system may include some volume measures, but should also include nonvolume-based measures such as those in the right column.

By incorporating activity drivers that capture other aspects of the production process besides volume, ABC will assign more indirect cost to products that require more setup time, more complex processing, more quality control, or more engineering and design.

See Exhibit 4.4 for the activity cost drivers that will be used to assign activity costs in our Toyota example. Machine hours is used as the driver for the machining and installation activity. The number of setups is used as the activity driver for the setup activity. The number of engineering hours is used as the driver to assign engineering and design

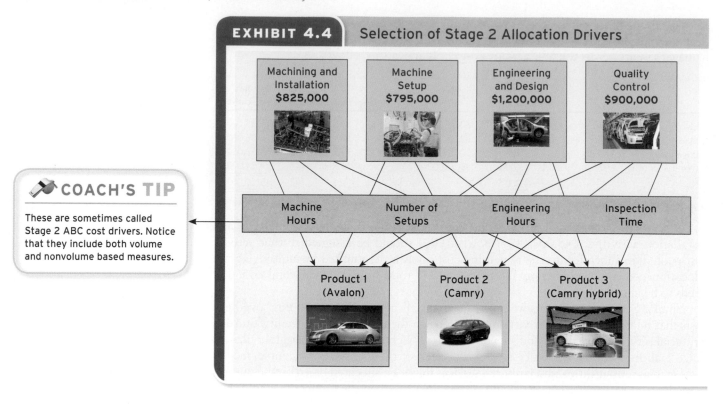

EXHIBIT 4.4 Selection of Stage 2 Allocation Drivers

costs. Inspection time is used to assign quality control costs. The Stage 2 allocations for each of these cost pools are discussed in the next section.

Assign Indirect Costs to Products or Services Based on Their Activity Demands

The next step is to assign the costs from the activity cost pools to the individual products using the Stage 2 activity drivers in Exhibit 4.4. Two methods can be used to assign indirect costs to individual products or services based on their activity requirements: activity rates and activity proportions. The two methods are mathematically equivalent and will provide identical results as long as there are no rounding errors in the rates or proportions. The method used depends on the type of information provided and whether complete information on all product or service lines is available.

Learning Objective 4
Assign activity costs to products or services (Stage 2) using activity rates.

Activity Rate Method   The first method involves computing an **activity rate** that is very similar to the predetermined overhead rate computed earlier. The only difference is that we now have an activity rate for each activity cost pool, calculated as follows:

$$\text{Activity Rate} = \frac{\text{Total Activity Cost}}{\text{Total Activity Driver}}$$

To illustrate the activity rate method, let's assign the cost of the first activity cost pool, machining and installing components. The total indirect cost assigned to this activity pool from Stage 1 was $825,000. In Stage 2, this total is assigned to the three products on the basis of machine hours. Assume that the total machine hours required by each of the three Toyota models is as follows:

	Avalon	Camry	Camry Hybrid	Total
Machine hours	3,000	10,500	1,500	15,000

The activity rate would be computed as:

$$\text{Activity Rate} = \frac{\$825,000}{15,000} = \$55 \text{ per machine hour}$$

For every hour of machine time, we need to charge $55 to cover the machine-related activity costs. To assign the cost to the products, we multiply the activity rate by the activity requirements of each individual product (see Exhibit 4.5)

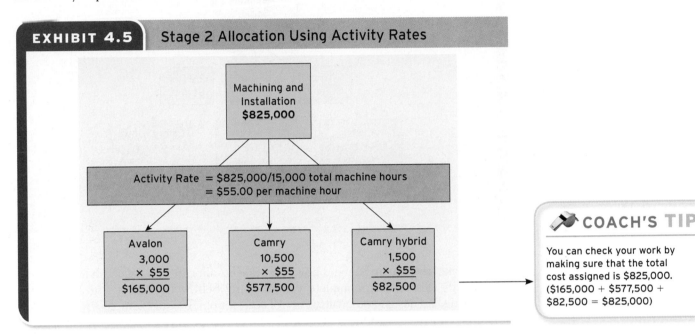

EXHIBIT 4.5 Stage 2 Allocation Using Activity Rates

Machining and Installation **$825,000**

Activity Rate = $825,000/15,000 total machine hours = $55.00 per machine hour

Avalon	Camry	Camry hybrid
3,000	10,500	1,500
× $55	× $55	× $55
$165,000	$577,500	$82,500

> **COACH'S TIP**
> You can check your work by making sure that the total cost assigned is $825,000. ($165,000 + $577,500 + $82,500 = $825,000)

Activity Proportion Method The second method for assigning activity costs to individual products is by calculating activity proportions or percentages. To illustrate this method, let's assign the total cost of the setup activity ($795,000), which will be allocated based on the number of setups. A setup occurs every time the company switches from producing one product to another. The batch size is the number of units produced after each setup. For example, if the Avalon is produced in batches of 250 units, it would take 400 batches (and 400 setups) to produce 100,000 units (100,000/250 = 400). How many setups will be required for the Camry, Camry hybrid, and in total?

> **Learning Objective 5**
> Assign activity costs to products or services (Stage 2) using activity proportions.

Annual Production Information	Avalon	Camry	Camry Hybrid	Total
Total number of units produced	100,000	350,000	50,000	500,000
Average batch size (units per batch)	250	1,000	200	
Number of setups	100,000/250 = 400	?	?	?

The number of setups is computed by dividing the number of units produced by the average batch size. The activity proportion (percentage) is calculated by dividing the number of setups for each product line by the total number of setups. For example, 400 of the 1,000 setups (40%) are for the Avalon. What is the proportion of setups for the Camry and Camry hybrid?

Annual Production Information	Avalon	Camry	Camry Hybrid	Total
Total number of setups	400	350	250	1,000
Proportion of setups	400/1,000 = 40%	?	?	

>
> **COACH'S TIP**
> The proportion for the Camry is 35 percent (350/1,000) and 25 percent (250/1,000) for the Camry hybrid.

To assign the $795,000 in machine setup cost, we multiply by the activity proportion (percentage of setups) for each product, as shown in Exhibit 4.6.

EXHIBIT 4.6   Stage 2 Allocation Using Activity Proportions

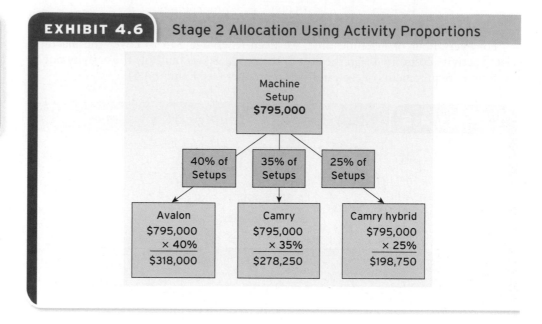

To make sure you understand how to do Stage 2 allocations using both activity rates and activity proportions, complete the following Self-Study Practice to allocate the engineering and design and quality control costs for our Toyota example.

Self-Study Practice

Assume the following activity cost and drivers for the engineering and design and quality control cost pools for Toyota.

Activity Cost Pool	Activity Cost	ACTIVITY COST DRIVERS (ENGINEERING AND INSPECTION HOURS)			
		Avalon	Camry	Camry Hybrid	Total
Engineering and design	$1,200,000	4,000	2,000	14,000	20,000
Quality control	900,000	3,000	2,000	5,000	10,000

1. Calculate an activity rate for engineering and design. Use this rate to assign the total engineering and design cost to the three products.

2. Calculate activity proportion for the quality control activity based on number of inspection hours. Use these percentages to assign the quality control costs to the three products.

After you are have finished, check your answers with the solution in the margin.

Solution to Self-Study Practice

2. Quality control

	Avalon	Camry	Camry Hybrid	Total
Inspection hours	3,000	2,000	5,000	10,000
Percentages	30%	20%	50%	100%
Quality control	× $900,000	× $900,000	× $900,000	× $900,000
	$270,000	$180,000	$450,000	$900,000

1. Engineering activity rate = $1,200,000/20,000 = $60 per engineering hour

	Avalon	Camry	Camry Hybrid	Total
Inspection hours	4,000	2,000	14,000	20,000
Activity rate	× $60	× $60	× $60	× $60
Inspection cost	$240,000	$120,000	$840,000	$1,200,000

To complete the Stage 2 ABC allocations, we need to add the cost of all four activities for each product line. The Stage 2 allocations for the four activity pools are summarized in the following table:

SUMMARY OF STAGE 2 ABC ALLOCATIONS (IN THOUSANDS)				
	Avalon	Camry	Camry Hybrid	Total
Machining and installation	$165,000	$ 577,500	$ 82,500	$ 825,000
Machine setup	318,000	278,250	198,750	795,000
Engineering and product design	240,000	120,000	840,000	1,200,000
Quality control	270,000	180,000	450,000	900,000
Total manufacturing overhead cost	$993,000	$1,155,750	$1,571,250	$3,720,000

COACH'S TIP

Notice that the total amount of overhead cost is the same as in the traditional costing example ($3,720,000). But under ABC, the Camry hybrid receives the highest total overhead allocation even though it is the lowest volume product. The reason is that this product is produced in small batches and requires a lot of engineering and product design as well as quality inspections.

To calculate the manufacturing overhead cost per unit, we need to divide the total manufacturing overhead by the number of units of each product as shown in the following table:

CALCULATING MANUFACTURING OVERHEAD COST PER UNIT				
	Avalon	Camry	Camry Hybrid	Total
Total manufacturing overhead cost (thousands)	$993,000	$1,155,750	$1,571,250	$3,720,000
Number of units produced (thousands)	÷ 100	÷ 350	÷ 50	
Manufacturing overhead cost per unit	9,930	3,302	31,425	

COMPARISON OF VOLUME-BASED AND ACTIVITY BASED COST SYSTEMS

See Exhibit 4.7 for a comparison of the results of ABC to the volume-based cost system described at the beginning of the chapter. Recall that the only difference is how each method assigns indirect, or manufacturing overhead, costs to each of the products.

The difference between the traditional value-based cost system and the ABC system relates to the volume and complexity of the three products and how these issues are accounted for in the costing system.

Recall that the Camry received the highest amount of total manufacturing overhead under the volume-based cost system because it required the most total direct labor hours. Although the Camry is a high-volume model, it is also the most basic or standard model produced at the Kentucky plant. The Avalon is a premium version of the Camry, and the Camry hybrid uses more innovative technology than the Camry.

The largest distortion occurs with the Camry hybrid. Although it is a low-volume product (and thus does not require as many total direct labor hours), it is produced in smaller batches and requires a disproportionate share of the setups, engineering and product design, and quality inspections. The result is that the Camry hybrid is dramatically undercosted under the volume-based cost system compared to ABC.

Learning Objective 6
Compare the results of a volume-based cost system to activity based costing.

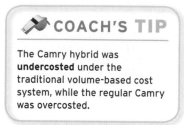

COACH'S TIP

The Camry hybrid was **undercosted** under the traditional volume-based cost system, while the regular Camry was overcosted.

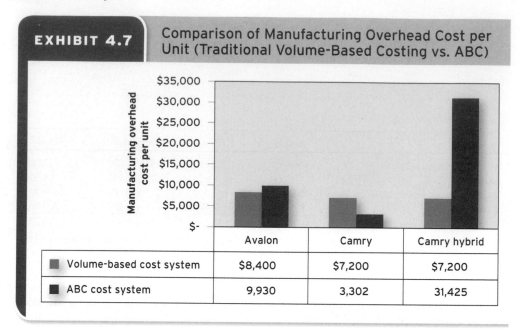

EXHIBIT 4.7	Comparison of Manufacturing Overhead Cost per Unit (Traditional Volume-Based Costing vs. ABC)

	Avalon	Camry	Camry hybrid
Volume-based cost system	$8,400	$7,200	$7,200
ABC cost system	9,930	3,302	31,425

CALCULATION OF TOTAL MANUFACTURING COST AND GROSS MARGIN

The only difference between ABC and traditional cost systems is the treatment of indirect costs, or manufacturing overhead. To compute the full manufacturing cost, we still need to add the direct materials and direct labor costs, which do not change as a result of the cost allocation method used.

To compute **total manufacturing cost per unit** using ABC, we add the manufacturing **overhead** cost per unit to the direct materials and direct labor costs that were provided earlier in the chapter and repeated here:

Per Unit Cost Information	Avalon	Camry	Camry Hybrid
Direct materials	$ 8,000	$ 7,000	$ 6,500
Direct labor	2,800	2,400	2,400
Manufacturing overhead (using ABC)	9,930	3,302	31,425
Total manufacturing cost per unit	$20,730	$12,702	$40,325

Subtracting the unit manufacturing costs from the unit sales prices results in the following gross margin analysis:

	Avalon	Camry	Camry Hybrid
Unit selling price	$28,000	$18,000	$35,000
Less: Manufacturing cost per unit	20,730	12,702	40,325
Gross profit per unit	$ 7,270	$ 5,298	($ 5,325)
Gross profit margin (% of sales)	26.0%	29.4%	(15.2%)

Exhibit 4.8 shows a comparison of the gross margin percentages of the products based on the traditional (volume-based) cost system and ABC.

The ABC analysis shows that the Camry is now the most profitable product with a 29.4 percent gross margin compared to 26 percent for the Avalon and negative 15.2 percent for the Camry hybrid. In this purely hypothetical example, the Camry hybrid is no longer the most profitable product but is actually unprofitable on a gross margin basis. **Gross margin** is the profit before any nonmanufacturing costs such as those for selling, distribution, dealerships, and corporate administration have been taken into account.

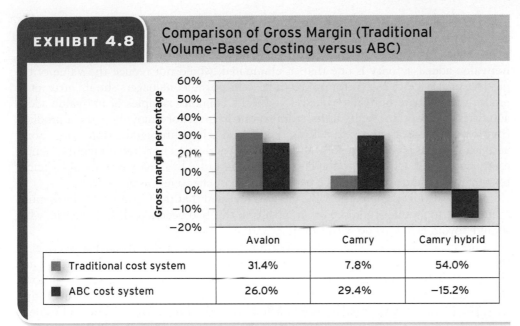

EXHIBIT 4.8	Comparison of Gross Margin (Traditional Volume-Based Costing versus ABC)

	Avalon	Camry	Camry hybrid
■ Traditional cost system	31.4%	7.8%	54.0%
■ ABC cost system	26.0%	29.4%	−15.2%

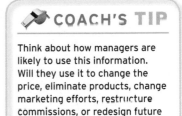

COACH'S TIP

Think about how managers are likely to use this information. Will they use it to change the price, eliminate products, change marketing efforts, restructure commissions, or redesign future products?

Although this example is not intended to reflect the realities of Toyota's production process, it does illustrate a common problem with volume-based cost systems. Such traditional cost systems tend to undercost low-volume products and overcost high-volume products. By focusing strictly on volume, traditional cost systems do not take into account other factors that drive cost, such as the complexity of the production process or the additional setup, design, and quality control activities required by newer or more innovative products.

Activity Based Management (ABM)

Activity based costing (ABC) is a method of assigning indirect costs to products or services based on the activities they require. **Activity based management** (ABM) encompasses all of the actions that managers take to improve operations or reduce costs based on the ABC data. To reap the benefits of ABC, managers must use it to manage the underlying activities and identify areas that would benefit from process improvements.

Learning Objective 7
Describe how managers use the results of activity based costing for activity based management.

The first step in any improvement program is to target areas that need improvement. Managers should start by asking the following questions:

1. What activities are performed?
2. How much does it cost to perform each activity?
3. Does the activity add value to the customer?

The first question focuses managers' attention on **activities** as the driver of cost within the organization. Managers who want to manage costs must manage the underlying activities. Reducing the number of activities required to perform a task can improve profit by either reducing costs (e.g., reduced workforce) or allowing more work to be performed for the same cost (e.g., increased capacity).

The second question focuses managers' attention on those activities that have the most potential for improvement. The activity rates identified by the ABC system provide insight into how much it costs to perform key activities. Managers can compare their activity rates with those of other firms in the industry or to the best performing firms in other industries, a process called **benchmarking**. Benchmarking can be used to pinpoint areas in which the company is ahead or behind the competition and provide managers incentives to improve their own operations. Alternatively, managers might decide to outsource some activities to an outside firm that can do it more cost effectively. The costs and benefits of outsourcing are discussed further in Chapter 7.

The third question relates to one of the most important steps in ABM, which is the identification and elimination of nonvalue-added activities. A **value-added activity** is one that enhances the perceived value of the product or service to the customer. A **nonvalue-added activity** is one that, if eliminated, would not reduce the value of the product or service to the customer. To the extent possible, managers should attempt to reduce or eliminate nonvalue-added activities. Common examples of nonvalue-added activities are reworking faulty units, storing units in inventory, moving parts or products from one place to another, expediting orders, and scheduling productions runs. Some activities such as preparing reports and complying with regulatory requirements are necessary but do not add value to the customer. As part of ABM, managers should attempt to streamline these activities to be performed as cost effectively as possible.

In our Toyota example, the ABC analysis revealed that the Camry hybrid was much more costly to produce than the other models. If this had been a realistic scenario, what should Toyota managers do with this information?

One possibility is for managers to rethink the pricing of the product or service. In this example the price of the Camry hybrid would have to be increased substantially, and it is not clear that customers would be willing to pay that premium even for an innovative product. In addition, improved pricing is not the real goal of ABC. In many industries, prices are set by the market, not based on the cost of the product. The real value of ABC is for cost management rather than pricing.

Another option managers may consider is eliminating products that are not profitable. Although this action may eventually need to be considered, managers should first try to make the product profitable. This approach is where ABC can really pay off in the form of activity based management. Let's look further at the Toyota example to see whether we can pinpoint areas for potential improvement through activity based management.

See Exhibit 4.9 for the key activities that affected the cost of the Camry hybrid in the ABC example.

COACH'S TIP

Although setups are often associated with manufacturing, they also occur in many service settings. For example, changing an airline flight crew is a type of setup activity. If you have ever sat on an airplane waiting for a new crew to arrive and get settled, you know that consumers do not value this activity.

From the airline's perspective, any time spent on the ground is nonvalue added. That is why airlines search for ways to load planes more efficiently.

COACH'S TIP

Think about why this product receives so much engineering and quality control costs. What actions could managers take based on this information? What about the other costs?

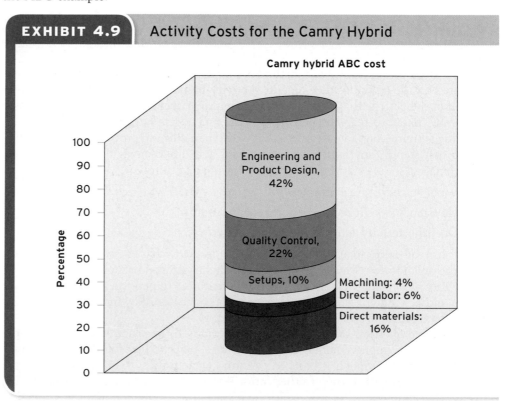

EXHIBIT 4.9   **Activity Costs for the Camry Hybrid**

Camry hybrid ABC cost

Engineering and Product Design, 42%

Quality Control, 22%

Setups, 10%

Machining: 4%
Direct labor: 6%

Direct materials: 16%

In the next section, we discuss various approaches to cost management that Toyota might use to manage the costs revealed by the ABC analysis, including life cycle cost management, total quality management, target costing, and just-in-time inventory management.

LIFE CYCLE COST MANAGEMENT

In pursuing cost management, managers need to set their cost reduction goals across all stages of the **product life cycle** including product introduction, growth, maturity, and eventual decline. Even if a product is unprofitable in the early stages of its life cycle, it may make up for it in later stages. Cost tends to be higher in the early stages of the product life cycle (as in the case of hybrid cars) while most of the revenues are earned in the growth and maturity stages. In today's digital age, product life cycles are becoming increasingly short (only a few years in the case of technology products), so managers must be able to estimate life cycle costs accurately to make good product introduction decisions.

In our Toyota example, a high percentage of the Camry hybrid's unit cost (42 percent) was from engineering and design activities. Why does the Camry hybrid receive such a disproportionate share of the engineering cost compared to the other two models? First, it is a newer product that uses innovative technology. It is not unexpected that more engineering effort would be devoted to a product that uses new technology. In addition, the Camry hybrid was the product with the lowest volume, so there are not as many units over which to spread the engineering and design cost. As the product reaches a more mature stage of its life cycle, the average unit cost should decrease as the company becomes more experienced with the new technology and gains economies of scale by producing and selling more units.

TOTAL QUALITY MANAGEMENT (TQM)

The second highest cost assigned to the Camry hybrid was for quality control, which was allocated on the basis of number of inspection hours. Are quality inspections a value-added or nonvalue-added activity? Although Toyota's customers clearly value quality (a hallmark of the Toyota brand), quality inspections themselves are not considered a value-added activity. Consumers care about the end quality of the product, not necessarily how that quality was achieved.

In managing quality costs, managers must balance four types of quality costs:

- **Prevention costs** are incurred to prevent quality problems from occurring in the first place. Examples include statistical process control, quality training, and other elements of total quality management (TQM). Although prevention activities are costly, most quality experts believe the most effective way to manage quality costs is to avoid problems in the first place.

- **Appraisal or inspection costs** are incurred to identify defective products before they get to the customer. Unfortunately, inspection activities do not prevent defects from happening again, and most managers now realize it is better to prevent mistakes than to find them.

- **Internal failure costs** result from defects that are caught **before** the product is shipped to the customer. These costs include scrap or discarded products, rework, and downtime caused by quality problems. The more effective a company's appraisal (inspection) activities, the better its chance of catching defects internally. Although costly, internal failures are preferred over external failures.

- **External failure costs** occur when a defective product makes its way into the customer's hands. These costs include warranty costs, recalls, product replacement, legal fees, and damage to the company's reputation due to poor quality. This approach to quality should be considered a last resort and eliminated to the extent possible.

One way that Toyota manages quality is by investing in prevention-related activities rather than inspection activities. As part of a quality initiative, managers can prepare a **quality cost report** that summarizes the activities and costs incurred to prevent, detect, and correct quality problems. The report helps managers understand their current approach to quality, spot potential problem areas, and identify opportunities for improvement.

COACH'S TIP

These quality costs are listed in order of preference. As part of TQM, managers are better off investing in prevention and appraisal costs than paying for external failure costs.

TARGET COSTING

Target costing is an approach to cost management that was first introduced at Toyota in 1959.[2] The basic idea behind target costing is to determine what the target cost **should be** to meet the market price and still provide a profit for the company's shareholders. Target costing is sometimes called **cost planning** because it requires managers to think about costs up front so that they can design and manufacture products at a cost that will satisfy both customers (through the market price) and shareholders (through a target profit).

The target cost should reflect all of the costs that will be incurred across the entire value chain. The **value chain** is the linked set of activities required to design, develop, produce, market, deliver, and provide service after the sale. It encompasses everything from product conception to eventual disposal of the product by the end customer.

Although managerial accounting often focuses on manufacturing costs, or those incurred as the product is being produced, as much as 90 percent of these costs are committed (unchangeable) by the time production starts. The goal of target costing is to determine the target cost of the product **before** manufacturing ever starts.

With target costing, the price is set by the market and reflects what consumers are willing to pay for a product or service. The target cost is the difference between the expected market price and the amount of profit needed to satisfy stakeholders.

Toyota uses target costing extensively to ensure that its products are profitable. As a simplified example, assume that Toyota is planning to introduce a new vehicle with the following estimates:

Market price	$30,000
Annual demand	20,000 units
Life cycle	3 years
Target profit	20% return on sales

The target cost is computed by subtracting the target profit from the market price as follows:

$$\text{Market Price } \$30,000 - \text{Target Profit } (20\% \times \$30,000) \ \$6,000 = \text{Target Cost } \$24,000$$

The $24,000 target cost is the most that can be spent on the product and still achieve the 20 percent return on sales (given a market sales price of $30,000). The target cost includes more than just manufacturing costs and must also cover designing, developing, making, and delivering the product to the end consumer.

The target cost should be based on the product's entire life cycle and should reflect any gains from continuous improvements that occur over its life cycle. A product is often more costly at the beginning of its life cycle than at the end. The goal of target costing is to make sure the target cost will be met across the product's entire life cycle.

Given the target unit cost, how much can Toyota spend on the new model across its entire life cycle and still meet the target cost?

$$\text{20,000 units per year} \times \text{3 years} \times \$24,000 = \$1,440,000,000$$

After the target cost is set, the next step is to determine whether it is feasible to design, develop, manufacture, and deliver the product at that cost. As shown in the following diagram, the cost reduction goal is set by comparing the target cost to the estimated cost as shown in Exhibit 4.10.

Under target costing, products should not be manufactured unless the estimated cost is less than the target cost. Remember that the target cost is based strictly on the market price and target profit. The estimated cost is based on the product's design and

---

[2]As noted, Robin Cooper and Tanaka, Toyota Motor Corporation: Target Costing System, Harvard Business School Case 9-197-031. Copyright Harvard Business School Publishing, 1997.

EXHIBIT 4.10	Target Costing

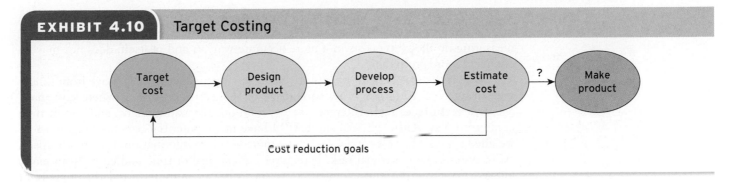

the company's existing manufacturing processes. If the estimated cost exceeds the target cost, further cost reduction is necessary by either redesigning the product, reengineering the process, or both. To achieve the cost reduction goals, managers from all areas (design, development, manufacturing, and accounting) must work together to find creative ways to achieve the target cost without affecting the end value to the consumer.

This process is very time consuming. Toyota's cost planning process begins at least four years before the product launch. This gives managers time to meet the cost reduction target through product redesign, process reengineering, supplier management, and other cost management techniques.

One important part of target costing is **value engineering**, which involves analyzing the market and estimating what consumers will be willing to pay for a product with specific features. For example, when introducing a new model with improved functionality (better fuel economy, more safety features, enhanced electronics), Toyota would need to estimate how much consumers will be willing to pay for these features. If consumers do not value certain features, they may be eliminated to meet the target cost.

Activity based management plays a key role in target costing by helping managers find ways to achieve the target cost while still providing the value and features consumers are willing to pay for. The key is to eliminate activities that do not add value to consumers. One way that manufacturing firms can reduce cost while improving quality and value is by streamlining operations and reducing unnecessary inventory.

JUST-IN-TIME (JIT)

Toyota was one of the first firms to adopt a **just-in-time (JIT)** approach to manufacturing. Under a JIT system, a company purchases materials and manufactures products based on customer demand. JIT is a demand–pull system in which materials and products are **pulled** through the manufacturing system based on customer demand. In a traditional manufacturing setting, products are **pushed** through the system and often end up sitting in inventory.

Most managers realize that inventory adds many more problems than it solves including inventory carrying costs and quality problems. To successfully implement a JIT strategy, a company must rethink almost everything it does. JIT requires an extreme commitment to quality and very strong relationships with suppliers and customers. Although few firms have realized the full potential of JIT, most companies that implement it experience a substantial decrease in ordering and warehousing costs as well as many benefits related to quality and flexibility.

One by-product of a JIT system is the elimination of many complications in product costing that inventory creates. Product costing is much easier in a JIT environment because there is no need to worry about how much cost must be reported as inventory (an asset) and how much should be reported as Cost of Goods Sold (on the income statement). This means that managerial accountants can switch roles from being measurement experts to being information providers and partners in management decision making.

SUMMARY OF ABC AND ABM

To summarize, activity based costing is a method of assigning indirect costs to products or services based on the activities they require. ABC uses both volume-based cost drivers (such as labor hours or machine hours) and nonvolume-based cost drivers (such as the number of setups, engineering hours, and inspections). The result should be a more accurate picture of the actual costs to produce products and serve customers. But measuring or allocating costs in a more accurate way, in and of itself, does not make a company more profitable.

To gain the true benefits of activity based costing, managers must move from simply **measuring** costs to finding ways to **manage** or reduce them. This is where cost management techniques such as target costing, total quality management, and just in time come into play. Although ABC and ABM have many potential benefits, they must be weighed against the costs of obtaining the more accurate information. Implementing an ABC system is not a trivial task. It requires a great deal of time and effort from many employees across the entire organization (not just accountants), and the support of upper management. Because of the unique nature of the drivers required by ABC, new types of data must be collected and added to the accounting system. Employees must spend time tracking the time spent on various activities, a task that many will consider nonvalue-added or a waste of time. In short, implementing and maintaining an activity based costing system can present a formidable challenge, and management must weigh its potential benefits against its costs.

DEMONSTRATION CASE

Grapeville Estates produces two types of wine. The first is a standard-variety chardonnay produced in large batches and aged for a relatively short period of time (about four months) in large metal containers (vats). The second wine is a limited-edition cabernet made in very small batches from premium grapes and then aged for more than three years in special French oak barrels to provide a particular taste. The barrels require significant maintenance between batches and can be used only a few times before they lose some of the oak flavor that they transfer to the wine.

The company currently uses a volume-based cost system with total manufacturing overhead cost of $375,000 applied to the two products at a rate of 150 percent of direct labor dollars. Assume the following production cost information for the most recent year:

	Standard Chardonnay	Vintage Cabernet
Number of bottles produced	200,000	25,000
Unit cost information		
Direct materials (grapes and bottles)	$2.00	$4.00
Direct labor	1.00	2.00
Manufacturing overhead	?	?
Manufacturing cost per unit	?	?

The company has conducted an ABC analysis and traced the manufacturing overhead cost to three activity cost pools, with the following cost and drivers.

Activity	Total Cost	Total Amount of Activity Driver		Activity Rate	
Purchasing and receiving materials (grapes)	$ 90,000	450,000	Pounds of grapes	?	per pound
Setting up to produce a new batch of wine	100,000	400	Number of batches	?	per batch
Fermenting and aging wine in barrels	80,000	200,000	Number of fermentation days	?	per fermentation day
Inspecting the wine for quality control	105,000	20,000	Number of inspections	?	per inspection
	$375,000				

The activities required by the two products follow:

	Standard Chardonnay	Vintage Cabernet
Pounds of grapes	400,000	50,000
Number of batches	200	200
Number of fermentation days	30,000	170,000
Number of inspections	2,000	18,000

Required:

1. Compute the manufacturing cost per bottle of the two products using the volume-based cost system.
2. Compute the activity rate for each of the four cost pools under ABC.
3. Compute the total manufacturing overhead cost that would be assigned to each product using ABC. Verify that the total cost sums to $375,000.
4. Compute the unit manufacturing cost of each product using ABC.
5. Compare the unit manufacturing cost under ABC with the current volume-based cost system. Which product was overcosted under the volume-based cost system compared to ABC and which was undercosted?
6. Explain why ABC provided different information than the current cost system.

See pages 154–155 for solution.

CHAPTER SUMMARY

Assign indirect cost to products or services using a single volume-based allocation measure. p. 135   **LO1**

- A traditional cost system assigns indirect (overhead) costs to products or services using a volume-based measure such as the number of direct labor hours, machine hours, or units produced. These systems, while simple, assume that all indirect costs are driven by volume and ignore other factors such as the complexity of the production process and other non-volume drivers of cost.

- Unlike traditional cost systems that rely strictly on volume-based allocation measures, ABC systems include measures that capture something other than the sheer volume of units produced or customers served.

Classify activities as unit, batch, product, customer, or facility level. p. 138   **LO2**

- Activity based costing systems capture the following types of activities:
  - Unit-level activities are performed for each individual unit.
  - Batch-level activities are performed for a group of units all at once.
  - Product-level activities are performed to support a general product line, not specific units or batches.
  - Customer-level activities are performed for a specific customer.
  - Facility-level or companywide activities are performed for the company overall and do not relate to specific products, customers, batches, or units.

Assign indirect costs to activity cost pools (Stage 1) and select a driver for each pool. p. 140   **LO3**

- The first stage of ABC is to assign indirect costs to activity cost pools. The goal is to create as few activity cost pools as possible while capturing the major activities performed.

- The next step is to identify an activity cost driver for each of the activity cost pools. The goal is to identify a driver that has a cause-and-effect relationship with the underlying activity that occurs in each activity cost pool.

Assign activity costs to products or services (Stage 2) using activity rates. p. 142   **LO4**

- An activity rate is computed for each cost pool by dividing the total indirect cost of the pool by the total quantity or amount of the cost driver.

- To assign the indirect cost to individual products or services, multiply the activity rate by the activity driver for each product or service.

Assign activity cost to products or services (Stage 2) using activity proportions. p. 143   **LO5**

- To calculate an activity proportion, divide the requirements of each individual product or service by the total quantity or amount of the activity driver.

- To assign the indirect cost to individual products or services, multiply the activity proportion by the total indirect cost.

LO6   **Compare the results of a volume-based cost system to activity based costing. p. 145**

- The only difference between a volume-based cost system and activity based costing is the assignment of indirect (overhead) costs to products or services.

- Volume-based cost systems tend to overcost high-volume simple products and undercost low-volume, customized, or complex products.

- By taking into account both volume and nonvolume drivers of costs, ABC should provide a more accurate picture of the cost of producing diverse products or serving customers with diverse needs.

LO7   **Describe how managers use the results of activity based costing for activity based management. p. 147**

- Activity based management (ABM) encompasses all actions that managers take to reduce costs or improve processes based on the ABC information.

- To benefit from ABC, managers must manage the underlying activities and engage in activity based management including the following:

  - Identifying and eliminating nonvalue-added activities.
  - Managing costs across the entire product life cycle.
  - Using target costing to design products and processes to meet customer demands and provide the necessary profit to stakeholders.
  - Reduce quality costs by engaging in total quality management (TQM).
  - Managing inventory costs by using just-in-time inventory.

SOLUTION TO DEMONSTRATION CASE

1.

	Standard Chardonnay	Vintage Cabernet
Direct materials (grapes and bottles)	$2.00	$4.00
Direct labor	1.00	2.00
Manufacturing overhead (150% of direct labor)	1.00 × 150% = 1.50	$2.00 × 150% = 3.00
Manufacturing cost per unit	$4.50	$9.00

2.

Activity	Total Cost	Total Amount of Activity Driver		Activity Rate	
Purchasing and receiving materials (grapes)	$ 90,000	450,000	($90,000/450,000) =	$0.20	per pound
Setting up to produce a new batch of wine	100,000	400	($100,000/400) =	$250	per batch
Fermenting and aging wine in barrels	80,000	200,000	($80,000/200,000) =	$0.40	per fermentation day
Inspecting the wine for quality control	105,000	20,000	($105,000/20,000) =	$5.25	per inspection
	$375,000				

3.

Activity Driver	Standard Chardonnay		Vintage Cabernet	
Pounds of grapes	$0.20 × 400,000 =	$ 80,000	$ 0.20 × 50,000 =	$ 10,000
Number of batches	$ 250 × 200 =	50,000	$ 250 × 200 =	50,000
Number of fermentation days	$ 0.40 × 30,000 =	12,000	$0.40 × 170,000 =	68,000
Number of inspections	$ 5.25 × 2,000 =	10,500	$ 5.25 × 18,000 =	94,500
Total		$152,500		$ 222,500

$152,500 + $222,500 = $375,000

4.

	Standard Chardonnay	Vintage Cabernet
Manufacturing overhead	$152,500	$222,500
Number of bottles produced	÷ 200,000	÷ 25,000
Manufacturing overhead cost per bottle	$ 0.76	$ 8.90

5.

	Standard Chardonnay	Vintage Cabernet
Direct materials (grapes and bottles)	$2.00	$ 4.00
Direct labor	1.00	2.00
Manufacturing overhead cost per bottle (from ABC)	0.76	8.90
Manufacturing cost per bottle (from ABC)	$3.76	$14.90
Manufacturing cost per bottle (current system) (from requirement 1)	$4.50	$ 9.00
Difference in existing system and ABC	$0.74	($ 5.90)

Under the volume-based cost system, the standard chardonnay was overcosted and the vintage cabernet was undercosted.

6. The current cost system captured only the volume of units produced. The ABC system captured other nonvolume-based drivers including the number of setups, fermentation days, and inspections. Even though the vintage cabernet is a low-volume product, it is produced in smaller batches and requires more fermentation days and more stringent quality control than the standard cabernet.

KEY TERMS

Activity Based Costing (ABC) (p. 137)
Activity Based Management (p. 147)
Activity Cost Driver (p. 141)
Activity Rate (p. 142)
Appraisal or Inspection Costs (p. 149)
Batch-Level Activities (p. 139)
Benchmarking (p. 147)
Customer-Level Activities (p. 138)

External Failure Costs (p. 149)
Facility or Companywide Activities (p. 138)
Internal Failure Costs (p. 149)
Just-in-Time (JIT) System (p. 151)
Nonvalue-Added Activity (p. 148)
Nonvolume-Based Cost Drivers (p. 141)
Prevention Costs (p. 149)

Product-Level Activities (p. 138)
Product Life Cycle (p. 149)
Quality Cost Report (p. 149)
Target Costing (p. 150)
Unit-Level Activities (p. 139)
Value-Added Activity (p. 148)
Value Engineering (p. 151)
Volume-Based Allocation Measure (p. 135)

See complete definitions in glossary at back of text.

QUESTIONS

1. What is an allocation base?
2. What is the difference between a volume allocation measure and a nonvolume allocation measure?
3. Explain the statement that traditional costing systems use volume-based allocation measures.
4. What are the potential negative consequences of a traditional volume-based costing system?
5. What types of business might use activity based costing?
6. How does activity based costing differ from traditional costing systems?
7. Describe the two stages of activity based costing.
8. Identify the categories (hierarchy) of activities in an activity based costing system.
9. Why must costs be classified into different categories for ABC? What is the basis for these categories?
10. Consider a construction company that builds semicustom homes. Give an example of each of the following

activities: facility level, product level, customer level, batch level, and unit level.
11. Explain the difference between the activity rate method and the activity proportion method of ABC.
12. Define activity based management and explain how it is related to activity based costing.
13. What is benchmarking? How does it benefit a company?
14. What is a nonvalue-added activity? Considering the construction company in question 10, give an example of a value-added and a nonvalue-added activity.
15. What are the four types of quality costs that comprise total quality management (TQM)?
16. What is target costing? How does activity based management play a role in target costing?
17. Explain the concept of a just-in-time inventory system. What is its primary benefit?
18. Briefly discuss the advantages and disadvantages of activity based costing and activity based management.

MULTIPLE CHOICE

Quiz 4
www.mhhe.com/whitecotton1e

1. Traditional (non-ABC) cost systems assign indirect (overhead) costs on the basis of:

   a. Nonvolume-based cost drivers.
   b. Unit- or volume-based cost drivers.
   c. Activity based cost drivers
   d. Facility-level cost drivers.

2. Both traditional and ABC cost systems focus on the assignment of:

   a. Direct costs.
   b. Indirect costs.
   c. Manufacturing costs.
   d. Nonmanufacturing costs.

3. Which of the following is a volume-based allocation measure?

   a. Number of units produced.
   b. Number of direct labor hours.
   c. Number of machine hours.
   d. All of the above.

4. Number of setups is an example of:

   a. Unit-level activity.
   b. Batch-level activity.
   c. Product-level activity.
   d. Facility-level activity.

5. Which of the following is not a facility-level activity?

   a. Maintenance on the factory building.
   b. Factory utilities.
   c. Research and development for a new product.
   d. Manufacturing supervision.

Use the following information for the next five questions:

Hi-Def Video Company makes two types of digital DVD players, economy and deluxe, with the following per unit cost information:

	Economy (8,000 units)	Deluxe (2,000 units)
Direct materials	$50	$100
Direct labor	25	25
Manufacturing overhead	?	?
Full manufacturing cost per unit	?	?

The company currently applies $1 million in manufacturing overhead to the two products on the basis of direct labor hours. Both products require two hours of direct labor.

6. What rate is currently used to apply manufacturing overhead to the two products?

   a. $100 per unit.
   b. $100 per direct labor hour.
   c. $50 per unit.
   d. $50 per direct labor hour.

7. Using the rate calculated in question 6, what is the full manufacturing cost per unit of the deluxe product?

   a. $50.
   b. $100.
   c. $175.
   d. $225.

Assume that High-Def has decided to implement an ABC system and has assigned the $1 million in manufacturing overhead to four activities, which will be assigned to the two products based on the following activity drivers:

Activity Pools	Activity Cost	Activity Driver	Activity Driver for Each Product Line	
			Economy	Deluxe
Materials handling	$ 250,000	Number of parts	40,000	60,000
Quality control	500,000	Number of inspections	8,000	12,000
Finishing	200,000	Number of direct labor hours	16,000	4,000
Packaging	50,000	Number of packages shipped	2,000	2,000
Total	$1,000,000			

8. What is the activity rate for the material handling activity cost pool?

   a. $ 2.50 per part.
   b. $ 4.00 per part.
   c. $ 8.00 per part.
   d. $10.50 per part.

9. Using the activity proportion method, how much of the quality control cost would be assigned to the economy model?

   a. 20% of $500,000 = $100,000.
   b. 40% of $500,000 = $200,000.
   c. 60% of $500,000 = $300,000.
   d. 80% of $500,000 = $400,000.

10. In comparing the results of ABC with the volume-based cost system (based on direct labor hours), which of the following statements is most likely to be true?

   a. The current cost system will overcost the deluxe model compared to ABC.
   b. The current cost system will undercost the economy model compared to ABC.
   c. The current cost system will overcost the economy model compared to ABC.
   d. Both *a* and *b* are true.

Answers to Multiple-Choice Questions located in back of the text.

MINI EXERCISES

M4-1 Comparing Traditional and ABC Systems

LO1, 6

Landau Company is considering a switch from its traditional costing system to an activity based system. It has compiled the following information regarding its product lines.

	Traditional Costing	ABC
Revenue	$325,000	$325,000
Overhead		
Product X	52,000	71,000
Product Y	50,000	31,000
	$102,000	$102,000

Explain why the overhead costs could be so different between the two costing systems.

M4-2 Identifying Cost Drivers in an ABC System

LO3

Zapex makes electronic components for handheld games and has identified several activities as components of manufacturing overhead: factory rent, factory utilities, quality inspections, material handling, machine setup, employee training, machine maintenance, inventory security costs, and supervisor salaries. For each activity that Zapex has identified, choose a cost driver to allocate that cost. Explain your reasoning.

M4-3 Identifying Cost Drivers in an ABC System

LO3

For each of the following activities, indicate the appropriate category (unit, batch, product, customer, or facility level) and suggest a possible cost driver for each pool.

1. Factory utilities.
2. Machine setups.
3. Research and development for a new product.
4. Sanding rough edges of the product.
5. Packaging the product for shipment.
6. Developing new packaging for a special order of 200 units.
7. Maintenance on equipment.
8. Assembling the product's component parts.
9. Material handling costs.
10. Quality control testing.

M4-4 Calculating Activity Rates

LO4

Bradshaw Corp. has identified three cost pools in its manufacturing process: equipment maintenance, setups, and quality control. Total cost assigned to the three pools is $143,000, $78,000, and $87,000, respectively. Cost driver estimates for the pools are 10,000 machine hours, 150 setups, and 450 quality inspections, respectively. Calculate the activity rate for each of Bradshaw's activity pools.

M4-5 Assigning Costs Using Activity Rates

LO4

Newkirk Co. has identified one of its cost pools to be quality control and has assigned $50,000 to that pool. Number of inspections has been chosen as the cost driver for this pool; Newkirk performs 25,000 inspections annually. Suppose Newkirk manufactures two products that consume 10,000 and 15,000 inspections each. Using activity rates, determine the amount of quality control cost to be assigned to each of Newkirk's product lines.

M4-6 Assigning Costs Using Activity Proportions

LO5

Refer to the information presented in M4-5. Suppose that Newkirk manufacturers only the two products mentioned and they consume 100 percent of the company's quality inspections. Using activity proportions, determine how much quality control cost will be assigned to each of Newkirk's product lines.

LO4   M4-7 Calculating Activity Rates for ABC System

Martinez, Inc., manufactures four lines of gardening carts and uses activity based costing to calculate product cost. Compute the activity rates for each of the following activity cost pools:

Activity Pool	Estimated Total Cost	Estimated Cost Driver
Machining	$326,000	13,000 machine hours
Setup	68,000	350 batches
Quality control	95,000	800 inspections

LO4   M4-8 Assigning Costs to Products Using Activity Rates

Refer to the information presented in M4-7. Suppose the flower child gardening cart requires 2,500 machine hours, 300 inspections, and 100 batches. Using the activity rates calculated in M4-7, determine the amount of overhead assigned to the flower child product line.

LO5   M4-9 Assigning Costs to Products Using Activity Proportions

Refer to the information presented in M4-7. Suppose the rosey posey gardening cart requires 4,750 machine hours, 215 inspections and 65 batches. Using activity proportions, determine the amount of overhead assigned to the rosey posey product line.

LO7   M4-10 Classifying Activities as Value Added or Nonvalue Added

Offtrack Corp. has identified the following activities in its manufacturing process. Indicate whether each activity is value added or nonvalue added.

> Product design research
> Materials handling
> Machining
> Assembly of components
> Finished goods inventory storage
> Rework after a quality inspection
> Painting end product
> Raw materials inventory storage

LO2   M4-11 Classifying Activities According to Level

Refer to the activities presented in M4-10. Classify each cost as facility, product, customer, batch, or unit level.

EXERCISES

LO6, 7   E4-1 Understanding the Complexity of ABC and Implications of Inaccurate Data

One of the disadvantages of activity based costing is the amount of information it requires. To reliably calculate costs using an ABC system, a company must have information about total overhead costs and how those costs are divided into various categories. ABC also requires data about a variety of cost drivers that are used to allocate the cost pools.

Required:

1. Explain how a company can accumulate this information. Include the identity of any persons responsible for providing the necessary data.
2. Explain how inaccuracies in the cost pool estimates or cost driver estimates would impact the company.

LO2   E4-2 Classifying Activities According to Level, Determining Value Added or Nonvalue Added

Summer Company manufactures flowerpots in several different sizes and has identified the following activities in its manufacturing process.

> Storing inventory
> Creating molds

Pouring plaster
Firing pots in kiln
Sanding and finishing
Painting
Performing quality control
Ordering materials
Delivering orders to customers
Insuring the manufacturing facility
Reconfiguring machinery between batches

Required:

1. Classify each activity listed as facility, product, customer, batch, or unit level.
2. Identify a cost driver for each activity listed.
3. Indicate whether each activity is value added or nonvalue added.

E4-3 Computing Activity Rates, Classifying Activities

LO2, 4

Francis Company uses three activity pools. Each pool has a cost driver where information follows:

Activity Pool and Amount	Cost Driver	Estimated Total of Cost Driver
Machining $250,000	Number of machine hours	80,000
Designing costs $65,000	Number of design hours	8,000
Setup costs $73,000	Number of batches	400

Required:

1. Compute the activity rate for each activity. Round to three decimal places.
2. Classify each activity as facility, product, customer, batch, or unit level.

E4-4 Assigning Costs Using Activity Rates

LO4

Refer to the information presented in E4-3. Suppose that Francis Company manufactures three products, A, B, and C. Information about these products follows:

	Product A	Product B	Product C
Number of machine hours	30,000	40,000	10,000
Number of design hours	3,200	1,800	3,000
Number of batches	50	75	275

Required:

1. Considering the information about these three products, comment on the likely complexity of the manufacturing process for each.
2. Using the activity rates calculated in E4-3, determine the amount of overhead assigned to each product.

E4-5 Assigning Costs Using Activity Proportions

LO5

Refer to the information presented in E4-3. Suppose that Francis Company manufactures three products. Information about its three products follows:

	Product A	Product B	Product C
Number of machine hours	30,000	40,000	10,000
Number of designer hours	3,200	1,800	3,000
Number of batches	50	75	275

Required:

1. Using activity proportions, determine the amount of overhead assigned to each product.
2. Compare these results with those obtained using activity rates in E4-4.
3. Considering the information about these three products, comment on the likely impact of using a traditional costing system.

LO3, 4   **E4-6 Calculating Activity Rates, Assigning Costs**

Titan Corp. has identified the following information:

Cost pools	
Material handling	$40,000
Machine maintenance	25,500
Cost drivers	
Number of material moves	800
Number of machine hours	75,000

Required:

1. Calculate Titan's activity rate for each cost pool.
2. Determine the amount of overhead assigned to Titan's products if they have the following requirements:

	Product A	Product B
Number of material moves	500	300
Number of machine hours	42,000	33,000

LO1   **E4-7 Calculating Traditional Overhead Rates, Assigning Costs**

Rawlings Corp. has two product lines, A and B. Rawlings has identified the following information about its overhead and potential cost drivers.

Total overhead	$75,000
Cost drivers	
Number of labor hours	2,500
Number of machine hours	46,000

Required:

1. Suppose the Rawlings Corp. uses a traditional costing system with number of labor hours as the cost driver. Determine the amount of overhead assigned to each product line if Product A requires 70% of the labor hours and Product B requires 30%.
2. Suppose Rawlings uses a traditional costing system with machine hours as the cost driver. Determine the amount of overhead assigned to each product line if Product A consumes 17,000 machine hours and Product B consumes 29,000.

LO3, 4   **E4-8 Calculating Activity Rates, Assigning Costs**

Refer to the information about Rawlings Corp. presented in E4-7. Rawlings has identified the following detailed information about its cost pools and cost drivers.

Cost pools	
Material handling	$60,000
Machine maintenance	$15,000
Cost drivers	
Number of material moves	500
Number of machine hours	46,000

Required:

1. Calculate Rawlings' activity rate for each cost pool.
2. Determine the amount of overhead assigned to Rawlings' products if they have the following requirements:

	Product A	Product B
Number of material moves	200	300
Number of machine hours	17,000	29,000

E4-9 Calculating Traditional Overhead Rates, Assigning Costs   LO1

Matson Company manufactures automobile floor mats. It currently has 2 product lines, the Standard and the Deluxe.

Matson has a total of $26,040 in overhead. It currently used a traditional cost system with overhead applied to the product on the basis of either direct labor (DL) hours or machine hours. Matson has compiled the following information about possible cost drivers and its two product lines.

Matson Company Total	Quantity/Amount Consumed by Standard Floor Mat Line	Quantity/Amount Consumed by Deluxe Floor Mat Line
1,000 DL hours	600 DL hours	400 DL hours
7,150 machine hours	3,000 machine hours	4,150 machine hours

Required:

1. Suppose Matson used a traditional costing system with direct labor hours as the cost driver. Determine the amount of overhead assigned to each product line.
2. Suppose Matson used a traditional costing system with machine hours as the cost driver. Determine the amount of overhead assigned to each product line.

E4-10 Assigning Costs Using Activity Rates   LO4

Refer to the information given in E4-9 regarding Matson Company. Suppose that Matson has conducted further research into its overhead and potential cost drivers. As a result, the company has compiled the following detailed information breaking total overhead into three cost pools

Activity Pools	Cost Driver	Cost Assigned to Pool	Quantity/Amount Consumed by Standard Floor Mat Line	Quantity/Amount Consumed by Deluxe Floor Mat Line
Material Handling	# moves	$ 2,500	40 moves	60 moves
Quality Control	# inspections	$ 9,240	600 inspections	720 inspections
Machine Maintenance	# machine hrs	$14,300	3,000 machine hours	4,150 machine hours

Required:

1. Calculate the activity rates for each cost pool assuming Matson uses an ABC system.
2. Calculate the amount of overhead that Matson will assign to the standard floor mat line.
3. Determine the amount of overhead Matson will assign to the deluxe product line.

E4-11 Comparing Traditional Costing Systems and Activity Based Costing   LO6

Refer to your solutions obtained in E4-9 and E4-10.

Required:

1. Discuss the costs and benefits to Matson of moving from a traditional costing system to an ABC system.
2. Compare the results of each potential traditional costing system to those obtained in the ABC approach.

LO3, 4, 5, 6   **E4-12 Assigning Costs Using Traditional System, ABC System**

Nixon makes two types of doghouse, plain and super. The company is currently using a traditional costing system with labor hours as the cost driver but is considering change to activity based costing. In preparation for the possible switch, Nixon has identified two cost pools: materials handling and setup. Pertinent data follow:

	Plain Doghouse	Super Doghouse
Number of labor hours	15,000	9,000
Number of material moves	300	450
Number of setups	40	80

Total estimated overhead costs are $150,000 of which $40,000 is assigned to the material handling cost pool and $110,000 is assigned to the setup cost pool.

Required:

1. Calculate the overhead assigned to the Plain Doghouse using the traditional costing system based on direct labor hours.
2. Calculate the overhead assigned to the Plain Doghouse using ABC. (Round activity rates or activity proportions to four decimal places if necessary.)
3. Was the Plain Doghouse over or under-costed by the traditional cost system compared to ABC?

LO1, 3, 4, 5, 6   **E4-13 Assigning Costs Using Traditional System, ABC System**

Refer to E4-12.

Required:

1. Calculate the overhead assigned to the Super Doghouse line using the traditional costing system based on direct labor hours.
2. Calculate the overhead assigned to the Super Doghouse line using an activity based costing system. (Round activity rates or activity proportions to four decimal places if necessary.)
3. Was the Super Doghouse over or undercosted by the traditional cost system compared to ABC?

LO1, 3, 4, 5, 6   **E4-14 Assigning Costs Using Traditional System, ABC System**

Dunnstreet produces two types of calculator, standard and deluxe. The company is currently using a traditional costing system with machine hours as the cost driver but is considering a move to activity based costing. In preparing for the possible switch, Dunnstreet has identified two cost pools: materials handling and setup. The collected data follow:

	Standard Model	Deluxe Model
Number of machine hours	25,000	30,000
Number of material moves	550	850
Number of setups	80	500

Total estimated overhead costs are $225,000 of which $70,000 is assigned to the material handling cost pool and $155,000 is assigned to the setup cost pool.

Required:

1. Calculate the overhead assigned to each product using the traditional cost system. Round the overhead rate to four decimal places if necessary.
2. Calculate the overhead assigned to each product using ABC. Round activity rates to four decimal places if necessary.

LO7   **E4-15 Describing the Benefits of JIT**

A number of manufacturers recently have moved to a JIT inventory system. JIT systems have a number of potential benefits but also can have negative consequences for a company whose suppliers are not dependable.

Required:

1. Discuss the reasons a company might implement a JIT system.
2. What are the potential benefits of a JIT system?

3. What are the potential negative consequences of a JIT system?

4. Discuss whether you believe the potential benefits outweigh the possible costs.

5. Name a company that has implemented JIT in recent years.

E4-16 **Calculating Target Cost**   L07

Radar Inc. has developed a new and improved widget. The company plans to sell the product through an existing Web site. Radar's marketing department believes the product will sell for $50. Radar's goal is a 40 percent profit margin on the widget.

Required:

1. If current prototypes cost $35 to produce, will Radar meet its profit goal?

2. Calculate the target cost necessary for Radar to earn 40 percent profit.

3. Suggest at least three areas that Radar might investigate for ways to cut the prototype cost enough to meet the target profit for this product.

E4-17 **Calculating Target Cost**   L07

Pawkins Company uses target costing to ensure that its products are profitable. Assume Pawkins is planning to introduce a new product with the following estimates:

Estimated market price	$1,200
Annual demand	100,000 units
Life cycle	5 years
Target profit	25% return on sales

Required:

1. Compute the target cost of this product.

2. Compute the target cost if Pawkins wants a 35 percent return on sales.

3. Compute the target cost if Pawkins wants a 10 percent return on sales.

E4-18 **Explaining the Concept of TQM**   L07

Your co-worker has come to you for help for several things the boss mentioned recently. Specifically, the boss was discussing the company's move to a TQM approach to its manufacturing process and repeatedly mentioned multiple types of quality costs and whether activities are value added or nonvalue added.

Required:

Explain each of these concepts to your co-worker. Include the relationship between these concepts and activity based management.

PROBLEMS–SET A    |ACCOUNTING

PA4-1 **Assigning Costs Using Traditional System, ABC System**   L01, 3, 4, 6

Larkspur Corp. manufactures bird feeders. It currently has two product lines, the standard and the deluxe. Larkspur has a total of $137,250 in overhead.

The company has identified the following information about its overhead activity pools and the two product lines:

Activity Pools	Cost Driver	Cost Assigned to Pool	Qty Consumed by Standard	Qty Consumed by Deluxe
Material handling	Number of moves	$ 3,500	20 moves	50 moves
Quality control	Number of inspections	$ 33,750	250 inspections	125 inspections
Machine maintenance	Number of machine hrs	$100,000	5,000 machine hours	5,000 machine hours

Required:

1. Suppose Larkspur used a traditional costing system with machine hours as the cost driver. Determine the amount of overhead assigned to each product line.

2. Calculate the activity rates for each cost pool in Larkspur's ABC system.

3. Calculate the amount of overhead that Larkspur will assign to the standard line if it uses an ABC system.

4. Determine the amount of overhead Larkspur will assign to the deluxe line if it uses an ABC system.

5. Compare the results for a traditional system with that of an ABC system. Which do you think is more accurate and why?

LO1, 3, 5, 6   **PA4-2** **Assigning Costs Using Traditional System, Assigning Costs Using Activity Proportions**

www.mhhe.com/whitecotton1e

HulaHug Corp., which manufactures hula hoops, currently has two product lines, the Roundabout and the Sassafras. HulaHug has total overhead of $131,200.

HulaHug has identified the following information about its overhead activity pools and the two product lines.

Activity Pools	Cost Driver	Cost Assigned to Pool	Quantity/Amount Consumed Roundabout Line	Quantity/Amount Consumed Sassafras Line
Material handling	Number of moves	$19,650	575 moves	425 moves
Quality control	Number of inspections	$78,750	6,000 inspections	4,500 inspections
Machine maintenance	Number of machine hours	$32,800	21,000 machine hours	20,000 machine hours

Required:

1. Suppose HulaHug used a traditional costing system with machine hours as the cost driver. Determine the amount of overhead assigned to each product line.

2. Calculate the activity proportions for each cost pool in HulaHug's ABC system.

3. Calculate the amount of overhead that HulaHug will assign to the Roundabout line if it uses an ABC system.

4. Determine the amount of overhead HulaHug will assign to the Sassafras line if it uses an ABC system.

5. Compare the results for a traditional system with an ABC system. Which do you think is more accurate and why?

LO3, 4   **PA4-3** **Selecting Cost Drivers, Assigning Costs Using Activity Rates**

Landon Company makes two models of children's playhouses, the Castle and the Mansion. Basic production information follows:

	Castle	Mansion
Direct materials cost per unit	$ 45	$ 72
Direct labor cost per unit	23	35
Sales price per unit	350	565
Expected production per month	700 units	400 units

Landon has monthly overhead of $219,000, which is divided into the following cost pools:

Setup costs	$ 86,000
Quality control	73,000
Maintenance	60,000
Total	$219,000

The company has also compiled the following information about the chosen cost drivers:

	Castle	Mansion	Total
Number of setups	42	58	100
Number of inspections	340	390	730
Number of machine hours	1,700	1,300	3,000

Required:

1. Suppose Landon used a traditional costing system with machine hours as the cost driver. Determine the amount of overhead assigned to each product line.
2. Calculate the production cost per unit for each of Landon's products under a traditional costing system.
3. Calculate Landon's gross margin per unit for each product under the traditional costing system.
4. Select the appropriate cost driver for each cost pool and calculate the activity rates if Landon wanted to implement an ABC system.
5. Assuming an ABC system, assign overhead costs to each product based on activity demands.
6. Calculate the production cost per unit for each of Landon's products in an ABC system.
7. Calculate Landon's gross margin per unit for each product under an ABC system.
8. Compare the gross margin of each product under the traditional system and ABC.

PA4-4 Selecting Cost Drivers, Assigning Costs Using Activity Rates

LO3, 4

www.mhhe.com/whitecotton1e

Gutierrez Company makes two models of portable camping stove, the Sportsman and the Expedition.

Basic production information follows:

	Sportsman	Expedition
Direct materials cost per unit	$20	$ 28
Direct labor cost per unit	$15	$ 19
Sales price per unit	$82	$105
Expected production per month	1,200 units	960 units

Gutierrez has monthly overhead of $11,180, which is divided into the following cost pools:

Setup costs	$ 2,600
Quality control	5,500
Maintenance	3,080
Total	$11,180

The company has also compiled the following information about the chosen cost drivers:

	Sportsman	Expedition	Total
Number of setups	14	26	40
Number of inspections	140	300	440
Number of machine hours	1,400	1,400	2,800

Required:

1. Suppose Gutierrez used a traditional costing system with machine hours as the cost driver. Determine the amount of overhead assigned to each product line.
2. Calculate the production cost per unit for each of Gutierrez's products under a traditional costing system.

3. Calculate Gutierrez's gross margin per unit for each product under the traditional costing system.

4. Select the appropriate cost driver for each cost pool and calculate the activity rates if Gutierrez wanted to implement an ABC system.

5. Assuming an ABC system, assign overhead costs to each product based on activity demands.

6. Calculate the production cost per unit for each of Gutierrez's products with an ABC system.

7. Calculate Gutierrez's gross margin per unit for each product under an ABC system.

8. Compare the gross margin of each product under the traditional system and ABC.

LO7   **PA4-5 Describing the Impact of ABM and TQM on a Company**

In recent years, the managerial concepts of activity based management (ABM), activity based costing (ABC), and total quality management (TQM) have received considerable attention from manufacturing and other companies. The development of a global economy as well as consumers' ability to shop around has led to increased competition in the market and pressure on companies to focus efforts on cost-cutting measures wherever possible.

Required:

1. Conduct online or library research for articles about companies that have successfully implemented ABM, TQM, and/or ABC within their organizations.

2. Read and briefly summarize at least three such articles.

3. Choose one of these companies and write a memo to your classmates outlining the company's implementation. Include their time lines, any problems encountered, and perceived benefits.

PROBLEMS–SET B

LO1, 3, 4, 6   **PB4-1 Assigning Costs Using Traditional System, ABC System**

Momentum Corp., which manufactures skateboards, currently has two product lines, the Standard and the Deluxe, and $29,000 in total overhead.

The company has identified the following information about its overhead activity pools and the two product lines:

Activity Pools	Cost Driver	Cost Assigned to Pool	Quantity/Amount Consumed Standard Line	Quantity/Amount Consumed Deluxe Line
Material handling	Number of moves	$ 1,400	100 moves	75 moves
Quality control	Number of inspections	$ 5,100	1,000 inspections	875 inspections
Machine maintenance	Number of machine hours	$22,500	8,000 machine hours	12,000 machine hours

Required:

1. Suppose Momentum used a traditional costing system with machine hours as the cost driver. Determine the amount of overhead assigned to each product line.

2. Calculate the activity rates for each cost pool in Momentum's ABC system.

3. Calculate the amount of overhead that Momentum will assign to the Standard line if it uses an ABC system.

4. Determine the amount of overhead Momentum will assign to the Deluxe line if it uses an ABC system.

5. Compare the results for the traditional system with those of the ABC system. Which do you think is more accurate and why?

PB4-2 Assigning Costs Using Traditional System, Assigning Costs Using   LO1, 3, 5, 6
      Activity Proportions

Wildwind Corp. is the manufacturer of wind chimes. It currently has two product lines, the Clear Tone and the Bella. Wildwind has $61,200 in total overhead.

    The company has identified the following information about its overhead activity pools and the two product lines.

Activity Pools	Cost Driver	Cost Assigned to Pool	Quantity/Amount Consumed ClearTone	Quantity/Amount Consumed Bella
Material handling	Number of moves	$15,300	235 moves	275 moves
Quality control	Number of inspections	$28,900	578 inspections	867 inspections
Machine maintenance	Number of machine hours	$17,000	18,000 machine hours	16,000 machine hours

Required:

1. Suppose Wildwind used a traditional costing system with machine hours as the cost driver. Determine the amount of overhead assigned to each product line.

2. Calculate the activity proportions for each cost pool in Wildwind's ABC system.

3. Calculate the amount of overhead that Wildwind will assign to the ClearTone product line if it uses an ABC system.

4. Determine the amount of overhead Wildwind will assign to the Bella product line if it uses an ABC system.

5. Compare the results for a traditional system with those of an ABC system. Which do you think is more accurate and why?

PB4-3 Selecting Cost Drivers, Assigning Costs Using Activity Rates   LO3, 4

Muffintop Company makes two models of snack cake, the poppyseed and the blueberry.
    Basic production information follows:

	Poppyseed	Blueberry
Direct materials cost per unit	$0.75	$0.85
Direct labor cost per unit	$0.25	$0.25
Sales price per unit	$2.50	$2.50
Expected production per month	140,000 units	190,00 units

Muffintop has monthly overhead of $135,000, which is divided into the following cost pools:

Setup costs	$ 50,000
Quality control	28,300
Maintenance	37,800
Engineering	18,900
Total	$135,000

The company has also compiled the following information about the chosen cost drivers:

	Poppyseed	Blueberry	Total
Number of setups required	40	60	100
Number of inspections	275	350	625
Number of machine hours	1,500	750	2,250
Number of Engineering hours	65	70	135

Required:

1. Suppose Muffintop used a traditional costing system with machine hours as the cost driver. Determine the amount of overhead assigned to each product line.
2. Calculate the production cost per unit for each of Muffintop's products under a traditional costing system.
3. Calculate Muffintop's gross margin per unit for each product under the traditional costing system.
4. Select the appropriate cost driver for each cost pool and calculate the activity rates if Muffintop wanted to implement an ABC system.
5. Assuming an ABC system, assign overhead costs to each product based on activity demands.
6. Calculate the production cost per unit for each of Muffintop's products with an ABC system.
7. Calculate Muffintop's gross margin per unit for each product under an ABC system.
8. Compare the gross margin of each product under the traditional system and ABC.

LO3, 4 **PB4-4 Selecting Cost Drivers, Assigning Costs Using Activity Rates**

Wayward Company makes two models of automobile navigation system, the SeldomLost and the NeverLost.

Its basic production information follows:

	SeldomLost	NeverLost
Direct materials cost per unit	$ 92	$115
Direct labor cost per unit	$ 51	$ 75
Sales price per unit	$390	$615
Expected production per month	4,000 units	9,000 units

Wayward has monthly overhead of $521,870, which is divided into the following cost pools:

Setup costs	$170,455
Quality control	203,775
Maintenance	65,700
Engineering	81,940
Total	$521,870

The company has also compiled the following information about the chosen cost drivers:

	SeldomLost	NeverLost	Total
Number of setups required	60	86	146
Number of inspections	975	675	1,650
Number of machine hours	350	650	1,000
Number of Engineering hours	352	612	964

Required:

1. Suppose Muffintop used a traditional costing system with machine hours as the cost driver. Determine the amount of overhead assigned to each product line.
2. Calculate the production cost per unit for each of Wayward's products under a traditional costing system.
3. Calculate Wayward's gross margin per unit for each product under the traditional costing system.
4. Select the appropriate cost driver for each cost pool and calculate the activity rates if Wayward wanted to implement an ABC system.
5. Assuming an ABC system, assign overhead costs to each product based on activity demands.

6. Calculate the production cost per unit for each of Wayward's products with an ABC system.
7. Calculate Wayward's gross margin per unit for each product under an ABC system.
8. Compare the gross margin of each product under the traditional system and ABC.

PB4-5 Defining Concepts of Target Costing, Just in Time, and Lean Manufacturing

LO7

In recent years, the managerial concepts of target costing, just-in-time inventory systems, and lean manufacturing processes have received considerable attention from manufacturing companies. Increased competition in the marketplace and growing pressure have led companies to focus efforts on cost-cutting measures wherever possible while still generating acceptable profits.

Required:

1. Briefly define each of these concepts.
2. Conduct online or library research for articles about companies that have successfully utilized target costing, just-in-time inventory systems, and/or implemented lean manufacturing practices.
3. Read and briefly summarize at least three such articles.
4. Choose one of these companies and write a memo to your classmates outlining the company's utilization or implementation of these concepts. Include their time line, any problems encountered, and perceived benefits.

SKILLS DEVELOPMENT CASES

S4-1 Researching Companies That Have Implemented Activity Based Costing

LO7

Review recent issues of business publications (e.g., *BusinessWeek, The Wall Street Journal*) for information about companies that have implemented activity based costing. Choose one company to research in detail.

Required:

Answer the following questions:

1. Briefly describe the company, its products, and its history.
2. If the company has multiple divisions or segments, has one or more of them implemented activity based costing (ABC)?
3. If one or more divisions or segments use ABC, what factor(s) prompted the decision to do so?
4. What type of costing system was utilized prior to the conversion to ABC?
5. Were any specific difficulties experienced during the switch?
6. What benefits has the company or one or more of its divisions or segments identified as a result of implementing ABC?
7. Did the move to an ABC system impact other areas of the company and/or result in changes to other aspects of its operation?
8. Does the company view the ABC implementation as successful?

S4-2 Applying ABC Concepts to an Existing Business

LO3, 7

Existing businesses are often sold when the owner wants to retire, relocate, or simply change fields. Peruse your local newspaper or an online resource such as craigslist classifieds for businesses being offered for sale in your area and choose one that you would be interested in purchasing. Your choice should be an existing business that is already in operation as opposed to a franchise or start-up business opportunity.

Required:

1. Write a brief summary of the business, its product(s) or service(s), and why you are interested in this particular company. Include a photocopy or printout of the original advertisement.
2. Make a list of the costs you expect in order to operate your new company. Separate these costs into product costs (materials, labor, and overhead) and period costs.

3. Describe the process you will use to determine the price you charge for products or services.

4. Consider the costs you identified as overhead in requirement 3 above. Group these overhead costs into pools and choose an activity driver for each pool. Explain the rationale behind your pools and the drivers chosen. How will this help you price the products or services that your business provides?

5. List 5 ways that this ABC system might help you evaluate and improve the performance or profitability of your company.

LO2, 6   **S4-3 Applying ABC to the Restaurant Industry**

Restaurants such as Subway© generally offer a limited number of food categories (subs, salads, wraps, etc.) that are similarly priced. On the other hand, a restaurant such as Applebee's will have a broader menu in which each entrée is individually priced. Consider the "behind the scenes" operation of each restaurant.

Required:

1. Assuming that the prices reflect the restaurants' cost, explain why these two restaurants price their products so differently.

2. How might a Subway store's overhead differ from Applebee's? How could these differences impact the restaurants' costing systems?

3. Briefly explain a process that each might use to estimate product costs. Include overhead costs as well as whether/how those might be pooled. For any cost pools, identify an appropriate cost driver.

LO7   **S4-4 Researching Time Driven ABC**

Recently, Robert Kaplan and Steven Anderson have outlined a revised version of activity based costing known as Time Driven Activity Based Costing (TDABC). This updated method is intended to overcome some of the shortcomings of ABC and the problems companies often faced with implementation.

Required:

1. Conduct online research of TDABC and briefly summarize this new approach.

2. Describe the following:
   (a) The authors' reasons for revising the original ABC process
   (b) How TDABC is an improvement over traditional ABC
   (c) The benefits expected by a company that implements TDABC

3. In your opinion, will TDABC accomplish the authors' goals? Explain.

4. Consider the relationship between ABC and activity based management. With that in mind, what limitations might a company implementing TDABC encounter as opposed to a traditional ABC system?

LO1, 6, 7   **S4-5 Applying ABC to Small Businesses**

Read the article "Yes, ABC Is for Small Business Too" by Douglas T. Hicks, *Journal of Accountancy*, August 1999.
(http://www.journalofaccountancy.com/Issues/1999/Aug/hicks.htm)

Required:

1. According to Hicks, why have small companies avoided ABC?

2. Explain Small Company's costing system prior to the implementation of ABC.

3. What aspects of Small's operation suggest that the traditional system might not accurately reflect production costs?

4. Briefly describe the changes that Small's ABC team made in the costing system.

5. What benefits did Small Company experience after implementing ABC?

6. Describe the change in management's attitude that Hicks noted following ABC.

CHAPTER 5

Cost Behavior

YOUR LEARNING OBJECTIVES

After completing this chapter, you should be able to:

LO1   Identify costs as either variable, fixed, step, or mixed.

LO2   Prepare a scattergraph to illustrate the relationship between total cost and activity.

LO3   Use the high-low method to analyze mixed costs.

LO4   Use least-squares regression to analyze mixed costs.

LO5   Prepare and interpret a contribution margin income statement.

Lecture Presentation–LP5
www.mhhe.com/whitecotton1e

FOCUS COMPANY: Starbucks Coffee

"Beyond a Cup of Coffee"

www.starbucks.com

A s you sit with your friends in your local Starbucks Coffee shop, the conversation quickly turns to spring break and your plans to escape to your favorite destination (beach, mountain, or city) for a few days of relaxation. Assume that the major costs of the trip will be transportation, food, entertainment, and a condo that will sleep six to eight people. In planning the trip, you find yourself asking the following questions:

- How much can I afford to spend on this vacation?
- Should I fly or drive to my destination?
- How many people must go on the trip to keep it affordable yet enjoyable?
- How many nights can I afford to stay and remain within my budget?

Answering these questions requires you to understand cost behavior, the topic of this chapter. Cost behavior relates to the way in which total and per unit costs change as a result of a change in something else. In the spring break example, costs of transportation, food, entertainment, and lodging all behave in different ways depending on the choice of flying or driving, the number of people on the trip, and the number of nights stayed. Understanding these cost behavior patterns is the key to helping you decide whether you can afford the trip, whether to drive or fly, how many nights to stay, and how many people to invite along.

In business, managers make a variety of decisions, such as what product or service to offer, what type of equipment to buy, how many workers to hire, how many units to produce, and whether to make or buy components. Managers must understand cost behavior in order to make these decisions. In this chapter and the next, we use a hypothetical Starbucks Coffee shop to illustrate the role of cost behavior in managerial decision making. We lay the foundation in this chapter by identifying cost behavior patterns and analyzing mixed costs. In the next chapter, we apply the cost behavior concepts to a managerial decision-making technique called cost-volume-profit analysis.

As always, we make a number of simplifying assumptions, but use of this familiar company should allow you to understand how to apply the concepts of cost behavior to a real-world business setting.

ORGANIZATION OF THE CHAPTER

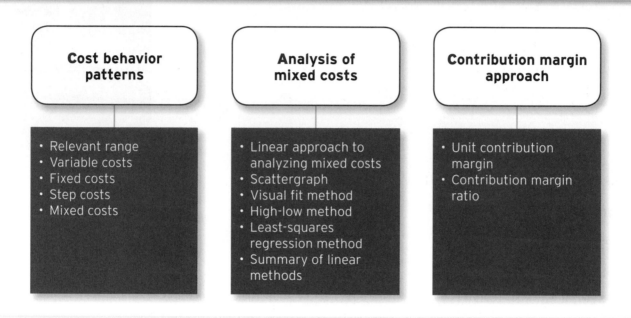

Cost behavior patterns	Analysis of mixed costs	Contribution margin approach
• Relevant range • Variable costs • Fixed costs • Step costs • Mixed costs	• Linear approach to analyzing mixed costs • Scattergraph • Visual fit method • High-low method • Least-squares regression method • Summary of linear methods	• Unit contribution margin • Contribution margin ratio

The previous four chapters described how to calculate the cost of a physical product such as a Tombstone pizza, Toll Brothers custom home, CK Mondavi wine, or Toyota automobile. The method used to determine the cost of these products depended on the type of product (job order costing for diverse products and process costing for homogeneous products) and the need to capture the underlying activities required to make the products (activity-based costing). Although the mechanics of the various costing methods differ, all have the same basic objective: to calculate the full manufacturing cost of each unit produced. This product costing information was used to determine Cost of Goods Sold (on the Income Statement) and the value of Work in Process Inventory and Finished Goods Inventory (on the Balance Sheet).

The costing systems described in the previous chapters were all examples of **full absorption costing**, a costing method that assigns **all manufacturing costs** to the product as it is being produced. Full absorption costing methods are based on GAAP's requirement that all manufacturing costs be treated as **product costs;** that is, all manufacturing costs must be traced to the product and included as inventory until the product is sold.

Although full absorption costing is required for external reporting, this method is not always useful for internal management decision making. For internal purposes, managers often need information that is based on cost behavior. In other words, managers need to know how costs will change as a result of a specific decision, such as introducing a new product, selling more units, or investing in automated equipment. In addition, full absorption costing methods can sometimes give managers incentives to "overproduce," or produce more units than the market demands. While doing so drives down the cost per unit and has a positive effect on short-term accounting profit, it may not be worth it in the long run because of increased inventory costs such as obsolescence, quality problems, storage, and insurance. The supplement to this chapter covers this limitation of full absorption costing as well as a more detailed discussion of the differences between full absorption and variable costing.

In this chapter, we shift gears from product costing to focus on **cost behavior.** Instead of classifying costs as either manufacturing (product) or nonmanufacturing (period) costs, we now classify costs based on **how they behave in response to a change in some measure of activity.** A solid understanding of cost behavior is the key to almost all of the managerial decision-making approaches discussed throughout the remainder of this book.

Cost Behavior Patterns

Cost behavior is defined as the way in which total cost behaves, or changes, when some measure of activity changes. Activities that cause total cost to change are referred to as **cost drivers**. Some of the most common activity measures include the number of direct labor hours, machine hours, units produced, and customers served. As you learned in Chapter 4, these are all examples of volume-based cost drivers. Other factors that drive cost, such as the number of setups, orders, and shipments, are examples of nonvolume-based cost drivers. For simplicity, we focus on how costs behave or change in response to changes in the number of units produced or customers served.

RELEVANT RANGE

When we analyze costs based on behavior, we must limit the range of analysis to the **relevant range**, or the range of activity over which we expect our assumptions about cost behavior to hold true. For example, we will use a straight line to describe the relationship between total cost and activity. In reality, the relationship between total cost and activity probably is not perfectly linear. However, as long as we limit our analysis to a fairly narrow range of activity—that is, the relevant range—we can **assume** that the relationship is linear and come close to estimating true cost behavior.

The relevant range also applies to fixed costs. When we say that a cost is fixed, it will only hold true over a limited range of activity. At some point, fixed costs must increase to accommodate more activity.

When analyzing cost behavior, it is important to limit the analysis to the relevant range and be aware that our conclusions may not be valid outside that range of activity.

VARIABLE COSTS

Variable costs are those that change **in total** in direct proportion to changes in activity. If activity increases by 50 percent, total variable costs should also increase by 50 percent. If activity decreases by 20 percent, total variable costs should also decrease by 20 percent. Examples of variable costs incurred by Starbucks Coffee include coffee beans, milk, sugar, cups, and paper products. All of these costs will increase, in total, as Starbucks sells more coffee drinks.

Although **total** variable costs change with activity, variable cost **per unit** remains constant. For example, the cost of coffee used in each cup should be the same regardless of how many cups are served. This ignores any discount that a company may receive by purchasing ingredients "in bulk," or in large quantities.

See Exhibit 5.1 for charts of how the total and per unit variable cost for ingredients such as coffee beans changes with the number of coffee drinks served.

As the graph in Exhibit 5.1 on the left shows, the total cost of ingredients increases in direct proportion to increases in the number of coffee drinks served. As the graph on

> **COACH'S TIP**
>
> You can think of the relevant range as a company's "normal" operating range. If we try to extend our analysis beyond the normal range, our assumptions may not hold true.

> **Learning Objective 1**
> Identify costs as either variable, fixed, step, or mixed.

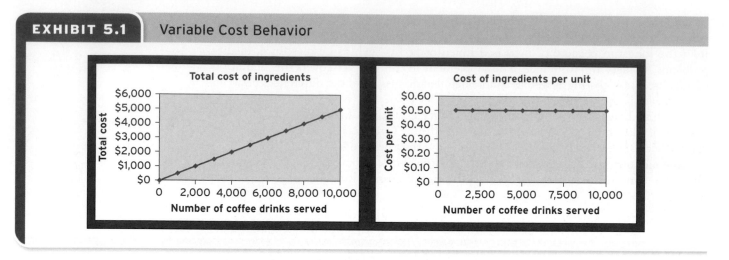

EXHIBIT 5.1 | Variable Cost Behavior

the right shows, however, the **per unit** cost of ingredients remains constant, regardless of how many drinks are served.

FIXED COSTS

Fixed costs remain the same **in total** regardless of activity level. For Starbucks Coffee fixed costs include rent, manager salaries, depreciation on equipment, and insurance. These costs remain the same, in total, regardless of how many coffee drinks are served each month. On a **per unit** basis, however, fixed costs decrease with increases in activity levels (see Exhibit 5.2).

The idea that unit fixed costs decrease with increases in activity levels is an important concept, but may give managers the mistaken impression that they can increase profits simply by increasing the number of units produced during a given time period. As an extreme example, imagine what would happen if a Starbucks manager decided to make as many cups of coffee as possible each day regardless of whether there were enough customers to buy them. Although doing so would drive down the unit cost of each cup, it would also result in a lot of coffee being thrown away, with no revenue from customers to cover the cost.

Although this example may seem far-fetched, it is not uncommon for managers to believe that they can drive down costs by producing as many units as possible. The difference is that in most companies, the unsold units are not thrown away at the end of the day like a cold cup of coffee. Instead, unsold units are stored in a warehouse as

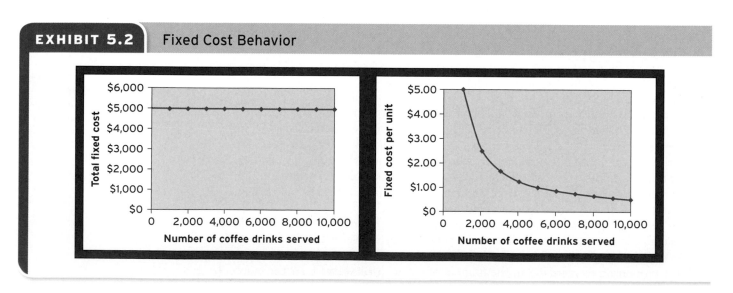

EXHIBIT 5.2 | Fixed Cost Behavior

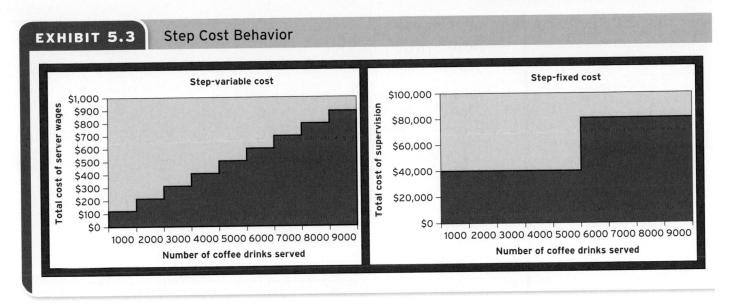

EXHIBIT 5.3 | Step Cost Behavior

inventory—a solution that adds unnecessary costs for insurance, storage, handling, and so on. The bottom line is that while increasing production lowers the average cost of each unit produced (because the fixed costs are spread over more units), it does not translate into increased profit unless sales also increase.

STEP COSTS

Step costs are fixed over a range of activity and then increase in a steplike fashion when a capacity limit is reached. Depending on the width of the steps, step costs may be treated as either step-variable or step-fixed costs, as shown in Exhibit 5.3.

As the graph on the left in Exhibit 5.3 shows, **step-variable costs** tend to be fixed over a fairly narrow range of activity and rise in multiple steps across the relevant range. At Starbucks Coffee, a step-variable cost includes the wages paid to servers. Starbucks relies heavily on part-time labor, and managers try to schedule more workers when more customers are expected. Once employees are on the job, however, they must be paid regardless of how many customers they serve. Because the steps are so narrow and the total cost increases with the number of coffee drinks served, Starbucks can treat the cost of server wages as a variable cost.

As the graph on the right side of Exhibit 5.3 shows, **step-fixed costs** are fixed over a much wider range of activity than step-variable costs. To allow more customers to be served, for example, Starbucks might hire an additional supervisor or rent additional space or equipment. Because these costs are fixed over a fairly wide range of activity, they are treated as fixed costs, at least within a limited range of activity.

MIXED COSTS

Mixed costs, also known as **semivariable costs,** have both a fixed and a variable component. The fixed portion represents the base amount that will be incurred regardless of activity. The variable cost is the amount that is based on activity or usage. An example of a mixed cost is a cell phone plan that has a fixed charge each month plus an additional charge for each minute of usage or each text message sent. Most utility expenses behave the same way. Companies incur a minimum charge each month regardless of activity, but the total utility expense increases with increased activity, measured by kilowatt hours or gallons of water used.

The next section shows how to separate the fixed and variable components of mixed costs. First take a moment to make sure you understand the difference between fixed, variable, step, and mixed costs by completing the following Self-Study Practice.

COACH'S TIP

Think of fixed costs as "buying" a limited amount of capacity. In the spring break example, renting the condo provides the capacity to sleep up to eight people. If more than eight come on the trip, it may be necessary to rent another unit, which will add more cost. Thus, the cost of lodging is "fixed" only within a limited range.

Self-Study Practice

1. Which of the following statements is true?
   a. If activity increases by 10 percent, total fixed cost will increase by 10 percent.
   b. If activity increases by 10 percent, per unit variable cost will increase by 10 percent.
   c. If activity increases by 10 percent, per unit fixed cost will decrease by 10 percent.
   d. If activity increases by 10 percent, total variable cost will increase by 10 percent.

2. For each row in the following table, indicate whether the cost is variable, fixed, step, or mixed.

	UNITS OF ACTIVITY				
	0 Units	100 Units	200 Units	300 Units	400 Units
Total cost of A	$ 0	$200	$400	$600	$800
Total cost of B	500	500	500	750	750
Total cost of C	350	400	450	500	550
Total cost of D	750	750	750	750	750

After you have finished, check your answers with the solutions in the margin.

Analysis of Mixed Costs

To make decisions, managers must be able to estimate how costs will change as a result of a specific decision, such as introducing a new product or producing more units. While it is fairly easy to predict what will happen for variable costs and fixed costs, mixed costs are more difficult because they contain both fixed and variable components.

Our goal in analyzing mixed costs is to identify how much of the cost is fixed and how much of it varies with a particular activity driver. We know from the previous section that variable and fixed costs behave differently, so it is important to sort out these two effects for managerial decision making. Later in the chapter, we introduce a decision-making framework called the contribution margin income statement. This framework, which classifies costs as either variable or fixed, provides the foundation for analyzing many managerial decisions.

LINEAR APPROACH TO ANALYZING MIXED COSTS

The three methods we use to analyze mixed costs are based on the **linearity assumption**, or the assumption that the relationship between total cost and activity can be approximated by a straight line, as shown in the following formulas:

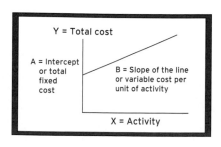

$$Y = A + B(X)$$

$$\text{Total Cost} = \text{Fixed Cost} + \text{Variable Cost per Unit} \times \text{Activity Level}$$

Y = Total cost

A = Intercept or total fixed cost

B = Slope of the line or variable cost per unit of activity

X = Activity

These terms are interpreted as follows.

- **Y** is total cost, which is shown on the vertical axis. It is called the **dependent variable** because we assume that Y is dependent on X.

- **X** is the activity that causes Y (total cost) to change. This variable is also called the **cost driver** or the **independent variable.**

- **A** is the amount of cost that will be incurred regardless of activity level (X), or the **total fixed cost.** This term is also called the **intercept term** or the **constant.**

- **B** indicates how much Y (total cost) will increase with each additional unit of X (activity). In other words, **B** is the **variable cost per unit of X** and is represented by the **slope** of the line.

SCATTERGRAPH

Learning Objective 2
Prepare a scattergraph to illustrate the relationship between total cost and activity.

The first step in analyzing mixed cost is to prepare a visual representation of the relationship between total cost and activity. A **scattergraph** is a graph with total cost plotted on the vertical (Y) axis and a measure of activity, or cost driver, plotted on the horizontal (X) axis. A scattergraph is useful for getting a "feel" for the data and helps answer preliminary questions such as whether the linear assumption is reasonable and whether there are unusual patterns or outliers in the data.

As an example, consider the following data showing total overhead cost (Y) and the number of customers served (X) for our hypothetical Starbucks location.

Month	Number of Customers Served (X)	Total Overhead Cost (Y)
January	9,000	$15,000
February	15,000	15,750
March	12,500	16,000
April	6,000	12,500
May	5,000	13,250
June	10,000	13,000

A scattergraph can be created by manually plotting data points on graph paper or by using a computer program such as Excel.

To prepare a scattergraph, plot the number of customers served on the horizontal (X) axis and total overhead cost on the vertical (Y) axis. See Exhibit 5.4 for an illustration of how to create a scattergraph of these data using Excel.

The resulting scattergraph (see Exhibit 5.5) reveals a slightly positive relationship between total overhead cost (Y) and the number of customers served (X). In general, as the number of customers increases, the total overhead cost also increases. Although the points do not fall in a perfect line, we can use a straight line to approximate, or estimate, the relationship.

Once a scattergraph has been created and we have confirmed that the relationship between total cost and activity is roughly linear, the next step is to fit a line through the data that will provide an estimate of total fixed cost (intercept) and variable cost per unit (slope). There are several ways to "fit the line":

- The **visual fit method** involves "eye balling" the data on the scattergraph and drawing a line through the graph to capture the relationship between total cost and activity. This method is simple and intuitive but is very subjective and does not provide very precise estimates of the intercept (fixed cost) and slope (variable cost per unit).

- The **high-low method** uses the two most extreme activity (X) observations to "fit the line." This method uses only two data points to solve for variable cost per unit (slope) and total fixed cost (intercept). We illustrate this method in detail in a later section.

- **Least-squares regression** is a statistical technique for finding the best fitting line based on all available data points. Although it is more complicated than the high-low method, a spreadsheet program such as Excel can be used to do the calculations.

EXHIBIT 5.4   Scattergraph Creation in Excel

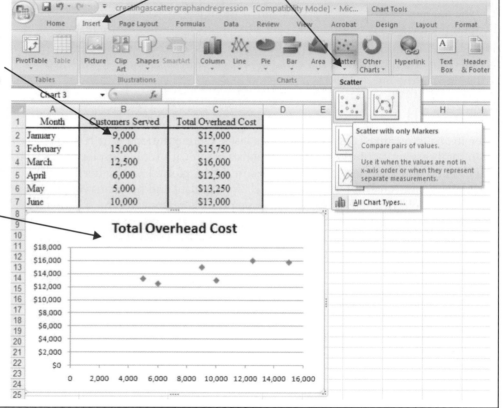

Step 1: Enter the data and highlight the information to include in the graph.

Step 2: Select Insert from the main menu and Scatter as the chart type.

Step 3: Edit and label the graph.

Month	Customers Served	Total Overhead Cost
January	9,000	$15,000
February	15,000	$15,750
March	12,500	$16,000
April	6,000	$12,500
May	5,000	$13,250
June	10,000	$13,000

COACH'S TIP

Draw a straight line through this data that you think best captures the relationship between total overhead cost (Y) and customers served (X).

The point where your line intercepts the Y axis is your estimate of the total fixed cost.

The slope of the line is your estimate of the variable cost per customer served.

EXHIBIT 5.5   Scattergraph of Total Overhead Cost (Y) and Customers Served (X)

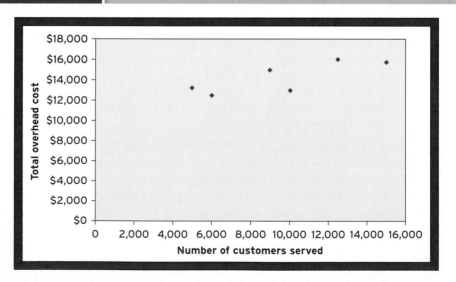

VISUAL FIT METHOD

To illustrate the visual fit method, try drawing a line through Exhibit 5.5 that you think best captures the relationship between total overhead cost and the number of customers served. Where does your line intercept the Y axis, and what does this value represent? Depending on how you drew your line, it will probably intercept the Y axis somewhere between $10,000 and $14,000. The intercept represents the amount of overhead cost that will be incurred even if no customers are served, or the total fixed cost. Some overhead costs, such as rent and insurance, will be incurred even if the store is closed and are therefore considered fixed costs.

If your line slopes upward, the total cost increases with the number of customers served, indicating a variable cost. The steeper the slope, the higher the variable cost per customer served, but it is difficult to determine the exact slope of the line by looking at the scattergraph.

As you can see, the visual fit method is very subjective and not very exact. The high-low method and least-squares regression will provide more precise estimates of the intercept (fixed cost) and slope of the line (variable cost per unit). The interpretation of the intercept and slope, however, is the same as for the visual fit method.

HIGH-LOW METHOD

The high-low method calculates the line based on the two most extreme activity (X) data points. Although it only uses two points, this approach may provide a reasonable estimate of the fixed and variable costs as long as the high and low data points represent the general trend in the data, which appears to be the case in this example.

The first step in the high-low method is to find the two most extreme activity (X) observations. The data we have been using for our Starbucks example follow:

Learning Objective 3
Use the high-low method to analyze mixed costs.

Month	Number of Customers Served (X)	Total Overhead Cost (Y)	
January	9,000	$15,000	
February	15,000	15,750	High X
March	12,500	16,000	
April	6,000	12,500	
May	5,000	13,250	Low X
June	10,000	13,000	

COACH'S TIP

Be sure to pick the highest and lowest X (customers served). Notice that this is not necessarily the same as the highest and lowest Y (total cost).

The high-low method will use the high (February) and low (May) data points to estimate the variable cost per unit and the total fixed cost. It ignores all of the other months.

The second step is to calculate the slope of the line based on the high and low data points. You may recall from your high school algebra class that the slope of a line is calculated as "rise over run," or the change in Y over the change in X. We use the same logic here to calculate how much total cost (Y) changes with a corresponding change in activity level (X).

$$\text{Variable Cost per Unit} = \frac{\text{Difference in Total Cost } (Y_1 - Y_2)}{\text{Difference in Activity } (X_1 - X_2)}$$

Applying this formula to the data from February and May results in the following:

$$\text{Variable Cost per Unit} = \frac{\$15,750 - \$13,250 = \$2,500}{15,000 - 5,000 = 10,000} = \$0.25 \text{ per Unit}$$

COACH'S TIP

Students sometimes wonder if it matters whether they subtract the high values from the low, or the low values from the high. As long as you use the same order for both the numerator and the denominator, the result will be the same.

This formula shows that total overhead cost increased by $2,500 when the number of customers served increased by 10,000. Thus, the slope of the line, or variable cost per unit, is $0.25 per customer served.

Now that we know the variable cost per unit (slope), the third step is to solve for total fixed cost (intercept) using the following equation:

$$\boxed{\begin{matrix}\text{Total}\\\text{Fixed Cost}\end{matrix}} = \boxed{\begin{matrix}\text{Total}\\\text{Cost}\end{matrix}} - \boxed{\begin{matrix}\text{Total Variable Cost}\\\text{(Variable Cost per Unit} \times \text{X)}\end{matrix}}$$

Because we now know that the variable cost is $0.25 per customer served we can use **either** the high **or** the low data point to solve for the fixed cost. The high and low data points for our Starbucks example follow.

Month	Number of Customers Served (X)	Total Overhead Cost (Y)	
February	15,000	$15,750	High X
May	5,000	13,250	Low X

First let's use the data from February to solve for the total fixed cost:

$$\boxed{\begin{matrix}\text{Total}\\\text{Fixed Cost}\end{matrix}} = \boxed{\begin{matrix}\text{Total Cost}\\\text{(February)}\\\$15,750\end{matrix}} - \boxed{\begin{matrix}\text{Total Variable Cost (February)}\\\$0.25 \times 15,000 \text{ Customers Served}\\\$3,750\end{matrix}} = \boxed{\$12,000}$$

We get exactly the same result if we use May instead:

$$\boxed{\begin{matrix}\text{Total}\\\text{Fixed Cost}\end{matrix}} = \boxed{\begin{matrix}\text{Total Cost}\\\text{(May)}\\\$13,250\end{matrix}} - \boxed{\begin{matrix}\text{Total Variable Cost (May)}\\\$0.25 \times 5,000 \text{ Customers Served}\\\$1,250\end{matrix}} = \boxed{\$12,000}$$

Regardless of whether we use the high (February) or low (May) data point, we get total fixed cost of $12,000.

See Exhibit 5.6 for a visual depiction of the results of the high-low method. Notice that the line is drawn so that it goes through the most extreme (high and low) values on the horizontal (X) axis. Notice also that the line intersects the Y axis at $12,000, which is the estimate of total fixed cost. Although it is difficult to determine the slope of the line from the graph, we know from the high-low formula that the variable cost (slope) is $0.25 per customer served.

To summarize, the high-low method estimates total overhead cost as follows:

$$\boxed{\begin{matrix}\text{Total}\\\text{Overhead}\\\text{Cost}\end{matrix}} = \boxed{\begin{matrix}\text{Total}\\\text{Fixed Cost}\\\$12,000\end{matrix}} + \boxed{\begin{matrix}\text{Total}\\\text{Variable Cost}\\\$.25 \times \text{Customers Served}\end{matrix}}$$

We can use this formula to predict total overhead cost in the future so long as we have an estimate of the number of customers to be served and it falls within the relevant range. For example, if Starbucks expects to serve 8,000 customers in July, it would budget for $12,000 in fixed overhead cost plus $2,000 ($0.25 × 8,000 customers) in variable costs for a total overhead of $14,000.

The high-low method is simple to apply, but it suffers from a major (and sometimes critical) defect. It utilizes only two data points. Generally, two points are not enough to produce reliable results. Additionally, periods in which the activity is unusually low or unusually high may produce inaccurate results. A cost formula that is estimated solely using data

EXHIBIT 5.6 | **High-Low Method Shown on the Scattergraph**

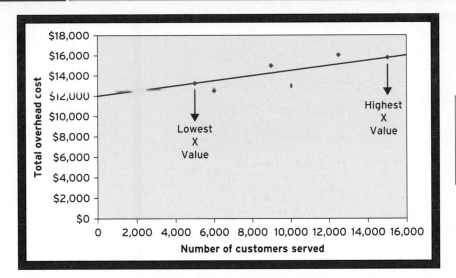

Notice that the line intercepts the Y axis at $12,000. The slope of the line is $0.25 per customer served.

from these unusual periods may seriously misrepresent the true cost relationship that holds during normal periods. Other methods of cost analysis that utilize a larger number of data points generally are more accurate than the high-low method. A manager who chooses to use the high-low method should do so with a full awareness of the method's limitations.

The next section illustrates the use of least-squares regression method, a linear approach that uses all available data to find the best fitting line. First, complete the following Self-Study Practice to make sure you understand how to estimate fixed and variable costs using the high-low method.

 Self-Study Practice

A travel agent has collected the following information regarding the number of reservations made and the total cost of running the agency for the past four months:

Month	Number of Reservations Booked	Total Cost
January	600	$41,000
February	400	32,000
March	860	55,000
April	740	56,000

Using the high-low method, determine the variable cost per reservation and the total fixed cost.

After you have finished, check your answers with the solutions in the margin.

Solution to Self-Study Practice
High (March): 860 reservations $55,000
Low (February): 400 reservations $32,000

Variable Cost = ($55,000 − $32,000) / (860 − 400) = $23,000 / 460
= $50 per reservation

Total Fixed Cost = $55,000 − ($50 × 860) = $12,000
or $32,000 − ($50 × 400) = $12,000

LEAST-SQUARES REGRESSION METHOD

Least-squares regression is a statistical technique that uses all of the available data to find the best fitting line. The best fitting line is the one that minimizes the sum of the squared errors, where error is the difference between the regression prediction and the actual data values, as shown in Exhibit 5.7.

Learning Objective 4
Use least-squares regression to analyze mixed costs.

EXHIBIT 5.7   Least-Squares Regression Approach

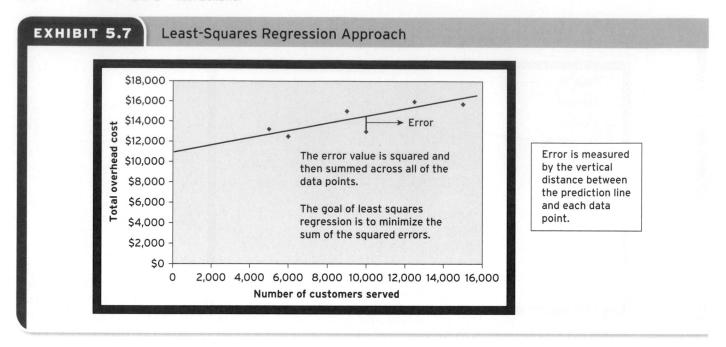

The error value is squared and then summed across all of the data points.

The goal of least squares regression is to minimize the sum of the squared errors.

Error is measured by the vertical distance between the prediction line and each data point.

The goal of least-squares regression is to find the line that minimizes the total squared value of the error terms.

Although the formulas for finding the line that minimizes the sum of squared error are cumbersome, computer programs and statistical packages make calculating least-squares regression very easy. It takes only a few clicks of the mouse to obtain regression results, but it is critical that you understand what the results mean and how to use them for managerial decision making.

Exhibit 5.8 shows how to calculate least-squares regression using Excel. Other computer programs and statistical calculators will produce similar output. The key is to correctly interpret the results. One word of caution is that we generally need more than six data points to get reliable regression results. But for simplicity and comparison, we use the same data that we used for the high-low method.

The regression method uses all available data to find the best fitting line or the one that minimizes the sum of the squared error around the regression line. The regression output also provides information about the "goodness of fit" of the model, or how well the regression line fits the data points. The most common measure of goodness of fit is the R square value. **R square** tells managers how much of the variability in the Y variable (total cost) is explained by the X variable (number of customers served). The closer the R squared value is to 1, the more reliable the results. In our Starbucks example, the number of customers served explains about 64 percent of the variation in total overhead cost, with the remaining 36 percent unexplained.

The regression output also provides an estimate of the total fixed cost (intercept) and variable cost per unit (slope of the line). In this example, the estimate of total fixed overhead cost is $11,181, and the estimate of the variable cost is $0.32 per customer served. Based on these regression results, we can estimate total overhead cost as follows:

$$\text{Total Overhead Cost} = \text{Total Fixed Cost } \$11{,}181 + \text{Total Variable Cost } \$0.32 \times \text{Number of Customers Served}$$

EXHIBIT 5.8   Steps for Calculating Regression in Excel

Step 1: Enter the data into Excel. Click on the data tab from the main menu.

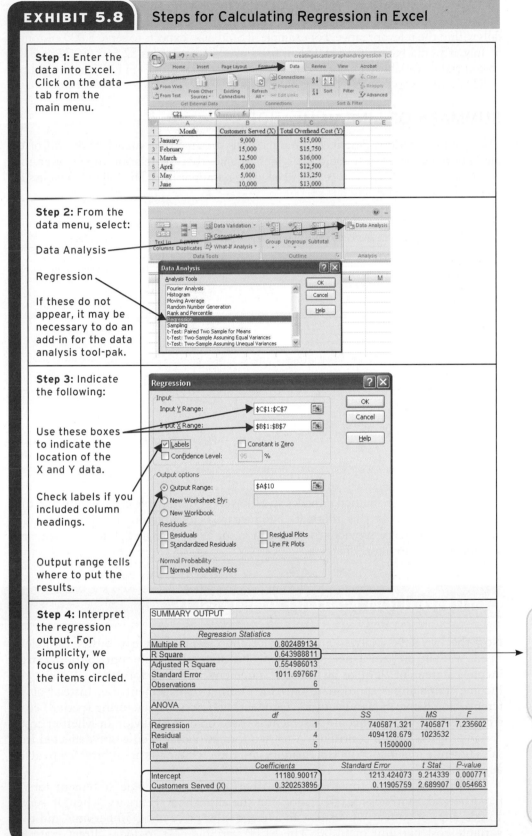

	A	B	C	D	E
1	Month	Customers Served (X)	Total Overhead Cost (Y)		
2	January	9,000	$15,000		
3	February	15,000	$15,750		
4	March	12,500	$16,000		
5	April	6,000	$12,500		
6	May	5,000	$13,250		
7	June	10,000	$13,000		

Step 2: From the data menu, select:

Data Analysis

Regression

If these do not appear, it may be necessary to do an add-in for the data analysis tool-pak.

Data Analysis

Analysis Tools

Fourier Analysis
Histogram
Moving Average
Random Number Generation
Rank and Percentile
Regression
Sampling
t-Test: Paired Two Sample for Means
t-Test: Two-Sample Assuming Equal Variances
t-Test: Two-Sample Assuming Unequal Variances

OK   Cancel   Help

Step 3: Indicate the following:

Use these boxes to indicate the location of the X and Y data.

Check labels if you included column headings.

Output range tells where to put the results.

Regression

Input

Input Y Range: $C$1:$C$7

Input X Range: $B$1:$B$7

☑ Labels   ☐ Constant is Zero

☐ Confidence Level: 95 %

Output options

◉ Output Range: $A$10
○ New Worksheet Ply:
○ New Workbook

Residuals

☐ Residuals   ☐ Residual Plots
☐ Standardized Residuals   ☐ Line Fit Plots

Normal Probability

☐ Normal Probability Plots

OK   Cancel   Help

Step 4: Interpret the regression output. For simplicity, we focus only on the items circled.

SUMMARY OUTPUT

Regression Statistics	
Multiple R	0.802489134
R Square	0.643988811
Adjusted R Square	0.554986013
Standard Error	1011.697667
Observations	6

ANOVA

	df	SS	MS	F
Regression	1	7405871.321	7405871	7.235602
Residual	4	4094128.679	1023532	
Total	5	11500000		

	Coefficients	Standard Error	t Stat	P-value
Intercept	11180.90017	1213.424073	9.214339	0.000771
Customers Served (X)	0.320253895	0.11905759	2.689907	0.054663

 **COACH'S TIP**

R square is a measure of the model's explanatory power. Higher values are better. Here, the number of customers explains about 64% of overhead cost.

 **COACH'S TIP**

Estimated fixed cost is $11,181. Estimated variable cost is $0.32 per customer served.

We can use the regression results to predict total overhead cost in the future so long as we have an estimate of the number of customers to be served and this level of activity falls within the relevant range. For example, if Starbucks expects to serve 8,000 customers in July, it would budget for $11,181 in fixed overhead cost plus $2,560 ($0.32 × 8,000 customers) in variable costs for a total overhead cost of $13,741 ($11,181 total fixed cost + $2,560 total variable cost).

SUMMARY OF LINEAR METHODS

The previous sections described three methods for analyzing mixed costs. All of the methods relied on a linear approach, which assumes that the relationship between total cost (Y) and activity (X) can be described using a straight line. The following table summarizes the three methods:

Method	Approach	Estimating Variable and Fixed Cost	Advantages	Limitations
Visual fit method	Draw a line through the scattergraph that captures the relationship between X and Y	Fixed Cost = Y Intercept Variable Cost = Slope of the Line	Simple and intuitive	Not very precise
High-low method	Use the highest and lowest X values to fit the line	Variable Cost per Unit $= \dfrac{(Y1 - Y2)}{(X1 - X2)}$ Fixed Cost = Total Cost − Variable Cost (based on either high or low X)	Simple and intuitive	Uses only two data points, which may not represent the general trend in the data
Least-squares regression	Use a statistical package to find the line that minimizes the sum of squared error terms	Intercept = Total Fixed Cost X Coefficient = Variable Cost per Unit of X	Uses all data points Easy to calculate in Excel	Requires more data and assumptions Proper interpretation of results is critical

Notice that each method provides an estimate of the variable cost per unit and total fixed cost. Next we use this information to prepare a contribution margin income statement. This statement provides the foundation for many managerial decision scenarios we will evaluate in future chapters.

Contribution Margin Approach

Learning Objective 5
Prepare and interpret a contribution margin income statement.

Now that we have analyzed cost behavior and classified costs as either variable or fixed, we can prepare a new type of income statement, the **contribution margin income statement**. Unlike an income statement intended for external users, this income statement is appropriate only for internal management use. Instead of differentiating between manufacturing (product) and nonmanufacturing (period) costs, a contribution margin income statement is based on cost behavior, or whether cost is variable or fixed. In a contribution margin format, variable costs are deducted from sales revenue to get contribution margin, and then fixed costs are subtracted to arrive at profit.

To illustrate, let's construct a contribution margin income statement for our hypothetical Starbucks Coffee shop for the month of February when it served 15,000 cups of coffee. We assume an average sales price of $2.50 per unit and total variable cost per unit of $1.00. The $1.00 variable cost includes direct materials (coffee, cups, etc.) and direct labor (server wages) plus the variable portion of the overhead cost (supplies, electricity, etc.). We assume that total fixed overhead costs are $12,000. Using this information, the contribution margin income statement would appear as follows:

STARBUCKS COFFEE Contribution Margin Income Statement For the Month of February 2009 15,000 Units Sold			
	Total	Per Unit	Percent of Sales
Sales revenue	$37,500	$2.50	100%
Less: Variable costs	15,000	1.00	40
Contribution margin	22,500	$1.50	60%
Less: Fixed costs	12,000		
Profit (loss)	$10,500		

Contribution margin is the difference between sales revenue and variable costs:

Contribution margin represents the amount left from sales revenue after variable costs have been covered to contribute toward fixed costs and profit. In this example, the total contribution margin earned on 15,000 units sold is $22,500 ($37,500 − $15,000). When the fixed costs of $12,000 are subtracted, the profit is $10,500.

The contribution margin income statement is not used for external reporting (GAAP). Rather, it provides a tool for managers to do "what-if" analysis or to analyze what will happen to profit if something changes. To do so, managers focus on either the unit contribution margin or the contribution margin as a percentage of sales.

UNIT CONTRIBUTION MARGIN

The **unit contribution margin** tells us how much each additional unit sold contributes to the bottom line. Because fixed costs do not change with volume (at least within the relevant range), each additional unit sold contributes $1.50 to profit.

What would happen if Starbucks sold 16,000 cups of coffee instead of 15,000? As long as this is within the relevant range of operations (i.e., fixed costs will not increase), we can quickly determine that an extra 1,000 units will add $1,500 (1,000 × $1.50) to the bottom line. We can verify this answer by creating a new contribution margin income statement based on 16,000 units, as follows:

STARBUCKS COFFEE Contribution Margin Income Statement For the Month of March 2009 16,000 Units Sold			
	Total	Per Unit	Percent of Sales
Sales revenue	$40,000	$2.50	100%
Less: Variable costs	16,000	1.00	40
Contribution margin	24,000	$1.50	60%
Less: Fixed costs	12,000		
Profit (loss)	$12,000		

In the next chapter, we use the unit contribution margin to address a number of scenarios involving the relationship between cost, volume, and profit.

CONTRIBUTION MARGIN RATIO

The contribution margin can also be stated as a ratio or percentage of sales. The **contribution margin ratio** is calculated as follows:

The contribution margin ratio tells managers how much contribution margin is generated by every dollar of sales. In this case, every dollar of sales generates $0.60 in contribution margin. Because total fixed costs do not change with changes in volume (at least within the relevant range), any change in contribution margin will fall directly to the bottom line.

As an example, assume Starbucks' manager is thinking of spending an extra $2,000 each month for local advertising. She believes the increased exposure will increase monthly sales revenue by $5,000. Should she do it?

Because we know that the contribution margin ratio is 60 percent, we can quickly determine that a $5,000 increase in sales revenue will increase the contribution margin by $3,000. Of course, fixed costs would go up by $2,000 for the additional advertising expense. The net effect on profit would be a $1,000 increase as follows:

Increased sales		$5,000
Less: Increased variable costs		2,000
Increased contribution margin	($5,000 × 60%)	3,000
Increased fixed expenses		2,000
Increased profit		1,000

In the next chapter, we use the contribution margin approach to evaluate how changes in product prices, sales volume, or costs affect contribution margin and thus profit. Take a moment to complete the following Self-Study Practice to make sure you understand how to prepare a contribution margin income statement.

> **COACH'S TIP**
>
> The contribution margin ratio provides a shortcut for determining the effect of an increase in sales on profit. Another way to find the effect is to prepare two contribution margin income statements and see whether profit increases or decreases. Although this approach takes longer, it is a good way to verify the calculations.

Self-Study Practice

In the same month that a company sold 750 units for $80 each, it reported total variable costs of $45,000 and total fixed expenses of $10,000.
Calculate the following:

1. Total contribution margin.
2. Contribution margin per unit.
3. Contribution margin ratio.
4. Profit (loss).

After you have finished, check your answers with the solutions in the margin.

Solution to Self-Study Practice

1. (750 × $80) − $45,000 = $15,000
2. $15,000/750 = $20
3. $20/$80 = 25%
4. $15,000 − $10,000 = $5,000

SUPPLEMENT 5: VARIABLE VERSUS FULL ABSORPTION COSTING

As explained in the first chapters of this book, GAAP requires that all manufacturing costs be treated as part of the cost of the product and counted as inventory until the product is sold. This approach is called **full absorption costing** because the product must "fully absorb" all costs incurred to produce it. The distinction between product and period costs is relevant only for companies that sell a physical product that can be stored as inventory. It is not relevant for service companies that do not store physical products as inventory.

As the name implies, **variable costing** is based on the distinction between variable costs and fixed costs. Variable costing is used only for internal decision making and does not meet GAAP external reporting requirements.

See Exhibit 5A.1 for a summary of the key differences between variable costing and full absorption costing.

EXHIBIT 5A.1 — Calculation and Uses of Full Absorption Costing and Variable Costing

	Full Absorption Costing	Variable Costing
Purpose	External financial reporting (GAAP)	Internal decision making
Cost classification	Manufacturing versus nonmanufacturing costs	Variable versus fixed costs
Income statement formulas	Sales	Sales
	− Cost of goods sold	− Variable costs
	Gross margin	**Contribution margin**
	− Nonmanufacturing expenses	− Fixed expenses
	Net income from operations	Net profit
Treatment of fixed manufacturing overhead	Divided between cost of goods sold and ending inventory	Expensed during the period incurred

---

Full absorption costing is based on the distinction between manufacturing and non-manufacturing costs. **Gross margin** is the difference between sales revenue and the cost of goods sold. For external reporting (GAAP), cost of goods sold reflects the full manufacturing cost of the units sold. The full manufacturing cost of units manufactured but not sold is counted as inventory on the balance sheet. Nonmanufacturing costs are expensed immediately and subtracted after gross margin to arrive at net operating income.

Variable costing captures the distinction between variable and fixed costs and ignores whether the costs are related to manufacturing or nonmanufacturing activities. The difference between sales revenue and variable costs is called **contribution margin.** Fixed costs are deducted after the contribution margin to arrive at net profit.

In terms of bottom line profitability, the two methods will provide the same results as long as production and sales are equal. The two methods can give different results, however, for any company that builds or depletes inventory. The next section illustrates the difference between full absorption costing and variable costing for a manufacturing company and shows how to reconcile the results of the two methods.

COACH'S TIP

Notice that gross margin and contribution margin are not the same. **Contribution margin** is the difference between sales revenue and variable costs; it is used only for internal reporting. **Gross margin** is the difference between sales revenue and the cost of goods sold; it appears on external financial statements.

Reconciling Variable and Full Absorption Costing

In terms of the effect on the bottom line, variable costing and full absorption costing have one critical difference: the treatment of fixed manufacturing overhead. Full absorption costing (GAAP) requires that all manufacturing cost, including fixed manufacturing overhead, be treated as a product cost, which means that the cost will be included in either cost of goods sold or inventory, depending on whether the product has been sold. Variable costing deducts all fixed costs, including fixed manufacturing overhead, during the period incurred.

To see how this difference can impact the bottom line, consider a company that produces and sells only one product. Assume this is the company's first month of operation, so it had no inventory on hand at the beginning of the month. Costs and production information follow.

Number of units produced	10,000
Number of units sold	8,000
Unit sales price	$ 100
Manufacturing Cost per Unit	
Direct materials	$ 25
Direct labor	15
Variable manufacturing overhead	5
Fixed manufacturing overhead ($200,000/10,000 units)	20
Full manufacturing cost per unit	$ 65
Nonmanufacturing Costs	
Variable selling expenses ($5 per unit sold)	$40,000
Fixed general and administrative costs	60,000

The following table shows the computation of profit under each method:

FULL ABSORPTION COSTING
Income Statement
Month 1

Sales Revenue (8,000 units × $100)	$800,000
Less: Cost of Goods Sold	
(8,000 units × $65)	520,000
Gross Margin	$280,000
Less: Selling Expenses ($5 per unit sold)	40,000
General and Administrative Expenses	60,000
Operating Profit	$180,000

VARIABLE COSTING
Income Statement
Month 1

Sales Revenue (8,000 units × $100)	$800,000
Less: Variable Cost of Goods Sold	
(8,000 × $45)	360,000
Variable Selling Expenses	
(8,000 × $5)	40,000
Contribution Margin	$400,000
Less: Fixed Manufacturing Overhead	200,000
General and Administrative Expenses	60,000
Operating Profit	$140,000

$40,000 difference in profit

The $40,000 difference in profit is due to the different treatment of fixed manufacturing overhead under the two costing methods. Full absorption costing requires that all manufacturing costs (including fixed manufacturing overhead) be spread over the number of units produced, but only a portion of the total manufacturing cost is reported as cost of goods sold. The remainder is reported as inventory (an asset) on the balance sheet.

In this example, the $200,000 fixed manufacturing overhead cost is spread over the 10,000 units produced for a fixed overhead rate of $20 per unit. This cost is then divided between the 8,000 units sold and the 2,000 units remaining in ending inventory. Because 2,000 units are not yet sold, full absorption costing reports $40,000 of the $200,000 in fixed overhead as an asset on the balance sheet rather than as an expense on the income statement. This cost is eventually expensed but not until the units are sold.

In contrast, variable costing deducts the entire $200,000 in fixed manufacturing overhead as an expense during the current period. The rationale is that the fixed cost will be incurred regardless of how many units are produced and sold. Thus, variable costing assigns $20 less to each of the 2,000 units in ending inventory, or a total of $40,000. This difference in the treatment of fixed manufacturing overhead explains the $40,000 difference in operating profit between the two methods.

In sum, the difference in profit between full absorption costing and variable costing is directly related to the fixed manufacturing overhead cost per unit and the change in ending inventory as in the following formula:

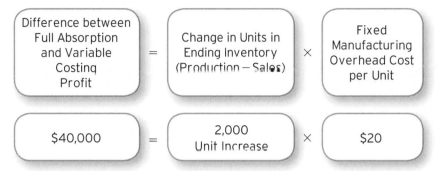

Difference between Full Absorption and Variable Costing Profit	=	Change in Units in Ending Inventory (Production − Sales)	×	Fixed Manufacturing Overhead Cost per Unit
$40,000	=	2,000 Unit Increase	×	$20

What would happen if, in the following month, the company produced exactly the number of units sold? We assume that sales demand remains constant at 8,000 units, but now the fixed manufacturing overhead must be spread over 8,000 units produced. The revised full manufacturing cost per unit follows:

Number of units produced	8,000
Number of units sold	8,000
Manufacturing Cost per Unit	
Direct materials	$ 25
Direct labor	15
Variable manufacturing overhead	5
Fixed manufacturing overhead ($200,000/8,000 units)	25
Full manufacturing cost per unit	$ 70

> **COACH'S TIP**
>
> Although total fixed cost remains the same, fixed cost per unit increases to $25, because fewer units were produced. The full manufacturing cost per unit is now $70.

If cost of goods sold is calculated based on the current period production cost of $70 per unit, profit under full absorption and variable costing would be calculated as follows:

FULL ABSORPTION COSTING
Income Statement
Month 2

Sales Revenue (8,000 units × $100)	$800,000
Less: Cost of Goods Sold	
(8,000 units × $70)	560,000
Gross Margin	$240,000
Less: Selling Expenses ($5 per unit sold)	40,000
General and Administrative Expenses	60,000
Operating Profit	$140,000

VARIABLE COSTING
Income Statement
Month 2

Sales Revenue (8,000 units × $100)	$800,000
Less: Variable Cost of Goods Sold	
(8,000 × $45)	360,000
Variable Selling Expenses	
(8,000 × $5)	40,000
Contribution Margin	$400,000
Less: Fixed Manufacturing Overhead	200,000
General and Administrative Expenses	60,000
Operating Profit	$140,000

No difference in profit

Notice that when production and sales are equal, there is no difference in profit between full absorption and variable costing. The reason is that all of the current period fixed manufacturing overhead costs are deducted (in full) on the income statement. Because all of the units produced were sold, none of the current period manufacturing costs can be deferred (or pushed into future periods) by being counted as inventory (an asset) on the balance sheet.

Finally, consider the case in which production is less than sales, or inventory is reduced. In month 3, assume that 8,000 units are sold, but only 6,000 were produced. The full manufacturing cost per unit would be computed as follows:

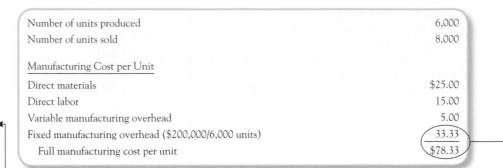

Number of units produced	6,000
Number of units sold	8,000
Manufacturing Cost per Unit	
Direct materials	$25.00
Direct labor	15.00
Variable manufacturing overhead	5.00
Fixed manufacturing overhead ($200,000/6,000 units)	33.33
Full manufacturing cost per unit	$78.33

COACH'S TIP

Although total fixed cost remains the same, fixed cost per unit increases to $33.33, which increases the full manufacturing cost per unit to $78.33.

To avoid rounding error, the full manufacturing cost per unit for the 6,000 units sold will be carried to four decimal places ($78.3333) in the calculation of cost of goods sold. The other 2,000 units sold were from the inventory created in month 1 when the full manufacturing cost was $65.00 per unit produced. Based on this information, profit under the two methods is calculated as follows:

FULL ABSORPTION COSTING
Income Statement
Month 3

Sales Revenue (8,000 units × $100)	$800,000
Less: Cost of Goods Sold	
6,000 units × $78.3333 = $470,000	
2,000 units × $65.0000 = $130,000	600,000
Gross Margin	$200,000
Less: Selling Expenses ($5 per unit sold)	40,000
General and Administrative Expenses	60,000
Operating Profit	$100,000

VARIABLE COSTING
Income Statement
Month 3

Sales Revenue (8,000 units × $100)	$800,000
Less: Variable Cost of Goods Sold	
(8,000 × $45)	360,000
Variable Selling Expenses	
(8,000 × $5)	40,000
Contribution Margin	$400,000
Less: Fixed Manufacturing Overhead	200,000
General and Administrative Expenses	60,000
Operating Profit	$140,000

$40,000 difference in profit

The $40,000 difference in profit is due to the 2,000 unit decrease in inventory multiplied by the fixed manufacturing cost per unit. Recall that the 2,000 units added to inventory in month 1 had a fixed manufacturing cost of $20 per unit. When these units are finally sold, there will be an extra $20 in cost of goods sold under full absorption costing compared to variable costing (which never attaches fixed costs to units produced, only those that are sold).

The following table summarizes the results of this example:

	Units Produced		Units Sold	Full Absorption Profit		Variable Costing Profit
Month 1	10,000	>	8,000	$180,000	>	$140,000
Month 2	8,000	=	8,000	140,000	=	140,000
Month 3	6,000	<	8,000	100,000	<	140,000

Notice that full absorption profit is different in each of the three months even though sales remain the same at 8,000 units. Full absorption profit is highest when the number of units produced is more than the number sold. The reason is that full absorption costing spreads the total manufacturing cost over the number of units produced, not the number of the units sold. This means that a portion of the fixed manufacturing overhead is counted as inventory (an asset), and therefore **not** expensed during the period incurred.

In contrast, variable costing shows the same profit each month. The reason is that variable costing always deducts the fixed manufacturing costs (in full) during the period incurred. This makes sense because the fixed cost will be incurred each period regardless of the number of units produced or sold.

This example illustrates a major limitation of full absorption costing. Although full absorption costing is required for external reporting (GAAP), managers should not necessarily use this method to guide their internal decisions. As this example shows, full absorption costing may lead managers to "overproduce," or produce more units than the market demands. While doing so may be good in the short run because the cost per unit decreases, the resulting inventory is very costly to maintain in terms of storage, handling, insurance, and potential obsolescence. In addition, inventory has many "hidden" costs, such as tied up working capital, reduced flexibility, and quality control problems.

In this hypothetical example, the inventory was built up and then depleted within a three-month period. In reality, managers may be reluctant to drive down inventory because of the negative effect it will have on full absorption (GAAP) profit (see month 3 income statement for an example). If managers continue to build inventory period after period, the inventory costs will continue to rise, further compounding the problem. These issues are avoided under variable costing because profit is a strict function of sales volume rather than production volume.

The illustration in Exhibit 5A.2 summarizes the relationship between production, sales, inventory, and profit under variable and full absorption costing.

EXHIBIT 5A.2   Effect of Changes in Inventory under Full Absorption Costing and Variable Costing

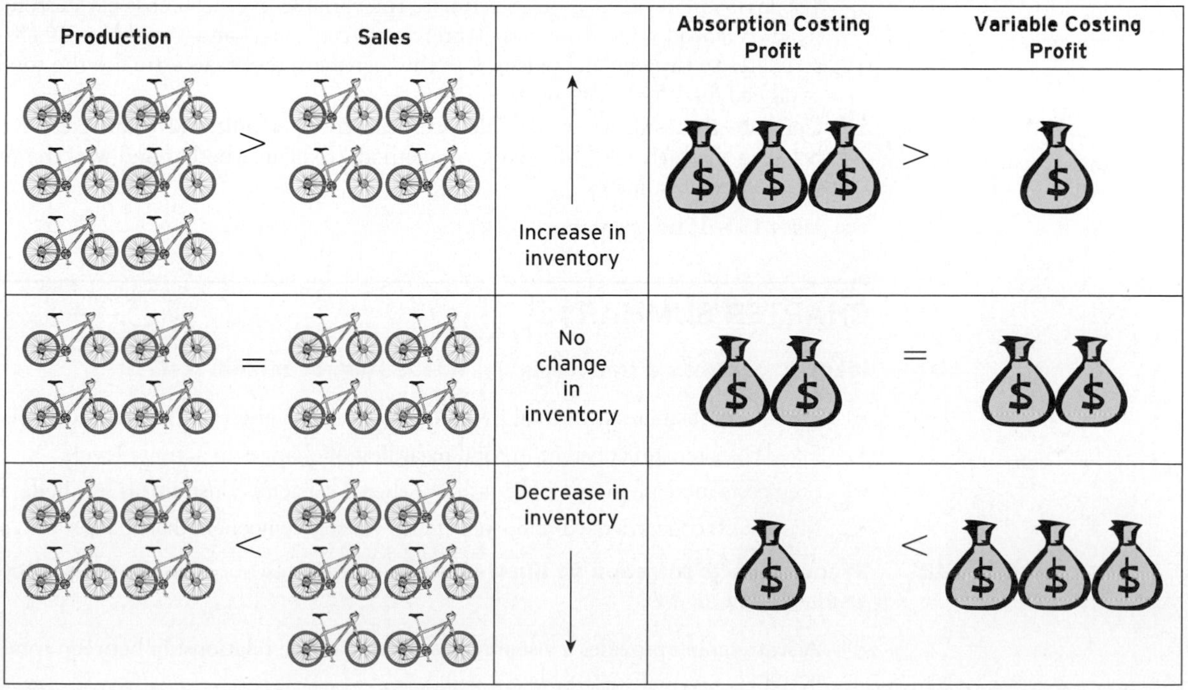

DEMONSTRATION CASE

The manager of a local bakery and café is trying to determine how its monthly costs vary with the number of customers served. The manager knows that direct material and direct labor costs tend to be higher when the bakery has more customers but is not sure about the indirect or "overhead" costs of running the business.

The following table shows the number of customers and total overhead cost for the past 12 months:

Month	Number of Customers (X)	Total Overhead Cost (Y)
January	1,200	$10,500
February	1,150	8,225
March	1,550	11,551
April	1,634	11,750
May	1,780	12,225
June	1,000	10,000
July	1,600	9,835
August	1,350	10,555
September	1,825	14,000
October	1,850	11,444
November	2,000	12,000
December	1,725	10,998

Required:

1. Give examples of indirect or overhead costs for a bakery café that would behave as a:
   a. Variable cost.
   b. Fixed cost.
   c. Step cost.
   d. Mixed cost.
2. Prepare a scattergraph to illustrate the relationship between total overhead cost (Y) and number of customers (X). What does this scattergraph tell you about the relationship between total overhead and number of customers served?
3. Use the high-low method to calculate the variable overhead cost per customer and total fixed overhead cost. Use the results to estimate total overhead for 1,500 customers.
4. Use least-squares regression to estimate the variable overhead cost per customer and total fixed overhead cost. Round the intercept (fixed cost) and variable cost (X-coefficient) estimates to two decimal places. Use the regression results to estimate the total amount of overhead for 1,500 customers.
5. Compare the estimate of variable overhead cost per unit and total fixed overhead costs between the high-low and regression methods. Explain whether and why the methods provide different estimates.

See pages 195–196 for solution.

CHAPTER SUMMARY

LO1   Identify costs as either variable, fixed, step, or mixed. p. 175

- Variable costs increase in total in direct proportion to increases in activity level.
- Fixed costs remain constant in total regardless of changes in activity level.
- Step costs increase in a steplike fashion when a capacity constraint is reached.
- Mixed costs contain a fixed component plus a variable component that changes with activity level.

LO2   Prepare a scattergraph to illustrate the relationship between total cost and activity. p. 179

- A scattergraph provides a visual representation of the relationship between total cost and activity.
- A scattergraph is created by plotting activity level on the horizontal (X) axis and total cost on the vertical (Y) axis.

- If the scattergraph suggests that the relationship between cost and activity is roughly linear, a straight line can be used to approximate that relationship.

- The slope of the line represents the variable cost per unit of activity.

- The intercept of the line represents the total fixed cost.

Use the high-low method to analyze mixed costs. p. 181   **LO3**

- The high-low method is one of three linear methods that can be used to estimate the relationship between total cost and activity. The high-low method steps are to:
  - Identify the two data points that represent the highest and lowest activity (X) levels.
  - Calculate the variable cost per unit by dividing the change in total cost across the high and low points by the change in activity level across the high and low points.
  - Calculate the total fixed cost by subtracting the total variable cost from the total cost at either the high or low point.

Use least-squares regression to analyze mixed costs. p. 183   **LO4**

- Least-squares regression uses all available data to find the best fitting line.

- The best fitting line is the one that minimizes the sum of squared errors, or the squared vertical distance between the data points and the regression line.

- The regression output provides an estimate of total fixed cost (intercept) and the variable cost per unit of X (X coefficient).

- Although least-squares regression is easily computed using a computer program such as Excel, properly interpreting the information is critical for managerial use.

Prepare and interpret a contribution margin income statement. p. 186   **LO5**

- Contribution margin is the difference between sales revenue and variable costs. The contribution margin can be expressed on a total, per unit, or as a percentage or ratio of sales.

- The unit contribution margin, which is the difference between a unit's selling price and its variable cost, indicates how profit will change as a result of selling one more or one less unit.

- The contribution margin ratio is computed by dividing the unit contribution margin by the unit selling price or by dividing the total contribution margin by total sales revenue. The contribution margin ratio shows how much a $1 increase in sales will affect the contribution margin and net operating income.

SOLUTION TO DEMONSTRATION CASE

1. Examples of indirect or overhead costs for a bakery and café:
   a. Variable costs: paper supplies, indirect materials, beverages
   b. Fixed costs: rent, insurance, taxes
   c. Step costs: supervisor salaries, baking equipment
   d. Mixed costs: utilities, janitorial service, equipment maintenance

2.

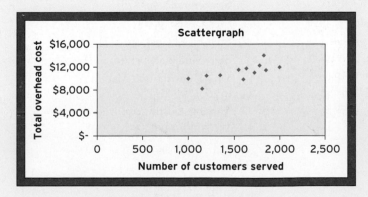

The relationship between total overhead cost and number of customers served appears to be somewhat positive and fairly linear. It appears to be a mixed cost because it has a fixed component (intercept) and a positive slope (variable cost).

3. The high-low method should be based on the high and low X (number of customers):

Month	Number of Customers (X)	Total Overhead Cost (Y)
June (low)	1,000	$10,000
November (high)	2,000	12,000
Difference	1,000	$ 2,000

Variable Overhead Cost per Unit = $2,000 / 1,000 = $2 per Customer
Fixed Overhead Cost (based on June) = $10,000 − (1,000 × $2) = $8,000
Fixed Overhead Cost (based on November) = $12,000 − (2,000 × $2) = $8,000
Estimated Total Overhead for 1,500 Customers = $8,000 + ($2 × 1,500) = $11,000

4. Least-squares regression results:

SUMMARY OUTPUT	
Regression Statistics	
Multiple R	0.72331837
R Square	0.523189464
Adjusted R Square	0.475508411
Standard Error	1046.579751
Observations	12
ANOVA	
	df
Regression	1
Residual	10
Total	11
	Coefficients
Intercept	$5,915.80
Number of Customers	$3.33

Estimated Total Overhead for 1,500 Customers = $5,915.80 + ($3.33 × 1,500) = $10,910.80

5. Comparison of high-low and regression

Method	Variable Overhead Cost per Customer	Total Fixed Overhead Cost
High Low	$2.00	$8,000.00
Regression	3.33	$5,915.80

The high-low method provides a higher estimate of total fixed cost (intercept) and a lower estimate of the variable cost per unit (slope of the line) compared to the regression results. The total fixed cost (intercept) is $8,000 for high-low compared to $5,915.80 for regression. The high-low line is also flatter (vc = $2.00) than the regression line based on all of the available data (vc = $3.33).

KEY TERMS

Contribution Margin (p. 187)

Contribution Margin Income Statement (p. 186)

Contribution Margin Ratio (p. 188)

Cost Behavior (p. 175)

Cost Driver (p. 175)

Dependent Variable (p. 179)

Full Absorption Costing (p. 174)

High-Low Method (p. 179)

Independent Variable (p. 179)

Least-Squares Regression (p. 179)

Linearity Assumption (p. 178)

Mixed Costs (p. 177)

Relevant Range (p. 175)

R Square (p. 184)

Scattergraph (p. 179)

Step Costs (p. 177)

Step-Fixed Cost (p. 177)

Step-Variable Cost (p. 177)

Unit Contribution Margin (p. 187)

Variable Costing (p. 189)

Visual Fit Method (p. 179)

See complete definitions in glossary at back of text.

QUESTIONS

1. Explain the difference between a variable cost, fixed cost, step cost, and mixed cost. Give an example of each.

2. Explain what happens to the following when activity level decreases:

   a. Total fixed cost.
   b. Total variable cost.
   c. Total mixed cost.
   d. Fixed cost per unit.
   e. Variable cost per unit.
   f. Mixed cost per unit.

3. What is the relevant range and why is it important?

4. Why is it important to separate the fixed and variable components of a mixed cost? What might happen if that were not done?

5. The formula for analyzing mixed costs is Y = A + B(X). Explain what each term represents.

6. Why is a scattergraph plot useful?

7. Describe the three methods of analyzing mixed costs. What are the strengths and weaknesses of each method? Will these methods always yield exactly the same results?

8. What does the R square value mean?

9. Why is a contribution margin income statement more useful to managerial decision makers than the income statement intended for external users?

10. Explain how to calculate total contribution margin, contribution margin per unit, and contribution margin ratio. What is the meaning of each?

11. When activity level increases, explain what happens to:

    a. Contribution margin per unit.
    b. Contribution margin ratio.
    c. Total contribution margin.
    d. Total fixed cost.
    e. Profit.

12. Explain the difference between absorption costing and variable costing. Why do internal users need variable costing?

13. What is the critical item that is treated differently in full absorption versus variable costing? Explain how each method treats it.

14. When will variable costing show the same profit as absorption costing?

15. Compare the full absorption and variable incomes when finished goods inventory increases and when it decreases.

MULTIPLE CHOICE

Quiz 5
www.mhhe.com/whitecotton1e

1. Which of the following increases when activity level increases?

   a. Total variable cost.
   b. Total fixed cost.
   c. Total mixed cost.
   d. Both a and c.

2. Which of the following is **not** a method used to separate mixed costs?

   a. Regression analysis.
   b. Break-even analysis.
   c. High-low method.
   d. Visual fit method.

3. Consider the following information for a local concession stand's first four weeks of operation:

Week	Number of Drinks Served	Total Cost
1	1,000	$2,500
2	2,000	3,250
3	1,750	3,000
4	2,250	3,200

Using the high-low method, what is the equation for total operating cost for this concession stand?

   a. Operating Cost = $1,750 + ($0.75 × Number of drinks served).
   b. Operating Cost = $1,000 + ($1.75 × Number of drinks served).
   c. Operating Cost = $1,940 + ($0.56 × Number of drinks served).
   d. Operating Cost = $1,750 + ($0.56 × Number of drinks served).

4. Bombay Co. sells handmade rugs. Its variable cost per rug is $30, and each rug sells for $50. What are Bombay's contribution margin per unit and contribution margin ratio?

   a. $20 and 40 percent.
   b. $30 and 60 percent.
   c. $20 and 60 percent.
   d. $30 and 40 percent.

5. Suppose you are given the following results from a least-squares regression performed on a local coffee shop's weekly cost data.

	Coefficients
Intercept	$836.07
X Variable 1 (customers served)	1.69

Which of the following statements is true?

a. Total weekly variable cost is $836.07.
b. The coffee shop incurs $1.69 in variable costs for each customer served.
c. Total weekly fixed costs are $836.07.
d. Both b and c are true.
e. None of the above is true.

6. Total contribution margin is

a. The difference between total variable cost and fixed cost.
b. The difference between sales and cost of goods sold.
c. The difference between sales and fixed cost.
d. The difference between sales and variable cost.
e. None of the above is true.

7. Which approach to analyzing mixed costs is most helpful in identifying data outliers?

a. Least-squares regression.
b. High-low method.
c. Contribution margin income statement.
d. Scattergraph.

8. Last year, Ritter Company sold 5,000 bird feeders for $20 each. Total fixed costs were $42,000, and Ritter's profit was $30,000. What was its total variable cost last year?

a. $28,000.   c. $70,000.
b. $58,000.   d. Cannot be determined.

9. Which of the following would be subtracted from total sales revenue when calculating contribution margin?

a. Factory machinery depreciation.
b. Direct materials used.
c. Factory supervisor's salary.
d. Office machinery depreciation.

10. Hathaway Corp. manufactures garden hoses. Last month, its ending inventory level increased. In comparing absorption costing to variable costing,

a. Both would show the same amount of profit.
b. Variable costing would show more profit.
c. Absorption costing would show more profit.
d. Effect on income cannot be determined.

Answers to Multiple-Choice Questions located in back of the text.

MINI EXERCISES

Mc Graw Hill connect | ACCOUNTING

LO1   **M5-1 Identifying Cost Behavior**

Martha Trent is trying to prepare a personal budget and has identified the following list of monthly costs. Identify each cost as fixed, variable, or mixed. Indicate a possible cost driver for any variable or mixed cost.

1. Rent.
2. Utilities.
3. Car payment.
4. Cell phone bill.
5. Gasoline.
6. Cable bill.
7. Groceries.
8. Dining out.

LO1   **M5-2 Identifying Cost Behavior**

Steve's Snow Cones is a small refreshment stand located near a football stadium. Its fixed expenses total $300 per week and the variable cost per snow cone is $0.35. Complete the following table for the various levels.

Number of snow cones	500	1,000	1,500
Total fixed cost			
Fixed cost per snow cone			
Total variable cost			
Variable cost per snow cone			
Total cost			
Cost per snow cone			

LO2   **M5-3 Preparing a Scattergraph**

Taylor's Tan-O-Rama is a local tanning salon. The following information reflects its number of appointments and total costs for the first half of the year:

Month	Number of Appointments	Total Cost
January	500	$5,400
February	600	5,900
March	1,000	6,700
April	450	5,675
May	300	5,328
June	350	5,325

Prepare a scattergraph by plotting Taylor's Tan-O-Rama's data on a graph. Then draw a line that you believe best fits the data points. Using the graph and line you have drawn, estimate the firm's total fixed cost per month.

M5-4 Analyzing Mixed Costs Using High-Low Method

LO3

Refer to the Tan-O-Rama data in M5-3. Using the high-low method, calculate the total fixed cost per month and the variable cost per tanning appointment. How does the estimate of fixed cost compare to what you estimated in M5-3?

M5-5 Analyzing Mixed Costs Using Least Squares Regression

LO4

Refer to the Tan-O-Rama data In M5-3. Suppose Taylor performed a least squares regression and obtained the following results:

	Coefficients
Intercept	4636.29
X Variable 1	2.03

Put Taylor's results into a linear equation format $(Y = A + BX)$ and explain what each component means. Compare the regression results to those obtained in M5-3 and M5-4. Which method is most accurate? Why?

M5-6 Calculating Contribution Margin and Contribution Margin Ratio

LO5

Refer to the Tan-O-Rama regression output given in M5-5. Suppose that the company charges $6 per tanning session. Calculate the contribution margin per unit and contribution margin ratio as well as the total contribution margin if the shop books 1,200 tanning sessions this month.

M5-7 Preparing a Scattergraph

LO2

Wendy's Widgets builds the world's best widgets. Information for the last eight months follows:

Month	Number of Widgets Produced	Total Cost
January	4,000	$7,000
February	2,250	5,000
March	3,500	6,250
April	4,300	7,750
May	1,875	5,000
June	3,000	6,250
July	1,500	4,250
August	2,500	5,750

Prepare a scattergraph by plotting Wendy's data on a graph. Then draw a line that you believe best fits the data points. Using the graph and line you have drawn, estimate Wendy's total fixed cost per month.

M5-8 Analyzing Mixed Costs Using High-Low Method

LO3

Refer to the Wendy's Widgets data in M5-7. Using the high-low method, calculate the total fixed cost per month and the variable cost per widget. How does the estimate of fixed cost compare to what you estimated in M5-7?

M5-9 Analyzing Mixed Costs Using Least-Squares Regression

LO4

Refer to the Wendy's Widgets data in M5-7. Suppose Wendy performed a least-squares regression and obtained the following results.

	Coefficients
Intercept	2718.59
X Variable 1	1.11

Put Wendy's results into a linear equation format $(Y = A + BX)$ and explain what each component means. Compare the regression results to those obtained in M5-7 and M5-8. Which method is most accurate? Why?

LO5   **M5-10 Preparing a Contribution Margin Income Statement**

Refer to the data for Wendy's Widgets in M5-7–M5-9. Suppose that Wendy's expect to sell 3,200 widgets during the month of September and that each widget sells for $2.75. Using this information along with the regression results given in M5-9, prepare Wendy's contribution margin income statement for the month of September.

LO5   **M5-11 Preparing a Contribution Margin Income Statement**

Following is relevant information for Sunsplash Smoothie Shop, a small business that serves fruit drinks.

Total fixed cost per month	$1,200.00
Variable cost per drink	1.25
Sales price per drink	4.75

During the month of June, Sunsplash sold 500 smoothies. Using the preceding information, prepare its contribution margin income statement for the month of June.

LO5   **M5-12 Calculating Contribution Margin and Contribution Margin Ratio**

Lezoli Enterprises sells handmade clocks. Its variable cost per clock is $6, and each clock sells for $15. Calculate Lezoli's contribution margin per unit and contribution margin ratio. Suppose Lezoli sells 2,000 clocks this year. Calculate the total contribution margin.

EXERCISES

LO1   **E5-1 Determining Cost Behavior and Calculating Expected Cost**

Tweety Company manufactures one model of birdbath, which is very popular. Tweety sells all units it produces each month. The relevant range is 0–1,500 units, and monthly production costs for the production of 1,000 units follow. Tweety's utilities and maintenance costs are mixed with the fixed components shown in parentheses.

Production Costs	Amount
Direct materials	$ 1,500
Direct labor	7,500
Utilities ($100 fixed)	650
Supervisor's salary	3,000
Maintenance ($280 fixed)	480
Depreciation	800

Required:

1. Identify each cost as variable, fixed, or mixed, and express each cost as a rate per month or per unit (or combination thereof). State any assumptions you make.
2. Determine the total fixed cost per month and the variable cost per unit for Tweety.
3. State Tweety's linear cost equation for a production level of 0–1,500 units.
4. Calculate Tweety's expected total cost if production increased to 1,200 units per month.

LO5   **E5-2 Calculating Contribution Margin and Contribution Ratio, Preparing Contribution Margin Income Statement**

Refer to the information for Tweety Company in E5-1. Suppose it sells each birdbath for $20.

Required:

1. Calculate the unit contribution margin and contribution margin ratio for each birdbath sold.
2. Prepare a contribution margin income statement assuming that Tweety produces and sells 1,400 units.

E5-3 Understanding Cost Behavior and Implications of Relevant Range   **LO1**

Refer to the information for Tweety Company in E5-1. Tweety Company's owner, Sylvester, believes that he can sell 2,000 birdbaths during the month of April and has predicted a contribution margin income of $16,320 as shown in the following contribution margin statement:

TWEETY COMPANY
Contribution Margin Income Statement
Expected for 2,000 Units

Sales Revenue (2,000 × $20.00)	$40,000
Less. Variable Costs (2,000 × $9.75)	19,500
Contribution Margin (2,000 × $10.25)	$20,500
Less: Fixed Costs	4,180
Income from Operations	$16,320

Required:

Explain to Sylvester why his prediction is incorrect. Be specific about his incorrect assumptions and give him as much detail as possible about what the accurate contribution margin statement would show.

E5-4 Analyzing Mixed Costs Using High-Low Method   **LO3**

Valley Dental Services is a specialized dental practice whose only service is filling cavities. Valley has recorded the following for the past nine months.

Month	Number of Cavities Filled	Total Cost
January	625	$2,800
February	700	2,900
March	500	2,100
April	425	2,000
May	450	2,200
June	300	1,700
July	375	1,800
August	550	2,400
September	575	2,600

Required:

1. Use the high-low method to estimate total fixed cost and variable cost per cavity filled. Using these estimates, calculate Valley's total cost for filling 500 cavities.
2. How closely does your estimate match the actual cost for March? Why would these be different?

E5-5 Analyzing Mixed Costs Using Scattergraph Method   **LO2**

Refer to the information in E5-4 regarding Valley Dental.

Required:

1. Create a scattergraph using Valley's activity and cost information and draw a line on the graph that you believe has the best fit.
2. Using this graph and best fitting line, estimate Valley Dental's total fixed cost.
3. Does your visual fit line differ from the one calculated using the high-low method? If so, why?

E5-6 Analyzing Mixed Costs Using Least-Squares Regression Method   **LO4**

Refer to the information in E5-4 regarding Valley Dental.

Required:

1. Perform a least squares regression using Valley's activity and cost information and state the linear cost equation (Y = A + BX).
2. Explain what each component of the cost equation represents.
3. Do the regression results differ from those obtained using the high-low and scattergraph methods? If so, why?

L05   **E5-7 Preparing Contribution Margin Income Statement**

Consider Valley Dental's cost equation results obtained in E5-6 using least-squares regression.

Required:

1. Determine Valley Dental's contribution margin per unit and contribution margin ratio if it charges $45 for each cavity filled.
2. Prepare a contribution margin income statement for October assuming Valley expects to fill 610 cavities during the month.

L02, 3, 4   **E5-8 Analyzing Mixed Costs Using Scattergraph, High-Low Method, and Least-Squares Regression**

Aspen, Inc., manufactures one model of computer desk. The following data are available regarding units shipped and total shipping costs.

Month	Number of Units Shipped	Total Shipping Cost
January	30	$3,600
February	60	2,300
March	40	1,700
April	20	1,200
May	70	2,300
June	80	2,700
July	50	2,000

Required:

1. Prepare a scattergraph of Aspen's shipping cost and draw the line you believe best fits the data.
2. Based on this graph, estimate Aspen's total fixed shipping costs per month.
3. Using the high-low method, calculate Aspen's total fixed shipping costs and variable shipping cost per unit.
4. Perform a least-squares regression analysis on Aspen's data.
5. Using the regression output, create a linear equation (Y = A + BX) for estimating Aspen's shipping costs.

L02, 3   **E5-9 Determining Cost Behavior, Analyzing Mixed Costs Using Scattergraph and High-Low Methods**

Camp Sunshine offers overnight summer camp programs for children ages 10–14 every summer during June and July. Each camp session is one week and can accommodate up to 100 children. The camp is not coed, so boys attend during the odd-numbered weeks and girls attend during the even-numbered weeks. While at the camp, participants make crafts, participate in various sports, help care for the camp's resident animals, have cookouts and hayrides, and help assemble toys for local underprivileged children.

The camp provides all food as well as materials for all craft classes and the toys to be assembled. One cabin can accommodate up to 10 children, and one camp counselor is assigned to each cabin. Three camp managers are on-site regardless of the number of campers enrolled.

Following is the cost information for Camp Sunshine's operations last summer:

Week	Number of Campers	Cost to Run Camp
1	45	$ 8,050
2	59	8,460
3	78	10,900
4	86	11,100
5	94	13,670
6	92	14,300
7	85	12,325
8	78	11,270

Required:

1. For each of the following items, identify whether the cost is variable, fixed, mixed, step-variable, or step-fixed. State any assumptions you make.
   a. Cost of meals for campers.
   b. Cost of camp counselor wages.
   c. Cost of crafting materials.
   d. Depreciation on the cabins.
   e. Feed for the camp animals.
   f. Electricity for the camp.
   g. Camp managers' salaries.
   h. Cost of toys to be assembled by campers.
   i. Housekeeping (e.g., cleaning cabins between sessions, laundering bed linens).

2. Prepare a scattergraph of Camp Sunshine's operating cost and draw the line you believe best fits the data.

3. Based on this graph, estimate Camp Sunshine's total fixed costs per month.

4. Using the high-low method, calculate Camp Sunshine's total fixed operating costs and variable operating cost per child.

5. Using the high-low method results, calculate the camp's expected operating cost if 85 children attend a session.

E5-10 Analyzing Mixed Costs Using Least-Squares Regression   LO4

Refer to the Camp Sunshine data presented in E5-9.

Required:

1. Perform a least-squares regression analysis on Camp Sunshine's data.

2. Using the regression output, create a cost equation (Y = A + BX) for estimating Camp Sunshine's operating costs.

3. Using the least-squares regression results, calculate the camp's expected operating cost if 85 children attend a session.

4. Compare this estimated cost to the actual cost incurred during week 7. Explain why these numbers might differ.

E5-11 Comparing High-Low Method and Least-Squares Regression Results   LO3, 4

Consider Camp Sunshine's cost estimated in E5-9 using the high-low method and E5-10 using regression. The two methods yielded very different results, especially in their estimates of fixed cost.

Required:

1. Describe the differences in the cost estimates generated by these two methods.
2. Explain why you believe the differences exist.
3. Explain which method is more reliable and why.

E5-12 Preparing Contribution Margin Income Statement   LO5

Consider Camp Sunshine's cost equation results obtained in E5-10 using least-squares regression. Suppose that Sunshine is contemplating staying open one additional week during the summer.

Required:

1. Determine Sunshine's contribution margin per camper if each camper pays $175 to attend the camp for a week.
2. Prepare a contribution margin income statement for week 9 assuming Sunshine expects to have 65 campers that week.
3. Explain whether Sunshine should add a ninth week to its schedule.

LO1, 5   **E5-13 Determining Cost Behavior, Preparing Contribution Margin Income Statement**

Paddle Away, Inc., makes one model of wooden canoe. Partial information for it follows:

Number of canoes produced and sold	450	600	750
Total costs			
Variable costs	$ 67,500	?	?
Fixed costs	150,000	?	?
Total costs	$217,500	?	?
Cost per unit			
Variable cost per unit	?	?	?
Fixed cost per unit	?	?	?
Total cost per unit	?	?	?

Required:

1. Complete the preceding table.
2. Identify three costs that would be classified as fixed costs and three as variable costs for Paddle Away.
3. Suppose Paddle Away sells its canoes for $500 each. Calculate the contribution margin per canoe and the contribution margin ratio.
4. Next year Paddle Away expects to sell 800 canoes. Prepare a contribution margin income statement for the company.

LO5   **E5-14 Calculating Contribution Margin and Contribution Ratio, Preparing Contribution Margin Income Statement**

Refer to the information presented in E5-13 for Paddle Away. Each of the following scenarios is a variation of Paddle Away's original data.

Required:

Prepare its contribution margin income statement for each independent scenario.

1. Paddle Away raises the sales price to $600 per canoe.
2. Both sales price and variable cost per unit increase by 10 percent.
3. Paddle Away cuts its fixed cost by 20 percent.

LO3, 5   **E5-15 Analyzing Mixed Costs Using High-Low Method, Preparing Contribution Margin Income Statement**

Cory Bryant runs a courier service in downtown Phoenix. He charges clients $0.50 per mile driven. Cory has determined that if he drives 3,000 miles in a month, his total operating cost is $875. If he drives 4,000 miles in a month, his total operating cost is $1,025.

Required:

1. Using the high-low method, determine Cory's variable and fixed operating cost components. Show this as a linear formula (Y = A + BX).
2. Prepare a contribution margin income statement for Cory's service assuming he drove 2,400 miles last month.

LO3, 5   **E5-16 Analyzing Mixed Costs Using High-Low Method and Preparing Contribution Margin Income Statement**

Frieda Carson delivers parts for several local auto parts stores. She charges clients $0.75 per mile driven. She has determined that if she drives 2,000 miles in a month, her average operating cost is $0.55 per mile. If Frieda drives 4,000 miles in a month, her average operating cost is $0.40 per mile.

Required:

1. Using the high-low method, determine Frieda's variable and fixed operating cost components. Show this as a linear cost formula (Y = A + BX).
2. Prepare a contribution margin income statement for the business last month when Frieda drove 1,500 miles.

E5-17 Understanding the Need for Variable Costing

Supplement

Your friend, Manuel Rodriguez, has been working as a staff accountant for Williams Company, a small local manufacturing company. His job responsibilities to date have entailed several aspects of financial accounting: preparing monthly financial statements for the owners/investors and the bank with which Williams maintains a line of credit. Manuel has been offered a promotion to cost accountant. In that capacity, he would be responsible for overseeing Williams' manufacturing facility and tracking all production costs. He would also be expected to generate a contribution margin income statement on a regular basis for company employees to use. Manuel has come to you for help in understanding the difference between this contribution margin statement and the ones he has prepared in the past.

Required:

Explain to Manuel the differences between these two income statement formats. Include in your explanation the basis for separating costs, targeted users, and information that can be obtained from each one.

E5-18 Comparing Full Absorption Costing and Variable Costing

Supplement

The following information pertains to the first year of operation for Sonic Boom Radios, Inc.

Number of units produced	3,000
Number of units sold	2,500
Unit sales price	$ 350
Direct materials per unit	70
Direct labor per unit	60
Variable manufacturing overhead per unit	10
Fixed manufacturing overhead ($225,000/3,000 units)	75
Variable selling expenses ($15/unit sold)	37,500
Fixed general and administrative expenses	65,000

Required:

Prepare Sonic Boom's full absorption costing income statement and variable costing income statement for the year.

PROBLEMS–SET A

Mc Graw Hill **connect**

|ACCOUNTING   L02, 3, 4

PA5-1 Analyzing Mixed Costs Using Scattergraph, High-Low, and Least-Squares Regression Methods

Garfield Company manufactures a popular brand of dog repellant known as DogGone It, which it sells in gallon-size bottles with a spray attachment. The majority of Garfield's business comes from orders placed by homeowners who are trying to keep neighborhood dogs out of their yards. Garfield's operating information for the first six months of the year follows:

Month	Number of Bottles Sold	Operating Cost
January	1,000	$10,500
February	1,400	15,740
March	1,750	15,800
April	2,400	19,675
May	3,480	27,245
June	3,625	34,755

Required:

1. Prepare a scattergraph of Garfield's operating cost and draw the line you believe best fits the data. Identify any potential outliers and explain your treatment of them.
2. Based on this graph, estimate Garfield's total fixed costs per month.
3. Using the high-low method, calculate Garfield's total fixed operating costs and variable operating cost per bottle.
4. Perform a least-squares regression analysis on Garfield's data.
5. Determine how well this regression analysis explains the data.
6. Using the regression output, create a linear cost equation (Y = A + BX) for estimating Garfield's operating costs.

LO2, 3, 4 **PA5-2 Analyzing Mixed Costs Using Scattergraph, High-Low, and Least Squares Regression Methods**

Larry's Sporting Goods is a locally owned store that specializes in printing team jerseys. The majority of its business comes from orders for various local teams and organizations. While Larry's prints everything from bowling team jerseys to fraternity/sorority apparel to special event shirts, summer league baseball and softball team jerseys are the company's biggest source of revenue.

A portion of Larry's operating information for the company's last year follows:

Month	Number of Jerseys Printed	Operating Cost
January	200	5,500
February	195	5,740
March	250	5,800
April	550	8,675
May	680	9,245
June	625	9,760
July	430	6,200
August	365	6,155
September	310	5,980
October	250	6,010
November	175	4,950
December	150	4,925

Required:

1. Prepare a scattergraph of Larry's operating cost and draw the line you believe best fits the data. Identify any potential outliers and explain your treatment of them.
2. Based on this graph, estimate Larry's total fixed costs per month.
3. Using the high-low method, calculate the store's total fixed operating costs and variable operating cost per uniform.
4. Using the high-low method results, calculate the store's expected operating cost if it printed 480 jerseys.
5. Perform a least-squares regression analysis on Larry's data.
6. Using the regression output, create a linear equation (Y = A + BX) for estimating Larry's operating costs.
7. Using the least-squares regression results, calculate the store's expected operating cost if it prints 625 jerseys.

LO3, 4, 5 **PA5-3 Analyzing Mixed Cost Using High-Low and Regression, Preparing and Interpreting Contribution Margin Income Statement**

Refer to your solutions for Larry's Sporting Goods in PA5-2.

Required:

1. Consider the pattern of Larry's activity and costs throughout the year. Would you consider this to be a seasonal business? Explain your answer and how this information could impact the relative proportion of fixed and variable costs for the store's business.
2. Using the cost estimates obtained with the high-low and regression methods, predict the store's operating costs for the upcoming months based on expected sales levels.

Month	Expected Number of Jerseys
January	240
February	180
March	300
April	590
May	710
June	660

3. Explain why there are differences between cost predictions based on high-low method and least-squares regression. Which do you think is more accurate? Why?

4. Using the regression results, prepare contribution margin income statements for January through June. Assume that the average sales price is $18 per jersey.

5. Based on the regression equation, what is Larry's expected fixed cost per month? What would Larry expect total annual fixed cost to be?

6. Suppose that the store's actual fixed cost last year was $51,000. Explain why this amount varies from the prediction based on the regression results.

PA5-4 Predicting Cost Behavior, Calculating Contribution Margin and Contribution Margin Ratio, Calculating Profit

LO5

www.mhhe.com/whitecotton1e

Overhill, Inc., produces one model of mountain bike. Partial information for the company follows.

Cost Data			
Number of bikes produced and sold	500	800	1,000
Total costs			
Variable costs	$125,000	$?	$?
Fixed costs per year	?	?	?
Total costs	?	?	?
Cost per unit			
Variable cost per unit	?	?	?
Fixed cost per unit	?	?	?
Total cost per unit	?	$543.75	?

Required:

1. Complete Overhill's cost data table.

2. Calculate Overhill's contribution margin ratio and its total contribution margin at each sales level indicated in the cost data table assuming the company sells each bike for $650.

3. Calculate profit at each of the sales levels assuming a sales price of $650.

PA5-5 Comparing Full Absorption and Variable Costing

Supplement

www.mhhe.com/whitecotton1e

Refer to the information for Overhill, Inc., in PA5-4. Additional information for Overhill's most recent year of operations follows:

Number of units produced	2,000
Number of units sold	1,300
Sales price per unit	$ 650.00
Direct materials per unit	110.00
Direct labor per unit	90.00
Variable manufacturing overhead per unit	40.00
Fixed manufacturing overhead ($235,000/2,000 units)	117.50
Variable selling expenses ($10 per unit sold)	13,000.00
Fixed general and administrative expenses	70,000.00

Required:

1. Without any calculations, explain whether Overhill's income will be higher with full absorption costing or variable costing.

2. Prepare a full absorption costing income statement and a variable costing income statement for Overhill. Assume there was no beginning inventory.

3. Compute the difference in profit between full absorption costing and variable costing. Reconcile the difference.

PA5-6 Comparing Full Absorption and Variable Costing

Happy Hula manufactures authentic Hawaiian hula skirts that are purchased for traditional Hawaiian celebrations, costume parties, and other functions. During its first year of business, the company incurred the following costs:

Variable Cost per Hula Skirt	
Direct materials	$ 7.35
Direct labor	2.50
Variable manufacturing overhead	1.05
Variable selling & administrative expenses	0.40
Fixed Cost per Month	
Fixed manufacturing overhead	$15,875
Fixed selling and administrative expenses	4,950

Happy Hula charges $30 for each skirt that it sells. During the first month of operation, it made 1,500 skirts and sold 1,375.

Required:

1. Assuming Happy Hula uses variable costing, calculate the variable manufacturing cost per unit for last month.
2. Prepare a variable costing income statement for last month.
3. Assuming Happy Hula uses full absorption costing, calculate the full manufacturing cost per unit for last month.
4. Prepare a full absorption costing income statement.
5. Compare the two income statements and explain any differences.
6. Suppose next month Happy Hula expects to produce 1,200 hula skirts and sell 1,300. Without any calculations, explain whether variable or full absorption costing will show a higher income.

PROBLEMS–SET B

PB5-1 Analyzing Mixed Costs Using Scattergraph, High-Low, and Least-Squares Regression Methods

Odie Company manufactures a popular brand of cat repellant known as Cat-B-Gone, which it sells in gallon-size bottles with a spray attachment. The majority of Odie's business comes from orders placed by homeowners who are trying to keep neighborhood cats out of their yards. Odie's operating information for the first six months of the year follows:

Month	Number of Bottles Sold	Operating Cost
January	800	$ 6,100
February	1,000	7,500
March	1,250	9,875
April	1,950	14,050
May	2,350	17,245
June	2,825	23,150

Required:

1. Prepare a scattergraph of Odie's operating cost and draw the line you believe best fits the data. Identify any potential outliers and explain your treatment of them.
2. Based on this graph, estimate Odie's total fixed costs per month.
3. Using the high-low method, calculate Odie's total fixed operating costs and variable operating cost per bottle.
4. Perform a least-squares regression analysis on Odie's data.
5. Determine how well this regression analysis explains the data.
6. Using the regression output, create a linear equation $(Y = A + BX)$ for estimating Odie's operating costs.

PB5-2 Analyzing Mixed Costs Using Scattergraph, High-Low, and Least-Squares Regression

Sigrid's Custom Graphics specializes in creating and painting store window advertisement displays. The majority of its business comes from local retailers and fast-food restaurants.

A portion of Sigrid's operating information for the past year follows:

Month	Number of Window Displays	Operating Cost
January	40	$1,530
February	42	1,720
March	66	2,100
April	75	2,675
May	80	3,250
June	83	3,760
July	81	3,270
August	87	3,155
September	80	2,980
October	58	2,090
November	67	1,950
December	77	2,925

Required:

1. Prepare a scattergraph of Sigrid's operating cost and draw the line you believe best fits the data. Identify any potential outliers and explain your treatment of them.

2. Based on this graph, estimate Sigrid's total fixed costs per month.

3. Using the high-low method, calculate Sigrid's total fixed operating costs and variable operating cost per window.

4. Using the high-low method results, calculate the expected operating cost for the business if it paints 96 windows.

5. Perform a least-squares regression analysis on Sigrid's data.

6. Using the regression output, create a linear equation (Y = A + BX) for estimating Sigrid's operating costs.

7. Using the least-squares regression results, calculate the store's expected operating cost if it paints 80 windows.

PB5-3 Analyzing Mixed Cost Using High-Low and Regression, Preparing and Interpreting Contribution Margin Income Statement

Refer to your solutions for Sigrid's Custom Graphics in PB5-2.

Required:

1. Consider the pattern of the company's activity and costs throughout the year. Would you consider this to be a seasonal business? Explain your answer and how this information could impact the relative proportion of fixed and variable costs for the business.

2. Using your cost estimates obtained with the high-low and regression methods, predict the store's operating costs for the upcoming months based on the following expected sales levels.

Month	Expected Number of Windows
January	44
February	48
March	70
April	76
May	87
June	85

3. Explain why there are differences between cost predictions based on high-low method and on least-squares regression. Which do you think is more accurate? Why?

4. Using the regression results, prepare contribution margin income statements for January through June. Assume that the business charges $80 per window on average.

5. Based on the regression equation, what is the expected fixed cost per month for the business? What would it expect total annual fixed cost to be?

6. Suppose that the actual fixed cost of the business last year was $7,320. Explain why this amount varies from the prediction based on regression results for Sigrid's.

LO5   **PB5-4 Predicting Cost Behavior, Calculating Contribution Margin and Contribution Margin Ratio, Calculating Profit**

CoverUp, Inc., produces one model of seat cover. Partial information for the company follows:

Cost Data			
Number of seat covers produced and sold	1,500	1,700	2,100
Total costs			
Variable costs	$?	$?	$15,750
Fixed costs per year	?	?	?
Total costs	?	?	?
Cost per unit			
Variable cost per unit	?	?	?
Fixed cost per unit	?	?	?
Total cost per unit	$31.00	?	?

Required:

1. Complete CoverUp's cost data table.
2. Calculate CoverUp's contribution margin ratio and its total contribution margin at each sales level indicated in the cost data table assuming the company sells each cover for $30.
3. Calculate profit at each of the sales levels assuming a sales price of $30.

Supplement   **PB5-5 Comparing Full Absorption and Variable Costing**

Refer to the information for CoverUp in PB5-4. Additional information for CoverUp's most recent year of operations follows:

Number of units produced	3,000
Number of units sold	2,800
Sales price per unit	$ 30.00
Direct materials per unit	3.00
Direct labor per unit	2.00
Variable manufacturing overhead per unit	1.50
Fixed manufacturing overhead ($15,000/3,000 units)	5.00
Variable selling expenses ($1 per unit sold)	2,800.00
Fixed general and administrative expenses	20,250.00

Required:

1. Without any calculations, explain whether CoverUp's income will be higher with full absorption costing or variable costing.
2. Prepare a full absorption costing income statement and a variable costing income statement for CoverUp. Assume there was no beginning inventory.
3. Compute the difference in profit between full absorption costing and variable costing. Reconcile the difference.

Supplement   **PB5-6 Comparing Full Absorption and Variable Costing**

Thyme2Cook manufactures garden planters for growing fresh herbs to use in cooking. Individuals as well as local restaurants purchase the planters. Recently, the company incurred the following costs:

Variable Cost per Planter	
Direct materials	$ 5.60
Direct labor	3.20
Variable manufacturing overhead	1.55
Variable selling & administrative expenses	0.65
Fixed Cost per Month	
Fixed manufacturing overhead	$12,125
Fixed selling and administrative expenses	8,640

Thyme2Cook charges $17 for each planter that it sells. During the first month of operation, it made 6,500 planters and sold 6,225.

Required:

1. Assuming Thyme2Cook uses variable costing, calculate the variable manufacturing cost per unit for last month.
2. Prepare a variable costing income statement for last month.
3. Assuming Thyme2Cook uses full absorption costing, calculate the full manufacturing cost per unit for last month.
4. Prepare a full absorption costing income statement.
5. Compare the two income statements and explain any differences.
6. Suppose next month Thyme2Cook expects to produce 6,000 planters and sell 5,475 of them. Without any calculations, explain whether variable or absorption costing will show a higher profit.

SKILLS DEVELOPMENT CASES

S5-1 Analyzing Cost Behavior and the Impact on Profit

LO1

Ink Spot, Inc., is a new business located in upstate New York. It prints promotional flyers for local businesses and distributes them at public places or area events. The flyers are either placed on the windshield of cars in parking lots or distributed by hand to people.

Ink Spot's owner, Dana Everhart, is facing a difficult decision. She could purchase a commercial printer and produce the flyers in house. However, the machinery, costing approximately $20,000, is quite expensive. The printer has an estimated useful life of four years and would be depreciated using the straight-line method with no salvage value. If Dana purchases the printer, she would also have to buy paper and toner for the machine and pay for maintenance or repairs as needed. She estimates that it would cost $0.02 per page to print the flyers herself.

Alternatively, Dana could pay a local printing company $0.05 per copy to print the flyers. She would incur no printing costs other than the $0.05 per page if she chooses this alternative. However, $0.05 per page is considerably more than Dana would have to pay for paper and toner if she owned a commercial printer.

Dana plans to charge customers $0.08 per page for each flyer Ink Spot distributes.

Required:

1. Why does Dana need to understand cost behavior? How does it impact Dana and her business?
2. Name at least three costs in addition to the cost of producing the flyers that a business such as Ink Spot would incur, and describe the cost behavior of each one.
3. Considering the decision Dana must make, determine the cost behavior of each alternative. For any mixed cost, determine the amount of each component as much as possible.
4. Discuss other factors about Ink Spot's operating environment that Dana should consider when deciding whether to make the flyers or buy them from a local printing company.
5. Discuss factors other than cost that Dana should consider.

CHAPTER 6

Cost-Volume-Profit Analysis

YOUR LEARNING OBJECTIVES

After completing this chapter, you should be able to:

LO1   Use cost-volume-profit analysis to find the break-even point.

LO2   Use cost-volume-profit analysis to determine the sales needed to achieve a target profit.

LO3   Compute the margin of safety.

LO4   Analyze how changes in prices and cost structure affect the cost-volume-profit relationships.

LO5   Calculate the degree of operating leverage and use it to predict the effect a change in sales has on profit.

LO6   Perform multiproduct cost-volume-profit analysis and explain how the product mix affects the analysis.

Lecture Presentation–LP6
www.mhhe.com/whitecotten1e

FOCUS COMPANY: Starbucks Coffee

"Beyond a Cup of Coffee"

www.starbucks.com

These days you don't have to go far to buy a cup of Starbucks Coffee. Started as a small coffee shop in Seattle's Pike Place Market more than three decades ago, Starbucks Coffee can now be found on street corners, college campuses, and airports across the country and abroad. Consider the following facts about Starbucks:

- From 2002–2007, Starbucks opened approximately five new locations every day. In 2008, the company realized it could not sustain that rate of growth and began closing locations.
- The average customer spends $4.05 per visit at Starbucks.
- Starbucks spends more on employee health insurance than on coffee beans.
- When Starbucks eliminated the 8-ounce cup from its menu (making the "tall" the new "small"), it increased revenue by 25 cents per cup with only 2 cents of added product cost.[1]

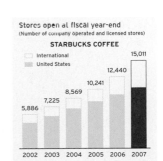

Stores open at fiscal year-end
(Number of company operated and licensed stores)
STARBUCKS COFFEE

□ International
▨ United States

2002: 5,886
2003: 7,225
2004: 8,569
2005: 10,241
2006: 12,440
2007: 15,011

How does Starbucks decide how much to charge for a cup of coffee, how many customers a particular location must serve to be profitable, and how changes in prices, costs, and product offerings affect the bottom line? This chapter introduces a decision-making approach that can help managers answer these and many other questions. Cost-volume-profit analysis is a decision-making tool that models how changes in prices, costs, volume, or product mix affect the bottom line.

Throughout this chapter, we use a hypothetical Starbucks coffee shop as our focus company. Initially, we limit our analysis to the sale of one type of product: coffee. Later in the chapter, we expand our analysis to show how to incorporate the other products that Starbucks sells, such as pastries, CDs, T-shirts, and appliances. As usual, we use hypothetical numbers for all of the examples, but they will give you a good idea of how to apply cost-volume-profit in a real-world situation.

---

[1]Taylor Clark, *Starbucked: A Double Tall Tale of Caffeine, Commerce, and Culture* (New York: Little, Brown and Company, 2007).

Cost-volume-profit analysis	Applications of cost-volume-profit analysis	Multiproduct cost-volume-profit analysis
• Assumptions of cost-volume-profit • Cost-volume-profit graph • Break-even analysis • Target profit analysis	• Margin of safety • Evaluating changes in prices • Changes in cost structure • Degree of operating leverage	• Weighted average contribution margin • Break-even analysis • Target profit analysis • Contribution margin ratio approach

Cost-Volume-Profit Analysis

Video 6-1
www.mhhe.com/whitecotton1e

Cost-volume-profit (CVP) analysis is a managerial decision-making tool that focuses on the relationships among product prices, the volume and mix of units sold, variable and fixed costs, and profit. The approach allows managers to see how a change in one or more of these variables will impact profitability while holding everything else constant.

Let's start with a simple but unrealistic scenario in which Starbucks sells only one type and size of coffee. Assume the price is $2.50 per unit and variable costs are $1.00 per unit. Recall from Chapter 5 that variable costs are incurred for each additional unit sold, such as the cost of coffee beans, cups, server wages, and electricity to run the coffee machines. Fixed costs are $12,000 per month including rent, insurance, equipment depreciation, salaries, and other costs that must be paid each month regardless of the number of customers served.

The following table shows how total revenue, variable costs, fixed costs, and profit will change depending on the volume of units sold. This table is based on the contribution margin income statement that was introduced in Chapter 5. This approach, which classifies costs as either variable or fixed, is key to analyzing cost-volume-profit relationships.

> **COACH'S TIP**
>
> Notice that the company had a loss at 5,000 units and a profit at 10,000. The break-even point is the number of units that would yield zero profit.

	Per Unit	VOLUME OF UNITS SOLD		
		5,000	10,000	15,000
Sales revenue	$2.50	$12,500	$25,000	$37,500
Variable costs	1.00	5,000	10,000	15,000
Contribution margin	1.50	$ 7,500	$15,000	$22,500
Fixed costs	—	12,000	12,000	12,000
Operating profit	—	($ 4,500)	$ 3,000	$10,500

Notice that total sales revenue, variable costs, and contribution margin increase in direct proportion to the number of units sold. Total fixed costs remain the same, however, at least within this limited range of sales volume (called the **relevant range**). At 5,000 units, the total contribution margin is less than total fixed costs, so the company has a loss. At 10,000 units, the total contribution margin is more than total fixed costs, so the company has a profit. Somewhere in between, the contribution margin equals total fixed costs, and the company would earn zero profit.

Assume that the Starbucks manager has the following questions:

- How many cups of coffee must be sold each month to break even, or earn zero profit?
- The owner (my boss) expects the business to earn $18,000 in profit each month. How do I achieve that?
- Last month we sold 15,000 cups of coffee and made a decent profit, but business has slowed down due to the bad economy. How much can sales drop before the business is "in the red," or losing money?
- I've been thinking about automating the customer order process. We could serve more coffee with fewer employees, but it would increase monthly expenses by $14,000. How many additional customers would I need to serve each day to justify this investment?
- If I expand our product offering to sell green tea, muffins, and sandwiches, how many customers do I need each month to break even? To earn $18,000 in profit?

Each of these questions can be addressed using cost-volume-profit analysis, but they require us to make some key assumptions. Our conclusions will be only as sound as the assumptions on which they are based.

ASSUMPTIONS OF COST-VOLUME-PROFIT ANALYSIS

CVP is based on the following assumptions:

1. A straight line can be used to describe how total cost and total revenue change across the relevant range of activity.
2. All costs can be accurately described as either fixed or variable.
3. Changes in total cost are due strictly to changes in the volume of units produced or customers served.
4. Production and sales are equal.
5. Companies that sell more than one product or service maintain a constant product or sales mix.

The first assumption continues the linear approach that we used in Chapter 5 to analyze cost behavior. Although total cost and activity are not always perfectly linear, a straight line should provide a reasonable approximation, at least within a limited range of activity called the relevant range.

The second assumption is that all costs can be classified as either variable or fixed. For mixed costs, or those that have both a fixed and variable component, we can use the high-low method or least-squares regression to separate the two effects.

The third assumption is that total costs change only as a result of a change in the number of units produced or customers served. We ignore other factors that can affect total cost, such as employee learning curves, productivity gains, and quantity discounts for buying in bulk.

The fourth assumption, that production equals sales, keeps inventory levels constant and avoids any difference in profit that can occur due to the accounting method used to value inventory.

The final assumption is needed to perform CVP in a multiproduct setting, which is addressed at the end of this chapter.

COST-VOLUME-PROFIT GRAPH

A cost-volume-profit graph, or **CVP graph**, is useful for visualizing the relationship between total revenue, total costs, the volume of units sold, and profit. Refer to Exhibit 6.1 for a CVP graph based on the revenue and cost information for Starbucks.

The total revenue (blue) line is based on the number of units sold multiplied by the unit sales price. The total cost (red) line represents the sum of the variable and fixed

EXHIBIT 6.1   Cost-Volume-Profit Graph

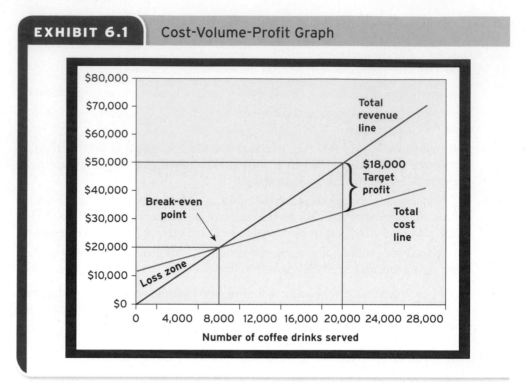

costs. Total fixed cost ($12,000) is shown as the point at which the line intercepts the Y axis. Conceptually, this is the amount of cost that would be incurred even if no coffee were sold. The unit variable cost ($1) is represented by the slope of the total cost line. This is the amount by which total cost increases with each additional unit sold.

The **break-even point** is the point at which the total revenue and total cost lines cross (leaving zero profit). In this example, the break-even point corresponds to 8,000 units or $20,000 in total revenue and total cost.

The difference between the total revenue and total cost lines is the profit (or loss). Anything below 8,000 units results in a loss because total costs exceed total revenue. Anything above 8,000 units results in a profit. For example, if Starbucks sells 20,000 units, it will earn a target profit of $18,000 ($50,000 in revenue − $32,000 in total costs).

Although the CVP chart is useful for conceptualizing the relationship between total revenue, fixed and variable costs, volume, and profit, we must use equations or formulas to compute the exact numbers. The next section illustrates how to calculate the break-even point and target profit numbers shown in the CVP graph.

BREAK-EVEN ANALYSIS

Break-even analysis is the simplest form of cost-volume-profit analysis. The goal of **break-even analysis** is to determine the level of sales (in either units or total sales dollars) needed to break even, or earn zero profit.

Several methods can be used to find the break-even point including:

1. Profit equation method.
2. Unit contribution margin method.
3. Contribution margin ratio method.

Each of these methods is illustrated in the following sections. When you have a solid understanding of how to find the break-even point, each approach can be easily modified to perform other types of CVP analysis, including a target profit.

Profit Equation Method

The profit equation method uses an equation in which profit is defined as the difference between total sales revenue and total fixed and variable costs as follows:

Profit Equation

Total Sales Revenue − Total Variable Costs − Total Fixed Costs = Profit

(Unit Price × Q) − (Unit Variable Costs × Q) − Total Fixed Costs = Profit

Where: Q = Quantity of unit sold

Notice that total sales revenue and variable costs are a function of the number of units sold (Q), while total fixed costs are independent of the number of units sold. In CVP analysis, we allow any single factor in the equation to vary while holding everything else constant to determine the ultimate effect on profit.

In our Starbucks example, the unit price is $2.50, the unit variable cost is $1.00, and the total fixed costs are $12,000.00.

To find the break-even point, we simply set the profit equation equal to zero and solve for the quantity of units (Q), as follows:

Break-Even Analysis

(Unit Price × Q) − (Unit Variable Costs × Q) − Fixed Costs = Profit

($2.50 × Q) − ($1.00 × Q) − $12,000 = 0

$1.50 Q = $12,000

Q = $12,000/$1.50

Q = 8,000

> **COACH'S TIP**
>
> To find the break-even point, set the profit equation equal to zero. If you want to earn a profit, set the equation to the target profit.

This analysis shows that Starbucks needs to sell 8,000 units to break even, or earn zero profit. To verify that this is correct, we can plug Q = 8,000 into the profit equation and make sure that profit is zero, as follows:

(Unit Price × Q) − (Unit Variable Costs × Q) − Fixed Costs = Profit

($2.50 × 8,000) − ($1.00 × 8,000) − $12,000 = 0

$20,000 − $8,000 − $12,000 = 0

Unit Contribution Margin Method

An alternative method to cost-volume-profit is based on the concept of the contribution margin. This method is mathematically equivalent to the profit equation method but nets the unit sales price and unit variable costs together to arrive at unit contribution margin, as follows:

	Per Unit
Sales price	$2.50
Less: Variable cost	1.00
Contribution margin	$1.50

The **unit contribution margin** tells us how much contribution margin is generated by each additional unit sold. The contribution margin is used to cover fixed costs, and whatever is left over is profit. Expressing the total contribution margin in terms of the number of units sold results in the following:

Unit Contribution Margin Approach

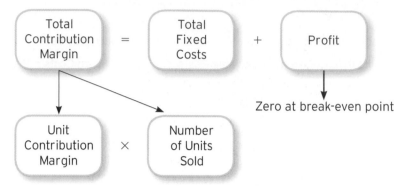

Zero at break-even point

At break even, the total contribution margin equals total fixed costs so that profit is zero. The break-even point can be calculated by dividing total fixed costs by the unit contribution margin, as follows:

$$\text{Break-Even Units} = \frac{\text{Total Fixed Costs}}{\text{Unit Contribution Margin}}$$

Applying this formula to our Starbucks example results in the following:

$$\text{Break-Even Units} = \$12,000/\$1.50 \text{ per Drink}$$
$$\text{Break-Even Units} = 8,000 \text{ Coffee Drinks}$$

This break-even formula shows that Starbucks needs to sell 8,000 coffee drinks per month to cover its fixed costs, with nothing left over as profit.

To translate break-even units into sales revenue, we multiply by the unit sales prices as follows:

$$\text{Break-Even Sales} = \text{Break-Even Units} \times \text{Unit Sales Price}$$
$$\text{Break-Even Sales} = 8,000 \text{ Units} \times \$2.50 = \$20,000$$

These numbers are consistent with the break-even point shown on the CVP graph in Exhibit 6.1. Starbucks will break even, or earn zero profit, at 8,000 units, or $20,000 in total sales revenue.

Contribution Margin Ratio Method

The third way to calculate the break-even point is based on the contribution margin (CM) ratio. Recall that the contribution margin ratio is calculated by dividing contribution margin by sales revenue, as follows:

	Per Unit	Percent of Sales
Sales price	$2.50	100%
Variable cost	1.00	40%
Contribution margin	$1.50	60% ($1.50/$2.50)

The contribution margin ratio tells us how much contribution margin is generated by each dollar of sales revenue. For every $1.00 in sales revenue, Starbucks will generate $0.60 in contribution margin. For example, if sales revenue is $1,000, contribution margin will be 60 percent of that amount, or $600.

At break even, the total contribution margin must equal total fixed costs, with nothing left as profit. To calculate break even in terms of sales revenue, we divide total fixed costs by the contribution margin ratio as in the following formula:

$$\text{Break-Even Sales} = \frac{\text{Total Fixed Costs}}{\text{Contribution Margin Ratio (\%)}}$$

Because Starbucks' CM ratio is 60 percent, the total sales needed to cover $12,000 in fixed costs can be calculated as follows:

$$\text{Break-Even Units} = \$12,000/60\%$$
$$\text{Break-Even Sales} = \$20,000$$

This is the same answer we found by multiplying 8,000 units by the $2.50 unit sales price. The contribution margin ratio simply provides a more direct way to calculate the sales revenue needed to break even.

At this point, you may be wondering why you need to calculate break even several different ways. If you understand each approach and how each relates to the others, you are more likely to understand the logic and concepts behind cost-volume-profit analysis. This will make it easier to apply the approach to scenarios other than break even. The second reason it is important to know different approaches is that managers must often deal with missing or incomplete information. For example, managers may not have ready access to the detailed price and quantity information needed to use the equation or unit contribution margin method. Managers are accustomed to dealing with information in terms of total sales dollars. This is particularly true when they deal with multiple products or services that have different unit prices, costs, and quantities. Although the unit contribution margin method is very intuitive, the contribution margin ratio method is more practical, particularly as the number of products or services increases.

TARGET PROFIT ANALYSIS

Although break-even analysis is a common starting point for performing CVP, most managers want to do more than just break even. They want to earn a profit. **Target profit analysis** is an extension of break-even analysis that allows managers to determine the number of units or total sales revenue needed to earn a target profit. To earn a target profit, the total contribution margin must be enough to cover the fixed costs **plus** the target profit as follows:

$$\boxed{\begin{array}{c}\text{Total}\\\text{Contribution}\\\text{Margin}\end{array}} = \boxed{\begin{array}{c}\text{Total}\\\text{Fixed}\\\text{Costs}\end{array}} + \boxed{\begin{array}{c}\text{Target}\\\text{Profit}\end{array}}$$

> **Learning Objective 2**
> Use cost-volume-profit analysis to determine the sales needed to achieve a target profit.

To determine the level of sales needed to earn a target profit, we simply modify the break-even formulas to include the target profit in the numerator, as follows:

$$\text{Target Units} = \frac{\text{Total Fixed Costs} + \text{Target Profit}}{\text{Unit Contribution Margin}}$$

$$\text{Target Sales} = \frac{\text{Total Fixed Costs} + \text{Target Profit}}{\text{Contribution Margin Ratio (\%)}}$$

For example, if the Starbucks manager wants to earn $18,000 in profit each month, the target units and target sales would be calculated as follows:

$$\text{Target Units} = \frac{\$12,000 + \$18,000}{\$1.50 \text{ per Drink}} = 20,000 \text{ Coffee Drinks}$$

$$\text{Target Sales} = \frac{\$12,000 + \$18,000}{60\%} = \$50,000$$

COACH'S TIP

The only difference between the target profit formula and the break-even formula is that the target profit formula adds the target profit to fixed costs. The amount in the denominator depends on whether you want to find the answer in units or total sales dollars.

This analysis shows that Starbucks needs to sell 20,000 units to cover $12,000 in fixed costs and still have $18,000 in profit. Remember that the company needs to sell 8,000 units to break even. Each additional unit contributes $1.50 in contribution margin and thus profit (because fixed costs don't change). Multiplying the unit contribution margin of $1.50 by 12,000 extra units (above break even) gives $18,000. The total sales revenue generated by 20,000 units is $50,000 (20,000 units × $2.50 unit price). You get the same $50,000 if you divide the fixed costs plus target profit by the contribution margin ratio of 60 percent.

To make sure you understand how to calculate the break-even point and target profit, complete the following Self-Study Practice.

Self-Study Practice

A company sells a product for $60 per unit. Variable costs are $36 per unit, and monthly fixed costs are $120,000. Answer the following questions.

1. What is the break-even point in units and in total sales dollars?
2. What is the contribution margin ratio?
3. What level of total sales would be required to earn a target profit of $60,000?

After you have finished, check your answers with the solutions in the margin.

Solution to Self-Study Practice

1. Break-Even Units = Fixed Costs/CM per unit
   = $120,000/($60 − $36) = 5,000 units
   Break-Even Sales Dollars = 5,000 units × $60 price = $300,000
2. CM Ratio = $24/$60 = 40%
3. Target Sales $= (Fixed Costs + Target Profit)/CM Ratio =
   ($120,000 + 60,000)/40% = $450,000

Applications of Cost-Volume-Profit Analysis

Learning Objective 3
Compute the margin of safety.

The previous section illustrated the two most common applications of cost-volume-profit analysis: break-even and target profit analysis. In this section, we extend this basic analysis to several other applications of cost-volume-profit analysis.

MARGIN OF SAFETY

The **margin of safety** is the difference between actual or budgeted sales and the break-even point. Think of the margin of safety as a buffer zone that identifies how much sales can drop before the business will suffer a loss. This application of CVP analysis is most relevant to companies that face a significant risk of **not** making a profit, such as start-up businesses or companies that face extreme competition or abrupt changes in demand. The formula for calculating the margin of safety is:

$$\text{Margin of Safety} = \text{Actual or Budgeted Sales} - \text{Break-Even Sales}$$

Existing companies base the margin of safety on prior period sales; new businesses base it on budgeted or expected sales. For example, if you were thinking of opening a new Starbucks location and had developed a business plan based on an anticipated or budgeted sales level, it would be wise to compare that level to the break-even point. Doing so would show you how much cushion you have between making a profit and suffering a loss.

To apply the margin of safety, let's assume that our hypothetical Starbucks location sold 15,000 coffee drinks during the most recent month (February) as shown in the following contribution margin income statement:

STARBUCKS COFFEE HOUSE Contribution Margin Income Statement For the Month of February 2009 15,000 Units Sold		
	Total	Per Unit
Sales revenue	$37,500	$2.50
Less: Variable costs	15,000	1.00
Contribution margin	22,500	$1.50
Less: Fixed costs	12,000	
Profit (Loss)	$10,500	

Notice that the company operated above the break-even point during February with sales of $37,500 and a profit of $10,500. Recall that the break-even point was 8,000 units, or $20,000 in total sales. Thus, the margin of safety is calculated as follows:

Margin of Safety	=	Actual or Budgeted Sales	−	Break- Even Sales
$17,500		$37,500		$20,000

Expressing the margin of safety as a percentage of actual or budgeted sales provides a better idea of how large this buffer zone is. In this case, the margin of safety as a percentage of February's actual sales is 46.7 percent ($17,500/$37,500). In other words, Starbucks' monthly sales could drop as much as $17,500 or 46.7 percent before the company would be "in the red," or losing money.

EVALUATING CHANGES IN PRICES

Managers can also use the cost-volume-profit framework to evaluate pricing decisions. Assume that Starbucks' manager is considering increasing the price of coffee to $4 with no effect on unit variable cost or total fixed costs. The following table summarizes the effect this proposed price increase would have on the unit contribution margin and contribution margin ratio:

	CURRENT PRICE		PROPOSED PRICE	
	Per Unit	Percent	Per Unit	Percent
Sales price	$2.50	100%	$4.00	100%
Variable cost	1.00	40%	1.00	25%
Contribution margin	$1.50	60%	$3.00	75%

> **COACH'S TIP**
>
> The proposed price increase will double the unit contribution margin ($1.50 to $3.00). This means the company will need to sell one-half as many units to break even.

Notice that both the unit contribution margin and the contribution margin ratio increase as a result of the price increase. We can use these revised numbers to evaluate the implications of the new pricing structure as illustrated in the following scenarios.

Scenario 1

Assume the manager expects the price increase to reduce monthly sales by 20 percent (from 15,000 units in February to 12,000 units). Is the price increase a good idea?

Because total fixed costs do not change, we can evaluate this decision by comparing the total contribution margin earned before and after the proposed price increase. Because the price increase is expected to impact the number of units sold, we multiply by the unit contribution margin to determine the effect on contribution margin, as follows:

Learning Objective 4
Analyze how changes in prices and cost structure affect the cost-volume-profit relationships.

	Current Price	Proposed Price
Unit contribution margin	$ 1.50	$ 3.00
Number of units	× 15,000	× 12,000
Total contribution margin	$22,500	$36,000
Difference	$13,500	

This analysis shows that total contribution margin will increase by $13,500 as a result of the proposed price increase. Because total fixed costs remain the same, this increase in contribution margin will fall to the bottom line.

Scenario 2

What if the manager is unsure how customers will react to the price increase? The manager wants to know what level of total sales revenue will be required to earn at least the same monthly profit as in February when the company earned $10,500.

To analyze this scenario, we can use the following formula:

$$\text{Target Sales} = \frac{\text{Total Fixed Costs} + \text{Target Profit}}{\text{Contribution Margin Ratio (\%)}}$$

Because fixed costs will remain at $12,000 and the profit before the price increase was $10,500, the target sales based on the new 75 percent contribution margin ratio would be computed as follows:

$$\text{Target Sales} = \frac{\$12,000 + \$10,500}{75\%}$$

$$\text{Target Sales} = \$30,000$$

This analysis shows that the company needs to earn $30,000 in total sales revenue to earn $10,500 in profit. Because the proposed sales price is $4, this translates into 7,500 units ($30,000/$4). You could get this same number by dividing the total fixed costs plus the target profit by the new unit contribution margin as follows:

$$\text{Target Units} = \frac{\text{Total Fixed Costs} + \text{Target Profit}}{\text{Unit Contribution Margin}}$$

$$\text{Target Units} = \frac{\$12,000 + \$10,500}{\$3.00}$$

$$\text{Target Units} = 7,500 \text{ units}$$

Before we continue, complete the following Self-Study Practice to make sure you can compute the margin of safety and analyze the effect of a price increase on CVP relationships.

Self-Study Practice

Last month's contribution margin income statement follows:

Contribution Margin Income Statement 10,000 Units Sold			
	Per Unit	Total	Percent of Sales
Sales price	$4.00	$40,000	100%
Variable cost	1.50	15,000	37.5%
Contribution margin	$2.50	25,000	62.5%
Fixed costs		10,000	
Profit		$15,000	

Break-Even Units = $10,000/$2.50 = 4,000 units
Break-Even Sales = $10,000/62.5% = $16,000

1. Compute last month's margin of safety in dollars and as a percentage of sales.

2. Assume the sales price increases by 25 percent with no effect on unit variable costs. Compute the new unit contribution margin and contribution margin ratio.

3. Given the price increase described in question 2, how many units must be sold to earn the same profit as last month?

After you have finished, check your answers with the solutions in the margin.

CHANGES IN COST STRUCTURE

Next we analyze how a change in cost structure affects the cost-volume-profit relationship. **Cost structure** refers to how a company uses variable costs versus fixed costs to perform its operations. Some companies have a relatively high proportion of variable costs such as direct materials and direct labor while others have relatively more fixed costs such as facilities, equipment, and supervision. Managers face many decisions that can affect their relative cost structure and have implications for cost-volume-profit analysis.

A common example is the decision to automate a process that is currently done manually. Automation typically reduces variable costs (by reducing direct labor) while increasing fixed costs (by increasing equipment depreciation, maintenance, and supervision).

Assume that Starbucks is considering investing in equipment that would allow customers to place their own order using a touch screen at the counter. The company could lease the machine for $14,000 per month (increasing monthly fixed costs from $12,000 to $26,000). The automation would save $0.70 in variable costs (from $1.00 to $0.30). The unit sales price will be $2.50 under either alternative. What level of volume would be needed to justify this expenditure?

One way to solve this problem is to use the profit equation method. Instead of setting a single profit equation equal to zero (to find break even), we set two profit equations equal to each other so that they yield the same profit. This is a type of **indifference point,** or point at which managers should be indifferent between the two alternatives because they yield the same profit.

The following equations are used to solve for the number of units at which profit will be the same with or without automation.

Profit Equation (before automation)	=	Profit Equation (after automation)
(Unit Price × Q) − (Unit VC × Q) − Fixed cost	=	(Unit Price × Q) − (Unit VC × Q) − Fixed cost
$2.50 Q − $1.00 Q − $12,000	=	$2.50 Q − $0.30 Q − $26,000
$1.50 Q − $12,000	=	$2.20 Q − $26,000
−$0.70 Q	=	−$14,000
Q	=	20,000

At a sales volume of 20,000 units, the company will make the same profit with or without automation. To verify that we did the algebra correctly, we can plug Q = 20,000 back into the profit equation to make certain the profit is the same:

Profit Equation (before automation)	=	Profit Equation (after automation)
(Unit Price × Q) − (Unit VC × Q) − Fixed cost	=	(Unit Price × Q) − (Unit VC × Q) − Fixed cost
$2.50 (20,000) − $1.00 (20,000) − $12,000	=	$2.50 (20,000) − $0.30 (20,000) − $26,000
$50,000 − 20,000 − $12,000	=	$50,000 − $6,000 − $26,000
$18,000	=	$18,000

At 20,000 units, profit will be $18,000 under either alternative. If volume is more than 20,000 units, the company will make a higher profit with the automated ordering system. But if volume is less than 20,000 units per month, profit will be higher without automation. See Exhibit 6.2 for a visual depiction of the effect of automation on the cost-volume-profit relationship.

As long as the manager expects demand to exceed 20,000 units per month, the investment in automation will result in increased profit. However, there is a greater risk with automation in the event that demand is not as large as expected. This risk is reflected in a measure called *degree of operating leverage*, which is discussed next.

DEGREE OF OPERATING LEVERAGE

In physics, a lever is a tool that allows a small amount of force to move a heavy object. In business, operating leverage is a multiplication factor that explains how a relatively small change in sales revenue can result in a larger effect on profit.

Degree of operating leverage measures the extent to which fixed costs can be used to translate (or magnify) a given change in sales volume into a larger change in profit.

Operating leverage of more than 1 (a magnification effect) occurs when a company utilizes fixed costs as the lever to turn a change in sales revenue into a larger change in profit. All else equal, the higher a company's fixed cost, the greater its degree of operating leverage.

Degree of operating leverage is calculated as follows:

$$\text{Degree of Operating Leverage} = \frac{\text{Contribution Margin}}{\text{Profit}}$$

To apply this formula, let's see how the trade-off of fixed and variable costs (through automation) affects Starbucks' degree of operating leverage. As a starting point, we use the indifference point of 20,000 units so that each method will provide the same starting profit, as follows:

	20,000 UNITS SOLD (NO AUTOMATION)		20,000 UNITS SOLD (AUTOMATION)	
	Per Unit	Total	Per Unit	Total
Sales price	$2.50	$50,000	$2.50	$50,000
Variable cost	1.00	20,000	0.30	6,000
Contribution margin	$1.50	$30,000	$2.20	$44,000
Fixed cost		12,000		26,000
Profit		$18,000		$18,000
Degree of Operating Leverage =		$30,000		$44,000
Contribution Margin/Profit		$18,000		$18,000
		1.67		2.44

EXHIBIT 6.2	**Effect of Automation on the CVP Relationships**

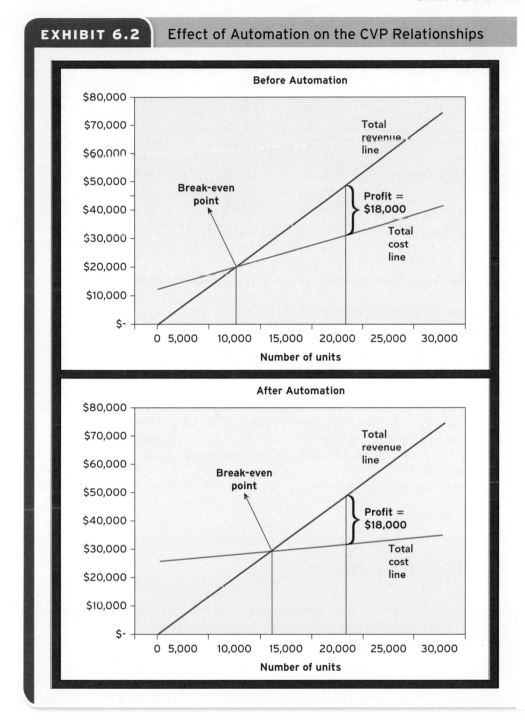

Although profit is the same at 20,000 units, the degree of operating leverage is higher with automation (2.44) than without it (1.67). The reason is that automation results in a trade-off between fixed and variable costs, which respond differently to changes in volume.

The degree of operating leverage is a multiplier that we can use to predict how a percentage change in sales revenue will translate into a percentage change in profit. In this example, if sales revenue increases by 10 percent, profit will increase by 16.7 percent (10% × 1.67) without automation or 24.4 percent (10% × 2.44) with it.

We can confirm this by creating a new contribution margin income statement under each scenario:

	NO AUTOMATION		AUTOMATION	
	Base Case	10 Percent Increase	Base Case	10 Percent Increase
Sales revenue	$50,000	$55,000	$50,000	$55,000
Variable cost	20,000	22,000	6,000	6,600
Contribution margin	$30,000	$33,000	$44,000	$48,400
Fixed cost	12,000	12,000	26,000	26,000
Profit	$18,000	$21,000	$18,000	$22,400
Percentage change in profit	$\dfrac{\$21,000-18,000}{\$18,000}$		$\dfrac{\$22,400-18,000}{\$18,000}$	
	16.7%		24.4%	

Starting at the same level of profit ($18,000), the company will experience a larger increase in profit with automation than without it.

Keep in mind that operating leverage works in both directions. It magnifies the effect of both increases and decreases in sales revenue. If sales decrease by 10 percent, the company will experience a more dramatic decline in profit with automation than without it. In general, a company with a high degree of operating leverage will experience greater swings in profit as a result of changes in sales revenue and is therefore considered riskier than a comparable company with a smaller degree of operating leverage. In making choices about cost structure, managers must consider both the rewards (potential for increased profit) and amount of risk (upside and downside) they are willing to bear.

Complete the following Self-Study Practice to make sure you understand the effect of cost structure on the degree of operating leverage and profit.

 ## Self-Study Practice

Alpha and Beta Companies make a similar product. Alpha makes the product manually; Beta uses robots to do much of the assembly. Last month, both companies sold 20,000 units and made the same profit as follows:

	Alpha (20,000 units)		Beta (20,000 units)	
	Per Unit	Total	Per Unit	Total
Sales price	$100	$200,000	$100	$200,000
Variable cost	60	120,000	20	40,000
Contribution margin	$ 40	80,000	$ 80	$160,000
Fixed cost		20,000		100,000
Profit		$ 60,000		$ 60,000

1. Calculate the degree of operating leverage for each company.

2. If sales increase by 10 percent, how much will profit increase for each company?

3. Which company is better positioned to withstand a decrease in demand? Why?

After you have finished, check your answers with the solutions in the margin.

Solution to Self-Study Practice

1. Degree of Operating Leverage (DOL) = Contribution Margin/Profit

   Alpha (DOL) = $80,000/$60,000 = 1.333

   Beta (DOL) = $160,000/60,000 = 2.667

2. Alpha profit will increase by 13.33 percent (10% × 1.333)

   Beta profit will increase by 26.67 percent (10% × 2.667)

3. Alpha is better positioned to withstand a decrease in demand because it has lower operating leverage. Beta has more fixed costs that are not easily reduced when demand drops.

Multiproduct Cost-Volume-Profit Analysis

In the previous examples, we simplified the CVP analysis by assuming that Starbucks sells only one type and size of coffee drink. But we all know that Starbucks and most other businesses offer more than one product or service. For example, Starbucks sells coffee, tea, pastries, sandwiches, salads, mugs, T-shirts, and other novelty items. Each of these items is likely to have a different price and unit cost, which makes the CVP analysis more complex.

> **Learning Objective 6**
> Perform multiproduct cost-volume-profit analysis and explain how the product mix affects the analysis.

The key to performing CVP analysis in a multiproduct setting is to make an assumption about the relative proportion of sales (in either units or total sales dollars) from each product or service line. The only caveat is that the analysis will be valid only for the assumed product or sales mix.

WEIGHTED AVERAGE CONTRIBUTION MARGIN

Let's start by stating the sales mix in terms of units, which will be used to calculate a **weighted average unit contribution margin.** The weighted average unit contribution margin is then used in place of the single product unit contribution margin in the cost-volume-profit analysis.

To illustrate, we can extend our Starbucks example to incorporate two product offerings, coffee and pastries. While still not a realistic scenario, this simple setting illustrates the concepts and techniques needed to apply CVP to even more product and service offerings. Assume the unit price and cost of the two products are as follows:

	Coffee	Pastries
Sales price	$2.50	$4.00
Variable cost	1.00	1.25
Unit contribution margin	$1.50	$2.75

Notice that pastries have a higher unit contribution margin ($2.75) than coffee ($1.50). We can calculate a weighted average of these two numbers, with the weight based on the relative proportion (mix) of units sold.

Assume that 60 percent of units sold are coffee and 40 percent pastries. Based on this product mix, the **weighted average unit contribution margin** would be calculated as follows:

	Coffee	Pastries
Unit contribution margin	$1.50	$2.75
Unit mix (weight)	× 60%	× 40%
	$0.90	$1.10
Weighted Average Unit Contribution Margin	$0.90 + $1.10 = $2.00	

The $2 weighted average unit contribution margin means that Starbucks will make an average of $2 in contribution margin for each unit sold, but ONLY if 60 percent of the units are coffee and 40 percent are pastries. This weighted average contribution margin can be used in place of the single product unit contribution margin in cost-volume-profit analysis.

BREAK-EVEN ANALYSIS

At break even, fixed costs must exactly equal the contribution margin. If we divide the total fixed costs by the weighted average unit contribution margin, the result tells us how many total units must be sold to break even. We then use the assumed product mix percentages to determine how many units of each product type must be sold.

Assuming Starbucks' monthly fixed costs are $12,000, the break-even point would be calculated as follows:

$$\text{Break-Even Units} = \frac{\text{Total Fixed Costs}}{\text{Weighted Average Unit CM}}$$

$$\text{Break-Even Units} = \frac{\$12,000}{\$2}$$

$$\text{Break-Even Units} = 6{,}000$$

This shows that 6,000 total units are required to break even. But how many of these units should be coffee and how many pastries? Because the $2 weighted average contribution margin was based on a 60 percent/40 percent product mix, we must use the same mix to determine the units of each individual product:

$$\text{Coffee Units} = 6{,}000 \times 60\% = 3{,}600$$
$$\text{Pastry Units} = 6{,}000 \times 40\% = 2{,}400$$

The company will break even if it sells 3,600 units of coffee and 2,400 units of pastries.

What would happen if the company sold 6,000 total units, but 3,000 (50%) were coffee and 3,000 (50%) were pastries? Would the company still break even? It would not because the break-even point was contingent on the 60/40 product mix. By shifting the product mix toward the pastry product (and away from coffee), the company will earn **more** contribution margin because each pastry contributes a higher contribution margin than coffee. Because fixed costs do not change, the company will earn a slight profit.

The next example shows how shifting the product mix toward coffee would affect the CVP analysis.

TARGET PROFIT ANALYSIS

Next, we extend the cost-volume-profit analysis to include a target profit. For this example, assume that Starbucks serves four coffee drinks for every pastry (or a 4:1 ratio). The new product mix is 80 percent coffee units and 20 percent pastry units. The weighted average unit contribution margin based on this product mix is calculated as follows:

COACH'S TIP

To calculate the new product mix use the following formulas:

$\frac{4}{5} = 80\%$ Coffee

$\frac{1}{5} = 20\%$ Pastries

	Coffee	Pastries
Unit contribution margin	$1.50	$2.75
Unit mix (weight)	× 80%	× 20%
	$1.20	$0.55
Weighted Average Unit Contribution Margin	$1.20 + $0.55 = $1.75	

Notice that the new weighted average unit contribution margin ($1.75) based on an 80/20 product mix is lower than the $2.00 unit contribution margin calculated in the previous example (using a 60/40 product mix). Because the coffee product is now weighted more heavily, the weighted average unit contribution margin is lower.

If the Starbucks manager wants to earn a monthly profit of $9,000 and monthly fixed costs remain at $12,000, how many coffee and pastry units must be sold? We use the same target profit formula as before but divide by the weighted average unit contribution margin:

$$\text{Target Units} = \frac{\text{Total Fixed Costs} + \text{Target Profit}}{\text{Weighted Average Unit CM}}$$

$$\text{Target Units} = \frac{\$12,000 + \$9,000}{\$1.75}$$

$$\text{Target Units} = 12,000$$

$$\text{Coffee Units} = 12,000 \times 80\% \text{ Mix} = 9,600$$
$$\text{Pastry Units} = 12,000 \times 20\% \text{ Mix} = 2,400$$

The company will earn $9,000 if it sells 9,600 coffee drinks and 2,400 pastries. We can confirm this result by preparing a contribution margin income statement as follows:

STARBUCKS COFFEE
Contribution Margin Income Statement
Based on Target Profit of $9,000

	Coffee (9,600 units)		Pastries (2,400 units)		Overall (12,000 units)
	Per Unit	Total	Per Unit	Total	Total
Sales revenue	$2.50	$24,000	$4.00	$9,600	$33,600
Variable cost	1.00	9,600	1.25	3,000	12,600
Contribution margin	$1.50	$14,400	$2.75	$6,600	21,000
Fixed cost					12,000
Profit					$ 9,000

This statement confirms the results of our target profit analysis. Profit will be $9,000 if the company sells 12,000 units, with 9,600 units of coffee (80 percent) and 2,400 units of pastries (20 percent).

CONTRIBUTION MARGIN RATIO APPROACH

We can also do multiproduct CVP analysis based on the **weighted average contribution margin ratio**. This approach is commonly used in business because managers often have aggregated information about revenue and costs by product line (as opposed to the detailed information about prices, volumes, etc).

Consider the following contribution margin statement for Starbucks. This is the same income statement we just prepared for a target profit of $9,000, but the numbers have been restated as a percentage of total sales revenue.

COACH'S TIP

$21,000/$33,600 = 62.5%
  This is the overall (weighted average) contribution margin ratio. On average, the company generates $0.625 for every $1.00 of sales.

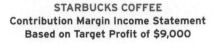

STARBUCKS COFFEE
Contribution Margin Income Statement
Based on Target Profit of $9,000

	Coffee		Pastries		Overall	
	Total	Percent	Total	Percent	Total	Percent
Sales revenue	$24,000	100%	$9,600	100%	$33,600	100%
Variable cost	9,600	40	3,000	31.25	12,600	37.5
Contribution margin	$14,400	60%	$6,600	68.75%	21,000	62.5%
Fixed cost					12,000	
Profit					$ 9,000	

The **weighted average contribution margin ratio** reflects the contribution margin ratios of the two products weighted according to the relative percentage of total sales revenue. In this example, the sales revenue mix is approximately 71.43 percent ($24,000/$33,600) from coffee and 28.57 percent ($9,600/$33,600) from pastries. The sales revenue mix is based on total sales revenue (dollars) not units.

The 62.5 percent overall or weighted average contribution margin ratio means that every dollar of sales revenue will generate an average of $0.625 in contribution margin. But this number only holds if the sales revenue mix is 71.43 percent coffee and 28.57 percent pastries.

Managers can use the 62.5 percent weighted average contribution margin ratio to determine how much total sales revenue is needed to break even or earn a target profit. Assume that the Starbucks' manager wants to earn a target profit of $15,000. Given the assumed sales mix, what is the total sales revenue needed to achieve this target profit?

To answer this question, we can use the target sales revenue formula, with the weighted average contribution margin ratio as the denominator:

$$\text{Target Sales} = \frac{\text{Total Fixed Costs} + \text{Target Profit}}{\text{Weighted Average CM Ratio}}$$

$$\text{Target Sales} = \frac{\$12,000 + \$15,000}{62.5\%}$$

$$\text{Target Sales} = \$43,200$$

Coffee Sales Revenue = $43,200 × 71.43% = $30,858
Pastry Sales Revenue = $43,200 × 28.57% = $12,342

Notice that we used the sales revenue mix (not the unit sales mix) to determine how much of the total sales revenue must come from coffee and pastries. Remember that the 62.5 percent weighted average contribution margin ratio was weighted according to the sales revenue mix, not the unit product mix.

If the company achieves this target sales revenue, it should earn $15,000 in target profit. We can confirm this result with the following contribution margin income statement:

	STARBUCKS COFFEE Contribution Margin Income Statement Based on Target Profit of $15,000					
	Coffee		Pastries		Overall	
	Total	Percent	Total	Percent	Total	Percent
Sales revenue	$30,858	100%	$12,342	100%	$43,200	100%
Variable cost	12,343	40	3,857	31.25	16,200	37.5
Contribution margin	$18,515	60%	$ 8,485	68.75%	27,000	62.5%
Fixed cost					$12,000	
Profit					$15,000	

The most important thing to remember when performing cost-volume-profit analysis in a multiproduct setting is to assume and maintain a constant product or sales mix. The mix can be stated in terms of the number of units sold (called the **product mix**) or as a percentage of total sales revenue (called the **sales mix**). The only difference between the two is the unit sales price (which is excluded from the product mix but included in the sales revenue mix). Either approach provides the same end result. Most students are more comfortable solving CVP problems in terms of units and then multiplying the result by the price to find total sales revenue. In the real world, however, managers often need to work with aggregated reports that are stated in dollars and percentages. In this sense, the contribution margin ratio approach is more valuable in the real world.

DEMONSTRATION CASE A (SINGLE PRODUCT)

In 2004, two young entrepreneurs realized that almost everyone loves cereal but no one ever eats it outside of their own home. So they opened Cereality, a cereal bar and café in the student union at Arizona State University. This innovative concept in fast food appealed to students and others who loved the idea of mixing Cocoa Puffs and Lucky Charms at almost any time of the day. Since then, Cereality franchises have opened at other college campuses around the country.

Based on market research, the young entrepreneurs decided to charge $3.75 for customers to create their own cereal combinations. They knew that costs such as cereal, milk, and paper products would vary with the number of customers but that other costs such as rent and insurance would be incurred each month even if the store were closed.

Assume the following cost structure for Cereality:

	Cereal
Unit sales price	$3.75
Unit variable cost	0.75
Unit contribution margin	$3.00
Monthly fixed costs	$6,000

Required:

1. How many customers must Cereality serve each month to break even?
2. How much total sales revenue must Cereality earn each month to break even?
3. If the owners want to earn an operating profit of $7,500 per month, how many customers must they serve?
4. If Cereality expects to serve 3,000 customers next month, what is the margin of safety in units? In total sales dollars? As a percentage of expected sales?

See page 233 for solution.

DEMONSTRATION CASE B (MULTIPRODUCT)

Cereality is considering adding a yogurt product to its cereal line with the following unit price and cost information:

	Cereal	Yogurt
Unit sales price	$3.75	$3.00
Unit variable cost	0.75	1.50
Unit contribution margin	$3.00	$1.50
Monthly fixed costs	$6,000	

Assume the product mix is four units of cereal for every one unit of yogurt.

Required:

1. Compute the weighted average unit contribution margin.
2. How many units of each product must be sold to break even?
3. Explain what would happen to the break-even point if the unit sales mix was 1:1.
4. Using the new sales mix of 1:1, how many units of each product must be sold to earn $7,500 per month?

See page 233 for solution.

CHAPTER SUMMARY

LO1   Use cost-volume-profit analysis to find the break-even point. p. 216

- The break-even point is the point at which contribution margin exactly equals fixed costs indicating that the company is making zero profit.
- To find the break-even point in units, divide total fixed costs by the unit contribution margin. This is the number of units needed to break even.
- To find the break-even point in sales dollars, divide total fixed costs by the contribution margin ratio. This identifies the total sales needed to break even.

LO2   Use cost-volume-profit analysis to determine the sales needed to achieve a target profit. p. 219

- For a business to earn a profit, its total contribution margin must be enough to cover fixed costs plus the desired target profit.
- To determine the number of units needed to earn a target profit, divide the target contribution margin (fixed cost plus target profit) by the unit contribution margin.
- To determine the total sales needed to earn a target profit, divide the target contribution margin (fixed cost plus target profit) by the contribution margin ratio.

LO3   Compute the margin of safety. p. 220

- The margin of safety is the difference between actual or budgeted sales and break-even sales. It indicates how much cushion there is between the current (or expected) level of sales and the break-even point.

Analyze how changes in prices and cost structure affect the cost-volume-profit relationships. p. 222   **LO4**

- To analyze how changes in prices or cost structure affect the cost-volume-profit relationships, we allow one thing to change while holding everything else constant.
- All else equal, an increase in the selling price will increase the contribution margin and lower the break-even point.
- Changing unit variable costs or total fixed costs also affects the cost-volume profit relationship.

Calculate the degree of operating leverage and use it to predict the effect a change in sales has on profit. p. 224   **LO5**

- Operating leverage occurs when a company uses fixed costs to leverage a relatively small change in sales revenue into a larger effect on profit.
- Degree of operating leverage is calculated as the ratio of contribution margin to profit. This number is the multiplication factor that explains how a percentage change in sales revenue translates into a percentage change in profit.

Perform multiproduct cost-volume-profit analysis and explain how the product mix affects the analysis. p.227   **LO6**

- The key to multiproduct cost-volume-profit analysis is to assume and maintain a constant product or sales mix.
- The weighted average unit contribution margin is calculated based on the relative proportion of units sold. It can be used to solve for the number of units needed to break even or earn a target profit.
- The weighted average contribution margin ratio is calculated based on the relative proportion of total sales revenue. It can be used to solve for the total revenue needed to break even or earn a target profit.

SOLUTION TO DEMONSTRATION CASE A (SINGLE PRODUCT)

1. Break-Even Units = Fixed Cost/Unit Contribution Margin
   = $6,000/$3.00 = 2,000 Customers

2. Break-Even Sales Dollar = Fixed Cost/Contribution Margin Ratio
   = $6,000/80% = $7,500

3. Target Units = (Fixed Costs + Target Profit)/Unit Contribution Margin
   = ($6,000 + $7,500)/$3.00 = 4,500 Units

4. Margin of Safety = 3,000 − 2,000 = 1,000 units; 1,000 × $3.75 = $3,750; $3,750/(2,000 × $3.75) = 50%

SOLUTION TO DEMONSTRATION CASE B (MULTIPRODUCT)

1. Weighted average contribution margin:

	Cereal	Yogurt
Unit contribution margin	$3.00	$1.50
Unit mix (weight)	× 80%	× 20%
	$2.40	$0.30
Weighted Average Unit Contribution Margin	$2.40 + $0.30 = $2.70	

2. Break-Even Units = Fixed Cost/Weighted Average Unit Contribution Margin
   = $6,000/$2.70 = 2,222 Total Units

   Cereal Units = 2,222 × 80% = 1,778 units

   Yogurt Units = 2,222 × 20% = 444 units

3. If the sales mix was 1:1, or 50 percent from each product, the break-even point would increase. The reason is that the unit sales mix would shift toward yogurt, which has a lower unit contribution margin than cereal. This means the company would need to sell more total units to break even.

4. New weighted average contribution margin:

	Cereal	Yogurt
Unit contribution margin	$3.00	$ 1.50
Unit mix (weight)	× 50%	× 50%
	$1.50	$ 0.75
Weighted Average Unit Contribution Margin	$1.50 + $0.75 = $2.25	

Target Units = (Fixed Cost + Target Profit)/Weighted Average Unit Contribution Margin
= ($6,000 + $7,500)/$2.25 = 6,000 Total Units

Cereal Units = 6,000 × 50% = 3,000 units

Yogurt Units = 6,000 × 50% = 3,000 units

Managerial Analysis Tools

Name of Measure	Formula
Contribution margin per unit	Unit Sales Price − Variable Cost per Unit or $\dfrac{\text{Total Contribution Margin}}{\text{Number of Units Sold}}$
Contribution margin ratio	$\dfrac{\text{Unit Contribution Margin}}{\text{Units Sales Price}}$ or $\dfrac{\text{Total Contribution Margin}}{\text{Total Sales Revenue}}$
Break-even units	$\dfrac{\text{Total Fixed Costs}}{\text{Unit Contribution Margin}}$
Break-even sales	Break-Even Units × Unit Sales Price or $\dfrac{\text{Total Fixed Costs}}{\text{Contribution Margin Ratio}}$
Target units	$\dfrac{\text{Total Fixed Costs + Target Profit}}{\text{Unit Contribution Margin}}$
Target sales revenue	Target Units × Unit Sales Price or $\dfrac{\text{Total Fixed Costs + Target Profit}}{\text{Contribution Margin Ratio}}$
Margin of safety	Actual or Budgeted Sales − Break-Even Sales
Margin of safety percentage	$\dfrac{\text{Actual or Budgeted Sales − Break Even Sales}}{\text{Actual or Budgeted Sales}}$
Degree of operating leverage	$\dfrac{\text{Contribution Margin}}{\text{Profit}}$

KEY TERMS

Break-Even Analysis (p. 216)
Break-Even Point (p. 216)
Cost-Volume-Profit (CVP) Analysis (p. 214)
CVP Graph (p. 215)

Margin of Safety (p. 220)
Target Profit Analysis (p. 219)
Weighted Average Unit Contribution Margin (p. 227)

Weighted Average Contribution Margin Ratio (p. 230)

See complete definitions in the glossary in the back of this text.

QUESTIONS

1. Identify and briefly describe the assumptions of CVP.
2. Why should managers create a CVP graph?
3. When considering a CVP graph, how is the break-even point shown?
4. Your supervisor has requested that you prepare a CVP graph for your company's product but does not understand its meaning or how changes would affect the graph. Explain to your supervisor how your graph would be affected by:
   a. an increase in the selling price.
   b. a decrease in variable cost per unit.
   c. an increase in fixed costs.
5. Why is it important for a company to know its break-even point? What happens to the break-even point if variable cost per unit decreases? If total fixed cost increases?
6. Explain the difference between unit contribution margin and contribution margin ratio.
7. A company's cost structure can have a high proportion of fixed costs or a high proportion of variable costs. Which cost structure is more vulnerable to decreases in demand? Why?
8. Explain the difference in calculating the break-even point in units and in dollars. How can one be used to double-check the other?
9. Apple Company and Baker Company are competitors in the same industry, producing the same product. They have similar variable costs per unit and selling prices, but Baker has more fixed costs. Explain the impact of this on each company's break-even point.
10. Bert Company and Ernie Company are competitors in the same industry. The companies produce the same product

and have the same amount of fixed costs and the same selling price per unit. However, Bert has higher variable cost per unit. Compare the break-even point of each company.

11. Explain the difference between break-even analysis and target profit analysis.
12. Explain margin of safety. Why is it important for managers to know their margin of safety?
13. Give an example of a company to which margin of safety is particularly important and explain why.
14. Explain how a decision to automate a manufacturing facility would likely impact a company's cost structure and its break-even point.
15. Explain degree of operating leverage and how it relates to fixed cost.
16. How does degree of operating leverage help managers predict changes in profit? In general, would you prefer a higher or lower degree of operating leverage?
17. Why is sales mix important to multiproduct CVP analysis? Explain how sales mix is factored into CVP analysis.
18. How is weighted average contribution margin calculated?
19. What will happen to a company's break-even point if the sales mix shifts to favor a product with a lower contribution margin per unit?
20. How do you use the weighted average contribution margin ratio in cost-volume-profit analysis?
21. Why is the weighted average contribution margin ratio approach commonly used in practice?
22. What is the difference between the product mix and the sales mix?

MULTIPLE CHOICE

1. Which of the following is **not** an assumption of CVP analysis?

   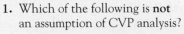
   Quiz 6
   www.mhhe.com/whitecotton1e

   a. A straight line can be used to approximate the relationship between cost and revenue within the relevant range.
   b. Production and sales are equal.
   c. Sales mix remains constant for any company selling more than one product.
   d. All costs can be accurately described as either fixed, variable, mixed, or step.

2. Contribution margin ratio is represented by
   a. (Sales − Fixed Cost)/Sales.
   b. (Sales − Variable Cost)/Sales.

   c. (Fixed Cost − Variable Cost)/Sales.
   d. Variable Cost/Sales.

3. When total contribution margin equals total fixed cost, a company has
   a. A net loss.
   b. Net income.
   c. Zero profit.
   d. Higher variable cost and fixed cost.

4. Baugh Company expects to sell 5,000 chairs for $10 per unit. The contribution margin ratio is 30 percent and Baugh will break even at this sales level. What are Baugh's fixed costs?
   a. $15,000.   c. $35,000
   b. $30,000.   d. None of the above.

5. Whistler Co. sells one model of radio. Suppose its cost per radio is $125 and its total fixed costs are $4,130. Each radio sells for $195. How many radios must Whistler sell to break even?

   a. 33.   **c.** 45.
   b. 21.   **d.** 59.

6. Recent information for Shady Co., which makes automobile sunscreens, follows:

Selling price per screen	$ 18
Total fixed cost per month	1,225
Variable cost per screen	7

   If Shady wants to earn $1,250 profit next month, how many screens must it sell?

   a. 109.   **c.** 186.
   b. 136.   **d.** 225.

7. Various information for Happy Camper Co., which makes sleeping bags, follows:

Selling price per bag	$ 30
Total fixed cost per month	2,250
Variable cost per bag	21
Last month's profit	1,260

   How many sleeping bags did the company sell last month?

   a. 159.   **c.** 140.
   b. 250.   **d.** 390.

8. Refer to the information in question 7 for Happy Camper. Suppose it decides to lower its selling price to $27. How many sleeping bags must it sell to match last month's profit?

   a. 585.   **c.** 780.
   b. 375.   **d.** 130.

9. Which of the following statements about a CVP graph is true?

   a. Total revenue is a downward-sloping line.
   b. Break even is the point at which the total revenue and total cost lines intersect.
   c. The dollar value of sales revenue and total cost are plotted on the horizontal (X) axis.
   d. The total cost line includes only fixed costs.

10. When performing multiproduct CVP analysis

   a. Sales mix is assumed to remain constant.
   b. An average contribution margin is used to determine the break-even point.
   c. Both *a* and *b* are true.
   d. The products must be analyzed separately.

Answers to Multiple-Choice Questions located in back of the text.

MINI EXERCISES

L01   **M6-1** **Calculating Contribution Margin, Contribution Margin Ratio**

Determine the missing amounts in the following table:

Unit Sales Price	Unit Variable Costs	Unit Contribution Margin	Contribution Margin Ratio
25.00	$10.00	?	?
?	12.00	24.00	?
40.00	?	?	25%

L01   **M6-2** **Calculating Contribution Margin and Contribution Margin Ratio, Finding Break-Even Point**

Lezoli Enterprises sells handmade clocks. Its variable cost per clock is $6, and each clock sells for $15. Calculate Lezoli's contribution margin per unit and contribution margin ratio. If the company's fixed costs total $6,660, determine how many clocks Lezoli must sell to break even.

L02   **M6-3** **Determining Sales Needed to Achieve a Target Profit**

Refer to the information presented in M6-2. How many units must Lezoli sell to earn a profit of at least $5,400?

L01, 4   **M6-4** **Analyzing Changes in Price Structure**

Refer to the information presented in M6-2. Suppose that Lezoli raises its price by 20 percent, but costs do not change. What is its new break-even point?

L01   **M6-5** **Finding Break-even Point**

Speedy Print makes advertising hangers that are placed on doorknobs. It charges $0.04 and estimates its variable cost to be $0.01 per hanger. Speedy's total fixed cost is $3,000 per month, which consists primarily of machinery depreciation and rent. Calculate the number of advertising hangers that Speedy must sell in order to break even.

M6-6 Calculating Break Even After Cost Structure Change

LO1, 4

Refer to the information presented in M6-5. Suppose that the cost of paper has increased and Speedy's variable cost per unit increases to $0.015 per hanger. Calculate its new break-even point assuming this increase is **not** passed along to customers.

M6-7 Calculating Margin of Safety

LO3

Allegra Company has sales of $167,000 and a break-even sales point of $123,000. Compute Allegra's margin of safety and its margin of safety ratio.

M6-8 Calculating Target Profit

LO2

Theodora Patel makes stuffed teddy bears. Recent information for her business follows:

Selling price per bear	$ 25.00
Total fixed cost per month	1,500.00
Variable cost per bear	15.00

If Theodora wants to earn $1,250 profit next month, how many bears will she have to sell?

M6-9 Identifying Margin of Safety

LO3

Refer to the information in M6-8 for Theodora Patel. If she sells 275 bears next month, determine the margin of safety in number of units, sales dollars, and percentage of sales.

M6-10 Calculating Degree of Operating Leverage

LO5

Refer to the information in M6-8 for Theodora Patel. Determine the degree of operating leverage if she sells 350 bears this month.

M6-11 Predicting Effects on Profit

LO4

Refer to the information in M6-8 for Theodora Patel. Suppose sales increase by 20 percent next month. Calculate the effect that increase will have on her profit.

M6-12 Analyzing Multiproduct CVP

LO6

Tien Company has two products: Product A has a contribution margin per unit of $4 and Product B has a contribution margin of $6 per unit. Calculate the weighted average contribution margin if Tien has a 50/50 sales mix. Explain how a shift in the sales mix would affect Tien's weighted average contribution margin and its break-even point.

M6-13 Analyzing Multiproduct CVP

LO6

Complete the following table

Product A Unit CM	Product B Unit CM	Sales Mix	Weighted Average Contribution Margin
$ 9.00	$ 8.00	30/70	?
2.50	4.20	80/20	?
15.75	11.90	40/60	?
45.60	55.50	65/35	?

M6-14 Analyzing Multiproduct CVP

LO6

Bradshaw manufactures two products. Information follows:

	Product A	Product B
Sales price	$13.50	$16.75
Variable cost per unit	$ 6.15	$ 6.85
Percentage of total sales	60%	40%

Calculate Bradshaw's weighted average contribution margin per unit.

M6-15 Analyzing Multiproduct CVP

LO6

Refer to the information presented in M6-14. Calculate the break-even point if Bradshaw's total fixed costs are $230,000.

LO6   **M6-16 Analyzing Multiproduct CVP**

Refer to the information presented in M6-14. Suppose that each product's sales price increases by 10 percent. Sales mix remains the same and total fixed costs are $230,000. Calculate the new break-even point for Bradshaw.

LO6   **M6-17 Analyzing Multiproduct CVP, Calculating Weighted Average, Contribution Margin Ratio**

Information for Kandar Company follows:

	Product A	Product B
Sales Revenue	$40,000	$60,000
− Total Variable Cost	12,000	21,000
Contribution Margin	$28,000	$39,000

Determine Kandar's (overall) weighted average contribution margin ratio.

LO6   **M6-18 Calculating Break-Even Sales Using Weighted Average Contribution Margin Ratio**

Refer to the information presented for Kandar Company in M6-17. Determine its break-even sales dollars if total fixed costs are $35,000.

LO5   **M6-19 Calculating Target Sales**

Refer to the information in M6-18 regarding Kandar Company. Determine target sales needed to earn a $25,000 target profit.

EXERCISES

LO1   **E6-1 Understanding CVP Relationships**

Suppose your sister works for a small real estate office as a receptionist. Her employer is possibly going to be forced to lay off several employees and explained that the company was not "breaking even" and that layoffs would start next month unless things change. The boss has also asked all employees to think of ways that the company could hit that magical break-even point and, ultimately, earn a profit. Your sister has come to you for help in understanding the boss's comments and wants suggestions to pass along.

Required:

1. Explain the following concepts and their relationships to your sister: break even, variable cost, fixed cost, contribution margin, and profit.
2. Help your sister identify five suggestions to offer the boss that would improve the company's performance.
3. Explain why just breaking even will not ensure that your sister keeps her job over the long term.

LO1, 2, 3   **E6-2 Determining Break-Even, Target Profit, Margin of Safety**

Pizza Pizazz is a local restaurant. Price and cost information follows:

Price per pizza	$ 13.00
Variable cost per pizza	
Ingredients	2.35
Direct labor	1.20
Overhead (box, etc.)	0.20
Fixed cost per month	$3,515.00

Required:

1. Determine Pizza Pizazz's break-even point in units and sales dollars.
2. Determine the restaurant's margin of safety if it currently sells 450 pizzas per month.
3. Determine the number of pizzas that Pizazz must sell to generate $2,000 in profit.

E6-3 Analyzing Changes in Price, Cost Structure, Degree of Operating Leverage **LO4, 5**

Refer to the information for Pizza Pizazz in E6-2.

Required:

1. Calculate Pizza Pizazz's new break-even point under each of the following independent scenarios:
   a. Sales price increases by $1.00 per pizza.
   b. Fixed costs increase by $500.00 per month.
   c. Variable costs decrease by $0.35 per pizza.
   d. Sales price decreases by $0.50 per pizza.

2. Refer to the original information presented in E6-2. Assume that Pizza Pizazz sold 400 pizzas last month. Calculate the company's degree of operating leverage.

3. Using the degree of operating leverage, calculate the impact on profit caused by a 10 percent increase in sales revenue.

E6-4 Calculating Contribution Margin and Contribution Margin Ratio; **LO1, 2**
    Identifying Break-Even Point, Target Profit

Paddle Away, Inc., makes one model of wooden canoe. Partial information for it follows.

Number of canoes produced and sold	450	600	750
Total costs			
Variable costs	$ 67,500	?	?
Fixed costs	150,000	?	?
Total costs	$217,500	?	?
Cost per unit			
Variable cost per unit	?	?	?
Fixed cost per unit	?	?	?
Total cost per unit	?	?	?

Required:

1. Complete the preceding table.
2. Suppose Paddle Away sells its canoes for $550 each. Calculate the contribution margin per canoe and the contribution margin ratio.
3. This year Paddle Away expects to sell 820 canoes. Prepare a contribution margin income statement for the company.
4. Calculate Paddle Away's break-even point in units and in sales dollars.
5. Suppose Paddle Away wants to earn $75,000 profit this year. Calculate the number of canoes that must be sold to achieve this target.

E6-5 Identifying Break-Even Point, Analyzing How Price Changes Affect **LO1, 2, 3, 4**
    Profitability; Calculating Margin of Safety, Target Profit

Refer to the information in E6-4 regarding Paddle Away.

Required:

1. Suppose that Paddle Away raises its selling price to $675 per canoe. Calculate its new break-even point in units and in sales dollars.
2. If Paddle Away sells 650 canoes, compute its margin of safety in units and as a percentage of sales. (Use the new sales price of $675.)
3. Calculate the number of canoes that Paddle Away must sell at $675 each to generate $100,000 profit.

E6-6 Analyzing Break Even, Preparing CVP Graph, Calculating Degree **LO1, 4, 5**
    of Operating Leverage, Predicting Effect of Price Structure Changes

Cory Bryant runs a courier service in downtown Phoenix. He charges clients $0.50 per mile driven. Cory has determined that if he drives 3,000 miles in a month, his total operating cost is $875. If he drives 4,000 miles in a month, his total operating cost is $1,025. Cory has used the high-low method (covered in Chapter 5) to determine that his monthly cost equation is: Total Monthly Cost = $425 + $0.15 per Mile Driven.

Required:

1. Determine how many miles Cory needs to drive to break even.
2. Calculate Cory's degree of operating leverage if he drives 4,200 miles.
3. Suppose Cory took a week off and his sales for the month decreased by 25 percent. Using the degree of operating leverage, calculate the effect this will have on his profit for that month.

LO2, 3   **E6-7 Calculating Contribution Margin, Contribution Margin Ratio, Margin of Safety**

Last month, Willsted Company sold 450 units for $25 each. During the month, fixed costs were $2,520 and variable costs were $7 per unit.

Required:

1. Determine the unit contribution margin and contribution margin ratio.
2. Calculate the break-even point in units and sales dollars.
3. Compute Willsted's margin of safety in units and as a percentage of sales.

LO1   **E6-8 Analyzing Break-Even Point, Preparing CVP Graph**

Peggy's Ribbon World makes award rosettes. Following is information about the company:

Variable cost per rosette	$ 1.10
Sales price per rosette	2.50
Total fixed costs per month	889.00

Required:

1. Determine how many rosettes Peggy's must sell to break even.
2. Calculate the break-even point in sales dollars.
3. Prepare a CVP graph for Peggy's assuming the relevant range is zero to 1,500 rosettes.

LO2, 3, 5   **E6-9 Calculating Target Profit, Margin of Safety, Degree of Operating Leverage**

Refer to the information regarding Peggy's Ribbon World in E6-8.

Required:

1. Suppose Peggy's would like to generate a profit of $800. Determine how many rosettes it must sell to achieve this target profit.
2. If Peggy's sells 1,100 rosettes, compute its margin of safety in units, in sales dollars, and as a percentage of sales.
3. Calculate Peggy's degree of operating leverage if it sells 1,100 rosettes.
4. Using the degree of operating leverage, calculate the change in Peggy's profit if it raises the sales price of each rosette by $0.50. (Assume costs do not change.)

LO5   **E6-10 Determining Contribution Margin from Degree of Operating Leverage**

Sonny Company and Cher Corp have degrees of operating leverage of 2.5 and 4.7, respectively. Both companies have net income of $80,000.

Required:

1. Without performing any calculations, discuss what the degrees of operating leverage tell us about the two companies.
2. Determine each company's total contribution margin.
3. Compare the companies' cost structures.

E6-11 Calculating Break Even, Degree of Operating Leverage

LO1, 5

Longview Company is considering automating its manufacturing facility. Company information before and after the proposed automation follows:

	Before Automation	After Automation
Sales Revenue	$198,000	$198,000
− Variable Cost	98,000	48,000
Contribution Margin	$100,000	$150,000
− Fixed Cost	15,000	58,000
Net Income	$ 85,000	$ 92,000

Required:

1. Calculate Longview's break-even sales dollars before and after automation.
2. Compute Longview's degree of operating leverage before and after automation.
3. Interpret the meaning of your calculations in requirement 2.

E6-12 Calculating Break Even with Different Cost Structures

LO5

Laurel Company and Hardy Inc. are separate companies that operate in the same industry. Following are variable costing income statements for the two companies showing their different cost structures:

	Laurel Co.	Hardy Inc.
Sales	$275,000	$275,000
Variable Costs	185,000	125,000
Contribution Margin	90,000	150,000
Fixed Costs	35,000	95,000
Net Income	$ 55,000	$ 55,000

Required:

1. Briefly describe the similarities and differences in these two companies.
2. Calculate the break-even sales dollars for each company.

E6-13 Calculating Degree of Operating Leverage

LO5

Refer to the information in M6-12 for Laurel Company and Hardy Inc.

Required:

1. Calculate each company's degree of operating leverage.
2. Explain why companies with the same total sales and net income have different degrees of operating leverage.
3. Compare these two companies' vulnerability to market fluctuations.

E6-14 Analyzing Multiproduct CVP

LO6

Robbie's Rent-A-Ride rents two models of automobiles: the standard and the deluxe. Information follows:

	Standard	Deluxe
Rental price per day	$25.00	$35.00
Variable cost per day	10.50	15.80

Robbie's total fixed cost is $18,500 per month.

Required:

1. Determine the contribution margin and contribution margin ratio per rental day for each model that Robbie's offers.
2. Which model would Robbie's prefer to rent? Explain your answer.

3. Calculate Robbie's break-even point if the sales mix is 50/50.
4. Calculate the break-even point if Robbie's sales mix changes so that the standard model is rented 75 percent of the time and the deluxe model is rented for only 25 percent.
5. Calculate the break-even point if Robbie's sales mix changes so that the standard model is rented 25 percent of the time and the deluxe model is rented for 75 percent.

LO6   E6-15 Analyzing Multiproduct CVP

Refer to the information presented in E6-14 for Robbie's Rent-A-Ride.

Required:

1. Determine Robbie's new break-even point in each of the following **independent** scenarios.
   a. Sales mix is 40/60.
   b. Sales price increases on both models by 20 percent. (Assume a sales mix of 50/50.)
   c. Fixed costs increase by $5,200. (Assume a sales mix of 50/50.)
   d. Variable costs increase by 30 percent.

LO6   E6-16 Analyzing Multiproduct CVP

BlueStar makes three models of camera lens. Its sales mix and contribution margin per unit follow:

	Percentage of Total Sales	CM per Unit
Lens A	25%	$40
Lens B	40	32
Lens C	35	45

Required:

1. Determine the weighted average contribution margin.
2. Determine the number of units of each product that BlueStar must sell to break even if fixed costs are $187,000.
3. Determine how many units of each product must be sold to generate a profit of $73,000.

LO6   E6-17 Analyzing Multiproduct CVP

Refer to the information in E6-16 for BlueStar. Suppose the sales mix has shifted to 40/30/30.

Required:

1. Determine the new weighted average contribution margin.
2. Determine the number of units of each product that BlueStar must sell to break even if fixed costs are $187,000.
3. Determine how many units of each product must be sold to generate a profit of $73,000.
4. Explain why these results differ from those calculated in E6-16.

LO5   E6-18 Multiproduct CVP Analysis

MoJo Corp. makes three models of insulated thermos. MoJo has $300,000 in total revenue and $180,000 total variable costs. Its sales mix is given below:

	Percentage of Total Sales
Thermos A	35%
Thermos B	45
Thermos C	20

Required:

1. Calculate the weighted average contribution margin ratio.
2. Determine the total sales revenue MoJo needs to break even if fixed costs are $75,000.
3. Determine the total sales revenue needed to generate a profit of $90,000.
4. Determine the sales revenue from each product needed to generate a profit of $90,000.

E6-19 Multiproduct CVP Analysis

LO5

Refer to the information in E6-18 for MoJo Corp. Suppose MoJo has improved its manufacturing process and expects total variable costs to decrease by 20 percent. The company expects sales revenue to remain stable at $300,000.

Required:

1. Calculate the new weighted average contribution margin ratio.
2. Determine total sales that MoJo needs to break even if fixed costs after the manufacturing improvements are $55,600.
3. Determine the total sales revenue that MoJo must generate to earn a profit of $90,000.
4. Determine the sales revenue from each product needed to generate a profit of $90,000.

PROBLEMS–SET A

|ACCOUNTING

LO1

www.mhhe.com/whitecotton1e

PA6-1 Calculating Contribution Margin, Contribution Margin Ratio, Break-Even Point

Overhill, Inc., produces one model of mountain bike. Partial information for the company follows:

Number of bikes produced and sold	500	800	1,000
Total costs			
Variable costs	$125,000	$?	$?
Fixed costs per year	?	?	?
Total costs	?	?	?
Cost per unit			
Variable cost per unit	?	?	?
Fixed cost per unit	?	?	?
Total cost per unit	?	$543.75	?

Required:

1. Complete the table.
2. Calculate Overhill's contribution margin ratio and its total contribution margin at each sales level indicated in the table assuming the company sells each bike for $650.
3. Consider the contribution margins just calculated and total fixed costs. Determine whether Overhill's break-even point will be more or less than 500 units.
4. Calculate Overhill's break-even point in units and sales dollars.

PA6-2 Analyzing Break-Even Point, Setting Target Profit Degree of Operating Leverage

LO1, 2, 4

Fred Carson delivers parts for several local auto parts stores. He charges clients $0.75 per mile driven. Fred has determined that if he drives 2,000 miles in a month, his average operating cost is $0.55 per mile. If he drives 4,000 miles in a month, his average operating cost is $0.40 per mile. Fred has used the high-low method (covered in Chapter 5) to determine that his monthly cost equation is: Total Cost = $600 + $0.25 per Mile.

Required:

1. Determine how many miles Fred needs to drive to break even.
2. Assume Fred drove 1,500 miles last month. Without making any additional calculations, determine whether he earned a profit or a loss last month.
3. Determine how many miles Fred must drive to earn $1,000 profit.
4. Prepare a contribution margin income statement assuming Fred drove 1,500 miles last month. Use this information to calculate Fred's degree of operating leverage.

PA6-3 Calculating Contribution Margin, Contribution Margin Ratio, Break-Even Point, Target Profit

LO1, 2

Cardinal Castles, Inc., makes one type of birdhouse that it sells for $30 each. Its variable cost is $14 per house, and its fixed costs total $13,840 per year. Cardinal currently has the capacity to produce up to 2,000 birdhouses per year, so its relevant range is zero to 2,000 houses.

Required:

1. Prepare a contribution margin income statement for Cardinal assuming it sells 1,100 birdhouses this year.
2. Without any calculations, determine Cardinal's total contribution margin if the company breaks even.
3. Calculate Cardinal's contribution margin per unit and its contribution margin ratio.
4. Calculate Cardinal's break-even point in number of units and in sales dollars.
5. Suppose Cardinal wants to earn $20,000 this year. Determine how many birdhouses it must sell to generate this amount of profit. Is this possible?
6. Prepare a cost-volume-profit graph for Cardinal including lines for both total cost and sales revenue. Clearly identify fixed cost and the break-even point on your graph.

LO1, 2, 3, 5 **PA6-4 Analyzing Break-Even Point, Target Profit Degree of Operating Leverage**

www.mhhe.com/whitecotton1e

Simpson Company produces one golf cart model. A partially complete table of company costs follows:

Number of golf carts produced and sold	600	800	1,000
Total costs			
Variable costs	$?	$400,000	$?
Fixed costs per year	?	500,000	?
Total costs	?	$900,000	?
Cost per unit			
Variable cost per unit	?	?	?
Fixed cost per unit	?	?	?
Total cost per unit	?	?	?

Required:

1. Complete the table.
2. Simpson sells its carts for $1,200 each. Prepare a contribution margin income statement for each of the three production levels given in the table.
3. Based on these three statements (and without any additional calculations), estimate Simpson's break-even point in units.
4. Calculate Simpson's break-even point in number of units and in sales dollars.
5. Assume Simpson sold 700 carts last year. Without performing any calculations, determine whether Simpson earned a profit last year.
6. Calculate the number of carts that Simpson must sell to earn $65,000 profit.
7. Calculate Simpson's degree of operating leverage if it sells 850 carts.
8. Using the degree of operating leverage, calculate the change in Simpson's profit if sales are 10 percent less than expected.

LO6 **PA6-5 Analyzing Multiproduct CVP, Break-Even Point, Target Profit, Margin of Safety**

Randolph Company produces two fountain pen models. Information about its products follows:

	Product A	Product B
Sales Revenue	$75,000	$125,000
− Variable Costs	22,000	38,000
Contribution Margin	$53,000	$ 87,000
Total units sold	5,000	5,000

Randolph's fixed costs total $78,500.

Required:

1. Determine Randolph's weighted average contribution margin and weighted average contribution margin ratio.
2. Calculate Randolph's break even in units and in sales dollars.

3. Calculate the number of units that Randolph must sell to earn a $150,000 profit.
4. Calculate Randolph's margin of safety and margin of safety as a percentage of sales if it sells 8,000 total pens.

PA6-6 Multiproduct CVP, Analyzing Break-Even Point, Target Profit, Degree of Operating Leverage

LO1, 5

SewFun Company produces two models of sewing basket. Information about SewFun's products is given below:

	Product A	Product B
Sales revenue	$28,000	$43,000
− Variable costs	11,400	18,000
Contribution margin	$16,600	$25,000
Total units sold	780	1,820

SewFun's fixed costs total $35,200.

Required:

1. Determine SewFun's weighted average contribution margin and weighted average contribution margin ratio.
2. Calculate SewFun's break-even units and break-even sales dollars.
3. Calculate the number of units of each product that will be sold at break even.
4. Calculate the total sales necessary for SewFun to earn a profit of $63,200.
5. Calculate the sales revenue generated from each product line if SewFun earns its target of $63,200 profit.
6. Calculate SewFun's degree of operating leverage.

PROBLEMS—SET B

PB6-1 Calculating Contribution Margin, Contribution Margin Ratio, Break-Even Point

LO1

CoverUp, Inc., produces one model of seat cover. Partial information for the company follows:

	1,500	1,700	2,100
Number of seat covers produced and sold			
Total costs			
Variable costs	$?	$?	$15,750
Fixed costs per year	?	?	?
Total costs	?	?	?
Cost per unit			
Variable cost per unit	?	?	?
Fixed cost per unit	?	?	?
Total cost per unit	$31.00	?	?

Required:

1. Complete the table.
2. Calculate CoverUp's contribution margin ratio and its total contribution margin at each sales level indicated in the table assuming the company sells each seat cover for $30.
3. Consider the contribution margins just calculated and total fixed costs for the company. Determine whether CoverUp's break-even point will be more or less than 1,500 units.
4. Calculate CoverUp's break-even point in units and sales dollars.

PB6-2 Preparing Contribution Margin Income Statement, Analyzing Break-Even Point, Setting Target Profit

LO1, 2

Tina Sutton delivers flowers for several local flower stores. She charges clients $0.85 per mile driven. Tina has determined that if she drives 1,200 miles in a month, her average operating cost is $0.70 per mile. If she drives 2,000 miles in a month, her average operating cost is $0.60 per mile.

Tina has used the high-low method (covered in Chapter 5) to determine that her monthly cost equation is: Total Cost = $300 + $0.45 per Mile.

Required:

1. Determine how many miles Tina needs to drive to break even.
2. Assume Tina drove 900 miles last month. Without making any additional calculations, determine whether she earned a profit or a loss for the month.
3. Prepare a contribution margin income statement assuming Tina drove 900 miles last month.
4. If Tina wants to earn $800 a month, determine how many miles she must drive.

LO1, 2   **PB6-3 Calculating Contribution Margin, Contribution Margin Ratio, Break-Even Point**

Hot Dog, Inc., makes one type of doggie sweater that it sells for $25 each. Its variable cost is $11 per sweater and its fixed costs total $8,600 per year. Hot Dog currently has the capacity to produce up to 1,000 sweaters per year, so its relevant range is zero to 1,000 sweaters.

Required:

1. Prepare a contribution margin income statement for Hot Dog assuming it sells 600 sweaters this year.
2. Without any calculations, determine Hot Dog's total contribution margin if the company breaks even.
3. Calculate Hot Dog's contribution margin per unit and its contribution margin ratio.
4. Calculate Hot Dog's break-even point in number of units and in sales dollars.
5. Suppose Hot Dog wants to earn $3,000 this year. Determine how many sweaters it must sell to generate this amount of profit. Is this possible?
6. Prepare a cost-volume-profit graph for Hot Dog including lines for both total cost and sales revenue. Clearly identify fixed cost and the break-even point on your graph.

LO1, 2, 5   **PB6-4 Preparing Contribution Margin Income Statement, Analyzing Break-Even Point Degree of Operating Leverage**

StaySafe Company produces one security door model. A partially complete table of its costs follows:

Number of doors produced and sold	400	500	700
Total costs			
Variable costs	$30,000	$?	$?
Fixed costs per year	65,000	?	?
Total costs	95,000	?	?
Cost per unit			
Variable cost per unit	?	?	?
Fixed cost per unit	?	?	?
Total cost per unit	?	?	?

Required:

1. Complete the table.
2. StaySafe sells its doors for $200 each. Prepare a contribution margin income statement for each of the three production levels in the table.
3. Based on these three statements (and without any additional calculations), estimate StaySafe's break-even point in units.
4. Calculate StaySafe's break-even point in number of units and in sales dollars.
5. Assume StaySafe sold 600 doors last year. Without performing any calculations, determine whether it earned a profit last year.
6. Calculate the number of doors that StaySafe must sell to earn a $10,000 profit.
7. Calculate StaySafe's degree of operating leverage if it sells 700 doors.
8. Using the degree of operating leverage, calculate the change in StaySafe's profit if sales are 20 percent more than expected. (Assume costs did not change.)

**PB6-5 Analyzing Multiproduct CVP, Break-Even Point, Target Profit, Margin   LO6
of Safety**

Lemming Company produces two backpack models. Information about its products follows:

	Product A	Product B
Sales revenue	$135,000	$77,000
− Variable costs	67,000	21,500
Contribution margin	$ 68,000	$55,500
Total units sold	15,000	5,000

Lemming's fixed costs total $51,700.

Required:

1. Determine Lemming's weighted average contribution margin and weighted average contribution margin ratio.
2. Calculate Lemming's break even in units and in sales dollars.
3. Calculate the number of units that Lemming must sell to earn a $95,000 profit.
4. Calculate Lemming's margin of safety and margin of safety as a percentage of sales if it sells 35,000 total backpacks.

**PB6-6 Multiproduct CVP, Analyzing Break-Even Point, Target Profit, Degree   LO1, 5
of Operating Leverage**

MowFun Company produces two models of electric lawnmower. Information about MowFun's products is given below:

	Product A	Product B
Sales revenue	$264,400	$396,600
− Variable costs	171,400	213,000
Contribution margin	$ 93,000	$183,600
Total units sold	300	500

MowFun's fixed costs total $82,980.

Required:

1. Determine MowFun's weighted average contribution margin and weighted average contribution margin ratio.
2. Calculate MowFun's break-even units and break-even sales dollars.
3. Calculate the number of units of each product that will be sold at break even.
4. Calculate the total sales necessary for MowFun to earn a profit of $172,305.
5. Calculate the sales revenue generated from each product line if MowFun earns its target of $172,305 profit.
6. Calculate MowFun's degree of operating leverage.

SKILLS DEVELOPMENT CASES

**S6-1 Evaluating the Effect of Decisions on Contribution Margin, Break Even,   LO4
Margin of Safety**

Companies must make many decisions regarding day-to-day business activities. For each of the following decision-making situations, discuss its impact on a company's contribution margin (both total and per unit), break-even point, margin of safety, and degree of operating leverage.

Required:

1.   Whether to pay employees a fixed salary or an hourly wage.
2.   Whether to pay commissions to salespeople.
3.   Whether to purchase a building or rent space.
4.   Whether to purchase component parts or manufacture them.
5.   Whether to create its own delivery department (including the purchase and maintenance of delivery vehicles) or contract with a delivery company.

LO1, 6   **S6-2 Researching Cost of Operating Vending Machine, Performing Cost-Volume-Profit Analysis, Multiproduct CVP**

Suppose you have decided to start a small business selling snacks from vending machines. You have secured a location for one candy vending machine in a local bookstore. Rental for the space will cost $200 per month.

Vending machines can be purchased at wholesale clubs such as Sam's Club and Costco. You can also purchase the snacks to stock the machines in bulk at warehouse clubs.

Required:

1.   Either visit a local warehouse club or review its Web site to determine the initial cost to purchase a snack vending machine.
2.   Assume you are initially going to have only one type of snack bar in your machine. What type of snack bar will you choose? If you purchase the bars in bulk, what is your cost per bar?
3.   How much will you charge for each bar sold?
4.   What is your contribution margin per bar? How many bars must you sell to cover the cost of the vending machine?
5.   When you have covered the initial investment, what will the monthly break-even point be in number of bars and in sales dollars?
6.   Repeat requirements 2–5 assuming you decided to have a drink vending machine instead of a snack machine. Remember to find the price for a beverage vending machine. You may assume rental for the vending machine space is $200 per month regardless of its type.
7.   Assume your machine can accommodate more than one product, for example, a snack machine that can dispense both chips and candy bars or a drink machine that offers both soda and water. Repeat requirements 2–5 assuming you have decided to offer two products. The products should have different prices, variable costs, and contribution margins. Perform the analyses for three levels of sales mix: 50/50, 30/70, and 70/30.

LO1, 2   **S6-3 Researching a Company Web Site, Performing Cost-Volume-Profit Analysis**

Pink Jeep Tours offers off-road tours to individuals and groups visiting the Southwestern U.S. hotspots of Sedona, Arizona, and Las Vegas, Nevada. Take a tour of the company's Web site at www.pinkjeep.com. Suppose you are the manager for the Pink Jeep office in Sedona. From the company Web site, choose two tours offered there. One tour should last all day, and the other should be a shorter tour of 2–4 hours.

For the following requirements, assume that each Jeep tour has four adult passengers plus a tour guide.

Required:

1.   List the various costs Pink Jeep would incur to offer each tour. Indicate whether each cost identified is variable, fixed, or mixed based on the number of tours offered.
2.   Briefly research each cost listed in requirement 1 and estimate its amount. Estimate variable costs on a per Jeep tour basis and fixed costs on a monthly basis. Break any mixed cost into variable and fixed components. State any assumptions that you must make when estimating these costs (and be aware that many assumptions must be made).

3. What is Pink Jeep's total variable cost for each tour? Does this cost differ for each type of tour? Explain.

4. Using the current tour prices listed on Pink Jeep's Web site, determine the contribution margin per Jeep tour for each tour type.

5. Assume Pink Jeep ran **only** the all-day excursion tour in the month of August. In this case, how many tours are needed to break even?

6. Assume Pink Jeep ran **only** the shorter tour during August. In this case, how many tours are needed to earn $30,000 in profit for the month?

CHAPTER 7

Incremental Analysis for Short-Term Decision Making

YOUR LEARNING OBJECTIVES

After completing this chapter, you should be able to:

LO1   Describe the five steps in the decision-making process.

LO2   Define and identify relevant costs and benefits.

LO3   Analyze a special-order decision.

LO4   Analyze a make-or-buy decision.

LO5   Analyze a decision to eliminate an unprofitable business segment.

LO6   Analyze a sell-or-process further decision.

LO7   Prioritize products to maximize short-term profit with constrained resources.

Lecture presentation—LP7
www.mhhe.com/whitecotton1e

FOCUS COMPANY: Mattel Toys

"The World's Premier Toy Brands"

www.mattel.com

In 1945, two friends named Matt and Elliot combined their names, money, and artistic talents to form the company Mattel. They started out producing picture frames but quickly expanded into dollhouse furniture. Matt soon left the business and Elliot's wife Ruth joined the management team. Based on their early success with dollhouse furniture, Elliot and Ruth decided to focus Mattel's efforts on producing and selling toys.

After more than a decade of satisfactory but not stellar performance, Mattel struck it big in 1959 with the introduction of Barbie, a doll named after Ruth and Elliot's own daughter Barbara. Since then, Barbie and her fabulous friends, clothes, and accessories have entertained generations of young girls and, no doubt, a few boys.

Today, Mattel's success hinges on much more than just Barbie dolls. The company has a huge portfolio of products for children of all ages, including Fisher Price toys, Matchbox cars and trucks, Hot Wheels, Mattel classic games, and American Girl dolls. Mattel has also had its share of controversy over the years including critics who question whether Barbie is an appropriate role model for young girls. More recently, Mattel experienced a wave of bad press when it recalled millions of toys that were manufactured in China and contained toxic levels of lead-based paint.

This chapter illustrates how Mattel managers can use managerial accounting information to make the following decisions:

- Whether to accept an order from a large university to produce a special Barbie doll who wears the school logo and colors.
- Whether to make or buy the packaging materials for the American Girl doll collection.
- Whether to eliminate one of its Power Wheels products.
- Whether to add more features to a remote control toy.
- Which products to produce given limited resources.

Although we use fictitious scenarios and numbers to address these questions, we make them as realistic as possible to illustrate how Mattel's managers might approach these and other decisions.

Managerial decision-making framework

- Steps in the decision-making process
- Relevant versus irrelevant costs and benefits
- Opportunity costs and capacity considerations

Incremental analysis for short-term decision making

- Special-order decisions
- Make-or-buy decisions
- Decisions to eliminate unprofitable business segments
- Sell-or-process further decisions
- Prioritization of products with constrained resources
- Summary of incremental analysis

Managerial Decision-Making Framework

Learning Objective 1
Describe the five steps in the decision-making process.

This section describes the general decision-making framework and introduces several important decision-making concepts. The remainder of the chapter applies this framework to a variety of short-term decision scenarios and illustrates how Mattel managers could use incremental analysis to address each decision problem.

STEPS IN THE DECISION-MAKING PROCESS

Exhibit 7.1 shows the five steps in the decision-making process. This general framework is adapted from other business disciplines and can be used to analyze a variety of decision problems.

Step 1: Identify the Decision Problem

The first step in the decision-making process is to identify the decision problem. See Exhibit 7.2 for a description of a decision problem that you may have encountered yourself: deciding where to live. You can apply the same type of analysis to many other personal decisions, such as deciding where to go to college or what kind of vehicle to buy. Later in this chapter, we apply a similar process to a variety of problems that managers face in the business world.

EXHIBIT 7.1	Managerial Decision-Making Process

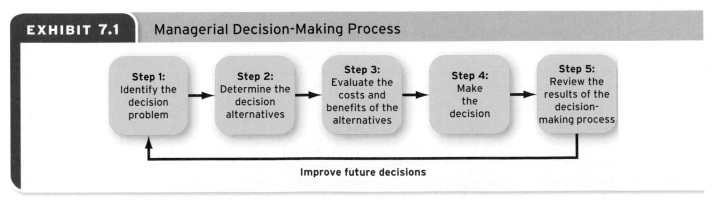

Step 1: Identify the decision problem → **Step 2:** Determine the decision alternatives → **Step 3:** Evaluate the costs and benefits of the alternatives → **Step 4:** Make the decision → **Step 5:** Review the results of the decision-making process

Improve future decisions

EXHIBIT 7.2	Application of the Five-Step Managerial Decision-Making Process to a Personal Decision

Step 1: Identify the decision problem.

Your freshman year living in the dorm is almost up and you must decide where you are going to live next year.

Step 2: Determine the decision alternatives.

You've narrowed it down to two options:
- Lease a 3-bedroom house with two roommates.
- Lease a 1-bedroom apartment.

Step 3: Evaluate the costs and benefits of the alternatives.

	3-Bedroom House	1-Bedroom Apartment	Difference in Cost
Rent	$1,800 / 3 = $600 per month	$800 per month	House is $200 per month cheaper.
Utilities	$450 / 3 = $150 per month	$150 per month	Cost is the same and therefore not relevant.
Advertising for roommates	$50	0	$50 one-time cost to find two roommates.
Gas and on-campus parking	$75 per month	Close enough to bike to school.	Apartment saves $75 in fuel and parking per month.

Quantitative Summary: The house is $125 less per month ($200 rent − $75 in gas and parking), but you will have to spend $50 to find two roommates.

Qualitative Factors: The house is large and has a great backyard for parties, but you are tired of sharing space with loud, messy roommates. You think you would enjoy the one-bedroom apartment, especially for studying and quiet entertaining.

Step 4: Make the decision.

You will have to make a trade-off between the cost advantages of the house and the qualitative advantages of the one-bedroom apartment. Let's assume you are on a very tight budget and decide to sign the lease on the house and begin the search for new roommates.

Step 5: Review the results of the decision-making process.

Looking back on the outcome, you will later determine whether your decision was a good one. If you were unable to find two good roommates, the decision may prove to be a bad one. If you find that your roommates are great and become lifelong friends, your decision was a good one. Either way, you are likely to learn something that will affect the way you make similar decisions in the future.

Step 2: Determine the Decision Alternatives

Once managers have identified the problem, the next step is to determine the possible solutions, called **decision alternatives**. This is a critical step because the remainder of the decision process hinges on the decision alternatives identified here. If a potential alternative is not included in this initial stage, it will not be included in the later phases of the analysis. The housing decision described in Exhibit 7.2 identified two potential decision alternatives: lease a house with two roommates or rent a one-bedroom apartment on your own. We ignored other potential alternatives such as living with parents or buying your own home; thus, these alternatives were not considered in the analysis.

Step 3: Evaluate the Costs and Benefits of the Alternatives

The primary focus in this chapter is the third step of the decision process, which involves comparing the costs and benefits of the decision alternatives identified in Step 2. For short-term decision making, we use a decision-making approach called **incremental analysis** or **differential analysis**. This approach is sometimes called **relevant costing** because it focuses only on those costs (and benefits) that are relevant to the decision at hand. The identification of relevant costs and benefits is discussed in more detail shortly.

Step 4: Make the Decision

Once managers have evaluated the costs and benefits of the decision alternatives, they are ready to make the decision. However, they will probably not base it strictly on the numerical analysis performed in Step 3. Managers should incorporate a variety of other factors, such as strategic issues, quality considerations, legal and ethical issues, and the like. For all of the decisions that we analyze throughout this chapter, we first perform a numerical or quantitative analysis to determine which alternative is "best" based strictly on the numbers. We then discuss what qualitative factors might come into play to influence managers' decisions. For example, in the housing scenario illustrated in Exhibit 7.2, the numeric analysis showed that sharing a house with two roommates was the least costly alternative (by about $125 per month). However, the apartment had other advantages (such as privacy and quiet) that might influence your decision about which housing alternative to choose.

Step 5: Review the Results of the Decision-Making Process

Once managers have made the decision based on the relevant costs and benefits identified in Step 3, as well as any additional qualitative factors in Step 4, they will eventually need to review the results of the decision-making process to determine whether they made the correct decision, or whether they should use a different decision-making approach in the future. The role of managerial accounting in helping managers evaluate performance to improve future decisions is discussed in detail in Chapters 10 and 11.

RELEVANT VERSUS IRRELEVANT COSTS AND BENEFITS

Learning Objective 2
Define and identify relevant costs and benefits.

The rest of this chapter focuses on the third step of the decision-making process, which involves comparing the costs and benefits of the decision alternatives. In particular, we want to compare only those costs and benefits that are **relevant** to the decision being made. Although the decision-making process should include consideration of both costs and benefits, our examples focus primarily on the **cost** side of the process. As you will see shortly, not all costs are relevant to a particular decision. Benefits are also incorporated only when they are relevant to the particular decision.

Relevant Costs

A **relevant cost** has the potential to influence a particular decision and will change depending on which alternative a manager selects. Costs that differ between decision alternatives are also called **differential costs** or **incremental costs**. In Exhibit 7.2, the difference in monthly rent between the house and the apartment was $200. Only the difference in cost was relevant to the decision of whether to rent the house or the apartment.

Another term for relevant cost is **avoidable cost**—that is, a cost that can be avoided by choosing one decision alternative instead of another. In Exhibit 7.2, the costs of fuel and on-campus parking could be avoided if you lived in an apartment near campus and could ride your bike to class. This cost was relevant to the decision because it differed between the two alternatives.

Irrelevant Costs

Irrelevant costs are those that will not impact a particular decision or differ between alternatives. Two types of cost do not change depending on the alternative selected and should therefore be ignored:

- **Costs that have already been incurred and are not relevant to future decisions,** called **sunk costs**. Because these costs have already been spent (that is, they are sunk), they will not change depending on which alternative the manager selects.
- **Costs that are the same regardless of the alternative the manager chooses.** In Exhibit 7.2, the monthly utility costs were estimated to be $150 regardless of whether you share the rental house or rent the apartment. Because the cost is the same for both options, it is not relevant to the decision and can be ignored.

OPPORTUNITY COSTS AND CAPACITY CONSIDERATIONS

An **opportunity cost** is the forgone benefit (or lost opportunity) of choosing to do one thing instead of another. We all face opportunity costs anytime we make a choice about what to do with our limited time or money. Similarly, business managers face opportunity costs when they are forced to choose one alternative over another because of limited resources such as cash, employee time, equipment availability, or space.

Capacity is a measure of the limit placed on a specific resource. It could be the number of people who will fit in a restaurant or an airplane, the number of employees who are available to serve clients, the amount of machine time that is available to make a product, or the amount of warehouse space that is available to store inventory.

If a company has **idle** or **excess capacity**, it has not yet reached the limit on its resources, and therefore opportunity costs are not relevant. When a company is operating at **full capacity**, the limit on one or more of its resources has been reached, and making the choice to do one thing means giving up the opportunity to do something else. At full capacity, opportunity costs become relevant and should be incorporated into the analysis.

In the next section, we apply the concept of relevant costs, or incremental analysis, to Mattel, the world's leading toy company. First make sure that you understand the decision-making process and can correctly identify relevant costs by completing the following Self-Study Practice.

 ## Self-Study Practice

1. Which of the following steps in the decision-making process are out of sequence?
   (a) Identify the decision problem.
   (b) Evaluate the costs and benefits of the alternatives.
   (c) Determine the decision alternatives.
   (d) Make the decision.
   (e) Review the results of the decision-making process.

2. Which of the following costs would **not** be relevant to the decision of whether to take the bus or drive your vehicle to school for a semester? Assume that you will continue to own your vehicle under either alternative.
   (a) The cost of the fuel you use driving to and from campus.
   (b) The cost of on-campus parking.
   (c) The wear and tear on your vehicle due to the extra mileage.
   (d) The time you could spend studying while traveling on the bus instead of driving to school.
   (e) The monthly cost of liability insurance on your vehicle.

After you have finished, check your answers with the solutions in the margin.

Solution to Self-Study Practice
1. (b) and (c) are reversed.
2. (e)

Incremental Analysis for Short-Term Decision Making

In this section, we illustrate how to use **incremental analysis** to analyze four common business decisions: special-order, make-or-buy, continue-or-discontinue, and sell-or-process further decisions. In the real world, the specific decisions managers need to make depend on a variety of factors, such as the type of business they are running, their level of responsibility, and the particular problem they are trying to solve. Nevertheless, the approach we use to address these problems can be applied to many other short-term managerial decisions.

Video 7-1
www.mhhe.com/whitecotton1e

SPECIAL-ORDER DECISIONS

Managers must often decide whether to accept or reject an order that is outside the scope of normal sales. These one-time or special orders are often offered at a lower price than customers normally pay for the product or service. The decision that managers must make is whether to accept or reject the offer. We can analyze this decision by comparing the incremental costs to the incremental benefits (revenue) of the special order.

As an example, assume that a major university has asked Mattel to produce a special University Barbie dressed in a sporty outfit and carrying a backpack with the school's logo and colors. The university bookstore has offered to buy 25,000 of these dolls at a

Learning Objective 3
Analyze a special-order decision.

COACH'S TIP

A key assumption in analyzing special orders is that they will not affect the production and sale of units sold through regular channels. That means the company must have the extra capacity (in terms of machines, people, etc.) to fill the special order without disrupting normal operations.

price of $7 each, which it would then sell in the bookstore and in alumni catalogs for a retail price of $15 each. Mattel **has excess capacity and can fill the order without affecting production of other Barbie dolls,** which are normally sold to toy stores and discount chains for $9 each. Assume the estimated cost to produce the University Barbie is as follows:

	Unit Cost
Direct materials (silicone rubber, clothing, accessories)	$3.50
Direct labor	1.00
Variable manufacturing overhead (indirect materials, power, etc.)	0.50
Fixed manufacturing overhead (factory rent, supervision, etc.)	2.50
Total manufacturing cost	$7.50

At first glance, it appears that Mattel should reject the offer because the $7.00 offer is less than the $7.50 it will cost to make the University Barbie. But is this analysis correct?

Recall that a relevant cost (1) occurs in the future; and (2) changes as a result of the decision. Do all of the costs that are included in the $7.50 meet these criteria? The answer is no. While the variable costs would increase as a result of the special order, the fixed costs would be incurred in either case. Thus, the fixed manufacturing overhead costs are not relevant to this decision and should be ignored.

Incremental Analysis (with Excess Capacity)

The incremental analysis of Mattel's special order decision follows:

Incremental Analysis of the Special Order for 25,000 University Barbie Dolls

	Per Unit	Total
Incremental revenue	$7.00	$175,000
Less: Incremental costs		
Direct materials	3.50	87,500
Direct labor	1.00	25,000
Variable overhead	0.50	12,500
Fixed overhead	—	—
Total incremental cost	5.00	125,000
Incremental profit	$2.00	$ 50,000

Notice that this incremental analysis does not include fixed manufacturing overhead costs. The reason these costs have been excluded is that fixed costs such as rent, insurance, and supervision would be incurred regardless of whether Mattel accepts the special order. Because the special order does not cause total fixed costs to increase, only the variable costs of producing the University Barbie are relevant. The special order price of $7 less $5 in variable cost means that each unit will generate $2 in incremental (extra) profit, for a total of $50,000 in incremental profit.

Qualitative Analysis

Two important cautions should be noted when making this type of short-term analysis. First, this analysis is valid only for one-time or special orders. Managers would not want to use incremental analysis to make long-term pricing decisions because prices must cover **all** costs if the company is to be profitable in the long run. Managers should also consider whether accepting the special order will impact the price that other customers are willing to pay for sales made through regular channels.

Second, this analysis is valid only if the company has excess, or idle, production capacity. If not, the company would not be able to fill the special order without canceling or deferring sales made through regular channels, resulting in lost sales or an opportunity cost. This assumes that capacity cannot be increased in the short run. Even if the company could expand capacity by renting more factory space or machines, it would not make sense to do so for a one-time or special order.

The following section illustrates how to incorporate opportunity costs when capacity is limited.

Incremental Analysis (without Excess Capacity)

Now assume that Mattel is operating at full production capacity and cannot fill the special order for 25,000 University Barbies without reducing production and sale of Barbies sold through "normal" channels. It normally sells the dolls to stores and discount chains for about $9 each. Should Mattel's managers accept a special-order price of $7?

In this case, we need to incorporate the opportunity cost of limited capacity. The opportunity cost can be measured as the contribution margin that would be lost on sales made through regular channels. Remember that contribution margin is the sales price minus all variable costs. We ignore fixed costs because they will not change in the short run. Assume the production costs of the regular Barbie dolls are similar to those of the University Barbie:

	Unit Cost
Direct materials (silicone rubber, clothing, accessories)	$3.50
Direct labor	1.00
Variable manufacturing overhead (indirect materials, power, etc.)	0.50
Fixed manufacturing overhead (factory, rent, supervision, etc.)	2.50
Total manufacturing cost	$7.50

Because Barbies sold through normal channels are priced at $9.00 and the variable cost per unit is $5.00 ($3.50 + $1.00 + $0.50), the contribution margin earned on a Barbie sold through regular channels is $4.00 ($9.00 price − $5.00 variable cost) per unit, or $100,000. Again, we ignore the fixed costs because they will be incurred regardless of the decision.

When the opportunity cost of lost sales is incorporated into the incremental analysis, we see that the incremental revenue from the special order is no longer enough to cover the incremental costs, as follows:

Incremental Analysis of the Special Order for 25,000 University Barbie Dolls	Per Unit	Total
Incremental revenue	$ 7.00	$ 175,000
Less: Incremental costs		
Direct materials	3.50	87,500
Direct labor	1.00	25,000
Variable overhead	0.50	12,500
Fixed overhead	—	—
Opportunity cost of lost sales	4.00	100,000
Total incremental cost	9.00	225,000
Incremental profit	$(2.00)	$ (50,000)

Notice that the incremental cost associated with the special order is $9 when the opportunity cost of lost sales is considered, which is more than the offer price of $7.00. The net result of accepting the order would be a $50,000 decrease in profit. When a company is operating at full capacity, managers should not accept a special order for less than the price they could get through normal channels. This quantitative analysis ignores other qualitative factors such as the chance to capture a new customer or expand into a new region. As always, the quantitative analysis must be balanced against these qualitative factors.

Complete the following Self-Study Practice to make sure you understand how to analyze special-order decisions.

💡 Self-Study Practice

Big Top Tent Company has received a special order for 10,000 units at a discounted price of $100 each. The product, which normally sells for $150, has the following manufacturing costs.

	Cost per Unit
Direct materials	$ 40
Direct labor	20
Variable manufacturing overhead	20
Fixed manufacturing overhead	30
Unit cost	$110

1. Assume Big Top has enough extra capacity to fill the order without affecting the production or sale of its product to regular customers. If Big Top accepts the offer, what effect will the order have on the company's short-term profit?

2. If Big Top is at full capacity, what price would be needed to cover all incremental costs, including opportunity costs?

After you have finished, check your answers with the solutions in the margin.

Learning Objective 4
Analyze a make-or-buy decision.

MAKE-OR-BUY DECISIONS

The next managerial decision we analyze is whether to perform a particular activity or function in-house or to purchase it from an outside supplier. Traditionally, these decisions have been called **make-or-buy decisions**, but more recently they have been referred to as **insourcing versus outsourcing decisions**. Almost any business function can be outsourced including production activities or support functions such as payroll, information technology, distribution, and technical support. The key question is whether the organization wants to perform the activities with its own resources and employees, or hire a third party to perform the activities.

To analyze a make/buy or insource/outsource decision, managers should compare the **relevant** costs of performing the activities internally to the cost of buying from an external supplier. In other words, managers should include only those costs that would change depending on whether the company outsources or not. As with any decision, managers must also consider whether there are opportunity costs or benefits lost by performing an activity internally rather than buying it externally.

To analyze a make-or-buy scenario, let's consider the packaging process at Mattel. The design, marketing, and production of appealing toys are Mattel's competitive strengths, so outsourcing less critical activities such as packaging might make sense.

Assume that Mattel currently performs all packaging of its American Girl collection in-house. The company produces a total of 200,000 dolls annually; cost data for the packaging process (not the dolls themselves) follow:

Internal Cost of Packaging 200,000 American Girl Dolls per Year		
	Annual Cost	**Unit Cost**
Packaging materials (cardboard, plastic, etc.)	$300,000	$1.50
Packaging direct labor	90,000	0.45
Indirect materials (glue, tape, etc.)	60,000	0.30
Packaging supervision	50,000	0.25
Other fixed manufacturing overhead	200,000	1.00
Total packaging cost	$700,000	$3.50

> **COACH'S TIP**
>
> When you see fixed costs stated on a per unit basis, be careful. What really counts is the total fixed cost and whether that total cost will change depending on the decision.

Mattel has been negotiating with an outside supplier to provide packaging for the American Girl dolls. After several discussions, the supplier has agreed to a price of $3 per unit for all packaging-related activities. The agreement includes a three-year contract for a minimum of 200,000 units per year.

Should Mattel continue to do its own packaging or outsource these activities to the supplier? To answer this question, Mattel should first consider whether all of the costs associated with the packaging activities are relevant. Another way to think about it is to consider which costs are **avoidable**, or can be eliminated by outsourcing.

All of the variable costs (packaging materials, direct labor, and indirect materials) are relevant, or avoidable, by outsourcing. This assumes, of course, that Mattel does not employ a union workforce, a factor that would make the elimination of direct labor more difficult. But what about the packaging supervision cost? Although supervision is considered a fixed cost, it is potentially avoidable if the supervision is directly related to the packaging process (i.e., the supervisor is not responsible for other activities). If so, Mattel could eliminate the position and perhaps convince the external supplier to hire the supervisor in order to maintain the existing production standards.

Other fixed manufacturing overhead includes costs such as depreciation on machines and the packaging department's share of common facility costs such as rent, utilities, insurance, and the like. These costs are probably not avoidable because they will be incurred regardless of the outsourcing decision. In addition, depreciation is a sunk cost that results from a prior decision to purchase capital equipment. You may recall from your financial accounting course that depreciation is calculated based on an asset's historical (sunk) cost or the amount paid at some point in the past. Tax implications related to depreciation are relevant for decision making, but for simplicity, these issues are not discussed or analyzed here.

The next question management must consider is whether keeping the packaging in-house has any opportunity costs. In other words, are there better uses for the resources currently devoted to packaging? If so, these potential benefits (opportunity costs) should be incorporated into the analysis.

Assume that Mattel's managers investigated further and learned the following:

Information Gathered	Manager's Analysis
• All costs directly related to the packaging activities including all direct and indirect materials, labor, and supervision could be avoided.	• Because these costs can be avoided, they should be considered a relevant cost of internal packaging.
• Other total fixed manufacturing overhead costs would remain unchanged.	• Because these costs will be incurred under either alternative, they should be excluded from the analysis.
• The factory space now used for packaging the American Girl Doll collection could be used to expand production of a popular product line. The expansion would generate an additional $150,000 in profit per year.	• Mattel will receive this benefit by outsourcing but not if it keeps the packaging in-house. This amount can be considered a benefit of outsourcing or an opportunity cost of insourcing, but not both.

Incremental Analysis

Based on the relevant cost analysis and additional information provided, an incremental cost analysis of this decision follows:

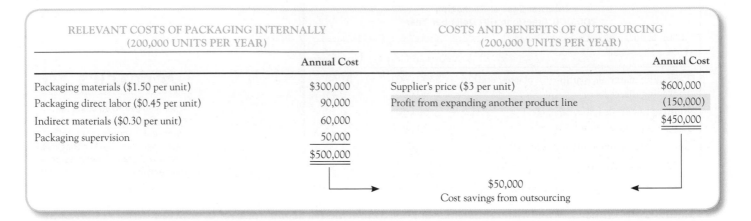

RELEVANT COSTS OF PACKAGING INTERNALLY (200,000 UNITS PER YEAR)		COSTS AND BENEFITS OF OUTSOURCING (200,000 UNITS PER YEAR)	
	Annual Cost		**Annual Cost**
Packaging materials ($1.50 per unit)	$300,000	Supplier's price ($3 per unit)	$600,000
Packaging direct labor ($0.45 per unit)	90,000	Profit from expanding another product line	(150,000)
Indirect materials ($0.30 per unit)	60,000		$450,000
Packaging supervision	50,000		
	$500,000		

$50,000
Cost savings from outsourcing

The relevant cost of internal packaging is $500,000 per year. This amount excludes the other fixed manufacturing overhead costs that would be incurred even if the company outsources the packaging.

The incremental analysis also includes $150,000 in potential profit that could be earned by expanding another product line. There are two ways to account for this factor. The table above shows this as a benefit of outsourcing or extra profit that could be gained by outsourcing. Alternatively, it could be considered an opportunity cost (lost benefit) of keeping the packaging in-house. In that case, the $150,000 in profit would have been added to the cost of in-house packaging instead of subtracted from the cost of outsourcing. Most students find it more intuitive to consider it as a benefit of outsourcing, but the end result (difference in cost) is the same in either case.

Overall, the incremental analysis shows that Mattel will save $50,000 per year by outsourcing the packaging to the external supplier.

Qualitative Analysis

Of course, quantitative analysis has its limitations. Before making a final decision, Mattel's managers would want to consider many other qualitative factors, such as the following:

- Will the quality of the packaging be as good, or even better, than Mattel can provide internally? Sometimes quality can be improved by outsourcing because the supplier specializes in the activity. For example, the supplier may have more experience with certain packaging technology, allowing Mattel to concentrate on designing and manufacturing the toys themselves.

- Will the supplier be reliable in delivering the packaging? If not, we may lose sales.

- What will happen if demand for the product rises above 200,000 units? Does the supplier have the capacity to meet the increased demand? Will the supplier charge a higher or lower price for the additional units?

- What will happen in three years? Will the supplier increase the price significantly? Going back to internal packaging would be difficult after the space has been converted for another purpose.

- What if the expected profit from expanding the other product line has been substantially over- or underestimated?

- Does outsourcing the packaging create any additional risks, such as those that Mattel experienced when outsourcing to Chinese companies (see the Spotlight on Decision Making on page 261)?

Spotlight On DECISION MAKING

Mattel Becomes the Poster Child for the Dangers of Outsourcing to China

Outsourcing occurs when a company hires a third party to do part of its work. Often the third party is located in a foreign country, such as India or China, where labor is much less expensive.

Although many companies have recently started outsourcing to control costs, Mattel has been producing its toys overseas for almost 50 years. Most of its toys are produced in "company-owned" plants in China where Mattel can maintain strict quality standards. But the company also outsources production of some toys to other Chinese manufacturers that may not maintain the same quality standards.

This decision came back to haunt Mattel in the fall of 2007 when the company was forced to recall millions of "toxic toys" that contained unsafe levels of lead-based paint. The costs to Mattel were high including consumer lawsuits, a drop in the company's stock price, sanctions by Congress, and a general loss in consumer and investor confidence.

The lesson is that outsourcing decisions must be made carefully and include an analysis of both the benefits and risks. Mattel's experience also highlights the need to build strict quality control standards into outsourcing agreements regardless of whether the outsourcing contract is with a company overseas or in the United States.

> The New York Times, September 29, 2007
> **Recalls Make Toy Shopping a Source of Anxiety**
>
> **Mattel issues a third toy recall**
> Los Angeles Times, September 5, 2007,
>
> St. Petersburg Times, August 15, 2007
> **Lead scare crosses all lines**
>
> **Fisher-Price recalls IM toys**
> CNN.com, August 1, 2007

To make sure you understand how to analyze insourcing versus outsourcing (make-or-buy) decisions, complete the following Self-Study Practice.

Self-Study Practice

Which of the following costs would **not** be relevant to the decision of whether to make a part internally or buy it from an outside supplier?

(a) Cost of materials needed to make the part internally.

(b) Cost of power to run the machines that make the part.

(c) Fact that the supplier does not maintain high-quality standards.

(d) Share of the rent on the factory (where several parts are made).

(e) Opportunity cost of the space currently used to produce the part.

After you have finished, check your answer with the solution in the margin.

Solution to Self-Study Practice

(d) (The rent on the factory will be incurred regardless and is therefore irrelevant.)

DECISIONS TO ELIMINATE UNPROFITABLE BUSINESS SEGMENTS

The next decision we consider is whether to eliminate a particular division or segment of the business. Businesses can be segmented (divided) in a number of ways, such as by product line, service offering, or geographic region. If a particular business segment is not performing as well as expected, managers may decide to eliminate it. These decisions are sometimes called **keep-or-drop** or **continue-or-discontinue decisions**. In deciding whether to eliminate a business segment, managers should consider which costs and benefits would change as a result of the decision. Because some of the costs may be incurred even if the segment is eliminated, we need to do an incremental analysis to determine the net effect on the bottom line.

> **Learning Objective 5**
> Analyze a decision to eliminate an unprofitable business segment.

Assume that Mattel produces three models of Power Wheels battery-powered vehicles: Jeep Wrangler 4×4, Barbie Mustang, and Dora the Explorer Jeep. Mattel's managers are considering dropping the Barbie Mustang because it is unprofitable with a $20,000 loss last year. Before deciding to eliminate the product, Mattel's managers should ask the following questions:

- What costs (and revenues) would change as a result of the decision to discontinue the Barbie Mustang?
- Would the costs (and revenues) of other product lines be affected by the decision to eliminate the Barbie Mustang?
- Are there alternative uses for the resources currently devoted to the Barbie Mustang (i.e., opportunity costs)?

The following segmented income statement shows the revenue and costs of the three models last year:

**Segment Data for Power Wheels Product Line
by Product Model**

	Jeep Wrangler 4×4	Barbie Mustang	Dora the Explorer Jeep	Total
Sales Revenue	$500,000	$150,000	$350,000	$1,000,000
Less: Variable Costs	200,000	100,000	140,000	440,000
Contribution Margin	$300,000	$ 50,000	$210,000	$ 560,000
Less: Direct Fixed Costs	50,000	40,000	30,000	120,000
Segment Margin	$250,000	$ 10,000	$180,000	$ 440,000
Less: Common Fixed Costs*	100,000	30,000	70,000	200,000
Profit	$150,000	$ (20,000)	$110,000	$ 240,000

*Common fixed costs are allocated to the three products as a percentage of total sales revenue.

This segmented income statement is based on the contribution margin approach introduced in Chapter 5. However, it has been expanded to include a new line item called **segment margin**, which is calculated as sales revenue less all costs that are directly attributable to the segment including variable costs and direct fixed costs. A **direct fixed cost** is one that can be attributed to a specific segment of the business. Examples are a machine used to produce only one type of product, a supervisor who is responsible for a specific division, and advertising aimed at a specific region or product line. Even though these costs are fixed, or independent of the number of units produced or sold, they relate to only one segment and thus could be avoided if the segment were eliminated.

Unlike direct fixed costs that relate to a specific segment, **common fixed costs** are shared by multiple segments and thus will be incurred even if a segment is eliminated. In evaluating segment profitability, managers should focus on the segment margin rather than the bottom-line profit margin. The segment margin tells managers how much incremental profit a segment generates that helps to cover common fixed costs and contribute to companywide profit. Although the Barbie Mustang is not profitable in terms of the bottom line, it generates $10,000 in segment margin, which helps cover the common fixed costs.

The second question managers must address is whether the elimination of one segment will affect the cost and revenues of other segments. For example, customers who were planning to buy the Barbie Mustang might purchase one of the other products instead.

Assume that the elimination of the Barbie Mustang will increase sales of the Dora the Explorer Jeep by 10 percent but have no effect on the Jeep 4×4. What effect would this have on overall company profit? Remember that variable costs increase in direct proportion to changes in sales, so both the sales revenue and variable costs of the Dora Explorer Jeep would increase by 10 percent. The net effect will be a 10 percent increase in the contribution margin of the Dora the Explorer Jeep.

The third question is whether any opportunity costs should be considered. Would the elimination of the Barbie Mustang free resources (people, space, or machines) that could be used in another way? Perhaps another product could be developed that would contribute more to profit than the Barbie Mustang. For the following incremental analysis, we assume that there are no alternative uses for the resources and thus no opportunity costs.

Incremental Analysis

Based on the information given in the previous section, we can prepare an incremental analysis of the decision to eliminate the Barbie Mustang, as follows:

Elimination of Barbie Mustang	
Lost sales revenue	($150,000)
Less: Avoidable variable costs	100,000
Less: Avoidable direct fixed costs	40,000
Lost segment margin	($ 10,000)
Effect on Dora Explorer (10% increase)	
Increased sales ($350,000 × 10%)	$ 35,000
Less: Increased variable cost ($140,000 × 10%)	(14,000)
Increased contribution margin ($210,000 × 10%)	$ 21,000
Net effect of eliminating the Barbie Mustang	$ 11,000

> **COACH'S TIP**
>
> You may notice that the format of the incremental analysis changes from decision to decision, and there is more than one way to work each problem.
> Unfortunately, there is no "set format" for doing incremental analysis. The key is to focus on what is the same in each analysis: the comparison of relevant or differential costs and benefits.

This analysis shows that Mattel will lose $10,000 in segment margin from the elimination of the Barbie Mustang but will gain an additional $21,000 in contribution margin from increased sales of the Dora the Explorer Jeep. The net effect is an $11,000 increase in profit. All other costs are irrelevant, and no opportunity costs are included in the decision analysis.

An alternative way to analyze this decision is to create a new segmented income statement for the company without the Barbie Mustang, as follows:

	Jeep Wrangler 4×4	Dora the Explorer Jeep	Total
Sales Revenue	$500,000	$350,000 × 110% = $385,000	$885,000
Less: Variable costs	200,000	140,000 × 110% = $154,000	354,000
Contribution margin	$300,000	210,000 × 110% = $231,000	$531,000
Less: Direct fixed costs	50,000	30,000	80,000
Segment Margin	$250,000	$201,000	$451,000
Less: Common fixed costs*	113,000	87,000	200,000
Profit	$137,000	$114,000	$251,000

*Common fixed costs were reallocated to the remaining two products as a percentage of total sales revenue.

A few important points about this segmented income statement should be noted:

- The sales, variable cost, and contribution margin of the Dora the Explorer Jeep increased by 10 percent. Total fixed costs did not change as a result of the increased sales.
- Common fixed costs remained at $200,000. This total cost is simply reallocated or distributed among the two remaining product lines on the basis of their new sales revenue.
- The total profit is $251,000 after the Barbie Mustang is eliminated. Total profit with the Mustang was $240,000. Thus, overall profit increased by $11,000 ($251,000 − $240,000). This is the same overall difference in profit calculated using the incremental analysis.

> **COACH'S TIP**
>
> Overall profit is now $251,000, which is $11,000 higher than the $240,000 earned with the Barbie Mustang.

Based strictly on the incremental analysis, Mattel should discontinue the Barbie Mustang to increase profit by $11,000 per year.

Qualitative Analysis

As in the other decision scenarios, the quantitative analysis is only a starting point for making the decision. Managers must always consider other important factors including the effect of the decision on customer loyalty and employee morale.

Managers must also think about the likely impact of discontinuation on other products and customers. The previous example involved **substitute products** or products that can be used in place of one another. In other words, consumers might choose the Dora the Explorer Jeep if the Barbie Mustang was not available. In that scenario, eliminating one product could boost sales of another product line.

But sometimes firms have **complementary products**, or products that are used together. Common examples include Brother printers and cartridges, computers and software programs, and Nintendo game systems and games. In the case of complementary products, eliminating one product can have a negative effect on the related product. When choosing to discontinue products, managers must carefully anticipate the effect on other related product lines.

Before continuing, complete the following Self-Study Practice to make sure you can analyze decisions to eliminate a business segment.

 ## Self-Study Practice

Big Top Tent Company is trying to decide whether to keep or drop one of its outdoor wedding tents. The company's segmented income statement shows that this product is generating a net loss, as follows:

Sales Revenue	$100,000
Variable Costs (canvas, ropes, and direct labor)	70,000
Contribution Margin	$ 30,000
Direct Fixed Costs (supervision)	10,000
Segment Margin	$ 20,000
Allocated Common Fixed Costs	30,000
Profit (Loss)	$(10,000)

The company estimates that eliminating this product line will increase the contribution margin on a related product line by $25,000. Based on this information, what impact would dropping the line have on the company's overall profitability?

(a) $5,000 increase.

(b) $10,000 increase.

(c) $25,000 increase.

(d) $35,000 decrease.

After you have finished, check your answers with the solutions in the margin.

SELL-OR-PROCESS FURTHER DECISIONS

The next managerial decision we consider is whether to sell a product "as is" or continue to refine it so that it can be sold for a higher price. Once again, we can analyze this decision by comparing the incremental costs and benefits of this decision. If the increased revenue is enough to offset the incremental cost, the company should process further; otherwise it is better off selling the product as is.

As an example, assume that Mattel has begun development of a remote control Hummer toy. So far, the company has spent a total of $250,000 on research and development. Based on the features that are currently included in the product, managers estimate that they could sell 100,000 units at a price of $15 each.

One of the product designers has suggested that additional features such as moveable parts, music, and lights be added to the toy. If the company spends an additional $100,000 on development, it could sell the enhanced product for $18 per unit. However, the enhanced product would have higher manufacturing costs because it would require additional components and more labor in the assembly and machining departments. The following table summarizes the expected costs and revenues from selling the product based on the current design versus selling it with the enhanced features:

	Current Design	Enhanced Design
Estimated demand	100,000 units	100,000 units
Estimated sales price	$15 per unit	$18 per unit
Estimated manufacturing costs (per unit)		
Direct materials	$3.00	$4.25
Direct labor	1.50	1.75
Variable manufacturing overhead	0.50	0.75
Fixed manufacturing overhead	2.00	2.00
Unit manufacturing costs	$7.00	$8.75
Research and development costs	$250,000	$350,000

Should the company sell the product as it is currently designed or spend more money to create the enhanced design? To answer this question, managers should compare the incremental revenue and incremental costs of the two alternatives as summarized in the following table:

Increased sales revenue 100,000 units × $3 ($18 − $15)	$300,000
Increased manufacturing costs 100,000 units × $1.75 ($8.75 − $7.00)	(175,000)
Increased research and development costs	(100,000)
Increased profit	$ 25,000

This analysis suggests that the company would make an additional $25,000 in profit by incorporating additional features into the toy. The increased sales revenue generated by the higher sales price is more than enough to offset the increase in development and manufacturing costs.

Notice, however, that the analysis incorporated no opportunity costs. By spending time enhancing the Hummer toy, Mattel's product designers may be sacrificing time that could be better spent designing new products that might earn even more profit. Whenever possible, managers need to incorporate these opportunity costs into the decision-making process.

PRIORITIZATION OF PRODUCTS WITH CONSTRAINED RESOURCES

As previously discussed, opportunity costs occur any time that resources are limited or constrained. The **constrained resource** could be anything that is needed to operate the business, such as cash, employees, machines, or facilities. When any of these resources is unable to meet demand, the company cannot produce enough products to fill customer orders, and managers must decide which products to produce or which customers to serve.

In the long term, companies can manage constrained resources by eliminating nonvalue-added activities such as rework and waiting, or by increasing the capacity of the constrained resources by hiring more workers, buying bigger or faster machines, or leasing additional space. All of these actions take time, however, and may result in higher cost.

In the short run managers can maximize profit by prioritizing products or customers based on the amount of contribution margin generated by the most constrained resource, called the **bottleneck**. The bottleneck limits the system's overall output and therefore determines how much contribution margin is lost due to limited resources. We focus on contribution margin because fixed costs do not change in the short run and are therefore irrelevant.

If labor is the most constrained resource, managers should focus on maximizing the amount of contribution margin earned per direct labor hour. If a machine is the most constrained resource, the focus should be on maximizing the amount of contribution margin per machine hour. Prioritizing in this way results in the highest possible short-term profit.

To illustrate, assume that one of Mattel's factories produces three types of toy cars with the following price, cost, and production information:

COACH'S TIP

The company needs 360,000 minutes of machine time to meet the full demand for all three products.

	Matchbox	Hot Wheels	Remote Control
Unit sales price	$5.00	$15.00	$25.00
Unit variable costs	2.00	7.00	10.00
Unit contribution margin	$3.00	$ 8.00	$15.00
Machine time required (minutes per unit)	6	10	20
Monthly demand (units)	10,000	10,000	10,000
Total machine requirements (minutes)	60,000	100,000	200,000

Assume the company has only 330,000 minutes of machine time available during the month but needs 360,000 minutes to meet the demand for all three products. How should Mattel's managers prioritize production of the three products?

To answer this question, we need to determine how much contribution margin is generated for each minute of machine time, which is the most constrained resource. These calculations follow:

	Matchbox	Hot Wheels	Remote Control
Unit contribution margin	$3.00	$8.00	$15.00
Machine time required (minutes per unit)	÷6	÷10	÷20
Contribution margin per minute of machine time	$0.50	$0.80	$ 0.75

Although the remote control product has the highest contribution margin per unit ($15.00), it also takes the most time to produce (20 minutes). This product yields $0.75 ($15.00/20) in contribution margin for every minute of machine time. In contrast, the Hot Wheels product generates $0.80 ($8.00/10) for each minute of machine time. The Matchbox product generates $0.50 ($3.00/6) per minute.

To maximize short-term profit, Mattel's managers should focus first on producing the Hot Wheels product because it generates $0.80 in contribution margin per minute. However, they should not produce more than the 10,000 units demanded because doing so would result in an unnecessary build up of inventory. Next they should produce the Remote Control product, which has the second highest contribution margin per machine hour. Whatever time is left can be devoted to the Matchbox product, which generates the lowest contribution margin per minute of machine time. These calculations follow:

	Matchbox	Hot Wheels	Remote Control
Priority	3	1	2
Demand (in units)	5,000	10,000	10,000
Machine time required (minutes per unit)	6	10	20
Total machine requirements (in minutes)	30,000	100,000	200,000

This analysis shows that Mattel should produce 10,000 Hot Wheels, 10,000 remote control cars, and 5,000 Matchbox cars. This combination of products will result in the most total contribution margin given the limited machine hours available. This analysis assumes that fixed costs will remain unchanged and that machine time is the most constrained resource or bottleneck. If the bottleneck shifts to another resource, such as labor or space, managers would need to repeat the analysis with the new bottleneck process.

SUMMARY OF INCREMENTAL ANALYSIS

This chapter applied incremental or relevant cost analysis to a number of short-term decisions. Although the decision problems were different, the same basic approach was used to analyze each decision. In all cases, we focused only on the relevant or incremental cost and benefits of the decision problem. Some common rules for analyzing relevant costs and benefits are summarized here:

- Relevant costs and benefits occur in the **future** and **differ** between the decision alternatives.
- Relevant costs are also sometimes called **avoidable** or **differential costs**—costs that will change based on the decision made.
- Variable costs are usually relevant to the decision because they vary with the number of units produced or sold.
- Fixed costs may not be relevant because they do not change with the number of units produced or sold.
- Fixed costs that are directly related to the decision may be avoidable and thus relevant.
- Common or allocated fixed costs are shared by multiple products or services and are generally not relevant.
- Opportunity costs are the lost benefit of choosing one alternative over another. These costs are relevant and occur when capacity is reached or resources are constrained. Opportunity costs can be treated either as a benefit of one option, or as a cost of the other, but not both.

The quantitative analysis provides a starting point for making decisions but must be balanced against other qualitative factors such as quality considerations, customer loyalty, employee morale, and many other important factors.

DEMONSTRATION CASE

Assume you need to buy a new vehicle. The junker that you paid $5,000 for two years ago has a current value of $1,500. You have narrowed the choice down to a used 2004 Jeep Cherokee with a blue book value of $8,000 and a new Hyundai Elantra with a sticker price of $12,995. You plan to drive either vehicle for at least five more years.

Required:

1. List the five steps in the decision-making process and briefly describe the key factors you would consider at each step.
2. Indicate whether each of the following factors would be relevant or irrelevant to your decision:
   (a) The $5,000 you paid for your junker two years ago.
   (b) The $1,500 your vehicle is worth today.

(c) The blue book value of the Jeep Cherokee.

(d) The sticker price of the Hyundai Elantra.

(e) The difference in fuel economy for the Jeep and the Hyundai.

(f) The cost of on-campus parking.

(g) The difference in insurance cost for the Jeep and the Hyundai.

(h) The difference in resale value five years from now for the Jeep and the Hyundai.

(i) The fact that the Hyundai comes with a warranty but the Jeep does not.

3. Consider only the costs you classified as irrelevant for #2 above.

(a) Would any of these costs be relevant if you were deciding whether to keep your present vehicle or buy a new one?

(b) Would any of these costs be relevant if you were deciding whether to get rid of your vehicle and ride your bike to work and school?

See page 269 for solution.

CHAPTER SUMMARY

LO1   Describe the five steps in the decision-making process. p. 252

- The managerial decision-making process has five steps:
  - Identify the decision problem.
  - Determine the decision alternatives.
  - Evaluate the costs and benefits of the alternatives.
  - Make the decision.
  - Review the results of the decision-making process.

LO2   Define and identify relevant costs and benefits. p. 254

- When making decisions, managers should focus only on costs and benefits that are relevant to the decision. To be relevant, a cost or benefit must meet the following criteria:

  - It must occur in the future, not the past. Sunk costs are never relevant.
  - The total amount of the cost or benefit must change depending on which alternative is selected.

- Relevant costs are sometimes called **differential costs**, **incremental costs**, or **avoidable costs**. Costs that will not change regardless of the alternative selected are irrelevant and should be ignored.

- Opportunity costs are the forgone (lost) benefits of choosing one alternative over another. Opportunity costs occur when resources are limited or when capacity constraints are reached and are relevant for decision making.

LO3   Analyze a special-order decision. p. 255

- A special order is outside the scope of normal sales. If the incremental revenue exceeds the incremental costs of filling the special order, it will increase short-term profitability.

- If a company has excess capacity, only the variable costs of filling the special order are relevant.

- Fixed costs do not change in the short run and are therefore not included in the incremental analysis.

- If a company is operating at full capacity, the opportunity cost of lost sales is relevant and should be incorporated into the incremental analysis.

LO4   Analyze a make-or-buy decision. p. 258

- Make-or-buy decisions involve deciding whether to perform a particular function in-house versus buying it from an outside supplier. They are also called in source versus outsource decisions.

- The relevant costs of making a product or providing a service internally include all variable costs plus any incremental fixed costs.

- The opportunity costs of making something internally include alternative uses for the internal resources.

- Many qualitative considerations including quality, reliability, and environmental concerns are also important in make-or-buy decisions.

LO5   Analyze a decision to eliminate an unprofitable business segment. p. 261

- Managers must often decide whether to eliminate a business segment that is not performing as well as expected.

- To decide whether to eliminate a segment, managers should focus on the segment margin, or the amount of profit generated by the segment after variable costs and direct fixed costs have been deducted.

- Common fixed costs would be incurred even if the segment is eliminated and are not relevant to the decision.

- Managers must also consider how elimination of the segment would affect other segments or product lines and whether alternative uses for the resources currently devoted to the business segment exist.

Analyze a sell-or-process further decision. p. 265   **LO6**

- A sell-or-process further decision determines whether to sell a product as is or continue to invest in it.

- The incremental revenue should be compared to the incremental cost of continuing to enhance the product or service.

Prioritize products to maximize short-term profit with constrained resources. p. 265   **LO7**

- A constrained resource occurs when its capacity is insufficient to meet the demands placed on it.

- The most constrained resource is also called the bottleneck, which limits the system's overall output.

- To maximize short-term profit, managers should prioritize products based on the amount of contribution margin earned per unit of time in the most constrained (bottleneck) process.

SOLUTION TO DEMONSTRATION CASE

1.

Factors to Considers	
Step 1: Identify the decision problem.	You need (or want) to buy another vehicle presumably because your old one is no longer fulfilling its purpose.
Step 2: Determine the decision alternatives.	What kind of vehicle should you buy (a car, a truck, an SUV)? Should you buy a new or a used vehicle? What is your price range? What fuel economy should the vehicle you buy offer? What other features are important to you?
Step 3: Evaluate the costs and benefits of the alternatives.	What is the difference in price for each alternative, fuel economy, cost of insurance, cost of maintenance, reliability ratings, future resale value, and other benefits or costs?
Step 4: Make the decision.	Which cost and qualitative considerations, such as style and function, outweigh the others?
Step 5: Review the results of the decision-making process.	Does the vehicle you purchased meet your needs? Is it reliable? Are you comfortable in it? Can you make the payments?

2.

    (a) Sunk cost.
    (b) Same under both options.
    (c) Relevant.
    (d) Relevant.
    (e) Relevant.
    (f) Same under both options.
    (g) Relevant.
    (h) Relevant.
    (i) Relevant.

3.

    (a) Yes, the $1,500 value of your current vehicle would be relevant because you could sell it under one option but not the other.
    (b) Yes, the cost of on-campus parking would be relevant because you could avoid it if you did not own a vehicle.

KEY TERMS

Avoidable Cost (p. 254)	Constrained Resource (p. 265)	Idle Capacity (p. 255)
Bottleneck (p. 266)	Differential Analysis (p. 254)	Incremental Analysis (p. 253)
Capacity (p. 255)	Differential Cost (p. 254)	Incremental Cost (p. 254)
Common Fixed Cost (p. 262)	Direct Fixed Cost (p. 262)	Segment Margin (p. 262)
Complementary Products (p. 264)	Excess Capacity (p. 255)	Substitute Products (p. 264)
	Full Capacity (p. 255)	

See complete definitions in glossary at back of text.

QUESTIONS

1. Briefly describe the five steps of the management decision-making process.

2. Suppose you are considering a part-time job to earn some extra spending money. List four factors that could affect that decision and would be included in Step 3 of your decision-making process.

3. Tom Ellis recently bought a plasma television and has since stated that he would not recommend it to others. This indicates that Tom has completed which step of the decision-making process?

4. What are the criteria for a cost to be considered relevant to any decision?

5. How is an avoidable cost related to a relevant cost?

6. Explain opportunity cost and give two opportunity costs of your decision to enroll in classes this semester.

7. Why should opportunity costs be factored into the decision-making process, and why is it often difficult to do?

8. Explain excess capacity and full capacity. Include the implications that each has for a company's production decisions.

9. How are the concepts of full capacity and opportunity cost interrelated?

10. What is a special-order decision? Why can managers ignore fixed overhead costs when making special-order decisions?

11. How might the acceptance of a special order have negative consequences for a company?

12. How does excess capacity impact a special-order decision?

13. Suppose that you are the manager of a local deli. Give an example of each of the following decisions that you might have to make and identify three factors that would be relevant to each decision:

    (a) Special order.
    (b) Make or buy.
    (c) Eliminating an unprofitable business segment.

14. Briefly describe three problems that might result from a decision to buy a component part from an external supplier. For each problem, identify one way to avoid or correct it.

15. How do opportunity costs affect make-or-buy decisions? How are opportunity costs shown in a make-or-buy analysis?

16. When a product line is eliminated, why aren't the total fixed costs associated with that line **not** automatically eliminated as well?

17. How might the decision to drop a product line affect a company's remaining products?

18. Briefly explain what happens to total variable costs when a product line is dropped.

19. Identify three opportunity costs that might result from a decision to eliminate a business segment.

20. Explain how a constrained resource impacts management decisions in both the long and the short term.

21. Why do decisions involving a constrained resource focus on contribution margin instead of profit margin?

MULTIPLE CHOICE

Quiz 7
www.mhhe.com/whitecotton1e

1. The decision-making approach in which a manager considers only costs and benefits that differ for alternatives is called:

    a. Incremental analysis.
    b. Outsourcing.
    c. Differential analysis.
    d. Either (*a*) or (*c*).

2. Which of the following is not a step of the management decision-making process?

    a. Review results of the decision-making process.
    b. Contact competitors who have made similar decisions.
    c. Evaluate the costs and benefits of the alternatives.
    d. Determine the decision alternatives.

3. Sunk costs are always

   a. Opportunity costs.
   b. Avoidable.
   c. Relevant.
   d. Irrelevant.

4. When making a one-time special-order decision, a company can ignore fixed overhead because

   a. The cost is not avoidable.
   b. The cost is avoidable.
   c. The cost cannot be determined.
   d. None of the above.

5. When making make-or-buy decisions, managers should consider

   a. Alternate uses for any facility currently being used to make the item.
   b. The costs of direct materials included in making the item.
   c. Qualitative factors such as whether the supplier can deliver the item on time and to the company's quality standards.
   d. All of the above.

6. Which of the following costs is not likely to be completely eliminated by a decision to drop a product line?

   a. The variable overhead traced to that product line.
   b. The cost of direct materials used to make the product.
   c. The common fixed costs allocated to that product line.
   d. All of the above will be completely eliminated.

7. Which of the following causes opportunity costs to become relevant to management decisions?

   a. Sunk cost.
   b. Operating at full capacity.
   c. Operating with idle or excess capacity.
   d. Avoidable costs.

8. Which of the following could be a constrained resource?

   a. Machine hours.
   b. Direct material.
   c. Factory space.
   d. All of the above.

9. When resources are constrained, managers should prioritize products in order to maximize.

   a. Contribution margin per unit of the constrained resource.
   b. Sales volume.
   c. Opportunity cost.
   d. Fixed cost per unit of the constrained resource.

10. Which of the following is not an important qualitative factor.

    a. Employee morale.
    b. Customer loyalty.
    c. Cost per unit.
    d. Quality considerations.

Answers to Multiple-Choice Questions located in back of the text.

MINI EXERCISES

M7-1 Matching Key Terms and Concepts to Definitions

LO1, 2, 3, 4, 5, 6

A number of terms and concepts from this chapter and a list of descriptions, definitions, and explanations follow. For each term listed on the left, choose at least one corresponding item from the right. Note that a single term may have more than one description and a single description may be used more than once or not at all.

_____ 1. Excess capacity.

_____ 2. Identify the decision problem.

_____ 3. Constrained resource.

_____ 4. Special-order decision.

_____ 5. Differential costs.

_____ 6. Evaluate the costs and benefits of alternatives.

_____ 7. Make-or-buy decision.

_____ 8. Sunk costs.

_____ 9. Opportunity costs.

_____ 10. Keep or drop decision.

_____ 11. Full capacity.

_____ 12. Avoidable costs.

(a) Short-term management decision made using differential analysis.

(b) Management decision in which lost revenue is compared to the reduction of costs to determine the overall effect on profit.

(c) Exists when a company has not yet reached the limit on its resources.

(d) Costs that have already been incurred.

(e) Management decision in which fixed manufacturing overhead is ignored as long as there is enough excess capacity to meet the order.

(f) Costs that can be avoided by choosing one option over another.

(g) Step 5 of the management decision-making process.

(h) Management decision in which relevant costs of making a product internally are compared to the cost of purchasing that product.

(i) Cost that is relevant to short-term decision making.

(j) Resource that is insufficient to meet the demands placed on it.

(k) First step of the management decision-making process.

(l) Costs that are always irrelevant to management decisions.

(m) Exists when a company has met its limit on one or more resources.

(n) Benefits given up when one alternative is chosen over another.

(o) Costs that change across decision alternatives.

(p) Step 3 of the management decision-making process.

LO2   **M7-2 Identifying Relevant and Irrelevant Costs**

Sarah Ramirez is considering taking a part-time job at a local clothing store. She loves the store and shops there often, but unfortunately, employee discounts are given only to full-time employees. If Sarah takes this job, she would have to withdraw from her Tuesday night basket-weaving class to work. Accepting the job would also mean that Sarah must give up her volunteer work at the local animal sanctuary, an activity that she enjoys a great deal. The new job would pay approximately $125 per week but would cost Sarah $15 per week in gas. Sarah would be able to keep her Saturday afternoon job at the library that pays $40 per week.

A list of factors that Sarah has identified follows. For each one, indicate whether it is relevant or irrelevant to Sarah's decision.

1. The $125 income from the new job.
2. The $40 income from the library.
3. The $50 nonrefundable registration fee Sarah paid for the basket-weaving class.
4. The $15 cost for gas.
5. The $75 per month that Sarah spends for clothing.
6. The time Sarah spends volunteering at the animal sanctuary.

LO2   **M7-3 Identifying Relevant and Irrelevant Costs**

The local summer baseball league wants to buy new uniforms for its teams. The current uniforms are quite old and will require $400 in repairs before they can be handed out to players next week for the upcoming season. The old uniforms will be replaced as soon as new ones can be purchased. League leaders have investigated several possible fund-raisers and have narrowed the choice to two options: candy sales and car washes. Each option can generate the $2,500 that the new uniforms would cost.

Option 1:

The candy sales option would require the league to purchase 2,000 candy bars at a cost of $0.75 each. The players and coaches would then sell the bars for $2.00 each. The league estimates that it would take about four weeks to sell the candy and collect all of the money.

Option 2:

The car wash option would require about $200 for buckets, sponges, soap, and towels. A local business has offered to donate the water (estimated at $300 total) and a location. The car washes would be held on Saturdays, and each team would be required to provide workers. Each car wash day is expected to generate $450 in proceeds, so the league expects that it would take six weeks to raise $2,500.

Required:

1. Several factors related to the league's choice follow. Indicate whether each factor is relevant or irrelevant to deciding which project to engage in and briefly explain your reason.
   (a) Repair costs for the old uniforms, $400.
   (b) Initial outlay to purchase the candy bars, $1,500.
   (c) Initial outlay to purchase car wash supplies, $200.
   (d) Cost of water for the car wash option, $300.
   (e) Cost of the new uniforms, $2,500.
   (f) Additional two weeks that the car wash option would require to raise the money.
2. List three qualitative factors that the league should consider in making its choice.

Questions M7-4 through M7-7 refer to Flyaway Company, which produces window fans.

LO2, 3   **M7-4 Analyzing a Special-Order Decision**

Flyaway Company has just received a one-time offer to purchase 10,000 units of its Breezy model for a price of $20 each. The Breezy model costs $25 to produce ($17 in variable costs and $8 of fixed overhead). Because the offer came during a slow production month, Flyaway has enough excess capacity to accept the order.

1. Should Flyaway accept the special order?
2. Determine the impact the special order would have on Flyaway's net income.

M7-5 Considering Impact of Full Capacity on Special-Order Decision

Explain how the analysis and decision in M7-4 would have been affected if Flyaway were operating at full capacity.

M7-6 Analyzing Unprofitable Business Segment Decision

Suppose that Flyaway Company also produces the Windy model fan, which currently has a net loss of $40,000 as follows:

	Windy Model
Sales revenue	$160,000
Less: Variable costs	130,000
Contribution margin	$ 30,000
Less: Direct fixed costs	20,000
Segment margin	$ 10,000
Less: Common fixed costs	50,000
Profit	$ (40,000)

Eliminating the Windy product line would eliminate $20,000 of direct fixed costs. The $50,000 of common fixed costs would be redistributed to Flyaway's remaining product lines.

Determine whether Flyaway should eliminate the Windy fan line and explain why or why not.

M7-7 Analyzing Make-or-Buy Decision

Flyaway Company also has the Cyclone fan model. It is the company's top-selling model with sales of 30,000 units per year. This model has a dual fan as well as a thermostat component that causes the fan to cycle on and off depending on the room temperature. Flyaway has always manufactured the thermostat component but is considering buying the part from a supplier.

It costs Flyaway $5 to make each thermostat ($3 variable and $2 fixed). Mostat Co. has offered to sell the component to Flyaway for $4. Flyaway's decision to purchase the part from Mostat would eliminate all variable costs but none of the fixed costs. Flyaway has no other possible uses for the area currently dedicated to the thermostat production.

Determine whether Flyaway should continue to make the thermostat or purchase the part from Mostat Co. Justify your answer.

M7-8 Identifying Capacity Impact on Special-Order Decisions

Your roommate, Joe Thompson, has taken a summer intern position at a local manufacturing company. Because he is a junior majoring in accounting, the company expects him to have a grasp of managerial accounting basics. However, Joe didn't attend class very often and made only a C− in managerial accounting. On his first day, the company president gave Joe a tour of the production facility and talked extensively about one of the company's direct materials becoming a constrained resource. Because Joe's entire internship is likely going to revolve around this limited resource and its impact on company decisions, he is in a panic to understand the concept.

Explain to Joe the terms *full capacity*, *excess capacity*, and *constrained resource*. Also briefly explain how a constrained resource could affect special-order and production decisions for his employer.

M7-9 Making Production Decisions with Constrained Resource

Juanita Poblamo makes large ceramic pots for use in outdoor landscape. She currently has two models, one square and the other round. Because of the size of Juanita's creations, only one pot can be fired in the kiln at a time. Information about each model follows:

	Square	Round
Sales price	$70	$90
Variable cost	$15	$20
Firing time	2 hours	3 hours

Assume that Juanita can sell as many pots as she can create but that she is limited as to the number of hours that the kiln can be run. Determine which model Juanita should produce and explain your answer.

LO2, 7   M7-10 Making Production Decision with Constrained Resource

Refer to the information presented in M7-9. Suppose that Juanita has developed a rectangular, medium-size ceramic pot. It requires 3 hours of kiln time; however, two medium-size pots can fit in the kiln at once. The medium-size pots would sell for $55 each and have variable cost of $10 per pot. Determine which type of pot Juanita should produce and explain your answer.

EXERCISES

LO1, 2   E7-1 Identifying Relevant Costs and Calculating Differential Costs

Maria Turner has just graduated from college with a degree in accounting. She had planned to enroll immediately in the master's program at her university but has been offered a lucrative job at a well-known company. The job is exactly what Maria had hoped to find after obtaining her graduate degree.

In anticipation of master's program classes, Maria has already spent $450 to apply for the program. Tuition is $8,000 per year, and the program will take two years to complete. Maria's expected salary after completing the master's program is approximately $60,000. If she pursues the master's degree, Maria would stay in her current home that is near the campus and costs $600 per month in rent. She would also remain at her current job that pays $25,000 per year. Additionally, Maria's immediate family is nearby. She spends considerable time with family and friends, especially during the holidays. This would not be possible if she accepts the job offer because of the distance from her new location.

The job Maria has been offered includes a salary of $50,000. She would have to relocate to another state, but her employer would pay the $5,000 for moving expenses. Maria's rent in the new location would be approximately $800 per month. The new location is a fast-growing, active city that offers a number of cultural activities that Maria would enjoy. The city is also home to Maria's favorite Major League Baseball team, and she would expect to buy season tickets.

Required:

1. Help Maria make her decision by categorizing the factors involved in making her choice. Complete the following chart regarding the factors in Maria's decision. A single factor may have multiple columns checked.

	Relevant	Irrelevant	Sunk Cost	Qualitative
$450 spent on application fee				
$8,000 per year tuition				
$60,000 salary with master's degree				
$600 per month current rent				
$25,000 current salary				
Time spent with family and friends				
$50,000 new salary				
$5,000 moving expenses				
$800 rent per month in new location				
Cultural activities in the new location				
Ability to have MLB season tickets				

2. For each item following, determine the differential amount in Maria's alternatives. For example, the incremental cost of tuition is $16,000 if Maria chooses to pursue the master's degree.

   (a) Rent.
   (b) Salary for the next two years.
   (c) Salary after two years.
   (d) Moving expenses.

The following information pertains to E7-2 through E7-6.

Electronic Playground, Inc. (EPI), manufactures and sells computer games. The company has several product lines based on the age range of the target market and the games marketing as educational or entertainment. EPI sells both individual games as well as packaged sets. All games are in CD format, and some utilize accessories such as steering wheels, electronic tablets, and hand controls. To date, EPI has developed and manufactured all CDs itself as well as the accessories and packaging for all of its products.

The gaming market has traditionally been targeted at teenagers and young adults. However, the increasing affordability of computers and the incorporation of computer activities into junior high and elementary school curriculums has led to a significant increase in sales to younger children. EPI has always included games for younger children but now wants to expand its business to capitalize on changes in the industry. The company currently has excess capacity and is investigating several possible ways to improve profitability.

E7-2 Analyzing a Special-Order Decision

LO2, 3

EPI has been approached by a fourth-grade teacher from Phoenix about the possibility of creating a specially designed game that would be customized for her classroom and environment. The teacher would like an educational game to correspond to her classroom coverage of the history of the desert Southwest and the state of Arizona in particular. EPI has not sold its products directly to teachers or school systems in the past, but its Marketing Department identified that possibility during a recent meeting.

The teacher has offered to buy 1,000 copies of the CD at a price of $5 each. EPI could easily modify one of its existing educational programs about U.S. history to accommodate the request. The modifications would cost approximately $500. A summary of the information related to production of EPI's current history program follows.

Direct materials	$ 1.25
Direct labor	0.50
Variable manufacturing overhead	2.25
Fixed manufacturing overhead	2.00
Total cost per unit	$ 6.00
Sales price per unit	$12.00

Required:

1. Determine the impact this special order would have on EPI's total profit.
2. Should EPI accept the special order?
3. Suppose that the special order had been to purchase 1,000 copies of the program for $4.50 each. What effect would that offer have on EPI's total profit?
4. Suppose that EPI is operating at full capacity. To accept the special order, it would have to reduce production of the history program. Assuming that fixed manufacturing overhead costs are unavoidable, at what price for the special order is EPI financially indifferent between the two options?
5. Explain why a company might accept a special order that did not increase profits.

E7-3 Analyzing a Make-or-Buy Decision

LO2, 4

EPI is considering outsourcing the production of the handheld control module used with some of its products. The company has received a bid from Control Freak Co. (CFC) to produce

10,000 units of the module per year for $15 each. The following information pertains to EPI's production of the control modules:

Direct materials	$ 8
Direct labor	3
Variable manufacturing overhead	2
Fixed manufacturing overhead	3
Total cost per unit	$16

EPI has determined that it could eliminate all variable costs if the control modules were produced externally, but none of the fixed overhead is avoidable. At this time, EPI has no specific use in mind for the space that is currently dedicated to the control module production.

Required:

1. Determine the impact this decision will have on EPI's annual income.
2. Should EPI buy the modules from CFC or continue to make them?
3. Suppose that the EPI space currently used for the modules could be utilized by a new product line that would generate $35,000 in annual profit. Does this change your recommendation to EPI? If so, how?

LO2, 5   E7-4 Analyzing the Decision to Eliminate Unprofitable Segment

EPI is considering eliminating a product from its ToddleTown Tours collection. This collection is aimed at children one to three years of age and includes "tours" of a hypothetical town. Two products, The Pet Store Parade and The Grocery Getaway, have impressive sales. However, sales for the third CD in the collection, The Post Office Polka, have lagged the others. Several other CDs are planned for this collection, but none is ready for production.

EPI's information related to the ToddleTown Tours collection follows:

Segmented Income Statement for EPI's ToddleTown Tours Product Lines

	Pet Store Parade	Grocery Getaway	Post Office Polka	Total
Sales Revenue	$50,000	$45,000	$15,000	$110,000
Variable Costs	23,000	19,000	10,000	52,000
Contribution Margin	27,000	26,000	5,000	58,000
Less: Direct Fixed Costs	4,800	3,100	1,500	9,400
Segment Margin	22,200	22,900	3,500	48,600
Less: Common Fixed Costs*	14,400	12,960	4,320	31,680
Profit	$ 7,800	$ 9,940	$ (820)	$ 16,920

*Allocated based on total sales dollars.

EPI has determined that elimination of the Post Office Polka (POP) program would not impact sales of the other two items. The remaining fixed overhead currently allocated to the POP product would be redistributed to the remaining two products.

Required:

1. Determine what would happen to the company's total profit if EPI drops the POP product. What is your recommendation about the elimination?
2. Suppose that $3,700 of the common fixed costs could be avoided if the POP product line were eliminated. Would your recommendation to EPI change? Why or why not?

LO2, 6   E7-5 Analyzing Sell-or-Process Further Decision

EPI educational products are currently sold without any supplemental materials. The company is considering the inclusion of instructional materials such as an overhead slide presentation, potential test questions, and classroom bulletin board materials for teachers. A summary of the expected costs and revenues for EPI's two options follows:

	CD Only	CD with Instructional Materials
Estimated demand	50,000 units	50,000 units
Estimated sales price	$20	$35
Estimated cost per unit		
Direct materials	$ 1.25	$ 1.75
Direct labor	0.50	4.25
Variable manufacturing overhead	2.25	5.50
Fixed manufacturing overhead	2.00	2.00
Unit manufacturing cost	$ 6.00	$13.50
Additional development cost		$65,000

Required:

1. Determine whether EPI should process the educational CDs further or sell them without instructional materials. Include the difference in net profit from processing the CDs further.
2. Suppose that choosing to process the CDs further will reduce the number of units sold to 35,000. Determine the impact on EPI's profit of the decision to process further.

E7-6 Identifying Qualitative Factors in Short-Term Decision Making

LO2, 3, 4, 5

Refer to E7-2 through E7-5.

Required:

Identify at least three qualitative factors that EPI should consider when making each decision.

E7-7 Analyzing Special-Order Decision

LO2, 6

Eclipse Company manufactures a variety of sunglasses. Production information for its most popular line, the Total Eclipse (TE), follows:

	Per Unit
Sales price	$37.50
Direct materials	$ 5.75
Direct labor	2.50
Variable manufacturing overhead	1.75
Fixed manufacturing overhead	4.00
Total manufacturing cost	$14.00

Suppose that Eclipse has been approached about making a special order for 2,000 units of custom TE sunglasses for a new semiprofessional volleyball league. All units in the special order would be produced in the league's signature colors with a specially designed logo emblem attached to the side of the glasses. The league has offered to pay $30.00 per unit in the special order. Additional costs for the special order total $1.50 per unit for mixing the special frame color and purchasing the emblem with the league's logo that will be attached to the glasses.

Required:

1. Assuming Eclipse has the idle capacity necessary to accommodate the special order, should it do so? Determine the impact this would have on Eclipse's net income.
2. Suppose Eclipse is currently operating its production facility at full capacity and accepting the special order would mean reducing production of its regular TE model. Determine whether Eclipse should accept the special order.
3. Determine the special order price per unit at which Eclipse is indifferent to accepting the special order.

LO2, 7   ### E7-8 Making Decisions with Constrained Resources

Barclay manufactures three types of stained glass window, cleverly named Products A, B, and C. Information about these products follows:

	Product A	Product B	Product C
Sales price	$35	$45	$75
Variable costs per unit	17	21	32
Fixed costs per unit	5	5	5
Required number of labor hours	0.5	0.8	1.25

Barclay currently is limited to 16,000 labor hours per month.

Required:

Assuming an infinite demand for each of Barclay's products, determine the company's preferred production. Justify your answer.

LO2, 7   ### E7-9 Making Decisions Involving Constrained Resource

Refer to the information presented in E7-8.

Barclay's Marketing Department has determined the following demand for its products:

Product A	18,000 units
Product B	12,000 units
Product C	4,000 units

Required:

Given the company's limited resource and expected demand, determine how many of each product Barclay should produce to maximize its profit.

PROBLEMS—SET A

Mc Graw Hill **connect** |ACCOUNTING

LO2, 3   ### PA7-1 Analyzing Special-Order Decision

www.mhhe.com/whitecotton1e

Sunblocker Corp. makes several varieties of beach umbrellas and accessories. It has been approached about producing a special order for custom umbrellas. The special-order umbrellas with the Randolph Industries logo would be distributed to participants at an upcoming convention sponsored by Randolph.

Randolph has offered to buy 1,500 of the No-More-Squint (NMS) umbrellas at a price of $8 each. Sunblocker currently has the excess capacity necessary to accept the offer. The following information is related to the production of the NMS umbrella:

Direct materials	$ 2.25
Direct labor	0.75
Variable manufacturing overhead	3.50
Fixed manufacturing overhead	2.50
Total cost	$ 9.00
Regular sales price	$19.00

Required:

1. Determine the impact this special order would have on Sunblocker's total profit.
2. Should Sunblocker accept the special order?
3. Suppose that the special offer had been to purchase 2,000 umbrellas for $7.50 each. What effect would the offer have on Sunblocker's total profit?

4. Assume that Sunblocker is operating at full capacity. Determine the special-order price per unit at which Sunblocker would be indifferent to accepting the special order.

PA7-2 Analyzing Make-or-Buy Decision

Sunblocker Corp. (see PA7-1) is considering outsourcing production of the umbrella tote bag included with some of its products. The company has received a bid from CarryAll Co. to produce 8,000 units per year for $6 each. Sunblocker has the following information about its own production of the tote bags:

Direct materials	$3
Direct labor	1
Variable manufacturing overhead	1
Fixed manufacturing overhead	2
Total cost per unit	$7

Sunblocker has determined that all variable costs could be eliminated by dropping production of the tote bags, but none of the fixed overhead is avoidable. At this time, Sunblocker has no specific use in mind for the space currently dedicated to producing the tote bags.

Required:

1. Determine the impact this decision would have on Sunblocker's annual income.
2. Should Sunblocker buy the tote bags from CarryAll or continue to make them?
3. Suppose that the space Sunblocker currently uses to make the bags could be utilized by a new product line that would generate $10,000 in annual profits. Does this change your recommendation to Sunblocker? If so, how?

PA7-3 Analyzing Decision to Eliminate Unprofitable Segment

Sunblocker Corp. (see PA7-1 and PA7-2) is considering eliminating a product from its Happy Sand line of beach umbrellas. This collection is aimed at people who spend time on the beach or have an outdoor patio near the beach. Two products, the Happy Day and Morning Sun umbrellas, have impressive sales. However, sales for the Rolling Surf model have been dismal.

Sunblocker's information related to the Happy Sand line follows:

Segmented Income Statement for Sunblocker's Happy Sand Beach Umbrella Products

	Happy Day	Morning Sun	Rolling Surf	Total
Sales Revenue	$60,000	$60,000	$30,000	$150,000
Variable Costs	34,000	31,000	23,000	88,000
Contribution Margin	$26,000	$29,000	7,000	$ 62,000
Less: Direct Fixed Costs	1,900	2,500	1,000	5,400
Segment Margin	$24,100	$26,500	$ 6,000	$ 56,600
Common Fixed Costs*	17,840	17,840	8,920	44,600
Profit	$ 6,260	$ 8,660	$(2,920)	$ 12,000

*Allocated based on total sales dollars.

Sunblocker has determined that eliminating the Rolling Surf model would cause sales of the Happy Day and Morning Sun models to increase by 10 percent and 15 percent, respectively. Variable costs for these two models would increase proportionately. However, none of the fixed cost allocated to the Rolling Surf model is avoidable. The fixed overhead currently allocated to this model would be redistributed to the remaining two products.

Required:

1. Determine what would happen to the company's total profit if Sunblocker were to drop the Rolling Surf product. What is your recommendation to Sunblocker?

2. Suppose that Sunblocker had no direct fixed overhead in its production information and the entire $50,000 of fixed cost was common fixed cost. Would your recommendation to Sunblocker change? Why or why not?

LO2, 6   PA7-4 Analyzing Sell-or-Process Further Decision

The Spinner model of Sunblocker Corp. (see PA7-1 through PA7-3) is currently manufactured as a very plain umbrella with no decoration. The company is considering changing this product to a much more decorative model by adding a silk-screened design and embellishments. A summary of the expected costs and revenues for Sunblocker's two options follows:

	Spinner Umbrella	Decorated Umbrella
Estimated demand	10,000 units	10,000 units
Estimated sales price	$8.00	$19.00
Estimated manufacturing cost per unit		
Direct materials	$1.25	4.75
Direct labor	0.50	3.25
Variable manufacturing overhead	0.50	2.50
Fixed manufacturing overhead	2.00	2.00
Unit manufacturing cost	$4.25	$12.50
Additional development cost		$15,000

Required:

1. Determine whether Sunblocker should process the Spinner umbrellas further or sell them without decoration. Include the difference in net profit from processing them further.

2. Suppose that choosing to process the umbrellas further would reduce estimated demand to 8,000. Determine the impact of the decision to process further on Sunblocker's profit.

LO2, 7   PA7-5 Making Decisions Constrained Resource

Lattie-Dah, Inc., is a small company that manufactures three versions of outdoor hammock. Unit information for its products follows:

	Hammock A	Hammock B	Hammock C
Sales price	$30	$40	$50
Direct materials	6	7	8
Direct labor	1	3	7
Variable manufacturing overhead	2	2	2
Fixed manufacturing overhead	3	4	5
Required number of labor hours	0.10	0.30	0.75
Required number of machine hours	3	2.50	2.0

Lattie-Dah has determined that it can sell a limited number of each hammock in the upcoming year. Expected demand for each model follows:

Hammock A	50,000 units
Hammock B	20,000 units
Hammock C	30,000 units

Required:

1. Suppose that direct labor hours has been identified as a constrained resource with a maximum of 26,000 hours available per year. Assuming an infinite demand for each of Lattie-Dah's products, determine the company's preferred production. Justify your answer.

2. If the number of direct labor hours is the only constrained resource, determine the number of units of each hammock that Lattie-Dah should produce to maximize its profit.

3. Suppose that the number of machine hours has been identified as the only constrained resource with a maximum of 230,000 hours available per year. Assuming unlimited demand for each of Lattie-Dah's products, determine the company's preferred production. Justify your answer.

4. If the number of machine hours is the only constrained resource, determine the number of units of each hammock that Lattie-Dah should produce to maximize its profit.

PROBLEMS—SET B

PB7-1 Analyzing a Special-Order Decision

LO2, 3

Woodchuck Corp. makes several varieties of wooden furniture. It has been approached about producing a special order for rocking chairs. A local senior citizens group would use the special-order chairs in a newly remodeled activity center.

The senior citizens have offered to buy 80 of the Rock-On chairs at a price of $70 each. Woodchuck currently has the excess capacity necessary to accept the offer. A summary of the information related to production of Woodchuck's Rock-On model follows:

Direct materials	$30
Direct labor	20
Variable manufacturing overhead	12
Fixed manufacturing overhead	11
Total cost	$73
Regular sales price	$99

Required:

1. What impact would this special order have on Woodchuck's total profit?
2. Should Woodchuck accept the special order?
3. Suppose that the special offer had been to purchase 100 rocking chairs for $65 each. What effect would that offer have on Woodchuck's total profit?
4. Assume Woodchuck is operating at full capacity. Determine the special-order price per unit at which Woodchuck would be indifferent to accepting the special order.

PB7-2 Analyzing a Make-or-Buy Decision

LO2, 4

Woodchuck Corp. (see PB7-1) is considering the possibility of outsourcing the production of upholstered chair pads included with some of its wooden chairs. The company has received a bid from Padalong Co. to produce 1,000 units per year for $9 each. Woodchuck has the following information about its own production of the chair pads:

Direct materials	$ 4
Direct labor	2
Variable manufacturing overhead	2
Fixed manufacturing overhead	3
Total cost per unit	$11

Woodchuck has determined that all variable costs could be eliminated by dropping production of the chair pads, but none of the fixed overhead is avoidable. At this time, Woodchuck has no specific use in mind for the space currently dedicated to producing the chair pads.

Required:

1. Determine the impact this decision would have on Woodchuck's annual income.
2. Should Woodchuck buy the chair pads from Padalong or continue to make them?

3. Suppose that a new product line that Woodchuck wants to develop could utilize the space currently used for the chair pads. What amount of income must the new product line generate for Woodchuck to outsource the chair pads?

LO2, 5 **PB7-3 Analyzing Decision to Eliminate Unprofitable Segment**

Woodchuck Corp. (see PB7-1 and PB7-2) is considering eliminating a product from its line of outdoor tables. Two products, the Oak-A and Fiesta tables, have impressive sales. However, sales for the Studio model have been dismal.

Information related to Woodchuck's outdoor table line follows:

Segmented Income Statement for Woodchuck's Outdoor Table Products

	Oak-A	Fiesta	Studio	Total
Sales Revenue	$110,000	$77,000	$33,000	$220,000
Variable Costs	77,000	52,000	24,000	153,000
Contribution Margin	$ 33,000	$25,000	9,000	$ 67,000
Less: Direct Fixed Costs	3,200	2,400	800	6,400
Segment Margin	$ 29,800	$22,600	$ 8,200	$ 60,600
Common Fixed Costs*	16,800	11,760	5,040	33,600
Profit	$ 13,000	$10,840	$ 3,160	$ 27,000

*Allocated based on total sales dollars.

Woodchuck has determined that eliminating the Studio model will cause sales of the Oak-A and Fiesta tables to increase by 20 percent and 5 percent, respectively. Variable costs for these two models will increase proportionately. Direct fixed costs are avoidable, but common fixed costs will remain unchanged.

Required:

1. Determine what would happen to the company's total profit if Woodchuck were to drop the Studio product. What is your recommendation to Woodchuck?
2. Suppose Woodchuck had $1,800 of direct fixed overhead that was traceable to the Studio model. Would your recommendation to Woodchuck change? Why or why not?

LO2, 6 **PB7-4 Analyzing Sell-or-Process Further Decision**

Woodchuck currently manufactures one model of very plain, unfinished oak bookcase. The company is considering changing this product by adding a long-wearing finish and more appealing trim. A summary of the expected costs and revenues for Woodchuck's two options follows:

	Unfinished Bookcase	Finished Bookcase
Estimated demand	8,000 units	8,000 units
Estimated sales price	$50.00	$90.00
Estimated cost per unit		
Direct materials	$11.00	$14.00
Direct labor	8.00	18.00
Variable manufacturing overhead	0.50	1.50
Fixed manufacturing overhead	5.00	5.00
Unit manufacturing cost	$24.50	$38.50
Additional implementation cost		$75,000

Required:

1. Determine whether Woodchuck should process the unfinished bookcases further or sell them unfinished. Include the difference in net profit from processing the bookcases further.

2. Suppose that choosing to process the bookcases further would reduce the number of units sold to 5,000. Determine the impact of the decision to process further on Woodchuck's profit.

PB7-5 Making Decisions Involving Constrained Resource

LO2, 7

Glowbright Company makes three types of long-burning scented candles. The models vary in terms of size and type of materials (fragrance, decorations, etc.). Unit information for Glowbright follows:

	Candle X	Candle Y	Candle Z
Sales price	$15.00	$18.00	$23.00
Direct materials	2.00	1.75	2.25
Direct labor	2.00	4.00	8.00
Variable manufacturing overhead	1.00	1.25	1.25
Fixed manufacturing overhead	2.00	2.00	2.50
Required number of pounds beeswax	1.0	1.50	1.75
Required number of labor hours	5.0	2.50	5.0

Glowbright has determined that it can sell a limited number of each candle in the upcoming year. Expected demand for the three models follows:

Candle X	22,000 units
Candle Y	8,000 units
Candle Z	15,000 units

Required:

1. Suppose that disease in the suppliers' hives has severely restricted the production of beeswax. Thus, beeswax has been identified as a constrained resource with a maximum of 41,000 pounds available per year. Assuming an unlimited demand for each of Glowbright's products, determine the company's preferred production. Justify your answer.

2. If the number of pounds of beeswax is the only constrained resource, determine the number of units of each candle that Glowbright should produce to maximize its profit.

3. Suppose that the number of labor hours has been identified as the only constrained resource with a maximum of 104,000 hours available per year. Assuming an infinite demand for each of Glowbright's products, determine the company's preferred production. Justify your answer.

4. If the number of labor hours is the only constrained resource, determine the number of units of each candle that Glowbright should produce to maximize its profit.

SKILLS DEVELOPMENT CASES

S7-1 Evaluating Decision to Eliminate Collegiate Sports Programs: Quantitative and Qualitative Considerations

LO3

Due to budget cutbacks, colleges and universities across the country are struggling to cut expenses. Frequent casualties of these money-saving decisions are organized sports teams. Suppose that a fictional college, West Tennessee State (WTS), has identified three teams to eliminate in its effort to cut costs: men's lacrosse, women's softball, and men's diving. A summary of each sport's annual revenue and costs follows:

	Men's Lacrosse	Women's Softball	Men's Diving
Revenue	$ 25,600	$ 37,800	$ 14,900
Less: Expenses			
Scholarships	150,000	130,000	40,000
Coaches salaries	53,000	49,700	62,800
Team travel	21,100	28,500	13,200
Venue maintenance	15,000	20,000	35,000
Equipment	4,300	2,800	800
Team support	16,600	11,200	6,300
Net Income (loss)	$(234,400)	$(204,400)	$(143,200)

The combined net loss from these three programs is $(582,000).

Required:

1. Do you think WTS would see an immediate improvement in its bottom line (loss) of ($582,000)? Why or why not?

2. Determine whether each individual line item would be completely eliminated, partially eliminated, or not eliminated. Label the items as avoidable, partially avoidable, or unavoidable, and explain any assumptions you made in determining the classification.

3. Research actual examples of colleges or universities that have eliminated sports programs. List five that have eliminated sports teams in the past three years and identify which teams were eliminated.

4. Major sports such as men's football and basketball are seldom, if ever, eliminated even though they generally have the highest dollar amount of expenses. Why are these sports retained? What other factors could affect which teams are eliminated?

5. Choose one of the institutions identified in requirement 3 to investigate in more detail. For that college or university, discuss the factors that led to its choice(s), the anticipated impact on direct participants (coaches, athletes, etc.), and the total amount of savings expected. Also include reactions from the student body and the local and college communities.

LO3 **S7-2 Evaluating Walmart's Decision to Eliminate Product Offerings: Quantitative and Qualitative Considerations**

During 2006 and 2007, Walmart decided to eliminate two long-standing components of its business: merchandise layaway and off-the-bolt sales of fabric (also called by-the-yard sales). Each of these decisions met with considerable controversy among Walmart customers.

Required:

1. Research these two Walmart decisions and write a brief paragraph explaining its point of view in making each decision. Include any information you can find about the profitability of the segment and possible plans for an alternative in the fabric decision.

2. Describe the "typical" Walmart customer who was most impacted by these decisions.

3. Write a brief paragraph from this typical customer's point of view explaining how Walmart's decision would impact the customer.

4. Identify three possible effects of each decision on other segments of Walmart's business. Be specific in terms of both the segment and the possible impact.

5. Consider a small rural community in an economically depressed area of the United States. How might each of these decisions impact the people in that community? Contrast this to the impact felt in larger urban areas of the country.

LO4 **S7-3 Researching Outsourcing Issues in National and Local Press**

Outsourcing, particularly to overseas companies, is a hot-button topic that has garnered much attention in the academic, national, and local business media.

Required:

1. Conduct an Internet search for articles about outsourcing. What are some of the major reasons that companies decide to outsource? What are the advantages and disadvantages of outsourcing from the perspective of the company and its stockholders, managers, employees, and local community?

2. Search for a recent article on outsourcing in a national business publication such as *Fortune*, *BusinessWeek*, or *The Wall Street Journal*. Briefly summarize the article's main points, including any outsourcing trends, companies making outsourcing decisions, or issues related to politics or the U.S. economy.

3. Search the archives of your local or regional newspaper for articles about outsourcing. Try to identify a specific company in your area that has outsourced part of its operations. Describe the part of the business that was outsourced. For example, did it outsource part of its manufacturing operation or a support function such as information technology or customer support? What likely factors came into play in making the decision? What impact, if any, will this decision have on customers, employees, and the local community?

4. Discuss whether you or someone you know has been personally affected by a company's decision to outsource.

CHAPTER 8

Capital Budgeting

YOUR LEARNING OBJECTIVES

After completing this chapter, you should be able to:

LO1 Calculate the accounting rate of return and describe its major weaknesses.

LO2 Calculate the payback period and describe its major weaknesses.

LO3 Calculate net present value and describe why it is superior to the other capital budgeting techniques.

LO4 Predict the internal rate of return and describe its relationship to net present value.

LO5 Use the net present value method to analyze mutually exclusive capital investments.

LO6 Use the profitability index to prioritize independent capital investment projects.

Lecture Presentation–LP8
www.mhhe.com/whitecotten1e

FOCUS COMPANY: Mattel Toys

"The World's Premier Toy Brands"

www.mattel.com

Assume you just finished a summer internship at a local business. Your supervisor was so impressed with your work that she offered you a full-time position starting immediately. If you take the job, you will not be able to stay in school for the two years you still need to graduate. You are considering the following options:

- Take the job, which will pay $25,000 per year.
- Stay in school, at a cost of $12,000 per year. Your expected salary upon graduation is $45,000.

What would you do? If you take the job, you would start earning a salary immediately. Getting paid today is always better than getting paid the same amount in the future! On the other hand, graduating with a college degree will allow you to earn more in the long run. How do you decide whether the long-term benefits are worth the short-term sacrifice (investment of time and money)?

This chapter discusses several techniques you can use to address this and other similar decisions. In business, we refer to these as **capital investment decisions**. A capital investment involves some up-front investment of cash that is expected to pay off in the future in the form of either increased revenue or cost savings. Capital budgeting is the process and set of tools that managers use to make capital investments decisions.

To illustrate the capital budgeting process, we continue the Mattel example we started in the last chapter. In the previous chapter, we used incremental analysis to evaluate a number of short-term decision scenarios. In this chapter, we consider long-term decisions that span multiple years. As always, we use fictitious scenarios and numbers but try to make them as realistic as possible to illustrate how Mattel's managers might approach the decisions.

Capital budgeting process	Time value of money	Applications of NPV
• Capital investment decisions • Cash flow versus accounting net income • Accounting rate of return • Payback period	• Discounted cash flow methods • Net present value (NPV) • Internal rate of return (IRR) • Summary of capital budgeting methods	• Decision case 1: Lease or buy equipment • Decision case 2: To automate or not to automate • Decision case 3: Prioritizing independent projects • Summary analysis of opening case decision

Video 8-1
www.mhhe.com/whitecotton1e

Capital Budgeting Process

Capital budgeting is the process that managers use to make capital investment decisions. These decisions involve an investment in major capital assets, such as new machinery, replacement machinery, new plants, new products, and research and development projects.[1] Examples of capital investment decisions that managers at Mattel might make include:

- Whether to invest in a project to develop a children's MP3 product for downloading children's books, music, and educational materials from Mattel's Web site.
- Whether it is more cost efficient to lease or buy a piece of machinery.
- Whether to invest in new technology that would save on future labor costs.
- How to prioritize limited funds for research and development projects.

CAPITAL INVESTMENT DECISIONS

In general, managers make two types of capital investment decisions:

- **Screening decisions** require managers to evaluate a proposed capital investment to determine whether it meets some minimum criteria. In other words, managers must decide whether a project is acceptable or not.
- **Preference decisions** require managers to choose from among a set of alternative capital investment opportunities. Because companies typically have limited funds to invest in capital projects, managers must prioritize and select from the available options.

---

[1] We use the term **capital assets** in a much broader sense than in financial accounting. For example, human capital is developed through education and on-the-job training. It is valuable capital, even though it is not counted as an asset on the balance sheet. Similarly, financial accounting (GAAP) does not allow companies to capitalize research and development expenses even though they require a major capital investment.

Capital investment decisions can also be categorized based on whether the projects are independent or mutually exclusive:

- **Independent projects** are unrelated to one another, so that investing in one project does not preclude or affect the choice about other alternatives. For example, if Mattel chooses to invest in a children's MP3 product, it could also invest in an unrelated product line (assuming sufficient funds are available for both investments).

- **Mutually exclusive projects** require making a choice among competing alternatives. For example, if Mattel is deciding whether to refurbish old equipment or invest in new equipment, managers would do one or the other (but not both).

This chapter describes four different methods that managers can use to evaluate capital investment decisions:

1. Accounting rate of return.
2. Payback period.
3. Net present value.
4. Internal rate of return.

The first two methods are commonly used and provide a useful screening tool for evaluating investment alternatives. However, they suffer from the limitations that they do not incorporate the time value of money. The last two methods are considered superior because they do incorporate the time value of money.

To illustrate the differences between the methods, we evaluate a hypothetical capital budgeting decision at Mattel. Assume that Mattel's managers are evaluating a proposal to invest in a children's MP3 product that would allow parents to download children's music, books, and educational products from Mattel's Web site. This new product, called the Learning Pod or L Pod, would require an up-front investment of $1 million. Based on preliminary market research and production cost estimates, Mattel has estimated that the product would generate $108,000 in net operating income over the next five years, as follows:

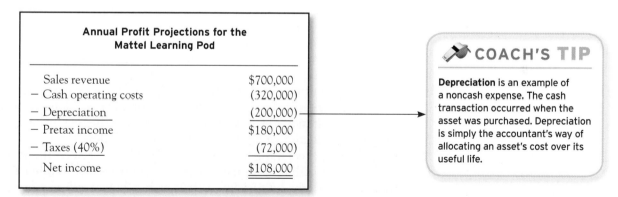

Annual Profit Projections for the Mattel Learning Pod

Sales revenue	$700,000
− Cash operating costs	(320,000)
− Depreciation	(200,000)
− Pretax income	$180,000
− Taxes (40%)	(72,000)
Net income	$108,000

COACH'S TIP

Depreciation is an example of a noncash expense. The cash transaction occurred when the asset was purchased. Depreciation is simply the accountant's way of allocating an asset's cost over its useful life.

The basic question that Mattel's managers must answer is whether this proposed project is worth the $1 million up-front investment. We can measure the benefit of the investment based on net income or cash flow. The difference between the two measures is discussed next because both will be used to evaluate Mattel's capital budgeting decision.

CASH FLOW VERSUS ACCOUNTING NET INCOME

You should recall from your previous accounting class that net income and cash flow are not the same thing. For accounting purposes, revenue is recognized when it is earned, not when cash is received. Similarly, expenses are recorded as they are incurred rather than when cash is paid. These differences between accounting income and cash flow are discussed in more detail in Chapter 12. In this chapter, we assume that the only difference between net income and cash flow is depreciation expense.

In the Mattel example, the original cost of the investment is $1 million. For accounting purposes, this cost will be depreciated over the five-year life of the assets, resulting in annual depreciation of $200,000. Depreciation is a noncash expense. Although the income statement includes $200,000 in depreciation expense, Mattel does not actually pay $200,000 in cash each year. Thus, to convert from net income to cash flow, we must **add** back the depreciation that was deducted in the computation of net income, as follows:

$$\boxed{\text{Net Income } \$108,000} + \boxed{\text{Depreciation } \$200,000} = \boxed{\text{Net Cash Flow } \$308,000}$$

Alternatively, we could have started at the top of the income statement with sales revenue and subtracted only the cash operating costs and taxes ($700,000 − $320,000 − $72,000 = $308,000). Notice that this "direct" approach also results in $308,000 in net cash flow per year.

The benefit of the project will be measured as $108,000 in annual net income, or $308,000 in annual net cash flow, depending on the capital budgeting method used.

ACCOUNTING RATE OF RETURN

The **accounting rate of return** is calculated as annual net income divided by the original investment in assets. This approach is also called the **annual rate of return**, **simple rate of return**, or **unadjusted rate of return**.

In the Mattel example, the project's annual net income of $108,000 is divided by the $1 million initial investment, for an accounting rate of return of 10.8 percent:

$$\boxed{\text{Net Income } \$108,000} / \boxed{\text{Initial Investment } \$1\text{ million}} = \boxed{\text{Accounting Rate of Return } 10.8\%}$$

To determine whether the project is acceptable (a screening decision), Mattel's managers would compare the 10.8 percent accounting rate of return to the minimum required rate of return, or **hurdle rate**. If Mattel's minimum required rate of return is less than 10.8 percent, the project is acceptable. If the required rate is more than 10.8 percent, the project is unacceptable.

The accounting rate of return is a simple and intuitive approach that is frequently used as a screening tool to evaluate capital investment decisions. However, it suffers from two major limitations. First, it does not incorporate the time value of money. Second, it is based on accounting net income rather than cash flow.

For years, accounting and finance experts have debated the relative merits of net income versus cash flow for making investment decisions. While research suggests that **both** are useful, the bottom line is that cash is king. Cash is more objective than net income, is not as easily manipulated, and is not influenced by accounting choices such as the method used to depreciate the capital assets.

The remaining capital budgeting techniques we consider are based on cash flow rather than net income. These methods are based on $308,000 in cash flow per year rather than $108,000 in accounting net income.

PAYBACK PERIOD

The **payback period** is the amount of time needed for a capital investment to "pay for itself." In the simplest case in which cash flows are equal each year, the payback period is calculated as follows:

In our Mattel example, the original investment is $1 million, and the net cash flow is estimated at $308,000 per year. Thus, the payback period is calculated as follows:

$$\boxed{\begin{array}{c}\text{Initial}\\\text{Investment}\\\text{\$1 million}\end{array}} \ / \ \boxed{\begin{array}{c}\text{Annual}\\\text{Net Cash Flow}\\\text{\$308,000}\end{array}} = \boxed{\begin{array}{c}\text{Payback}\\\text{Period}\\\text{3.25 years}\end{array}}$$

A payback period of 3.25 tells managers that the project is expected to pay for itself in a little over three years. In general, projects with shorter payback periods are considered safer investments than those with longer payback periods. The payback method provides a very useful initial screening tool based on how long it will take for the project to recoup its original investment. For example, managers might have a rule of thumb that projects must pay back the original investment within at least five years before they are considered further.

The payback method is a little more complicated when the cash flows are not equal in each year. In this case, the payback must be computed on a year-by-year basis by subtracting the net cash flow from the unpaid investment balance each year until the entire investment is eventually paid back. For example, if the net cash flows for the Mattel project are expected to be $250,000, $300,000, $340,000, $375,000 and $400,000 in years 1–5, respectively, the payback period would be calculated as follows:

Year	Initial Investment		Annual Net Cash Flow		Unpaid Investment
1	$1000,000	−	$250,000	=	$750,000
2	750,000	−	300,000	=	450,000
3	450,000	−	340,000	=	110,000
4	110,000	−	375,000	=	(265,000)
5	N/A		N/A		N/A

> **COACH'S TIP**
>
> The unpaid investment is the amount that still needs to be paid back after each year. It hits zero sometime between three and four years.

This analysis shows that the payback is somewhere between three and four years. If we assume the net cash flow is uniform during the fourth year, the exact payback would be estimated as follows:

$$\text{3 years} + (\$110,000/\$375,000) = 3.293 \text{ years}$$

The payback method is relatively simple and is commonly used to determine how long it will take for a project to recoup its initial investment. However, it does not incorporate the time value of money, and it ignores any cash flows that occur after the end of the payback period. The final two methods we discuss explicitly incorporate the time value of money.

But first, take the following Self-Study Practice to make sure you understand the accounting rate of return and payback method.

Self-Study Practice

Timberland Company is considering investing $1,000,000 in a project that is expected to generate $175,000 in net income for the next five years. The assets will be depreciated over five years for an annual depreciation expense of $200,000.

1. Calculate the accounting rate of return.
2. Calculate the payback period.

After you have finished, check your answers with the solutions in the margin.

Time Value of Money

The time value of money is critical to many business decisions. You have probably already had some exposure to time value of money concepts in other business classes. On a personal level, you encounter time value of money issues anytime you must take out a loan to buy a car or house, to pay for tuition, or when you invest money in a savings account or CD. Because the time value of money is so important to capital budgeting decisions, the next section provides a brief review of the concepts. The supplement to this chapter provides more detail on the topic and shows how to calculate present and future values that incorporate the time value of money.

Spotlight On DECISION MAKING

Buying a home is one of the most important investment decisions most people make during their lives. For this investment, the time value of money is reflected in home mortgage rates. The following graph below shows the fluctuation in average mortgage rates from 1963-2008.

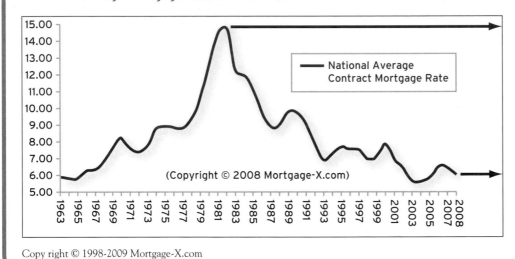

(Copyright © 2008 Mortgage-X.com)

Mortgage rates were at a historic high in the early 1980s, approaching an average of 15 percent.

By 2009, mortgage rates had dropped below 5 percent. Unfortunately, when housing prices fell, many people realized they could not afford their home in spite of extremely low interest rates.

The **time value of money** is the simple idea that the value of money changes over time because it can be invested to earn interest. Given a choice between receiving $1,000 today or $1,000 a year from now, which would you prefer? You should have answered today because you could invest the money and have even more in the future. For example, if you invest $1,000 at 10 percent interest, you would have $1,100 [$1,000 × (1 + 10%)] a year from now.

The time value of money becomes even more powerful due to a force called **compounding**, where interest is earned on top of interest. For example, if you invested $1,000 at 10 percent interest for three years and the interest was compounded annually, you would have $1,331 at the end of three years, as follows:

Year	Amount at Start of Year	+	Interest during the Year	=	Amount at End of Year
1	$1,000	+	$1,000 × 10% = $100	=	$1,100
2	1,100	+	1,100 × 10% = 110	=	1,210
3	1,210	+	1,210 × 10% = 121	=	1,331

This is an example of a **future value** problem. In such problems, we know how much money we have today and we want to know what it will be worth at some point in the future.

In **present value** problems, we know how much money we will have (or need to have) at some point in the future, and the goal is to determine the value of that money in today's (present value) dollars. Instead of compounding (adding interest on top of interest), present value problems involve **discounting** future cash flows back to their equivalent value in today's (present value) dollars. Discounting is exactly the opposite of the compounding. Just as interest builds up over time through compounding, discounting involves backing out the interest to determine the present value.

The following diagram summarizes the difference between future value and present value problems

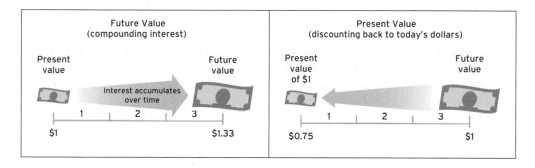

These examples illustrate how a single cash flow can be compounded to arrive at a future value, or discounted to arrive at a present value. But time value of money problems often involve cash flows that occur across a number of years. A stream of cash flows that occurs equally across time is called an **annuity**. We can use the same compounding and discounting concepts to determine the future or present value of a stream of cash flows (annuity) as follows:

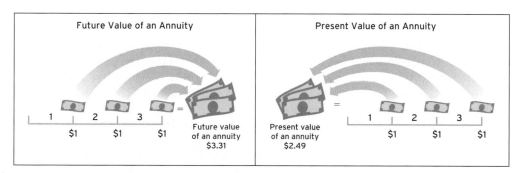

The supplement to this chapter describes in more detail how to calculate future and present values for a single amount and for an annuity. If you need a refresher on these topics, you should review the supplement, paying particular attention to the present value calculations. These present value concepts are at the heart of the capital budgeting techniques presented in the remainder of this chapter.

DISCOUNTED CASH FLOW METHODS

Discounted cash flow methods incorporate the time value of money. As with any quantitative analysis, it requires making some assumptions, which are summarized here:

- All future cash flows happen at the end of the year. In reality, companies receive and pay out cash throughout the year. But for simplicity, we assume that all cash flows happen at the end of the year.

- Cash inflows are immediately reinvested in another project to earn a similar rate of return. In reality, the projects available for reinvestment will have varying rates of return. At a minimum, the funds should be reinvested to earn the minimum required rate of return.

- All cash flows can be projected with 100% certainty. In general, the further the cash flow extends into the future, the more uncertain it is. But we assume that all cash flows are known with certainty.

Managers must be aware of these assumptions and understand how they affect the analysis and conclusions. Later in the chapter we illustrate how managers can use sensitivity or "what if" analysis to analyze how changing the underlying assumptions will affect the analysis and decisions.

NET PRESENT VALUE (NPV)

The **net present value (NPV) method** compares the present value of a project's future cash flows to the initial cash outflow. The difference between the present value of the cash inflows and outflows is called the **net present value**.

Before we can apply the NPV method, we need to know the **discount rate**, or the rate that will be used to discount the future cash flows to reflect the time value of money. The rate used to compute the net present value is sometimes called the **required rate of return**, **minimum rate of return**, or **hurdle rate**. Conceptually, the discount rate should reflect the company's **cost of capital**, which is a function of its after tax cost of debt and equity financing. In general terms, a positive NPV means that a proposed project will generate a return in excess of the cost of capital, creating economic value for the company and its shareholders. A negative net present value means that the project will not cover the cost of capital and will reduce the firm's economic value. The following rules are used to make screening decisions using the net present value method.

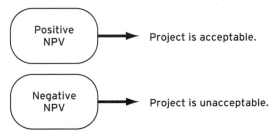

Let's apply the NPV method to Mattel's potential investment in the L Pod project. Recall that the project requires an initial investment of $1 million and is expected to generate $308,000 in cash flow for each of the next five years. Assume that Mattel's cost of capital or required rate of return is 12 percent. To calculate the NPV manually, we can use the present value of a $1 factors shown in Table 8.2 (on page 305) with $n = 1$–5 and $i = 12$ percent. Based on this information, the NPV would be calculated as follows:

Year	Cash Flow		PV of $1 (12%)		Present Value
0	$(1,000,000)		—		$(1,000,000)
1	308,000	×	0.8929	=	275,013
2	308,000	×	0.7972	=	245,538
3	308,000	×	0.7118	=	219,234
4	308,000	×	0.6355	=	195,734
5	308,000	×	0.5674	=	174,759
			Net present value	=	$ 110,278

Because the cash flows occur evenly throughout the life of the project, we could have used the PV of an annuity (from Table 8.4) to compute the NPV as follows:

Year	Cash Flow		PV of an Annuity (12%)		Present Value
0	(1,000,000)		—		$(1,000,000)
1–5	308,000	×	3.6048	=	1,110,278
			Net present value	=	$ 110,278

The present value tables are useful for showing how the NPV method actually works. In reality, managers are likely to use a financial calculator or computer program to do the calculations. Exhibit 8.1 shows how to use Excel to calculate NPV.

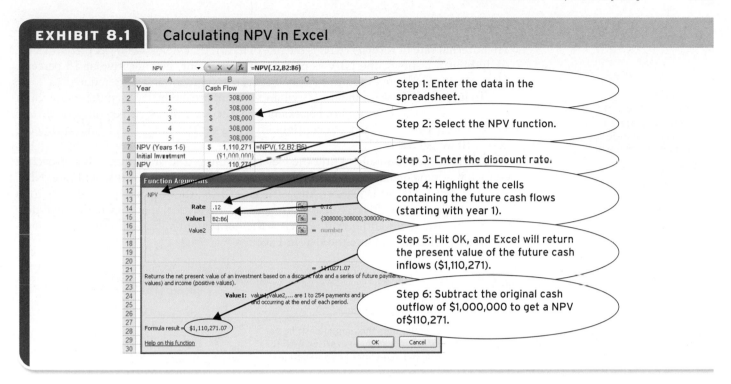

EXHIBIT 8.1	Calculating NPV in Excel

Step 1: Enter the data in the spreadsheet.

Step 2: Select the NPV function.

Step 3: Enter the discount rate.

Step 4: Highlight the cells containing the future cash flows (starting with year 1).

Step 5: Hit OK, and Excel will return the present value of the future cash inflows ($1,110,271).

Step 6: Subtract the original cash outflow of $1,000,000 to get a NPV of $110,271.

Using Excel to compute the net present value gives an NPV of $110,271. This is very close to the $110,278 obtained using the present value tables. The $7 difference is due to rounding in the present value tables.

Regardless of the method used, the investment has a positive NPV. Mattel's managers should view this as an acceptable investment because the future cash flows more than compensate for the 12 percent cost of capital that is inherent in the discount rate.

What would happen if the discount rate had been 14 percent? Would the NPV increase or decrease? It would decrease because the future cash flows would be more heavily discounted to reflect the increased time value of money. Exhibit 8.2 shows how the NPV for the project will change as the discount rate changes.

Notice that the NPV decreases as the discount rate increases. Remember that discounting future cash flows is just the opposite of earning compound interest. When the interest rate is high, you have to invest less money today to have a certain amount of money in the future. Similarly, as the discount rate increases, the future cash flows are more heavily discounted and thus worth less in today's (present value) dollars.

> **COACH'S TIP**
>
> Follow these steps in Excel and see if you can get the NPV of $110,271. Then repeat using a discount rate of 14%.

EXHIBIT 8.2	Net Present Values at Various Discount Rates

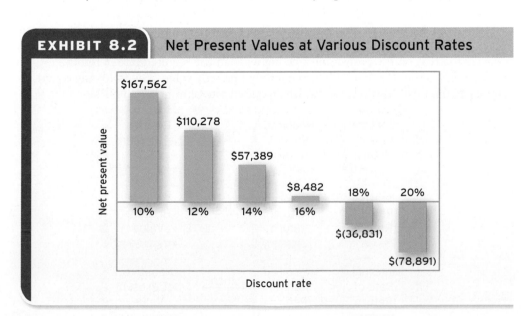

> **COACH'S TIP**
>
> Notice that the NPV is positive at 16 percent and negative at 18 percent. The internal rate of return (IRR) is the discount rate that would yield a NPV of zero.
>
> What would you estimate the IRR to be based on this graph?

INTERNAL RATE OF RETURN (IRR)

The **internal rate of return (IRR)** is the rate of return that yields a zero net present value. As Exhibit 8.2 shows, the NPV is positive at 16 percent, but negative at 18 percent. Thus, the internal rate of return must be between 16 percent and 18 percent.

To find the IRR, we could use a trial-and-error approach by trying different discount rates until we get a NPV of zero. For example, a discount rate of 17 percent would yield an NPV of ($14,601). We could continue to try to get the exact IRR by narrowing the rate until we get a zero NPV.

Although it is difficult to find the exact IRR using trial and error, this approach is useful for helping managers understand the relationship between the discount rate, NPV, and IRR. But if managers want to know the exact IRR, they are likely to use Excel or a financial calculator to do the calculation. Even so, it is critical that they understand how to interpret the result and how it relates to the net present value. Exhibit 8.3 illustrates the steps needed to compute the IRR in Excel.

> **Learning Objective 4**
> Predict the internal rate of return and describe its relationship to net present value.

EXHIBIT 8.3   Calculating IRR Using Excel

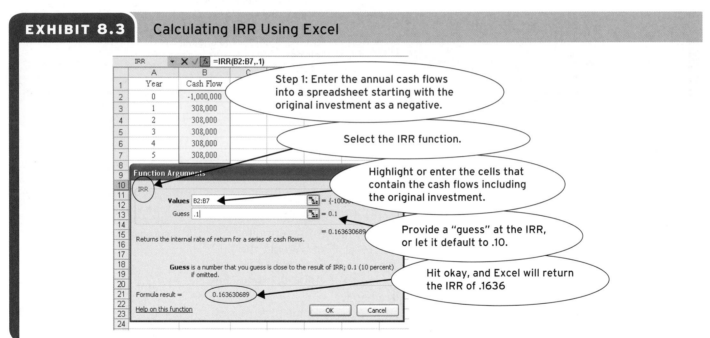

Following these steps gives an IRR of 16.36 percent for our Mattel example. Notice that this falls within the 16–17 percent range we determined using trial and error.

As you can see, the IRR is closely related to the NPV method. The NPV uses the company's required rate of return as the discount rate to determine whether the present value of the future cash flows is enough to cover the required rate of return. If the NPV is positive, the IRR on the project must be higher than the required rate of return.

The IRR is the rate that will yield a zero net present value. The following equations summarize the relationship between IRR, required rate of return, and NPV.

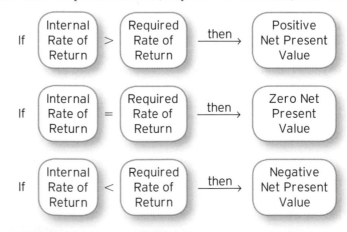

SUMMARY OF CAPITAL BUDGETING METHODS

See Exhibit 8.4 for a summary of the four capital budgeting methods.

EXHIBIT 8.4	Comparison of the Capital Budgeting Methods

Method	Formula	Advantages	Disadvantages
Accounting rate of return	$ARR = \left(\dfrac{Net\ Income}{Investment}\right)$	• Simple • Intuitive	• Does not incorporate the time value of money • Some argue cash is a better measure of investment performance than net income
Payback method	$Payback = \left(\dfrac{Investment}{Annual\ Cash\ Flow}\right)$	• Simple • Intuitive	• Does not incorporate the time value of money • Ignores anything that happens after the payback period
Net present value	$NPV = \left(\begin{array}{l}PV\ of\ Future\ Cash\\ Flows - Original\\ Investment\end{array}\right)$	• Incorporates the time value of money	• May be difficult to determine the appropriate discount rate • Ignores qualitative factors that may be important to the decision
Internal rate of return	$IRR = NPV\ of\ Zero$	• Incorporates the time value of money	• Assumes that cash flows are reinvested at the internal rate of return, which may not be realistic • Ignores qualitative factors that may be important to the decision

To make sure you understand the four capital budgeting techniques, complete the following Self-Study Practice.

 Self-Study Practice

1. Which of the following statements regarding the four capital budgeting methods is **true?** You may select more than one answer.
   a. Both the accounting rate of return and the payback period consider the time value of money.
   b. Both the accounting rate of return and the payback period are based on accounting measures rather than on cash flow.
   c. Both the NPV method and the IRR ignore the time value of money.
   d. The accounting rate of return is based on net income; the other three methods are based on cash flow

2. Jackson Company's required rate of return is 10 percent. The NPV of a project using the 10 percent discount rate is $(15,333). Which of the following statements regarding the NPV and IRR is **true?** You may select more than one answer.
   a. The present value of the project's future cash flows is more than the original cost of the investment.
   b. The present value of the project's future cash flows is less than the original cost of the investment.
   c. The IRR on this project is less than 10 percent.
   d. The IRR on this project is more than 10 percent.

After you have finished, check your answers with the solutions in the margin.

Applications of NPV

Learning Objective 5
Use the net present value method to analyze mutually exclusive capital investments.

The final section of this chapter illustrates how to apply the NPV method to several capital investment decisions. These examples are slightly more complex than the simple scenario analyzed in the previous section, and include both uneven cash flows and different types of cash inflows and outflows. They also illustrate how managers would evaluate mutually exclusive and independent capital investment projects. A mutually exclusive project involves an "either/or" choice, such as whether to lease or buy equipment. Managers will do one or the other, but not both.

DECISION CASE 1: LEASE OR BUY EQUIPMENT

A common investment decision is whether to purchase or lease a capital asset such as a building or piece of equipment. In your personal life, you may have faced similar decisions when deciding whether to lease or buy a personal asset such as a home or a car.

To illustrate, assume that Mattel plans to replace an office copy machine with a new model. The office manager is trying to decide whether to buy the machine outright or lease it from a copier company. He has gathered the following information about the two options:

Purchase Option		Lease Option	
Purchase price	$20,000	Annual lease payment	$6,000
Annual operating costs (paper, toner, maintenance, etc)	$ 1,000	(includes all supplies and maintenance)	
Useful life	4 years	Contract length	4 years
Salvage value	$ 4,000		

The copier would cost $20,000 to purchase. The annual operating costs for paper, toner, and maintenance are estimated to be $1,000. The copier is expected to last four years at which point it will have an estimated salvage or residual value of $4,000.

The company could lease the same machine from a copy company that would provide the machine and all operating supplies and maintenance for a contract price of $6,000 per year.

If Mattel's discount rate (cost of capital) is 10 percent, should the company lease or buy the copier? We can use the net present value method to compare the cost of each option in present value terms. The option with the lowest cost (on a net present value basis) is preferred.

The following table shows the net present value of the two options using a 10 percent discount rate. The discount factors can be found in Table 8.2 (on page 305) with n = 1, 2, 3, 4 and i = 10 percent.

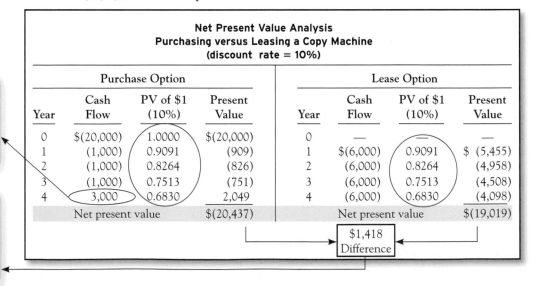

**Net Present Value Analysis
Purchasing versus Leasing a Copy Machine
(discount rate = 10%)**

	Purchase Option				Lease Option		
Year	Cash Flow	PV of $1 (10%)	Present Value	Year	Cash Flow	PV of $1 (10%)	Present Value
0	$(20,000)	1.0000	$(20,000)	0	—	—	—
1	(1,000)	0.9091	(909)	1	$(6,000)	0.9091	$ (5,455)
2	(1,000)	0.8264	(826)	2	(6,000)	0.8264	(4,958)
3	(1,000)	0.7513	(751)	3	(6,000)	0.7513	(4,508)
4	3,000	0.6830	2,049	4	(6,000)	0.6830	(4,098)
	Net present value		$(20,437)		Net present value		$(19,019)

$1,418
Difference

 **COACH'S TIP**

Cash flow is different in year 4 because of the salvage value. $4,000 salvage − $1,000 operating costs

COACH'S TIP

Leasing is less costly than buying on a net present value basis. The difference in NPV is $1,418 in favor of leasing.

Of course, this analysis is contingent on a number of assumptions, including the 10 percent discount rate, the four-year decision horizon, and the $4,000 estimated salvage value. A change in any of these assumptions could reverse the decision. When analyzing capital investment decisions, managers should perform **sensitivity analysis** to see whether changing the underlying assumptions would affect the decision. For example, if the discount rate were 6 percent instead of 10 percent, the purchase option would have a lower NPV than leasing as follows:

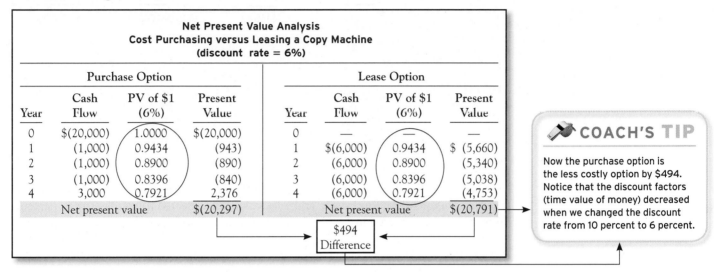

Net Present Value Analysis
Cost Purchasing versus Leasing a Copy Machine
(discount rate = 6%)

	Purchase Option				Lease Option		
Year	Cash Flow	PV of $1 (6%)	Present Value	Year	Cash Flow	PV of $1 (6%)	Present Value
0	$(20,000)	1.0000	$(20,000)	0	—	—	—
1	(1,000)	0.9434	(943)	1	$(6,000)	0.9434	$ (5,660)
2	(1,000)	0.8900	(890)	2	(6,000)	0.8900	(5,340)
3	(1,000)	0.8396	(840)	3	(6,000)	0.8396	(5,038)
4	3,000	0.7921	2,376	4	(6,000)	0.7921	(4,753)
	Net present value		$(20,297)		Net present value		$(20,791)

$494
Difference

COACH'S TIP

Now the purchase option is the less costly option by $494. Notice that the discount factors (time value of money) decreased when we changed the discount rate from 10 percent to 6 percent.

Building a spreadsheet in Excel makes doing this type of sensitivity analysis much easier. It is also important to perform sensitivity analysis on the other assumptions, including the salvage value and useful life. If the machine were estimated to be worth more than $4,000 at the end of four years or if Mattel were able to use the copier for a longer period of time, the purchase option would be less costly and could potentially reverse the decision.

Finally, we should note that we ignored the tax implications of owning versus leasing the copier. These issues are covered in advanced managerial accounting and corporate finance textbooks.

DECISION CASE 2: TO AUTOMATE OR NOT TO AUTOMATE

The next decision we examine is the investment in automation or technology. Examples of possible investments include:

- Investing in robots to reduce direct labor costs.
- Investing in bar code or radio frequency identification (RFID) technology to reduce inventory costs and improve the flow of material through production.
- Investing in computerized accounting systems to save on record-keeping costs.

Each of these investments requires a major up-front investment that is expected to save costs in the long run. We can use the NPV method to compare the future cost savings (on a present value basis) to the initial investment.

As an example, assume that Mattel is thinking of renovating the facility that produces Power Wheel battery-operated vehicles. The renovation would include the installation of robots to install parts, assemble the product, and automate the packaging process.

This $10 million investment is expected to have the following effects:

- The total time to produce each unit (cycle time) would decrease, which will increase the capacity of the plant by 20 percent. There is sufficient demand to sell all additional units produced at the current unit sales price of $150.
- The company will be able to reduce direct labor cost per unit by 30 percent.
- Factory supervision costs will increase by $500,000 per year.
- The estimated useful life of the new equipment is six years, at which point it will have a residual value of $1,000,000. Straight-line depreciation of the assets will be $1,500,000 per year [($10,000,000 − 1,000,000)/6 years].

The following table summarizes these effects on net income:

EFFECT OF AUTOMATION ON MATTEL'S POWER WHEELS' DIVISION					
	CURRENT (NO AUTOMATION)		PROPOSED (AUTOMATION)		DIFFERENCE
Production and sales volume	100,000 units		120,000 units		20,000 units
	Per Unit	Total	Per Unit	Total	Total
Sales revenue	$150	$15,000,000	$150	$18,000,000	$3,000,000
Variable costs					
Direct materials	$ 25		$ 25		
Direct labor	50		35		
Variable manufacturing overhead	10		10		
Total variable manufacturing costs	85	8,500,000	70	8,400,000	100,000
Contribution margin	$ 65	6,500,000	$ 80	9,600,000	3,100,000
Fixed manufacturing costs		2,500,000		4,500,000	(2,000,000)
Net income		$ 4,000,000		$ 5,100,000	$1,100,000

The shaded portion of the table highlights the variables that are expected to change as a result of automation. Production and sales volume is expected to increase by 20 percent, from 100,000 to 120,000 units. Direct labor costs are expected to decrease by 30 percent, from $50 to $35 ($50 × 70%). Fixed costs are expected to increase by $2,000,000, including $500,000 for factory supervision and $1,500,000 for depreciation. The net effect of these changes is that automation is expected to increase annual net income by $1,100,000.

Let's calculate the NPV of this investment using a 12 percent discount rate. Remember that the net present value method is based on cash flow rather than net income. Thus, we need to add back the depreciation (a noncash expense) to net income to get net cash flow (1,100,000 + 1,500,000 = 2,600,000). We also need to incorporate the initial investment (at time zero) and the salvage value of the machinery at the end of six years. This analysis is summarized in the following table:

Year	Investment/ Salvage Value	Net Income	Add Back Depreciation	Net Cash Flow	PV of $1 (12%)	Present Value
0	$(10,000,000)	—	—	$(10,000,000)	1	$(10,000,000)
1		$1,100,000	$1,500,000	2,600,000	0.8929	2,321,540
2		1,100,000	1,500,000	2,600,000	0.7972	2,072,720
3		1,100,000	1,500,000	2,600,000	0.7118	1,850,680
4		1,100,000	1,500,000	2,600,000	0.6355	1,652,300
5		1,100,000	1,500,000	2,600,000	0.5674	1,475,240
6	1,000,000	1,100,000	1,500,000	3,600,000	0.5066	1,823,760
				Net Present Value		$ 1,196,240

The positive NPV of $1,196,240 means that the proposed investment in automation will generate a return in excess of the 12 percent cost of capital. Any return in excess of the cost of capital is acceptable and will create economic wealth for the firm. Once again, however this analysis is contingent on a number of assumptions and ignores the effect of taxes.

DECISION CASE 3: PRIORITIZING INDEPENDENT PROJECTS

Learning Objective 6
Use the profitability index to prioritize independent capital investment projects.

The previous decision scenarios involved mutually exclusive capital investment decisions. For example, choosing to lease the copy machine would eliminate the option of purchasing. Similarly, choosing to automate the production facility precludes the option of staying with the status quo.

Other investment decisions involve choosing among independent projects, where accepting one does not necessarily preclude accepting another unrelated project. However, managers typically have limited funds to invest and therefore must prioritize their investment resources.

To prioritize independent projects, we cannot simply compare their NPVs, which are stated as absolute dollar values. This makes comparing projects of different sizes difficult. Although the IRR is a relative measure of performance, it assumes that the cash flows will be reinvested to earn the same IRR, which is unlikely to be true for independent investments.

Managers should prioritize capital investment projects based on a factor called the profitability index. The **profitability index** is computed as follows:

$$\text{Profitability Index} = \text{Present Value of Future Cash Flows} \; / \; \text{Initial Investment}$$

A profitability index higher than 1 means that a project has a positive NPV because the present value of the future cash flows (numerator) is higher than the initial investment (denominator). A profitability index less than 1 means that the NPV is negative.

To illustrate, assume Mattel's managers are trying to decide how to prioritize their limited research and development budget. They are considering the following independent projects:

	Project A	Project B	Project C
Present value of future cash flows	$600,000	$810,000	$1,200,000
Initial investment	300,000	450,000	800,000
Net present value	$300,000	$360,000	$ 400,000
Profitability index	$\frac{\$600,000}{\$300,000} = 2.0$	$\frac{\$810,000}{\$450,000} = 1.8$	$\frac{\$1,200,000}{\$800,000} = 1.5$

How should Mattel prioritize these three projects? If they base the decision strictly on the NPV, project C would be given highest priority because it has the highest NPV. However, project C also requires the largest investment.

The profitability index considered both the present value of the future cash flows (benefits) and the initial investment (cost). Notice that project A has the highest profitability index, followed by project B, and then project C. The profitability index allows managers to prioritize projects based on how much NPV is generated per dollar of investment.

The profitability index is conceptually similar to the method used to prioritize constrained or bottleneck resources in the previous chapter. In this example the limited resource is cash. The profitability index measures the amount of long-term value (represented by the present value of future cash flows) that is generated per unit of the scarce resource (investment of cash).

SUMMARY ANALYSIS OF OPENING CASE DECISION

We started this chapter by asking whether you would accept a $25,000 job offer or stay in school two more years (at a cost of $12,000 per year) so that you could graduate and get a higher paying job (at $45,000 per year). After completing this chapter, you should now understand several different ways you could analyze this personal decision. Let's take a look at what your cash flows would look like under each option for the next 10 years:

Year	OPTION 1: TAKE THE JOB Salary	OPTION 2: STAY IN SCHOOL Tuition/Books	OPTION 2: STAY IN SCHOOL Salary	Difference in Cash Flow
1	$25,000	$(12,000)		$(37,000)
2	25,000	(12,000)		(37,000)
3	25,000		$45,000	20,000
4	25,000		45,000	20,000
5	25,000		45,000	20,000
6	25,000		45,000	20,000
7	25,000		45,000	20,000
8	25,000		45,000	20,000
9	25,000		45,000	20,000
10	25,000		45,000	20,000

COACH'S TIP

Try using these numbers to compute the accounting rate of return, payback period, NPV, and IRR. What decision would you make? What assumptions did you make?

In this example, you would have to invest $37,000 per year for the next two years to earn an additional $20,000 per year for the following eight years. If we apply the four capital budgeting methods from the chapter to this information, it reveals the following:

- **Accounting rate of return.** Starting in year 3, you would earn $20,000 more income per year on your $74,000 investment in the first 2 years. This is a simple rate of return (accounting rate of return) of 27 percent ($20,000/$74,000).

- **Payback period.** It will take between three and four years **after** graduation to pay back the $74,000 investment you make in the first two years ($74,000 / $20,000 = 3.7 years).

- **Net present value.** You need to know the cost of financing your education, which you could estimate based on the interest rate you are paying for loans or the interest you could be earning if you invested in mutual funds. Assuming your cost of capital is 6 percent, the net present value on your investment over 10 years is $42,968. This is how much better off you will be in today's dollars over the next 10 years if you stay in school rather than taking the job.

- **Internal rate of return.** The internal rate of return on this investment is 18.31 percent. Notice that it is much higher than the 6 percent required rate of return or cost of financing your education. This is the rate of return you will make over the next 10 years if you can continue to invest and earn this type of return on your education.

As you can see, each of these methods provides slightly different information, is based on different assumptions, and has strengths and weaknesses. This analysis ignored other important factors such as your personal tax rate, opportunities for promotions and raises over time, and qualitative factors such as which job would bring you more personal fulfillment. In reality, it is very important to factor these issues into the decision process as well. The four capital budgeting techniques discussed in this chapter provide a starting point for the analysis but must be combined with many other important factors.

SUPPLEMENT 8: TIME VALUE OF MONEY

This supplement provides additional details on how to use present value and future value tables to incorporate the time value of money. Although you can use a calculator or computer to do the computations, you need to understand where the numbers come from. In some business situations, you will know the dollar amount of a cash flow that occurs in the future and will need to determine its value now. This type of situation is known as a **present value** problem. The opposite situation occurs when you know the dollar amount of a cash flow that occurs today and need to determine its value at some point in the future, which requires solving a **future value** problems. The following table illustrates the basic difference between present value and future value problems:

	Now	Future
Present value	?	$1,000
Future value	$1,000	?

Present and future value problems may involve two types of cash flow: a single payment or an annuity (a fancy word for a series of equal cash payments). Thus, you need to learn how to deal with four different situations related to the time value of money:

1. Future value of a single payment.
2. Present value of a single payment.
3. Future value of an annuity.
4. Present value of an annuity.

Computing Future and Present Values of a Single Amount

Future Value of a Single Amount   In problems involving the future value of a single amount, you will be asked to calculate how much money you will have in the future as the result of investing a certain amount right now. If you were to receive a gift of $10,000, for instance, you might decide to put it in a savings account and use the money as a down payment on a house after you graduate. The future value computation would tell you how much money you will have from this gift when you graduate. To solve a future value problem, you need to know three items:

1. Amount to be invested.
2. Interest rate (i) the amount will earn.
3. Number of periods (n) in which the amount will earn interest.

The future value concept is based on compound interest, which simply means that interest is calculated on top of interest. Thus, the amount of interest for each period is calculated using the principal plus any interest earned in prior periods. Graphically, the calculation of the future value of $1 for three periods at an interest rate of 10 percent may be represented as follows:

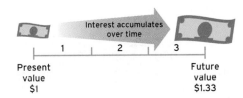

Assume that on January 1, 2010, you deposit $1,000 in a savings account at 10 percent annual interest compounded annually. At the end of three years, the $1,000 will have increased to $1,331 as follows:

Year	Amount at Start of Year	+	Interest during the Year	=	Amount at End of Year
1	$1,000	+	$1,000 × 10% = $100	=	$1,100
2	1,100	+	1,100 × 10% = 110	=	1,210
3	1,210	+	1,210 × 10% = 121	=	1,331

You can avoid the detailed arithmetic by referring to Table 8.1.

TABLE 8.1   Future Value of $1

Periods	2%	3%	3.75%	4%	4.25%	5%	6%	7%	8%
0	1.	1.	1.	1.	1.	1.	1.	1.	1.
1	1.02	1.03	1.0375	1.04	1.0425	1.05	1.06	1.07	1.08
2	1.0404	1.0609	1.0764	1.0816	1.0868	1.1025	1.1236	1.1449	1.1664
3	1.0612	1.0927	1.1168	1.1249	1.1330	1.1576	1.1910	1.2250	1.2597
4	1.0824	1.1255	1.1587	1.1699	1.1811	1.2155	1.2625	1.3108	1.3605
5	1.1041	1.1593	1.2021	1.2167	1.2313	1.2763	1.3382	1.4026	1.4693
6	1.1262	1.1941	1.2472	1.2653	1.2837	1.3401	1.4185	1.5007	1.5869
7	1.1487	1.2299	1.2939	1.3159	1.3382	1.4071	1.5036	1.6058	1.7138
8	1.1717	1.2668	1.3425	1.3686	1.3951	1.4775	1.5938	1.7182	1.8509
9	1.1951	1.3048	1.3928	1.4233	1.4544	1.5513	1.6895	1.8385	1.9990
10	1.2190	1.3439	1.4450	1.4802	1.5162	1.6289	1.7906	1.9672	2.1589
20	1.4859	1.8061	2.0882	2.1911	2.2989	2.6533	3.2071	3.8697	4.6610

Periods	9%	10%	11%	12%	13%	14%	15%	20%	25%
0	1.	1.	1.	1.	1.	1.	1.	1.	1.
1	1.09	1.10	1.11	1.12	1.13	1.14	1.15	1.20	1.25
2	1.1881	1.2100	1.2321	1.2544	1.2769	1.2996	1.3225	1.4400	1.5625
3	1.2950	1.3310	1.3676	1.4049	1.4429	1.4815	1.5209	1.7280	1.9531
4	1.4116	1.4641	1.5181	1.5735	1.6305	1.6890	1.7490	2.0736	2.4414
5	1.5386	1.6105	1.6851	1.7623	1.8424	1.9254	2.0114	2.4883	3.0518
6	1.6771	1.7716	1.8704	1.9738	2.0820	2.1950	2.3131	2.9860	3.8147
7	1.8280	1.9487	2.0762	2.2107	2.3526	2.5023	2.6600	3.5832	4.7684
8	1.9926	2.1436	2.3045	2.4760	2.6584	2.8526	3.0590	4.2998	5.9605
9	2.1719	2.3579	2.5580	2.7731	3.0040	3.2519	3.5179	5.1598	7.4506
10	2.3674	2.5937	2.8394	3.1058	3.3946	3.7072	4.0456	6.1917	9.3132
20	5.6044	6.7275	8.0623	9.6463	11.5231	13.7435	16.3665	38.3376	86.7362

COACH'S TIP

Future value of $1 at 10% interest for 3 years = 1.3310.

Using Table 8.1, you quickly determine how much money you will have after 3 years if you invest $1,000 today, as follows:

$$\$1,000 \times 1.3310 = \$1,331$$

Note that the increase of $331 is due to the time value of money.

Present Value of a Single Amount   The **present value** of a single amount is the value to you today of receiving some amount of money in the future. For instance, you might be offered an opportunity to invest in a financial instrument that would pay you $1,000 in three years. Before you decide whether to invest, you would want to determine the present value of the instrument.

To compute the present value of an amount to be received in the future, we must discount (a procedure that is the opposite of compounding) at i interest rate for n periods. In discounting, the interest is subtracted rather than added as it is in compounding. Graphically, the present value of $1 due at the end of the third period with an interest rate of 10 percent can be represented as follows:

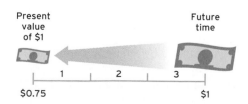

Assume that today is January 1, 2010, and you have the opportunity to receive $1,000 cash on December 31, 2012 (three years from today). At an interest rate of 10 percent per year, how much is the $1,000 payment worth to you on January 1, 2010 (today)? You could discount the amount year by year, but it is easier to use Table 8.2, Present Value of $1.

TABLE 8.2	Present Value of $1

Periods	2%	3%	3.75%	4%	4.25%	5%	6%	7%	8%
1	0.9804	0.9709	0.9639	0.9615	0.9592	0.9524	0.9434	0.9346	0.9259
2	0.9612	0.9426	0.9290	0.9246	0.9201	0.9070	0.8900	0.8734	0.8573
3	0.9423	0.9151	0.8954	0.8890	0.8826	0.8638	0.8396	0.8163	0.7938
4	0.9238	0.8885	0.8631	0.8548	0.8466	0.8227	0.7921	0.7629	0.7350
5	0.9057	0.8626	0.8319	0.8219	0.8121	0.7835	0.7473	0.7130	0.6806
6	0.8880	0.8375	0.8018	0.7903	0.7790	0.7462	0.7050	0.6663	0.6302
7	0.8706	0.8131	0.7728	0.7599	0.7473	0.7107	0.6651	0.6227	0.5835
8	0.8535	0.7894	0.7449	0.7307	0.7168	0.6768	0.6274	0.5820	0.5403
9	0.8368	0.7664	0.7180	0.7026	0.6876	0.6446	0.5919	0.5439	0.5002
10	0.8203	0.7441	0.6920	0.6756	0.6595	0.6139	0.5584	0.5083	0.4632
20	0.6730	0.5537	0.4789	0.4564	0.4350	0.3769	0.3118	0.2584	0.2145

Periods	9%	10%	11%	12%	13%	14%	15%	20%	25%
1	0.9174	0.9091	0.9009	0.8929	0.8850	0.8772	0.8696	0.8333	0.8000
2	0.8417	0.8264	0.8116	0.7972	0.7831	0.7695	0.7561	0.6944	0.6400
3	0.7722	0.7513	0.7312	0.7118	0.6931	0.6750	0.6575	0.5787	0.5120
4	0.7084	0.6830	0.6587	0.6355	0.6133	0.5921	0.5718	0.4823	0.4096
5	0.6499	0.6209	0.5935	0.5674	0.5428	0.5194	0.4972	0.4019	0.3277
6	0.5963	0.5645	0.5346	0.5066	0.4803	0.4556	0.4323	0.3349	0.2621
7	0.5470	0.5132	0.4817	0.4523	0.4251	0.3996	0.3759	0.2791	0.2097
8	0.5019	0.4665	0.4339	0.4039	0.3762	0.3506	0.3269	0.2326	0.1678
9	0.4604	0.4241	0.3909	0.3506	0.3329	0.3075	0.2843	0.1938	0.1342
10	0.4224	0.3855	0.3522	0.3220	0.2946	0.2697	0.2472	0.1615	0.1074
20	0.1784	0.1486	0.1240	0.1037	0.0868	0.0728	0.0611	0.0261	0.0115

To determine how much $1,000 to be received in three years is worth in today's dollars, we simply multiply by the PV of $1 factor for $n = 3$ and $i = 10$ percent, as follows:

COACH'S TIP

Present value of $1 discounted at 10% interest for 3 years = .7513.

$$\$1,000 \times 0.7513 = \$751.30$$

What does a PV of $751.30 mean? It is the amount you would pay now to have the right to receive $1,000 at the end of three years, assuming an interest rate of 10 percent. Conceptually, you should be indifferent between having $751.30 today and receiving $1,000 in three years. If you had $751.30 today but wanted $1,000 in three years, you could simply deposit the money in a savings account that pays 10 percent interest, and it would grow to $1,000 in three years.

What if you could earn only 6 percent instead of 10 percent interest? Would the present value increase or decrease? To answer this, we would take the same approach using Table 8.2 except that the interest rate would change to $i = 6$ percent. Referring to Table 8.2, we see the present value factor for $i = 6$ percent, $n = 3$, is 0.8396. Thus, the present value of $1,000 to be received at the end of three years, assuming a 6 percent interest rate, would be $839.60 ($1,000 × 0.8396). Notice that when we assume a 6 percent interest rate, the present value is higher than when we assumed a 10 percent interest rate. The reason for this difference is that, to reach

$1,000 three years from now, you would now need to deposit more money in a savings account if it earns 6 percent interest than if it earns 10 percent interest.

Self-Study Practice

1. If the interest rate in a present value problem increases from 8 percent to 10 percent, will the present value increase or decrease?

2. What is the present value of $10,000 to be received 10 years from now if the interest rate is 5 percent, compounded annually?

3. If $10,000 is deposited now in a savings account that earns 5 percent interest compounded annually, how much will it be worth 10 years from now?

After you have finished, check your answers with the solution in the margin.

Computing Future and Present Values of an Annuity

Instead of a single payment, many business problems involve multiple cash payments over a number of periods. An **annuity** is a series of consecutive payments characterized by:

1. An equal dollar amount each interest period.
2. Interest periods of equal length (year, half a year, quarter, or month).
3. An equal interest rate each interest period.

Examples of annuities include monthly payments on a car or house, yearly contributions to a savings account, and monthly pension benefits.

Future Value of an Annuity   If you are saving money for some purpose, such as remodeling your home or taking a vacation, you might decide to deposit a fixed amount of money in a savings account each month. The future value of an annuity tells you how much money will be in your savings account at some point in the future.

The future value of an annuity includes compound interest on each payment from the date of payment to the end of the term of the annuity. Each new payment accumulates less interest than prior payments because the number of periods in which to accumulate interest decreases. The future value of an annuity of $1 for three periods at 10 percent may be represented graphically as:

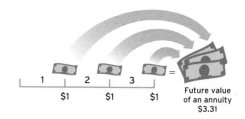

Assume that each year for three years, you deposit $1,000 cash into a savings account that earns 10 percent interest per year. You make the first $1,000 deposit on December 31, 2010, the second one on December 31, 2011, and the third and last one on December 31, 2012. The first $1,000 deposit earns compound interest for two years (for a total principal and interest of $1,210); the second deposit earns interest for one year (for a total principal and interest of $1,100). The third deposit earns no interest because it was made on the day that the balance is computed. Thus, the total amount in the savings account at the end of three years is $3,310 ($1,210 + $1,100 + $1,000).

To calculate the future value of this annuity, we could compute the interest on each deposit. However, a faster way is to refer to Table 8.3, Future Value of an Annuity of $1:

TABLE 8.3	Future Value of an Annuity of $1								
Periods*	2%	3%	3.75%	4%	4.25%	5%	6%	7%	8%
1	1.	1.	1.	1.	1.	1.	1.	1.	1.
2	2.02	2.03	2.0375	2.04	2.0425	2.05	2.06	2.07	2.08
3	3.0604	3.0909	3.1139	3.1216	3.1293	3.1525	3.1836	3.2149	3.2464
4	4.1216	4.1836	4.2307	4.2465	4.2623	4.3101	4.3746	4.4399	4.5061
5	5.2040	5.3091	5.3893	5.4163	5.4434	5.5256	5.6371	5.7507	5.8666
6	6.3061	6.4684	6.5914	6.6330	6.6748	6.8019	6.9753	7.1533	7.3359
7	7.4343	7.6625	7.8386	7.8983	7.9585	8.1420	8.3938	8.6540	8.9228
8	8.5830	8.8923	9.1326	9.2142	9.2967	9.5491	9.8975	10.2598	10.6366
9	9.7546	10.1591	10.4750	10.5828	10.6918	11.0266	11.4913	11.9780	12.4876
10	10.9497	11.4639	11.8678	12.0061	12.1462	12.5779	13.1808	13.8164	14.4866
20	24.2974	26.8704	29.0174	29.7781	30.5625	33.0660	36.7856	40.9955	45.7620
Periods*	9%	10%	11%	12%	13%	14%	15%	20%	25%
1	1.	1.	1.	1.	1.	1.	1.	1.	1.
2	2.09	2.10	2.11	2.12	2.13	2.14	2.15	2.20	2.25
3	3.2781	3.3100	3.3421	3.3744	3.4069	3.4396	3.4725	3.6400	3.8125
4	4.5731	4.6410	4.7097	4.7793	4.8498	4.9211	4.9934	5.3680	5.7656
5	5.9847	6.1051	6.2278	6.3528	6.4803	6.6101	6.7424	7.4416	8.2070
6	7.5233	7.7156	7.9129	8.1152	8.3227	8.5355	8.7537	9.9299	11.2588
7	9.2004	9.4872	9.7833	10.0890	10.4047	10.7305	11.0668	12.9159	15.0735
8	11.0285	11.4359	11.8594	12.2997	12.7573	13.2328	13.7266	16.4991	19.8419
9	13.0210	13.5975	14.1640	14.7757	15.4157	16.0853	16.7856	20.7989	25.8023
10	15.1929	15.9374	16.7220	17.5487	18.4197	19.3373	20.3037	25.9587	33.2529
20	51.1601	57.2750	64.2028	72.0524	80.9468	91.0249	102.4436	186.6880	342.9447

* There is one payment each period.

The future value of your three deposits of $1,000 each can be computed as follows:

$$\$1,000 \times 3.3100 = \$3,310$$

COACH'S TIP

Future value of a $1 annuity for 3 years at 10% interest = 3.31

Spotlight On DECISION MAKING

The Power of Compounding Compound interest is a remarkably powerful economic force. In fact, the ability to earn interest on interest is the key to building economic wealth. If you save $1,000 per year for the first 10 years of your career, you will have more money when you retire than it you saved $15,000 per year for the last 10 years of your career. This surprising outcome occurs because the money you save early in your career will earn more interest than the money you save at the end of your career. If you start saving money now, the majority of your wealth will not be the money you saved but the interest your money was able to earn over time.

The accompanying chart illustrates the power of compounding over a brief 10-year period. If you deposit $1 each year in an account earning 10 percent interest, at the end of just 10 years, only 63 percent of your balance will be made up of money you have saved. The rest will be interest you have earned. After 20 years, only 35 percent of your balance will be from saved money. The lesson associated with compound interest is that even though saving money is difficult, you should start now.

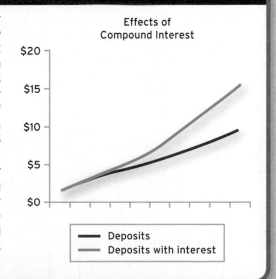

Effects of Compound Interest

— Deposits
— Deposits with interest

Present Value of an Annuity The present value of an annuity is the value now of a series of equal amounts to be received (or paid out) for some specified number of periods in the future. A good example is a retirement program that offers employees a monthly income after retirement. The present value of an annuity of $1 for three periods at 10 percent can be represented graphically as:

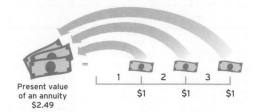

Present value
of an annuity
$2.49

1   2   3
$1 $1 $1

Assume you are to receive $1,000 cash on each December 31 for three years: 2010, 2011, and 2012. How much would the sum of these three $1,000 future amounts be worth on January 1, 2010, assuming an interest rate of 10 percent per year? One way to determine this is to use Table 8.2 to calculate the present value of each single amount as follows:

			FACTOR FROM TABLE 8.2		
Year	Amount		$i = 10\%$		Present Value
1	$1,000	×	0.9091 ($n = 1$)	=	$ 909.10
2	$1,000	×	0.8264 ($n = 2$)	=	826.40
3	$1,000	×	0.7513 ($n = 3$)	=	751.30
			Total present value	=	$2,486.80

Alternatively, we can compute the present value of this annuity more easily by using Table 8.4 as follows:

TABLE 8.4	Present Value of Annuity of $1

Periods*	2%	3%	3.75%	4%	4.25%	5%	6%	7%	8%
1	0.9804	0.9709	0.9639	0.9615	0.9592	0.9524	0.9434	0.9346	0.9259
2	1.9416	1.9135	1.8929	1.8861	1.8794	1.8594	1.8334	1.8080	1.7833
3	2.8839	2.8286	2.7883	2.7751	2.7620	2.7232	2.6730	2.6243	2.5771
4	3.8077	3.7171	3.6514	3.6299	3.6086	3.5460	3.4651	3.3872	3.3121
5	4.7135	4.5797	4.4833	4.4518	4.4207	4.3295	4.2124	4.1002	3.9927
6	5.6014	5.4172	5.2851	5.2421	5.1997	5.0757	4.9173	4.7665	4.6229
7	6.4720	6.2303	6.0579	6.0021	5.9470	5.7864	5.5824	5.3893	5.2064
8	7.3255	7.0197	6.8028	6.7327	6.6638	6.4632	6.2098	5.9713	5.7466
9	8.1622	7.7861	7.5208	7.4353	7.3513	7.1078	6.8017	6.5152	6.2469
10	8.9826	8.5302	8.2128	8.1109	8.0109	7.7217	7.3601	7.0236	6.7101
20	16.3514	14.8775	13.8962	13.5903	13.2944	12.4622	11.4699	10.5940	9.8181

Periods*	9%	10%	11%	12%	13%	14%	15%	20%	25%
1	0.9174	0.9091	0.9009	0.8929	0.8550	0.8772	0.8696	0.8333	0.8000
2	1.7591	1.7355	1.7125	1.6901	1.6681	1.6467	1.6257	1.5278	1.4400
3	2.5313	2.4869	2.4437	2.4018	2.3612	2.3216	2.2832	2.1065	1.9520
4	3.2397	3.1699	3.1024	3.0373	2.9745	2.9137	2.8550	2.5887	2.3616
5	3.8897	3.7908	3.6959	3.6048	3.5172	3.4331	3.3522	2.9906	2.6893
6	4.4859	4.3553	4.2305	4.1114	3.9975	3.8887	3.7845	3.3255	2.9514
7	5.0330	4.8684	4.7122	4.5638	4.4226	4.2883	4.1604	3.6046	3.1611
8	5.5348	5.3349	5.1461	4.9676	4.7988	4.6389	4.4873	3.8372	3.3289
9	5.9952	5.7590	5.5370	5.3282	5.1317	4.9464	4.7716	4.0310	3.4631
10	6.4177	6.1446	5.8892	5.6502	5.4262	5.2161	5.0188	4.1925	3.5705
20	9.1285	8.5136	7.9633	7.4694	7.0248	6.6231	6.2593	4.8696	3.9539

* There is one payment each period.

 COACH'S TIP

Present value of $1 annuity at 10% for 3 years = 2.4869.

$1,000 × 2.4869 = $2,487 (rounded)

You should be indifferent between receiving $2,487 today and receiving $1,000 at the end of each of the next 3 years.

DEMONSTRATION CASE

Maddox Company is considering investing $800,000 in a new project. Projected annual revenues, expenses, and profit for the next four years follow:

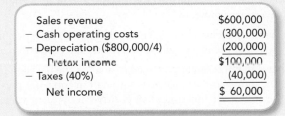

Sales revenue	$600,000
− Cash operating costs	(300,000)
− Depreciation ($800,000/4)	(200,000)
Pretax income	$100,000
− Taxes (40%)	(40,000)
Net income	$ 60,000

The project's assets are expected to have no salvage value at the end of four years. The company's required rate of return is 12 percent.

Required:

1. Compute the accounting rate of return.
2. Compute the payback period.
3. Compute the four-year NPV using a 12 percent discount rate.
4. Without computing the exact IRR, explain whether it would be higher or lower than the 12 percent required rate of return.
5. Compute the exact IRR using Excel.

See page 310 for solution.

CHAPTER SUMMARY

Calculate the accounting rate of return and describe its major weaknesses. p. 290   LO1

- The accounting rate of return is calculated as net income/original investment.
- The major weakness of the accounting rate of return is that it does not incorporate the time value of money. It is also the only capital budgeting method that uses net income rather than cash flow to measure the benefits of a potential investment.

Calculate the payback period and describe its major weaknesses. p. 290   LO2

- The payback method computes the amount of time it will take for a capital investment to "pay for itself" or earn back enough cash to cover the original investment.
- The major weakness of the payback method is that it does not incorporate the time value of money. It also ignores all cash flows that occur after the payback period is over.

Calculate net present value and describe why it is superior to the other capital budgeting techniques. p. 294   LO3

- The net present value method compares the present value of future cash flows to the original investment.
- Future cash flows are converted to a present value basis to reflect the required rate of return or cost of capital.
- The net present value method is preferred over the accounting rate of return and payback period because it incorporates the time value of money.
- The net present value method is preferred over the internal rate of return method because it assumes that cash flows are reinvested at the required rate of return rather than the internal rate of return.

Predict the internal rate of return and describe its relationship to net present value. p. 296   LO4

- The internal rate of return is the return that will yield a zero net present value.
- If the internal rate of return is higher than the required rate of return, the net present value will be positive.

- If the internal rate of return is less than the required rate of return, the net present value will be negative.

LO5   Use the net present value method to analyze mutually exclusive capital investments. p. 298

- The net present value method can be used to compare and make a choice between mutually exclusive capital investment projects.

- An example of a mutually exclusive choice is the decision to lease or buy an asset. The option with the lowest net present value is preferred from a pure cost perspective.

- The net present value method can also be used to analyze the decision to invest in automation. In this case, the future cost savings from automation (on a net present value basis) are compared to the cost of the investment. A positive net present value suggests that the investment in the project is acceptable; otherwise it is unacceptable.

LO6   Use the profitability index to prioritize independent capital investment projects. p. 300

- The profitability index should be used to prioritize investment in independent projects when investment funds are limited.

- The profitability index is computed as the present value of future cash flows divided by the original investment.

- A profitability index greater than 1 means that a project has a positive net present value. A profitability index less than 1 means that a project has a negative net present value.

- The profitability index tells you how much benefit (measured as the present value of future cash flows) is generated for each dollar of investment.

SOLUTION TO DEMONSTRATION CASE

1. Accounting rate of return = $60,000/$800,000 = 7.5%
2. Payback period = $800,000/($60,000 + $200,000) = 3.08 years
3.

Year	Cash Flow	Present Value Factor (12% Discount)	Present Value
0	($ 800,000)	—	$(800,000)
1–4	$ 60,000 + $ 200,000 = $260,000 ×	3.0373*	789,698
		Net present value =	$ (10,302)

* PV of annuity of $1 for $n = 4$, $i = 12\%$.

4. Because the NPV is negative at a discount rate of 12 percent, the IRR must be less than 12 percent.
5. The exact IRR is 11.3879 percent.

KEY TERMS

See complete definitions in glossary at back of text.

QUESTIONS

1. Explain the difference between screening decisions and preference decisions.

2. What is the difference between independent projects and mutually exclusive projects? Give an example of each from your own experiences.

3. Briefly explain what the time value of money means.

4. Which capital budgeting methods incorporate the time value of money and which do not? Which are considered superior, and why?

5. What is a company's hurdle rate? How is it relevant to capital budgeting?

6. How do cash flow and net income differ? Explain why this difference is important to capital budgeting.

7. In everyday terms, explain what information the payback period provides about an investment.

8. What do a positive net present value (NPV) and a negative NPV indicate about an investment?

9. When would you use an annuity factor in a net present value calculation instead of a present value factor for a single cash flow?

10. Explain how the internal rate of return (IRR) and net present value (NPV) are related. If a project has an NPV of $50,000 using a 10 percent discount factor, what does this imply about that project's IRR?

11. Why is the net present value method generally preferred over the internal rate of return method?

12. Briefly explain how the profitability index is calculated and interpreted.

13. Explain the basic difference between future value and present value.

14. If you deposited $10,000 in a savings account that earns 10 percent, how much would you have at the end of 10 years?

15. If you hold a valid contract that will pay you $8,000 cash 10 years from now and the going rate of interest is 10 percent, what is its present value?

16. What is an annuity?

17. Use Tables 8.1 to 8.4 to complete the following schedule:

	Table Values		
	$i = 5\%$, $n = 4$	$i = 10\%$, $n = 7$	$i = 14\%$, $n = 10$
FV of $1			
PV of $1			
FV of annuity of $1			
PV of annuity of $1			

MULTIPLE CHOICE

Quiz 8
www.mhhe.com/whitecotton1e

1. Which of the following requires managers to determine whether a proposed capital investment meets some minimum criterion?

   a. Preference decision.
   b. Screening decision.
   c. Cash payback period.
   d. None of the above.

2. ABC Company is considering a $500,000 investment to automate its production process. The new equipment will allow ABC to save $75,000 each year in labor costs. What is this project's payback period?

   a. 4.00 years.   c. 6.67 years.
   b. 5.67 years.   d. 8.00 years.

3. What is the accounting rate of return for a project that requires an investment of $725,000 and yields total net income of $320,000 over four years?

   a. 11%.   c. 19.75%.
   b. 12.5%.   d. 44%.

4. When choosing among several independent projects that are **not** mutually exclusive, managers should

   a. Rely primarily on the accounting rate of return.
   b. Compare their net present values regardless of the projects' sizes.

   c. Calculate the profitability index of each project for comparison.
   d. Rely solely on the internal rates of return for comparison.

5. When deciding whether to lease or buy a long-term asset, managers should

   a. Flip a coin.
   b. Compare the net present value of the two options.
   c. Consider only the cash outflows.
   d. Always choose to buy a long-term asset.

6. Which of the following methods ignore the time value of money?

   a. Payback method and accounting rate of return.
   b. Payback method and internal rate of return.
   c. Accounting rate of return and net present value.
   d. Net present value and profitability index.

7. Discounted cash flow methods are considered superior to nondiscounting methods because

   a. Discounting methods recognize the time value of money.
   b. Discounting methods are simpler to calculate.
   c. Discounting methods are always based on accounting measurements of net income and investment.
   d. Both (a) and (c) are correct.

8. Jennings Company has evaluated a project and found that its internal rate of return is approximately 13.5 percent. Suppose Jennings' cost of capital is 12 percent. What, if anything, can you infer about the net present value (NPV) of this project?

   a. The NPV is less than zero.
   b. The NPV is more than zero.
   c. The NPV is exactly zero.
   d. Nothing can be determined about the project's NPV.

9. Which of the following is a characteristic of an annuity?

   a. An equal dollar amount each interest period.
   b. Interest periods of equal length.
   c. An equal interest rate each interest period.
   d. All of the above.

10. Which of the following statements is true?

   a. When the interest rate increases, the present value of a single amount decreases.
   b. When the number of interest periods increases; the present value of a single amount increases.
   c. When the interest rate increases, the present value of an annuity increases.
   d. None of the above.

> Answers to Multiple-Choice Questions located in back of the text.

MINI EXERCISES

LO1, 2, 3 **M8-1 Matching Key Terms and Concepts to Definitions**

A number of terms and concepts from this chapter and a list of descriptions, definitions, and explanations follow. For each term listed on the left, choose at least one corresponding item from the right. Note that a single term may have more than one description and a single description may be used more than once or not at all.

_____ 1. Time value of money
_____ 2. Profitability index
_____ 3. Payback period
_____ 4. Net present value method
_____ 5. Future value
_____ 6. Preference decision
_____ 7. Internal rate of return method
_____ 8. Screening decision
_____ 9. Accounting rate of return

a. Discounting method of capital budgeting.

b. Estimate of the average annual return on investment that a project will generate.

c. Capital budgeting method that identifies the discount rate that generates a zero net present value.

d. Decision that requires managers to evaluate potential capital investments to determine they meet a minimum criterion.

e. Only capital budgeting method based on accounting income instead of cash flow.

f. Ratio of the present value of future cash flows divided by the initial investment.

g. Value of a cash flow that happens today will be worth at some point in the future.

h. Concept recognizing that cash received today is more valuable than cash received in the future.

i. Decision that requires a manager to choose from a set of alternatives.

j. How long it will take for a particular capital investment to pay for itself.

k. Capital budgeting technique that compares the present value of the future cash flows for a project to its original investment.

LO1 **M8-2 Calculating Accounting Rate of Return**

What is the accounting rate of return for a project that is estimated to yield total income of $390,000 over three years and costs $865,000?

M8-3 Calculating Payback Period   LO2

A project has estimated annual net cash flows of $60,000 and is estimated to cost $390,000. What is the payback period?

M8-4 Calculating Accounting Rate of Return, Payback Period   LO1, 2

Milo Company is considering the purchase of new equipment for its factory. It will cost $250,000 and have a $50,000 salvage value in five years. The annual net income from the equipment is expected to be $30,000, and depreciation is $40,000 per year. Calculate and evaluate Milo's annual rate of return and payback period for the equipment.

M8-5 Calculating Net Present Value   LO3

Lemur Company is considering a project that has estimated annual net cash flows of $35,000 for six years and is estimated to cost $150,000. Lemur's hurdle rate is 8 percent. Determine the net present value of the project and whether it is acceptable to Lemur.

M8-6 Determining Internal Rate of Return   LO4

Cistar Company is considering a project that is estimated to cost $236,500 and provide annual net cash flows of $57,523 for the next five years. What is the internal rate of return for this project?

M8-7 Calculating Net Present Value, Predicting Internal Rate of Return   LO3, 4

Otis Company has the following information about a potential capital investment:

Initial investment	$400,000
Annual cash inflow	$ 70,000
Expected life	10 years
Cost of capital	11%

1. Calculate and evaluate the net present value of this project.
2. Without any calculations, explain whether the internal rate of return on this project is more or less than 11 percent.

M8-8 Calculating Profitability Index   LO6

Womac Corp. is considering three projects. Project A has a present value of $265,000 and an initial investment of $120,000. Project B has a present value of $400,000 and an initial investment of $220,000. Project C has a present value of $115,000 and an initial investment of $30,000. Using the profitability index, determine how Womac should prioritize these projects.

M8-9 Computing Present Value of Complex Contract   Supplement

As a result of a slowdown in operations, Mercantile Stores is offering employees who have been terminated a severance package of $100,000 cash; another $100,000 to be paid in one year; and an annuity of $30,000 to be paid each year for 20 years. What is the present value of the package assuming an interest rate of 8 percent?

M8-10 Computing Present Value of Complex Contract   Supplement

You plan to retire in 20 years. Calculate whether it is better for you to save $25,000 a year for the last 10 years before retirement or $15,000 for each of the 20 years. Assume you are able to earn 10 percent interest on your investments.

EXERCISES   ![McGraw Hill] connect™ |ACCOUNTING

E8-1 Calculating Accounting Rate of Return,   LO1, 2
       Payback Period

Midway Printing Co. is considering the purchase of new electronic printing equipment. It would allow Midway to increase its net income by $60,000 per year. Other information about this proposed project follows:

Initial investment	$300,000
Useful life	5 years
Salvage value	$100,000

Required:

Calculate and evaluate the following for Midway:
1. Accounting rate of return.
2. Payback period.

LO1, 2 **E8-2 Calculating Accounting Rate of Return, Payback Period**

Norton Car Wash Co. is considering the purchase of a new facility. It would allow Norton to increase its net income by $90,000 per year. Other information about this proposed project follows:

Initial investment	$425,000
Useful life	8 years
Salvage value	$ 50,000

Required:

Calculate and evaluate the following for Norton:
1. Accounting rate of return.
2. Payback period.

LO3, 4 **E8-3 Calculating Net Present Value, Internal Rate of Return**

Lancer Corp. has the following information available about a potential capital investment:

Initial investment	$1,300,000
Annual net income	$ 200,000
Expected life	8 years
Salvage value	$ 350,000
Lancer's cost of capital	10%

Required:

1. Calculate the project's net present value.
2. Without making any calculations, determine whether the internal rate of return (IRR) is more or less than 10 percent.
3. Calculate the net present value using a 20 percent discount rate.
4. Estimate the project's IRR.

LO1, 2, 3, 4 **E8-4 Calculating Accounting Rate of Return, Payback Period, Net Present Value**

Lenny's Limousine Service (LLS) is considering the purchase of two Hummer limousines. Various information about the proposed investment follows:

Initial investment (2 limos)	$600,000
Useful life	8 years
Salvage value	$100,000
Annual net income generated	$ 48,000
LLS's cost of capital	12%

Required:

Help LLS evaluate this project by calculating each of the following:
1. Accounting rate of return.
2. Payback period.
3. Net present value.
4. Based on your calculation of net present value, what would you estimate the project's internal rate of return to be?

E8-5 Analyzing Relationship between Net Present Value and Internal Rate of Return

LO3, 4

Consider the relationship between a project's net present value (NPV), its internal rate of return (IRR), and a company's cost of capital. For each scenario that follows, indicate the relative value of the unknown. If cost of capital is unknown, indicate whether it would be higher or lower than the stated IRR. If NPV is unknown, indicate whether it would be higher or lower than zero. Project 1 is shown as an example.

	Net Present Value	Cost of Capital	Internal Rate of Return
Project 1	<0	13%	<13%
Project 2	>0	?	10
Project 3	?	14	12
Project 4	>0	10	?
Project 5	<0	?	9
Project 6	?	9	10

E8-6 Comparing Options Using Present Value Concepts

Supplement

After hearing a knock at your front door, you are surprised to see the Prize Patrol from a large, well-known magazine subscription company. It has arrived with the good news that you are the big winner, having won "$20 million." You have three options:

(a) Receive $1 million per year for the next 20 years.
(b) Have $8 million today.
(c) Have $2 million today and receive $700,000 for each of the next 20 years.

Your financial adviser tells you that it is reasonable to expect to earn 10 percent on investments.

Required:

1. Calculate the present value of each option.
2. Determine which option you prefer and explain your reasoning.

E8-7 Deciding to Lease or Buy

LO3, 5

Your friend Jose is trying to decide whether to buy or lease his next vehicle. He has gathered information about each option but is not sure how to compare the alternatives. Purchasing a new vehicle will cost $26,500, and Jose expects about $500 per year in maintenance costs. He would keep the vehicle for five years and estimates the salvage value to be $8,500. Alternatively, Jose could lease the same vehicle for five years at a cost of $4,200 per year including maintenance. Assume a discount rate of 10 percent.

Required:

1. Determine the net present value of Jose's options.
2. Advise Jose which option he should choose and explain your reasoning.

E8-8 Comparing Projects Using Profitability Index

LO6

Dayton Corp has $2 million to invest in new projects. The company's managers have presented a number of possible options that the board must prioritize. Information about the projects follows:

	Project A	Project B	Project C	Project D
Initial investment	$550,000	$230,000	$ 790,000	$ 945,000
Present value of future cash flows	765,000	415,000	1,200,000	1,560,000

Required:

1. Is Dayton able to invest in all of these projects simultaneously? Explain.
2. Calculate the profitability index for each project and prioritize them for Dayton.

Supplement   **E8-9 Computing Growth in Savings Account: Single Amount**

On January 1, 2009, you deposited $6,000 in a savings account. The account will earn 10 percent annual compound interest, which will be added to the fund balance at the end of each year.

Required (round to the nearest dollar):

1.   What will be the balance in the savings account at the end of 10 years?
2.   What is the total interest for the 10 years?
3.   How much interest revenue did the fund earn in 2009 and in 2010?

Supplement   **E8-10 Computing Future Value of Annual Deposits**

You are saving for a Porsche Carrera Cabriolet, which currently sells for nearly half a million dollars. Your plan is to deposit $15,000 at the end of each year for the next 10 years. You expect to earn 5 percent each year.

Required:

1.   Determine how much you will have saved after 10 years.
2.   Determine the amount saved if you were able to deposit $17,500 each year.
3.   Determine the amount saved if you deposit $15,000 each year, but with 8 percent interest.

PROBLEMS–SET A

LO1, 2, 3, 4   **PA8-1 Calculating Accounting Rate of Return, Payback Period, Net Present Value**

www.mhhe.com/whitecotton1e

Hot Air Highlights (HAH) is considering the purchase of two new hot air balloons so that it can expand its desert sunset tours. Various information about the proposed investment follows:

Initial investment (for two hot air balloons)	$500,000
Useful life	10 years
Salvage value	$ 50,000
Annual net income generated	$ 42,000
HAH's cost of capital	11%

Required:

Help HAH evaluate this project by calculating each of the following:
1.   Accounting rate of return.
2.   Payback period.
3.   Net present value (NPV).
4.   Recalculate the NPV assuming HAH's cost of capital is 15 percent.
5.   Based on your calculation of NPV, what would you estimate the project's internal rate of return to be?

LO1, 2, 3, 5   **PA8-2 Making Automation Decision**

Soldrum Company is considering automating its production facility. The initial investment in automation would be $12 million, and the equipment has a useful life of 10 years with a residual value of $1 million. The company will use straight-line depreciation. Soldrum could expect a production increase of 40,000 units per year and a reduction of 20 percent in the labor cost per unit.

	Current (no automation)		Proposed (automation)	
Production and sales volume	80,000 units		120,000 units	
	Per Unit	Total	Per Unit	Total
Sales revenue	$90	?	$90	?
Variable costs				
Direct materials	$18		$18	
Direct labor	25		?	
Variable manufacturing overhead	10		10	
Total variable manufacturing costs	53		?	
Contribution margin	$37	?	$42	?
Fixed manufacturing costs		1,250,000		2,350,000
Net income		?		?

Required:

1. Complete the preceding table showing the totals and summarize the difference in the alternatives.

2. Determine the project's accounting rate of return.

3. Determine the project's payback period.

4. Using a discount rate of 15 percent, calculate the net present value (NPV) of the proposed investment.

5. Recalculate the NPV using a 10% discount rate.

6. Would you advise Soldrum to invest in the automation?

PA8-3 Comparing, Prioritizing Multiple Projects

LO1, 2, 3, 5, 6

Allister Company has a number of potential capital investments. Because these projects vary in nature, initial investment, and time horizon, management is finding it difficult to compare them.

Project 1: Retooling Manufacturing Facility

This project would require an initial investment of $5 million. It would generate $750,000 in additional cash flow each year. The new machinery has a useful life of eight years and a salvage value of $500,000.

Project 2: Purchase Patent for New Product

The patent would cost $3,400,000, which would be fully amortized over five years. Production of this product would generate $1,200,000 additional annual net income for Allister.

Project 3: Purchase a New Fleet of Delivery Trucks

Allister could purchase 25 new delivery trucks at a cost of $75,000 each. The fleet would have a useful life of 10 years, and each truck would have a salvage value of $5,000. Purchasing the fleet would allow Allister to expand its customer territory resulting in $500,000 of additional net income per year.

Required:

1. Determine each project's accounting rate of return.

2. Determine each project's payback period.

3. Using a discount rate of 10 percent, calculate the net present value of each project.

4. Determine the profitability index of each project and prioritize the projects for Allister.

L01, 2, 3, 4

www.mhhe.com/whitecotton1e

PA8-4 Calculating Accounting Rate of Return, Payback Period, Net Present Value

Wing Walker Aces (WWA), Inc., is considering the purchase of a small plane to use in its wing-walking demonstrations and aerial tour business. Various information about the proposed investment follows:

Initial investment	$110,000
Useful life	10 years
Salvage value	$ 10,000
Annual net income generated	$ 5,400
WWA's cost of capital	10%

Required:

Help WWA evaluate this project by calculating each of the following:
1. Accounting rate of return.
2. Payback period.
3. Net present value (NPV).
4. Recalculate WWA's NPV assuming the cost of capital is 6 percent.
5. Based on your calculations of NPV, what would you estimate the project's internal rate of return to be?

Supplement

PA8-5 Comparing Options Using Present Value Concepts

After completing a long and successful career as senior vice president for a large bank, you are preparing for retirement. After visiting the human resources office, you have found that you have several retirement options you can receive:

a. An immediate cash payment of $1 million.
b. Payment of $60,000 per year for life (your remaining life expectancy is 20 years).
c. Payment of $50,000 per year for 10 years and then $70,000 per year for life (this option is intended to give you some protection against inflation).

You believe you can earn 8 percent on your investments.

Required:

1. Calculate the net present value of each option.
2. Explain which option you prefer and why.

PROBLEMS—SET B

L01, 2, 3, 4

PB8-1 Calculating Accounting Rate of Return, Payback Period, Net Present Value

Ted's Taxi Company (TTC) is considering the purchase of four new taxicabs. Various information about the proposed investment follows:

Initial investment (for 4 vehicles)	$220,000
Useful life	5 years
Salvage value	$ 20,000
Annual net income generated	$ 27,000
TTC's cost of capital	9%

Required:

Help TTC evaluate this project by calculating each of the following:
1. Accounting rate of return.
2. Payback period.
3. Net present value (NPV).

4. Recalculate the NPV assuming the cost of capital is 15 percent.
5. Based on your calculations of NPV, what would you estimate the project's internal rate of return to be?

PB8-2 Making Automation Decision

Praton Company is considering automating its production facility. The initial investment in automation would be $8,000,000 and the equipment has a useful life of eight years with a residual value of $1,500,000. The company will use straight-line depreciation. Praton could expect a production increase of 20,000 units per year and a reduction of 40 percent in the labor cost per unit.

	Current (no automation)		Proposed (automation)	
Production and sales volume	60,000 units		80,000 units	
	Per Unit	Total	Per Unit	Total
Sales revenue	$70	?	$70	?
Variable costs				
Direct materials	$15		$15	
Direct labor	20		?	
Variable manufacturing overhead	7		7	
Total variable manufacturing costs	42		?	
Contribution margin	$28	?	$36	?
Fixed manufacturing costs		800,000		1,612,500
Net income		?		?

Required:

1. Complete the preceding table showing the totals and summarize the difference in the alternatives.
2. Determine the project's accounting rate of return.
3. Determine the project's payback period.
4. Using a discount rate of 15 percent, calculate the net present value (NPV) of the proposed investment.
5. Recalculate the NPV using a discount rate of 10 percent.
6. Would you advise Praton to invest in the automation?

PB8-3 Comparing, Prioritizing Multiple Projects

Franklin Company has a number of potential capital investments. Because these projects vary in nature, initial investment, and time horizon, Franklin's management is finding it difficult to compare them.

Project 1: Retooling Manufacturing Facility

This project would require an initial investment of $7,600,000. It would generate $975,000 in additional cash flow each year. The new machinery has a useful life of seven years and a salvage value of $600,000.

Project 2: Purchase Patent for New Product

The patent would cost $7,500,000, which would be fully amortized over 10 years. Production of this product would generate $1,650,000 additional annual net income for Franklin.

Project 3: Purchase a New Fleet of Delivery Vans

Franklin could purchase 10 new delivery vans at a cost of $25,000 each. The fleet would have a useful life of 10 years, and each van would have a salvage value of $2,500. Purchasing the fleet would allow Franklin to expand its delivery area resulting in $30,000 of additional net income per year.

Required:

1. Determine each project's accounting rate of return and compare the projects.
2. Determine each project's payback period and compare the projects.
3. Using a discount rate of 10 percent, calculate the net present value of each project.
4. Determine the profitability index of each project and prioritize the projects for Franklin.

LO1, 2, 3, 4 **PB8-4 Calculating Accounting Rate of Return, Payback Period, Net Present Value**

Titan Production Co. is considering an investment in new machinery for its factory. Various information about the proposed investment follows:

Initial investment	$750,000
Useful life	6 years
Salvage value	$120,000
Annual net income generated	$ 66,000
Titan's cost of capital	11%

Required:

Help Titan evaluate this project by calculating each of the following:

1. Annual rate of return.
2. Payback period.
3. Net present value (NPV).
4. Recalculate Titan's NPV assuming its cost of capital is 12 percent.
5. Based on your calculations of NPV, what would you estimate the project's internal rate of return to be?

Supplement **PB8-5 Comparing Options Using Present Value Concepts**

After incurring a serious injury caused by a manufacturing defect, your friend has sued the manufacturer for damages. The manufacturer made your friend three offers to settle the lawsuit;

(a) Receive an immediate cash payment of $100,000.
(b) Receive $6,000 per year for life (your friend's remaining life expectancy is 20 years).
(c) Receive $5,000 per year for 10 years and then $7,000 per year for life (this option is intended to compensate your friend for increased aggravation of the injury over time).

Your friend can earn 8 percent interest and has asked you for advice.

Required:

1. Calculate the net present value of each option.
2. Explain which option your friend should prefer and why.

SKILLS DEVELOPMENT CASES

LO3 **S8-1 Analyzing Personal Decision to Pursue Graduate Degree**

Assume your friend Greg Ellis is thinking of getting an MBA. He is a resident of Arizona and is currently earning $45,000 per year. One of the schools Greg is considering is Brigham Young University (BYU) in Provo, Utah. He went to the Forbes Web site and used the "Should You Get an M.B.A." decision tool to calculate the "five-year gain" from getting an MBA at BYU. The results of that analysis follow.

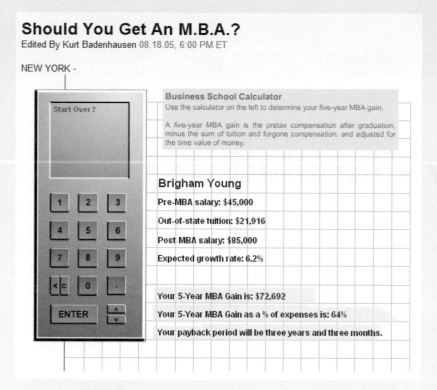

Should You Get An M.B.A.?

Edited By Kurt Badenhausen 08.18.05, 6:00 PM ET

NEW YORK -

Business School Calculator

Use the calculator on the left to determine your five-year MBA gain.

A five-year MBA gain is the pretax compensation after graduation, minus the sum of tuition and forgone compensation, and adjusted for the time value of money.

Brigham Young

Pre-MBA salary: $45,000

Out-of-state tuition: $21,916

Post-MBA salary: $85,000

Expected growth rate: 6.2%

Your 5-Year MBA Gain is: $72,692

Your 5-Year MBA Gain as a % of expenses is: 64%

Your payback period will be three years and three months.

Source: http://www.forbes.com/2005/08/16/cz_05mba_business_schools_gain_calulator.html

Greg was pleased to see that his five-year gain from getting an MBA was $72,692 and that the payback time on his investment would be just over three years. He is also considering a few other options:

- Getting a degree at Arizona State University (ASU) where he would qualify for in-state tuition. Greg believes his post-MBA salary would be the same with a degree from ASU as with one from BYU.

- Getting a degree at Harvard University. Greg believes he would be able to earn a higher starting salary (estimated at $100,000) with a Harvard degree.

Required:

1. Go to the Forbes Web site and calculate the five-year gain from getting an MBA at ASU. State any assumption you are asked to make. Explain what factors caused the five-year gain to be higher or lower at ASU than at BYU.

2. Go to the Forbes Web site and calculate the five-year gain from getting an MBA at Harvard. State any assumption you are asked to make. Explain what factors caused the five-year gain to be higher or lower at Harvard than at BYU.

3. The Forbes decision tool considers both out-of-pocket costs and opportunity costs. Give examples of each.

4. The Forbes decision tool also considers the time value of money. Without making specific calculations, explain how the time value of money is likely to differ for the Harvard and ASU alternatives. Remember that the up-front tuition is likely to be much lower at ASU than at Harvard, but the future benefits in terms of salary are likely to be higher at Harvard than ASU. How would these differences affect the time value of money?

5. Is the $45,000 pre-MBA salary relevant to Greg's decision about whether to go to Harvard, ASU, or BYU? Why or why not?

6. Suppose instead that Greg was trying to decide whether to continue with his current career path or get an MBA. Is his current salary relevant to this decision? Why or why not?

Budgetary Planning

YOUR LEARNING OBJECTIVES

After completing this chapter, you should be able to:

LO1   Describe the phases of the planning and control process.

LO2   List the key benefits of budgeting.

LO3   Explain the behavioral effects of budgets and provide guidelines for implementing a budget.

LO4   Describe the major components of the master budget and their interrelationships.

LO5   Prepare the following components of the operating budget:

    a. Sales budget.

    b. Production budget.

    c. Raw materials purchases budget.

    d. Direct labor budget.

    e. Manufacturing overhead budget.

    f. Cost of goods sold budget.

    g. Selling and administrative expense budget.

    h. Budgeted income statement.

LO6   Prepare the cash budget and describe the other financial budgets required to prepare a budgeted balance sheet.

Lecture Presentation–LP9
www.mhhe.com/whitecotton1e

FOCUS COMPANY: Cold Stone Creamery

"Because the world deserves better ice cream."

www.coldstonecreamery.com

Have you ever spent time planning a major event, such as a graduation party, bar or bat mitzvah, or wedding? If so, you probably realize the importance of having a budget to guide your decisions about where to hold the event, how many people to invite, and what food to serve. These and many other decisions affect the cost and success of any event.

Business managers use budgets in a similar way. Rather than budgeting for a one-time event, however, managers use budgets to plan their ongoing operations so they will be able to meet the organization's short-term and long-term objectives. Both profit-oriented and nonprofit organizations use budgets. The only difference is whether their short- and long-term objectives are oriented to earning a profit or reaching some nonprofit objective such as providing education, feeding the poor, or improving health care.

In this chapter, we describe the budgeting process in a company that many of you may be familiar with, Cold Stone Creamery. Founded in 1988 by two ice cream lovers in Tempe, Arizona, Cold Stone Creamery now has more than 1,500 locations in countries around the world including Korea and Japan. The company's employees prepare delicious, custom-made ice cream creations on a piece of cold granite by mixing freshly made ice cream with a wide variety of high-quality ingredients. Consumers may choose one of Cold Stone's best-selling flavors, such as Peanut Butter Cup Perfection or Cheesecake Fantasy, or create their own unique flavor choosing from dozens of mix-ins, such as nuts, candy, cookies, and fruit. A Harvard business student has estimated that the average person would need more than 421 lifetimes to try more than 11.5 million possible Cold Stone Creamery creations—but only by starting on the day he or she was born!

In this chapter, we prepare an entire master budget for a hypothetical Cold Stone Creamery location. In the next chapter, we determine whether Cold Stone Creamery achieved its budget by comparing actual to budgeted results. First, let's cover some basic concepts in budgeting.

Role of budgets in the planning and control cycle

- Planning process
- Benefits of budgeting
- Behavioral effects of budgets
- Components of the master budget

Preparation of the operating budgets

- Sales budget
- Production budget
- Raw materials purchases budget
- Direct labor budget
- Manufacturing overhead budget
- Budgeted cost of goods sold
- Selling and administrative expense budget
- Budgeted income statement

Preparation of the financial budgets

- Cash budget
- Budgeted balance sheet
- Budgeting in non-manufacturing firms

Role of Budgets in the Planning and Control Cycle

Learning Objective 1
Describe the phases of the planning and control process.

Video 9-1
www.mhhe.com/whitecotton1e

In the first chapter of this book, we introduced the four functions of management: planning, organizing, directing/leading, and control. This process, which is illustrated in Exhibit 9.1, is sometimes referred to as the **planning and control cycle**.

Planning is the forward-looking phase of the planning and control process that involves setting long-term objectives and defining short-term tactics that will help to achieve them. Once the plan is in place, managers must begin **organizing**, or arranging for the necessary resources needed to achieve the plan. An important part of the organizing process is the creation of a **budget**, a detailed plan that translates the company's objectives into financial terms. It involves identifying the resources and expenditures that will be required over a limited planning horizon (typically a year), which can be broken into shorter periods (for example, months or quarters). The next step, **directing/leading**, involves all actions managers must take to implement the plan including motivating employees to achieve results. As you will learn shortly, a budget can have either motivating or demotivating effects on behavior, depending on how it is implemented. As the plan is implemented, the managerial accounting system keeps track of the actual results, which are used later in the control process. The **control** function is the backward-looking part of the planning and control cycle. In this phase, managers compare actual to budgeted results to determine whether the objectives set during the planning stage were achieved. If not, managers can take corrective action where necessary. We focus more closely on the control process in Chapter 10 by calculating variances that compare actual to budgeted results.

EXHIBIT 9.1	Functions of Management

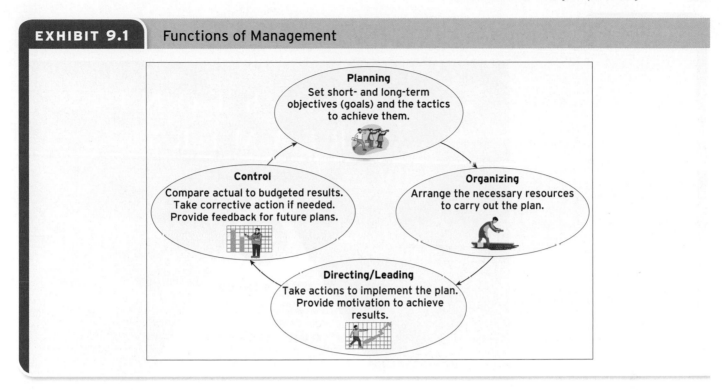

PLANNING PROCESS

The starting point of the planning process is managers' **strategic plan** or vision of what they want the organization to achieve over the long term. The strategic plan is then translated into long-term and short-term objectives, along with the tactics that will be used to achieve those objectives. A **long-term objective** is a specific goal that managers want to achieve over the long term, typically 5 to 10 years. A **short-term objective** is a specific goal that managers need to achieve in the short-run to reach their long-term goals. **Tactics** are the specific actions or mechanisms managers use to achieve the objectives.

For example, assume a company's long-term objective is to gain a 50 percent market share over the next five years. A short-term objective might be to increase sales revenue by 10 percent during the next year. One possible tactic for achieving that goal would be to increase the amount spent on advertising and promotion to generate additional sales.

Consider Cold Stone Creamery's strategic vision, called the "Pyramid of Success 2010," which is shown in Exhibit 9.2. This strategic plan, which was set in 2005, identifies what the company wanted to achieve by the year 2010. The top of the pyramid shows the company's strategic vision, which was to become "the #1 best-selling ice cream brand in America by December 31, 2009." This goal represents a specific long-term objective. To achieve this long-term goal, managers then set their short-term objectives and tactics. Although Cold Stone Creamery's objectives and tactics are not available to the general public (or its competitors), we can get a sense of their nature by examining the other levels of the pyramid.

The pyramid indicates that Cold Stone Creamery's daily purpose was to sell more ice cream, to more people, more often, in more locations so that the Cold Stone community can profit by making people happy. This suggests that the company's short-term objectives should be based on growth rates for sales revenue, profit, the number of new stores opened, and market share. In addition to these financial objectives, Cold Stone's success depends on its ability to introduce appealing new ice cream products and to hire and retain employees who can keep customers happy by providing the "ultimate ice cream experience." Thus, the company's planning and control system should include objectives for new product development, employee training and retention, and customer satisfaction. In Chapter 11, we discuss the importance of developing nonfinancial measures to track performance in these areas.

COACH'S TIP

The terms **budgeted, predicted, estimated, forecasted, anticipated, expected,** and **planned** are used interchangeably to reflect the future-oriented nature of the budgeting process.

| EXHIBIT 9.2 | Cold Stone Creamery's Strategic Vision: Pyramid of Success 2010 |

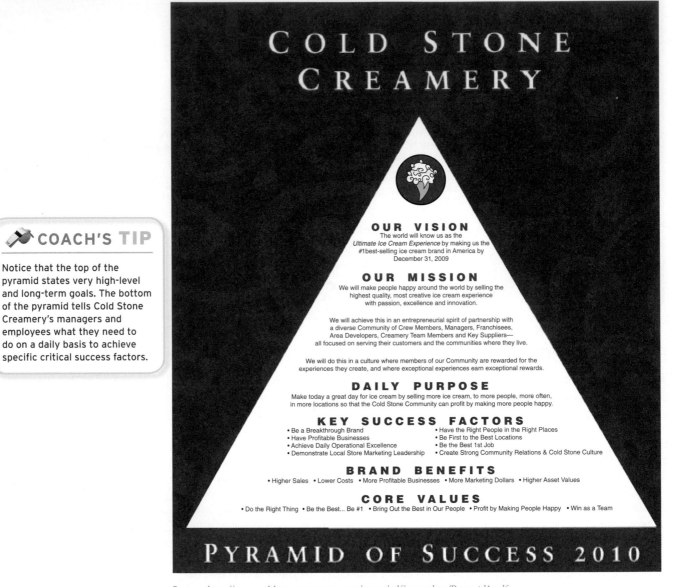

Source: http://www.coldstonecreamery.com/assets/pdf/secondary/Pyramid1.pdf.

BENEFITS OF BUDGETING

Budgeting has several benefits (see Exhibit 9.3). **One of the major advantages of budgeting is that it forces managers to look to the future.** In your own life, you or your parents may have prepared a budget to help save for college, a future vacation, or retirement. In business, budgets force managers to look ahead and address potential problems. For example, a budget can help managers plan to ensure they always have enough cash on hand to pay the company's bills or to avoid running out of inventory during periods of peak demand.

Budgets also play an important communication role within organizations. They provide a mechanism for managers to share expectations and priorities for the future. Because budgets span the entire organization, they also require managers from different functional areas to communicate and coordinate their activities.

EXHIBIT 9.3 | Benefits of Budgeting

Thinking ahead	Communication	Motivation
• Forcing managers to look ahead and state their goals for the future • Providing lead time to solve potential problems	• Communicating management's expectations and priorities • Promoting cooperation and coordination between functional areas of the organization	• Providing motivation for employees to work toward organizational objectives • Providing a benchmark for evaluating performance

Finally, **budgets serve an important role in motivating and rewarding employees**. If a budget is implemented correctly, it should motivate employees to work hard to meet the company's objectives. **Budgets also provide a useful benchmark for evaluating and rewarding employee performance**. We discuss the motivational effects of budgets in the next section; their role in performance evaluation is addressed in the next two chapters.

BEHAVIORAL EFFECTS OF BUDGETS

Although budgets are intended to motivate employees to work hard to achieve the organization's goals, they can sometimes create unintended effects. The way in which managers and employees behave in response to budgets depends, in large part, on how goals and budgets are set. Two considerations are especially critical: the relative difficulty of meeting goals and the degree of employee participation in establishing goals.

In setting budgetary goals, finding the right level of difficulty is important. Research suggests that **budgets that are tight but attainable are more likely to motivate people** than budgets that are either too easy or too difficult to achieve. Think about your own personal goals. If the goal is too easy, you will not have to work very hard to achieve it. If you set your goal too high, however, you may quickly become frustrated and give up. Similarly, managers must try to find the "just-right" level of difficulty in setting budgetary goals so that they have motivating rather than demotivating effects on employee behavior.

Involving employees at all levels of the organization in the budgeting process is also important. **Participative budgeting** allows employees throughout the organization to have input into the budget-setting process. This bottom-up approach to budgeting can be contrasted with a **top-down approach** in which top management sets the budget and imposes it on lower levels of the organization. In general, **a participative approach is more likely to motivate people to work toward an organization's goals than a top-down approach**.

One downside to participative budgeting is that employees may try to build a little extra cushion, or **budget slack**, into their budgets. They can do so by understating expected sales or overstating budgeted expenses, making it more likely that they will look good by coming in under budget for expenses or over budget for revenues. Budgets can also create a "use-it-or-lose-it" mentality that encourages managers to spend their entire budget to avoid a reduction in resources the next budget period. Many of these

> **Learning Objective 3**
> Explain the behavioral effects of budgets and provide guidelines for implementing a budget.

dysfunctional behaviors can be minimized by implementing the following budget-setting guidelines:

- **Use different budgets for planning than for performance evaluation**. Although budget slack can make planning difficult, it provides a way for managers to hedge against uncertainty that may affect their performance evaluation. Some slack can be beneficial, particularly in organizations that face major fluctuations in demand or costs that are beyond the manager's control.
- **Use a continuous, or rolling budget, approach**. Under continuous budgeting, the company maintains a rolling budget that always extends a certain period into the future. When one budget period passes, another is automatically added at the end. This approach keeps managers in continuous planning mode, always looking into the future and helps avoid the budget games that are played at the end of a budget period.
- **Use a zero-based budgeting approach**. Under zero-based budgeting, the entire budget must be constructed from scratch each period rather than starting with the last period's actual results. While time-consuming, it makes managers justify their budget each year.

Spotlight On ETHICS

Playing Budget Games

Managers who are evaluated and rewarded for meeting budgetary goals may engage in game playing. For example, a sales manager who has reached his or her sales quota for the week may try to defer sales to a future period by telling customers to come back later to make their purchase. Managers may even be tempted to postdate orders so that they **appear** to have been made in a different time period. Alternatively, a salesperson who has not met his or her quota may cut prices at the end of the period to increase sales volume and meet the sales goal.

By engaging in these tactics, managers are putting their own self-interest ahead of the organization's objectives. Although the complete elimination of such budget games is difficult to achieve, organizations must try to design their budgets and control systems to minimize these dysfunctional behaviors.

As this discussion indicates, managers must take a variety of behavioral factors into account in designing and implementing a budget system. There is not a "one-size-fits-all" solution to budgeting. The best approach depends on the nature of the business environment, type of organization, and tasks that managers must perform within the organization.

Before continuing, take a moment to make sure you understand the basic principles of budgeting by completing the following Self-Study Practice.

 Self-Study Practice

Which of the following statements is (are) false? You may select more than one answer.

1. Planning is the forward-looking phase of the planning and control cycle; control is the backward-looking phase of the cycle.
2. Short-term objectives are the specific goals that managers would like to achieve; tactics are the specific mechanisms they will use to achieve those goals.
3. Employees are more likely to be motivated by a top-down approach to budgeting than by a participative approach.
4. The creation of budget slack is not a problem for planning purposes, but it may cause problems in evaluating employees' performance.

After you have finished, check your answers with the solutions in the margin.

Solution to Self-Study Practice
Statements 3 and 4 are false.

COMPONENTS OF THE MASTER BUDGET

The **master budget** is a comprehensive set of budgets that covers all phases of an organization's planned activities for a specific period. Within the master budget, individual budgets can be classified as either operating budgets or financial budgets. See Exhibit 9.4 for an illustration of the components of the master budget. Note that each component either is based on or provides input for another component.

Operating budgets cover the organization's planned operating activities for a particular period including expected sales, production, raw materials purchases, direct labor, manufacturing overhead, and selling and administrative expenses. When all of these operating budgets are combined, they form a **budgeted income statement**.

Financial budgets focus on the financial resources needed to support operations including cash receipts and disbursements, capital expenditures, and financing. Note that each of the financial budgets relates in some way either to an asset (for example, cash and capital purchases) or to liabilities and equity (for example, financing activities). Thus, the financial budgets are used to create a **budgeted balance sheet**.

> **Learning Objective 4**
> Describe the major components of the master budget and their interrelationships.

> **COACH'S TIP**
>
> Notice that the sales budget affects almost all other budgets in the master budget. If the sales forecast is wrong, the rest of the master budget will be incorrect.

EXHIBIT 9.4	Components of the Master Budget

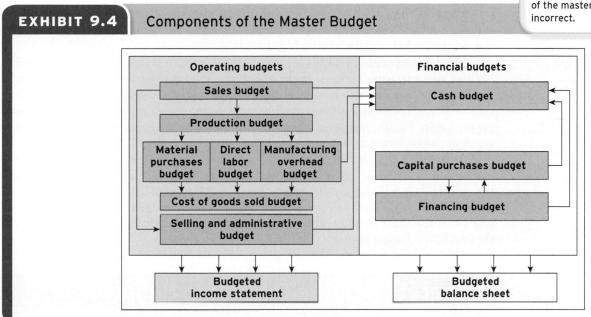

The starting point for preparing the master budget is the **sales budget** or **sales forecast**, which provides an estimate of the number of units to be sold and the total sales revenue to be generated each period. Various sources are used to determine the sales forecast including:

- Actual sales for the preceding period.

- Research on overall industry trends.

- Input from top management about target sales objectives (for example, market share goals).

- Input from research and development about new product introductions, new features of existing products, and so on.

- Planned marketing activities (for example, advertising and sales promotions).

Sales managers use all of these factors to determine their best estimate of future sales, which is reflected in the sales budget.

After the sales budget is set, managers prepare the **production budget** to show how many units must be produced each period. The number of units to be produced may differ from the number of units to be sold depending on the company's **inventory budget**, which shows planned levels of finished goods, work in process, and raw materials inventories at the beginning and end of each period.

Based on the production budget, managers can estimate the materials, labor, and manufacturing overhead costs needed to meet production.

- The **raw materials purchases budget** estimates the amount of raw materials needed to meet production goals given planned levels of raw materials inventory.

- The **direct labor budget** estimates the amount of direct labor needed to meet production needs.

- The **manufacturing overhead budget** estimates how much manufacturing overhead cost will be incurred to support budgeted production.

These manufacturing cost budgets are combined to calculate the **budgeted manufacturing cost per unit**, which is used to determine the **budgeted cost of goods sold**. This cost is calculated by multiplying the budgeted manufacturing cost per unit by budgeted units sales.

Based on the sales budget, managers can also prepare a **selling and administrative expense budget**, which identifies how much should be spent on selling and administrative costs to achieve planned sales levels.

All of the operating budgets are combined to form a budgeted income statement. Each of the operating budgets, starting with the sales budget, becomes a line item in the budgeted income statement. Managers then subtract the budgeted cost of goods sold, which incorporates all budgeted manufacturing costs, to arrive at the **budgeted gross margin**. Finally, managers subtract budgeted selling and administrative expenses to arrive at the budgeted operating profit (before taxes).

Note in Exhibit 9.4 that all operating budgets are connected in some way to one or more financial budgets. The primary financial budget that we prepare in this chapter is the **cash budget**, which provides information about budgeted cash receipts and disbursements. Based on the cash budget and the other financial budgets, we can prepare a **budgeted balance sheet** to summarize the company's assets, liabilities, and owners' equity at the end of the budget period.

Preparation of the Operating Budgets

In this section, we prepare the operating budgets for a hypothetical Cold Stone Creamery location. Although we make a number of simplifying assumptions and the numbers do not necessarily represent Cold Stone's actual cost of operations, the objective of this example is to show the structure of the various operating budgets and how they relate to one another.

SALES BUDGET

Learning Objective 5a
Prepare the sales budget.

The starting point for the master budget is the sales forecast or sales budget. The sales department typically provides this information based on a variety of sources, including prior sales, industry trends, and planned marketing activities.

Budgeted sales revenue is calculated by multiplying the number of units expected to be sold by the budgeted sales price. See Exhibit 9.5 for Cold Stone Creamery's sales budget for each quarter of 2011.

Notice that budgeted unit sales are high during the summer months and low during the winter months. The budgeted sales price is expected to remain constant at an average of $5 per unit for total budgeted sales revenue of $425,000.

EXHIBIT 9.5	Sales Budget				

	Quarter 1 Jan.–Mar.	Quarter 2 Apr.–June	Quarter 3 July–Sept.	Quarter 4 Oct.–Dec.	Yearly Total
Budgeted unit sales	15,000	20,000	27,000	23,000	85,000
Budgeted sales price	× $ 5.00	× $ 5.00	× $ 5.00	× $ 5.00	× $ 5.00
Budgeted sales revenue	$75,000	$100,000	$135,000	$115,000	$425,000

PRODUCTION BUDGET

The production budget is based on the sales budget and the amount of inventory the company wants to have on hand at the beginning and end of each period. If the company is planning to build inventory, production needs to be more than sales. If the company is planning to reduce its inventory, production should be less than sales. The relationship between budgeted production, sales, and beginning and ending inventory is summarized in the following formula:

Learning Objective 5b
Prepare the production budget.

$$\text{Budgeted Production Units} = \text{Budgeted Unit Sales} + \text{Budgeted Ending Finished Goods Inventory} - \text{Budgeted Beginning Finished Goods Inventory}$$

In the past, manufacturing companies held substantial inventories of finished goods inventory, which created a marked difference between the sales budget and the production budget. Today, however, companies such as Dell and Nike are moving toward a make-to-order approach in which the final product is manufactured to fill a specific customer order. In these companies, the production and sales budget are virtually the same.

Cold Stone Creamery is a make-to-order company that produces its ice cream creations at the customer's request. Thus, the company holds virtually no finished goods inventory except the "grab and go" containers that Cold Stone stocks for customers who want to enjoy a frozen creation at home. Traditional manufacturing companies maintain a much larger finished goods inventory that acts as a buffer between expected sales and production. To make our example more consistent with that of a traditional manufacturing company, we assume that **Cold Stone Creamery maintains an ending finished goods inventory equal to 5 percent of the current period's budgeted sales**. See Exhibit 9.6 for the resulting production budget based on this assumption and the sales budget from Exhibit 9.5.

> **COACH'S TIP**
>
> Today, many service businesses and manufacturing companies produce their products and services to order. These companies have no finished goods inventory, so the sales budget and the production budget are identical.

EXHIBIT 9.6	Production Budget				

	Quarter 1 Jan.–Mar.	Quarter 2 Apr.–June	Quarter 3 July–Sept.	Quarter 4 Oct.–Dec.	Yearly Total
Budgeted unit sales (from Exhibit 9.5)	15,000	20,000	27,000	23,000	85,000
+ Budgeted ending inventory 5% of current period budgeted sales	+ 750*	+ 1,000	+ 1,350	+ 1,150	+ 1,150
− Budgeted beginning inventory	− 900†	− 750	− 1,000	− 1,350	− 900
Budgeted production	14,850	20,250	27,350	22,800	85,250

* Ending inventory for quarter 1 = 15,000 × 5% = 750
† Beginning inventory for quarter 1 is assumed to be 900 units

As expected, production is budgeted to be highest during the summer months when budgeted sales are at their highest. Notice that the ending finished goods inventory is calculated as 5 percent of the current period sales. In quarter 1, ending inventory is budgeted at 750 units (15,000 units $\times$ 5 percent). This ending inventory value becomes the beginning inventory value for the next quarter.

RAW MATERIALS PURCHASES BUDGET

Learning Objective 5c
Prepare the raw materials purchases budget.

Next managers must budget for the purchase of raw materials. This budget depends on budgeted production needs and on planned levels of beginning and ending raw materials inventory. The formula follows:

$$\begin{array}{c}\text{Budgeted} \\ \text{Raw Materials} \\ \text{Purchases}\end{array} = \begin{array}{c}\text{Budgeted} \\ \text{Production} \\ \text{Units}\end{array} + \begin{array}{c}\text{Budgeted Ending} \\ \text{Raw Materials} \\ \text{Inventory}\end{array} - \begin{array}{c}\text{Budgeted Beginning} \\ \text{Raw Materials} \\ \text{Inventory}\end{array}$$

COACH'S TIP

Notice that the formula for budgeted raw materials purchases is very similar to the one for budgeted production. The only difference is that it starts with production (not sales) and adjusts for beginning and ending raw materials inventory.

In these formulas, always add the ending inventory and subtract the beginning inventory.

Let's apply this formula to the primary ingredients used to make ice cream: milk, cream, and sugar. The superpremium ice cream made at Cold Stone Creamery contains a relatively high proportion of cream (as opposed to milk) compared to most commercially manufactured ice cream. The specific mix of ingredients is what creates the ice cream's rich and creamy taste and its relatively high price (because cream is more expensive than milk). In reality, Cold Stone Creamery would prepare a separate budget for each of these major ingredients. However, for simplicity, we combine the purchase of milk, cream, and sugar into a single budget. We assume that each Cold Stone creation requires a total of 10 ounces of milk, cream, and sugar, and that the average price of this ingredient mix is $0.05 per ounce. Because of the company's emphasis on freshness and quality, managers want to keep the inventory of raw materials to a minimum. For illustration purposes, we assume that Cold Stone Creamery plans its purchase of raw materials so that the ending inventory equals 3 percent of **next period's** production needs. See Exhibit 9.7 for Cold Stone Creamery's raw materials purchases budget based on these assumptions.

EXHIBIT 9.7	**Raw Materials Purchases Budget (milk, sugar, and cream)**				

	Quarter 1 Jan.–Mar.	Quarter 2 Apr.–June	Quarter 3 July–Sept.	Quarter 4 Oct.–Dec.	Yearly Total
Budgeted production (from Exhibit 9.6)	14,850	20,250	27,350	22,800	85,250
Materials requirement (1 per unit)	$\times$ 10 oz.	$\times$ 10 oz.	$\times$ 10 oz.	$\times$ 10 oz.	$\times$ 10 oz.
Total material needed for production	148,500	202,500	273,500	228,000	852,500
+ Planned ending inventory (3% of next month's production needs)	+ 6,075*	+ 8,205	+ 6,840	+ 3,510‡	+ 3,510
− Planned beginning inventory (3% of current month's production needs)	− 4,455†	− 6,075	− 8,205	− 6,840	− 4,455
Total purchases of raw materials	150,120	204,630	272,135	224,670	851,555
Average cost per ounce	$\times$ $ 0.05	$\times$ $ 0.05	$\times$ $ 0.05	$\times$ $ 0.05	$\times$ $ 0.05
Budgeted cost of raw materials purchases	$ 7,506	$ 10,232	$ 13,607	$ 11,234	$ 42,578

* Ending inventory for quarter 1 = 202,500 $\times$ 3% = 6,075
† Beginning inventory for quarter 1 = 148,500 $\times$ 3% = 4,455
‡ Ending inventory for quarter 4 is assumed to be 3,510 ounces, but cannot be determined based on information given

Notice that raw materials purchases are based on budgeted **production** (not sales). We multiply budgeted production by the materials requirement per unit (10 ounces) to find the total amount of materials needed for production. Then we add the budgeted ending raw materials inventory and subtract the beginning raw materials inventory to determine how much ice cream to purchase. In this case, the ending inventory is based on 3 percent of **next period's** production needs, so the first quarter ending inventory equals 3 percent of second quarter production needs. This ending value of inventory becomes the beginning inventory for the next period.

Cold Stone Creamery would construct similar budgets for all other raw materials including the various candies and nuts used to make its ice cream creations. For this example, we assume the budgeted cost of these additional ingredients is about 40 percent of the cost of the milk, sugar, and cream (see Exhibit 9.8).

EXHIBIT 9.8	**Total Raw Materials Purchases**				
	Quarter 1 Jan.–Mar.	Quarter 2 Apr.–June	Quarter 3 July–Sept.	Quarter 4 Oct.–Dec.	Yearly Total
Total purchases of milk, sugar, and cream	$ 7,506	$10,232	$13,607	$11,233	$42,578
Total purchases of mix-in ingredients*	3,002	4,093	5,443	4,493	17,031
Total cost of raw materials purchases	$10,508	$14,325	$19,050	$15,726	$59,609

* Assumed to be 40 percent of the cost of milk, sugar, and cream

DIRECT LABOR BUDGET

Next we can determine how much direct labor must be hired to support budgeted production levels. We assume each Cold Stone Creamery creation requires 0.10 hour (6 minutes) of labor time including the time needed to take customers' orders, mix and serve the ice cream, and take customers' payments, as well as cleanup time and employee breaks. See Exhibit 9.9 for the resulting direct labor budget assuming an average labor rate of $8 per hour.

Learning Objective 5d
Prepare the direct labor budget.

EXHIBIT 9.9	**Direct Labor Budget**				
	Quarter 1 Jan.–Mar.	Quarter 2 Apr.–June	Quarter 3 July–Sept.	Quarter 4 Oct.–Dec.	Yearly Total
Budgeted production (from Exhibit 9.6)	14,850	20,250	27,350	22,800	85,250
Direct labor requirements (.010 hour per unit)	× 0.10 hr.	× 0.10 hr.	× 0.10 hr.	× 0.10 hr.	× 0.10 hr.
Total direct labor hours required	1,485	2,025	2,735	2,280	8,525
Direct labor cost per hour	× $ 8.00	× $ 8.00	× $ 8.00	× $ 8.00	× $ 8.00
Total direct labor cost	$11,880	$16,200	$21,880	$18,240	$68,200

MANUFACTURING OVERHEAD BUDGET

Next we can prepare the manufacturing overhead budget. Although Cold Stone Creamery is not a traditional manufacturing company, it does create and serve a physical product. Thus, we define manufacturing overhead as all costs other than direct materials and direct labor that the company must incur to make the ice cream and serve it to customers. This includes the costs of rent, depreciation on equipment, and other indirect costs such as utilities and paper supplies. It does not include selling costs, such as advertising and promotion, or administrative costs for legal counsel, accounting services, insurance, franchise fees, and so on. These nonmanufacturing costs are included in the selling and administrative expense budget.

Learning Objective 5e
Prepare the manufacturing overhead budget.

EXHIBIT 9.10 | Manufacturing Overhead Budget

	Quarter 1 Jan.–Mar.	Quarter 2 Apr.–June	Quarter 3 July–Sept.	Quarter 4 Oct.–Dec.	Yearly Total
Budgeted production	14,850	20,250	27,350	22,800	85,250
Variable overhead rate	× $ 0.10	× $ 0.10	× $ 0.10	× $ 0.10	× $ 0.10
Total variable manufacturing overhead cost	$ 1,485	$ 2,025	$ 2,735	$ 2,280	$ 8,525
Fixed manufacturing overhead	8,525	8,525	8,525	8,525	34,100
Total budgeted manufacturing overhead cost	$10,010	$10,550	$11,260	$10,805	$42,625

Some manufacturing overhead costs, such as those for indirect materials and paper supplies, vary with the number of units produced. Other costs, such as those for rent and depreciation, are incurred regardless of the number of units produced. We assume Cold Stone Creamery's variable manufacturing overhead cost is $0.10 per unit produced and the fixed manufacturing overhead cost is $8,525 per quarter. Refer to Exhibit 9.10 for the resulting manufacturing overhead cost budget.

Notice that the variable manufacturing overhead cost is highest during the summer when production is highest, but fixed manufacturing overhead cost is constant each period.

BUDGETED COST OF GOODS SOLD

Budgeted cost of goods sold should reflect all costs required to manufacture the product including raw materials, direct labor, and manufacturing overhead. See Exhibit 9.11 for the calculation of the budgeted cost of each unit produced based on the manufacturing cost budgets in Exhibits 9.8 through 9.10.

EXHIBIT 9.11 | Budgeted Manufacturing Cost per Unit

Budgeted cost of milk, sugar and cream (10 ounces × $0.05 per ounce)	$0.50
Budgeted cost of mix-in ingredients (40% of the cost of milk, sugar and cream)	0.20
Budgeted direct labor (.10 hours × $8.00 per hour)	0.80
Budgeted variable manufacturing overhead ($0.10 per unit)	0.10
Budgeted fixed manufacturing overhead ($34,100 per year/85,250 units produced)	0.40
Budgeted manufacturing cost per unit	$2.00

Learning Objective 5f
Prepare the cost of goods sold budget.

Notice that all variable manufacturing costs were calculated based on the variable manufacturing overhead cost per unit, but fixed manufacturing overhead cost was calculated based on the total annual cost and yearly production. Fixed manufacturing overhead costs do not change with production levels. Calculating the fixed manufacturing overhead cost on a yearly basis avoids fluctuations in average unit cost due to seasonal changes in production levels.

When we multiply the budgeted manufacturing cost of $2.00 by budgeted units sales, we arrive at budgeted cost of goods sold (Exhibit 9.12).

EXHIBIT 9.12 | Budget Cost of Goods Sold

	Quarter 1 Jan.–Mar.	Quarter 2 Apr.–June	Quarter 3 July–Sept.	Quarter 4 Oct.–Dec.	Yearly Total
Budgeted unit sales (from Exhibit 9.5)	15,000	20,000	27,000	23,000	85,000
Budgeted manufacturing cost per unit	× $ 2.00	× $ 2.00	× $ 2.00	× $ 2.00	× $ 2.00
Budgeted cost of goods sold	$30,000	$40,000	$54,000	$46,000	$170,000

Notice that budgeted cost of goods sold is based on the number of units expected to be sold (not produced). The budgeted cost of units produced but not sold will appear on the budgeted balance sheet as Finished Goods Inventory.

SELLING AND ADMINISTRATIVE EXPENSE BUDGET

The last operating budget we need to prepare is the selling and administrative expense budget, which includes all costs related to selling the product (such as advertising and promotion) and managing the business (such as franchise fees, legal counsel, accounting services, and insurance). We assume that Cold Stone Creamery's selling costs are budgeted at 5 percent of sales revenue. Fixed administrative expenses are estimated to be $10,000 per quarter. The resulting selling and administrative expense budget is shown in Exhibit 9.13.

> **Learning Objective 5g**
> Prepare the selling and administrative expense budget.

EXHIBIT 9.13   Selling and Administrative Expense Budget

	Quarter 1 Jan.–Mar.	Quarter 2 Apr.–June	Quarter 3 July–Sept.	Quarter 4 Oct.–Dec.	Yearly Total
Budgeted sales revenue (from Exhibit 9.5)	$75,000	$100,000	$135,000	$115,000	$425,000
5% of sales revenue	× $ 0.05	× $ 0.05	× $ 0.05	× $ 0.05	× $ 0.05
Variable selling expenses	3,750	5,000	6,750	5,750	21,250
Fixed administrative expenses	10,000	10,000	10,000	10,000	40,000
Budgeted selling and administrative expense	$13,750	$ 15,000	$ 16,750	$ 15,750	$ 61,250

BUDGETED INCOME STATEMENT

Finally, we can combine all of the operating budgets to form a budgeted income statement for Cold Stone Creamery (Exhibit 9.14).

> **Learning Objective 5h**
> Prepare the budgeted income statement.

EXHIBIT 9.14   Budgeted Income Statement

COLD STONE CREAMERY
Budgeted Income Statement
For the Year Ended December 31, 2011

	Quarter 1 Jan.–Mar.	Quarter 2 Apr.–June	Quarter 3 July–Sept.	Quarter 4 Oct.–Dec.	Yearly Total
Budgeted sales revenue (from Exhibit 9.5)	$75,000	$100,000	$135,000	$115,000	$425,000
Less: Budgeted cost of good sold (from Exhibit 9.12)	30,000	40,000	54,000	46,000	170,000
Budgeted gross margin	45,000	60,000	81,000	69,000	255,000
Less: Budgeted selling and administrative expenses (from Exhibit 9.13)	13,750	15,000	16,750	15,750	61,250
Budgeted operating income	$31,250	$ 45,000	$ 64,250	$ 53,250	$193,750

Before you move to the financial budgets, take a moment to make sure you understand the key relationships among the operating budgets by completing the following Self-Study Practice.

Self-Study Practice

1. Taylor Made's sales forecast for the next four quarters follows:

	Quarter 1	Quarter 2	Quarter 3	Quarter 4
Sales forecast (units)	12,000	14,000	15,000	18,000

If the company wants to maintain a finished goods inventory equal to 20 percent of sales for the next quarter, how many units should it produce during the second quarter?

2. Calico Coat Company's production budget follows:

	Quarter 1	Quarter 2	Quarter 3	Quarter 4
Budgeted production (units)	15,000	13,000	14,000	12,000

Each unit requires 5 yards of raw materials at a cost of $3 per yard. The company plans its raw materials purchases so that ending raw materials inventory equals 10 percent of the current quarter's production needs. At the beginning of the first quarter, 5,000 yards of materials were on hand.

What is the budgeted cost of raw materials purchases for the first quarter?

After you have finished, check your answers with the solutions in the margin.

Preparation of the Financial Budgets

As mentioned earlier, the financial budgets focus on the financial resources needed to support the company's operations including cash receipts and disbursements, capital purchases, and financing. Take a moment to review the relationship between the financial budgets and the operating budgets by reviewing Exhibit 9.4 on page 329. In this section, we concentrate on two financial budgets, the cash budget and the budgeted balance sheet.

CASH BUDGET

Learning Objective 6
Prepare the cash budget and describe the other financial budgets required to prepare a budgeted balance sheet.

The cash budget helps managers plan ahead to make certain they have enough cash on hand to meet their operating needs. It also helps them determine whether they need to borrow money to finance operations or whether they should invest excess cash to earn interest.

The cash budget is a future-oriented version of the statement of cash flows, which summarizes the amount of cash flowing into and out of the business during a given period of time. In this chapter, we focus primarily on the cash flows that arise from operating activities, which are directly related to the operating budgets described previously. The only financing activity we consider is the potential need for a short-term bank loan to maintain a minimum cash balance. Chapter 12 provides additional information about cash flows that stem from investing or other financing activities.

The basic form of the cash budget follows:

Beginning Cash Balance + Budgeted Cash Collections − Budgeted Cash Payments +/− Cash Borrowed or Repaid = Ending Cash Balance

Budgeted cash collections are based on the sales budget, while budgeted cash payments are based on all of the operating expense budgets including the raw materials purchases, direct labor, manufacturing overhead, and selling and administrative expense budgets. Remember, however, that sales revenue is not the same as cash. Sales are recognized when revenue is earned, not when cash is received. Similarly, expenses are recorded when incurred, which may not correspond to the time that cash is paid.

The first step in preparing the cash budget is to calculate budgeted cash collections. In reality, most of Cold Stone Creamery's customers pay with cash or credit card. Credit card transactions are converted to cash almost instantaneously less a transaction fee paid to the credit card company. But many businesses make sales "on account" and allow customers to pay weeks or even months later.

To illustrate how to budget for cash collections over multiple budget periods, let's take a closer look at the last quarter of Cold Stone Creamery's budget period. Assume that the fourth quarter budgeted sales revenue of $115,000 (from Exhibit 9.5) is broken down by month as follows:

	October	November	December
Budgeted sales revenue	$60,000	$45,000	$10,000

For purposes of illustration, assume that only 40 percent of Cold Stone's revenue is from cash sales. The other 60 percent is from sales on credit, which is collected as follows:

- 75 percent of credit sales collected in the month of sale.
- 25 percent of credit sales collected in the month following the sale.

Assume September sales were $35,000. The portion of September sales collected **during** October would be $5,250 ($35,000 × 60 percent on credit × 25 percent collected in the month following the sale). See Exhibit 9.15 for budgeted cash collections for October, November, and December.

EXHIBIT 9.15	**Budgeted Cash Collections**		

	October	November	December
Budgeted sales revenue	$60,000	$45,000	$10,000
Cash sales (40% of budgeted sales)	24,000	18,000	4,000
Credit sales (60% of budgeted sales)			
Collected in month of sale (75%)	27,000	20,250	4,500
Collected the following month (25%)	5,250	9,000	6,750
Budgeted cash collections	$56,250	$47,250	$15,250

October's cash sales equal 40 percent of budgeted sales revenue ($60,000 × 40% = $24,000). The remaining 60 percent of sales is on credit, some of which will be collected during October and the remainder during November. The portion of October's credit sales that will be collected **during** October is $27,000 ($60,000 × 60% × 75%). The remaining 25 percent of October's credit sales is budgeted to be collected in November ($60,000 × 60% × 25% = $9,000). Similarly, a portion of November's credit sales will be collected during December.

The second step in calculating the cash budget is to prepare a schedule of cash outflows, or payments, for operating expenses. To do so, we need to know when Cold Stone Creamery pays for items such a raw materials, direct labor, manufacturing overhead, and selling and administrative expense, which may not correspond to the period in which these expenses are incurred.

To continue our Cold Stone Creamery example, assume that budgeted raw material purchases for the fourth quarter of the year (from Exhibit 9.8) are reported by month as follows:

	October	November	December
Raw materials purchases	$6,000	$6,000	$3,726

Assume the following:

- 20 percent of raw materials are paid for during the month of purchase.
- 80 percent of raw materials are paid for in the month following purchase.
- September raw materials purchases were $20,000.

During October, Cold Stone would pay for 80 percent of the raw materials that it purchased in September ($20,000 × 80% = $16,000) plus 20 percent of the purchases made in October ($6,000 × 20 percent = $1,200). Similar calculations would be made for November and December, as follows:

	October	November	December
Raw materials purchases	$ 6,000	$6,000	$3,726
20% paid for in month of purchase	1,200	1,200	745
80% paid for in the following month	16,000	4,800	4,800
Cash paid for raw materials	$17,200	$6,000	$5,545

Cold Stone would make similar calculations for all other operating expenses including direct labor, manufacturing overhead, and selling and administrative expenses. For simplicity, we assume Cold Stone pays for all other operating costs during the month incurred.

The final adjustment needed to calculate cash payments is to adjust for any depreciation expense that is included in the operating expense budgets. As you learned in Chapter 8, depreciation is a noncash expense. Although depreciation expense was included in the operating budgets and budgeted income statement, it should be **excluded** from the cash budget. Assume that the operating budgets described previously included $1,000 in depreciation expense per month. This amount needs to be deducted from the budgeted operating expenses to calculate budgeted cash payments. See Exhibit 9.16 for budgeted cash payments for October, November, and December.

EXHIBIT 9.16   Budgeted Cash Payments

	October	November	December
Cash paid for raw materials	$17,200	$ 6,000	$ 5,545
Cash paid for direct labor	7,000	6,000	5,240
Manufacturing overhead	3,305	3,500	4,000
Selling and administrative expenses	6,000	5,000	4,750
Less depreciation (noncash expense)	(1,000)	(1,000)	(1,000)
Budgeted cash payments	$32,505	$19,500	$18,535

The final step in preparing the cash budget is to combine the cash collections and cash payments into the overall cash budget to determine their effect on the balance in the Cash account. The cash budget allows Cold Stone managers to determine whether they will have enough cash to pay their obligations or whether they need to borrow money to finance their operations.

Assume the following additional information, which is reflected in the cash budget in Exhibit 9.17.

- At the beginning of October, the balance in the Cash account was $50,000.

- Cold Stone Creamery has an agreement with the bank that it can borrow and repay cash as needed to maintain a minimum cash balance of $50,000. At the beginning of the year, the company had borrowed $100,000 to finance the start-up of the business.

- By the end of the third quarter (beginning of October), the company still owed $50,000 on this revolving line of credit.

EXHIBIT 9.17 Cash Budget

	October	November	December
Beginning cash balance	$50,000	$50,000	$51,495
Plus: Budgeted cash collections (from Exhibit 9.15)	56,250	47,250	15,250
Less: Budgeted cash payments (from Exhibit 9.16)	(32,505)	(19,500)	(18,535)
Cash balance before financing	73,745	77,750	48,210
Cash borrowed (repaid)	(23,745)*	(26,255)†	1,790‡
Ending cash balance	$50,000	$51,495	$50,000

* Cash surplus of $23,745 used to pay down $50,000 loan.
† Unpaid balance on loan is $50,000 − $23,745 = $26,255.
‡ Need to borrow $1,790 (50,000 − $48,210) in December.

In October, budgeted cash collections were more than cash payments, allowing Cold Stone Creamery to pay off $23,745 of the bank loan and still maintain a $50,000 cash balance. The amount owed to the bank after October is $26,255 ($50,000 − $23,745).

During November, Cold Stone expects to generate enough excess cash to pay off the remainder of the loan with enough left over to increase the cash balance to $51,495 ($77,750 − $26,255). Notice that the cash balance at the end of November is the beginning balance in December's cash budget.

In December, cash collections ($15,250) were less than cash payments ($18,535). The balance in the Cash account before financing is $48,210, so Cold Stone needs to borrow $1,790 to maintain a $50,000 minimum cash balance. It would repay this amount in January if cash collections exceed cash payments.

In this example, we assumed that the excess cash generated each month would be used to pay down an existing operating loan. Managers often need short-term loans to finance their start-up operations or to respond to seasonal fluctuations in sales revenue.

In other situations, managers may decide to invest excess cash in short- or long-term investments. For example, if the cash balance continues to build, Cold Stone's managers may decide to invest some of it in an interest-bearing certificate of deposit (CD). Before they tie up cash in this type of investment, managers must be able to predict or forecast how much cash they will need in the coming months. The cash budget is crucial for helping managers plan their short-term financing and investing needs.

The ending balance of cash along with other assets, liabilities, and equity accounts appears on the budgeted balance sheet, which is discussed next. First, take the following Self-Study Practice to make certain you can calculate cash collections and payments.

⚡ Self-Study Practice

1. Big Ben Clock Company's budget for first two months of the year included the following:

	January	February
Budgeted sales revenue	$120,000	$140,000
Budgeted raw material purchases	80,000	70,000
All other expenses	20,000	30,000

Other information follows:

- 60 percent of sales are received in cash. The remaining 40 percent of sales is on credit, collected as follows: 30 percent in month of sale, 65 percent the following month, 5 percent never collected.

- 80 percent of raw materials purchases is paid for in the month of purchase and the remainder in the following month.

- All other expenses are paid in cash with the exception of $5,000 in monthly depreciation expense.

Based on this information, calculate Big Ben's budgeted cash collections and payments for February.

After you have finished, check your answers with the solutions in the margin.

BUDGETED BALANCE SHEET

The final budget that we discuss is the **budgeted balance sheet**. Just as the operating budgets were combined into a pro forma (forward-looking) income statement, the financial budgets can be combined into a pro forma (forward-looking) balance sheet.

Several of the budgets prepared in the previous sections affect the year-end balance sheet as summarized here:

- The $50,000 ending cash balance (Exhibit 9.17) would appear as an asset on the budgeted balance sheet.

- Budgeted sales revenue for December was $10,000, 60% of which was on credit (Exhibit 9.15). Only 75% of credit sales are collected in the month of sales, leaving 25% uncollected at the end the month. Therefore accounts receivable on December 31 is $1,500 (10,000 × 60% × 25%).

- Any raw materials, work in process, or finished goods on hand at the end of the year would be shown as inventory on the balance sheet. The production budget (Exhibit 9.6) showed 1,150 units in finished goods inventory at year-end. These units would be valued at the budgeted manufacturing cost per unit of $2, resulting in Finished Goods Inventory of $2,300 (1,150 × $2).

- The raw materials purchases budget (Exhibit 9.7) showed 3,510 ounces of raw materials on hand at the end of the year. This Raw Materials Inventory would be valued at the $0.05 purchase price per ounce, or $175.50 (3,510 × $0.05).

Solution to Self-Study Practice

Cash Collections

		February
February cash sales	60% × $140,000	$ 84,000
February credit collections	40% × 30% × $140,000	16,800
January credit collections	40% × 65% × $120,000	31,200
Total cash collections		$132,000

Cash Payments

		February
February raw materials purchases	80% × $70,000	$56,000
January raw materials purchases	20% × $80,000	16,000
Cash paid for other expenses	30,000 − $5,000	25,000
Total cash payments		$97,000

- Raw materials purchased but not yet paid for would appear as a liability on the year-end balance sheet. The cash payment budget (Exhibit 9.16) showed that 80 percent of December's raw materials purchases of $3,726 would not be paid until January. The balance owed to the supplier (80% × $3,726 = $2,980.80) would appear as Accounts Payable on the year-end balance sheet.

- The budgeted net income of $193,750 (Exhibit 9.14) would flow through to the Owner's Equity account. Assuming a beginning balance of $67,455 and no dividends or owner withdrawals, the balance on December 31 would be budgeted at $261,205 ($193,750 + $67,455).

- Although not described here, most companies prepare a capital purchases budget and financing budget that would affect other elements of the budgeted balance sheet such as long-term assets and long-term liabilities.

See Exhibit 9.18 for Cold Stone Creamery's budgeted balance sheet.

EXHIBIT 9.18	Budgeted Balance Sheet

COLD STONE CREAMERY
Budgeted Balance Sheet
December 31, 2011

Assets		Liabilities	
Cash	$ 50,000	Accounts Payable	$ 2,981
Accounts Receivable	1,500	Short-Term Bank Loan	1,790
Raw Materials Inventory	176	Long-Term Liabilities	200,000
Finished Goods Inventory	2,300	Total Liabilities	$204,771
Long-Term Assets	412,000	Owner's Equity	261,205
Total Assets	$465,976	Total Liabilities and Owner's Equity	$465,976

The most important lesson to take away from the budgeted balance sheet is that it is based on many other financial and operating budgets that were prepared throughout the budget period. The end result of the budgeting process is a set of pro forma financial statements, including a budgeted income statement, statement of cash flows, and budgeted balance sheet. Each of these budgets provides managers valuable information to use for planning, managing operations, and making investing and financing decisions.

BUDGETING IN NONMANUFACTURING FIRMS

As noted at the beginning of this chapter, all organizations can benefit from budgeting regardless of whether it is a for-profit or not-for-profit business, a service firm, merchandiser, or manufacturer. However, the types of budgets prepared change depending on the type of firm.

Although Cold Stone Creamery is not a traditional manufacturing company, it does make and serve a physical product. In contrast, a service business such as a real estate company, law firm, or hair salon does not create and store a physical product. Thus, service firms do not need to prepare production budgets, inventory budgets, or manufacturing overhead budgets, but they do need to prepare budgets to predict sales revenue, labor costs, supplies, and other nonmanufacturing expenses such as commissions and advertising.

Budgets for merchandising firms also differ from both manufacturing and service firms. Recall that a merchandising company purchases finished goods for resale. As such, one of the primary operating budgets a merchandiser needs to prepare is the merchandise purchases budget. This budget is very similar to the raw materials purchases budget in Exhibit 9.7. However, instead of considering production needs and raw materials inventory, the merchandise purchases budget is based on budgeted sales and the need to maintain adequate levels of finished goods inventory as follows:

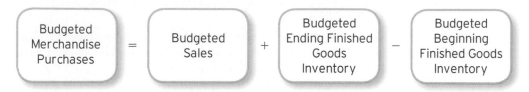

The other major difference between merchandising and manufacturing firms' budgets is that merchandising firms do not have raw materials, direct labor, or manufacturing overhead expense budgets.

DEMONSTRATION CASE A

Operating Budgets

Sky High Parachute Company manufactures and sells parachutes to adventure companies. The company's sales forecast for the coming year follows:

	Quarter 1	Quarter 2	Quarter 3	Quarter 4
Budgeted sales (units)	40,000	35,000	45,000	50,000

Other budgeted information follows:

- The budgeted sales price for each parachute is $1,000.
- The company budgets production so that ending finished goods inventory equals 10 percent of the next quarter's budgeted sales.
- Each parachute requires 20 square yards of a specialty material that costs $15 per square yard.
- The company purchases raw materials so that 10 percent of each quarter's production needs are left over at the end of the quarter to be used as beginning inventory in the next quarter. At the beginning of the first quarter, 70,000 square yards of material were on hand.
- Each parachute requires 15 hours of direct labor at a rate of $12 per hour.
- Manufacturing overhead costs are budgeted at $1 million per quarter plus $50 per unit produced.
- Selling and administrative expenses are budgeted at $500,000 per quarter plus 10 percent of total sales revenue.

Required:

Prepare the following operating budgets for quarters 1–3. (You do not have enough information to prepare all of the budgets for quarter 4.)

1. Sales budget.
2. Production budget.
3. Raw materials purchases budget.
4. Direct labor budget.
5. Manufacturing overhead budget.
6. Selling and administrative expense budget.

See page 345 for solution.

DEMONSTRATION CASE B

Cash Budget

Assume that Sky High Parachute Company's budgeted income statement is as follows:

	Quarter 1	Quarter 2	Quarter 3	Quarter 4
Budgeted sales revenue	$40,000,000	$35,000,000	$45,000,000	$50,000,000
Budgeted cost of goods sold	15,600,000	13,650,000	17,550,000	19,500,000
Budgeted gross margin	24,400,000	21,350,000	27,450,000	30,500,000
Budgeted selling and administrative expenses	4,500,000	4,000,000	5,000,000	5,500,000
Budgeted income from operations	$19,900,000	$17,350,000	$22,450,000	$25,000,000

Budgeted sales revenue is collected as follows:

- 60 percent of sales revenue is collected in cash.
- The remainder of sales is on credit and is collected as follows:
  - During the quarter of sale, 35 percent.
  - During the quarter following the sale, 60 percent.
  - Uncollected, 5 percent.

Cost of goods sold (manufacturing costs) consists of the following:

- Materials purchases represent 70 percent of cost of goods sold. The company pays for 40 percent of materials during the quarter of purchase and the remainder the next quarter.
- The remaining 30 percent of cost of goods sold is made up of direct labor and manufacturing overhead including $400,000 in depreciation (a noncash expense). All of the cash disbursements for direct labor and overhead are paid during the quarter incurred.
- Selling and administrative expenses are paid in the quarter after they are incurred.

Required:

Prepare the following schedules for quarters 2, 3, and 4.

1. Cash collections.
2. Cash payments.
3. Cash budget.

Note: You do not have enough information to prepare the cash budget for quarter 1, so assume its ending cash balance is $500,000.

See page 346 for solution.

CHAPTER SUMMARY

Describe the phases of the planning and control process. p. 324   LO1

- Planning is the forward-looking phase of the managerial process. It involves setting long- and short-term objectives and identifying the tactics that will be used to achieve them.
- Organizing involves arranging for the necessary resources needed to achieve the plan including the preparation of a budget.
- Directing/leading is the action phase of the managerial process. It involves implementing the objectives developed in the planning phase including motivating employees to achieve the objectives.
- Control is the backward-looking phase of the managerial process. It involves comparing actual results to budgeted amounts and taking corrective action if necessary.

List the key benefits of budgeting. p. 326   LO2

- Budgeting has several benefits:
  - Forces managers to plan ahead.
  - Serves as a basis for communication throughout the organization.
  - Motivates employees to work toward the organization's goals.

LO3 **Explain the behavioral effects of budgets and provide guidelines for implementing a budget. p. 327**

- Budgets can create a number of behavioral effects that should be considered in designing and implementing a budgetary control system.
- Budgets that are tight but attainable are more likely to motivate people to work hard than budgets that are either too easy or impossible to achieve.
- Participative budgeting allows individuals to provide input into the budget-setting process. However, it may lead to the creation of budget slack.
- Using different budgets for planning than for evaluating performance, rolling budgets and zero-based budgets can mitigate some of the game playing that occurs in the budgeting process.

LO4 **Describe the major components of the master budget and their interrelationships. p. 329**

- The master budget is a comprehensive set of budgets that covers all phases of an organization's planned activities for a specific period.
- The master budget contains two types of budgets: operating budgets and financial budgets.
- Operating budgets include all budgets needed to prepare a budgeted income statement including the sales budget, production budget, raw materials purchases budget, direct labor budget, manufacturing overhead budget, and selling and administrative expense budget.
- Financial budgets provide information about financial resources and obligations needed to prepare a budgeted balance sheet. These include the cash budget, inventory budget, capital expenditures budget, and financing budget.

LO5 **Prepare the following components of the operating budget. p. 330–335**

- **Sales budget.** The starting point of the budgeting process is the development of the sales budget. It is based on a variety of inputs and affects all other components of the master budget.
- **Production budget.** This budget is based on the sales budget and the planned levels of beginning and ending finished goods inventory.
- **Raw materials purchases budget.** This budget is based on the production budget and the planned levels of beginning and ending raw materials inventory.
- **Direct labor budget.** This budget is based on the production budget and shows how much labor is required to produce (or serve) each unit.
- **Manufacturing overhead budget.** This budget is based on the production budget and provides information about expected variable and fixed manufacturing overhead costs.
- **Cost of goods sold budget.** This budget is based on the budgeted manufacturing cost per unit multiplied by budgeted unit sales.
- **Selling and administrative expense budget.** This budget is based on the sales budget and provides information about expected selling and administrative expenses.
- All of the operating budgets can be combined to prepare a **budgeted income statement**.

LO6 **Prepare the cash budget and describe the other financial budgets required to prepare a budgeted balance sheet. p. 336**

- The **cash budget** is a future-oriented version of the statement of cash flows. This budget helps managers determine whether they need to borrow money to finance operations or whether they should invest excess cash to earn interest.
- The first step in preparing the cash budget is to prepare a schedule of cash collection based on the sales budget and an estimate of how and when cash will be received from customers.
- The second step in preparing the cash budget is to prepare a schedule of cash payments for all operating expenses based on when those costs will be paid.
- The final step in preparing the cash budget is to compute the ending balance of the Cash account based on the beginning balance, cash collections, and cash payments. This helps managers determine whether they need to borrow money to maintain a minimum cash balance.
- The ending balance of cash appears on the **budgeted balance sheet** along with the budgeted balances for all other asset, liability, and equity accounts.

SOLUTION TO DEMONSTRATION CASE A

1.

	Quarter 1	Quarter 2	Quarter 3	Quarter 4
Sales forecast (units)	40,000	35,000	45,000	50,000
Price per unit	× $ 1,000	× $ 1,000	× $ 1,000	× $ 1,000
Sales budget (dollars)	$40,000,000	$35,000,000	$45,000,000	$50,000,000

2.

	Quarter 1	Quarter 2	Quarter 3	Quarter 4
Unit sales forecast (from requirement 1)	40,000	35,000	45,000	50,000
Plus: Desired ending inventory	3,500	4,500	5,000	
Less: Planned beginning inventory	4,000	3,500	4,500	
Production budget (units)	39,500	36,000	45,500	

3.

	Quarter 1	Quarter 2	Quarter 3
Production budget (from requirement 2 in units)	39,500	36,000	45,500
Raw materials requirements (per unit in sq. yards)	× 20	× 20	× 20
Total raw materials needed for production (sq. yards)	790,000	720,000	910,000
Plus: Desired ending inventory	79,000	72,000	91,000
Less: Planned beginning inventory	70,000	79,000	72,000
Budgeted raw materials purchases (sq. yards)	799,000	713,000	929,000
Budgeted cost per square yard	× $ 15	× $ 15	× $ 15
Total raw materials purchases	$11,985,000	$10,695,000	$13,935,000

4.

	Quarter 1	Quarter 2	Quarter 3
Production budget (from requirement 2 in units)	39,500	36,000	45,500
Direct labor requirements (hours per unit)	× $ 15	× $ 15	× $ 15
Total labor hours required	592,500	540,000	682,500
Direct labor rate (per hour)	× $ 12	× $ 12	× $ 12
Total direct labor cost	$7,110,000	$6,480,000	$8,190,000

5.

	Quarter 1	Quarter 2	Quarter 3
Production budget (from requirement 2 in units)	39,500	36,000	45,500
Variable overhead rate ($50 per unit)	× $ 50	× $ 50	× $ 50
Variable overhead budget	$1,975,000	$1,800,000	$2,275,000
Fixed overhead budget	1,000,000	1,000,000	1,000,000
Total manufacturing overhead budget	$2,975,000	$2,800,000	$3,275,000

6.

	Quarter 1	Quarter 2	Quarter 3
Sales budget (from requirement 1)	$40,000,000	$35,000,000	$45,000,000
	× 0.10	× 0.10	× 0.10
Variable selling expenses (10% of sales dollars)	4,000,000	3,500,000	4,500,000
Fixed selling expenses	500,000	500,000	500,000
Budgeted selling and administrative expenses	$ 4,500,000	$ 4,000,000	$ 5,000,000

SOLUTION TO DEMONSTRATION CASE B

1.

	Quarter 1	Quarter 2	Quarter 3	Quarter 4
Budgeted sales revenue (given)	$40,000,000	$35,000,000	$45,000,000	$50,000,000
Budgeted cash receipts				
Cash sales (60% of current quarter sales)		$21,000,000	$27,000,000	$30,000,000
Credit sales collected in current quarter (40% of current quarter sales × 35%)		4,900,000	6,300,000	7,000,000
Credit sales collected in following quarter (40% of previous quarter sales × 60%)		9,600,000	8,400,000	10,800,000
Budgeted cash receipts		$35,500,000	$41,700,000	$47,800,000

2.

	Quarter 1	Quarter 2	Quarter 3	Quarter 4
Budgeted cost of goods sold (given)	$15,600,000	$13,650,000	$17,550,000	$19,500,000
Raw materials purchases (70% of cost of goods sold)	10,920,000	9,555,000	12,285,000	13,650,000
Direct labor and manufacturing overhead (30% of cost of goods sold)	4,680,000	4,095,000	5,265,000	5,850,000
Budgeted selling and administrative expenses (given)	4,500,000	4,000,000	5,000,000	5,500,000
Cash payments for:				
Raw materials paid for in current quarter (40% of current quarter purchases)		$ 3,822,000	$ 4,914,000	$ 5,460,000
Raw materials paid for in next quarter (60% of previous quarter purchases)		6,552,000	5,733,000	7,371,000
Direct labor and overhead (Less: $400,000 in depreciation)		3,695,000	4,865,000	5,450,000
Selling and administrative expenses		4,500,000	4,000,000	5,000,000
Budgeted cash payments		$18,569,000	$19,512,000	$23,281,000

3.

	Quarter 1	Quarter 2	Quarter 3	Quarter 4
Beginning balance of cash		$ 500,000	$17,431,000	$39,619,000
Plus: Budgeted cash receipts		35,500,000	41,700,000	47,800,000
Less: Budgeted cash disbursements		(18,569,000)	(19,512,000)	(23,281,000)
Ending balance of cash	$500,000	$17,431,000	$39,619,000	$64,138,000

KEY TERMS

See complete definitions in glossary at back of text.

QUESTIONS

1. Briefly describe why budgetary planning is important to managers.

2. What role do budgets play in the planning and control cycle?

3. What is a strategic plan, and how does it relate to short- and long-term goals?

4. Suppose that your strategic plan is to retire comfortably at the age of 55. List several long-term objectives, short-term objectives, and tactics that would enable you to accomplish this goal.

5. Identify and briefly discuss the benefits of budgeting.

6. Suppose a company chooses not to develop budgets. Describe three potential negative consequences of this decision.

7. What are the advantages and disadvantages of participative budgeting compared to top-down budgeting?

8. What is budgetary slack and why might it be detrimental to a company?

9. Briefly explain how each of the following helps to minimize dysfunctional behaviors caused by budgeting:

   (a) Different budgets for different purposes.
   (b) Continuous budgeting.
   (c) Zero-based budgeting.

10. What is the master budget, and what are its components?

11. Explain why the sales budget is the starting point for a company's budgeting process. Which budgets does the sales budget affect? Which budgets are not affected by the sales budget?

12. What sources does a company utilize to determine its sales forecast? What could happen if one of the sources used is inaccurate?

13. What are the components of the operating budget?

14. What are the components of the financial budget?

15. How are the cash budget and the budgeted balance sheet interrelated?

16. Why is the preparation of a cash budget important?

17. In preparing a cash budget, why must an adjustment be made for depreciation expenses?

18. What is the ultimate goal or end result of a company's entire budgeting process?

19. How does the budgeting process differ for a service company than for a manufacturing company?

20. How is a merchandiser's budgeting process different from that of a manufacturing company?

MULTIPLE CHOICE

1. Budgets help companies

   a. Meet short-term objectives.
   b. Meet long-term objectives.
   c. Both a and b.
   d. None of the above.

Quiz 9
www.mhhe.com/whitecotton1e

2. Which phases of the management process are impacted by budgeting?

   a. Planning.   c. Control.
   b. Directing/leading. d. All of the above.

3. Which of the following statements is true?

   a. GAAP requires all companies to prepare budgets.
   b. Only newly formed companies need budgets.
   c. Most service firms prepare production budgets.
   d. Most companies would benefit from budgeting.

4. Shasta Company plans to double its profits in five years. This is an example of a

   a. Long-term objective.
   b. Short-term objective.
   c. Tactic.
   d. Sales forecast.

5. Which of the following is **not** considered a direct benefit of budgeting?

   a. Better communication.
   b. Motivating employees.
   c. Developing new product lines.
   d. Forcing managers to think ahead.

6. Which of the following budgets would be prepared earliest in a company's budgeting process?

   a. Budgeted income statement.
   b. Budgeted balance sheet.
   c. Raw materials purchases budget.
   d. Production budget.

7. Which of the following budgets is affected by the sales budget?

   a. Direct labor budget.
   b. Cash receipts and disbursements budget.
   c. Selling and administrative budget.
   d. All of the above.

8. ABC Company expects to sell 100,000 units of its primary product in January. Expected beginning and ending finished goods inventory for January are 20,000 and 45,000 units, respectively. How many units should ABC produce?

   a. 100,000.   c. 75,000.
   b. 125,000.   d. 35,000.

9. Which of the following is **not** considered an operating budget?

   a. Cash budget.
   b. Budgeted income statement.
   c. Selling and administrative expense budget.
   d. Raw materials purchases budget.

10. Raya Company is calculating its expected cash receipts for the month of June. This should **not** include

    a. Cash sales made during June.
    b. Credit sales made during May.
    c. Credit sales made during June.
    d. Credit sales made during July.

Answers to Multiple-Choice Questions located in back of the text.

MINI EXERCISES

LO1   **M9-1 Explaining the Role of Managerial Accounting in the Planning and Control Cycle**

Your boss believes that the three management functions of planning, directing/leading, and control are unrelated. He also thinks that managerial accounting has no role in any of the functions. Is your boss correct? Explain why or why not.

LO2   **M9-2 Describing Advantages of Budgetary Planning**

Calypso Cal (CC), which manufactures surfboards, has a "Live today, worry about tomorrow later" motto. In keeping with this philosophy, CC has not set any long-term or short-term objectives or budgets for the company. Describe three potential consequences of CC's philosophy.

LO4   **M9-3 Classifying, Components of Master Budget**

Classify each of the following budgets as an operating (O) or financing (F) budget.

 a. Cash receipts and disbursements budget
 b. Sales budget
 c. Raw materials purchases budget
 d. Selling and administrative expense budget
 e. Budgeted balance sheet
 f. Manufacturing overhead budget
 g. Direct labor budget
 h. Budgeted income statement
 i. Production budget

LO5a   **M9-4 Preparing Sales Budget**

Ranger Company estimates that unit sales of its weather radios will be 8,000 in October; 8,200 in November; and 9,350 in December. Prepare Ranger's sales budget for the fourth quarter assuming each unit sells for $27.50.

LO5c   **M9-5 Preparing Purchases Budget**

Pascall Corp. expects to sell 1,300 units of its camera bags in March and 900 units in April. Each unit sells for $110. Pascall's ending inventory policy is 40 percent of the following month's sales. Pascall pays its supplier $50 per unit. Prepare Pascall's purchases budget for March.

LO5c   **M9-6 Preparing Raw Materials Purchases Budget**

CubbyHole, Inc., manufactures wooden shelving units for collecting and sorting mail. The company expects to produce 310 units in July and 400 units in August. Each unit requires 10 feet of wood at a cost of $1.20 per foot. CubbyHole wants to always have 300 feet of wood on hand in materials inventory. Prepare CubbyHole's raw materials purchases budget for July and August.

LO5d   **M9-7 Preparing Direct Labor Budget**

Refer to the information in M9-6 for CubbyHole, Inc. Each unit requires 1.5 hours of direct labor, and labor wages average $9 per hour. Prepare CubbyHole's direct labor budget for July and August.

LO5e   **M9-8 Preparing Manufacturing Overhead Cost Budget**

Damon Company expects sales of its headphones to be $200,000 in the first quarter and $236,000 in the second quarter. Its variable overhead is approximately 17 percent of sales, and fixed overhead costs are $52,000 per quarter. Prepare Damon's manufacturing overhead budget for the first two quarters.

LO6g   **M9-9 Preparing Selling and Administrative Expense Budget**

Affleck, Inc., expects sales of its housing for electric motors to be $83,000, $79,000, and $88,000 for January, February, and March, respectively. Its variable selling and administrative expenses are 9 percent of sales, and fixed selling and administrative expenses are $11,000 per month. Prepare Affleck's selling and administrative expense budget for January, February, and March.

LO6   **M9-10 Preparing Schedule of Cash Receipts**

Clooney Company expects sales for the first three months of next year to be $200,000, $235,000 and $298,000, respectively. Clooney expects 40 percent of its sales to be cash and the remainder to be credit sales. The credit sales will be collected as follows: 70 percent in the month of the sale and 30 percent in the following month. Prepare a schedule of Clooney's cash collections for the months of February and March.

EXERCISES

E9-1 Understanding Behavioral Effects of Budgeting

|ACCOUNTING   **LO3**

Samantha is the production manager for Wentworth Company. Each year, she is involved in the company's budgeting process. Company President Leslie has asked Samantha to submit the facility's budgeted production for the upcoming year. Leslie's typical process is to take the budget that Samantha provides and add 10 percent to it. That amount then becomes Samantha's target production level for the upcoming year. Additionally, Samantha can earn a bonus only if the facility exceeds the budgeted production level.

Required:

1. Explain any incentive Samantha might have to be dishonest with Leslie about the production level she thinks the facility can achieve.
2. Explain the impact Samantha's inaccurate production estimates could have on other company employees.

E9-2 Classifying, Ordering Components of the Master Budget

LO4

Organize the following budgets in order of preparation by placing the number before it and indicate how each would be affected by a sales forecast that is understated.

_____ Cash receipts and disbursements budget.

_____ Selling and administrative expense budget.

_____ Manufacturing overhead budget.

_____ Raw materials purchases budget.

_____ Budgeted balance sheet.

_____ Sales budget.

_____ Direct labor budget.

_____ Budgeted income statement.

_____ Budgeted cost of goods sold.

_____ Production budget.

E9-3 Calculating Unknowns Based on Production, Sales, Beginning and Ending Inventory Values

LO5b

Complete the following table.

NUMBER OF UNITS			
Production	Sales	Ending Inventory	Beginning Inventory
?	500	100	75
800	?	90	125
750	675	?	80
900	1,200	100	?
665	?	225	160
845	795	305	?

E9-4 Calculating Sales and Production Budgets

LO5a, b

Rainwater Corp. expects to sell 600 umbrellas in May and 400 in June. Each umbrella sells for $15. Rainwater's beginning and ending finished goods inventories for May are 75 and 50 units, respectively. Ending finished goods inventory for June will be 60 units.

Required:

1. Prepare Rainwater's sales budget for May and June.
2. Prepare Rainwater's production budget for May and June.

LO5c, e   **E9-5 Preparing Raw Materials Purchases and Manufacturing Overhead Budgets**

Refer to the information in E9-4 for Rainwater Corp. Each umbrella requires a total of $3.50 in direct materials that includes an opening mechanism that the company purchases from a supplier at a cost of $2.00 each. Rainwater wants to have 30 mechanisms on hand at May 1, 20 mechanisms at May 31, and 25 mechanisms at June 30. Additionally, Rainwater's fixed manufacturing overhead is $1,000 per month, and variable manufacturing overhead is $1.25 per unit produced.

Required:

1. Prepare Rainwater's May and June raw materials purchases budget for these mechanisms.
2. Prepare Rainwater's manufacturing overhead budget for May and June.

LO5d   **E9-6 Preparing Direct Labor Budget**

Refer to the information in E9-4 for Rainwater Corp. Suppose that each umbrella takes 0.20 direct labor hours to produce and Rainwater pays its workers $9 per hour.

Required:

Prepare Rainwater's direct labor budget for May and June.

LO5f   **E9-7 Preparing Cost of Goods Sold Budget**

Refer to E9-4 through E9-6 for Rainwater Corp. Use the information and solutions presented to complete the requirements.

Required:

1. Determine Rainwater's budgeted manufacturing cost per umbrella. (**Note:** Assume that fixed overhead per unit is $2.)
2. Prepare Rainwater's budgeted cost of goods sold for May and June.

LO5g   **E9-8 Preparing Selling and Administrative Expense Budget**

In addition to the information in E9-4 through E9-7 regarding Rainwater Corp., the following data are available:

• Selling costs are expected to be 6 percent of sales.
• Fixed costs per month total $1,200.

Required:

Prepare Rainwater's selling and administrative expense budget for May and June.

LO5h   **E9-9 Preparing Budgeted Income Statement**

Use the information and solutions from E9-4 through E9-8 for Rainwater Corp.

Required:

Prepare Rainwater's budgeting income statement for the months of May and June.

LO6   **E9-10 Calculating Cash Receipts**

Refer to information in E9-4 for Rainwater Corp. It expects the following unit sales for the third quarter:

July	525
August	490
September	450

Sixty percent of Rainwater's sales are cash. Of the credit sales, 50 percent is collected in the month of the sale, 45 percent is collected during the following month, and 5 percent is never collected.

Required:

Calculate Rainwater's total cash receipts for August and September.

E9-11 Preparing Production, Purchases Budgets

LO5b, c

Farlow Inc. has the following projected sales for the next four months:

Month	Sales in Units
April	3,580
May	3,875
June	4,620
July	4,135
August	3,950

At March 31, 2,148 units of finished goods are expected in inventory. Farlow's finished goods inventory policy is to have 60 percent of the next month's sales on hand at the end of each month. Direct material costs $3.10 per pound, and each unit requires 2 pounds. Raw materials inventory policy is to have 50 percent of the next month's production needs on hand at the end of each month. Raw materials on hand at March 31 totaled 3,757 pounds.

Required:

1. Prepare a production budget for April, May, and June.
2. Prepare a purchases budget for April and May.

E9-12 Preparing Direct Labor Budget

LO5d

Deadpin Corp. manufactures two styles of leather bowling bag, the Nerd and Supernerd. Budgeted production levels for October follow:

	Nerd	Supernerd
Production	2,500 bags	3,250 bags

Two departments, Cutting and Sewing, produce the bowling bags. Direct labor hours needed for each style are as follows:

	Cutting	Sewing
Nerd	0.1 hour per bag	0.3 hour per bag
Supernerd	0.2 hour per bag	0.5 hour per bag

Hourly direct labor rates are $12 for the Cutting department and $15 for Sewing.

Required:

Prepare Deadpin's direct labor budget for October.

E9-13 Preparing Selling and Administrative Expense Budget

LO5g

The following information is available for Revelle Company.

- Sales price per unit is $80.
- November and December, sales were budgeted at 3,100 and 3,550 units, respectively.
- Variable costs are 11 percent of sales (6 percent commission, 2 percent advertising, 3 percent shipping).
- Fixed costs per month are sales salaries, $5,000; office salaries, $2,500; depreciation, $2,500; building rent, $3,500; insurance, $1,500; and utilities, $800.

Required:

Prepare Revelle's selling and administrative expense budgets for November and December.

LO5h　**E9-14　Preparing Budgeted Income Statement**

Omar Company has compiled the following data for the upcoming year.

- Sales are expected to be 15,000 units at $35.75 each.
- Direct materials requires 2 pounds per unit at $1.50 per pound.
- Direct labor requires 1.5 hours per unit at $12.50 per hour.
- Manufacturing overhead is $3.00 per unit.
- Beginning raw material inventory is $3,500.00.
- Ending raw material inventory is $4,100.00.
- Raw material costs $1.50 per pound.
- Selling and administrative costs totaled $135,870.00.

Required:

1. Prepare Omar's cost of goods sold budget.
2. Prepare Omar's budgeted income statement.

LO6　**E9-15　Preparing Cash Budget**

Garcia Company has the following information for the month of March.

Cash balance, March 1	$15,575
Collections from customers	34,650
Paid to suppliers	22,300
Manufacturing overhead	6,100
Direct labor	8,250
Selling and administrative expenses	4,200

Garcia pays wages in the month incurred. Manufacturing overhead includes $1,200 for machinery depreciation, but the amount for selling and administrative expenses is exclusive of depreciation. Additionally, Garcia also expects to sell a piece of property for $15,000 during March.

Required:

Prepare Garcia's cash budget for the month of March.

LO6　**E9-16　Calculating Cash Receipts**

Wright Company makes 75 percent of its sales in cash. Credit sales are collected as follows: 65 percent in the month of sale and 35 percent in the month following the sale.

　　Wright's budgeted sales for upcoming months follow:

June	$22,500
July	25,000
August	23,000
September	21,000

Required:

Compute Wright's expected cash receipts for August.

LO6　**E9-17　Preparing Cash Budget**

Sonora Clothing Company is a retail company that sells hiking and other outdoor gear specially made for the desert heat. It sells to individuals as well as local companies that coordinate adventure getaways in the desert for tourists. The following information is available for several months of the current year.

Month	Sales	Purchases	Cash Expenses Paid
May	$ 90,000	$ 70,000	$24,000
June	115,000	95,000	29,500
July	130,000	120,000	38,250
August	125,000	80,000	34,700

The majority of Sonora's sales (70 percent) are cash, but a few of the excursion companies purchase on credit. Of the credit sales, 40 percent are collected in the month of sale and 60 percent are collected in the following month. All of Sonora's purchases are on account with 55 percent paid in the month of purchase and 45 percent paid the following month.

Required:

1. Prepare a schedule of cash collections for July and August.
2. Prepare a schedule of cash payments for July and August.

PROBLEMS–SET A

 |ACCOUNTING   LO5a, b, c, d, e, f, g

PA9-1 **Preparing Operating Budgets**

www.mhhe.com/whitecotton1e

Bamboo You, Inc. This company manufactures bamboo picture frames that sell for $20 each. Each frame requires 4 linear feet of bamboo, which costs $1.50 per foot. Each frame takes approximately 30 minutes to build, and the labor rate averages $10.00 per hour.

Bamboo You has the following inventory policies:

Ending finished goods inventory should be 40 percent of the next month's sales.

Ending raw materials inventory should be 30 percent of the next month's production.

Expected unit sales (frames) for the upcoming months follow:

March	275
April	250
May	300
June	400
July	375
August	425

Variable manufacturing overhead is incurred at a rate of $0.25 per unit produced. Annual fixed manufacturing overhead is estimated to be $7,200 ($600 per month) for an expected production of 4,000 units for the year. Selling and administrative expenses are estimated at $650 per month plus $0.60 per unit sold.

Required:

Prepare the following for Bamboo You, Inc., for the second quarter (April, May, and June). Include each month as well as the quarter 2 total for each budget.

1. Sales budget.
2. Production budget.
3. Raw materials purchases budget.
4. Direct labor budget.
5. Manufacturing overhead cost budget.
6. Budgeted cost of goods sold.
7. Selling and administrative expenses budget.

PA9-2 **Preparing Budgeted Income Statement**

LO5h

www.mhhe.com/whitecotton1e

Refer to the information in PA9-1.

Required:

Prepare Bamboo You's budgeted income statement for quarter 2.

LO6

www.mhhe.com/whitecotton1e

PA9-3 Preparing Cash Budget

Refer to the information in PA9-1. Bamboo You, Inc., had $9,800 cash on hand at April 1. Of its sales, 70 percent is in cash. Of the credit sales, 40 percent is collected during the month of the sale, and 60 percent is collected during the month following the sale.

Of direct material purchases, 80 percent is paid for during the month purchased and 20 percent is paid in the following month. Raw materials purchases for March 1 totaled $2,000. All other operating costs are paid during the month incurred. Monthly fixed manufacturing overhead includes $150 in depreciation.

Required:

Prepare the following for Bamboo You for quarter 2:
1. Budgeted cash receipts. Include each month (April–June) as well as quarter 2 totals.
2. Budgeted cash payments.
3. Cash budget.

LO5a, b, c, d

PA9-4 Preparing Operating Budget Components

Black & Decker (B&D) manufactures a wide variety of tools and accessories. One of its more popular items is a cordless power handisaw. Use the following fictitious information about this product line to complete the problem requirements. Each handisaw sells for $40. B&D expects the following unit sales.

January	2,000
February	2,200
March	2,700
April	2,500
May	1,900

B&D's ending finished goods inventory policy is 25 percent of the next month's sales.

Suppose each handisaw takes approximately 0.75 hours to manufacture, and B&D pays an average labor wage of $16.50 per hour.

Each handisaw requires a plastic housing that B&D purchases from a supplier at a cost of $7.00 each. The company has an ending raw materials inventory policy of 20 percent of the following month's production requirements. Materials other than the housing unit total $4.50 per handisaw.

Manufacturing overhead for this product includes $72,000 annual fixed overhead (based on production of 27,000 units) and $1.10 per unit variable manufacturing overhead. B&D's selling expenses are 7 percent of sales dollars, and administrative expenses are fixed at $18,000 per month.

Required:

Prepare the following for the first quarter:
1. Sales budget.
2. Production budget.
3. Raw materials purchases budget for the plastic housings.
4. Direct labor budget.

LO5f, g

PA9-5 Preparing Operating Budget Components

Refer to the information presented in PA9-4 regarding Black & Decker's handisaw.

Required:

Prepare the following for the first quarter:
1. Cost of goods sold budget.
2. Selling and administrative expense budget.
3. Budgeted income statement for the handisaw product.

PROBLEMS—SET B

PB9-1 **Preparing Operating Budgets**

LO5a, b, c, d, e, f, g

Flying High Company manufactures kites that sell for $15.00 each. Each kite requires 2 yards of lightweight canvas, which costs $0.50 per yard. Each kite takes approximately 45 minutes to build, and the labor rate averages $8.00 per hour.

Flying High has the following inventory policies:

Ending finished goods inventory should be 30 percent of next month's sales.

Ending raw materials inventory should be 20 percent of next month's production.

Expected kite sales for the upcoming months are:

March	850
April	700
May	650
June	720
July	830
August	760

Variable manufacturing overhead is incurred at a rate of $0.30 per unit produced. Annual fixed manufacturing overhead is estimated to be $9,000 ($750 per month) for an expected production of 9,000 units for the year. Selling and administrative expenses are estimated at $820 per month plus $0.75 per unit sold.

Required:

Prepare the following for Flying High for the second quarter (April, May, and June). Include each month as well as the quarter 2 total in each budget.

1. Sales budget.
2. Production budget.
3. Raw materials purchases budget.
4. Direct labor budget.
5. Manufacturing overhead budget.
6. Budgeted cost of goods sold.
7. Selling and administrative expenses budget.

PB9-2 **Preparing Budgeted Income Statement**

LO5h

Refer to the information in PB9-1.

Required:

Prepare Flying High's budgeted income statement for quarter 2.

PB9-3 **Preparing Cash Budget**

LO6

Refer to the information in PB9-1. Flying High Company had $12,200 cash on hand at April 1. Of its sales, 80 percent is cash. Of the credit sales, 60 percent is collected during the month of the sale and 40 percent is collected during the month following the sale.

Of raw material purchases, 70 percent is paid for during the month purchased, and 30 percent is paid in the following month. Raw materials purchases for March totaled $800. All other operating costs are paid during the month incurred. Monthly fixed manufacturing overhead includes $280 in depreciation.

Required:

Prepare the following for quarter 2:

1. Budgeted cash receipts. Include each month (April–June) as well as quarter 2 totals.
2. Budgeted cash payments.
3. Cash budget.

PB9-4 **Preparing Operating Budget Components**

Black & Decker (B&D) manufactures a wide variety of tools and accessories. One of its more popular craft-related items is the cord free glue gun. Use the following fictitious information about this product to complete the problem requirements. Each glue gun sells for $25. B&D expects the following unit sales.

January	8,000
February	7,400
March	8,700
April	9,500
May	9,150

B&D's ending finished goods inventory policy is 30 percent of the following month's budgeted sales.

Suppose each glue gun takes approximately 0.5 hours to manufacture, and B&D pays an average labor wage of $16.50 per hour.

Each glue gun requires a heating element that B&D purchases from a supplier at a cost of $1.25 each. The company has an ending raw materials inventory policy of 40 percent of the following month's production requirements. Materials other than the heating elements total $3.25 per glue gun.

Manufacturing overhead for this product includes $96,900 annual fixed overhead (based on production of 102,000 units) and variable manufacturing overhead of $0.80 per unit. B&D's selling expenses are 5 percent of sales dollars, and administrative expenses for this product are fixed at $17,500 per month.

Required:

Prepare the following for the first quarter.

1. Sales budget.
2. Production budget.
3. Raw materials purchases budget for the heating element.
4. Direct labor budget.

PB9-5 **Preparing Operating Budgets Components**

Refer to the information presented in PB9-4 regarding Black & Decker's glue gun product.

Required:

Prepare the following for the first quarter:

1. Cost of goods sold budget.
2. Selling and administrative expense budget.
3. Budgeted income statement for the glue gun product.

SKILLS DEVELOPMENT CASES

S9-1 **Evaluating Impact of Corporate Culture and Pressure to Meet the Numbers in Accounting Reporting Environment**

In 1995, *BusinessWeek* ran a cover story entitled "Blind Ambition: How the Pursuit of Results Got Out of Hand at Bausch and Lomb." The two-part article details a number of games Bausch and Lomb (B&L) managers played to artificially achieve short-term results at the expense of long-term value.

The "numbers-oriented" culture at B&L was far from unique as evidenced by the high-profile accounting scandals that occurred during the past decade. Since then, numerous reforms, including the Sarbanes-Oxley Act of 2002, have been implemented to improve the corporate reporting environment.

Required:

1. Find *BusinessWeek*'s "Blind Ambition" article on the Internet. Read it and list five specific examples of actions that B&L managers took to artificially boost short-term results.

2. Were the actions taken at B&L unethical, illegal, or both? What was the likely impact on long-term results and stockholder value?

3. Explain how the corporate culture at B&L may have contributed to managers' pressure to achieve budgetary results.

4. How did the bonus and compensation systems affect the behavior of individual B&L managers?

5. Conduct an Internet search on the Sarbanes-Oxley Act. What was its intent? Did it include any requirements aimed at improving corporate culture as a means to reduce fraudulent reporting?

S9-2 Interviewing, Writing a Real-World Budget Process Report

LO2, 3

Budgets can be used in almost any type of organization including large corporations, small businesses, government organizations, universities, churches, and student clubs.

Required:

Choose any local organization and interview two people who are involved in its budget process. Try to choose one person who actually worked on preparing the budget (e.g., an accountant or the treasurer) and another person who is affected by the budget (e.g., a person in charge of spending the budget, or an employee who is evaluated based on his or her ability to meet budgetary goals).

1. Based on your interviews, write a brief description of the budgeting process within this organization. The description should be a factual account of the steps taken to develop and distribute the budget without any qualitative evaluations of the process. You should identify the type of budgeting (top down or participative) and the personnel involved in the budgeting process as well as any recent and/or anticipated adjustments to the process and the overall importance management place on budgets.

2. Separately consider each of the people you interviewed. How satisfied does each seem with the organization's budgeting process? What step(s) of the process were they the most and least satisfied with? Did either of your interviewees identify a particular step of the process that has been troublesome?

3. Suppose the organization you investigated has retained you as a consultant. Based on the information compiled from the organization and your knowledge from this course, what recommendations would you make to this organization regarding its budgeting process?

S9-3 Researching Online Budget Tools

LO2, 3

Numerous personal financial planning or budgeting tools are available on the Internet, many of them free. Choose at least two different online budgeting sites and input information for a typical person of your age. (**Note:** You may either create a fictitious profile or use your own personal information. If you choose to use your personal data, be sure to read the sites' privacy policies.)

Required:

1. Use each tool to develop a monthly budget.
2. Compare and contrast the two online budgeting tools. Do you prefer aspects of one over the other? Are there things that you dislike? Explain.
3. How helpful do you think such tools are in personal financial management? What are the pros and cons?

CHAPTER 10

Budgetary Control

YOUR LEARNING OBJECTIVES

After completing this chapter, you should be able to:

LO1   Describe the standard-setting process and explain how standard costs relate to budgets and variances.

LO2   Prepare a flexible budget and show how total costs change with sales volume.

LO3   Calculate and interpret the direct materials price and quantity variances.

LO4   Calculate and interpret the direct labor rate and efficiency variances.

LO5   Calculate and interpret the variable overhead rate and efficiency variances.

LO6   Calculate and interpret the fixed overhead spending variance.

Lecture Presentation—LP10
www.mhhe.com/whitecotton1e

FOCUS COMPANY: Cold Stone Creamery

"Because the World Deserves Better Ice Cream."

www.coldstonecreamery.com

The previous chapter described the role of budgets in the planning and control process. This chapter discusses the use of variances in the control phase of that process. A **variance** is simply the difference between actual and budgeted results. Variances act as signals to managers that their planned results are (or are not) being achieved.

Think of the planning and control process in terms of flying an airplane. Before takeoff, the pilot must file a flight plan that describes where the plane is going and how the pilot will get it there. The flight plan is similar to the role of a budget in business. The budget states where the business needs to go in the future and how managers plan to get it there.

Likewise, the system of signals that guide pilots and air traffic controllers during the flight serves as a control mechanism. Just as the pilot monitors the plane's instrument panel to follow these signals, managers keep a close eye on key indicators, including variances, to determine whether they are on track to achieve their plan. If they go too far off course, managers need a signal that they should take corrective action.

In the last chapter, you began the study of the planning and control process by preparing a master budget for a hypothetical Cold Stone Creamery location. In this chapter, we continue this example by calculating Cold Stone's cost variances for direct materials, direct labor, and manufacturing overhead. We also discuss how to prepare a different kind of budget, the flexible budget, which serves as a benchmark for calculating variances. First, you need to become familiar with standard cost systems, the basis for these budgets and variances.

Standard cost systems	Master budget versus flexible budget	Direct material and direct labor variances	Manufacturing overhead cost variances
• Ideal versus attainable standards • Types of standards • Standard cost card	• Flexible budget as a benchmark • Volume variance versus spending variance • Favorable versus unfavorable variances	• Variance framework • Direct materials variances • Direct labor variances	• Variable manufacturing overhead variances • Fixed manufacturing overhead spending variance • Summary of variances

Standard Cost Systems

A **standard cost system** is the foundation of a managerial control system. The key difference between a standard cost system and the cost systems covered in earlier chapters is that costs are recorded at standard rather than actual amounts. The standards are set in advance to reflect what managers think cost **should** be. Managers can then use the standard costs to create budgets, set prices for products and services, and make a variety of other decisions.

IDEAL VERSUS ATTAINABLE STANDARDS

Standards can be set at varying levels of difficulty or achievability. The most extreme case is an **ideal standard**, or one that can be achieved only under perfect or ideal conditions. An example is the performance standard of a world-class athlete, such as a 4-minute mile. Standards that are almost impossible to achieve are unlikely to motivate people to work hard to achieve them. At the other end of the spectrum is an **easily attainable standard**, or one that can be met without much effort. Research suggests that tight but attainable standards—the happy medium between these two extremes—are best for motivating individuals to work hard.

What these general guidelines mean to a particular business depends on the type of task and the person performing it. Imagine, for example, that you just started training for a 10-K charity run. You can run a 10-minute mile with relative ease but would like to improve your running time. It probably would not be realistic to set a 4-minute mile as your performance standard because most people are not physically capable of achieving that ideal standard. What standard would motivate you to train hard without being so difficult that it would cause you to give up? This type of standard is sometimes called a "stretch goal"—one you must stretch yourself to achieve. Similarly, organizations should set standard costs so that they are difficult but not impossible to achieve. To foster continuous improvement, the standards should increase in difficulty over time, just as you would decrease your target running time as your strength and training improve.

COACH'S TIP

Managers should set standards at realistic levels that allow a certain amount of downtime for preventive maintenance, employee breaks, training, and the like. Failure to build these factors into the standards can reduce performance over the long run because of machine breakdowns, low employee morale, and high turnover rates.

Video 10-1
www.mhhe.com/whitecotton1e

TYPES OF STANDARDS

Standard cost systems rely on two types of standards, quantity standards and price standards:

Learning Objective 1
Describe the standard-setting process and explain how standard costs relate to budgets and variances.

	Definition	Examples
Quantity standard	The amount of input that should go into a single unit of the product	Number of ounces of aluminum in a Coca Cola can Number of tons of steel in a Ford F-150 truck Number of yards of denim in a pair of Levi's 550 jeans
Price standard	The price that should be paid for a specific quantity of input	Price per ounce of aluminum Price per ton of steel Price per yard of denim

Notice that these standards are stated in terms of the quantity and price of the **input** (ounces, tons, or yards) that **should** be required to create a single unit of output. Similar quantity and price standards are developed for direct labor and other inputs. The quantity standard for direct labor is the amount of time (in hours, minutes, or seconds) that workers **should** take to produce a single unit of product. The price standard for labor, called the **standard labor rate**, is the expected hourly cost of labor including employee taxes and benefits.

As mentioned in the previous section, we calculate variances by comparing actual costs to budgeted or standard costs. Although we often use the terms **standard** and **budget** interchangeably, they have slightly different meanings. Standards are expressed at a very detailed level to reflect the cost and quantity of the **inputs** that go into a product or service. A simple example of an input is the amount of flour needed to make a cake. A budget, on the other hand, is the total dollar amount that we expect to spend to achieve a certain level of **output**. In other words, a budget depends not only on the standards that are stated in terms of the input but also on the level of output, such as the number of cakes that will be made. As you will see shortly, we can develop different budgets for different levels of output, but the standards we use to develop those budgets remain the same.

Video 10-2
www.mhhe.com/whitecotton1e

STANDARD COST CARD

The price standard is multiplied by the quantity standard for each input to get the **standard unit cost**. Then all standard costs are summarized on a **standard cost card**, a form that shows what the company **should** spend to make a single unit of product based on expected production and sales for the coming period. Exhibit 10.1 shows a hypothetical standard cost card for Cold Stone Creamery.

EXHIBIT 10.1	Standard Cost Card for Cold Stone Creamery

	Standard Quantity	Standard Price (Rate)	Standard Unit Cost
Direct costs			
Ice cream*	10 oz.	$0.05 per oz.	$0.50
Mix-in ingredients	2 oz.	0.10 per oz.	0.20
Direct labor	.10 hrs.	8.00 per hr.	0.80
Manufacturing overhead costs			
Variable manufacturing overhead (based on number of direct labor hours)	.10 hrs.	1.00 per hr.	0.10
Fixed manufacturing overhead $6,000/15,000 units = $0.40 per unit			0.40
Standard manufacturing cost per unit			$2.00

COACH'S TIP

You may wonder how companies set their price and quantity standards. Managers use many types of information including historical data, industry averages, and the results of process studies to determine how much time and money they **should** spend to make a product.

* In reality, Cold Stone Creamery purchases milk, cream, and sugar and uses these raw ingredients to make fresh ice cream at each individual store. For simplicity, we assume that the ice cream is purchased from a regional distribution center.

According to the standard cost card, Cold Stone should use 10 ounces of ice cream and 2 ounces of mix-in ingredients (fruits, candy, nuts) to make each unit of product. The standard price is $0.05 per ounce for ice cream and $0.10 per ounce for mix-ins, which results in a standard unit cost for materials of $0.70 ($0.50 + $0.20).

The direct labor standard assumes that employees can produce and serve an average of 10 units per hour—including the time needed to prepare, serve, and clean up after each customer as well as an allowance for training time, breaks, and the like. Converting this direct labor standard to a per unit basis produces a standard amount of time to produce each unit of 0.10 hours (6 minutes). Because the standard labor rate (including taxes and benefits) is $8.00 per hour, the standard direct labor cost per unit is $0.80.

Variable manufacturing costs are applied to the product at a rate of $1.00 per direct labor hour. When this standard variable overhead rate is multiplied by the standard quantity of 0.10 labor hours per unit, we get a standard unit cost of $0.10 for variable overhead. Fixed overhead costs are budgeted at $6,000 per month, which is spread over the 15,000 units we expect to produce and sell, resulting in a fixed manufacturing overhead cost of $0.40 per unit. Adding all of these standard cost components, we arrive at a standard manufacturing cost of $2.00 per unit.

Master Budget versus Flexible Budget

In the last chapter, you prepared an entire master budget for Cold Stone Creamery. Recall that the master budget is an integrated set of operating and financial budgets reflecting what managers expect to achieve in a future accounting period. The starting point for preparing the master budget is the sales forecast, or the company's best estimate of future sales. All other components of the master budget are based on the sales forecast including the production budget, the raw materials purchases budget, the direct labor budget, the manufacturing overhead budget, and the selling and administrative expense budget.

The master budget is an example of a **static budget**—that is, a budget that is based on a single (fixed) estimate of sales volume. Because predicting sales volume with 100 percent certainty is impossible, managers often find it useful to prepare a **flexible budget** that shows how budgeted costs and revenues will change across different levels of sales volume. As you should recall from Chapter 5, variable costs are those that change (in total) in response to a change in production or sales volume. Fixed costs are those that remain the same (in total) regardless of production or sales volume. For simplicity, we assume that production and sales are equal. See Exhibit 10.2 for a flexible budget for Cold Stone Creamery's manufacturing costs.

EXHIBIT 10.2 | Preparation of the Master and Flexible Budgets

The master budget is based on managers' best estimate of sales volume (15,000 units) multiplied by the standard unit cost.

	Standard Unit Cost (from Exhibit 10.1)	Flexible Budget (12,000 units)	Master Budget (15,000 units)	Flexible Budget (18,000 units)
Variable manufacturing costs:				
Ice cream	$ 0.50	$ 6,000	$ 7,500	$ 9,000
Mix-in ingredients	0.20	2,400	3,000	3,600
Direct labor	0.80	9,600	12,000	14,400
Variable manufacturing overhead	0.10	1,200	1,500	1,800
Fixed manufacturing overhead	0.40	6,000	6,000	6,000
Total manufacturing costs	$ 2.00	$ 25,200	$ 30,000	$ 34,800

The flexible budget shows how total costs are expected to change if sales are lower (12,000 units) or higher (18,000 units) than expected.

Two points are important to keep in mind when preparing a flexible budget. **First, total variable costs change in direct proportion to changes in volume.** For example, if Cold Stone's sales volume increases from 15,000 units to 18,000 units (see Exhibit 10.2), the budgeted cost of ice cream increases from $7,500 to $9,000. The 20 percent increase in sales volume (3,000/15,000 = 20%) produces a 20 percent increase in total cost of ice cream ($1,500/$7,500 = 20%). The same effect will occur for all other variable costs.

Second, total fixed costs remain the same regardless of volume. Cold Stone's budgeted fixed cost is held constant at $6,000 in the master budget and flexible budget columns shown in Exhibit 10.2. However, the fixed cost per unit of $0.40 shown on the standard cost card is only true for the master budget sales volume of 15,000 units ($6,000/15,000 = $0.40).

Before we continue, complete the following Self-Study Practice to make sure you understand how to prepare a flexible budget.

 ## Self-Study Practice

Assume that Papa John's standard unit cost and master budget for 20,000 units are as follows:

	Standard Unit Cost	Master Budget (20,000 units)	Flexible Budget (25,000 units)
1. Pizza dough	$0.80	$16,000	
2. Pizza sauce	0.20	4,000	
3. Direct labor	1.00	20,000	
4. Variable manufacturing overhead	0.25	5,000	
5. Fixed manufacturing overhead	0.50	10,000	
	$2.75	$55,000	

Prepare a flexible budget for 25,000 units and enter the amounts in the Flexible Budget column.

After you have finished, check your answers with the solutions in the margin.

FLEXIBLE BUDGET AS A BENCHMARK

The flexible budget is a useful benchmark for evaluating managerial performance. In general, we rely on the master budget for planning, or forward-looking purposes, and on the flexible budget for control, or backward-looking purposes. See Exhibit 10.3.

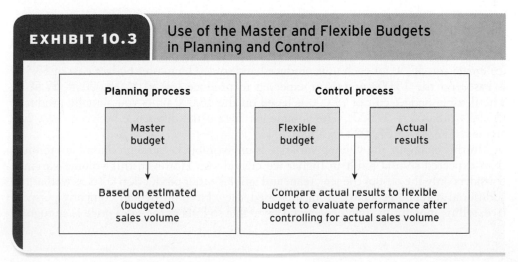

EXHIBIT 10.3 Use of the Master and Flexible Budgets in Planning and Control

To illustrate the importance of the flexible budget for performance evaluation, assume you are a Cold Stone Creamery manager, and it is your responsibility to control the cost of the ice cream used to make Cold Stone creations. Based on the master budget sales forecast of 15,000 units, your ice cream budget was set at $7,500 ($0.50 per unit × 15,000 units). After the budget period, you learned that the actual cost of ice cream was $8,000, or $500 higher than budgeted. Based on this information, how would your boss evaluate your performance at controlling ice cream costs?

To answer this question, we need to think about the two possible reasons that the actual cost might have been higher than budgeted:

- You may have spent more than $0.50 for each unit of ice cream.
- You may have produced more than 15,000 units.

What if we knew that your store actually produced and sold 18,000 units of ice cream? Would that knowledge change how your boss evaluates your performance at controlling ice cream costs? In this case, we can attribute the increased cost to the increase in volume. In fact, you actually spent **less** than $0.50 per unit on ice cream.

The lesson here is that to evaluate cost control, we cannot just compare actual results to the master budget because the difference can be due to either spending or volume. The flexible budget allows us to separate the effects of spending from volume.

VOLUME VARIANCE VERSUS SPENDING VARIANCE

The only difference between the master budget and the flexible budget is the volume used to create each budget. Thus, any comparison of the master budget to the flexible budget creates a **volume variance** that represents the difference between actual and budgeted volume. **Spending variances** are calculated by comparing actual costs to the flexible budget (not the master budget). Because both numbers are based on the same volume, this provides an "apples to apples" comparison of spending.

COACH'S TIP

Spending variances are calculated by comparing actual costs to the flexible budget. The master budget is used to calculate volume variances, not spending variances.

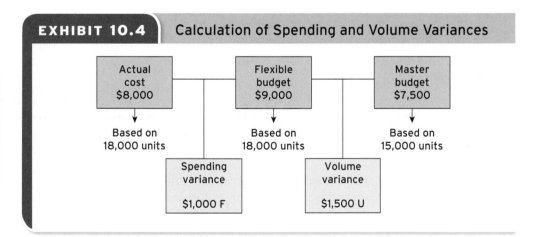

EXHIBIT 10.4   Calculation of Spending and Volume Variances

See Exhibit 10.4 for a comparison of the master and flexible budget based on the ice cream example presented in the previous section. Remember that your budget for ice cream was $0.50 for each unit produced and sold. The master budget cost of $7,500 is based on the 15,000 units you expected to produce ($0.50 × 15,000 = $7,500). The flexible budget cost of $9,000 is based on the 18,000 units you actually produced ($0.50 × 18,000 = $9,000). The volume variance is the difference between these two amounts ($9,000 − $7,500 = $1,500).

In this example, the volume variance is unfavorable because producing more units than expected **should** result in higher ice cream cost. However, this volume variance considers only the cost of the ice cream and ignores other production costs as well as the additional revenue generated from increased sales. From an overall company perspective, selling more units than expected is favorable so long as the sales price is enough to cover the increased variable costs. We do not consider revenue variances in this chapter, but they are covered in more advanced managerial accounting texts.

Exhibit 10.4 also includes a comparison of actual ice cream costs to the flexible budget.

Recall that you actually spent $8,000 on ice cream to produce 18,000 units. The flexible budget shows that it **should** have cost $9,000 to produce 18,000 units (18,000 × $0.50). The difference between actual cost and the flexible budget is a favorable spending variance of $1,000 ($9,000 − $8,000). It is favorable because you spent less on ice cream than the flexible budget allowed. Notice that volume is held constant between these two numbers at 18,000 units. So, the entire variance can be attributed to your **spending** on ice cream as opposed to the volume of units produced. There are at least two possible explanations for this favorable spending variance. Perhaps you were able to negotiate a reduced price for the ice cream. Or perhaps employees skimped on the amount of ice cream they put into each Cold Stone Creation. In the next section, we calculate price and quantity variances that break the overall spending variance into more detailed components so that we can hold a specific manager responsible for it.

COACH'S TIP

In calculating variances, we always isolate the effect of a single factor while holding all other factors constant. Doing so makes it easier to assign responsibility to the manager who has control over that factor.

FAVORABLE VERSUS UNFAVORABLE VARIANCES

Cost variances are calculated by comparing actual costs to the flexible budget. A **favorable variance** (F) occurs when actual costs are less than budgeted costs. An **unfavorable variance** (U) occurs when actual costs are more than budgeted costs. Common causes of favorable and unfavorable variances include the following:

Causes of Favorable (F) Variances	Causes of Unfavorable (U) Variances
• Paying a lower price than expected for direct materials	• Paying a higher price than expected for direct materials
• Using less direct materials than expected	• Using more direct materials than expected
• Paying a lower rate than expected for direct labor	• Paying a higher rate than expected for direct labor
• Taking less time to produce a unit than expected	• Taking more time than expected to produce a unit
• Paying less than expected for manufacturing overhead costs	• Paying more than expected for manufacturing overhead costs
• Using less of a variable overhead resource than expected	• Using more of a variable overhead resource than expected
• Using more of a fixed overhead resource than expected	• Using less of a fixed overhead resource than expected

COACH'S TIP

The words **favorable** and **unfavorable** do not necessarily indicate good and bad performance. Rather, they reflect a difference between actual and standard costs. Sometimes a favorable variance can signal bad performance and an unfavorable variance can indicate good performance.

In the remainder of this chapter, we calculate cost variances that illustrate each of these potential causes.

Direct Material and Direct Labor Variances

We can use the same basic framework to calculate variances for direct materials and direct labor costs. This framework allows us to separate the overall spending variance into two unique components: a price variance and a quantity variance.

VARIANCE FRAMEWORK

The price variance relates to the amount **paid** for a particular **input** that goes into the final product. For Cold Stone Creamery, the direct inputs to the final product are ice cream, mix-in ingredients, and employee time. The price variance compares the price actually paid for each of these inputs to the standard price that **should have** been paid. Notice that when we talk about price in this context, we are talking about the amount paid for something (cost), not the price we charged the final customer (revenue). Thus, the price variance for direct materials and direct labor is really a cost variance.

The quantity variance relates to the quantity of **input** used to make the final product. For Cold Stone, the quantity of input can be measured in terms of **ounces** of ice cream and mix-in ingredients or **hours** of employee time. For simplicity, we assume that the quantity of input purchased equals the quantity used. That way we don't need to worry about changes in inventory, which complicates the calculations.

Exhibit 10.5 illustrates the framework used to analyze direct cost variances.

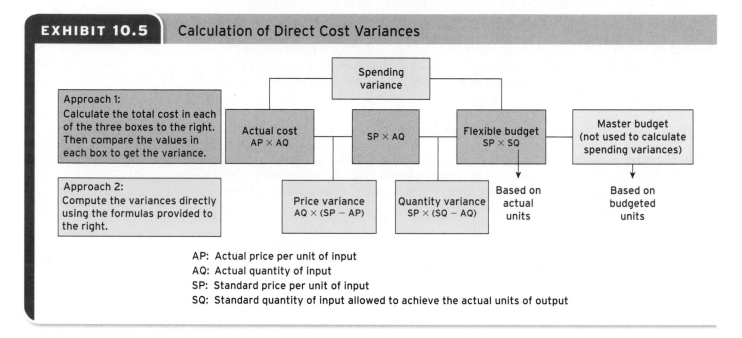

EXHIBIT 10.5   Calculation of Direct Cost Variances

AP: Actual price per unit of input
AQ: Actual quantity of input
SP: Standard price per unit of input
SQ: Standard quantity of input allowed to achieve the actual units of output

Direct cost variances can be calculated in two ways. The first approach is to calculate the total cost in each of the boxes shown in Exhibit 10.5. Then calculate the difference (variance) between each box by subtracting one value from the other. The second approach is to use the formulas provided in Exhibit 10.5 shown here:

$$\text{Price Variance} = [(SP \times AQ) - (AP \times AQ)] = AQ \times (SP - AP)$$
$$\text{Quantity Variance} = [(SP \times SQ) - (SP \times AQ)] = SP \times (SQ - AQ)$$

Notice that each variance formula allows only one factor (either price or quantity) to vary while holding the other factor constant. Isolating the variance this way allows managers to identify the specific cause of the variance so that a specific manager can be held responsible for it.

DIRECT MATERIALS VARIANCES

In an earlier example, we learned that Cold Stone Creamery had a $1,000 unfavorable spending variance for ice cream. Let's see if we can determine a more specific cause of that variance. The standard cost for Cold Stone's ice cream is as follows:

Direct Costs	Standard Quantity	Standard Price	Standard Unit Cost
Ice cream	10 oz.	$0.05 per oz.	$0.50

Cold Stone's actual results were as follows:

- Produced and sold 18,000 units.
- Purchased and used 200,000 ounces of ice cream at a total cost of $8,000.

Let's start by identifying the following terms:

Actual price: $8,000/200,000 = $0.04 per ounce.

Actual quantity: 200,000 ounces.

Standard price: $0.05 per ounce.

Standard quantity: 10 ounces per unit × 18,000 actual units = 180,000 ounces.

The **direct materials price variance** is the difference between the actual price and the standard price for direct materials multiplied by the actual quantity of direct materials purchased. In this case, the actual price of ice cream was $0.04 per ounce; the standard price was $0.05 per ounce. To get the price variance, we need to multiply the $0.01 price difference by the 200,000 ounces that were actually purchased.

The **direct materials quantity variance** is the difference between the actual quantity and the standard quantity of direct materials used, multiplied by the standard price. This variance is sometimes called the **direct materials usage variance**. Because the standard quantity is 10 ounces of ice cream for each unit produced, the standard quantity allowed for 18,000 units is 180,000 ounces. However, the company actually used 200,000 ounces. To get the quantity variance, we need to multiply the difference of 20,000 ounces by the $0.05 standard price.

Entering these numbers into Exhibit 10.5 provides the variances in Exhibit 10.6.

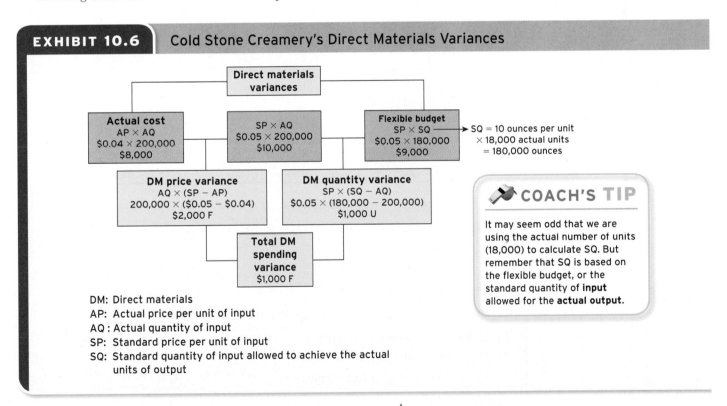

EXHIBIT 10.6 Cold Stone Creamery's Direct Materials Variances

DM: Direct materials
AP: Actual price per unit of input
AQ: Actual quantity of input
SP: Standard price per unit of input
SQ: Standard quantity of input allowed to achieve the actual units of output

We can draw two conclusions from this diagram. First, the direct materials price variance is $2,000 (F) favorable because the company paid $0.01 less than the standard cost for the 200,000 ounces of materials purchased. **The direct materials purchasing manager is responsible for the direct materials price variance.** A favorable price variance is not always good, however. Although it has a positive effect on short-term spending, it could have a negative effect over the long term if customers can detect a difference in product quality. What are some potential explanations for this favorable price variance? Perhaps the purchasing manager purchased lower quality ingredients or negotiated a reduced

price, or perhaps the company received a quantity discount that was not factored into the standard price. Alternatively, it may simply reflect a market fluctuation in the price of ice cream much the same way that dairy prices fluctuate at the grocery store.

Second, the direct materials quantity variance is $1,000 unfavorable because the company used 200,000 ounces of ice cream to make 18,000 units when the standard allowed only 10 ounces per unit, or 180,000 total ounces. **The production manager is typically responsible for the direct materials quantity variance**—in this case, the manager who oversees the employees who make and serve the ice cream creations. What are some potential explanations for this unfavorable usage variance? Perhaps employees put too much ice cream into each unit, or perhaps the standard quantity does not account for ice cream given away to customers in taste tests or thrown away at the end of the day. Managers would need to investigate further to determine the exact cause, but the variance gives them a starting point for their investigation.

The **direct materials spending variance** combines the direct materials price and quantity variances. Because the price variance is $2,000 favorable and the quantity variance is $1,000 unfavorable, we net them to get a $1,000 favorable spending variance. Notice that this is the same number we calculated in Exhibit 10.4 (page 364) by comparing actual costs to the flexible budget. Now, however, we have a better idea of **why** the company had a favorable spending variance for ice cream. These variances provide feedback to managers that they may need to change their behavior. Alternatively, the variances may signal that the company's standards need to be updated to reflect new pricing or production methods.

Before you continue, complete the following Self-Study Practice to see whether you can calculate the direct materials variances for Cold Stone Creamery's mix-in ingredients.

 ## Self-Study Practice

Cold Stone Creamery's standard cost card for mix-in ingredients follows:

Direct Costs	Standard Quantity	Standard Price	Standard Unit Cost
Mix-in ingredients	2 oz.	$0.10 per oz.	$0.20

Actual results were as follows:

- Produced and sold 18,000 units.
- Purchased and used 35,000 ounces of mix-in ingredients at a total cost of $4,200 ($0.12 per ounce).

Calculate the following variances and label them as favorable (F) or unfavorable (U):

1. Direct materials price variance.
2. Direct materials quantity variance.
3. Direct materials spending variance.

After you have finished, check your answers with the solutions in the margin.

DIRECT LABOR VARIANCES

Learning Objective 4
Calculate and interpret the direct labor rate and efficiency variances.

The method for calculating direct labor variances is similar to the direct materials variances with a few modifications:

- Because the price of direct labor is based on the direct labor rate, **the price variance for labor is called the direct labor rate (not price) variance.**

Solution to Self-Study Practice

1. DM Price Variance = AQ × (SP − AP) = 35,000 × ($0.10 − $0.12) = $700 U
2. DM Quantity Variance = SP × (SQ − AQ) = $0.10(36,000 − 35,000) = $100 F
3. DM Spending Variance = $700 Unfavorable − $100 Favorable = $600 U

- Because direct labor quantity is measured in hours, **the quantity variance for labor is called the direct labor efficiency variance**.

Let's use Exhibit 10.7 to analyze Cold Stone Creamery's actual and standard direct labor costs.

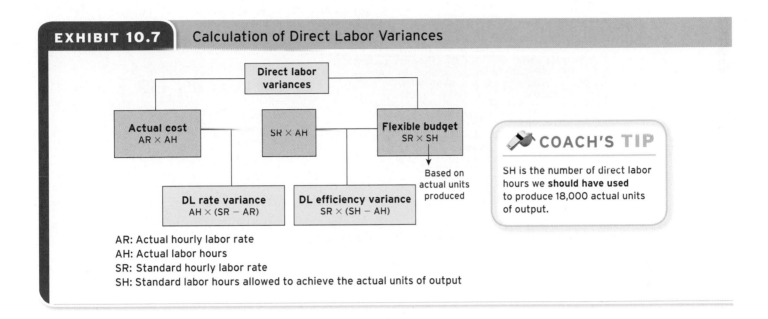

EXHIBIT 10.7 | **Calculation of Direct Labor Variances**

COACH'S TIP

SH is the number of direct labor hours we **should have used** to produce 18,000 actual units of output.

AR: Actual hourly labor rate
AH: Actual labor hours
SR: Standard hourly labor rate
SH: Standard labor hours allowed to achieve the actual units of output

The labor portion of Cold Stone's standard cost card follows:

Input	Standard Quantity	Standard Rate	Standard Unit Cost
Direct labor	0.10 hrs.	$8.00 per hr.	$0.80

COACH'S TIP

Try using these numbers in Exhibit 10.7 to see whether you can calculate the variances yourself. Then look at the answers in Exhibit 10.8.

Cold Stone's actual results were as follows:

- Actual number of units produced was 18,000.
- Actual direct labor costs were $16,500 for 2,000 hours.

Let's start by filling in the following terms:

Actual labor rate: $16,500/2,000 hours = $8.25 per hour.

Actual labor hours: 2,000 hours.

Standard labor rate: $8.00 per hour.

Standard labor hours: 0.10 hours × 18,000 units = 1,800 hours.

The **direct labor rate variance** is the difference between the actual labor rate and the standard labor rate multiplied by the actual number of labor hours. The **direct labor efficiency variance** is the difference between the actual number of labor hours and the standard number of labor hours multiplied by the standard labor rate. Cold Stone's direct labor standard indicates that an employee should take 0.10 hours (6 minutes) to produce a single unit of output. Because Cold Stone's employees produced 18,000 units, they should have required only 1,800 direct labor hours. Actually, employees worked 2,000 direct labor hours to produce 18,000 units.

Using these numbers in the framework shown in Exhibit 10.7 gives the results in Exhibit 10.8.

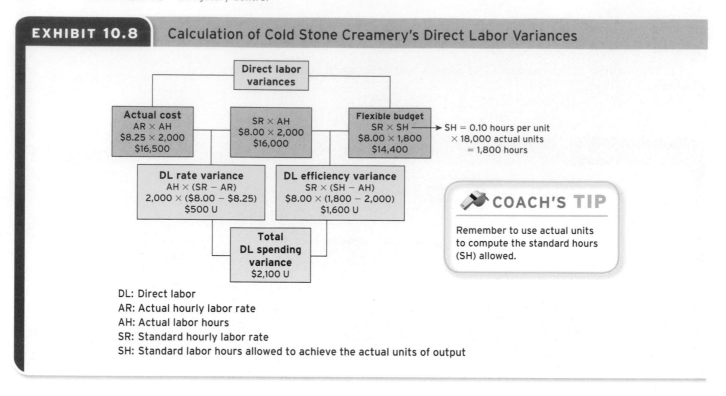

EXHIBIT 10.8   Calculation of Cold Stone Creamery's Direct Labor Variances

DL: Direct labor
AR: Actual hourly labor rate
AH: Actual labor hours
SR: Standard hourly labor rate
SH: Standard labor hours allowed to achieve the actual units of output

The direct labor rate variance is $500 unfavorable because the company paid $0.25 more per hour than the standard labor rate for the 2,000 actual labor hours worked. **Holding an individual manager responsible for the direct labor rate variance is difficult** because many factors can influence the variance including labor market conditions, how and when workers were hired and promoted, and turnover rates in the organization. In this case, the variance is unfavorable because the actual labor rate ($8.25) was slightly higher (on average) than the standard rate ($8.00). The market wage rate may have increased, but the standard wage rate may not have been adjusted to reflect that market reality.

The direct labor efficiency variance is unfavorable because workers took 200 more hours than they **should** have to produce 18,000 units. When we multiply the 200 extra hours by the standard labor rate of $8.00 per hour, we get an unfavorable efficiency variance of $1,600. **The production manager is responsible for the direct labor efficiency variance.** A variety of factors can affect this variance including how quickly workers can make the product and how closely production can be matched with customer demand. Unlike a traditional manufacturing firm, which can use inventory to keep production levels stable, Cold Stone Creamery cannot produce its product until a customer walks through the door. Having employees standing around with no customers to serve will negatively affect the direct labor efficiency variance. This variance can signal to managers that the staffing schedule should be modified.

The **direct labor spending variance** is the sum of the direct labor rate and direct labor efficiency variances. In this case both variances are unfavorable, so we add them together to determine the unfavorable spending variance of $2,100 ($500 U + $1,600 U = $2,100 U). The direct labor spending variance represents the combined effect of the direct labor rate and efficiency variances on direct labor costs.

Manufacturing Overhead Cost Variances

Because manufacturing overhead costs cannot be traced directly to specific units, they must be **applied** to products using a predetermined overhead rate and an allocation measure (cost driver) such as direct labor hours. The standard overhead rates are estimated before the accounting period begins based on budgeted costs and budgeted levels of the overhead cost drivers. Overhead is then applied to specific units during the period by multiplying the budgeted (standard) rate by the standard quantity of the cost driver.

This is a key difference between a standard cost system and the "normal" cost system described in Chapters 2–4. In these earlier chapters, we established a predetermined manufacturing overhead rate based on budgeted costs and budgeted levels of the cost drivers. Then we applied overhead cost to products by multiplying the overhead rate by the **actual** value of the cost driver. In a standard cost system, we multiply the budgeted (standard) overhead rate by the **standard** value of the cost driver.

The overall difference (variance) between actual and applied manufacturing overhead is still called **over-** or **underapplied overhead**. Now, however, we can separate the overall variance into more detailed variances to gain some insight into **why** manufacturing overhead costs were over- or underapplied. As you will see shortly, our interpretation of these overhead variances changes significantly depending on whether the overhead cost is variable or fixed.

Video 10-3
www.mhhe.com/whitecotton1e

VARIABLE MANUFACTURING OVERHEAD VARIANCES

Variable manufacturing overhead costs include indirect materials such as cleaning supplies and paper products, as well as the power to run machines and other incidental costs that vary with some activity driver. In this chapter, we assume these costs vary in direct proportion to direct labor hours—a realistic assumption for a labor-oriented business such as Cold Stone Creamery. As you learned in earlier chapters, however, overhead costs can vary with many other factors including number of machine hours and nonvolume activity drivers such as the number of setups, material-handling transactions, and the like. Companies that use activity based costing would do a separate analysis for each activity cost driver (a task that is beyond the scope of this book).

Because we assume that variable overhead (VOH) costs are driven by direct labor hours (DLH), we can simply substitute the variable overhead rate for the direct labor rate in the direct labor variance framework.

Let's apply this framework to our Cold Stone Creamery example. The variable manufacturing overhead standards are as follows:

Learning Objective 5
Calculate and interpret the variable overhead rate and efficiency variances.

	Standard Quantity	Standard Rate	Standard Unit Cost
Variable manufacturing overhead applied at $1.00 per direct labor hour	0.10 hrs	$1.00 per hr.	$0.10

The company's actual results were as follows:

- Actual units produced were 18,000.
- Actual direct labor hours were 2,000.
- Actual variable overhead costs were $1,800.

Let's start by identifying the following terms:

Actual VOH rate: $1,800/2,000 hours = $0.90 per hour.

Actual DLH: 2,000 hours.

Standard VOH rate: $1.00 per hour.

Standard DLH: .10 hours × 18,000 units = 1,800 hours.

The **variable overhead rate variance** is the difference between the actual variable overhead rate and the standard variable overhead rate multiplied by the actual value of the cost driver (DLH). In this case, the actual cost of variable overhead is $0.90 per direct labor hour, and the standard variable overhead rate is $1.00 per direct labor hour. The **variable overhead efficiency variance** is the difference between the number of actual direct labor hours used and the number of standard direct labor hours multiplied by the standard VOH rate. In this case, the actual hours was 2,000, but only 1,800 hours should have been required to produce 18,000 units. See Exhibit 10.9 for the calculation of the variable overhead variances.

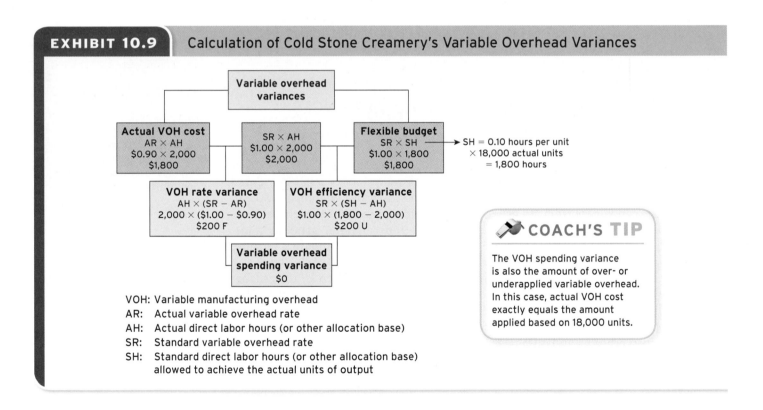

EXHIBIT 10.9   Calculation of Cold Stone Creamery's Variable Overhead Variances

COACH'S TIP

The VOH spending variance is also the amount of over- or underapplied variable overhead. In this case, actual VOH cost exactly equals the amount applied based on 18,000 units.

The variable overhead rate variance is favorable because the actual variable overhead rate ($0.90) was less than the standard variable overhead rate ($1.00). When we multiply the $0.10 difference by 2,000 actual direct labor hours, we get a favorable variable overhead rate variance of $200. What caused this variance? Managers may have paid less for variable overhead items (cleaning supplies, napkins, or power) than the standard allows, or the relationship between variable overhead cost and direct labor hours may not be perfectly proportional. Even if the variable overhead costs are partially driven by direct labor hours, other factors are likely to influence spending on variable overhead costs.

The variable overhead efficiency variance is unfavorable because the company used 200 more direct labor hours than **should** have been needed to produce

18,000 units. Multiplying the 200 extra hours by the $1 standard variable overhead rate gives a $200 unfavorable variable overhead efficiency variance. Although this variance is called the **variable overhead efficiency variance**, it is really driven by the efficiency (or inefficiency) of the underlying cost driver (that is, direct labor hours). This variance is a mirror image of the direct labor efficiency variance. The assumption is that as managers use more direct labor hours, they also incur additional variable overhead costs.

The variable overhead spending variance is the sum of the variable overhead rate variance and the variable overhead efficiency variance. In this case, it is zero because the $200 favorable variable overhead rate variance exactly offsets the $200 unfavorable variable overhead efficiency variance.

Before you continue, complete the following Self-Study Practice to make sure you can calculate the direct labor and variable overhead variances.

 Self-Study Practice

Papa John's standard cost card for direct labor and variable overhead includes the following costs.

Direct costs	Standard Quantity	Standard Rate
Direct labor	.3 hrs.	$10.00 per hr.
Variable overhead	.3 hrs.	2.50 per hr.

Actual results were as follows:

- The number of units sold and produced was 15,000.
- The direct labor cost was $38,000 for 4,000 hours ($9.50 per hour).
- The variable overhead cost was $12,000 for 4,000 hours ($3.00 per hour).

Calculate the following variances and label them as favorable or unfavorable:

1. Direct labor rate variance.
2. Direct labor efficiency variance.
3. Direct labor spending variance.
4. Variable overhead rate variance.
5. Variable overhead efficiency variance.
6. Variable overhead spending variance.
7. Briefly explain the relationship between the direct labor efficiency variance and the variable overhead efficiency variance.

After you have finished, check your answers with the solutions in the margin.

Solution to Self-Study Practice

1. DL Rate Variance: AH × (SR − AR) = 4,000 × ($10.00 − $9.50) = $2,000 F
2. DL Efficiency Variance: SR × (SH − AH) = $10.00 × (4,500 − 4,000) = $5,000 F
3. DL Spending Variance = $2,000 F + $5,000 F = $7,000 F
4. VOH Rate Variance: AH × (SR − AR) = 4,000 × ($2.50 − $3.00) = $2,000 U
5. VOH Efficiency Variance: SR × (SH − AH) = $2.50 × (4,500 − 4,000) = $1,250 F
6. VOH Spending Total Variance = $2,000 U + $1,250 F = $750 U
7. The DL efficiency and the VOH efficiency variances are both driven by the difference between actual labor hours and standard labor hours. The VOH efficiency variance is 25 percent of the DL efficiency variance because the VOH is based on DL hours.

FIXED MANUFACTURING OVERHEAD SPENDING VARIANCE

The model used to analyze direct materials, direct labor, and variable overhead variances does not apply to fixed manufacturing overhead costs. In general, fixed manufacturing overhead costs are less "controllable" than variable costs. Fixed manufacturing overhead costs such as rent, machine depreciation, and factory supervision are incurred to provide the capacity to perform work, but the total fixed cost does not vary with volume within that range of capacity. Even so, managers need to budget for total fixed costs, and it

Learning Objective 6
Calculate and interpret the fixed overhead spending variance.

is possible that the actual amount spent will be higher or lower than budgeted due to factors other than volume.

The **fixed overhead spending variance**, also called the **fixed overhead budget variance**, is calculated by comparing actual fixed overhead costs to budgeted fixed overhead costs. For example, if Cold Stone Creamery budgeted for $6,000 in fixed manufacturing overhead but actually spent $6,300, it would report a $300 unfavorable fixed overhead spending variance, as follows:

This $300 unfavorable spending variance could be due to an unexpected rise in the cost of rent, insurance, supervision, or other fixed costs.

There are other variances that relate to the method used to **apply** fixed manufacturing costs to individual products or customers. Even though the costs are considered "fixed," we still use a fixed overhead rate to apply the full manufacturing cost to individual units. Depending on how accurately we estimate the fixed overhead rate, the amount of fixed overhead applied is likely to differ from the amount budgeted. These fixed overhead volume variances are covered in the supplement to this chapter.

SUMMARY OF SPENDING VARIANCES

In this chapter, we calculated many different variances. You are probably beginning to suffer from calculation overload. How in the world are you going to remember how to calculate all these variances? Exhibit 10.10 provides a summary of all of the variances calculated in this chapter, along with a definition of the terms used in the formulas.

Of course, calculating the variance is only part of it. Tips for understanding and interpreting the variances follow:

- Variances are always calculated by comparing actual results to budgeted or standard results. Variances signal managers that they are (or are not) achieving their plans so they can take corrective action if necessary.

- Companies try to hold specific managers responsible for specific variances while removing the effects of factors that are beyond managers' control.

- The formulas for variances allow only one factor such as price, quantity, or volume to change, while holding everything else constant at either actual or standard values (depending on the type of variance).

- The driving factor for the variance always appears in parentheses in the formula and in the name of the variance. If you forget the name of a particular variance, just look at the terms in parentheses to determine the cause of the variance.

- Try not to memorize rules or rely on formulas to determine whether a variance is favorable or unfavorable; just think about it. Spending or using more of a variable resource is unfavorable. Using more of a fixed resource is favorable because it drives down the fixed cost per unit.

EXHIBIT 10.10	Summary of Variance Formulas and Terminology

Variance	Formula
DM Price Variance	$AQ \times (SP - AP)$
DM Quantity Variance	$SP \times (SQ - AQ)$
DM Spending Variance	Sum of DM Price and DM Quantity Variances
DL Rate Variance	$AH \times (SR - AR)$
DL Efficiency Variance	$SR \times (SH - AH)$
DL Spending Variance	Sum of DL Rate and DL Efficiency Variances
VOH Rate Variance	$AH \times (SR - AR)$
VOH Efficiency Variance	$SR \times (SH - AH)$
VOH Spending Variance	Sum of VOH Rate and VOH Efficiency Variances
Over or Underapplied VOH	Same as VOH Spending Variance
FOH Spending Variance	Budgeted − Actual FOH Costs
FOH Budget Variance	Same as FOH Spending Variance

Where:

DM: Direct materials

DL: Direct labor

VOH: Variable manufacturing overhead

FOH: Fixed manufacturing overhead

AP: Actual price of input

AQ: Actual quantity of input

SP: Standard price of input

SQ: Standard quantity of input allowed for actual units produced

AR: Actual labor rate (or VOH rate for VOH variances)

AH: Actual labor hours

SR: Standard labor rate (or standard VOH rate for VOH variances)

SH: Standard labor hours allowed for actual units produced

EXHIBIT 10.11	Summary of Spending Variances for Cold Stone Creamery

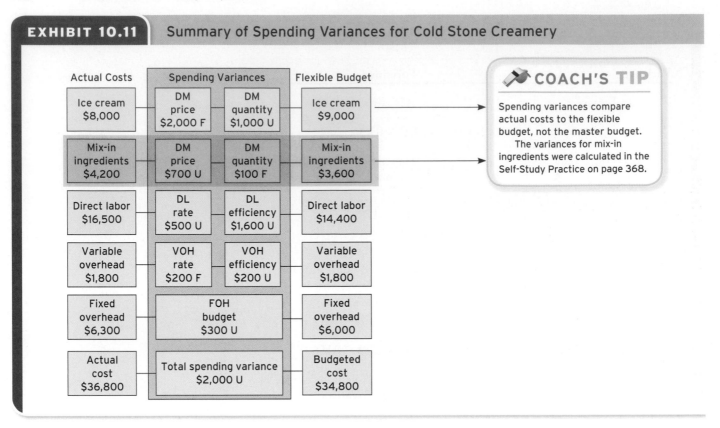

COACH'S TIP

Spending variances compare actual costs to the flexible budget, not the master budget. The variances for mix-in ingredients were calculated in the Self-Study Practice on page 368.

Finally, you need to understand how all of the variances fit together. See Exhibit 10.11 for a summary of all of the spending variances calculated in this chapter and how they can be used to explain the difference in Cold Stone Creamery's actual and budgeted results.

In a standard cost system, costs are initially recorded at standard (not actual) amounts, but eventually the accounting system needs to be adjusted to reflect the actual costs. At the end of the accounting period, the variances are used to adjust from standard to actual cost. In addition to the spending variances shown in Exhibit 10.11, the accounting system would also record the fixed overhead volume variances described in Supplement 10A. The detailed journal entries used to record manufacturing costs and variances in a standard cost system are discussed in Supplement 10B.

SUPPLEMENT 10A: FIXED MANUFACTURING OVERHEAD VOLUME AND CAPACITY VARIANCES

The chapter explained how to calculate spending variances by comparing actual costs to the flexible budget. This supplement describes other types of variances that result from the method used to apply fixed manufacturing overhead costs.

Although fixed manufacturing costs are, in theory, independent of volume, these costs must be assigned to individual units using a fixed overhead rate that is set in advance. The fixed overhead rate is computed by dividing budgeted total fixed overhead cost by some measure of activity, such as the number of units or the number of direct labor hours. The question is whether the denominator in the fixed overhead rate should be based on budgeted volume or some other measure such as practical capacity.

If actual volume differs from the value used in the denominator of the fixed overhead rate, it will create a fixed overhead volume variance. A volume variance has nothing to do with how much managers spent on fixed costs. It simply reflects the accuracy of the denominator used to compute the fixed overhead rate. The interpretation of the variance depends on the type of measure that was used in the denominator of the fixed overhead rate. Two common methods for computing fixed overhead rates and the resulting variances are discussed next.

Fixed Overhead Rate Based on Budgeted Volume

One of the most common methods for calculating the fixed overhead rate is based on budgeted production volume. In our Cold Stone Creamery example, total fixed overhead costs were budgeted at $6,000, and the master budget was based on planned production of 15,000 units. Based on this information, the fixed overhead rate was calculated as follows:

> Budgeted Fixed Overhead Rate = $6,000/15,000 Units = $0.40 per Unit

COACH'S TIP

The fixed overhead volume variance is sometimes called the "denominator variance" because it relates to the denominator used in the fixed overhead rate.

Cold Stone Creamery would apply fixed overhead at a rate of $0.40 per unit produced. This rate is intended to cover all of the "fixed" costs of production such as rent, depreciation, supervision, and insurance. The amount of fixed overhead applied will only equal $6,000 if the company actually produces 15,000 units. If Cold Stone produces anything other than 15,000 units, the amount of fixed overhead applied will differ from the $6,000 budgeted. For example, if Cold Stone produces 18,000 actual units, will it apply too much or too little fixed manufacturing overhead? The total amount applied will be $7,200 ($0.40 × 18,000 units), which is $1,200 higher than the $6,000 budgeted.

The difference between applied and budgeted fixed overhead is called the **fixed overhead (FOH) volume variance** and is computed as follows:

$$\text{Fixed Overhead Volume Variance} = \begin{array}{c}\text{Applied FOH}\\ \text{FOH Rate} \times\\ \text{Actual Volume}\end{array} - \begin{array}{c}\text{Budgeted FOH}\\ \text{FOH Rate} \times\\ \text{Budgeted Volume}\end{array}$$

Notice that the only difference between applied and budgeted fixed overhead is the volume of units produced (actual versus budgeted). The fixed overhead rate is the same in both. Thus, an alternative way to compute the fixed overhead volume variance is as follows:

$$\text{Fixed Overhead Volume Variance} = \begin{array}{c}\text{FOH Rate}\\ \times\\ (\text{Actual Volume} - \text{Budgeted Volume})\end{array}$$

In our Cold Stone example, the fixed overhead volume variance is computed as follows:

$$\text{Fixed Overhead Volume Variance} = \begin{array}{c}\$0.40\\ \times\\ (18,000 \text{ units} - 15,000 \text{ units})\end{array} = \begin{array}{c}\$1,200\\ \text{Favorable}\end{array}$$

Cold Stone Creamery expected to produce 15,000 units, but actually produced 18,000 units. Multiplying the 3,000 additional units by the $0.40 fixed overhead rate results in a $1,200 favorable volume variance. It is favorable because producing more units than expected drives down the fixed cost per unit (getting more volume from the same total cost). But remember that the total fixed cost does not change with volume. From an overall company perspective, a favorable volume variance results in higher profit only if the increased revenue from the units sold is enough to cover the increased variable costs.

When fixed overhead rates are based on budgeted production, total over- or underapplied fixed manufacturing overhead is the sum of the fixed overhead spending variance and fixed overhead volume variance. Earlier in the chapter, we calculated the fixed overhead spending variance of $300 unfavorable (see Exhibit 10.11). The fixed overhead volume variance was $1,200 favorable, for a total fixed overhead variance of $900 favorable. Favorable means that actual fixed overhead were less than applied, or overapplied by $900. These variances are summarized in Exhibit 10A.1.

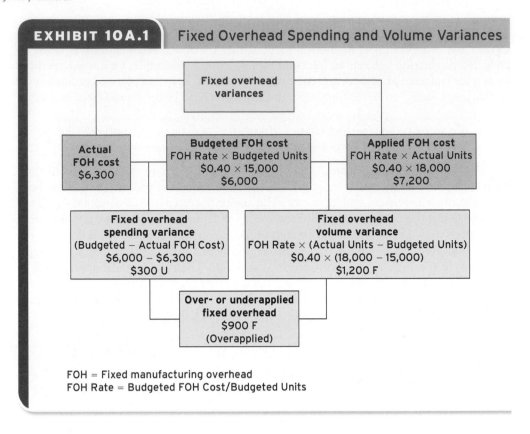

EXHIBIT 10A.1 Fixed Overhead Spending and Volume Variances

Fixed overhead variances

| Actual FOH cost $6,300 | Budgeted FOH cost FOH Rate × Budgeted Units $0.40 × 15,000 $6,000 | Applied FOH cost FOH Rate × Actual Units $0.40 × 18,000 $7,200 |

Fixed overhead spending variance (Budgeted − Actual FOH Cost) $6,000 − $6,300 $300 U

Fixed overhead volume variance FOH Rate × (Actual Units − Budgeted Units) $0.40 × (18,000 − 15,000) $1,200 F

Over- or underapplied fixed overhead $900 F (Overapplied)

FOH = Fixed manufacturing overhead
FOH Rate = Budgeted FOH Cost/Budgeted Units

Fixed Overhead Rate Based on Practical Capacity

Although fixed overhead rates are often based on budgeted production levels, most experts agree that a better approach is to base fixed overhead rates on practical capacity. **Practical capacity** is the volume that **could be** achieved under normal (not ideal) operating conditions. Practical capacity allows some downtime for necessary activities such as employee training, shift changes, breaks, and preventive maintenance.

Fixed overhead costs are incurred to provide (supply) an organization with the capacity to produce units or serve customers. Basing the fixed overhead rate on the amount of capacity supplied (as opposed to the amount of capacity actually used or consumed) prevents the fixed overhead rate from fluctuating due to changes in demand. Basing fixed costs on the amount of capacity supplied also highlights the cost of unutilized or unused capacity for management attention (and potential action).

As an example, assume that budgeted fixed overhead of $6,000 provides Cold Stone Creamery the practical capacity to produce and serve up to 20,000 ice cream creations per month. Even though the company expected to produce only 15,000 units per month, we should base the fixed overhead rate on the amount of practical capacity supplied (i.e., 20,000 units). The fixed overhead rate based on practical capacity would be computed as follows:

Fixed Overhead Rate = $6,000/20,000 units = $0.30 per unit

The fixed overhead rate based on practical capacity is $0.30 per unit. Notice that this is less than the $0.40 fixed overhead rate calculated previously based on expected or budgeted production of 15,000 units. If the company produces anything other than 20,000 units, it will have fixed overhead capacity variance. There are two types of capacity variances: one that is calculated in advance of the budget period (based on budgeted production volume of 15,000 units) and the other that is calculated after the budget period (based on actual production of 18,000 units). This is consistent with the general approach described in the chapter in which the master budget is based on budgeted production and variances are computed after the fact by comparing actual to budgeted results (flexible budget).

Before the budget period starts, managers calculate the expected (planned) cost of unused capacity as follows:

$$
\begin{array}{c}
\text{Expected} \\
\text{(Planned)} \\
\text{Capacity Variance}
\end{array}
=
\begin{array}{c}
\text{FOH Rate} \\
\times \\
\text{(Budgeted Volume} - \text{Practical Capacity)}
\end{array}
$$

Recall that Cold Stone's practical capacity is 20,000 units, but the master budget was based on planned production of 15,000 units. In this case, the planned capacity variance would be computed as follows:

$$
\begin{array}{c}
\text{Expected} \\
\text{(Planned)} \\
\text{Capacity Variance}
\end{array}
=
\begin{array}{c}
\$0.30 \\
\times \\
\text{(15,000 units} - \text{20,000 units)}
\end{array}
=
\begin{array}{c}
\$1,500 \\
\text{Unfavorable}
\end{array}
$$

The planned (expected) cost of unused capacity is $1,500 unfavorable. It is unfavorable because the company planned to produce fewer units than the amount of practical capacity available. This capacity variance tells managers that $1,500 (5,000 units × $0.30) of the total fixed manufacturing overhead cost is expected to be unused or underutilized. This information may encourage managers to find creative ways to utilize their capacity resources (e.g., increase sales) or to downsize capacity if demand is not expected to increase in the future (e.g., reduce fixed costs).

After the budget period is over, managers calculate the unexpected (unplanned) portion of the capacity variance by comparing actual to budgeted results, as follows:

$$
\begin{array}{c}
\text{Unexpected} \\
\text{(Unplanned)} \\
\text{Capacity Variance}
\end{array}
=
\begin{array}{c}
\text{FOH Rate} \\
\times \\
\text{(Actual Volume} - \text{Budgeted Production)}
\end{array}
$$

In our Cold Stone example, actual production was 18,000 units and budgeted production was 15,000 units. Multiplying the 3,000 unit difference by the fixed overhead rate gives the unexpected (unplanned) capacity variance:

$$
\begin{array}{c}
\text{Unexpected} \\
\text{(Unplanned)} \\
\text{Capacity Variance}
\end{array}
=
\begin{array}{c}
\$0.30 \\
\times \\
\text{(18,000 units} - \text{15,000 units)}
\end{array}
=
\$900 \text{ Favorable}
$$

Notice that this formula is the same as the volume variance presented earlier except that the fixed overhead rate is now based on **practical capacity**. This capacity variance is favorable because the company produced more units than expected and thus utilized more of the practical capacity than initially planned.

The total capacity variance is the sum of the planned and unplanned capacity variances, as follows:

In this example, the company expected to have a $1,500 unfavorable capacity variance, but actual utilization of capacity was $900 better than expected. The total capacity variance is $600 unfavorable because actual production was still 2,000 units below practical capacity (2,000 units × $0.30 = $600).

When fixed overhead costs are applied based on practical capacity, over- or underapplied fixed manufacturing overhead is the sum of the fixed overhead spending variance ($300 U) and the total fixed overhead capacity variance ($600 U), or $900 U (underapplied). These variances are summarized in Exhibit 10A.2.

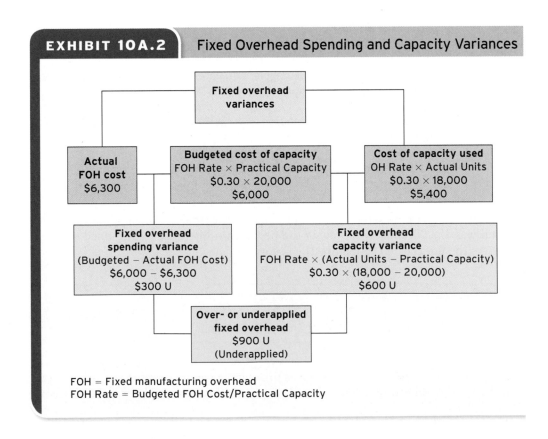

EXHIBIT 10A.2 Fixed Overhead Spending and Capacity Variances

SUPPLEMENT 10B: RECORDING STANDARD COSTS AND VARIANCES IN A STANDARD COST SYSTEM

This supplement describes the journal entries used to record manufacturing costs and variances in a standard cost system. In preparing journal entries for a standard cost system, keep in mind these common rules:

- The initial debit to an inventory account (Raw Materials, Work in Process, or Finished Goods) and the eventual debit to Cost of Goods Sold should be based on standard, not actual, cost.

- Actual costs should be credited to cash, payables, or other appropriate accounts such as accumulated depreciation or prepaid assets.

- The difference between the standard cost (debit) and the actual cost (credit) should be recorded as the cost variance.

- Unfavorable variances should appear as debit entries; favorable variances should appear as credit entries.

- At the end of the accounting period, all variances should be closed to the Cost of Goods Sold account to adjust from standard cost to the actual cost.

Recall from earlier chapters that manufacturing costs are initially recorded in inventory and are later recognized as Cost of Goods Sold as in Exhibit 10B.1.

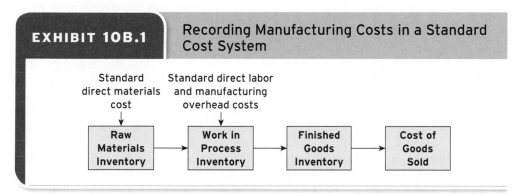

EXHIBIT 10B.1   Recording Manufacturing Costs in a Standard Cost System

A standard cost system initially records manufacturing costs at the standard rather than the actual amounts. Thus, the journal entries used to record manufacturing costs always involve a debit to an inventory account or to Cost of Goods Sold for the standard amount.

We illustrate this process using the variances we calculated for Cold Stone Creamery. Because the company does not make the product until a customer orders it, there is no need to keep Work in Process or Finished Goods Inventory accounts. Instead, we can bypass those accounts and transfer raw materials costs directly from the Raw Materials Inventory account to the Cost of Goods Sold account. Similarly, we can record direct labor and manufacturing overhead costs directly in the Cost of Goods Sold account (see Exhibit 10B.2).

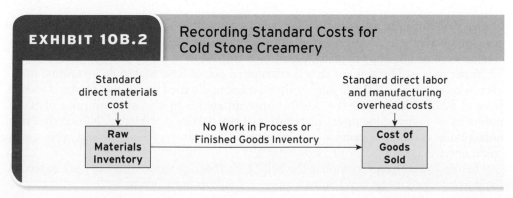

EXHIBIT 10B.2   Recording Standard Costs for Cold Stone Creamery

Direct Materials Costs

Let's start with the entry to record the purchase of raw materials. Assume Cold Stone's price and quantity standards for ice cream are as follows:

Direct Costs	Standard Quantity	Standard Price	Standard Unit Cost
Ice cream	10 oz.	$0.05 per oz.	$0.50

During the period, the purchasing manager bought 200,000 ounces of ice cream on account for a total of $8,000 (an average price of $0.04 per ounce). The journal entry to record the purchase of raw materials follows:

COACH'S TIP

Notice that the variance is the "plug figure" that makes the debits and credits balance. Here the actual cost (credit) is less than the standard cost (debit), resulting in a favorable (credit) variance.

	Debit	Credit
Raw Materials Inventory (200,000 × $0.05)	10,000	
Direct Materials Price Variance (200,000 × $0.01) ..		2,000
Accounts Payable (200,000 × $0.04)		8,000

Notice that the debit to Raw Materials Inventory is based on the standard price per unit of $0.05, but the credit to Accounts Payable is based on the actual price of $0.04 per unit. The difference between the actual price and the standard price is the direct materials price variance calculated earlier by multiplying the $0.01 difference in price by 200,000 ounces of ice cream. This variance is favorable because the actual price was less than the standard price. Notice that the favorable variance appears as a credit.

Next let's record the journal entry to transfer the cost of the ice cream out of Raw Materials Inventory and into Cost of Goods Sold. During the period, Cold Stone's employees used 200,000 ounces of ice cream to produce 18,000 units. The entry to transfer the cost of the ice cream from Raw Materials Inventory to Cost of Goods Sold is:

COACH'S TIP

A debit entry reflects an unfavorable variance. The quantity of materials actually taken from Raw Materials Inventory (a credit) was more than the standard quantity that should have been used to make 18,000 units (a debit).

	Debit	Credit
Cost of Goods Sold (180,000 ounces × $0.05)	9,000	
Direct Materials Quantity Variance (20,000 × $0.05)......	1,000	
Raw Materials Inventory (200,000 × $0.05).............		10,000

Notice that the amount debited to Cost of Goods Sold is based on what it **should have cost** the company to produce 18,000 units. Because each unit requires 10 ounces of ice cream, we multiply the standard quantity of 180,000 ounces by the standard price of $0.05 per ounce. The amount that is transferred out of Raw Materials Inventory, however, is based on the 200,000 ounces that were actually used multiplied by the standard price of $0.05. Multiplying the 20,000 ounce difference by the standard price of $0.05 results in an unfavorable direct materials quantity variance of $1,000. Notice that this unfavorable variance appears as a debit entry; a favorable variance would appear as a credit entry.

Before you continue, complete the Self-Study Practice to see whether you can record the purchase and use of Cold Stone Creamery's mix-in ingredients.

Self-Study Practice

Cold Stone Creamery's standard cost card for mix-in ingredients follows.

Direct Costs	Standard Quantity	Standard Price	Standard Unit Cost
Mix-in ingredients	2 oz.	$0.10 per oz.	$0.20

Actual results were as follows:

- Purchased 35,000 ounces of mix-in ingredients at a total cost of $4,200, or an average cost of $0.12 per ounce.
- Used 35,000 ounces of mix-in ingredients to produce the 18,000 units sold.

Prepare the journal entries to record the purchase of raw materials and the transfer of their cost to the Cost of Goods Sold account.

After you have finished, check your answers with the solutions in the margin.

Solution to Self-Study Practice

Purchase of Raw Materials

Raw Materials Inventory (35,000 × $0.10)	3,500	
Direct Materials Price Variance	700	
Accounts Payable (35,000 × $0.12)		4,200

Transfer to Cost of Goods Sold When Used

Cost of Goods Sold (36,000 × $0.10)	3,600	
Direct Materials Quantity Variance	100	
Raw Materials Inventory (35,000 × $0.10)		3,500

Direct Labor and Manufacturing Overhead Costs

The entries to record direct labor and manufacturing overhead costs are simpler than those to record direct materials costs because the cost can be recorded directly into Cost of Goods Sold.

The entry to record direct labor costs is:

	Debit	Credit
Cost of Goods Sold (1,800 hrs. × $8.00 per hr.)	14,400	
Direct Labor Rate Variance [2,000 × ($8.00 − 8.25)]	500	
Direct Labor Efficiency Variance [$8.00 × (1,800 − 2,000)] ..	1,600	
Wages Payable or Cash (2,000 hrs. × $8.25 per hr.)........		16,500

The entry to record variable manufacturing overhead costs is:

	Debit	Credit
Cost of Goods Sold (1,800 hrs. × $1.00 per hr.)	1,800	
Variable Overhead Efficiency Variance [$1.00 × (1,800 − 2,000)]	200	
Variable Overhead Rate Variance [2,000 × ($1.00 − $0.90)]		200
Wages Payable, Cash, etc. (2,000 hrs. × $0.90 per hr.)		1,800

For this example, we assume that fixed overhead rate of $0.40 was based on budgeted production, as described in Supplement 10A. The entry to record fixed manufacturing overhead costs is:

	Debit	Credit
Cost of Goods Sold (18,000 units × $0.40 per unit).........	7,200	
Fixed Overhead Spending Variance ($6,000 − $6,300) ...	300	
Fixed Overhead Volume Variance (18,000 − 15,000 units) × $0.40		1,200
Salaries Payable or Cash		6,300

Cost of Goods Sold and Cost Variance Summary

After all variances have been recorded, the Cost of Goods Sold and variance summary accounts appear as follows:

Cost of Goods Sold				Cost Variance Summary				
Ice cream	9,000			Ice cream quantity variance	1,000	2,000	Ice cream price variance	
Mix-ins	3,600			Mix-in price variance	700	100	Mix-in quantity variance	
Direct labor	14,400			DL rate variance	500	200	VOH rate variance	
Var. mfg. overhead	1,800			DL efficiency variance	1,600	1,200	FOH volume variance	
Fixed mfg. overhead	7,200			VOH efficiency variance	200			
Standard cost	36,000			FOH spending variance	300			
Variance adjustment	800	←				Balance	800	
Actual cost of goods sold	36,800							

COACH'S TIP

In the real world, each of the variances would appear in a separate account so that a specific manager can monitor and attempt to control the variance.

Notice that Cost of Goods Sold is based initially on the standard cost of $36,000. The standard cost card shown at the beginning of this chapter (see Exhibit 10.1 on page 361) indicated that each unit produced should cost $2.00. Because Cold Stone Creamery sold 18,000 units, the cost of goods sold is initially valued at the standard cost of $36,000 (18,000 × $2.00). At the end of the budget period, the variances are used to adjust from standard to actual cost of $36,800.

The Cost Variance Summary account indicates how much higher or lower the actual costs were compared to the standard costs. Overall, Cold Stone Creamery had more unfavorable variances than favorable variances, resulting in a debit (U) balance of $800. At the end of the accounting period, each individual variance is closed to Cost of Goods Sold, which has the net effect of increasing its amount by $800.

The combined entry to close the variance accounts to Cost of Goods Sold is:

	Debit	Credit
Ice Cream Price Variance	2,000	
Mix-In Quantity Variance	100	
Variable Overhead Rate Variance	200	
Fixed Overhead Volume Variance	1,200	
Cost of Goods Sold	800	
Ice Cream Quantity Variance		1,000
Mix-In Price Variance		700
Direct Labor Rate Variance		500
Direct Labor Efficiency Variance		1,600
Variable Overhead Efficiency Variance		200
Fixed Overhead Spending Variance		300

Notice that the closing entry debits the favorable variances to eliminate their credit balance and credits the unfavorable variances to eliminate their debit balance. The "plug figure" that makes the debits and credits equal is used to increase or decrease the Cost of Goods Sold account. In this case, we debited (increased) Cost of Goods Sold by $800, which raises it from the standard cost of $36,000 to the actual cost of $36,800.

Closing the variance accounts directly to Cost of Goods Sold is the easiest and most common method of adjusting for variances. However, if a company has significant Work in Process or Finished Goods Inventory, adjusting those accounts may also be necessary. That treatment of the variance accounts, which is rare in practice, is beyond the scope of this textbook.

DEMONSTRATION CASE

Bunko Beds produces bunk beds for children. It sells the beds through Pottery Barn Kids and other retail outlets. The standard cost of producing one of Bunko's most popular beds follows:

STANDARD COST CARD FOR BUNKO BEDS			
	Standard Quantity	Standard Price (Rate)	Standard Unit Cost
Direct materials (1 × 12" treated pine)	50 ft.	$ 2.50 per ft.	$125.00
Direct labor	5 hrs.	10.00 per hr.	50.00
Manufacturing overhead costs			
Variable manufacturing overhead (based on direct labor hours)	5 hrs.	5.00 per hr.	25.00
Fixed manufacturing overhead $120,000/3,000 units = $40 per unit			40.00
Standard manufacturing cost per unit			$240.00

Bunko's master budget was based on planned production and sale of 3,000 beds. Actual results were as follows:

- Produced 2,500 beds.
- Purchased and used 130,000 feet of direct materials at a total cost of $312,000.
- Total direct labor cost was $123,750 for 11,250 hours.
- Variable overhead cost was $54,000.
- Fixed overhead cost was $115,000.

Required:

Calculate the following variances and label them as favorable (F) or unfavorable (U).

1. Direct materials variances:
   a. Direct materials price variance.
   b. Direct materials quantity variance.
   c. Direct materials spending (total) variance.

2. Direct labor variances:
   a. Direct labor rate variance.
   b. Direct labor efficiency variance.
   c. Direct labor spending (total) variance.

3. Variable manufacturing overhead variances:
   a. Variable overhead rate variance.
   b. Variable overhead efficiency variance.
   c. Variable overhead spending (total) variance.

4. Fixed manufacturing overhead variances:
   a. Fixed overhead spending variance.

See page 387 for solution.

CHAPTER SUMMARY

Describe the standard-setting process and explain how standard costs relate to budgets and variances. p. 361   **LO1**

- Standard costs, which are set at the beginning of the accounting period to reflect what management believes costs **should be**, should be set so that they are difficult but not impossible to achieve.
- The standard price is the amount that **should** be paid for a particular quantity of input.
- The standard quantity is the amount of input that **should** be used to produce a single unit of output.

- Budgeted costs are based on the standard costs for inputs multiplied by a specific level of output.

- Variances are the difference between actual and budgeted or standard costs.

LO2   Prepare a flexible budget and show how total costs change with sales volume. p. 362

- A master budget is a static budget based on estimated or budgeted sales volume.

- A flexible budget shows how total costs are expected to change if actual sales are more or less than expected.

- A flexible budget is used to evaluate managerial performance after the fact by separating the effect of spending (that is, cost control) from the effect of volume.

- Spending variances are calculated by comparing actual costs to the flexible budget.

- Volume variances are calculated by comparing the flexible budget to the master budget.

LO3   Calculate and interpret the direct materials price and quantity variances. p. 366

- The direct materials price variance is driven by the difference between the actual and the standard price paid for direct materials.

- The direct materials quantity variance is driven by the difference between the actual quantity and the standard quantity of materials used in production. The standard quantity should be based on the actual volume of output.

- The direct materials purchasing manager is responsible for the direct materials price variance. The production manager is responsible for the direct materials quantity (usage) variance.

- The direct materials spending variance is the sum of the direct materials price and direct materials quantity variances.

LO4   Calculate and interpret the direct labor rate and efficiency variances. p. 368

- The direct labor rate variance is driven by the difference in the actual direct labor rate and the standard direct labor rate.

- The direct labor efficiency variance is driven by the difference between the actual number of labor hours and the standard number of labor hours allowed for the actual volume of output.

- Assigning responsibility for the direct labor rate variance is difficult as several managers and departments can affect it. The production manager is responsible for the direct labor efficiency variance.

- The direct labor spending variance is the sum of the direct labor rate and direct labor efficiency variances.

LO5   Calculate and interpret the variable overhead rate and efficiency variances. p. 371

- The variable overhead rate variance is driven by the difference between the actual variable overhead cost and the standard variable overhead cost per unit of the allocation base (such as direct labor hours).

- When variable overhead is based on direct labor hours, the variable overhead efficiency variance is driven by the difference between the actual number of labor hours and the standard number of labor hours allowed for production. It is a mirror image of the direct labor efficiency variance.

- The variable overhead spending variance is the sum of the variable overhead rate and the variable overhead efficiency variances.

LO6   Calculate and interpret the fixed overhead spending variance. p. 373

- The fixed overhead spending variance is the difference between actual fixed overhead cost and budgeted fixed overhead cost.

SOLUTION TO DEMONSTRATION CASE

1.   Direct materials variances:

AQ = 130,000 ft.

AP = $312,000/130,000 = $2.40 per ft.

SQ = 50 ft. × 2,500 actual units = 125,000 ft.

SP = $2.50 per ft.

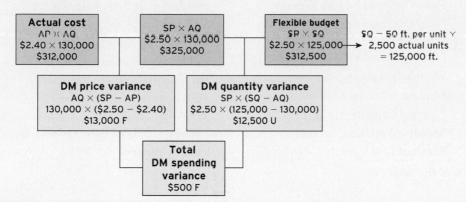

2.   Direct labor variances:

AH = 11,250 hrs.

AR = $123,750/11,250 = $11 per hr.

SH = 5 hrs. × 2,500 actual units = 12,500 hrs.

SR = $10 per hr.

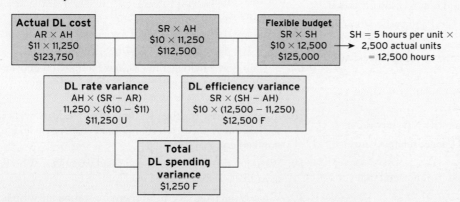

3.   Variable manufacturing overhead variances:

AH = 11,250

AR = $54,000/11,250 = $4.80 per hour

SH = 5 hrs. × 2,500 units = 12,500

SR = $5.00 per hour

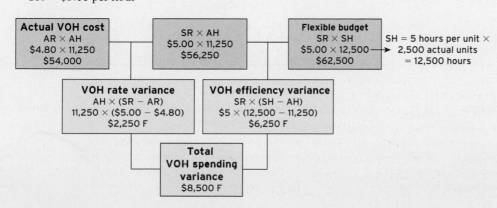

4. Fixed manufacturing overhead spending variance:

Actual FOH = $115,000

Budgeted FOH = $120,000

Fixed Overhead Spending Variance = $120,000 − $115,000 = $5,000 F

KEY TERMS

Direct Labor Efficiency Variance (p. 369)

Direct Labor Rate Variance (p. 369)

Direct Labor Spending Variance (p. 370)

Direct Materials Price Variance (p. 367)

Direct Materials Quantity Variance (p. 367)

Direct Materials Spending Variance (p. 368)

Easily Attainable Standard (p. 360)

Favorable Variance (p. 365)

Fixed Overhead Budget Variance (p. 374)

Fixed Overhead Spending Variance (p. 374)

Fixed Overhead Volume Variance (p. 377)

Flexible Budget (p. 362)

Ideal Standard (p. 360)

Practical Capacity (p. 378)

Spending Variances (p. 364)

Standard Cost Card (p. 361)

Standard Cost System (p. 360)

Standard Unit Cost (p. 361)

Static Budget (p. 362)

Unfavorable Variance (p. 365)

Variance (p. 359)

Variable Overhead Efficiency Variance (p. 372)

Variable Overhead Rate Variance (p. 372)

Volume Variance (p. 364)

See complete definitions in glossary at back of the text.

QUESTIONS

1. Briefly describe the difference between budgetary planning and control.

2. What are standard costs? When are they set?

3. Explain a standard cost system and how a company uses it.

4. What is the difference between ideal and easily attainable standards?

5. What type of standard is best for motivating individuals to work hard?

6. Briefly describe the two types of standards on which a standard cost system relies.

7. What is a standard cost card, and why is it important?

8. How do the terms standard and budget relate to one another and how do they differ?

9. Explain what the terms favorable variance and unfavorable variance mean.

10. How do the master budget, flexible budget, and static budget differ from one another?

11. What type of variance is created by comparing the master budget to the flexible budget?

12. What type of variance is calculated by comparing actual costs to the flexible budget?

13. The spending variance can be separated into two components. Name and briefly describe them.

14. What are the two direct materials variances? Who is most likely responsible for each of these?

15. Explain how a manager might make a trade-off between the direct materials price and the direct materials quantity variances.

16. What are the two direct labor variances? Who is most likely responsible for each of these?

17. Explain how a manager might make a trade-off between the direct labor rate and the direct labor efficiency variances.

18. In terms of how overhead is applied to products, what is the key difference between a normal cost system and a standard cost system?

19. What are the two variable overhead variances? Who is most likely responsible for each of these?

20. What is the fixed overhead spending variance? Who is most likely responsible for it?

21. Suppose you have determined a favorable fixed overhead spending variance of $1,000. How would you interpret that variance?

22. What does the term practical capacity mean? How does it differ from budgeted?

23. What happens to all of the variances that have been recorded during a period?

MULTIPLE CHOICE

1. In general, variances tell managers
    a. Nothing.
    b. Whom to promote and whom to fire.
    c. Whether budgeted goals are being achieved.
    d. Which departments are running at full capacity.

Quiz 10

www.mhhe.com/whitecotton1e

2. In distinguishing between budgets and standards, which of the following is true?
    a. The terms mean exactly the same thing.
    b. Standards are used to develop budgets.
    c. Budgets are used to develop standards.
    d. Budgets and standards are unrelated.

3. Variances are always noted as favorable or unfavorable. What do these terms indicate?

   a. Whether actual results are more or less than standard or budgeted amounts.
   b. Whether the manager in a particular department is doing a good job.
   c. Whether a company is performing as well as its competitors.
   d. All of the above.

4. What type of budget is an integrated set of operating and financial budgets that reflects managements' expectations for a given sales level, and what type shows how budgeted costs and revenues will change across different levels of sales volume?

   a. Flexible budget, master budget.
   b. Standard budget, flexible budget.
   c. Master budget, static budget.
   d. Master budget, flexible budget.

5. When evaluating performance in a standard cost system, actual results are compared to

   a. The flexible budget.
   b. The master budget.
   c. The variances.
   d. Last year's actual results.

6. Spending variances may be separated into

   a. Price and quantity variances.
   b. Price and volume variances.
   c. Volume and quantity variances.
   d. Quantity and quality variances.

7. Temecula Company has calculated its direct materials price variance to be $1,000 favorable and its direct materials quantity variance to be $3,000 unfavorable. Which of the following could explain both of these variances?

   a. The production manager has recently hired more skilled laborers.
   b. The purchases manager bought less expensive raw materials but they were of lower quality.
   c. A machine in the factory malfunctioned resulting in considerable wasted raw materials.
   d. The purchases manager bought higher quality materials.

8. In producing its product, Ranger Company used 1,500 hours of direct labor at an actual cost of $15 per hour. The standard for Ranger's production level is 1,400 hours at $14 per hour. What is Ranger's direct labor rate variance?

   a. $1,500 favorable.   c. $1,500 unfavorable.
   b. $1,400 favorable.   d. $1,400 unfavorable.

9. Refer to the preceding question about Ranger Company. In producing its product, Ranger Company used 1,500 pounds of direct materials at an actual cost of $1.50 per pound. The standard for Ranger's production level was 1,400 pounds at $1.40 per pound. What is Ranger's direct materials quantity variance?

   a. $150 favorable.
   b. $140 favorable.
   c. $150 unfavorable.
   d. $140 unfavorable.

10. An unfavorable fixed overhead volume or capacity variance indicates that a company

   a. Manufactured fewer units than it expected.
   b. Manufactured more units than it expected.
   c. Underestimated its total fixed overhead cost.
   d. Overestimated its total fixed overhead cost.

Solution to Multiple-Choice Questions located in back of the text.

MINI EXERCISES

M10-1 Creating Grading Scale Based on Ideal, Tight but Attainable, Easily Attainable Standards LO1

Consider the grading scale for a university class that has 500 possible points. The possible course grades are A, B, C, D, and F. Create a grading scale for the class that would fall into each of the following categories: an ideal standard, an easily attainable standard, and a tight but attainable standard. What are the implications for student motivation?

M10-2 Explaining Costs That Change with Flexible Budget Activity LO2

When preparing a company's flexible budget, which manufacturing cost(s) will change as the volume increases or decreases? Which manufacturing cost(s) will not change as the volume changes?

M10-3 Describing How to Set Standards in Standard Cost System LO1

Dabney Company manufactures widgets and would like to use a standard cost system. Explain how Dabney will determine the standards for direct materials and direct labor to use in its costing system.

M10-4 Calculating Unknown Values for Direct Labor Variances LO4

For each of the following independent cases, fill in the missing amounts in the table.

Case	Direct Labor Rate Variance	Direct Labor Efficiency Variance	Direct Labor Spending Variance
A	$ 750 F	$1,200 F	$?
B	2,000 U	?	3,500 U
C	1,000 F	?	1,800 U
D	?	500 F	2,500 U
E	?	1,100 U	1,950 U
F	650 F	1,150 U	?

LO3   M10-5 Interpreting Direct Materials Cost Variances

Phantom Corp. has calculated its direct materials price and quantity variances to be $500 favorable and $800 unfavorable, respectively. Phantom's production manager believes that these variances indicate that the purchasing department is doing a good job but production is doing a poor job. Explain whether the production manager's conclusions are correct.

LO3   M10-6 Calculating Direct Materials Cost Variances

Randolph, Inc., has determined a standard direct materials cost per unit of $6 (2 feet × $3 per foot). Last month, Randolph purchased and used 4,200 feet of direct materials for which it paid $12,180. The company produced and sold 2,000 units during the month. Calculate the direct materials price, quantity, and spending variances.

LO4   M10-7 Calculating Direct Labor Cost Variances

Clayton Corp. has determined a standard labor cost per unit of $12 (1 hour × $12 per hour). Last month, Clayton incurred 1,900 direct labor hours for which it paid $23,940. The company also produced and sold 2,000 units during the month. Calculate the direct labor rate, efficiency, and spending variances.

LO5   M10-8 Calculating Variable Manufacturing Overhead Variances

Montour Company has determined a standard variable overhead rate of $1.10 per direct labor hour and expects 1 labor hour per unit produced. Last month, Montour incurred 1,900 actual direct labor hours in the production of 2,000 units. The company has also determined that its actual variable overhead rate is $1.20 per direct labor hour. Calculate the variable overhead rate and efficiency variances as well as the total amount of over- or underapplied variable overhead.

LO6   M10-9 Calculating Fixed Manufacturing Overhead Spending Variance

LaPaz Company's standard fixed overhead rate is based on budgeted fixed manufacturing overhead of $9,000 and budgeted production of 30,000 units. Actual results for the month of October reveal that LaPaz produced 28,000 units and spent $9,200 on fixed manufacturing overhead costs. Calculate LaPaz's fixed overhead spending variance.

Supplement 10A   M10-10 Calculating Fixed Manufacturing Overhead Volume Variance

Refer to M10-9 for LaPaz Company. Calculate LaPaz's fixed overhead rate and the fixed overhead volume variance.

Supplement 10B   M10-11 Preparing Journal Entries to Record Direct Material Costs, Variances

During May, Willett Corp. purchased direct materials for 4,250 units at a total cost of $61,625. Willett's standard direct materials cost is $14 per unit. Prepare the journal entry to record this transaction.

Supplement 10B   M10-12 Preparing Journal Entries to Record Direct Labor Costs, Variances

Bowman Company reported the following information for the month of November. The standard cost of labor for the month was $38,000, but actual wages paid were $40,000. Bowman has calculated its direct labor rate and efficiency variances to be $2,500 unfavorable and $500 favorable, respectively. Prepare the necessary journal entry to record Bowman's direct labor cost for the month assuming that standard labor costs are recorded directly to Cost of Good Sold.

EXERCISES

 |ACCOUNTING

E10-1 Calculating Unknown Values for Direct Materials, Direct Labor Variances   LO3, 4

Three Pigs Company manufactures cast-iron barbeque cookware. During a recent windstorm, it lost some of its cost accounting records. Three Pigs has managed to reconstruct portions of its standard cost system database but is still missing a few pieces of information.

	Direct Materials	Direct Labor
Standard amount per pan produced	2.5 lb.	1.25 hr.
Standard cost	$4.00 per lb.	$16.00 per hr.
Actual amount used per pan produced	2.4 lb.	1.20 hr.
Actual cost	$4.10 per lb.	$15.50 per hr.
Actual number of pans produced and sold	2,500 pans	2,500 pans
Direct materials price variance	?	
Direct materials quantity variance	?	
Direct materials spending variance	?	
Direct labor rate variance		?
Direct labor efficiency variance		?
Direct labor spending variance		?

Required:

Use the information in the table to determine the unknown amounts. You may assume that Three Pigs does not keep any raw materials on hand.

E10-2 Preparing Flexible Budget for Manufacturing Costs   LO2

Follett Company makes handwoven blankets. The company's master budget appears in the first column of the table.

	Master Budget (5,000 units)	Flexible Budget (4,000 units)	Flexible Budget (6,000 units)	Flexible Budget (7,000 units)
Direct materials	$ 7,500			
Direct labor	20,000			
Variable manufacturing overhead	8,000			
Fixed manufacturing overhead	18,000			
Total manufacturing cost	$53,500			

Required:

Complete the table by preparing Follett's flexible budget for 4,000, 6,000, and 7,000 units.

E10-3 Interpreting Direct Materials Price, Quantity Variances   LO3

Cody's Collar Company makes custom leather pet collars. The company expects each collar to require 1.5 feet of leather and predicts leather will cost $2.25 per foot. Suppose Cody's made 60 collars during February. For these 60 collars, the company actually averaged 1.6 feet of leather per collar and paid $2.00 per foot.

Required:

1. Compute the standard direct materials cost per unit.
2. Without performing any calculations, determine whether the direct materials price variance will be favorable or unfavorable.
3. Without performing any calculations, determine whether the direct materials quantity variance will be favorable or unfavorable.
4. Give a potential explanation for this pattern of variances.
5. Where would you begin to investigate the variances?
6. Calculate the direct materials price and quantity variances.

E10-4 Calculating Direct Materials and Direct Labor Variances

Rub-a-Dub Dogs is a local pet grooming shop owned by Max Aslett. Max has prepared the following standard cost card for each dog bath given:

	Standard Quantity	Standard Rate	Standard Unit Cost
Direct costs			
Shampoo	2 oz.	$0.10 per oz.	$0.20
Water	20 gal.	0.05 per gal.	1.00
Direct labor	.75 hr.	9.00 per hr.	6.75

During the month of July, Max's employees gave 345 baths. The actual results were 725 ounces of shampoo used (total cost $87), 6,500 gallons of water used (cost of $390), and labor costs for 250 hours (cost of $2,300).

Required:

1. Calculate Rub-a-Dub Dogs' direct materials variances for both shampoo and water for the month of July.
2. Calculate Rub-a-Dub Dogs' direct labor variances for the month of July.
3. Identify a possible cause of each variance.

E10-5 Preparing Journal Entries to Record Direct Materials, Direct Labor Costs, Variances

Refer to the information presented in E10-4 regarding Rub-a-Dub Dogs.

Required:

Prepare journal entries to record Rub-a-Dub's July direct materials and labor transactions. (**Hint:** Record all costs directly to Cost of Goods Sold.)

E10-6 Calculating Direct Materials, Direct Labor Variances

Lucky Charm Company makes handcrafted silver charms that attach to jewelry such as a necklace or bracelet. Each charm is adorned with two crystals of various colors. Standard costs follow:

	Standard Quantity	Standard Price (Rate)	Standard Unit Cost
Direct costs			
Silver	0.25 oz.	$20.00 per oz.	$ 5.00
Crystals	2	0.25 per each	0.50
Direct labor	1.5 hrs.	15.00 per hr.	22.50

During the month of January, Lucky Charm made 1,500 charms. The company used 350 ounces of silver (total cost of $7,350) and 3,050 crystals (total cost of $701.50), and paid for 2,400 actual direct labor hours (cost of $34,800).

Required:

1. Calculate Lucky Charm's direct materials variances for silver and crystals for the month of January.
2. Calculate Lucky Charm's direct labor variances for the month of January.
3. Identify a possible cause of each variance.

E10-7 Preparing Journal Entries to Record Direct Materials, Direct Labor Costs, Variances

Refer to the information in E10-6 regarding Lucky Charm Company.

Required:

Prepare journal entries to record Lucky Charm's January direct materials and labor transactions. (**Hint:** Record all costs directly to Cost of Goods Sold.)

E10-8 Calculating and Interpreting Direct Material Variances   LO3

Easy Roller, Inc., manufactures plastic mats to use with rolling office chairs. Its standard cost information for last year follows:

	Standard Quantity	Standard Price (Rate)	Standard Unit Cost
Direct costs			
Plastic	12 sq ft.	$ 0.75 per sq. ft.	$9.00
Direct labor	.25 hr.	12.00 per hr.	3.00
Variable manufacturing overhead		1.20 per direct labor hour	0.30
Fixed manufacturing overhead ($360,000/900,000 units)			0.40

Easy Roller had the following actual results for the past year.

Number of units produced and sold	1,000,000
Number of square feet of plastic used	11,800,000
Cost of plastic purchased and used	$ 8,260,000
Number of labor hours worked	245,000
Direct labor cost	$ 2,891,000
Variable overhead cost	$ 318,500
Fixed overhead cost	$ 355,000

Required:

Calculate Easy Roller's direct materials price and quantity variances.

E10-9 Calculating, Interpreting Direct Material Variances   LO5

Refer to the information presented in E10-8 for Easy Roller.

Required:

Calculate Easy Roller's direct labor rate and efficiency variances.

E10-10 Calculating, Interpreting Direct Material Variances   LO5

Refer to the information presented in E10-8 for Easy Roller.

Required:

Calculate Easy Roller's variable overhead rate and efficiency variances and its over- or underapplied variable overhead.

E10-11 Calculating, Interpreting Fixed Manufacturing Overhead Spending, Volume Variances   LO6, Supplement 10A

Refer to the information presented in E10-8 for Easy Roller.

Required:

Calculate Easy Roller's fixed overhead spending and volume variances and its over- or underapplied fixed overhead.

E10-12 Preparing Journal Entries to Record Direct Material, Direct Labor, Variable Overhead Costs and Variances   Supplement 10B

Refer to the information presented in E10-8 for Easy Roller.

Required:

Prepare the journal entry to record the following for Easy Roller:

1. Direct materials costs and related variances. Assume the company purchases raw materials as needed and does not maintain any ending inventories.
2. Direct labor and related variances.
3. Variable overhead costs and related variances.

Supplement 10B

E10-13 Preparing Journal Entries to Record Fixed Manufacturing Overhead Cost, Variances

Refer to the information presented in E10-8 for Easy Roller.

Required:

Prepare the journal entry to record Easy Roller's fixed manufacturing overhead transactions assuming that overhead is applied using a fixed overhead rate based on budget production.

LO5

E10-14 Calculating Variable Manufacturing Overhead Variances

Slim Shady Company (SSC) manufactures lampshades. It applies variable overhead on the basis of direct labor hours. Information from SSC's standard cost card follows:

	Standard Quantity	Standard Rate	Standard Unit Cost
Variable manufacturing overhead	0.5	$0.80	$0.40

During August, SSC had the following actual results

Units produced and sold	25,000
Actual variable overhead	$ 9,490
Actual direct labor hours	13,000

Required:

Compute SSC's variable overhead rate variance, variable overhead efficiency variance, and over- or underapplied variable overhead.

Supplement 10B

E10-15 Preparing Journal Entries to Record Variable Manufacturing Overhead Cost, Variances

Refer to the information in E10-14 regarding Slim Shady Company.

Required:

Prepare the journal entry to record SSC's variable manufacturing overhead transactions for August.

LO6, Supplement 10A

E10-16 Calculating Fixed Manufacturing Overhead Spending, Volume Variances

Slim Shady Company (SSC) in E10-14 calculates a fixed overhead rate based on budgeted fixed overhead of $30,000 and budgeted production of 24,000 units. Actual results were as follows:

Number of units produced and sold	25,000
Actual fixed overhead	$29,000

Required:

Calculate the following for SSC:
1. Fixed overhead rate based on budgeted production.
2. Fixed overhead spending variance.
3. Fixed overhead volume variance.
4. Over- or underapplied fixed overhead.

Supplement 10B

E10-17 Preparing Journal Entries to Record Fixed Manufacturing Overhead Cost, Variances

Refer to the information in E10-16 regarding Slim Shady Company.

Required:

Prepare the journal entry to record SSC's fixed manufacturing overhead transactions for August assuming that overhead is applied using a fixed overhead rate based on budget production.

E10-18 Calculating Fixed Manufacturing Overhead Capacity Variances

LO6, Supplement 10A

Crystal Ball Company (CBC) bases its fixed overhead rate on practical capacity of 30,000 units per year. Budgeted and actual results for the most recent year follow:

	Budgeted	Actual
Fixed manufacturing overhead	$600,000	$510,000
Number of units produced	20,000	23,000

Required:

Calculate the following for CBC:

1. Fixed overhead rate based on practical capacity.
2. Fixed overhead spending variance.
3. Expected (planned) capacity variance.
4. Unexpected (unplanned) capacity variance.
5. Total over- or underapplied fixed manufacturing overhead

E10-19 Calculating Variable Manufacturing Overhead Variances

LO5

ClearView Company manufactures clear plastic CD cases. It applies variable overhead based on the number of machine hours used. Information regarding ClearView's overhead for the month of December follows:

	Standard Quantity	Standard Rate	Standard Unit Cost
Variable manufacturing overhead	0.1 machine hours per case	$0.50 per machine hour	$0.05

During December, ClearView had the following actual results.

Number of units produced and sold	625,000
Actual variable overhead cost	$ 30,240
Actual machine hours	63,000

Required:

Compute ClearView's variable overhead rate variance, variable overhead efficiency variance, and over- or underapplied variable overhead.

E10-20 Preparing Journal Entries to Record Variable Manufacturing Overhead Cost, Variances

Supplement 10B

Refer to the information in E10-19 regarding ClearView Company.

Required:

Prepare the journal entry to record ClearView's variable manufacturing overhead transactions for December.

E10-21 Calculating Fixed Manufacturing Overhead Volume Variances

LO6, Supplement 10A

ClearView Company calculates a fixed overhead rate based on budgeted fixed overhead of $180,000 and budgeted production of 600,000 units. Actual results were as follows:

Number of units produced and sold	625,000
Actual fixed overhead	$195,000

Required:

Calculate the following for ClearView:

1. Fixed overhead rate based on budgeted production.
2. Fixed overhead spending variance.

3. Fixed overhead volume variance.
4. Over- or underapplied fixed overhead.

Supplement 10B   **E10-22 Preparing Journal Entries to Record Fixed Manufacturing Overhead Cost, Variances**

Refer to the information presented in E10-21 regarding ClearView Company.

Required:

Prepare the journal entry to record ClearView's fixed overhead transactions for December.

LO6, Supplement 10A   **E10-23 Calculating Fixed Manufacturing Overhead Capacity Variances**

Crystal Ball Company (CBC) bases its fixed overhead rate on practical capacity of 80,000 units per year. Budgeted and actual results for the most recent year follow:

	Budgeted	Actual
Fixed manufacturing overhead	$540,000	$550,000
Number of units produced	70,000	77,000

Required:

Calculate the following for CBC:

1. Fixed overhead rate based on practical capacity.
2. Fixed overhead spending variance.
3. Expected (planned) capacity variance.
4. Unexpected (unplanned) capacity variance.
5. Total over- or underapplied fixed manufacturing overhead.

PROBLEMS—SET A

LO3, 4, 5   **PA10-1 Calculating Direct Material, Direct Labor, Variable Overhead Variances**

www.mhhe.com/whitecotton1e

Drink Well, Inc., manufactures custom-ordered commemorative beer steins. Its standard cost information follows:

	Standard Quantity	Standard Price (Rate)	Standard Unit Cost
Direct costs			
Clay	1.5 lbs.	$ 1.60 per lb.	$ 2.40
Direct labor	1.5 hrs.	12.00 per hr.	18.00
Variable MOH		1.20 per direct labor hour	1.80
Fixed MOH ($250,000/100,000 units)			2.50

Drink Well had the following actual results last year:

Number of units produced and sold	110,000
Number of pounds of clay used	180,000
Cost of clay	$ 279,000
Number of labor hours worked	150,000
Direct labor cost	$1,950,000
Variable overhead cost	$ 195,000
Fixed overhead cost	$ 295,000

Required:

Calculate the following for Drink Well:

1. Direct materials price, quantity, and total spending variances.
2. Direct labor rate, efficiency, and total spending variances.
3. Variable overhead rate, efficiency, and total spending variances.

PA10-2 Calculating Fixed Manufacturing Overhead Spending, Volume Variances   LO6, Supplement 10A

Refer to the information for Drink Well in PA 10-1.

Required:

Compute the following for Drink Well:

1. Fixed overhead spending variance.
2. Fixed overhead volume variance.
3. Total over- or underapplied fixed manufacturing overhead.

PA10-3 Preparing Journal Entries to Record Direct Material, Direct Labor,   Supplement 10B
    Variable Manufacturing Overhead

Refer to the information in PA10-1 for Drink Well.

Required:

Prepare the journal entry to record the following for Drink Well:

1. Direct materials costs and related variances. Assume the company purchases raw materials as needed and docs not maintain any ending inventories.
2. Direct labor and related variances.
3. Variable overhead costs and related variances.

PA10-4 Preparing Journal Entries to Record Fixed Manufacturing Overhead   Supplement 10B
    Costs, Variances

Refer to the information in PA10-1 for Drink Well.

Required:

Prepare the journal entry to record Drink Well's fixed manufacturing overhead costs and related variances for last year.

PA10-5 Calculating Direct Materials, Direct Labor, Variable Manufacturing   LO3, 4, 5
    Overhead

eXcel

www.mhhe.com/whitecotton1e

Darting Around Company manufactures dartboards. Its standard cost information follows:

	Standard Quantity	Standard Price (Rate)	Standard Unit Cost
Direct costs			
Cork board	2.5 sq. ft.	$ 2.00 per sq. ft.	$ 5.00
Direct labor	1 hr.	14.00 per hr.	14.00
Variable manufacturing overhead		.50 per direct labor hour	0.50
Fixed manufacturing overhead ($20,000/80,000 units)			0.25

Darting Around has the following actual results for the month of September:

Number of units produced and sold	70,000
Number of square feet of corkboard used	180,000
Cost of corkboard used	$378,000
Number of labor hours worked	75,000
Direct labor cost	$975,000
Variable overhead cost	$ 36,000
Fixed overhead cost	$ 25,000

Required:

Calculate the following for Darting Around:

1. Direct materials price, quantity, and total spending variances.
2. Direct labor rate, efficiency, and total spending variances.
3. Variable overhead rate, efficiency, and total spending variances.

LO6, Supplement 10A

PA10-6 Calculating Fixed Manufacturing Overhead Spending, Volume Variances

Refer to the information in PA 10-5.

Required:

Calculate the following for Darting Around:

1.   Fixed overhead spending variance.
2.   Fixed overhead volume variance.
3.   Total over- or underapplied fixed manufacturing overhead.

Supplement 10B

PA10-7 Preparing Journal Entries to Record Direct Material, Direct Labor, Variable Manufacturing Overhead

Refer to the information in PA10-5 for Darting Around Company.

Required:

Prepare the journal entry to record the following for Darting Around:

1.   Direct materials costs and related variances. Assume the company purchases raw materials as needed and does not maintain any ending inventories.
2.   Direct labor and related variances.
3.   Variable overhead costs and related variances.

Supplement 10B

PA10-8 Preparing Journal Entries to Record Fixed Manufacturing Overhead Costs, Variances

Refer to the information in PA10-5 for Darting Around.

Required:

Prepare the journal entry to record Darting Around's fixed manufacturing overhead costs and related variances for last year.

LO3, 4

PA10-9 Calculating Direct Materials, Direct Labor Variances

www.mhhe.com/whitecotton1e

Catch a Wave Company manufactures surfboards. Its standard cost information follows:

	Standard Quantity	Standard Price (Rate)	Standard Unit Cost
Direct costs			
Fiberglass	15 sq. ft.	$ 5 per sq. ft.	$ 75.00
Direct labor	10 hrs.	15 per hr.	150.00
Variable manufacturing overhead		6 per direct labor hour	60.00
Fixed manufacturing overhead ($20,000/250 units)			80.00

Catch a Wave has the following actual results for the month of June:

Number of units produced and sold	260
Number of square feet of fiberglass used	4,100
Cost of fiberglass used	$22,550
Number of labor hours worked	2,550
Direct labor cost	$39,525
Variable overhead cost	$14,790
Fixed overhead cost	$20,500

Required:

Calculate the following for Catch a Wave:

1.   Direct materials price, quantity, and total spending variances.
2.   Direct labor rate, efficiency, and total spending variances.

PA10-10 **Preparing Journal Entries to Record Direct Materials, Direct Labor,**
        Variable Manufacturing Overhead

Refer to the information in PA10-9 for Catch a Wave.

Required:

Prepare the journal entries to record the following for Catch a Wave:

1. Direct materials costs and related variances. Assume the company purchases raw materials as needed and does not maintain any ending inventories.
2. Direct labor and related variances.

PROBLEMS–SET B

PB10-1 **Calculating Direct Material, Direct Labor, Variable Manufacturing**
        Overhead

CandleGlow, Inc., manufactures scented pillar candles. Its standard cost information for the month of February follows:

	Standard Quantity	Standard Price (Rate)	Standard Unit Cost
Direct costs			
Wax	15 oz.	$ 0.05 per oz.	$0.75
Direct labor	0.25 hr.	14.00 per hr.	3.50
Variable manufacturing overhead		0.40 per direct labor hour	0.10
Fixed manufacturing overhead ($10,000/40,000 units)			0.25

CandleGlow has the following actual results for the month of February:

Number of units produced and sold	35,000
Number of ounces of wax purchased and used	530,000
Cost of wax used	$ 31,800
Number of labor hours worked	9,000
Direct labor cost	$123,750
Variable overhead cost	$ 3,300
Fixed overhead cost	$ 9,700

Required:

Calculate the following for CandleGlow:

1. Direct materials price, quantity, and total spending variances.
2. Direct labor rate, efficiency, and total spending variances.
3. Variable overhead rate, efficiency, and total spending variances.

PB10-2 **Calculating Fixed Manufacturing Overhead Spending**
        and Volume Variances

Refer to the information for CandleGlow in PB 10-1.

Required:

Compute the following for CandleGlow:

1. Fixed overhead spending variance.
2. Fixed overhead volume variance.
3. Total over- or underapplied fixed manufacturing overhead.

Supplement 10B **PB10-3 Preparing Journal Entries to Record Direct Material, Direct Labor, Variable Manufacturing Overhead**

Refer to the information in PB10-1 for CandleGlow.

Required:

Prepare the journal entry to record the following for CandleGlow:

1. Direct materials costs and related variances. Assume the company purchases raw materials as needed and does not maintain any ending inventories.
2. Direct labor and related variances.
3. Variable overhead costs and related variances.

Supplement 10B **PB10-4 Preparing Journal Entries to Record Fixed Manufacturing Overhead Costs, Variances**

Refer to the information in PB10-1 for CandleGlow.

Required:

Prepare the journal entry to record CandleGlow's fixed manufacturing overhead costs and related variances for last year.

LO3, 4, 5 **PB10-5 Calculating Direct Materials, Direct Labor, Variable Manufacturing Overhead**

Gotta Cotta, Inc., manufactures basic terra cotta planters. Its standard cost information for the past year follows:

	Standard Quantity	Standard Price (Rate)	Standard Unit Cost
Direct costs			
Clay	2 lbs.	$ 0.80 per lb.	$1.60
Direct labor	0.5 hr.	12.00 per hr.	6.00
Variable manufacturing overhead		0.40 per direct labor hour	0.20
Fixed manufacturing overhead ($480,000/800,000 units)			0.60

Gotta Cotta has the following actual results for the past year:

Number of units produced and sold	750,000
Number of pounds of clay used	1,450,000
Cost of clay purchased and used	$1,087,500
Number of labor hours worked	375,000
Direct labor cost	$3,937,500
Variable overhead cost	$ 157,500
Fixed overhead cost	$ 505,000

Required:

Calculate the following for Gotta Cotta:

1. Direct materials price, quantity, and total spending variances.
2. Direct labor rate, efficiency, and total spending variances.
3. Variable overhead rate, efficiency, and total spending variances.

LO6, Supplement 10A **PB10-6 Calculating Fixed Manufacturing Overhead Spending, Volume Variances**

Refer to the information for Gotta Cotta in PB 10-5.

Required:

Compute the following for Gotta Cotta:

1. Fixed overhead spending variance
2. Fixed overhead volume variance.
3. Over- or underapplied fixed manufacturing overhead.

PB10-7 Preparing Journal Entries to Record Direct Materials, Direct Labor, Variable Manufacturing Overhead   Supplement 10B

Refer to the information in PB10-5 for Gotta Cotta.

Required:

Prepare the journal entry to record the following for Gotta Cotta:

1. Direct materials costs and related variances. Assume the company purchases raw materials as needed and does not maintain any ending inventories.
2. Direct labor and related variances.
3. Variable overhead costs and related variances.

PB10-8 Preparing Journal Entries to Record Fixed Manufacturing Overhead Costs, Variances   Supplement 10B

Refer to the information in PB10-5 for Gotta Cotta.

Required:

Prepare the journal entry to record Gotta Cotta's fixed manufacturing overhead costs and related variances for last year.

PB10-9 Calculating Variable Manufacturing Overhead, Fixed Manufacturing Overhead Variances   LO5, 6, Supplement 10A

Catch a Wave Company manufactures surfboards. Its standard cost information follows.

	Standard Quantity	Standard Price (Rate)	Standard Unit Cost
Direct costs			
Fiberglass	15 sq. ft.	$ 5 per sq. ft.	$ 75.00
Direct labor	10 hr.	15 per hr.	150.00
Variable manufacturing overhead		6 per direct labor hour	60.00
Fixed manufacturing overhead ($20,000/250 units)			80.00

Catch a Wave has the following actual results for the month of June:

Number of units produced and sold	260
Number of square feet of fiberglass used	4,100
Cost of fiberglass used	$22,550
Number of labor hours worked	2,550
Direct labor cost	$39,525
Variable overhead cost	$14,790
Fixed overhead cost	$20,500

Required:

Calculate the following variances for Catch a Wave.

1. Variable overhead rate variance.
2. Variable overhead efficiency variance.

3. Total over- or underapplied variable overhead.

4. Fixed overhead spending (budget) variance.

5. Fixed overhead volume variance.

6. Total over- or underapplied fixed overhead.

Supplement 10B   **PB10-10 Preparing Journal Entries to Record Variable and Fixed Manufacturing Overhead Variances**

Refer to the information in PB10-9 for Catch a Wave.

Required:

Prepare journal entries to record the following for Catch a Wave:

1. Variable overhead costs and related variances.

2. Fixed overhead costs and related variances.

SKILLS DEVELOPMENT CASES

LO1   **S10-1 Evaluating Managerial Performance by Comparing Actual to Budgeted Results**

Suppose Acore Pharmaceuticals has four sales representatives assigned to the State of Arizona. These sales reps are responsible for visiting physicians in their assigned area, introducing the company's current or upcoming products, providing samples, getting feedback about the products, and generating sales. Each sales rep is given an expense budget that includes samples of Acore's products, travel expenses related to the company vehicle that Acore provides, and entertainment expenses such as buying meals or hosting small "meet and greet" receptions.

The following table includes both budgeted and actual amounts for each sales rep for the first half of the current year. As you can see, each was allotted the same amount of resources and expected to generate the same amount of sales for the six-month period.

	Samples		Travel		Entertainment		Sales	
Sales Rep	Budget	Actual	Budget	Actual	Budget	Actual	Budget	Actual
Terry	$7,200	$ 4,200	$18,000	$28,000	$4,800	$1,900	$90,000	$ 78,000
Maria	7,200	15,500	18,000	12,000	4,800	9,900	90,000	130,000
Samantha	7,200	2,900	18,000	18,000	4,800	4,600	90,000	43,000
Abraham	7,200	5,300	18,000	16,200	4,800	4,500	90,000	92,000

Required:

1. Calculate the expense and sales variances for each rep. Evaluate each of them and rank them in order of performance. Explain your rationale for these rankings. Suppose $100,000 in bonuses is available to be split among these sales reps. How would you allocate the money to them?

2. Now suppose that you find additional information about the territories to which Acore's Arizona reps are assigned. (If you're not familiar with Arizona, you can find a map at www.mapofarizona.net.)

   • Terry has the northern Arizona territory that includes everything north of Phoenix between the California and New Mexico borders. This territory encompasses a large amount of Native American reservation land as well as the Grand Canyon National Park. Flagstaff is the largest city in the territory.
   • Maria has the Phoenix area that includes the Phoenix metropolitan area and all suburbs (Glendale, Scottsdale, Mesa, and Sun City).
   • Samantha's Southwestern Arizona territory includes all areas south and west of Phoenix. Yuma is the largest city in this region.
   • Abraham's southeastern Arizona area includes everything south and east of Phoenix. Tucson is included in this territory.

Does this new information change your evaluation of Acore's Arizona sales reps? If so, how? Does your allocation of the bonus money change as a result of the additional information? If so, explain how.

3. Do you need any other information to evaluate these employees' performances for the first half of the year?

4. What, if any, adjustments would you make to the budgets for the remainder of the year?

5. Do you think that Acore's policy of allocating the same amount of expenses and expected sales to the four sales reps is adequate? What factors would you use in setting budgets for next year?

S10-2 Developing Standard Costs Using Time Studies, Incentives to Distort Standard

LO1

To be able to use a standard costing system, a company must develop standards that will serve as the guide for the amount of a resource (e.g., direct materials, direct labor) that should be consumed in the production of a unit. One way to accomplish this is to conduct a time or process study that examines the work of one individual whose results are then used as the standard. This standard serves as a base against which actual results will be compared and ultimately affects performance evaluations.

Suppose you work for an ice packaging service company and your job is to fill each plastic bag with 7 pounds of crushed ice and close the bag with a metal fastener. These bags are then delivered to local grocery and convenience stores for sale. Assume also you were chosen as the subject for a time or process study. Because some amount of spillage is normal, the study will measure the amount of ice each bag has. Your time to fill and fasten each bag will also be measured. These numbers will then serve as company standards for everyone within the company doing your job.

Required:

1. Is there any motivation for you to intentionally spill some ice or to purposefully take longer than normal to fill and/or fasten the bag?

2. How might these standards affect employees (including you) later?

3. How might the company mitigate this problem?

S10-3 Investigating Use of Variance Analysis, Variances in the Construction Industry

LO1

The variances calculated in this chapter are not appropriate for every organization. Industries and/or individual companies must often develop and use variances that make the most sense for evaluating performance for their specific circumstances. The construction industry is one example.

Required:

1. Go to http://www.constructionequipment.com/article/CA6568297.html and read the article that explains how budget variances can be used in the construction industry.

2. Explain how and why construction equipment costs are separated into owning costs and operating costs.

3. If you were a manager for this company, how would you interpret and evaluate the company's performance for each class of equipment?

4. Does this manner of evaluation make sense for a construction company? Why or why not?

5. Give examples of two other companies or industries that would use different variances than those calculated in this chapter.

CHAPTER 11

Decentralized Performance Evaluation

YOUR LEARNING OBJECTIVES

After completing this chapter, you should be able to:

LO1   List and explain the advantages and disadvantages of decentralization.

LO2   Describe the different types of responsibility centers and explain how managers in each type are evaluated.

LO3   Compute and interpret an investment center's return on investment.

LO4   Compute and interpret an investment center's residual income.

LO5   Describe the four dimensions of the balanced scorecard and how they are used to evaluate managerial performance.

LO6   Explain how transfer prices are set in decentralized organizations.

Lecture Presentation–LP11
www.mhhe.com/whitecotton1e

FOCUS COMPANY: Blockbuster

"Is Opportunity Knocking for You?"

www.blockbuster.com

T hink about the last time you rented a movie. Did you go to your neighborhood rental store such as Blockbuster or get it from an online rental service such as Netflix? The battle between Blockbuster and Netflix has been raging for more than a decade. Founded in 1986, Blockbuster Inc. became the world's largest provider of in-home movie entertainment. The company has struggled in recent years and many industry experts have predicted the demise of Blockbuster and other "bricks and mortar" rental stores due to competition from online rental services such as Netflix, the increasingly affordable cost of DVDs, and rapid advances in technology for downloadable movies. To survive in this rapidly changing industry, Blockbuster's managers must improve the company's performance going forward.

As you read this chapter, put yourself in the shoes of a stakeholder at Blockbuster and ask yourself the following questions:

- As a customer of Blockbuster, how would you rate the company's performance?

- If you were a manager at a local Blockbuster store (responsible for all aspects of store management), how would your boss measure your performance?

- If you were a manager in Blockbuster's distribution warehouse (responsible for shipping DVDs to individual stores), how would your boss measure your performance?

- If you were a senior executive at Blockbuster (responsible for developing and delivering entertainment using new delivery channels), how would your boss measure your performance?

- If you owned stock in Blockbuster, how would you measure the company's performance?

Each of these questions involves measuring or evaluating the performance of a manager, a segment of the business, or the entire company. As the questions indicate, performance can be measured in different ways depending on what and who is being evaluated.

In this chapter, we present a variety of methods for measuring the performance of business units and managers. To do so, we apply the techniques to Blockbuster and its various divisions. Although most of the details and the numbers we use in our examples are hypothetical, they are intended to illustrate the techniques that Blockbuster and other companies use to evaluate the performance of its managers and business units.

ORGANIZATION OF THE CHAPTER

Decentralization of responsibility	Evaluation of investment center performance	Transfer pricing
• Responsibility centers • Cost centers • Revenue centers • Profit centers • Investment centers	• Return on investment (ROI) • Residual income • Return on investment versus residual income • Limitations of financial performance measures • Balanced scorecard	• Market-price method • Cost-based method • Negotiation

Decentralization of Responsibility

Video 11-1
www.mhhe.com/whitecotton1e

As children, most of us couldn't wait to grow up and do everything our parents told us we were too young to do—drive a car, stay out late, date, or get a job. It didn't take long, though, to realize that all that freedom comes with a great deal of responsibility. Responsibility is the "state of being responsible, accountable or answerable." With responsibility comes the authority to make decisions for ourselves, to take action on behalf of others, and, ultimately, to be held accountable for both our decisions and our actions.

In business, employees are given the responsibility and authority to make decisions on behalf of their employer. How do organizations make sure that employees act responsibly or make decisions that are in the organization's best interest? The methods they use are not very different from the ones parents use to monitor and control their children, including setting clear rules and guidelines for conduct, directly observing behavior, indirectly measuring the decisions being made, and evaluating the outcome of those decisions.

Think, for example, about how parents teach their children to drive. They establish clear rules of conduct, such as how fast, when and where to drive, and how many passengers can be in the car. At first, they may insist on being in the car with the new driver (direct observation). Many parents also enroll their children in a driver's education course and receive report cards that assess their children's driving skills (indirect observation). At some point, parents must trust that their children have learned the rules of the road and will drive responsibly. Even so, parents may still check the odometer from time to time, install a GPS unit, or use some other means of indirect monitoring. These choices about how to monitor and control behavior have implications for trust in the parent/child relationship.

Organizations face similar issues as they try to ensure that managers are making responsible decisions—those that are in the best interests of the organization. The approach organizations use depends, in part, on how decision-making authority is delegated throughout the organization.

In a **decentralized organization**, decision-making authority is spread throughout the organization, and managers are given a great deal of autonomy to decide how to manage their individual units. In a **centralized organization**, decision-making authority is kept at the very top of the organization. Top executives make all strategic and operational decisions and charge lower-level managers with implementing those decisions.

In deciding how much decision-making authority to delegate, organizations must weigh the advantages and disadvantages of decentralization. See Exhibit 11.1 for a summary of the pros and cons of decentralization.

EXHIBIT 11.1	**Advantages and Disadvantages of Decentralization**

Centralized decisions

Decentralized decisions (organization wide)

Advantages of decentralization	Disadvantages of decentralization
• Recognizes that managers have specialized knowledge and can react quickly to local information • Allows the development of managerial expertise • Fosters competition among divisions • Allows top managers to focus on strategic issues	• May be less efficient and involve duplicate resources • Allows managers the opportunity to make decisions that are good for themselves or their division but which are not in the best interests of the organization overall

In most organizations, the distinction between centralized and decentralized operations is not an either-or matter but a question of **how much** decision-making authority to delegate. As companies grow, become geographically dispersed, or begin to offer more diversified products and services, keeping all decision-making authority at the top of the organization may not be possible or even desirable.

When decision-making authority is decentralized, the organization must find a way to monitor and evaluate managerial performance in much the same way that parents monitor and evaluate their children's driving behavior. Ideally, the company's performance measurement system should be designed so that the manager's goals and incentives are aligned with the organization's goals and objectives. Unfortunately, that is much easier said than done and is not always achieved in practice.

COACH'S TIP

As children grow up, parents must begin to let them make their own decisions. Similarly, as organizations grow in size, managers are often given more decision-making authority.

In the next section, we use Blockbuster Inc. to illustrate a variety of methods for measuring and evaluating managerial responsibility. Consider the simplified organizational chart for Blockbuster Inc. in Exhibit 11.2. To manage this large, geographically dispersed company, Blockbuster must delegate decision-making responsibility throughout the organization. The next section discusses some of the methods Blockbuster can use to measure and evaluate managerial performance in these various business segments.

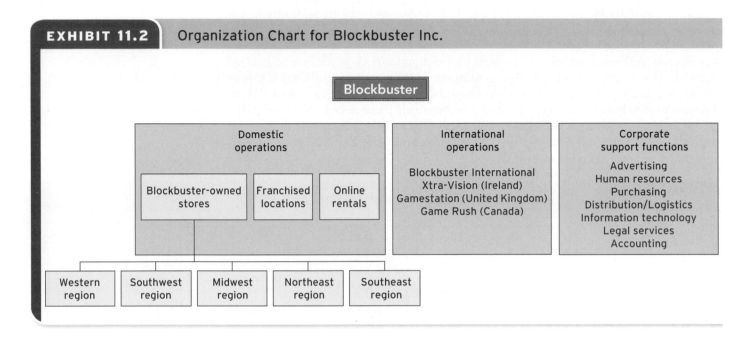

EXHIBIT 11.2 Organization Chart for Blockbuster Inc.

RESPONSIBILITY CENTERS

Responsibility accounting gives managers authority and responsibility for a particular part of the organization and then evaluates them based on that area of responsibility. The part of the organization for which managers are responsible is called a **responsibility center**. It can be established based on business function, product or service offerings, or geographic area.

Exhibit 11.2 shows that Blockbuster is divided into segments (divisions) based on all three characteristics: business support functions such as human resources, legal services, and accounting; service offerings including Blockbuster-owned stores, franchised stores, and online rentals; and geographic areas such as international, domestic, and regional. Many of these areas could be broken down further. For example, each of the geographic regions could be divided into districts, cities, towns, and individual stores.

One of the most important concepts in responsibility accounting is the **controllability principle**, which states that managers should be held responsible only for what they can control. The four different types of responsibility centers vary according to what the business manager can control and, thus, what he/she should be held responsible for:

- The manager of a **cost center** is responsible for controlling **cost**.
- The manager of a **revenue center** is responsible for generating **revenue**.
- The manager of a **profit center** is responsible for **profit** (revenue − cost).
- The manager of an **investment center** is responsible for **profit** (revenue − cost) and the **investments of assets**.

We next discuss each responsibility center and some common measures used to evaluate managerial performance in each.

COST CENTERS

Cost center managers have the authority to incur costs to support their areas of responsibility. All of Blockbuster's corporate support functions listed in Exhibit 11.2 would be treated as cost centers, including advertising, human resources, purchasing, distribution and logistics, information technology, legal services, and accounting. Note that these centers do not generate revenue directly from customers, although they can have an indirect impact on sales. For example, dollars spent on advertising should have an impact on the generation of revenue.

To understand the responsibilities of cost center managers, consider the following actual job descriptions posted recently on Blockbuster.com:

Cost Center Managers	Job Description/Responsibilities
Distribution Center Manager	• Responsible for the operation and management of the Distribution Center. • Supervise warehouse employees and provide training to ensure that productivity standards are met or exceeded. • Responsible for planning and management of the daily work activities of one or more departments within the warehouse (i.e., processing, returning, and packing) to performance metrics in the areas of throughput, cost, and customer service.
Human Resource Manager	• Manage the field Human Resources function within a specified area of responsibility. • Provide strategic direction and coaching to District Managers on the succession planning and development of employees. • Partner with region, district, and store management on HR related issues and with corporate HR on training and recruiting issues.

> **COACH'S TIP**
>
> Notice that these job descriptions tell employees what they will be responsible for and how they will be evaluated.

One of the primary tools that cost center managers use to monitor and measure performance is the budgetary control system and cost variances described in the last two chapters. However, cost center managers are responsible for more than just controlling costs. Usually they are also responsible for providing a high level of service to the rest of the organization whether in distribution, human resources, accounting, legal services, or some other internal function. Later in this chapter, we discuss the use of the **balanced scorecard** to assess how well managers perform on dimensions other than cost, including internal processes, customer service, and employee satisfaction and turnover.

REVENUE CENTERS

Revenue center managers are responsible for generating revenues within their areas of the organization. The following revenue center positions were posted recently on Blockbuster.com:

Revenue Center Managers	Job Description/ Responsibilities
Sales Manager	• Overall responsibility for meeting sales goals set by the strategic sales plan. • Responsible for implementing sales processes for training, communicating, and tracking progress. • Interact with customers in person and on the phone and utilize the computerized point of sale system to complete both credit and cash transactions and maintain member accounts.

| Customer Care Associate | • Manage service interactions by exhibiting a superior level of customer service and quality. Win back profitable customers through effective negotiations. |
| | • Take personal ownership of meeting average handle time, response time, and contract resolution rates to ensure service level agreements are met while effectively communicating value and service offerings to build and retain current membership base. |

Revenue center managers generally receive sales targets or quotas for a particular period of time and are evaluated based on whether they meet those targets. Later in this chapter, we use the balanced scorecard to incorporate other measures for evaluating revenue center managers including customer satisfaction, customer retention, and customer turnover.

PROFIT CENTERS

Profit center managers are responsible for generating a profit (revenue − cost) within their area of the business such as a store, district, region, division, or other business segment. Because they are responsible for both costs and revenues, profit center managers often supervise revenue and cost center managers. Consider the following profit center positions posted recently on Blockbuster.com:

Profit Center Positions	Job Description/Responsibilities [Blockbuster]
Store Manager (Tempe, AZ)	• Hire, train, and develop store employees. Schedule, organize, and direct assignments.
	• Resolve customer problems or complaints by determining optimal solutions.
	• Ensure interior and exterior of store is maintained to company standards.
	• Utilize labor management tools including effective scheduling to maximize productivity, profitability, and margins.
	• Analyze store's financial data and take action to grow revenues, control costs, and ensure appropriate inventory management (maintain product and sell-through merchandise inventories) to achieve sales and profit goals.
Regional Director of Operations (Seattle)	• General Manager responsible for the results of the overall regional business unit.
	• Responsible for maximizing earnings through the growth of rental and retail sales revenues, effective control of expenses, and the use of leadership and mentoring skills to maximize team performance.
	• Provide coaching, vision, and direction to the Region management team, monitor and manage performance, and develop strategies and people to achieve Region growth, service, and financial goals.

The most common method of evaluating a profit center manager is based on the **segmented income statement**. This type of income statement was introduced in Chapter 7 to evaluate whether a business segment should be continued or discontinued. The segment margin is useful for evaluating the performance of a profit center manager because it separates those costs that are within the segment manager's control from those costs that are outside of the manager's control. **Remember that managers should be held accountable only for those costs that are within their control**.

Segment margin is calculated as sales revenue less all costs that are directly attributable to a particular business segment, including variable costs and direct fixed costs. A **direct fixed cost** is incurred by the business segment and is therefore within the segment manager's control. Even though these costs are fixed, or independent of the volume of units produced or sold, they are incurred to support a specific business segment and are therefore considered within the segment manager's control. In contrast, **common fixed costs** are typically incurred at a higher level of the organization and are therefore outside the segment manager's control.

In evaluating a profit center manager, we should focus on the segment margin rather than the bottom-line profit margin, which includes costs that the manager cannot control. As an example, the following hypothetical segmented income statement reports on Blockbuster's Seattle District, which includes several retail stores in the area:

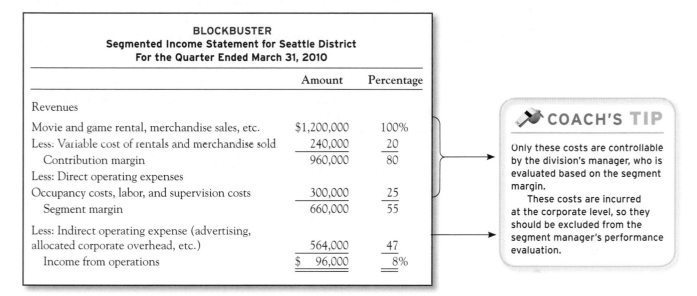

BLOCKBUSTER Segmented Income Statement for Seattle District For the Quarter Ended March 31, 2010	Amount	Percentage
Revenues		
Movie and game rental, merchandise sales, etc.	$1,200,000	100%
Less: Variable cost of rentals and merchandise sold	240,000	20
Contribution margin	960,000	80
Less: Direct operating expenses		
Occupancy costs, labor, and supervision costs	300,000	25
Segment margin	660,000	55
Less: Indirect operating expense (advertising, allocated corporate overhead, etc.)	564,000	47
Income from operations	$ 96,000	8%

> **COACH'S TIP**
>
> Only these costs are controllable by the division's manager, who is evaluated based on the segment margin.
> These costs are incurred at the corporate level, so they should be excluded from the segment manager's performance evaluation.

Notice that the variable costs of rentals and merchandise sold as well as the direct operating expenses of occupancy (rent), labor, and supervision are all directly attributable to the Seattle District. Thus, those costs are deducted from sales revenue to find the segment margin. Notice that indirect costs, such as advertising and allocated corporate overhead, are deducted **after** segment margin. Those costs are incurred at corporate headquarters and allocated to the individual divisions, so they should not be included in the segment margin. In short, a profit center manager should be evaluated based on the segment margin, not bottom-line profit because the segment margin includes only those costs that are within the manager's control.

INVESTMENT CENTERS

Investment center managers are responsible for generating a **profit** (revenue − cost) **and** investing **assets.** To understand the difference between a profit center manager and an investment center manager, consider two types of Blockbuster store: company-owned stores and franchised locations. Blockbuster Inc. owns and operates about 80 percent of the individual stores in the United States. For these company-owned stores, senior executives at corporate headquarters make all major investment decisions, including new store openings and store closings, adopting new technologies, and other decisions requiring major investments of capital. Because the lower-level managers at Blockbuster-owned stores do not make decisions concerning the investment of assets, they are profit center mangers, not investment center managers.

The other 20 percent of Blockbuster stores are franchised locations owned by other companies or individuals. The owners of these stores pay a franchise fee in exchange for the use of Blockbuster's name, national advertising and promotion, and other benefits such as access to the company's proprietary software. The owners/managers of franchised stores make their own decisions about where to locate, how much money to invest in physical assets and local advertising, and how to price their products. The following excerpt is from a recent annual report from Blockbuster.

As the report notes, the owner/manager of a franchised Blockbuster store has significantly more responsibility than the manager of a company-owned Blockbuster store. Because the owner-managers of franchised stores have control over the investment of assets, they are considered investment center managers.

The next section focuses on the evaluation of investment center performance. First, complete the following Self-Study Practice to make sure that you understand the differences between the four types of responsibility centers.

 ## Self-Study Practice

Which of the following statements about responsibility centers is (are) true? You may select more than one answer.

1. Cost center managers are responsible for generating sales in their area of the business.

2. Revenue center managers are responsible for controlling costs and generating revenue in their area of the business.

3. Profit center managers are responsible for controlling costs and generating revenue but not for investing assets.

4. Investment center managers are responsible for investing assets but not for controlling costs or generating revenue.

5. None of these statements is true.

After you have finished, check your answers with the solutions in the margin.

Solution to Self-Study Practice
The only true statement is 3.

Evaluation of Investment Center Performance

Learning Objective 3
Compute and interpret an investment center's return on investment.

As described in the previous section, investment center managers are responsible for generating profit and investing assets. As such, they will be evaluated based on their ability to generate enough profit to compensate for the investment in assets. Next we discuss two common measures for evaluating investment center performance: return on investment and residual income.

RETURN ON INVESTMENT (ROI)

The most common method of evaluating investment center performance is by using the rate of return on invested assets. Also called return on invested assets, the **return on investment (ROI)** is calculated as follows:

$$\text{Return on Investment (ROI)} = \frac{\text{Operating Income}}{\text{Average Invested Assets}}$$

ROI is calculated as operating profit divided by average invested assets. Thus, the higher a segment's operating profit is relative to its investment base, the higher its ROI.

Consider the following data for two hypothetical Blockbuster segments.

COMPARISON OF RETURN ON INVESTMENT FOR TWO BLOCKBUSTER BUSINESS SEGMENTS	Blockbuster Western Region	Blockbuster Online Rentals Division
Operating Income	$ 120,000	$ 600,000
Average invested assets	$2,000,000	$2,000,000
Return on Investment	6%	30%

Notice that the two divisions have the same level of investment, with average assets of $2,000,000. Yet Online Rentals generates a much higher operating profit ($600,000) and, thus, has a higher ROI (30 percent) than the Western Region (6 percent). This comparison of the two ROIs is a good starting point for evaluating the two investment centers, but it does not provide much information about **why** Online Rentals has a higher ROI.

To really understand ROI, we need to break it into two separate components: **investment turnover** and **profit margin**:

$$\text{Return on Investment (ROI)} = \text{Investment Turnover} \times \text{Profit Margin}$$

$$\frac{\text{Operating Income}}{\text{Average Invested Assets}} = \frac{\text{Sales Revenue}}{\text{Average Invested Assets}} \times \frac{\text{Operating Income}}{\text{Sales Revenue}}$$

Developed by executives at DuPont in the early 1900s, the formula is often referred to as the **DuPont method**. **Investment turnover** is the ratio of sales revenue to average invested assets; **profit margin** is the ratio of operating profit to sales revenue. Essentially, the DuPont formula shows that to increase ROI, managers must either generate more sales revenue from their assets (investment turnover) or keep a larger percentage of sales revenue as profit (profit margin).

Applying the DuPont method to Blockbuster's two segments provides the following results:

COMPARISON OF RETURN ON INVESTMENT, PROFIT MARGIN, AND INVESTMENT TURNOVER FOR TWO BLOCKBUSTER BUSINESS SEGMENTS	Blockbuster Western Region	Blockbuster Online Rentals Division
Sales revenue	$3,000,000	$6,000,000
Less: Operating expenses	(2,880,000)	(5,400,000)
Operating income	120,000	600,000
Average invested assets	2,000,000	2,000,000
Investment Turnover = $\dfrac{\text{Sales Revenue}}{\text{Average Invested Assets}}$	$\dfrac{3,000,000}{2,000,000} = 1.5$	$\dfrac{6,000,000}{2,000,000} = 3$
Profit Margin = $\dfrac{\text{Operating Income}}{\text{Sales Revenue}}$	$\dfrac{120,000}{3,000,000} = 4\%$	$\dfrac{600,000}{6,000,000} = 10\%$
ROI = $\dfrac{\text{Operating Income}}{\text{Average Invested Assets}}$	$\dfrac{120,000}{2,000,000} = 6\%$	$\dfrac{600,000}{2,000,000} = 30\%$
ROI = $\dfrac{\text{Investment}}{\text{Turnover}} \times \dfrac{\text{Profit}}{\text{Margin}}$	$1.5 \times 4\% = 6\%$	$10\% \times 3 = 30\%$

COACH'S TIP

Online Rentals generates more revenue than the Western Region from the same amount of invested assets.

Online Rentals earns more profit as a percentage of sales than the Western Region.

The combined effect is a much higher return on investment for Online Rentals than for the Western Region.

This analysis shows that two factors are driving the difference in ROI for Blockbuster's two segments. The relationship between investment turnover, profit margin, and return on investment is shown graphically in Exhibit 11.3

EXHIBIT 11.3	Investment Turnover, Profit Margin, and Return on Investment

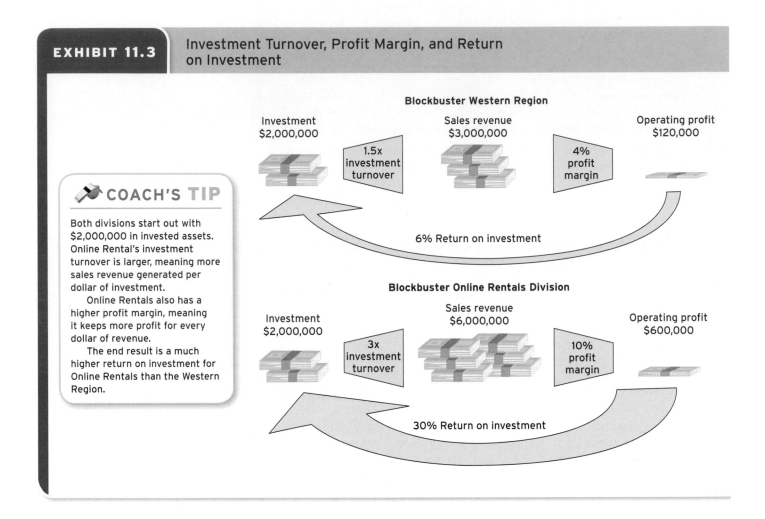

Blockbuster Western Region

Investment $2,000,000 — 1.5x investment turnover — Sales revenue $3,000,000 — 4% profit margin — Operating profit $120,000

6% Return on investment

Blockbuster Online Rentals Division

Investment $2,000,000 — 3x investment turnover — Sales revenue $6,000,000 — 10% profit margin — Operating profit $600,000

30% Return on investment

COACH'S TIP

Both divisions start out with $2,000,000 in invested assets. Online Rental's investment turnover is larger, meaning more sales revenue generated per dollar of investment.

Online Rentals also has a higher profit margin, meaning it keeps more profit for every dollar of revenue.

The end result is a much higher return on investment for Online Rentals than the Western Region.

Two factors affect a division's return on investment. The first factor is the amount of sales revenue generated for every dollar of investment. The investment turnover ratio shows how efficiently assets are used to generate sales revenue. The Western Region generates sales equal to 1.5 times its investment base; Online Rentals generates twice that amount—3 times its investment base—from the same level of investment.

The second factor that drives the difference in ROI is profit margin. The profit margin shows how much of a segment's sales revenue remains as operating profit after the operating costs have been covered. Online Rentals generates $0.10 in operating profit for every dollar of sales; the Western Region generates only $0.04 for every dollar of sales. This difference in profit margin is rooted in the different cost structures of the two segments. Blockbuster's bricks and mortar stores tend to have relatively high fixed costs (for rental space, utilities, and other overhead costs); Online Rentals has higher variable costs (for mailing movies back and forth to customers).

Multiplying the investment turnover by the profit margin gives the ROI, which can be reinvested in the company or paid out to the owners. In sum, Online Rentals generates more sales revenue from the same level of investment **and** keeps a higher percentage of that sales revenue as operating profit. The end result is that the Online Rentals' ROI (30 percent) is much higher than that for the Western Region (6 percent).

To make sure you understand how to calculate ROI, profit margin, and investment turnover, complete the following Self-Study Practice.

Self-Study Practice

Consider the following sample data for Blockbuster's Midwestern Region:

Sales	$1,000,000
Operating expenses	900,000
Operating income	100,000
Average invested assets	400,000

1. Compute the region's ROI, profit margin, and investment turnover.
2. Show how the ROI is related to profit margin and investment turnover.

After you have finished, check your answers with the solutions in the margin.

Solution to Self-Study Practice
1. ROI = $100,000/$400,000 = 25%
   Profit margin = $100,000/$1,000,000 = 10%
   Investment turnover = $1,000,000/$400,000 = 2.5
2. ROI = Profit Margin ×
         Investment Turnover
       = 10% × 2.5 = 25%

RESIDUAL INCOME

An alternative measure for evaluating an investment center's performance, called residual income, involves making a comparison between operating profit and the minimum required rate of return. Recall from Chapter 8 that organizations set the minimum required rate of return, sometimes called the **hurdle rate**, in order to cover the company's cost of capital. **Residual income** is the difference between the operating profit and the minimum profit the organization must earn to cover the hurdle rate as in the following formula:[1]

Learning Objective 4
Compute and interpret an investment center's residual income.

COACH'S TIP

The **hurdle rate** is the minimum return that the organization requires on invested assets. It is also called the required rate or **cost of capital**.

Let's compute the residual incomes for the two hypothetical Blockbuster's segments using a hurdle rate of 10 percent:

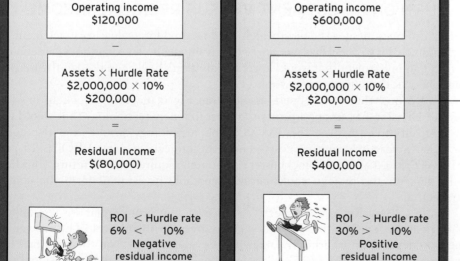

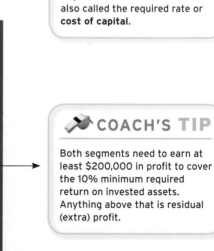

COACH'S TIP

Both segments need to earn at least $200,000 in profit to cover the 10% minimum required return on invested assets. Anything above that is residual (extra) profit.

---

[1]A closely related technique for evaluating investment center performance is known as economic value **added**, or EVA™. This approach, which was devised by Stern, Stewart and Co., measures the economic wealth that is created when a company's operating income exceeds its cost of capital. Conceptually, EVA is very similar to residual income, but it requires a number of complex adjustments that are beyond the scope of this textbook.

Notice that the Western Region has a negative residual income of $(80,000). In other words, the region's operating profit is not high enough to cover its 10 percent hurdle rate. Recall that the Western Region's ROI is only 6 percent—4 percent less than the 10 percent required rate of return. Multiplying the region's $2,000,000 average invested assets by the 4 percent shortfall in its ROI (compared to the hurdle rate), gives the same result: a negative residual income of $80,000.

Online Rentals' residual income is $400,000. This is the additional profit that is being earned, over and above the 10 percent hurdle rate. Recall that the Online Rentals Division is earning a 30 percent ROI. Multiplying the extra 20 percent return (over and above the 10 percent hurdle rate) by the division's $2,000,000 investment gives the same result: a residual income of $400,000.

Before you continue, complete the following Self-Study Practice to make sure you understand how to calculate residual income and its relationship to ROI.

 Self-Study Practice

Consider the following hypothetical data for Blockbuster's Midwest Region:

Operating income	$100,000
Average Invested assets	$400,000
ROI	25%

1. Using a hurdle rate of 10 percent, compute the division's residual income.
2. Explain how the residual income is related to the 25 percent ROI.

After you have finished, check your answers with the solution in the margin.

Solution to Self-Study Practice

1. Residual Income = Operating Income − (Invested Assets × Hurdle Rate) = $100,000 − ($400,000 × 10%) = $60,000
2. The 25 percent ROI is higher than the 10 percent hurdle rate: Excess of 15% × $400,000 Invested Assets = $60,000 Residual Income.

RETURN ON INVESTMENT VERSUS RESIDUAL INCOME

Return on investment is the most widely used method for evaluating investment center performance. However, it has one major disadvantage: It can sometimes cause managers to reject an investment that would lower the division's ROI even though the investment might benefit the company as a whole.

To see how that can happen, assume that the manager of Blockbuster's Online Rentals Division has an opportunity to invest in a new technology that would require an up-front investment of $1,000,000. The technology would save the company $150,000 a year in operating costs. Thus, the project's expected ROI is 15 percent ($150,000/$1,000,000). If Blockbuster's minimum required rate of return (hurdle rate) is 10 percent, the project would be an acceptable investment from the company's perspective.

From Online Rentals' perspective, however, the project may be less appealing. Will the manager of Online Rentals want to invest in the project? The answer to this question depends on whether the manager is evaluated based on the division's ROI or its residual income. The proposed project would generate a positive residual income because it would earn more than the required 10 percent hurdle rate. However, it would have a negative impact on the division's ROI because the 15 percent return is less than the division's current ROI of 30 percent. If the manager invests in this project, the division's ROI will drop from 30 percent to 25 percent, as shown in the following table.

EFFECT OF THE PROPOSED PROJECT ON ONLINE RENTALS'
RETURN ON INVESTMENT AND RESIDUAL INCOME

Return on Investment analysis		Status Quo (without project)	Effect of Proposed Project	If Project Is Accepted
$\dfrac{\text{Operating Income}}{\text{Average Invested Assets}} = \text{Return on Investment}$		$\dfrac{\$600,000}{\$3,000,000} =$	$\dfrac{150,000}{\$1,000,000} =$	$\dfrac{\$750,000}{\$3,000,000} =$
		30%	15%	25%
Residual Income analysis				
Operating Income		$600,000	$150,000	$750,000
Required Profit (10% of average invested assets)		(200,000)	(100,000)	(300,000)
Residual Income		$400,000	$ 50,000	$450,000

COACH'S TIP

Notice that the project would have a negative effect on Online Rentals' ROI because its rate of return would be less than the current ROI of 30 percent.

The project would generate a positive residual income, however, because its return is higher than the company's required rate of return, 10 percent.

This example shows how a responsibility accounting system can create **goal incongruence**, or conflict between a manager and the organization as a whole. A manager who is evaluated based on ROI may not be willing to invest in a project that is in the best interest of the company simply because doing so would have a negative impact on the manager's own performance evaluation. The residual income method helps to align the manager's goals with the organization's objective of earning a minimum ROI of 10 percent. Regardless of the division's current ROI, its residual income will increase as long as the manager invests only in projects that exceed the company's minimum required return.

LIMITATIONS OF FINANCIAL PERFORMANCE MEASURES

Both ROI and residual income are lagging indicators of financial performance. In other words, they are based on historical information taken from a company's financial statements including past sales revenue, operating income, and assets. These measures tell how well a company or a division did in the past but not necessarily how well it will do in the future.

Unfortunately, many of the actions that managers take to improve a company's financial performance in the short run can prove harmful to the organization over the long run. Examples include cutting back on research and development, reducing employee training, and using less expensive materials to make a product. While all of these decisions will improve short-run financial results, they will likely hurt the company in the long term through reduced sales, quality problems, customer complaints, and increased warranty expenses. To avoid these problems, organizations should evaluate and reward managers based on more than just short-term financial results. The next section discusses the balanced scorecard, a performance measurement system designed to focus managers' attention on a broader set of performance metrics rather than short-term financial results.

BALANCED SCORECARD

The **balanced scorecard** is a comprehensive performance measurement system that translates an organization's vision and strategy into a set of operational performance metrics. The balanced scorecard measures organizational performance on four key dimensions:

- **Customer perspective**. How do we want our customers to see us?
- **Learning and growth perspective**. How will we sustain our ability to change and improve?
- **Internal business processes**. What internal processes will we require to meet the needs of our customers, employees, and shareholders?
- **Financial perspective**. How do we satisfy our shareholders, regulators, and other stakeholders?

For each of these dimensions, managers must devise specific objectives, measures, and targets that can be used to measure performance and identify what needs to be done to improve in the future. These objectives, measures, and targets should be communicated

Learning Objective 5
Describe the four dimensions of the balanced scorecard and how they are used to evaluate managerial performance.

Video 11-2
www.mhhe.com/whitecotton1e

to managers throughout the organization so that everyone knows what needs to be done to achieve long-term success, not just short-term financial results.

See the sample balanced scorecard for Blockbuster in Exhibit 11.4. Notice that the center of the scorecard is the company's strategic vision. Each of the four categories surrounding the vision has specific objectives and measures used to track performance toward those objectives.

EXHIBIT 11.4	Balanced Scorecard for Blockbuster Inc.

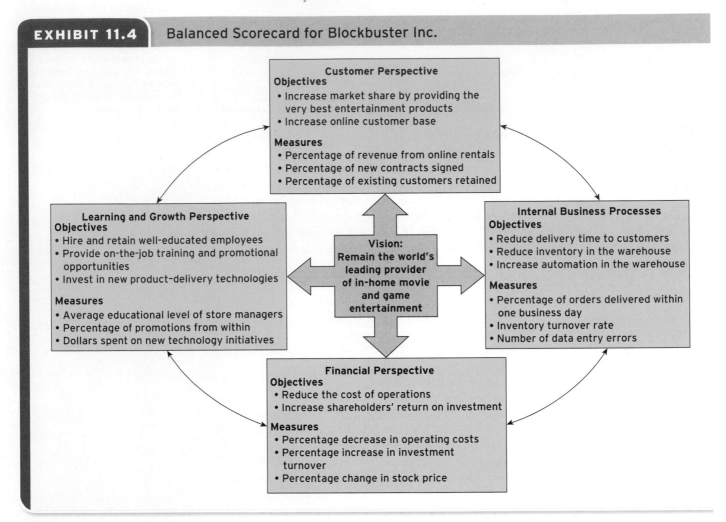

Customer Perspective
Objectives
- Increase market share by providing the very best entertainment products
- Increase online customer base

Measures
- Percentage of revenue from online rentals
- Percentage of new contracts signed
- Percentage of existing customers retained

Learning and Growth Perspective
Objectives
- Hire and retain well-educated employees
- Provide on-the-job training and promotional opportunities
- Invest in new product–delivery technologies

Measures
- Average educational level of store managers
- Percentage of promotions from within
- Dollars spent on new technology initiatives

Vision:
Remain the world's leading provider of in-home movie and game entertainment

Internal Business Processes
Objectives
- Reduce delivery time to customers
- Reduce inventory in the warehouse
- Increase automation in the warehouse

Measures
- Percentage of orders delivered within one business day
- Inventory turnover rate
- Number of data entry errors

Financial Perspective
Objectives
- Reduce the cost of operations
- Increase shareholders' return on investment

Measures
- Percentage decrease in operating costs
- Percentage increase in investment turnover
- Percentage change in stock price

In this example, Blockbuster's strategic vision is to remain the world's leading provider of in-home movies and gaming. To remain competitive in this rapidly changing industry, Blockbuster's managers cannot continue to operate as they have in the past, relying primarily on Blockbuster's neighborhood stores or mail order delivery. Instead, the company must invest in new technologies that will allow it to deliver downloadable movies and games directly to consumers.

Each perspective of the balanced scorecard should include objectives that support the overall vision and strategy, along with specific metrics that will be used to measure performance on the objectives. In addition, the objectives and metrics included in the balanced scorecard should have a cause-and-effect relationship where performance in one area of the scorecard ultimately affects performance in the others.

Assume that one of Blockbuster's strategies for achieving its vision is to invest in new technologies for delivering entertainment products through cable or Internet service providers. The company should include a metric in the learning and growth perspective of the scorecard to measure performance in this area. Eventually, investments in new product technologies should result in improved internal business processes such as reduced delivery time to customers, reduced inventory of movies and games in traditional (e.g., DVD) format, and reduced investment in "bricks and mortar" locations. Faster delivery time and improved technology should result in improved customer service, which would be measured by the percentage of existing customers retained and new customer sales. Ultimately, these improved internal business processes and customer metrics will affect the company's financial performance, which is measured by traditional financial metrics such as the company's stock price or ROI. Notice that performance on the financial metrics lags behind the other measures, which are leading indicators of future performance.

The causal linkages between the various elements of the balanced scorecard are summarized in Exhibit 11.5.

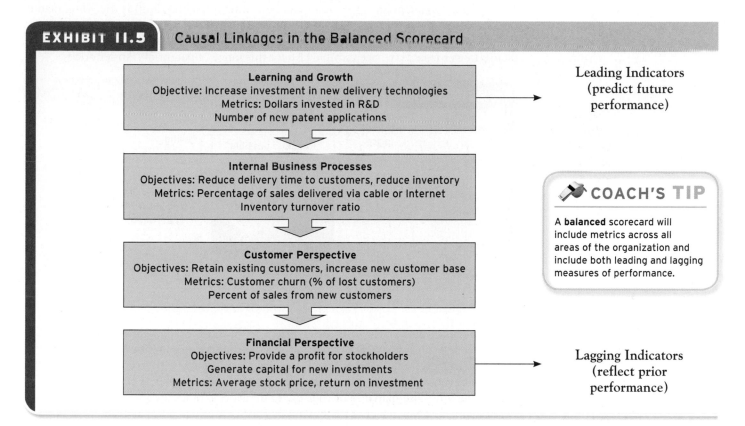

EXHIBIT 11.5 Causal Linkages in the Balanced Scorecard

Learning and Growth
Objective: Increase investment in new delivery technologies
Metrics: Dollars invested in R&D
Number of new patent applications

Internal Business Processes
Objectives: Reduce delivery time to customers, reduce inventory
Metrics: Percentage of sales delivered via cable or Internet
Inventory turnover ratio

Customer Perspective
Objectives: Retain existing customers, increase new customer base
Metrics: Customer churn (% of lost customers)
Percent of sales from new customers

Financial Perspective
Objectives: Provide a profit for stockholders
Generate capital for new investments
Metrics: Average stock price, return on investment

Leading Indicators (predict future performance)

Lagging Indicators (reflect prior performance)

COACH'S TIP
A **balanced** scorecard will include metrics across all areas of the organization and include both leading and lagging measures of performance.

Although the balanced scorecard is a useful tool for linking a company's strategic vision to operational metrics, it can be very time consuming to implement and requires involvement of employees at all levels of the organization. In addition, while the metrics in the balanced scorecard are intended to focus managers' attention on the company's long-term strategy, managers are often motivated by short-term financial results. For example, managers often receive bonuses based on achieving short-term financial results. Unless the company's incentive and reward system is redesigned to focus on long-term results, the balanced scorecard may not serve its intended purpose. Incentive systems that emphasize team-based performance rather than individual performance are more consistent with a balanced scorecard approach to performance measurement.

The next section discusses other issues that arise in decentralized organizations when managers of competing divisions buy and sell goods and services from one another.

Transfer Pricing

The final issue we consider in this chapter is how decentralized organizations deal with the transfer or sale of goods and services between divisions. A **transfer price** is the amount that one division charges when it sells goods or services to another division of the same company. Transfers happen quite often in today's business environment because many large corporations are composed of several relatively independent business units all owned by the same parent company. Business transactions between units or divisions of the same company are called **related-party transactions**.

Learning Objective 6
Explain how transfer prices are set in decentralized organizations.

Video 11-3
www.mhhe.com/whitecotton1e

Perhaps the easiest way to think about transfer prices is in terms of the deal you would get if you bought something from a relative. Maybe you want to buy a car from your brother-in-law's dealership, a meal at your cousin's restaurant, or a cut and style at your sister's hair salon. How much would you expect to pay for a product or service when buying from a relative? At a minimum, you should be willing to pay for any variable costs that your relative incurs. For example, if your brother, an auto mechanic, agrees to repair your car, you should at least be willing to pay for the parts. The minimum transfer price is called the "floor." The maximum amount you should be willing to pay (ceiling) is the going market rate for the product or service. In other words, you should not be willing to pay more for the product or service than you would if you bought it elsewhere or the amount that a complete stranger would pay. See Exhibit 11.6 for this range of potential transfer prices.

> ### COACH'S TIP
>
> In transfer pricing, the seller would like to charge the full market price, while the buyer would prefer to pay only variable costs. Managers often negotiate to a "fair" price somewhere in between.

EXHIBIT 11.6	Range of Potential Transfer Prices

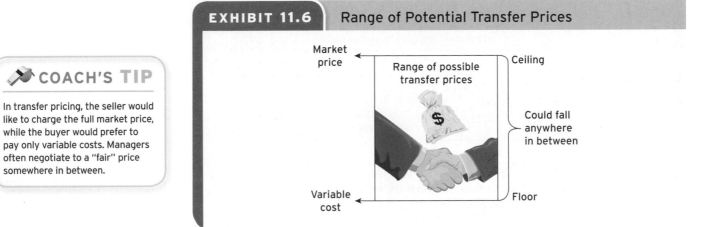

The same rules apply to transfer prices in decentralized organizations. The only difference is that the managers of decentralized business units are not necessarily friendly relatives. In fact, if managers are evaluated based on their ability to control costs and/or generate revenue, their goals may be diametrically opposed even if they do work in the same company. The manager of the selling division is motivated to sell at the highest possible price; the manager of the buying division is motivated to pay the lowest possible cost. Although the transfer price does not really matter from the overall company's perspective,[2] it can make a big difference to individual managers. As in the famous line from the film *The Godfather*, "It's not personal, it's just business."

As a simple example, assume Blockbuster has a controlling interest in the hypothetical company Popcorn Ltd., which manufactures bags of microwave popcorn for sale in large buckets at Blockbuster and other movie rental stores. Popcorn Ltd. operates as a free-standing business unit of Blockbucker Inc. and its managers are evaluated as profit center managers.

Assume that Popcorn Ltd.'s costs to produce a single case (24 packs) of microwave popcorn are as follows.

POPCORN LTD. **Cost to Produce 1 Case (24 packs) of Microwave Popcorn**		
Direct materials	$1.00	
Direct labor	0.25	$1.50
Variable overhead	0.25	
Fixed overhead ($350,000/100,000 unit capacity)	3.50	
Full manufacturing cost	$5.00	
The external market price (for non-Blockbuster buyers) is $ 10.00.		

---

[2]Transfer prices **can** have a major impact on multinational companies due to variations in tax rates from one country to the next. The tax implications of transfer prices are extremely complex and are beyond the scope of this textbook.

The manager of Blockbuster's Midwest Region has approached Popcorn Ltd. to buy popcorn for that region. What price should Popcorn Ltd. charge the Midwest Region for a case of popcorn?

There are three different ways to determine transfer prices: the market price method, the cost-based method, and negotiation.

MARKET-PRICE METHOD

The market price is the price that would be paid if the product or service were purchased from another supplier, or sold to an unrelated party. It is the maximum price that a buyer should be willing to pay. In this example, the market price is $10 per case of popcorn. The problem with using the market price as a transfer price is that the buyer has no incentive to purchase from within the company and so may consider buying from an outside supplier. For example, if your car dealer brother-in-law expects you to pay full market price, you may choose to buy a car from someone else.

In the Blockbuster example, if the buying division (Midwest Region) decides to buy from an outside supplier, the selling division (Popcorn Ltd.) loses the opportunity to profit from the sale just as your brother-in-law would lose the opportunity to earn a commission on your new car. As a result, the company as a whole may suffer. The only time that using a market price as a transfer price makes sense is when the selling division is operating at full capacity and cannot fill the order without giving up sales to external customers. If Popcorn Ltd. is already selling all the popcorn it can produce for $10 per case, for example, selling to the Midwest Region at a lower price would not make sense. The company would be losing more profitable business.

If the selling division has **excess capacity,** however, it can make a profit by selling at any price above the variable cost. (Remember that the total fixed cost is constant and does not change depending on the number of units produced and sold, at least within a limited range.) In this example, we assume Popcorn Ltd. has sufficient capacity to fill the Midwest Region's order without incurring additional fixed costs or losing sales to other customers. In that case, Popcorn Ltd. should be willing to sell the popcorn for less than the market price (see Exhibit 11.7). In the next section, we use the cost-based method to determine a transfer price for the popcorn.

EXHIBIT 11.7   **Range of Transfer Prices for Blockbuster Popcorn**

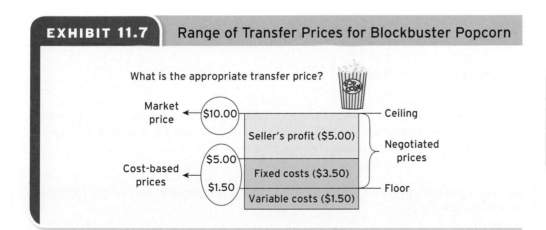

What is the appropriate transfer price?

Market price	$10.00		Ceiling
Cost-based prices	$5.00	Seller's profit ($5.00)	Negotiated prices
	$1.50	Fixed costs ($3.50)	Floor
		Variable costs ($1.50)	

COACH'S TIP

A "fair" transfer price falls somewhere between the market price (ceiling) and variable cost (floor).

COST-BASED METHOD

The cost-based method uses a cost measure such as variable cost or full cost as the basis for setting the transfer price. At a minimum, the selling division should recover the incremental (that is, variable) costs of producing and selling the product. In this example, the transfer price should be no less than the variable cost of $1.50 per case of popcorn. Another option is to base the transfer price on the full manufacturing cost of $5.00 per case, which covers both variable and fixed costs.

Many companies use a "cost-plus" transfer price. For example, Blockbuster might have a policy of making all internal transfers at the full manufacturing cost plus 10 percent. If so, the transfer price per case of popcorn would be $5.00 + (10% of $5.00) = $5.50. If the transfer price were set at $5.50, both buyer and seller would benefit from the transfer. The buying division (Midwest Region) would pay $5.50 per case, a $4.50 savings compared to the market price of $10.00. The selling division (Popcorn Ltd.) would make $5.50 minus $1.50 in variable costs for an incremental profit of $4.00 per case.

NEGOTIATION

A final option is to let divisional managers negotiate transfer prices. In this method, the negotiated price should fall somewhere between the variable cost ($1.50) and the full market price ($10.00). As in any negotiation, the final price will depend on the relative power of the buyer and seller, their negotiation skills, and how much inside information each has about the other division's cost, capacity, and demand.

Again, think of how you negotiate when buying a car. You should not be willing to pay more than the market price, which we assume is the sticker price. The dealer should not be willing to accept less than the variable cost; otherwise, the dealership will lose money on the sale. Knowing the variable cost of the car would certainly help you bargain. On the other hand, if the dealer knows you really want the car and has another customer who is ready to buy it, you will be in a less powerful bargaining position.

Negotiating transfer prices can be time consuming and can force managers of the same parent company to act as adversaries. To avoid such situations, companies may dictate that the buying and selling divisions split the difference so that each receives an equal benefit from the internal transfer. In our example, the transfer price would be midway between the $10.00 market price and the $1.50 in variable costs, or $5.75. This approach creates a win–win situation for the managers: The buying division saves $4.25 per case ($10.00 − $5.75) by buying from inside, and the selling division makes an extra $4.25 per case ($5.75 − $1.50) in incremental profit.

To make sure you understand how to set transfer prices, complete the following Self-Study Practice.

 ## Self-Study Practice

Kraft Foods owns both Tombstone Pizza and Kraft Cheese. Assume that Tombstone Pizza (the buyer) has approached Kraft Cheese (the seller) to ask for a special deal on the cheese used to produce Tombstone's frozen pizza.

Which of the following statements is true?

1. The minimum price the seller should accept is the variable cost of producing and selling the cheese.

2. The maximum price the buyer should pay is the market price.

3. Both statements above are true.

4. None of these statements is true.

After you have finished, check your answers with the solutions in the margin.

DEMONSTRATION CASE

Consider the following data for two divisions of Peter Piper Pizza:

	Northwest Region	Southwest Region
Average invested assets	$ 6,000,000	$6,000,000
Sales revenue	$18,000,000	$9,000,000
Less: Operating expenses	(17,460,000)	(8,100,000)
Operating income	$ 540,000	$ 900,000

Required:

1. Compute the investment turnover, profit margin, return on investment, and residual income for each division. Assume a 10 percent hurdle rate.

2. Explain the relationship between each division's residual income and its return on investment.

3. The manager of the Southwest Region has the opportunity to invest an additional $2,000,000 in a project expected to generate additional operating income of $220,000 per year. Calculate Southwest's new return on investment and residual income if the manager accepts the project.

4. Would Southwest's manager, who is evaluated based on the region's ROI, want to invest in the project? If the evaluation were based on the region's residual income? Why or why not?

See page 425 for solution.

CHAPTER SUMMARY

List and explain the advantages and disadvantages of decentralization. p. 406　　**LO1**

- Decentralization is the delegation of decision-making authority to managers at all levels of the organization.

- The advantages of decentralization include the ability to make decisions more quickly based on local information; the development of managerial expertise; increased competition among managers; and the increased opportunity for upper management to focus on strategic issues.

- The disadvantages of decentralization include the potential for duplicating resources and for making suboptimal decisions (those that are not made in the best interests of the organization as a whole).

Describe the different types of responsibility centers and explain how managers in each type are evaluated. p. 408　　**LO2**

- **Cost center:** Managers are responsible for controlling costs within their area of responsibility, such as distribution, advertising, accounting, or human resources. Cost center managers are evaluated based on their ability to stay within budget and provide the necessary support to the organization.

- **Revenue center:** Managers are responsible for generating sales revenue within their area of responsibility, such as a store, a district, or a region. They are evaluated based on their ability to meet sales quotas and other measures of success, such as customer retention.

- **Profit center:** Managers are responsible for earning a profit within their area of responsibility through both revenue generation and cost control. They are typically evaluated based on a measure such as segment margin, which includes only those costs that are within the segment manager's direct control.

- **Investment center:** Managers are responsible for both profit (revenue − cost) and the investment of assets. They are evaluated based on measures that include both profit and investment, such as return on investment and residual income.

LO3 **Compute and interpret an investment center's return on investment. p. 412**

- Return on investment (ROI) is the most common measure for evaluating investment center performance.

- ROI equals the investment center's operating profit divided by its average investment in assets.

- The DuPont formula shows that ROI equals the profit margin multiplied by the investment turnover ratio.

- Profit margin is the amount of profit generated for every dollar of sales revenue.

- Investment turnover is the amount of sales revenue generated for every dollar of invested assets.

- Companies can increase ROI by either increasing the profit margin (by reducing costs without reducing sales) or increasing the asset turnover rate (by increasing sales without increasing assets).

LO4 **Compute and interpret an investment center's residual income. p. 415**

- Residual income is an alternative measure for evaluating an investment center's performance.

- Residual income equals the difference between an investment center's operating profit and the minimum profit it must make to cover its hurdle rate (that is, the minimum rate of return on its assets).

- Managers can earn residual income by investing in projects that earn more than the minimum required rate of return (or hurdle rate).

LO5 **Describe the four dimensions of the balanced scorecard and how they are used to evaluate managerial performance. p. 417**

- The balanced scorecard is a comprehensive performance measurement system that translates the organization's vision and strategy into a set of operational performance measures.

- The balanced scorecard measures operational performances on four key dimensions: consumer perspective, learning and growth perspective, internal business processes, and financial perspective.

- The customer perspective focuses on the customer through measures such as customer retention, customer satisfaction, and market share.

- The learning and growth perspective focuses on the organization's ability to change and improve through measures such as the amount of money spent on research and development and employee education and training.

- The internal business perspective focuses on the internal processes required to meet customer needs through measures of on-time-delivery, quality, and internal process efficiency.

- The financial perspective focuses on traditional financial measures of performance, such as return on investment, residual income, sales revenue, and profit.

LO6 **Explain how transfer prices are set in decentralized organizations. p. 419**

- A transfer price is the price charged when one unit or division of a company sells goods or services to another unit or division of the same company.

- The maximum transfer price is the external market price, or the amount that would be charged to an unrelated party.

- The minimum transfer price is the variable cost (to the seller) of selling to the other division.

- Cost-based transfer prices can be set based on variable cost, full cost, or cost plus some percentage markup.

- Transfer prices can also be set through negotiation between the buying and selling divisions.

SOLUTION TO DEMONSTRATION CASE

1.

		Northwest Region	Southwest Region
Investment Turnover	$= \dfrac{\text{Sales Revenue}}{\text{Average Invested Assets}}$	$\dfrac{18,000,000}{6,000,000} = 3$	$\dfrac{9,000,000}{6,000,000} = 1.50$
Profit Margin	$= \dfrac{\text{Operating Income}}{\text{Sales Revenue}}$	$\dfrac{540,000}{18,000,000} = 3\%$	$\dfrac{900,000}{9,000,000} = 10\%$
Return on Investment	$= \dfrac{\text{Operating Income}}{\text{Average Invested Assets}}$	$\dfrac{540,000}{6,000,000} = 9\%$	$\dfrac{900,000}{6,000,000} = 15\%$
Operating Income		540,000	900,000
Minimum Required Profit (10% of Average Invested Assets)		(600,000)	(600,000)
Residual Income		(60,000)	300,000

2. The Northwest Region has a negative residual income because its return on investment, which is 9 percent, is less than the 10 percent hurdle rate; 1 percent of $6,000,000 = $(60,000).

The Southwest Region has a positive residual income because its return on investment, which is 15 percent, is higher than the 10 percent hurdle rate; 5 percent of $6,000,000 = $300,000.

3.

	Southwest Region (before project)	Proposed Project	Southwest Region (if project is accepted)
Return on Investment Analysis			
$\dfrac{\text{Operating Income}}{\text{Average Invested Assets}} = \text{Return on Investment}$	$\dfrac{\$900,000}{\$6,000,000} = 15\%$	$\dfrac{\$220,000}{\$2,000,000} = 11\%$	$\dfrac{\$1,120,000}{\$8,000,000} = 14\%$
Residual Income Analysis			
Operating Income	$900,000	$220,000	$1,120,000
Minimum Required Profit (10% of Average Invested Assets)	(600,000)	(200,000)	(800,000)
Residual Income	$300,000	$ 20,000	$ 320,000

4. If the evaluation is based on the region's return on investment (ROI), Southwest's regional manager probably would **not** want to invest in the project because it would lower the division's ROI. The project's expected ROI of 11 percent is less than the division's current ROI of 15 percent. Thus, investing the extra $2,000,000 would lower the region's ROI to 14 percent.

However, if the evaluation is based on the region's residual income, the manager **would** want to invest in the project because it would increase the region's residual income. Residual income will increase as long as the project's return (11 percent) is higher than the minimum required rate of return (10 percent).

KEY TERMS

Balanced Scorecard (p. 417)

Centralized Organization (p. 407)

Controllability Principle (p. 408)

Cost Center (p. 408)

Decentralized Organization (p. 407)

DuPont Method (p. 413)

Goal Incongruence (p. 417)

Investment Center (p. 408)

Investment Turnover (p. 413)

Profit Center (p. 408)

Profit Margin (p. 413)

Related-Party Transactions (p. 419)

Residual Income (p. 415)

Responsibility Accounting (p. 408)

Responsibility Center (p. 408)

Return on Investment (ROI) (p. 412)

Revenue Center (p. 408)

Segmented Income Statement (p. 410)

Transfer Price (p. 419)

See complete definitions in glossary at back of text.

QUESTIONS

1. Explain how centralized and decentralized companies differ. What are the advantages and disadvantages of each?

2. Why does decentralization create the need for responsibility accounting in an organization?

3. What is the controllability principle and why is it crucial to responsibility accounting?

4. Name the four types of responsibility centers and describe the managers' responsibilities and authority in each.

5. Briefly explain the difference between segment margin and bottom-line profit margin.

6. Why are profit center managers evaluated on segment margin instead of overall company income?

7. How do investment center managers differ from profit center managers?

8. What role do return on investment and residual income play in responsibility accounting?

9. Return on investment may be separated into two components. Name them and describe what each can tell you.

10. Explain how relying on return on investment for performance evaluation of investment center managers could lead to goal incongruence.

11. How is residual income calculated?

12. Briefly explain a company's hurdle rate including how it is set and how it is used in evaluating investment center performance.

13. What benefit does residual income offer in comparison to return on investment when evaluating performance?

14. What are the primary limitations of financial measures of performance?

15. Other than the one(s) mentioned in the text, give an example of an action that management might take to improve financial performance in the short run that could prove detrimental in the long run.

16. Explain the balanced scorecard approach to performance evaluation. What advantages does this approach have over using only financial measurements?

17. What are the four dimensions of a balanced scorecard? What does each dimension represent?

18. Why must a company consider its incentive and reward system when implementing a balanced scorecard approach?

19. Why are incentive systems that emphasize team-based performance more consistent with a balanced scorecard approach?

20. What is a transfer price?

21 Explain why two managers for the same company may be diametrically opposed to each other when considering a transfer price.

22. Explain the meaning of minimum and maximum transfer prices and identify who (the buyer or the seller) would determine each.

23. What is the market-price method of transfer pricing?

24. What does the term excess capacity mean? How does excess capacity affect a transfer price?

25. Describe the cost-based method of transfer pricing.

26. What are negotiated transfer prices? Explain two possible disadvantages of allowing managers to negotiate a transfer price.

MULTIPLE CHOICE

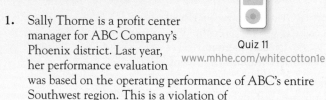

Quiz 11
www.mhhe.com/whitecotton1e

1. Sally Thorne is a profit center manager for ABC Company's Phoenix district. Last year, her performance evaluation was based on the operating performance of ABC's entire Southwest region. This is a violation of

   a. The hurdle rate principle.
   b. The controllability principle.
   c. The balanced scorecard approach.
   d. Negotiated transfer pricing rules.

2. Responsibility centers include

   a. Cost centers.
   b. Profit centers.
   c. Investment centers.
   d. All of these.

3. Which of the following statements is true?

   a. A profit center manager is responsible for investing company assets.
   b. A cost center manager should be evaluated based on sales revenue.

   c. A profit center manager should be evaluated based on return on investment.
   d. An investment center manager is responsible for costs, revenue, and the investment of assets.

4. Which of the following is most likely to be classified as a cost center manager?

   a. Accounting manager.
   b. Sales manager.
   c. Regional manager.
   d. All of these are cost center managers.

5. Return on investment and residual income are useful for evaluating

   a. Cost center managers.
   b. Revenue center managers.
   c. Profit center managers.
   d. Investment center managers.

6. Return on investment can be separated into

   a. Investment turnover and profit margin.
   b. Profit margin and residual income.
   c. Investment turnover and residual income.
   d. Profit margin and operating income.

7. Raymond Calvin is an investment center manager for XYZ Corp. and is evaluated solely on the return on investment for his division. Which of the following will improve Raymond's evaluation?

    a. Increasing the amount invested in assets while keeping operating income the same.
    b. Increasing the amount of operating income while keeping invested assets the same.
    c. Decreasing the amount invested in assets while keeping operating income the same.
    d. Either b or c.

8. Which of the following statements is true?

    a. Return on investment considers a company's hurdle rate for investments.
    b. Residual income considers a company's hurdle rate for investments.

    c. Projects may be rejected based on return on investment even though they produce positive residual income.
    d. Both b and c.

9. Which of the following is not a component of the balanced scorecard method of measuring performance?

    a. Customer perspective.
    b. Management perspective.
    c. Learning and growth perspective.
    d. Internal business processes.

10. Transfer price could be based on:

    a. Variable costs.
    b. Full cost.
    c. Market price.
    d. Any of the above.

> Answers to Multiple-Choice Questions located in back of the text.

MINI EXERCISES

M11-1 Describing Difference in Centralized and Decentralized Organizations

LO1

Lupe Bornes recently graduated from college and received job offers in management from two different companies. The positions are similar in terms of title, salary, and benefits, but the companies vary in organizational structure. Alpha Company is centralized while Beta Company is decentralized. Explain to Lupe what he can infer about each company and how it is likely to affect his position within each one.

M11-2 Describing Structure of Real-World Organizations Responsibility Centers

LO2

Responsibility centers can be created in a variety of ways. Give a real-world example of a company whose responsibility centers would likely be created on the basis of each of the following: functional area, product line, and geographic area.

M11-3 Applying Balanced Scorecard to Real-World Company

LO5

Consider the manager of your local Applebee's restaurant. Using a balanced scorecard approach, identify three measures for each of the four dimensions of the balanced scorecard.

Applebee's

M11-4 Applying Balanced Scorecard to Online Company

LO5

Choose a company that has an online sales segment; it can be a company that operates entirely online or a brick-and-mortar store with an online site. Assuming a balanced scorecard approach, identify five specific measures that the company could use to measure performance from the customer perspective. For each measure identified, indicate how that information would be obtained.

M11-5 Calculating Return on Investment, Residual Income

LO3, 4

Kettle Company has sales of $450,000, operating income of $250,000, average invested assets of $800,000, and a hurdle rate of 10 percent. Calculate Kettle's return on investment and its residual income.

M11-6 Calculating Return on Investment, Residual Income

LO3, 4

Lowry Company has sales of $125,000, cost of goods sold of $70,000, operating expenses of $20,000, average invested assets of $400,000, and a hurdle rate of 8 percent. Calculate Lowry's return on investment and its residual income.

LO3, 4   **M11-7 Calculating Return on Investment, Residual Income**

Rally Corp's Eastern Division has sales of $190,000, cost of goods sold of $110,000, operating expenses of $35,000, average invested assets of $900,000, and a hurdle rate of 12 percent. Calculate the Eastern Division's return on investment and its residual income.

LO3, 4   **M11-8 Impact of New Investment on ROI, Residual Income**

The Alpha Division of Mayfield Company had an operating income of $135,000 and net assets of $560,000. Mayfield has a required rate of return of 14 percent. Alpha has an opportunity to increase operating income by $32,000 with a $92,000 investment in assets. Compute Alpha Division's return on investment and residual income currently and if it undertakes the project.

LO2, 6   **M11-9 Describing Transfer Pricing Implications**

Assume that your cousin Matilda Flores manages a local glass shop that was recently bought by a company that produces custom picture frames. As a result, Matilda will soon be providing glass to the Frame Division. She has heard upper management mention a transfer price but does not understand what this term means or how it might affect her division. Briefly explain transfer pricing to Matilda and how it will impact her division's performance in the future.

LO6   **M11-10 Identifying Minimum, Maximum Transfer Prices**

Lancaster Company has two divisions, A and B. Division A manufactures a component that Division B uses. The variable cost to produce this component is $1.50 per unit; full cost is $2.00. The component sells on the open market for $5.00. Assuming Division A has excess capacity, what is the lowest price Division A will accept for the component? What is the highest price that Division B will pay for it?

LO6   **M11-11 Calculating Cost-Plus Transfer Price**

Bellows Company has two divisions, X and Y. Division X manufactures a wheel assembly that Division Y uses. The variable cost to produce this assembly is $4.00 per unit; full cost is $5.00. The component sells on the open market for $9.00. What will the transfer price be if Bellows uses a pricing rule of variable cost plus 40 percent?

LO6   **M11-12 Negotiating Transfer Prices**

Prigett Company is considering allowing the managers of its two divisions to negotiate a transfer price for the component that Division A manufactures and sells to Division B. Identify the range of possible transfer prices that could result from the negotiation. Briefly describe benefits and possible negative consequences of allowing the managers to negotiate a transfer price.

EXERCISES

LO1, 2, 5   **E11-1 Explaining Relationships among Decentralization, Responsibility Accounting, Controllability, Balanced Scorecard**

Assume you are the vice president of operations for a local company. Your company is in the process of converting from a small, centralized organization in which its president makes all decisions to a larger, geographically dispersed one with decentralized decision-making authority.

Required:

Write a brief memo to other company managers explaining how decentralization, responsibility accounting, controllability, and the balanced scorecard method of performance evaluation are all related. Include the most obvious changes the managers are likely to see as this transition takes place and how it will impact their performance evaluations in the future.

LO2   **E11-2 Identifying Responsibility Center Types**

Required:

Match the most likely type of responsibility center classification to each of the following positions. You may use a classification once, more than once, or not at all.

Employment Positions	Possible Responsibility Center Classification
____ Sales manager	a. Cost center
____ Regional manager	b. Revenue center
____ Company president	c. Profit center
____ Purchasing manager	d. Investment center
____ Human resources manager	
____ Chief financial officer	
____ Production facility manager	

E11-3 Finding Unknowns Using Return on Investment, Profit Margin, Investment Turnover

LO3

Tuttle Company recently had a computer malfunction and lost a portion of its accounting records. The company has reconstructed some of its financial performance measurements including components of the return on investment calculations.

Required:

Help Tuttle rebuild its information database by completing the following table:

Return on Investment	Profit Margin	Investment Turnover
?	5%	1.1
14%	?	2.0
3%	4%	?
23%	?	0.4

E11-4 Finding Unknowns Using Return on Investment, Profit Margin, Investment Turnover

LO3

Norshon Company recently had a computer malfunction and lost a portion of its accounting records. The company has reconstructed some of its financial performance measurements including components of the return on investment calculations.

Required:

Help Norshon rebuild its information database by completing the following table:

Return on Investment	Profit Margin	Investment Turnover	Operating Income	Sales Revenue	Average Invested Assets
?	?	?	$ 35,000	$ 700,000	$1,400,000
?	10%	0.40	100,000	?	2,500,000
?	15%	1.25	?	2,000,000	?
12%	?	2.00	?	500,000	?

E11-5 Calculating Return on Investment, Residual Income, Determining Effect of Changes in Sales, Expenses, Invested Asset, Hurdle Rate on Each

LO3, 4

Mancell Company has sales of $500,000, cost of goods sold of $370,000, other operating expenses of $50,000, average invested assets of $1,400,000, and a hurdle rate of 8 percent.

Required:

1. Determine Mancell's return on investment (ROI), investment turnover, profit margin, and residual income.

2. Several possible changes that Mancell could face in the upcoming year follow. Determine each scenario's impact on Mancell's ROI and residual income. (**Note:** Treat each scenario independently.)

   a. Company sales and cost of goods sold increase by 30 percent.
   b. Operating expenses decrease by $10,000.
   c. Operating expenses increase by 20 percent.
   d. Average invested assets increase by $300,000.
   e. Mancell changes its hurdle rate to 12 percent.

LO3, 4   **E11-6 Calculating Return on Investment, Residual Income, Determining Effect of Changes in Sales, Expenses, Invested Asset, Hurdle Rate on Each**

LaTreme Company has sales of $1,210,000, cost of goods sold of $735,000, other operating expenses of 148,000, average invested assets of $5,335,000, and a hurdle rate of 13 percent.

Required:

1. Determine LaTreme's return on investment (ROI), investment turnover, profit margin, and residual income.

2. Several possible changes that LaTreme could face in the upcoming year follow. Determine each scenario's impact on LaTreme's ROI and residual income. (**Note:** Treat each scenario independently.)

   a. Company sales and cost of goods sold increase by 15 percent.
   b. Operating expenses increase by $73,000.
   c. Operating expenses decrease by 10 percent.
   d. Average invested assets decrease by $285,000
   e. LaTreme changes its hurdle rate to 9 percent.

LO3, 4   **E11-7 Evaluating Managerial Performance Using Return on Investment, Residual Income**

Francis Corp. has two divisions, Eastern and Western. The following information for the past year is for each division:

	Eastern Division	Western Division
Sales	$ 600,000	$ 900,000
Cost of goods sold and operating expenses	450,000	600,000
Operating Income	$ 150,000	$ 300,000
Average invested assets	$1,000,000	$1,500,000

Francis has established a hurdle rate of 9 percent.

Required:

1. Compute each division's return on investment (ROI) and residual income for last year. Determine which manager seems to be performing better.

2. Suppose Francis is investing in new technology that will increase each division's operating income by $144,000. The total investment required is $1,600,000, which will be split evenly between the two divisions. Calculate the ROI and return on investment for each division after the investment is made.

3. Determine whether both managers will support the investment. Explain how their support will differ depending on which performance measure (ROI or residual investment) is used.

LO3, 4   **E11-8 Evaluating Managerial Performance Using Return on Investment, Residual Income**

Sullivan Company has three divisions, Larry, Moe, and Curly. The company has a hurdle rate of 5 percent. Selected operating data of the three divisions follow:

	Larry	Moe	Curly
Sales	$ 325,000	$220,000	$ 298,000
Cost of goods sold	216,000	123,000	202,000
Miscellaneous operating expenses	45,000	36,000	39,000
Allocated corporate expenses	18,000	12,000	16,500
Average invested assets	1,300,000	970,000	1,025,000

Required:

1. Compute the return on investment for each division.
2. Compute the residual income for each division.

E11-9 **Developing Balanced Scorecard**   L05

Choose a company with which you regularly do business. Assume you have been hired as a consultant to help overhaul its performance evaluation system.

Required:

1. Briefly outline a balanced scorecard approach that could be used to evaluate the performance of the company's managers.
2. For each of the four perspectives, identify three metrics that could be part of the balanced scorecard.
3. Explain the reasoning behind each metric that you choose.

E11-10 **Describing Balanced Scorecard Objectives and Perspectives**   L05

Your brother-in-law, Fred Miles, has just taken a new position as the plant manager of a local production facility. He has been told that the company uses a balanced scorecard approach to evaluate its managers. Fred is not familiar with this approach because his previous experience as a production manager focused only on whether the plant met the company's budgeted production.

Required:

1. Briefly explain to Fred how performance evaluations at his new company will differ from those at his previous company.
2. Give Fred five possible objectives that the new company will use in addition to production level in evaluating his performance. For each objective that you identify, be sure to indicate a plausible metric for measuring it.

E11-11 **Understanding Transfer Price Importance**   L06

Refer to E11-10 Suppose Fred's plant manufactures a component used by another division of the organization. He has approached you for help in understanding why everyone seems to be making such a big deal about the transfer price that he plans to charge for the component. Fred's comment was, "Transfer prices do not impact the amount of profit earned by the company as a whole, so they don't affect me. I don't care what transfer price is used."

Required:

1. Explain whether Fred is correct or incorrect.
2. Explain to Fred why he should care about the transfer price that is chosen.

E11-12 **Determining Transfer Price**   L06

The Fabrication Division of Hawking Company manufactures an antenna component used by the Electronics Division. This antenna is also sold to external customers for $35 per unit. Variable costs for the antenna are $17 per unit and fixed cost is $7 per unit. Hawking executives would like for the Fabrication Division to transfer 8,000 units to the Electronics Division at a price of $25 per unit.

Required:

1. Assume the Fabrication Department is operating at full capacity. Explain whether it should accept the transfer price proposed by management.
2. Identify the minimum transfer price that the Fabrication Division will accept and explain why.

E11-13 **Determining Transfer Price**   L06

Refer to the information presented in E11-12. Assume that the Fabrication Division has enough excess capacity to accommodate the request.

Required:

1. Explain whether the Fabrication Division should accept the $25 transfer price proposed by management.

2. Calculate the effect on Fabrication Division's net income if it accepts the $25 transfer price.

LO6   **E11-14 Determining Transfer Price**

Refer to the information presented in E11-12, but assume that the Electronics Department requires the antenna to be made from a specific blend of metals. This would raise the variable cost per unit to $27.

Required:

1. Explain whether the Fabrication Department should accept the $25 transfer price proposed by management.

2. Determine the minimum transfer price that it will accept.

3. Determine the mutually beneficial transfer price so that the two divisions equally split the profits from the transfer.

LO6   **E11-15 Determining Minimum, Maximum, Negotiated Transfer Prices**

Coleman Company is a lumber company that also manufactures custom cabinetry. It is made up of two divisions, Lumber and Cabinetry. The Lumber Division is responsible for harvesting and preparing lumber for use; the Cabinetry Division produces custom-ordered cabinetry. The lumber produced by the Lumber Division has a variable cost of $1.00 per linear foot and full cost of $1.50. Comparable quality wood sells on the open market for $3.00 per linear foot.

Required:

1. Assume you are the manager of the Cabinetry Division. Determine the maximum amount you would pay for lumber.

2. Assume you are the manager of the Lumber Division. Determine the minimum amount you would charge for the lumber if you have excess capacity. Repeat assuming you have no excess capacity.

3. Assume you were the president of Coleman. Determine a mutually beneficial transfer price.

4. Explain the possible consequences of simply letting the two division managers negotiate a price.

LO6   **E11-16 Identifying Minimum, Maximum Transfer Prices, Determining Effect on Each Division's Profit**

Womack Company is made up of two divisions, A and B. Division A produces a widget that Division B uses in the production of its product. Variable cost per widget is $0.50; full cost is $0.70. Comparable widgets sell on the open market for $1.10 each. Division A can produce up to 2 million widgets per year but is currently operating at only 50 percent capacity. Division B expects to use 100,000 widgets in the current year.

Required:

1. Determine the minimum and maximum transfer prices.

2. Calculate Womack Company's total benefit of having the widgets transferred between these divisions.

3. If the transfer price is set at $0.50 per unit, determine how much profit Division A will make on the transfer. Determine how much Division B will save by not purchasing the widgets on the open market.

4. If the transfer price is set at $1.10 per unit, determine how much profit Division A will make on the transfer. Determine how much Division B will save by not purchasing the widgets on the open market.

5. What transfer price would you recommend to split the difference?

PROBLEMS–SET A

**PA11-1 Calculating Return on Investment,
Residual Income, Determining Effect of Changes in Sales, Expenses,
Invested Asset, Hurdle Rate on Each**

LO3, 4

www.mhhe.com/whitecotton1e

Longview Company has the following information available for the past year:

	Northern Division	Southern Division
Sales	$1,200,000	$1,800,000
Cost of goods sold and operating expenses	900,000	1,300,000
Operating Income	$ 300,000	$ 500,000
Average invested assets	$1,000,000	$1,500,000

The company's hurdle rate is 8 percent.

Required:

1. Calculate return on investment (ROI) and residual income for each division for last year.
2. Recalculate ROI and residual income for each division for each independent situation that follows:
   a. Operating income increases by 10 percent.
   b. Operating income decreases by 10 percent.
   c. The company invests $250,000 in each division, an amount that generates $100,000 additional income per division.
   d. Longview changes its hurdle rate to 6 percent.

**PA11-2 Calculating Unknowns, Predicting Relationship among Return
on Investment, Residual Income, Hurdle Rates**

LO3, 4

The following is partial information for Dupre Company's most recent year of operation. It manufactures pet toys and categorizes its operations into two divisions, Cat and Dog.

	Cat Division	Dog Division
Sales revenue	?	$600,000
Average invested assets	$2,000,000	?
Operating income	$ 160,000	$150,000
Profit margin	20%	?
Investment turnover	?	0.2
Return on investment	?	?
Residual income	$ 40,000	$ (30,000)

Required:

1. Without making any calculations, determine whether each division's return on investment is above or below Dupre's hurdle rate. How can you tell?
2. Determine the missing amounts in the preceding table.
3. What is Dupre's hurdle rate?
4. Suppose Dupre has the opportunity to invest additional assets to help expand the company's market share. The expansion would require an average investment of $2 million and would generate $140,000 in additional income. From Dupre's perspective, is this a viable investment? Why or why not?
5. Suppose the two divisions would equally share the investment and profits from the expansion project. If return on investment is used to evaluate performance, what will each division manager think about the proposed project?
6. In requirement 5, will either manager's preference change if residual income is used to measure division performance? Explain your answer.

LO3, 4 **PA11-3 Evaluating Managerial Performance, Proposed Project Impact on Return on Investment, Residual Income**

Oswego Company has three divisions: A, B, and C. The company has a hurdle rate of 7 percent. Selected operating data of the three divisions are as follows:

	Division A	Division B	Division C
Sales	$1,255,000	$ 920,000	$ 898,000
Cost of goods sold	776,000	675,000	652,000
Miscellaneous operating expenses	64,000	52,000	53,100
Allocated corporate expenses	48,000	41,000	41,500
Average invested assets	4,150,000	3,860,000	3,215,000

Oswego is considering an expansion project in the upcoming year that will cost $5 million and return $400,000 per year. The project would be implemented by only one of the three divisions.

Required:

1. Compute the ROI for each division.
2. Compute the residual income for each division.
3. Rank the divisions according to the ROI and residual income of each.
4. Compute the return on the proposed expansion project. Is this an acceptable project?
5. Without any additional calculations, state whether the proposed project would increase or decrease each division's ROI.
6. Compute the new ROI and residual income for each division if the project was implemented within that division.

LO6 **PA11-4 Identifying Minimum, Maximum, Mutually Beneficial Transfer Prices**

Rideaway Corp. is a high-end bicycle manufacturing company that produces mountain bikes. Soft Saddle is a division of Rideaway that manufactures bicycle seats. SoftSaddle's seats are used in Rideaway's bikes and are sold to other bike manufacturers. Cost information per seat follows:

Variable cost	$22.00
Full cost	27.00
Market price	40.00

In addition, its capacity data follow:

Capacity per year	40,000 seats
Current production level	30,000 seats

Required:

1. Assuming Rideaway produces 3,000 bikes per year, determine the overall benefit of using seats from SoftSaddle instead of purchasing them externally.
2. Determine the maximum price that the bike production facility would be willing to pay to purchase the seats from SoftSaddle. How is the overall benefit divided between the two divisions if this transfer price is used?
3. Determine the minimum that SoftSaddle will accept as a transfer price. How is the overall benefit divided between the two divisions if this transfer price is used?
4. Determine the mutually beneficial transfer price for the bicycle seats.
5. How would your answer change if SoftSaddle were currently operating at capacity?

LO6 **PA11-5 Identifying Minimum, Maximum, Mutually Beneficial Transfer Prices**

Travel Well, Inc., manufactures a variety of luggage for airline passengers. The company has several luggage production divisions as well as a wholly owned subsidiary, SecureLock, that manufactures small padlocks used on luggage. Each piece of luggage that Duffle Bag Division produces has two padlocks for which it previously paid the going market price of $3 each. Financial information for Travel Well's Duffle Bag Division and for SecureLock follow:

	Duffle Bag Division	SecureLock
Sales		
4,500 bags × $150 each	$675,000	
200,000 locks × $3.00 each		$600,000
Variable expenses		
4,500 bags × $85.00 each	382,500	
200,000 locks × $0.60 each		120,000

SecureLock has a production capacity of 250,000 locks.

Required:

1. Determine how much Travel Well will save on each padlock if the Duffle Bag Division obtains them from SecureLock instead of an external supplier.
2. Determine the maximum and minimum transfer prices for the padlocks. Who sets these?
3. Suppose Travel Well has set a transfer price policy of variable cost plus 50 percent for all related-party transactions. Determine how much each party will benefit from the internal transfer.
4. Determine the mutually beneficial transfer price.

PROBLEMS–SET B

PB11-1 Calculating Return on Investment, Residual Income, Determining Effect   LO3, 4
         of Changes in Sales, Expenses, Invested Asset, Hurdle Rate on Each

Pascall Company has the following information available for the past year:

	Eastern Division	Western Division
Segment sales	$2,200,000	$1,300,000
Segment cost of goods sold and operating expenses	1,700,000	1,000,000
Segment income	$ 500,000	$ 300,000
Average invested assets	$3,800,000	$2,500,000

The company's hurdle rate is 10 percent.

1. Determine Pascall's return on investment (ROI) and residual income for each division for last year.
2. Recalculate Pascall's ROI and residual income for each division for each independent situation that follows:
   a. Operating income increases by 10 percent.
   b. Operating income decreases by 10 percent.
   c. The company invests $400,000 in each division, an amount that generates $80,000 additional income per division.
   d. Pascall changes its hurdle rate to 15 percent.

PB11-2 Calculating Unknowns, Predicting Relationship among Return   LO3, 4
         on Investment, Residual Income, Hurdle Rates

The following is partial information for Xavier Company's most recent year of operation. Xavier manufactures children's shoes and categorizes its operations into two divisions, Girls and Boys.

	Girls Division	Boys Division
Sales revenue	$2,000,000	?
Average invested assets	?	$1,000,000
Operating income	$ 500,000	$ 300,000
Profit margin	?	15%
Investment turnover	1.0	?
Return on investment	?	?
Residual income	$ 260,000	$ 180,000

Required:

1. Without making any calculations, determine whether each division's return on investment is above or below Xavier's hurdle rate. How can you tell?

2. Determine the missing amounts in the preceding table.

3. What is Xavier's hurdle rate?

4. Suppose Xavier has the opportunity to invest additional assets to help expand the company's market share. The expansion would require an investment of $4 million and would generate $800,000 in additional income. From Xavier's perspective, is this a viable investment? Why or why not?

5. Suppose the two divisions would equally share the investment and profits from the expansion project. If return on investment is used to evaluate performance, what will each division think about the proposed project?

6. In requirement 5, will either manager's preference change if residual income is used to measure division performance? Explain your answer.

LO3, 4 **PB11-3 Evaluating Managerial Performance, Impact of Proposed Project on Return on Investment, Residual Income**

Landau Company has three divisions, X, Y, and Z. The company has a hurdle rate of 8 percent. Selected operating data of the three divisions follow:

	Division X	Division Y	Division Z
Sales	$ 458,000	$ 560,000	$ 486,000
Cost of goods sold	316,000	313,925	233,600
Miscellaneous operating expenses	58,000	72,000	42,000
Allocated corporate expenses	29,000	39,000	35,500
Average invested assets	1,600,000	2,110,000	1,315,000

Landau is considering an expansion project in the upcoming year that will cost $3,500,000 and return $525,000 per year. The project would be implemented by only one of the three divisions.

Required:

1. Compute the ROI for each division.

2. Compute the residual income for each division.

3. Rank the divisions according to the ROI and residual income of each.

4. Compute the return on the proposed expansion project. Is this an acceptable project to Landau?

5. Without any additional calculations, state whether the proposed project would increase or decrease each division's ROI.

6. Compute the new ROI and residual income for each division if the project was implemented within that division.

PB11-4 Identifying Minimum, Maximum, Mutually Beneficial Transfer Prices   LO6

Snuggle Up Company produces outdoor gear. ZipIt is a division of Snuggle that manufactures unbreakable zippers used in Snuggle's gear and sold to other manufacturers. Cost information per zipper follows:

Variable cost	$0.80
Full cost	1.10
Market price	3.00

In addition, ZipIt's capacity data follow:

Capacity per year	2,000,000 zippers
Current production level	1,500,000 zippers

Required:

1. Assuming Snuggle produces 300,000 sleeping bags per year, what is the overall benefit of using zippers from ZipIt instead of purchasing them externally?
2. Determine the maximum price that the sleeping bag production facility would be willing to pay to purchase the zippers from ZipIt. How is the overall benefit divided between the two divisions if this transfer price is used?
3. Determine the minimum that ZipIt will accept as a transfer price. How is the overall benefit divided between the two divisions if this transfer price is used?
4. Determine the mutually beneficial transfer price for the zippers.
5. How would your answer change if ZipIt were currently operating at capacity?

PB11-5 Identifying Minimum, Maximum, Mutually Beneficial Transfer Prices   LO6

H2-Oh! produces bottled water. The company recently purchased PlastiCo., a manufacturer of plastic bottles. In the past, H2-Oh! has purchased plastic bottles on the open market at $0.25 each. Financial information for the past year for H2-Oh! and PlastiCo. follows:

	H2-Oh!	PlastiCo.
Sales		
500,000 units × $2.00 each	$1,000,000	
1,200,000 units × $0.25 each		$300,000
Variable expenses		
500,000 units × $0.25 each	125,000	
1,200,000 units × $0.05 each		60,000

PlastiCo has a production capacity of 2 million units.

Required:

1. Determine how much H2-Oh! will save on each bottle if it obtains them from PlastiCo. instead of an external supplier.
2. Determine the maximum and minimum transfer prices for the plastic bottles. Who sets these?
3. Suppose H2-Oh! has determined a transfer price rule of variable cost plus 40 percent for all related-party transactions. Determine how much each party will benefit from the internal transfer.
4. Determine the mutually beneficial transfer price.

SKILLS DEVELOPMENT CASES

LO6

S11-1 Researching Effect of Transfer Prices on Taxes

The problems surrounding transfer pricing are not limited to internal decisions. Companies' transfer prices can have huge implications well beyond departmental profits including significant tax implications.

In September 2006, the U.K.-based pharmaceutical giant, Glaxo SmithKline (GSK) settled an ongoing dispute with the U.S. Internal Revenue Service. In doing so, GSK agreed to pay $3.4 billion in back taxes and interest. This was the largest single tax dispute in U.S. history.

Required:

Research the GSK dispute and write a two-page memo summarizing the central issues of the dispute. Include in your summary the position of each side (IRS and GSK) as well as GSK's explanation for the settlement and any impact on company shareholders.

LO5

S11-2 Researching Use of Balanced Scorecard in Business

This chapter discussed the use of the balanced scorecard for evaluating managerial and organizational performance. Many companies have adopted this performance measurement in recent years.

Required:

Research or visit a company that has implemented the balanced scorecard and write a brief report of its experience. You should include information such as when the company implemented the balanced scorecard, what performance measurement approach it had used previously, any difficulties it experienced with the implementation, and the benefits received from the new method.

LO1

S11-3 Explaining Impact of Organizational Structure, Budgetary Processes on Employee Morale

In the last several chapters, you have learned about many aspects of organizational structure, budgeting, and performance evaluation. None of these company characteristics operates in isolation: They all interrelate to form an organization's culture and influence employee morale. The following table has several combinations of organizational structure and budgeting preparation style:

Organizational Structure	Budget Creation Process
Centralized	Administered
Decentralized	Participative
Centralized	Participative
Decentralized	Administered

Required:

For each combination in the table, write a brief paragraph summarizing both the potential advantages and disadvantages for a company using the combination. Consider the impact on managers and other employees as well as the potential impact on outside parties such as customers or other organizational stakeholders.

LO6

S11-4 Identify Transfer Pricing Issues in Practice

Blockbusters's online rental service (www.blockbuster.com) allows customers to return a limited number of movies to their local Blockbuster store to exchange for a free movie rental.

1. Visit Blockbuster.com and identify a service plan that allows for this type of movie exchange. How many movies can customers exchange each month, and what is the monthly fee?

2. Describe the transfer pricing issue that arises between Blockbuster.com and the local Blockbuster store. Explain how one division is providing services to another division. Should the local Blockbuster store earn revenue on this type of transaction? Why or why not?

3. Visit or call the manager of your local Blockbuster store. Try to find out the nature of any revenue sharing agreement for these exchange transactions. If the manager cannot reveal the terms of the actual agreement, ask how much the manager thinks the store should receive for a movie exchange, and why. Does it matter whether the movie exchange is a new release or an older title?

4. What are the variable costs to the Blockbuster store of participating in a movie exchange? How much would you estimate the variable cost to be?

5. Are there any opportunity costs of a movie exchange?

6. What do you think is a "fair" transfer price for a movie exchange?

CHAPTER 12

Reporting and Interpreting the Statement of Cash Flows

YOUR LEARNING OBJECTIVES

After completing this chapter, you should be able to:

LO1   Identify cash flows arising from operating, investing, and financing activities.

LO2   Report cash flows from operating activities, using the indirect method.

LO3   Report cash flows from investing activities.

LO4   Report cash flows from financing activities.

LO5   Interpret cash flows from operating, investing, and financing activities.

LO6   Report and interpret cash flows from operating activities, using the direct method

Lecture Presentation–LP12
www.mhhe.com/whitecotton1e

FOCUS COMPANY: Under Armour

www.underarmour.com

H ave you ever studied your bank statements to see how much money you bring in and pay out during a typical month? You don't have to be a financial genius to know that if you are spending more than you earn, your savings will quickly disappear, and you will need to get a loan or some other source of financing to see you through.

Most businesses face the same issues you do. In 2007, for example, Under Armour Inc.– famous for its frictionless sportswear–reported a net cash outflow from day-to-day operating activities. To ensure the company's long-term survival, managers had to stay on top of this change in the cash situation. Fortunately, the company had saved a great deal of cash in prior years. Managers were also able to negotiate some new loans to keep the business from running out of cash. By 2008, the company had turned things around and was again experiencing a positive net cash inflow from its operations.

Investors and creditors also monitor a company's cash inflows and outflows to predict whether they are likely to receive dividends and other amounts they are owed. They find information for making such predictions in the statement of cash flows. Similar to your personal bank statement, the statement of cash flows reports changes in the company's cash situation.

Statement of cash flows	Preparing the statement of cash flows	Interpreting the statement of cash flows
• Business activities and cash flows • Classifying cash flows • Relationship to other financial statements	• Direct and indirect reporting of operating cash flows • Determining operating cash flows (indirect method) • Cash flows from investing and financing activities	• Evaluating cash flows • Determining operating cash flows (direct method)

Statement of Cash Flows

BUSINESS ACTIVITIES AND CASH FLOWS

Learning Objective 1
Identify cash flows arising from operating, investing, and financing activities.

Video 12.1
www.mhhe.com/whitecotton1e

Accountants measure profitability based on net income, or the difference between revenue and expenses. Under the accrual method of accounting, revenue is always recognized when earned, and expenses are matched against the revenue they help create, regardless of when cash is actually received or paid.

Although net income is an extremely useful measure of a company's profitability, managers are often more concerned about cash flow than accounting net income. Even a profitable business can fail if managers do not have enough cash on hand to pay the bills. If a business is not generating sufficient cash from operations, managers may need to generate funds from other sources, such as selling off assets, borrowing money, or issuing stock.

Neither the income statement nor the balance sheet provides managers with the information they need to fully understand the changes in cash flow and the source of those changes. The balance sheet shows a company's cash balance at a point in time, but it doesn't explain the activities that caused changes in its cash. Cash may have been generated by the company's day-to-day operations, by the sale of the company's buildings, or by the negotiation of new loans. The income statement doesn't explain changes in cash because it focuses on just the operating results of the business, excluding cash that is received or paid when taking out or paying down loans, issuing or buying the company's own stock, and selling or investing in long-lived assets. Also, the timing of cash receipts and payments may differ from the accrual-based income statement, which reports revenues when they are earned and expenses when they are incurred. Under Armour, for example, reported a hefty amount of net income in each quarter of 2008, yet its related cash flows were negative in two of those four quarters. Such differences between net income and cash flows are the reason that GAAP requires every company to report a statement of cash flows.

The statement of cash flows shows each major type of business activity that caused a company's cash to increase or decrease during the accounting period. For purposes of this statement, cash is defined to include cash and cash equivalents. Cash equivalents are short-term, highly liquid investments purchased within three months of maturity. They are considered equivalent to cash because they are both (1) readily convertible to known amounts of cash, and (2) so near to maturity that their value is unlikely to change.

Spotlight On ETHICS

Cash Isn't Estimated

Critics of accrual-based net income claim it can be manipulated because it relies on many estimates (of bad debts, inventory market values, assets' useful lives), but cash flows do not involve estimates so they are not easily manipulated. A cash balance changes only when cash has been received or paid. One particularly dramatic illustration of the subjectivity of net income, but not cash, involved the bankruptcy of a department store chain operated by the W. T. Grant Company. Through biased estimates, the company reported net income for nine consecutive years but then shocked everyone when it declared bankruptcy and shut down the following year. At the time, a statement of cash flows wasn't required. Had it been required, the company would have reported negative operating cash flows in seven of the ten years.

James A. Largay, III, and Clyde P. Stickney, "Cash Flows, Ratio Analysis and the W.T. Grant Company Bankruptcy," *Financial Analysts Journal* 36, no. 4: 51–54, July/August 1980.

CLASSIFYING CASH FLOWS

The statement of cash flows requires that all cash inflows and outflows be classified as relating to the company's operating, investing, or financing activities. This classification of cash flows is useful because most companies experience different cash flow patterns as they develop and mature. Financial statement users are interested in a company's ability to generate operating cash flows that will allow it to continue investing in additional assets and repay the financing it originally obtained. Creditors and investors will tolerate poor operating cash flows for only so long before they stop lending to or investing in the company. For any company to survive in the long run, the amount of cash generated through daily operating activities has to exceed the amount spent on them.

A condensed version of Under Armour's statement of cash flows is presented in Exhibit 12.1. Don't worry about the details in the three cash flow categories yet. For now, focus on the categories' totals. Notice that each category can result in net cash inflows (represented by a positive number) or net cash outflows (represented by a negative number by using brackets). The sum of these three categories ($79 − $38 + $21 = $62) represents the overall change in cash on the balance sheet between the beginning and end of the period ($62 + $40 = $102).

Under Armour's 2008 cash flows in Exhibit 12.1 suggest the company is financially healthy. The company generated $79 million cash from its day-to-day operations. This money allowed Under Armour to invest $38 million in additional long-term assets and, combined with $21 million of net cash inflow from financing activities, build its cash balance at the end of the year. To learn the specific causes of these cash flows, you would consider the details of each category, as we will do now.

EXHIBIT 12.1   Under Armour's Condensed Statement of Cash Flows

UNDER ARMOUR, INC. Statement of Cash Flows For the Year Ended December 31, 2008		Explanations
(in millions)		
Cash Flows from Operating Activities		Cash flows related to day-to-day activities
Net income	$ 38	Positive net income (NI) generates cash inflow
Depreciation	16	Depreciation decreased NI but didn't decrease cash
Changes in operating assets and liabilities	25	Differences in the timing of net income and cash flows
Net cash provided by operating activities	79	Indicates overall cash impact of operating activities
Cash Flows Used in Investing Activities		Cash flows related to long-term assets
Purchase of equipment	(36)	Cash was used to purchase equipment
Purchase of intangible and other assets	(2)	Cash was used to purchase intangibles
Net cash used in investing activities	(38)	Indicates overall cash impact of investing activities
Cash Flows from Financing Activities		Cash flows from transactions with lenders, investors
Additional borrowings of long-term debt	16	Cash received from borrowing
Payments on long-term debt	(7)	Cash used to repay amounts previously borrowed
Proceeds from stock issuance	12	Cash received from issuing stock
Net cash provided by financing activities	21	Indicates overall cash impact of financing activities
Net Change in Cash and Cash Equivalents	62	$79 + $(38) + $21 = $62.
Cash and cash equivalents, beginning of year	40	Cash balance at beginning of the period
Cash and cash equivalents, end of year	$102	Cash balance at end of the period (on balance sheet)

 **COACH'S TIP**

Cash flows from operating activities (cash flows from operations) are cash inflows and outflows related to components of net income.

Operating Activities

Cash flows from operating activities (or **cash flows from operations**) are the cash inflows and outflows related directly to the revenues and expenses reported on the income statement. Operating activities involve day-to-day business activities with customers, suppliers, employees, landlords, and others. Typical cash flows from operating activities include:

Inflows	Outflows
Cash provided by	*Cash used for*
Collecting from customers	Purchasing services (electricity, etc.) and goods for resale
Receiving dividends	Paying salaries and wages
Receiving interest	Paying income taxes
	Paying interest

The difference between these cash inflows and outflows is reported on the statement of cash flows as a subtotal, Net Cash Provided by (Used for) Operating Activities.

Investing Activities

 **COACH'S TIP**

Cash flows from investing activities are cash inflows and outflows related to the sale or purchase of investments and long-lived assets.

Cash flows from investing activities are the cash inflows and outflows related to the purchase and disposal of investments and long-lived assets. Typical cash flows from investing activities include:

Inflows	Outflows
Cash provided by	*Cash used for*
Sale or disposal of property, plant, and equipment	Purchase of property, plant, and equipment
Sale or maturity of investments in securities	Purchase of investments in securities

The difference between these cash inflows and outflows is reported on the statement of cash flows as a subtotal, Net Cash Provided by (Used in) Investing Activities.

Financing Activities

Cash flows from financing activities include exchanges of cash with stockholders and cash exchanges with lenders (for principal on loans). Common cash flows from financing activities include:

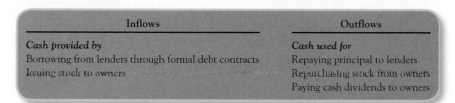

Inflows	Outflows
Cash provided by	*Cash used for*
Borrowing from lenders through formal debt contracts	Repaying principal to lenders
Issuing stock to owners	Repurchasing stock from owners
	Paying cash dividends to owners

The difference between these cash inflows and outflows is reported on the statement of cash flows as a subtotal, Net Cash Provided by (Used in) Financing Activities.

One way to classify cash flows into operating, investing, and financing categories is to think about the balance sheet accounts to which the cash flows relate. **Although exceptions exist, a general rule is that operating cash flows cause changes in current assets and current liabilities, investing cash flows affect noncurrent assets, and financing cash flows affect noncurrent liabilities or stockholders' equity accounts.**[1] Exhibit 12.2 shows how this general rule relates the three sections of the statement of cash flows (SCF) to each of the main sections of a classified balance sheet.

EXHIBIT 12.2 Relationships between Classified Balance Sheet and Statement of Cash Flows (SCF) Categories

SCF Categories	Classified Balance Sheet Categories	
Operating	Current assets	Current liabilities
Investing	Noncurrent assets	Noncurrent liabilities
Financing		Stockholders' equity

Self-Study Practice

Brunswick Corporation produces the Life Fitness line of gym equipment. A listing of some of its cash flows follows. Indicate whether each item is disclosed in the operating activities (O), investing activities (I), or financing activities (F) section of the statement of cash flows.

☐ *a.* Stock issued to stockholders.   ☐ *d.* Purchase of plant and equipment.

☐ *b.* Collections from customers.   ☐ *e.* Purchase of investment securities.

☐ *c.* Interest paid on debt.   ☐ *f.* Cash dividends paid.

After you have finished, check your answers with the solutions in the margin.

---

[1]Intermediate accounting courses discuss in detail exceptions to this general rule. Exceptions include investing activities that affect current assets (for example, short-term investments) and financing activities that affect current liabilities (for example, dividends payable and short-term notes payable).

RELATIONSHIP TO OTHER FINANCIAL STATEMENTS

The statement of cash flows is intended to provide a cash-based view of a company's business activities during the accounting period. It uses the same transactions that are reported in the income statement and balance sheet but converts them from the accrual basis to a cash basis. This conversion involves analyzing the income statement and the changes in balance sheet accounts, and relating these changes to the three cash flow categories. To prepare a statement of cash flows, you need the following:

1. **Comparative balance sheets**, showing beginning and ending balances, used in calculating the cash flows from all activities (operating, investing, and financing).
2. **A complete income statement**, used primarily in calculating cash flows from operating activities.
3. **Additional data** concerning selected accounts that increase and decrease as a result of investing and/or financing activities.

The approach to preparing the cash flow statement focuses on changes in the balance sheet accounts. It relies on a simple rearrangement of the balance sheet equation:

$$\text{Assets} = \text{Liabilities} + \text{Stockholders' Equity}$$

First, assets can be split into cash and all other assets, which we'll call **noncash assets:**

$$\text{Cash} + \text{Noncash Assets} = \text{Liabilities} + \text{Stockholders' Equity}$$

If we move the noncash assets to the right side of the equation, we get

$$\text{Cash} = \text{Liabilities} + \text{Stockholders' Equity} - \text{Noncash Assets}$$

Given this relationship, the **changes** in cash between the beginning and end of the period must equal the **changes** in the amounts on the right side of the equation between the beginning and end of the period:

$$\text{Change in Cash} = \text{Change in (Liabilities} + \text{Stockholders' Equity} - \text{Noncash Assets)}$$

This equation says that **changes in cash must be accompanied by and can be accounted for by the changes in liabilities, stockholders' equity, and noncash assets.**

Preparing the Statement of Cash Flows

Based on the idea that the change in cash equals the sum of the changes in all other balance sheet accounts, we use the following steps to prepare the statement of cash flows:

1. **Determine the change in each balance sheet account.** From this year's ending balance, subtract this year's beginning balance (i.e., last year's ending balance).

2. **Identify the cash flow category or categories to which each account relates.** Use Exhibit 12.2 as a guide, but be aware that some accounts may include two categories of cash flows. Retained Earnings, for example, can include both financing cash flows (paying dividends) and operating cash flows (generating net income). Similarly, Accumulated Depreciation can be affected by operating activities (depreciation for using equipment in daily operations) as well as investing activities (disposing of equipment).

3. **Create schedules that summarize operating, investing, and financing cash flows.**

We will follow these three steps to prepare a statement of cash flows for Under Armour for the year ended December 31, 2008. Step 1 requires that we subtract each account's beginning balance from its ending balance, as we have done in the right side of Exhibit 12.3. Next, for step 2, we indicated whether each account's cash flows relate to operating (O), investing (I), and/or financing (F) activities. Notice that Cash is not classified as O, I, or F, because Cash is not reported in these three sections but instead appears at the bottom of the statement of cash flows, as shown earlier in Exhibit 12.1. Step 3 in preparing a statement of cash flows is explained in the following sections.

DIRECT AND INDIRECT REPORTING OF OPERATING CASH FLOWS

Two alternative methods may be used when presenting the operating activities section of the statement of cash flows:

1. The **direct method** reports the total cash inflow or outflow from each main type of transaction (that is, transactions with customers, suppliers, employees, etc.). The difference between these cash inflows and outflows equals the Net Cash Provided by (Used in) Operating Activities.

2. The **indirect method** starts with net income from the income statement and adjusts it by eliminating the effects of items that do not involve cash (for example, depreciation) and including items that do have cash effects. Adjusting net income for these items yields the amount of Net Cash Provided by (Used in) Operating Activities.

> **COACH'S TIP**
>
> The **direct method** reports the components of cash flows from operating activities as gross receipts and gross payments. The **indirect method** of presenting the operating activities section of the cash flow statement adjusts net income to compute cash flows from operating activities.

Direct Method		Indirect Method	
Cash collected from customers	$ 738	Net Income	$38
Cash paid to suppliers of inventory	(369)	Depreciation	16
Cash paid to employees and suppliers of services	(251)		
Cash paid for interest	(7)	Changes in current assets and liabilities	25
Cash paid for income tax	(32)		
Net cash provided by (used in) operating activities	$ 79	Net cash provided by (used in) operating activities	$79

The point to remember about the direct and indirect methods is that they are simply different ways to arrive at the same number. **Net cash flows provided by (used in) operating activities is always the same under the direct and indirect methods.** Also, the choice between the two methods affects only the operating activities section of the statement of cash flows, not the investing and financing sections.

Spotlight On THE WORLD

Direct vs. Indirect Method Presentation

GAAP and IFRS currently allow companies to use either the direct or indirect method. The FASB and IASB have recently proposed removing this choice and allowing only the direct method. If adopted, this proposal would significantly change the way companies report their statement of cash flows. Currently, about 99 percent of large U.S. companies, including Under Armour, use the indirect method.

We focus on the indirect method in the following section because it is currently the most commonly used method in the United States. The direct method, which may be required by GAAP and IFRS in the future, is presented in the last section of this chapter.

EXHIBIT 12.3   Information for Preparing a Statement of Cash Flows

UNDER ARMOUR, INC.
Balance Sheet*

(in millions)	December 31, 2008*	December 31, 2007*	Step ① Change	Step ② Related Cash Flow Section
Assets				
Current Assets:				
Cash and Cash Equivalents	$102	$ 40	+62	Cash
Accounts Receivable	81	94	−13	O
Inventories	182	166	+16	O
Prepaid Expenses	31	22	+9	O
Total Current Assets	396	322		
Equipment	120	84	+36	I
Less: Accumulated Depreciation	(47)	(31)	−16	O (I = 0; see note 2 below)
Intangible and Other Assets	18	16	+2	I
Total Assets	$487	$391		
Liabilities and Stockholders' Equity				
Current Liabilities:				
Accounts Payable	$ 72	$ 55	+17	O
Accrued Liabilities	61	41	+20	O
Total Current Liabilities	133	96		
Long-Term Debt	23	14	+9	F
Total Liabilities	156	110		
Stockholders' Equity:				
Contributed Capital	175	163	+12	F
Retained Earnings	156	118	+38	O (F = 0; see note 1 below)
Total Stockholders' Equity	331	281		
Total Liabilities and Stockholders' Equity	$487	$391		

UNDER ARMOUR, INC.
Income Statement*
For the Year Ended December 31, 2008

(in millions)	
Net Sales	$725
Cost of Goods Sold	370
Gross Profit	355
Operating Expenses:	
Selling, General, and Administrative Expenses	262
Depreciation Expense	16
Total Operating Expenses	278
Income from Operations	77
Interest Expense	7
Net Income before Income Tax Expense	70
Income Tax Expense	32
Net Income	$ 38

Additional data

1. No dividends were declared or paid.
2. No disposals or impairments of equipment or intangibles occurred.
3. Equipment costing $36 million and intangibles costing $2 million were purchased with cash.
4. Long-term debt of $7 million was paid and $16 million in new loans was issued.
5. Shares of stock were issued for $12 million.

*Certain balances have been adjusted to simplify the presentation.

DETERMINING OPERATING CASH FLOWS (INDIRECT METHOD)

When using the indirect method, the schedule of operating activities has the following format.

> Net income
> Items included in net income that do not involve cash
>   + Depreciation
> Changes in current assets and current liabilities
>   + Decreases in current assets
>   − Increases in current assets
>   − Decreases in current liabilities
>   + Increases in current liabilities
> _____
> Net cash flow provided by (used in) operating activities

Net income. The schedule starts with net income, as reported on the last line of the company's income statement. By starting with net income, it's as if we are assuming all revenues resulted in cash inflows and all expenses resulted in cash outflows. Because we know this is not true, however, we must adjust net income to eliminate items that are included in net income but do not involve cash and to include items that were excluded from net income but do involve cash.

+Depreciation. Recall from Chapter 8 that depreciation is a noncash expense. In other words, it is an expense that was subtracted on the income statement, but which does not affect cash. By adding depreciation back, we **eliminate** the effect of having deducted it in the income statement.

+ Decreases in current assets. Adding decreases in current assets serves two purposes. First, it **eliminates** the effects of some transactions that decreased net income but did not affect cash in the current period. For example, when Supplies are used, net income decreases but cash is not affected. To eliminate these noncash effects from our cash flow computations, we must add back decreases in Supplies and other current assets. Second, adding decreases in current assets allows us to **include** the cash effects of other transactions that did not affect net income in the current period but did increase cash. For example, Cash increases when Accounts Receivable are collected. These cash inflows are captured by adding the amount by which this current asset had decreased.

− Increases in current assets. Subtracting increases in current assets similarly serves two purposes. First, it **eliminates** the effects of transactions that increased net income but did not affect cash in the current period. For example, net income increases when a company provides services on account, but cash is not affected. To eliminate these noncash effects, we subtract increases in current assets. Second, subtracting increases in current assets allows us to **include** the cash effects of other transactions that did not affect net income in the current period but did decrease cash. For example, Cash decreases when a company prepays its insurance or rent, but net income isn't affected until these assets are used up. These cash outflows can be captured by subtracting the increase in these current assets.

− Decreases in current liabilities. Subtracting decreases in current liabilities serves two purposes. First, it **eliminates** the effects of transactions that increased net income but did not affect cash. For example, a company decreases Unearned Revenue and increases net income in the current period when it fulfills its prior obligations to provide services, but cash is not affected. To eliminate these noncash effects, we subtract decreases in current liabilities. Second, subtracting decreases in current liabilities allows us to **include** the cash effects of other transactions that did not affect net income in the current period but did decrease cash. For example, Cash decreases when a company pays wages that were incurred and expensed in a previous period. These cash outflows are captured by subtracting decreases in current liabilities.

+ Increases in current liabilities. Adding increases in current liabilities serves two purposes. First, it **eliminates** the effects of transactions that decreased net income but did not affect cash. For example, when interest is accrued, a company decreases net income but its cash is not affected. To eliminate these noncash effects, we must add back increases in current liabilities. Second, adding increases in current liabilities allows us to **include** the cash effects of other transactions that did not affect net income in the current period but did increase cash. For example, Cash and Unearned Revenue increase when the company receives cash in advance of providing services. Adding the increase in current liabilities captures these cash inflows.

Under Armour's Operating Cash Flow—Indirect Method

The preceding approach to preparing an operating cash flow schedule can be applied to Under Armour's information in Exhibit 12.3. By taking the amount of the change in each account marked by an O in Exhibit 12.3, we have prepared an operating cash flow schedule for Under Armour in Exhibit 12.4. Understanding the causes of increases or decreases in each current asset and current liability is the key to understanding the logic behind the items in the schedule. Take your time reading the following explanations and make sure you understand the reasons for each item.

Net Income + Depreciation Net income and depreciation are always the first two lines to appear in a statement of cash flows prepared using the indirect method. They begin the process of converting net income to operating cash flows. They also begin the process of explaining the change in Cash by accounting for changes in the other balance sheet accounts. In the case of Under Armour, the $38 million of net income fully accounts for the change in Retained Earnings (the company had no dividends). Similarly, the $16 million of depreciation accounts for the change in Accumulated Depreciation (the company had no disposals).[2]

Decrease in Accounts Receivable Accounts Receivable increases when sales are made on account and it decreases when cash is collected from customers. An overall decrease in this account, then, implies that cash collections were greater than sales on account. To convert from the lower sales number that is included in net income to the higher cash collected from customers, we add the difference ($13 million).

COACH'S TIP

The depreciation addback is not intended to suggest that depreciation creates an increase in cash. Rather, it's just showing that depreciation does not cause a decrease in cash. This is a subtle, but very important, difference in interpretation.

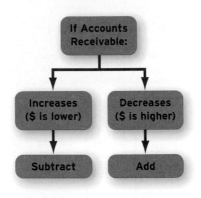

[2]Amortization and impairment losses are handled in exactly the same way as depreciation. Gains and losses on fixed asset disposals also are dealt with in a similar manner and are discussed in chapter Supplement 12A.

EXHIBIT 12.4	Under Armour's Schedule of Operating Cash Flows

Items	Amount (in millions)	Explanations
Net income	$38	Starting point, from the income statement
Items included in net income that do not involve cash		
+ Depreciation	16	Depreciation is a noncash expense
Changes in current assets and current liabilities		
+ Decrease in Accounts Receivable	13	Cash collections greater than sales on account
− Increase in Inventories	(16)	Purchases greater than cost of goods sold
− Increase in Prepaid Expenses	(9)	Prepayments greater than related expenses
+ Increase in Accounts Payable	17	Purchases greater than payments to suppliers
+ Increase in Accrued Liabilities	20	Cash payments less than accrued expenses
Net cash flow provided by (used in) operating activities	$79	Overall increase in cash from operations

Another way to remember whether to add or subtract the difference is to think about whether the overall change in the account balance is explained by a debit or credit. If the change in the account is explained by a debit, the adjustment in the cash flow schedule is reported like a corresponding credit to cash (subtracted). In Under Armour's case, the decrease in Accounts Receivable is explained by a credit, so the adjustment in the cash flow schedule is reported like a debit to cash (an increase), as follows.

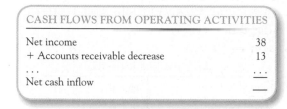

CASH FLOWS FROM OPERATING ACTIVITIES	
Net income	38
+ Accounts receivable decrease	13
. . .	. . .
Net cash inflow	·:·

Accounts Receivable (A)			
Beg. bal.	94		
		13	Decrease
End. bal.	81		

Increase in Inventory   The income statement reports the cost of merchandise sold during the period, but cash flow from operating activities must report cash purchases of inventory. As shown in the T-account on the left, purchases of goods increase the balance in inventory, and recording merchandise sold decreases the balance in inventory.

Inventories (A)	
Beg. bal.	
Purchases	Cost of goods sold
End. bal.	

Inventories (A)		
Beg. bal.	166	
Increase	16	
End. bal.	182	

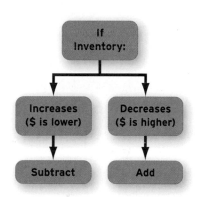

Under Armour's $16 million inventory increase means that the amount of purchases is more than the cost of goods sold. The increase (the extra purchases) must be subtracted from net income to convert to cash flow from operating activities in Exhibit 12.4. (A decrease would be added.)

Increase in Prepaid Expenses   The income statement reports expenses of the period, but cash flow from operating activities must reflect the cash payments. Cash prepayments increase the balance in prepaid expenses, and recording of expenses decreases the balance in prepaid expenses.

Prepaid Expenses (A)	
Beg. bal.	
Cash prepayments	Used-up / expensed
End. bal.	

Prepaid Expenses (A)		
Beg. bal.	22	
Increase	9	
End. bal.	31	

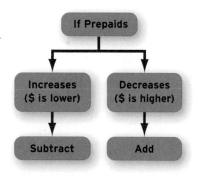

Under Armour's $9 million increase in Prepaid Expenses means that this period's cash prepayments were more than expenses. These extra cash prepayments must be subtracted in Exhibit 12.4. (A decrease would be added.)

Increase in Accounts Payable   Cash flow from operations must reflect cash purchases, but not all purchases are for cash. Purchases on account increase Accounts Payable and cash paid to suppliers decreases Accounts Payable.

Accounts Payable (L)	
	Beg. bal.
Cash payments	Purchases on account
	End. bal.

Accounts Payable (L)		
	Beg. bal.	55
	Increase	17
	End. bal.	72

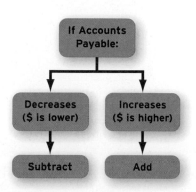

Accounts Payable increased by $17 million, which means that cash payments to suppliers were less than purchases on account. This increase in Accounts Payable (cash payments are less than purchases) must be added in Exhibit 12.4. (A decrease would be subtracted.)

Increase in Accrued Liabilities   The income statement reports all accrued expenses, but the cash flow statement must reflect only the actual payments for expenses. Recording accrued expenses increases the balance in Accrued Liabilities and cash payments for the expenses decreases Accrued Liabilities.

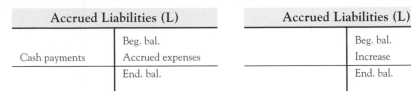

Accrued Liabilities (L)			Accrued Liabilities (L)	
	Beg. bal.		Beg. bal.	41
Cash payments	Accrued expenses		Increase	20
	End. bal.		End. bal.	61

Under Armour's Accrued Liabilities increased by $20 million, which indicates that more expenses were accrued than paid. Consequently, this difference (representing less cash paid) must be added back in Exhibit 12.4. (A decrease would be subtracted.)

By scanning Exhibit 12.3 on page 448, you can see that you have now considered the changes in all balance sheet accounts that relate to operating activities (marked by the letter O). The last step in determining the net case flows from operating activities is to calculate a total. As shown in Exhibit 12.4, the combined effect of all operating cash flows is a net cash inflow of $79 million.

Now that you have seen how to compute operating cash flows using the indirect method, take a moment to complete the following Self-Study Practice.

If Accrued Liabilities:

Decreases ($ is lower) → Subtract

Increases ($ is higher) → Add

🔆 Self-Study Practice

Indicate whether the following items taken from Brunswick Corporation's cash flow statement would be added (+), subtracted (−), or not included (0) in the reconciliation of net income to cash flow from operations.

- [ ] *a.* Decrease in inventories.
- [ ] *b.* Increase in accounts payable.
- [ ] *c.* Depreciation expense.
- [ ] *d.* Increase in accounts receivable.
- [ ] *e.* Increase in accrued liabilities.
- [ ] *f.* Increase in prepaid expenses.

After you have finished, check your answers with the solutions in the margin.

Solution to Self-Study Practice
a. +, *b.* +, *c.* +, *d.* −, *e.* +, *f.* −

CASH FLOWS FROM INVESTING AND FINANCING ACTIVITIES

In addition to cash flow from operations, the statement of cash flows provides information about cash flows from investing and financing activities.

Under Armour's Investing Cash Flow Calculations

Learning Objective 3
Report cash flows from investing activities.

To prepare the investing section of the statement of cash flows, you must analyze accounts related to long-lived tangible and intangible assets.[3] Unlike the analysis of operating activities, where you were concerned only with the *net* change in selected balance sheet

---

[3]Investing activities also include investments in other companies. Although not shown here, the cash flows for investments are similar to those shown in this section for equipment and intangible assets.

accounts, an analysis of investing (and financing) activities requires that you identify and separately report the causes of *both* increases and decreases in account balances. The following relationships are the ones that you will encounter most frequently:

Related Balance Sheet Accounts	Investing Activity	Cash Flow Effect
Property, Plant, and Equipment	Purchase of property, plant, and equipment for cash	Outflow
	Sale of property, plant, and equipment for cash	Inflow
Intangible Assets	Purchase of intangible assets	Outflow
	Sale of intangible assets	Inflow

Under Armour's balance sheet (Exhibit 12.3) shows two investing assets (noted with an I) that changed during the year: Equipment and Intangible Assets.

Equipment   To determine the cause of the change in the Equipment account, accountants would examine the detailed accounting records for equipment. Purchases of equipment increase the account, and disposals of equipment decrease it. The additional data in Exhibit 12.3 indicates that Under Armour purchased equipment for $36 million cash. This purchase is a cash outflow, which we subtract in the schedule of investing activities in Exhibit 12.5. In our example, this purchase fully accounts for the change in the Equipment balance, as shown in the Equipment T-account. Thus, we can assume that Under Armour did not dispose of any equipment during the year. Chapter Supplement 12A explains how disposals of property, plant, and equipment affect the statement of cash flows.

Equipment (A)			
Beg. bal.	84		
Purchases	36	Disposals	0
End. bal.	120		

EXHIBIT 12.5	Under Armour's Schedule of Investing Cash Flows

Items	Amount (in millions)	Explanations
Purchase of equipment	$(36)	Payment of cash for equipment
Purchase of intangible and other assets	(2)	Payment of cash for intangibles
Net cash provided by (used in) investing activities	(38)	Subtotal for the statement of cash flows

Intangible and Other Assets   A similar approach is used to determine cash flows associated with intangible assets. Analysis of Under Armour's detailed records indicates that the company did not have any reductions in its intangible assets as a result of disposals, impairments, or amortization during the year. However, Under Armour did purchase intangible assets for $2 million cash, as noted in the additional data in Exhibit 12.3. This cash outflow is subtracted in the schedule of investing activities in Exhibit 12.5.

Under Armour's Financing Cash Flow Calculations

This section of the cash flow statement includes changes in liabilities owed to owners (Dividends Payable) and financial institutions (Notes Payable and other types of debt), as well as changes in stockholders' equity accounts. Interest is considered an operating

Learning Objective 4
Report cash flows from financing activities.

activity so it is excluded from financing cash flows. The following relationships are the ones that you will encounter most often:

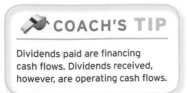

Related Balance Sheet Accounts	Financing Activity	Cash Flow Effect
Notes Payable	Borrowing cash from bank or other financial institutions	Inflow
	Repayment of loan principal	Outflow
Bonds Payable	Issuance of bonds for cash	Inflow
	Repayment of bond face value	Outflow
Contributed Capital	Issuance of stock for cash	Inflow
	Repurchase of stock with cash	Outflow
Retained Earnings	Payment of cash dividends	Outflow

To compute cash flows from financing activities, you should review changes in all debt and stockholders' equity accounts. Increases and decreases must be identified and reported separately. Under Armour's balance sheet in Exhibit 12.3 indicates that Long-Term Debt and Contributed Capital changed during the period as a result of financing cash flows (noted with an F).

Long-Term Debt   The additional data in Exhibit 12.3 indicates that Long-Term Debt was affected by both cash inflows and outflows, as shown in the T-account below. These cash flows are reported separately in the schedule of financing activities shown in Exhibit 12.6.

Long-Term Debt (L)			
		Beg. bal.	14
Repayments	7	Borrowings	16
		End. bal.	23

EXHIBIT 12.6   Under Armour's Schedule of Financing Cash Flows

Items	Amount (in millions)	Explanations
Additional borrowings of long-term debt	$16	Cash received when new loan obtained
Repayments on long-term debt	(7)	Cash paid on loan principal
Proceeds from stock issuance	12	Cash received from stockholders for new stock
Net cash provided by financing activities	21	Subtotal for the statement of cash flows

Contributed Capital   Under Armour did not repurchase stock during the year, but it did issue stock for $12 million cash. This stock issuance fully accounts for the change in Contributed Capital, as shown in the following T-account. This cash inflow is listed in the schedule of financing activities in Exhibit 12.6.

Contributed Capital (SE)		
	Beg. bal.	163
	Stock issued	12
	End. bal.	175

Retained Earnings   Net income increases Retained Earnings and dividends decrease Retained Earnings. Net income has already been accounted for as an operating cash flow. In Under Armour's case, no dividends were declared or paid in 2008 (see the additional data in Exhibit 12.3). As shown in the following T-account, dividends would have decreased Retained Earnings, had they been declared; their payment would have been reported as a cash outflow in the financing section of the statement of cash flows.

Retained Earnings (SE)			
		Beg. bal.	118
Dividends	0	Net income	38
		End. bal.	156

Under Armour's Statement of Cash Flows

Now that you have determined the cash flows for the three main types of business activities in Exhibits 12.4, 12.5, and 12.6, you can prepare the statement of cash flows in a proper format. Exhibit 12.7 shows the statement of cash flows for Under Armour using the indirect method. Notice that the net increase (decrease) subtotal combines cash flows from operating, investing, and financing activities to produce an overall net change in cash. This net change is added to the beginning cash balance to arrive at the ending cash balance, which is the same cash balance as reported on the balance sheet.

EXHIBIT 12.7	**Under Armour's Statement of Cash Flows (Indirect Method)**

UNDER ARMOUR, INC.
Statement of Cash Flows*
For the Year Ended December 31, 2008

(in millions)

Cash Flows from Operating Activities	
Net income	$ 38
Adjustments to reconcile net income to net cash provided by operating activities:	
Depreciation	16
Changes in current assets and current liabilities	
Accounts Receivable	13
Inventories	(16)
Prepaid Expenses	(9)
Accounts Payable	17
Accrued Liabilities	20
Net cash provided by (used in) operating activities	79
Cash Flows from Investing Activities	
Purchase of equipment	(36)
Purchase of intangible and other assets	(2)
Net cash provided by (used in) investing activities	(38)
Cash Flows from Financing Activities	
Additional borrowings of long-term debt	16
Payments on long-term debt	(7)
Proceeds from stock issuance	12
Net cash provided by (used in) financing activities	21
Net increase (decrease) in cash and cash equivalents	62
Cash and cash equivalents at beginning of period	40
Cash and cash equivalents at end of period	$102
Supplemental Disclosures	
Cash paid for interest	$ 7
Cash paid for income tax	32

COACH'S TIP

If you have difficulty remembering the order in which to report operating (O), investing (I), and financing (F) cash flows, say to yourself, "O, IF only I could remember!"

*Certain amounts have been adjusted to simplify the presentation.

COACH'S TIP

When doing homework problems, assume that all changes in noncurrent account balances are caused by cash transactions (unless the problem also describes changes caused by noncash investing and financing activities).

Supplemental Disclosures   In addition to their cash flows, all companies are required to report material investing and financing transactions that did not have cash flow effects (called **noncash investing and financing activities**). For example, the purchase of a $10,000 piece of equipment with a $10,000 note payable to the supplier does not cause either an inflow or an outflow of cash. As a result, these activities are not listed in the three main sections of the statement of cash flows. This important information is normally presented for users in a supplementary schedule to the statement of cash flows or in the financial statement notes. Supplementary information must also disclose (for companies using the indirect method) the amount of cash paid for interest and for income taxes. An example of this disclosure is shown at the bottom of Exhibit 12.7.

Interpreting the Statement of Cash Flows

Learning Objective 5
Interpret cash flows from operating, investing, and financing activities.

Unlike the income statement, which summarizes its detailed information in one number (net income), the statement of cash flows does not provide a summary measure of cash flow performance. Instead, it must be evaluated in terms of the cash flow pattern suggested by the subtotals of each of the three main sections. As we discussed at the beginning of this chapter, expect different patterns of cash flows from operating, investing, and financing activities depending on how well established a company is. An established, healthy company will show positive cash flows from operations, which are sufficiently large to pay for replacing current property, plant, and equipment and to pay dividends to stockholders. Any additional cash (called **free cash flow**) can (a) be used to expand the business through additional investing activities, (b) be used for other financing activities, or (c) simply build up the company's cash balance. After considering where the company stands in relation to this big picture, you should then look at the details within each of the three sections.

EVALUATING CASH FLOWS

The operating activities section indicates how well a company is able to generate cash internally through its operations and management of current assets and current liabilities. Most analysts believe this is the most important section of the statement because, in the long run, operations are the only continuing source of cash. Investors will not invest in a company if they do not believe that cash generated from operations will be available to pay dividends or expand the company. Similarly, creditors will not lend money or extend credit if they believe that cash generated from operations will be insufficient to repay them.

When evaluating the operating activities section of the statement of cash flows, consider the absolute amount of cash flow (is it positive or negative?), keeping in mind that operating cash flows have to be positive over the long run for a company to be successful. Also, look at the relationship between operating cash flows and net income, using a ratio called the Quality of Income Ratio.

Accounting Decision Tools		
Name of Measure	**Formula**	**What It Tells You**
Quality of income ratio	Net Cash Flow from Operating Activities / Net Income	• Whether operating cash flows and net income are in sync • A ratio near 1.0 means operating cash flows and net income are in sync

The quality of income ratio measures the portion of income that was generated in cash. All other things equal, a quality of income ratio near 1.0 indicates a high likelihood that revenues are realized in cash and that expenses are associated with cash outflows.

This ratio is most useful when compared to industry competitors or to prior periods. Any major deviations (say below 0.5 or above 1.5) should be investigated. In some cases, a deviation may be nothing to worry about, but in others, it could be the first sign of big problems to come. Four potential causes of deviations to consider include:

1. **Seasonality**. As in Under Armour's case, seasonal variations in sales and inventory levels can cause the ratio to fluctuate from one quarter to the next. Usually, this isn't a cause for alarm.

2. **The corporate life cycle (growth in sales)**. New companies often experience rapid sales growth. When sales are increasing, accounts receivable and inventory normally increase faster than the cash flows being collected from sales. This often reduces operating cash flows below net income, which, in turn, reduces the ratio. This isn't a major problem, provided that the company can obtain cash from financing activities until operating activities begin to generate more positive cash flows.

3. **Changes in revenue and expense recognition**. Most cases of fraudulent financial reporting involve aggressive revenue recognition (recording revenues before they are earned) or delayed expense recognition (failing to report expenses when they are incurred). Both of these tactics cause net income to increase in the current period, making it seem as though the company has improved its performance. Neither of these tactics, though, affects cash flows from operating activities. As a result, if revenue and expense recognition policies are changed to boost net income, the quality of income ratio will drop, providing one of the first clues that the financial statements might contain errors or fraud.

4. **Changes in working capital management**. Working capital is a measure of the amount by which current assets exceed current liabilities. If a company's current assets (such as accounts receivable and inventories) are allowed to grow out of control, its operating cash flows and quality of income ratio will decrease. More efficient management will have the opposite effect. To investigate this potential cause more closely, use the inventory and accounts receivable turnover ratios described in the next chapter.

Spotlight On BUSINESS DECISIONS

Quality of Income Deteriorates Prior to Bankruptcy

Lehman Brothers Holdings, Inc., was one of the largest and most profitable financial services companies in the world. But cash flow and working capital management problems led to the company's bankruptcy only a month before the stock market crash of 2008. The following comparison of Lehman's net income and net operating cash flows reveals the company's problems:

(in billions)	2006	2007	2008
Net income	$ 3.3	$ 4.0	$ 4.2
Net cash provided by (used in) operating activities	(12.2)	(36.4)	(45.6)

Another key issue that analysts assess using the statement of cash flows is the company's ability to generate enough cash internally to purchase new long-term assets. The capital acquisitions ratio is commonly used to determine the extent to which purchases of Property, Plant, and Equipment (PPE) were financed from operating activities (without the need for outside debt or equity financing or the sale of investments or other long-term assets). A ratio greater than 1.0 indicates that, all else equal, outside financing was not needed to replace equipment in the current period. Assuming this continues in the future, the higher a company's capital acquisitions ratio, the less likely that external financing will be needed to fund future expansion.

Accounting Decision Tools		
Name of Measure	**Formula**	**What It Tells You**
Capital acquisitions ratio	$\dfrac{\text{Net Cash from Operations}}{\text{Cash Paid for PPE}}$	• Whether operating cash flows are sufficient to pay for PPE purchases • A higher ratio means less need for external financing

The cash paid for property, plant, and equipment (used in the bottom part of the ratio) is reported in the investing activities section of the statement of cash flows. These expenditures can vary greatly from year to year, so the ratio typically is calculated as an average over a longer period, for instance, three years. When calculating the ratio, enter these expenditures as positive amounts (without brackets).

In Exhibit 12.8, we present the three-year average capital acquisitions ratio for Under Armour. The ratio shows that, over the past three years, Under Armour has financed about 79% of its purchases of property, plant, and equipment with cash generated from operating activities.

Because equipment needs differ dramatically across industries (for example, consider Under Armour versus Google), a particular company's ratio should be compared only with its prior years' figures or with other companies in the same industry. Also, while a high ratio can indicate strong cash flows, it also might suggest a failure to update plant and equipment, which can limit a company's ability to compete in the future. The main point is that you have to interpret the ratio in relation to the company's other activities and business strategy.

EXHIBIT 12.8 | **Capital Acquisition Ratio Computation**

Company	(in millions)	Relevant Information				Average 2006–08 Ratio Calculation
		2008	**2007**	**2006**	**Average**	
Under Armour	Net operating cash	$79	$(25)	$11	$22	$\dfrac{\$22}{28} = 0.79$ or 79%
	Cash for PPE	36	34	15	28	

 Self-Study Practice

The relevant cash flows for NIKE, Inc., are shown below. Calculate the capital acquisitions ratio for NIKE and compare it to Under Armour's ratio in Exhibit 12.8.

(in billions)	2008	2007	2006	Average	Ratio
Cash flow from operating activities	$1.9	$1.9	$1.7	$☐	☐
Purchases of property, plant, and equipment	0.4	0.3	0.3	0.3	

After you have finished, check your answers with the solutions in the margin.

Solution to Self-Study Practice

$1.8 ÷ $0.3 = 6.0 or 600%

Nike's operations generated six times more cash than was spent on Property, Plant, and Equipment. This suggests Nike has more free cash flow than Under Armour to use for other purposes, such as paying dividends and repaying loans.

DETERMINING OPERATING CASH FLOWS (DIRECT METHOD)

Earlier in this chapter, we discussed the indirect method of presenting a company's statement of cash flows. This method computes operating cash flows indirectly, by adding and subtracting items from Net Income. Because these items, by themselves, don't mean a lot, analyses of operating cash flows are limited to using just the overall Net Cash Provided by (Used for) Operating Activities. In contrast, the direct method of presentation provides more detailed information on each input into overall operating cash flows, which allows analysts to conduct more detailed analyses.

Exhibit 12.9 presents Under Armour's statement of cash flows using the direct method. Because this method lists each operating cash flow component, it allows more detailed analyses of operating cash flows. For example, the direct method would allow Under Armour's managers to determine that a 10 percent increase in product costs in 2008 would have required an additional cash outflow to inventory suppliers of $36.9 million (= 10% × $369 million). To cover these additional cash outflows, Under Armour could raise prices by 5 percent, which would generate a $36.9 million (= 5% × $738 million) cash inflow from customer collections.

EXHIBIT 12.9	**Under Armour's Statement of Cash Flows (Direct Method)**

UNDER ARMOUR, INC. Statement of Cash Flows For the Year Ended December 31, 2008		Explanations
(in millions)		
Cash Flows from Operating Activities		Cash flows related to day-to-day activities
Cash collected from customers	$738	Cash collected on account and from any cash sales
Cash paid to suppliers of inventory	(369)	Cash paid in the current period to acquire inventory
Cash paid to employees and suppliers of services	(251)	Cash paid for salaries, wages, utilities, rent, etc.
Cash paid for interest	(7)	Separate reporting of these items fulfills the role of
Cash paid for income tax	(32)	the supplemental disclosures in Exhibit 12.7
Net cash provided by (used in) operating activities	79	Indicates overall cash impact of operating activities
Cash Flows from Investing Activities		Cash flows related to long-term assets
Purchase of equipment	(36)	Cash was used to purchase equipment
Purchase of intangible and other assets	(2)	Cash was used to purchase intangibles
Net cash provided by (used in) investing activities	(38)	Indicates overall cash impact of investing activities
Cash Flows from Financing Activities		Cash flows from transactions with lenders, investors
Proceeds from long-term debt	16	Cash received from borrowing
Payments on long-term debt	(7)	Cash used to repay amounts previously borrowed
Proceeds from stock issuances	12	Cash received from issuing stock
Net cash provided by (used in) financing activities	21	Indicates overall cash impact of financing activities
Net Change in Cash and Cash Equivalents	62	$79 + $(38) + $21 = $62
Cash and cash equivalents, beginning of year	40	Cash balance at beginning of the period
Cash and cash equivalents, end of year	$102	Cash balance at end of the period (on balance sheet)

The direct method also provides financial statement users with more information to identify potential relationships between cash inflows and outflows. An increase in some activities, such as sales, generally leads to an increase in cash inflows from customers and cash outflows to inventory suppliers. However, an increase in sales activity only loosely affects other cash outflows, such as interest paid on loans. Knowing the detailed components of operating cash flows allows analysts to more reliably predict a company's future cash flows.[4]

In the remainder of this section, we describe how to prepare the statement of cash flows using the direct method. We focus on preparing just the operating activities section. For instructions on preparing the investing and financing activities sections, which are identical under both the direct and indirect methods, see pages 452–456.

Reporting Operating Cash Flows with the Direct Method

> **Learning Objective 6**
> Report and interpret cash flows from operating activities, using the direct method.

The direct method presents a summary of all operating transactions that result in either a debit or a credit to cash. It is prepared by adjusting each revenue and expense on the income statement from the accrual basis to the cash basis. We will complete this process for all of the revenues and expenses reported in the Under Armour income statement in Exhibit 12.3 to show the calculations underlying the operating cash flows in Exhibit 12.9. Notice that, with the direct method, we work directly with each revenue and expense listed on the income statement and ignore any totals or subtotals (such as net income).

Converting Sales Revenues to Cash Inflows   When sales are recorded, Accounts Receivable increases, and when cash is collected, Accounts Receivable decreases. This means that if Accounts Receivable decreases by $13 million, then cash collections were $13 million more than sales on account. To convert sales revenue to the cash collected, we need to add $13 million to Sales Revenue. The following flowchart shows this visually:

Using information from Under Armour's income statement and balance sheet presented in Exhibit 12.3, we compute cash collected from customers as follows:

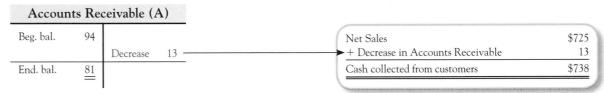

Accounts Receivable (A)			
Beg. bal.	94		
		Decrease	13
End. bal.	81		

Net Sales	$725
+ Decrease in Accounts Receivable	13
Cash collected from customers	$738

Converting Cost of Goods Sold to Cash Paid to Suppliers   Cost of goods sold represents the cost of merchandise sold during the accounting period, which may be more or less than the amount of cash paid to suppliers during the period. In Under Armour's case, Inventory increased during the year, because the company bought more merchandise than it sold. If the company paid cash to suppliers of inventory, it would have paid more cash to suppliers than the amount of Cost of Goods Sold. So, the increase in Inventory must be added to Cost of Goods Sold to compute cash paid to suppliers.

Typically, companies buy inventory on account from suppliers (as indicated by an Accounts Payable balance on the balance sheet). Consequently, we need to consider more than just the change in Inventory to convert Cost of Goods Sold to cash paid to

---

[4]Steven F. Orpurt and Yoonseok Zang, "Do Direct Cash Flow Disclosures Help Predict Future Operating Cash Flows and Earnings?" *The Accounting Review* 84, no. 3, 893–936 (May 2009).

suppliers. The credit purchases and payments that are recorded in Accounts Payable must also be considered. Credit purchases increase Accounts Payable, and cash payments decrease it. The overall increase in Accounts Payable reported by Under Armour in Exhibit 12.3 indicates that cash payments were less than credit purchases, so the difference must be subtracted in the computation of total cash payments to suppliers. In other words, to fully convert Cost of Goods Sold to a cash basis, you must consider changes in both Inventory and Accounts Payable in the following manner:

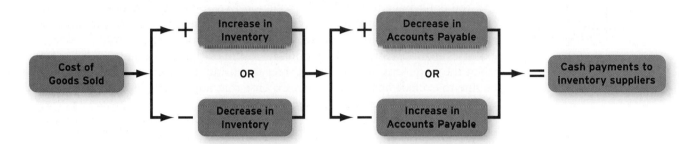

Using information from Exhibit 12.3, we compute cash paid to suppliers as follows:

Cost of Goods Sold	$370
+ Increase in Inventory	16
− Increase in Accounts Payable	(17)
Cash paid to inventory suppliers	$369

Inventories (A)

Beg. bal.	166		
Increase	16		
End. bal.	182		

Accounts Payable (L)

		Beg. bal.	55
		Increase	17
		End. bal.	72

Converting Operating Expenses to a Cash Outflow   The total amount of an expense on the income statement may differ from the cash outflow associated with that activity. Some amounts, like prepaid rent, are paid before they are recognized as expenses. When prepayments are made, the balance in the asset Prepaid Expenses increases. When expenses are recorded, Prepaid Expenses decreases. When we see Under Armour's prepaids increase by $9 million during the year, it means the company paid more cash than it recorded as operating expenses. This amount must be added in computing cash paid to service suppliers for operating expenses.

Some other expenses, like wages, are paid for after they are incurred. In this case, when expenses are recorded, the balance in Accrued Liabilities increases. When payments are made, Accrued Liabilities decreases. When Under Armour's Accrued Liabilities increase by $20 million, it means the company paid that much less cash than it recorded as operating expenses. This amount must be subtracted when computing cash paid to employees and service suppliers for operating expenses.

Generally, operating expenses such as Selling, General, and Administrative Expenses can be converted from the accrual basis to the cash basis in the following manner:

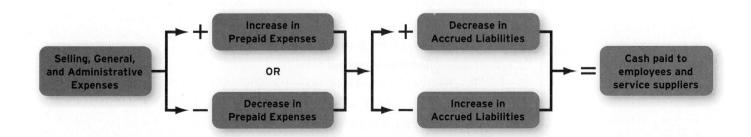

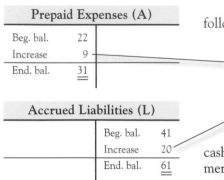

Prepaid Expenses (A)	
Beg. bal.	22
Increase	9
End. bal.	31

Accrued Liabilities (L)	
Beg. bal.	41
Increase	20
End. bal.	61

Using information from Exhibit 12.3, we can compute the total cash paid as follows:

Selling, General, and Administrative Expenses	$262
+ Increase in Prepaid Expenses	9
− Increase in Accrued Liabilities	(20)
Cash paid to employees and suppliers of services	$251

You don't have to convert Depreciation Expense on the income statement to the cash basis for the statement of cash flows because depreciation doesn't involve cash. It is merely reporting previously incurred costs as an expense in the current period. Noncash expenses like depreciation (or, similarly, revenues that don't affect cash) are omitted when the statement of cash flows is prepared using the direct method. Because of this, be sure to exclude any Depreciation Expense that might have been included in Selling, General, and Administrative Expenses.

The next account listed on the income statement in Exhibit 12.3 is Interest Expense of $7 million. Because the balance sheet does not report Interest Payable, we will assume all of the interest was paid in cash. Thus, interest expense equals interest paid.

Interest Expense	$7
No change in Interest Payable	0
Cash paid for interest	$7

The same logic can be applied to income taxes. Under Armour presents Income Tax Expense of $32 million. Exhibit 12.3 does not report an Income Tax Payable balance, so we assume income tax paid is equal to income tax expense.

Income Tax Expense	$32
No change in Income Tax Payable	0
Cash paid for income tax	$32

You have now seen, in this section, how to determine each amount reported in the operating activities section of a statement of cash flows prepared using the direct method. For a quick check on your understanding of this material, complete the following Self-Study Practice.

 Self-Study Practice

Indicate whether the following items taken from a cash flow statement would be added (+), subtracted (−), or not included (0) when calculating cash flow from operations using the direct method.

☐ *a.* Cash paid to suppliers.

☐ *b.* Payment of dividends to stockholders.

☐ *c.* Cash collections from customers.

☐ *d.* Purchase of plant and equipment for cash.

☐ *e.* Payments of interest to lenders.

☐ *f.* Payment of taxes to the government.

After you have finished, check your answers with the solutions in the margin.

Solution to Self-Study Practice

a. −, *b.* 0, *c.* +, *d.* 0, *e.* −, *f.* −

SUPPLEMENT 12A: REPORTING SALES OF PROPERTY, PLANT, AND EQUIPMENT (INDIRECT METHOD)

Whenever a company sells property, plant, and equipment (PPE), it records three things: (1) decreases in the PPE accounts for the assets sold, (2) an increase in the Cash account for the cash received on disposal, and (3) a gain if the cash received is more than the book value of the assets sold (or a loss if the cash received is less than the book value of the assets sold). The only part of this transaction that qualifies for the statement of cash flows is the cash received on disposal. This cash inflow is classified as an investing activity, just like the original equipment purchase.

Okay, that seems straightforward, so why do we have a separate chapter supplement for this kind of transaction? Well, there is one complicating factor. Gains and losses on disposal are included in the computation of net income, which is the starting point for the operating activities section when prepared using the indirect method. So, just as we had to fill in the hole that depreciation created on the income statement, we also have to fill in any holes created by losses reported on disposals of PPE. This means the operating activities section of an indirect method statement of cash flows will add back any losses deducted on the income statement. As the following example shows, the flip side is true for gains on disposal (they are subtracted).

To illustrate, assume that Under Armour sold a piece of its manufacturing equipment for $7 million. The equipment originally cost $15 million and had $10 million of accumulated depreciation at the time of disposal. The disposal would have been analyzed and recorded as follows (in millions):

1 Analyze

	Assets		=	Liabilities	+	Stockholders' Equity	
Cash		+7				Gain on Disposal	+2
Accumulated Depreciation		+10					
Equipment		−15					

2 Record

dr Cash	7	
dr Accumulated Depreciation	10	
cr Equipment		15
cr Gain on Disposal		2

The $7 million inflow of cash would be reported as an investing activity. The $10 million and $15 million are taken into account when considering changes in the Accumulated Depreciation and Equipment account balances. Lastly, the $2 million Gain on Disposal was included in net income, so we must remove (subtract) it in the operating activities section of the statement. Thus, the disposal would affect two parts of the statement of cash flows:

Cash flows provided by (used in) operating activities	
Net income	$38
Adjustments to reconcile net income to net cash from operations:	
. . .	. . .
Gain on disposal of property, plant, and equipment	(2)
. . .	. . .
Net cash provided by (used in) operating activities	. . .
Cash provided by (used in) investing activities	
Additions to property, plant, and equipment	. . .
Cash received from disposal of property, plant, and equipment	15
. . .	. . .
Net cash provided by (used in) investing activities	. . .

SUPPLEMENT 12B: SPREADSHEET APPROACH (INDIRECT METHOD)

As situations become more complex, the analytical approach that we used to prepare the statement of cash flows for Under Armour becomes cumbersome and inefficient. In actual practice, many companies use a spreadsheet approach to prepare the statement of cash flows. The spreadsheet is based on the same logic that we used in the main body of the chapter. The spreadsheet's primary advantage is that it offers a more systematic way to keep track of information. You may find it useful even in simple situations.

Exhibit 12B.1 shows the Under Armour spreadsheet, which we created as follows:

1. Make four columns to record dollar amounts. The first column is for the beginning balances for items reported on the balance sheet, the next two columns reflect debit and credit changes to those balances, and the final column contains the ending balances for the balance sheet accounts.

2. Enter each account name from the balance sheet in the far left of the top half of the spreadsheet.

3. As you analyze changes in each balance sheet account, enter the explanation of each item to be reported on the statement of cash flows in the far left of the bottom half of the spreadsheet.

Changes in the various balance sheet accounts are analyzed in terms of debits and credits in the top half of the spreadsheet with the corresponding debits and credits being recorded in the bottom half of the spreadsheet in terms of their impact on cash flows. The changes in balance sheet accounts other than cash contribute to explaining the change in the Cash account.

Let's go through each of the entries on the spreadsheet for Under Armour shown in Exhibit 12B.1, starting with the first one shown in the bottom half of the spreadsheet (all amounts in millions).

a. Net income of $38 is shown as an inflow in the operating activities section, with the corresponding credit going to Retained Earnings in the top half of the spreadsheet (to show that net income increased Retained Earnings).

b. Depreciation Expense of $16 is added back to net income because this type of expense does not cause a cash outflow when it is recorded. The corresponding credit explains the increase in the Accumulated Depreciation account during the period.

c. The decrease in Accounts Receivable means that cash collections from customers were more than sales on account. Net income includes the sales number, so to adjust up to the actual cash collected, we add the extra amount. This appears in our spreadsheet as if it is a debit to Cash and a corresponding credit to Accounts Receivable.

d. This entry reconciles the purchases of Inventory with Cost of Goods Sold. It is subtracted from net income because more inventory was purchased than was sold.

e. This entry reconciles the prepayment of expenses with their expiration. It is subtracted from net income because cash payments for new prepayments are more than the amounts that were reported as expenses when they expired.

f. This entry reconciles cash paid to suppliers with purchases on account. It is added because more was purchased on account than was paid in cash.

g. This entry reconciles the accrual of liabilities for operating expenses with payments for these expenses. The increase in Accrued Liabilities is added because the cash paid for accrued liabilities was less than the expenses accrued. The debit to Cash corresponds to the net credit to Accrued Liabilities.

h. This entry records the cash purchases of new equipment.

i. This entry records the cash purchase of intangibles.

j. This entry records cash provided by borrowing additional long-term debt.

COACH'S TIP

Think of the statement of cash flows (in the bottom half of the spreadsheet) as a big Cash T-account.

EXHIBIT 12B.1 **Spreadsheet to Prepare Statement of Cash Flows, Indirect Method**

UNDER ARMOUR, INC.
Statement of Cash Flow Spreadsheet
For the Year Ended December 31, 2008

(in millions)	Beginning Balances, December 31, 2007	Analysis of Changes Debit		Credit		Ending Balances, December 31, 2008
Items from Balance Sheet						
Cash and Cash Equivalents (A)	40	(m)	62			102
Accounts Receivable (A)	94			(c)	13	81
Inventories (A)	166	(d)	16			182
Prepaid Expenses (A)	22	(e)	9			31
Equipment (A)	84	(h)	36			120
Accumulated Depreciation (xA)	31			(b)	16	47
Intangible and Other Assets (A)	16	(i)	2			18
Accounts Payable (L)	55			(f)	17	72
Accrued Liabilities (L)	41			(g)	20	61
Long-Term Debt (L)	14	(k)	7	(j)	16	23
Contributed Capital (SE)	163			(l)	12	175
Retained Earnings (SE)	118			(a)	38	156

		Cash Inflows		Outflows		Subtotals
Statement of Cash Flows						
Cash flows from operating activities:						
Net income		(a)	38			
Adjustments to reconcile net income to cash provided by operating activities:						
Depreciation		(b)	16			
Changes in current assets and current liabilities:						
Accounts Receivable		(c)	13			
Inventories				(d)	16	
Prepaid Expenses				(e)	9	
Accounts Payable		(f)	17			
Accrued Liabilities		(g)	20			
						79
Cash flows from investing activities:						
Purchase of equipment				(h)	36	
Purchase of intangible and other assets				(i)	2	
						(38)
Cash flows from financing activities:						
Additional borrowings of long-term debt		(j)	16			
Payments of long-term debt				(k)	7	
Proceeds from stock issuance		(l)	12			
						21
Net decrease in Cash and Cash Equivalents				(m)	62	
			132		132	62

k. This entry records cash used to repay long-term debt.

l. This entry records the cash received from issuing stock.

m. This entry shows that the change in cash (in the top part of the spreadsheet) is accounted for by the net cash flows listed in the bottom part of the spreadsheet.

Check to see that Debits = Credits in your spreadsheet, because if they don't, you've missed something along the way. The bottom part of the spreadsheet can be used to prepare the formal statement of cash flows shown in Exhibit 12.7.

DEMONSTRATION CASE A: INDIRECT METHOD

During a recent quarter (ended March 31), Brunswick Corporation reported net income of $3,800 (all numbers in thousands). The balance in cash and cash equivalents at the beginning of the quarter (on January 1) was $351,400, and at the end of the quarter on March 31 was $280,000. The company also reported the following activities:

a. Borrowed $2,200 of debt.
b. Accounts receivable increased by $40,300.
c. Paid $31,800 in cash for purchase of property, plant, and equipment.
d. Recorded depreciation of $35,600.
e. Salaries payable increased by $10,210.
f. Other accrued liabilities decreased by $35,000.
g. Prepaid expenses decreased by $14,500.
h. Inventories increased by $20,810.
i. Accounts payable decreased by $10,200.
j. Issued stock to employees for $400 in cash.

Required:

Based on this information, prepare the cash flow statement using the indirect method. Evaluate the cash flows reported in the statement.

See page **468** for solution.

DEMONSTRATION CASE B: DIRECT METHOD

During a recent quarter (ended March 29), Cybex International reported that its cash and cash equivalents had increased from $216 on December 31 to $469 on March 29 (all amounts in thousands). The company also indicated the following:

a. Paid $13,229 to suppliers for inventory purchases.
b. Borrowed $2,400 from one of the company's main stockholders.
c. Paid $554 in cash for purchase of property, plant, and equipment.
d. Reported sales on account of $20,608. The company reported Accounts Receivable of $13,628 at the beginning of the quarter and $12,386 at the end of the quarter.
e. Paid operating expenses to employees and suppliers of services totaling $6,188.
f. Cash payments for interest totaled $1,060.
g. Made payments of $2,625 for principal owed on long-term debt.
h. Paid $284 cash for other financing activities.
i. Paid $57 cash for income taxes.

Required:

Based on this information, prepare the cash flow statement using the direct method. Evaluate the cash flows reported in the statement.

See page **469** for solution.

CHAPTER SUMMARY

Identify cash flows arising from operating, investing, and financing activities. p. 442

LO1

- The statement has three main sections: Cash flows from operating activities, which are related to earning income from normal operations; Cash flows from investing activities, which are related to the acquisition and sale of productive assets; and Cash flows from financing activities, which are related to external financing of the enterprise.

- The net cash inflow or outflow for the period is the same amount as the increase or decrease in cash and cash equivalents for the period on the balance sheet. Cash equivalents are highly liquid investments purchased within three months of maturity.

Report cash flows from operating activities, using the indirect method. p. 449

LO2

- The indirect method for reporting cash flows from operating activities reports a conversion of net income to net cash flow from operating activities.

- The conversion involves additions and subtractions for (1) noncash expenses (such as depreciation expense) and revenues that do not affect current assets or current liabilities, and (2) changes in each of the individual current assets (other than cash) and current liabilities (other than debt to financial institutions, which relates to financing).

Report cash flows from investing activities. p. 452

LO3

- Investing activities reported on the cash flow statement include cash payments to acquire fixed assets and investments and cash proceeds from the sale of fixed assets and investments.

Report cash flows from financing activities. p. 453

LO4

- Cash inflows from financing activities include cash proceeds from issuance of debt and common stock. Cash outflows include cash principal payments on debt, cash paid for the repurchase of the company's stock, and cash dividend payments. Cash payments associated with interest are a cash flow from operating activities.

Interpret cash flows from operating, investing, and financing activities. p. 456

LO5

- A healthy company will generate positive cash flows from operations, some of which will be used to pay for purchases of property, plant, and equipment. Any additional cash (called free cash flow) can be used to further expand the business, to pay down some of the company's debt, or simply build up the cash balance. A company is in trouble if it is unable to generate positive cash flows from operations in the long run because eventually creditors will stop lending to the company and stockholders will stop investing in it.

- Two common ratios for assessing cash flows are the quality of income ratio and the capital acquisitions ratio.

Accounting Decision Tools

Name of Measure	Formula	What It Tells You
Quality of income ratio	$\dfrac{\text{Net Cash Flow from Operating Activities}}{\text{Net Income}}$	• Whether operating cash flows and net income are in sync • A ratio near 1.0 means operating cash flows and net income are in sync
Capital acquisitions ratio	$\dfrac{\text{Net Cash Flow from Operating Activities}}{\text{Cash Paid for PPE}}$	• Whether operating cash flows are sufficient to pay for PPE purchases • A higher ratio means less need for external financing

LO6 **Report and interpret cash flows from operating activities, using the direct method. p. 460**

- The direct method for reporting cash flows from operating activities accumulates all of the operating transactions that result in either a debit or a credit to cash into categories. The most common inflows are cash received from customers and dividends and interest on investments. The most common outflows are cash paid for purchase of services and goods for resale, salaries and wages, income taxes, and interest on liabilities. It is prepared by adjusting each item on the income statement from an accrual basis to a cash basis.

SOLUTION TO DEMONSTRATION CASE A: INDIRECT METHOD

BRUNSWICK CORPORATION
Statement of Cash Flows
For the Quarter Ended March 31

≋ BRUNSWICK

(in thousands)

Cash Flows from Operating Activities	
Net income	$ 3,800
Adjustments	
Depreciation	35,600
Change in Accounts Receivable	(40,300)
Change in Inventories	(20,810)
Change in Prepaid Expenses	14,500
Change in Accounts Payable	(10,200)
Change in Salaries Payable	10,210
Change in Other Accrued Liabilities	(35,000)
Net cash provided by (used in) operating activities	(42,200)
Cash Flows from Investing Activities	
Additions to property, plant, and equipment	(31,800)
Net cash provided by (used in) investing activities	(31,800)
Cash Flows from Financing Activities	
Proceeds from debt borrowings	2,200
Proceeds from issuance of stock to employees	400
Net cash provided by (used in) financing activities	2,600
Increase (decrease) in Cash and Cash Equivalents	(71,400)
Cash and Cash Equivalents, January 1	351,400
Cash and Cash Equivalents, March 31	$280,000

Despite reporting profits this quarter, the company has negative cash flows from operations. This is caused primarily by build-ups of accounts receivable and inventories, with no corresponding reduction in spending for accounts payable and other accrued liabilities. This is potentially troublesome because it suggests the company may be encountering difficulties in selling its products and when collecting on past sales. In addition to the drain on cash for operating activities, the company also spent over $30 million for additional property, plant, and equipment. Financing activities had relatively little effect on cash flows during the period. The company entered this quarter with lots of cash (over $350 million) and, despite the shortfall in cash flow, still has lots remaining to finance future activities.

SOLUTION TO DEMONSTRATION CASE B: DIRECT METHOD

CYBEX INTERNATIONAL
Statement of Cash Flows
For the Quarter Ended March 29

⊂CYBEX

(in thousands)

Cash Flows from Operating Activities

Cash collected from customers ($13,628 + $20,608 − $12,386)	$21,850
Cash paid to suppliers of inventory	(13,229)
Cash paid to employees and suppliers of services	(6,188)
Cash paid for interest	(1,060)
Cash paid for income taxes	(57)
Net cash flow provided by operating activities	1,316
Cash Flows from Investing Activities	
Additions to property, plant, and equipment	(554)
Net cash flow provided by (used in) investing activities	(554)
Cash Flows from Financing Activities	
Proceeds from borrowing from a related party (stockholder)	2,400
Repayment of long-term debt principal	(2,625)
Payments for other financing activities	(284)
Net cash flow provided by (used in) financing activities	(509)
Increase (decrease) in Cash and Cash Equivalents	253
Cash and Cash Equivalents, December 31	216
Cash and Cash Equivalents, March 29	$ 469

Cybex reported a net inflow of $1,316 cash from operating activities during the quarter. These cash flows were more than enough to pay for the property, plant, and equipment purchased this quarter, as indicated by its capital acquisitions ratio of 2.38 ($1,316 ÷ $554). Some of the extra cash from operations that was not used to purchase property, plant, and equipment (also called free cash flow) could be used to pay down debt or to increase the company's cash balance. The financing activities section suggests that the company paid down a significant amount of long-term debt ($2,625), in part by borrowing funds from a related party ($2,400). Borrowing from a related party (particularly a major stockholder) is unusual, which would prompt analysts to investigate further. The company's quarterly report explains that its lenders had demanded immediate repayment of their loans because the company had violated its debt covenants. A major stockholder loaned money to the company so that it could make this repayment.

KEY TERMS

Cash Flows from Financing Activities p. 445
Cash Flows from Investing Activities p. 444

Cash Flows from Operating Activities (Cash Flows from Operations) p. 444

Direct Method p. 447
Indirect Method p. 447

See complete definitions in glossary at back of text.

QUESTIONS

1. Compare the purposes of the income statement, the balance sheet, and the statement of cash flows.

2. What information does the statement of cash flows report that is not reported on the other required financial statements?

3. What are cash equivalents? How are they reported on the statement of cash flows?

4. What are the major categories of business activities reported on the statement of cash flows? Define each of these activities.

5. What are the typical cash inflows from operating activities? What are the typical cash outflows from operating activities?

6. Describe the types of items used to compute cash flows from operating activities under the two alternative methods of reporting.

7. Under the indirect method, depreciation expense is added to net income to report cash flows from operating activities. Does depreciation cause an inflow of cash?

8. Explain why cash outflows during the period for purchases and salaries are not specifically reported on a statement of cash flows prepared using the indirect method.

9. Explain why a $50,000 increase in inventory during the year must be included in computing cash flows from operating activities under both the direct and indirect methods.

10. Loan covenants require that E-Gadget Corporation (EGC) generate $200,000 cash from operating activities each year. Without intervening during the last month of the current year, EGC will generate only $180,000 cash from operations. What are the pros and cons of each of the following possible interventions: (a) pressuring customers to pay overdue accounts, (b) delaying payment of amounts owing to suppliers, and (c) purchasing additional equipment to increase depreciation?

11. As a junior analyst, you are evaluating the financial performance of Digilog Corporation. Impressed by this year's growth in sales (20% increase), receivables (40% increase), and inventories (50% increase), you plan to report a favorable evaluation of the company. Your supervisor cautions you that those increases may signal difficulties rather than successes. When you ask what she means, she just says you should look at the company's statement of cash flows. What do you think you will find there? What are the cash flow effects when a company's receivables and inventories increase faster than its sales?

12. What are the typical cash inflows from investing activities? What are the typical cash outflows from investing activities?

13. What are the typical cash inflows from financing activities? What are the typical cash outflows from financing activities?

14. What are noncash investing and financing activities? Give one example. How are noncash investing and financing activities reported on the statement of cash flows?

15. (Supplement 12A) How is the sale of equipment reported on the statement of cash flows using the indirect method?

MULTIPLE CHOICE

Quiz 12
www.mhhe.com/whitecotton1e

1. Where is the overall change in cash shown in the statement of cash flows?
   a. In the top part, before the operating activities section.
   b. In one of the operating, investing, or financing activities sections.
   c. In the bottom part, following the financing activities section.
   d. None of the above.

2. In what order do the three sections of the statement of cash flows appear when reading from top to bottom?
   a. Financing, investing, operating.
   b. Investing, operating, financing.
   c. Operating, financing, investing.
   d. Operating, investing, financing.

3. Total cash inflow in the operating section of the statement of cash flows should include which of the following?
   a. Cash received from customers at the point of sale.
   b. Cash collections from customer accounts receivable.
   c. Cash received in advance of revenue recognition (unearned revenue).
   d. All of the above.

4. If the balance in Prepaid Expenses increased during the year, what action should be taken on the statement of cash flows when following the indirect method, *and why?*
   a. The change in the account balance should be subtracted from net income, because the net increase in Prepaid Expenses did not impact net income but did reduce the cash balance.
   b. The change in the account balance should be added to net income, because the net increase in Prepaid Expenses did not impact net income but did increase the cash balance.

   c. The net change in Prepaid Expenses should be subtracted from net income, to reverse the income statement effect that had no impact on cash.
   d. The net change in Prepaid Expenses should be added to net income, to reverse the income statement effect that had no impact on cash.

5. Which of the following would not appear in the investing section of the statement of cash flows?
   a. Purchase of inventory.
   b. Sale of investments.
   c. Purchase of land.
   d. All of the above would appear in the investing section of the statement of cash flows.

6. Which of the following items would not appear in the financing section of the statement of cash flows?
   a. The issuance of the company's own stock.
   b. The repayment of debt.
   c. The payment of dividends.
   d. All of the above would appear in the financing section of the statement of cash flows.

7. Which of the following is not added when computing cash flows from operations using the indirect method?
   a. The net increase in accounts payable.
   b. The net decrease in accounts receivable.
   c. The net decrease in inventory.
   d. All of the above should be added.

8. If a company engages in a material noncash transaction, which of the following is required?
   a. The company must include an explanatory narrative or schedule accompanying the statement of cash flows.
   b. No disclosure is necessary.

c. The company must include an explanatory narrative or schedule accompanying the balance sheet.

d. It must be reported in the investing and financing sections of the statement of cash flows.

9. The *total* change in cash as shown near the bottom of the statement of cash flows for the year should agree to which of the following?

a. The difference in Retained Earnings when reviewing the comparative balance sheet.

b. Net income or net loss as found on the income statement.

c. The difference in cash when reviewing the comparative balance sheet.

d. None of the above.

10. Which of the following is a ratio used to assess the extent to which operating cash flows are sufficient to cover replacement of property, plant, and equipment?

a. Free cash flow.   c. Current ratio.

b. Capital acquisitions ratio.   d. Quality of income ratio.

> Answers to the Multiple-Choice Questions located in back of the text.

MINI EXERCISES

|ACCOUNTING

M12-1 Identifying Companies from Cash Flow Patterns

LO1, 5

Based on the cash flows shown, classify each of the following cases as a growing start-up company (S), a healthy established company (E), or an established company facing financial difficulties (F).

	Case 1	Case 2	Case 3
Cash provided by (used for) operating activities	$ 3,000	$(120,000)	$80,000
Cash provided by (used for) investing activities	(70,000)	10,000	(40,000)
Cash provided by (used for) financing activities	75,000	75,000	(30,000)
Net change in cash	8,000	(35,000)	10,000
Cash position at beginning of year	2,000	40,000	30,000
Cash position at end of year	$10,000	$ 5,000	$40,000

M12-2 Matching Items Reported to Cash Flow Statement Categories (Indirect Method)

LO1, 2

The Buckle, Inc., operates 387 stores in 39 states, selling brand name apparel like Lucky jeans and Fossil belts and watches. Some of the items included in its 2008 statement of cash flows presented using the *indirect method* are listed here. Indicate whether each item is disclosed in the operating activities (O), investing activities (I), or financing activities (F) section of the statement or (NA) if the item does not appear on the statement.

The Buckle, Inc.

_____ 1. Purchase of investments.

_____ 2. Proceeds from issuance of stock.

_____ 3. Purchase of property and equipment.

_____ 4. Depreciation.

_____ 5. Accounts payable (decrease).

_____ 6. Inventories (increase).

M12-3 Determining the Effects of Account Changes on Cash Flows from Operating Activities (Indirect Method)

LO2

Indicate whether each item would be added (+) or subtracted (−) in the computation of cash flow from operating activities using the indirect method.

_____ 1. Depreciation.

_____ 2. Inventories decrease.

_____ 3. Accounts payable decrease.

_____ 4. Accounts receivable increase.

_____ 5. Accrued liabilities increase.

M12-4 Computing Cash Flows from Operating Activities (Indirect Method)

LO2

For each of the following independent cases, compute cash flows from operating activities. Assume the list below includes all balance sheet accounts related to operating activities.

	Case A	Case B	Case C
Net income	$200,000	$ 20,000	$360,000
Depreciation expense	40,000	150,000	80,000
Accounts receivable increase (decrease)	100,000	(200,000)	(20,000)
Inventory increase (decrease)	(50,000)	(100,000)	50,000
Accounts payable increase (decrease)	(110,000)	120,000	70,000
Accrued liabilities increase (decrease)	60,000	(220,000)	(80,000)

LO2 **M12-5 Computing Cash Flows from Operating Activities (Indirect Method)**

For the following two independent cases, show the cash flows from operating activities section of the 2010 statement of cash flows using the indirect method.

	Case A		Case B	
	2010	2009	2010	2009
Sales Revenue	$10,000	$9,000	$21,000	$18,000
Cost of Goods Sold	6,000	5,500	12,000	11,000
Gross Profit	4,000	3,500	9,000	7,000
Depreciation Expense	1,000	1,000	2,000	1,500
Salaries Expense	2,500	2,000	5,000	5,000
Net Income	500	500	2,000	500
Accounts Receivable	300	400	750	600
Inventories	600	500	790	800
Accounts Payable	800	700	800	850
Salaries Payable	1,000	1,200	200	250

LO3 **M12-6 Computing Cash Flows from Investing Activities**

Based on the following information, compute cash flows from investing activities under GAAP.

Cash collections from customers	$800	Sale of investments	300
Purchase of used equipment	350	Dividends received	100
Depreciation expense	200	Interest received	200

LO4 **M12-7 Computing Cash Flows from Financing Activities**

Based on the following information, compute cash flows from financing activities under GAAP.

Purchase of investments	$ 250
Dividends paid	800
Interest paid	400
Additional borrowing from bank	2,000

LO3, 4 **M12-8 Reporting Noncash Investing and Financing Activities**

Which of the following transactions would be considered noncash investing and financing activities?

_____ 1. Additional borrowing from bank.

_____ 2. Purchase of equipment with investments.

_____ 3. Dividends paid in cash.

_____ 4. Purchase of a building with a promissory note.

LO5 **M12-9 Interpreting Cash Flows from Operating, Investing, and Financing Activities**

Quantum Dots, Inc., is a nanotechnology company that manufactures "quantum dots," which are tiny pieces of silicon consisting of 100 or more molecules. Quantum dots can be used to illuminate very small objects, enabling scientists to see the blood vessels beneath a mouse's skin ripple with each heartbeat, at the rate of 100 times per second. Evaluate this research intensive company's cash flows, assuming the following was reported in its statement of cash flows.

	Current Year	Previous Year
Cash Flows from Operating Activities		
Net cash provided by (used for) operating activities	$ (50,790)	$(46,730)
Cash Flows from Investing Activities		
Purchases of research equipment	(250,770)	(480,145)
Proceeds from selling all short-term investments	35,000	—
Net cash provided by (used for) investing activities	(215,770)	(480,145)
Cash Flows from Financing Activities		
Additional long-term debt borrowed	100,000	200,000
Proceeds from stock issuance	140,000	200,000
Cash dividends paid	—	(10,000)
Net cash provided by (used for) financing activities	240,000	390,000
Net increase (decrease) in cash	(26,560)	(136,875)
Cash at beginning of period	29,025	165,900
Cash at end of period	$ 2,465	$ 29,025

M12-10 Calculating and Interpreting the Capital Acquisitions Ratio LO5

Capital Corporation reported the following information in its statement of cash flows:

	2008	2009	2010
Net cash flow from operating activities	$35,000	$32,000	$23,000
Purchases of property, plant, and equipment	31,818	22,857	20,325

Calculate, to one decimal place, the average capital acquisitions ratio for the period covering 2008–2010 and the capital acquisitions ratio for *each* year during the period. What does this analysis tell you about the company's need for using external financing to replace property, plant, and equipment?

M12-11 Calculating and Interpreting the Quality of Income Ratio LO5

Dan's Products, Inc., reported net income of $80,000, depreciation expense of $2,000, and cash flow from operations of $60,000. Compute the quality of income ratio. What does the ratio tell you about the company's accrual of revenues and/or deferral of expenses?

M12-12 Matching Items Reported to Cash Flow Statement Categories LO1, 6
         (Direct Method)

Prestige Manufacturing Corporation reports the following items in its 2010 statement of cash flows presented using the direct method. Indicate whether each item is disclosed in the operating activities (O), investing activities (I), or financing activities (F) section of the statement under GAAP or (NA) if the item does not appear on the statement.

____ 1. Payment for equipment purchase.   ____ 4. Proceeds from issuance of stock.

____ 2. Repayments of bank loan.   ____ 5. Interest paid.

____ 3. Dividends paid.   ____ 6. Receipts from customers.

M12-13 Computing Cash Flows from Operating Activities (Direct Method) LO6

For each of the following independent cases, compute cash flows from operating activities using the direct method. Assume the list below includes all items relevant to operating activities.

	Case A	Case B	Case C
Sales revenue	$70,000	$55,000	$95,000
Cost of goods sold	35,000	32,000	65,000
Depreciation expense	10,000	2,000	10,000
Other operating expenses	5,000	13,000	8,000
Net income	20,000	8,000	12,000
Accounts receivable increase (decrease)	(1,000)	4,000	3,000
Inventory increase (decrease)	2,000	0	(4,000)
Accounts payable increase (decrease)	0	3,000	(2,000)
Accrued liabilities increase (decrease)	1,000	(2,000)	1,000

LO6   **M12-14 Computing Cash Flows from Operating Activities (Direct Method)**

Refer to the two cases presented in M12-5, and show the cash flow from operating activities section of the 2010 statement of cash flows using the direct method.

EXERCISES

LO1, 2   **E12-1 Matching Items Reported to Cash Flow Statement Categories (Indirect Method)**

NIKE, Inc.

NIKE, Inc., is the best-known sports shoe, apparel, and equipment company in the world because of its association with sports stars such as LeBron James. Some of the items included in its recent statement of cash flows presented using the *indirect method* are listed here.

Indicate whether each item is disclosed in the operating activities (O), investing activities (I), or financing activities (F) section of the statement or (NA) if the item does not appear on the statement.

_____ 1. Additions to long-term debt.

_____ 2. Depreciation.

_____ 3. Additions to property, plant, and equipment.

_____ 4. Increase (decrease) in notes payable. (The amount is owed to financial institutions.)

_____ 5. (Increase) decrease in other current assets.

_____ 6. Cash received from disposal of property, plant, and equipment.

_____ 7. Reductions in long-term debt.

_____ 8. Issuance of stock.

_____ 9. (Increase) decrease in inventory.

_____ 10. Net income.

LO2   **E12-2 Understanding the Computation of Cash Flows from Operating Activities (Indirect Method)**

Suppose your company sells services of $150 in exchange for $100 cash and $50 on account.

Required:

1. Show the journal entry to record this transaction.
2. Identify the amount that should be reported as net cash flow from operating activities.
3. Identify the amount that would be included in net income.
4. Show how the indirect method would convert net income (requirement 3) to net cash flow from operating activities (requirement 2).
5. What general rule about converting net income to operating cash flows is revealed by your answer to requirement 4?

LO2   **E12-3 Understanding the Computation of Cash Flows from Operating Activities (Indirect Method)**

Suppose your company sells services for $300 cash this month. Your company also pays $100 in wages, which includes $20 that was payable at the end of the previous month and $80 for wages of this month.

Required:

1. Show the journal entries to record these transactions.
2. Calculate the amount that should be reported as net cash flow from operating activities.
3. Calculate the amount that should be reported net income.
4. Show how the indirect method would convert net income (requirement 3) to net cash flow from operating activities (requirement 2).
5. What general rule about converting net income to operating cash flows is revealed by your answer to requirement 4?

E12-4 Understanding the Computation of Cash Flows from Operating Activities (Indirect Method)   LO2

Suppose your company sells services of $150 in exchange for $100 cash and $50 on account. Depreciation of $40 also is recorded.

Required:

1. Show the journal entries to record these transactions.
2. Calculate the amount that should be reported as net cash flow from operating activities.
3. Calculate the amount that should be reported net income.
4. Show how the indirect method would convert net income (requirement 3) to net cash flow from operating activities (requirement 2).
5. What general rules about converting net income to operating cash flows is revealed by your answer to requirement 4?

E12-5 Understanding the Computation of Cash Flows from Operating Activities (Indirect Method)   LO2

Suppose your company sells goods for $300, of which $200 is received in cash and $100 is on account. The goods cost your company $125 in a previous period. Your company also recorded wages of $70, of which only $30 has been paid in cash.

Required:

1. Show the journal entries to record these transactions.
2. Calculate the amount that should be reported as net cash flow from operating activities.
3. Calculate the amount that should be reported net income?
4. Show how the indirect method would convert net income (requirement 3) to net cash flow from operating activities (requirement 2).
5. What general rules about converting net income to operating cash flows is revealed by your answer to requirement 4?

E12-6 Preparing and Evaluating a Simple Statement of Cash Flows (Indirect Method)   LO2, 5

Suppose your company's income statement reports $105 of net income, and its comparative balance sheet indicates the following.

	Beginning	Ending
Cash	$ 35	$205
Accounts Receivable	75	175
Inventory	260	135
Total	$370	$515
Wages Payable	$ 10	$ 50
Retained Earnings	360	465
Total	$370	$515

Required:

1. Prepare the operating activities section of the statement of cash flows, using the indirect method.
2. Identify the most important cause of the difference between the company's net income and net cash flow from operating activities.

LO1, 2, 5   **E12-7 Preparing and Evaluating a Simple Statement of Cash Flows (Indirect Method)**

Suppose the income statement for Goggle Company reports $70 of net income, after deducting depreciation of $35. The company bought equipment costing $60 and obtained a long-term bank loan for $60. The company's comparative balance sheet, at December 31, indicates the following.

	2009	2010	Change
Cash	$ 35	$205	
Accounts Receivable	75	175	
Inventory	260	135	
Equipment	500	560	
Accumulated Depreciation	(45)	(80)	
Total	$825	$995	
Wages Payable	$ 10	$ 50	
Long-Term Debt	445	505	
Contributed Capital	10	10	
Retained Earnings	360	430	
Total	$825	$995	

Required:

1. Calculate the change in each balance sheet account, and indicate whether each account relates to operating, investing, and/or financing activities.
2. Prepare a statement of cash flows using the indirect method.
3. In one sentence, explain why an increase in accounts receivable is subtracted.
4. In one sentence, explain why a decrease in inventory is added.
5. In one sentence, explain why an increase in wages payable is added.
6. Are the cash flows typical of a start-up, healthy, or troubled company? Explain.

LO2   **E12-8 Reporting Cash Flows from Operating Activities (Indirect Method)**

The following information pertains to Guy's Gear Company:

Sales		$80,000
Expenses:		
Cost of Goods Sold	$50,000	
Depreciation Expense	6,000	
Salaries Expense	12,000	68,000
Net Income		$12,000
Accounts Receivable decrease	$ 5,000	
Merchandise Inventory increase	8,000	
Salaries Payable increase	500	

Required:

Present the operating activities section of the statement of cash flows for Guy's Gear Company using the indirect method.

LO2, 5   **E12-9 Reporting and Interpreting Cash Flows from Operating Activities from an Analyst's Perspective (Indirect Method)**

New Vision Company completed its income statement and balance sheet for 2010 and provided the following information:

Service Revenue		$66,000
Expenses:		
Salaries	$42,000	
Depreciation	7,300	
Utilities	7,000	
Other	1,700	58,000
Net Income		$ 8,000
Decrease in Accounts Receivable	$12,000	
Bought a small service machine	5,000	
Increase in Salaries Payable	9,000	
Decrease in Other Accrued Liabilities	4,000	

Required:

1. Present the operating activities section of the statement of cash flows for New Vision Company using the indirect method.
2. Of the potential causes of differences between cash flow from operations and net income, which are the most important to financial analysts?

E12-10 Reporting and Interpreting Cash Flows from Operating Activities   **LO2, 5**
        from an Analyst's Perspective (Indirect Method)

Pizza International, Inc., operates 700 family restaurants around the world. The company's annual report contained the following information (in thousands):

Operating Activities			
Net loss	$(9,482)	Decrease in accounts payable	2,282
Depreciation	33,305	Decrease in accrued liabilities	719
Increase in receivables	170	Increase in income taxes payable	1,861
Decrease in inventories	643	Reduction of long-term debt	12,691
Increase in prepaid expenses	664	Additions to equipment	29,073

Required:

1. Based on this information, compute cash flow from operating activities using the indirect method.
2. What were the major reasons that Pizza International was able to report positive cash flow from operations despite having a net loss?
3. Of the potential causes of differences between cash flow from operations and net income, which are the most important to financial analysts?

E12-11 Inferring Balance Sheet Changes from the Cash Flow Statement   **LO2**
        (Indirect Method)

Colgate-Palmolive was founded in 1806. Its statement of cash flows reported the following information (in millions) for the year ended December 31, 2008:

Colgate-Palmolive

Operating Activities	
Net Income	$1,957
Depreciation	348
Cash effect of changes in	
Accounts Receivable	(70)
Inventories	(135)
Accounts Payable	125
Other	13
Net Cash Provided by Operations	$2,238

Required:

Based on the information reported in the operating activities section of the statement of cash flows for Colgate-Palmolive, determine whether the following accounts increased or decreased during the period: Accounts Receivable, Inventories, and Accounts Payable.

E12-12 Inferring Balance Sheet Changes from the Cash Flow Statement   **LO2**
        (Indirect Method)

The statement of cash flows for Apple Inc. contained the following information (in millions) for the year ended September 27, 2008:

Apple Inc.

Operating Activities	
Net Income	$4,834
Depreciation	473
Changes in current assets and current liabilities	
Accounts Receivable	(785)
Inventories	(163)
Accounts Payable	596
Unearned Revenue	5,642
Other adjustments	(1,001)
Net Cash Provided by Operations	$9,596

Required:

For each of the four current asset and liability accounts listed in the operating activities section of the statement of cash flows, determine whether the account balances increased or decreased during the period.

LO1, 2, 3, 4, 5   **E12-13 Preparing and Evaluating a Statement of Cash Flows (Indirect Method) from Comparative Balance Sheets and Income Statements**

Consultex, Inc., was founded in 2007 as a small financial consulting business. The company had done reasonably well in 2007–2009, but started noticing its cash dwindle early 2010. In January 2010, Consultex had paid $16,000 to purchase land and repaid $2,000 principal on an existing promissory note. In March 2010, the company paid $2,000 cash for dividends and $1,000 to repurchase Consultex stock that had previously been issued for $1,000. To improve its cash position, Consultex borrowed $5,000 by signing a new promissory note in May 2010 and also issued stock to a new private investor for $12,000 cash. Comparative balance sheets and income statements for the most recent fiscal year are presented below.

CONSULTEX, INC.
Balance Sheet
October 31

	2010	2009
Assets		
Cash	$11,000	$14,000
Accounts Receivable	14,000	12,000
Prepaid Rent	2,000	3,000
Land	26,000	10,000
Total Assets	$53,000	$39,000
Liabilities and Stockholders' Equity		
Wages Payable	$ 2,000	$ 3,000
Income Taxes Payable	1,000	1,000
Notes Payable (long-term)	15,000	12,000
Contributed Capital	20,000	9,000
Retained Earnings	15,000	14,000
Total Liabilities and Stockholders' Equity	$53,000	$39,000

CONSULTEX, INC.
Income Statement
For the Year Ended October 31

	2010	2009
Sales Revenue	$158,000	$161,000
Wages Expense	98,000	97,000
Rent Expense	36,000	30,000
Other Operating Expenses	19,700	20,000
Income before Income Tax Expense	4,300	14,000
Income Tax Expense	1,300	4,200
Net Income	$ 3,000	$ 9,800

Requirements:

1. Prepare a properly formatted Statement of Cash Flows for Consultex, Inc., for the year ended October 31, 2010 (using the indirect method).
2. What one thing can Consultex reasonably change in 2011 to avoid depleting its cash?

**E12-14 Analyzing Cash Flows from Operating Activities (Indirect Method)   LO2, 5
and Calculating and Interpreting the Quality of Income Ratio**

The 2008 annual report for PepsiCo contained the following information for the period (in   PepsiCo
millions):

Net income	$5,142	Increase in prepaid expense	68
Cash dividends paid	2,541	Increase in accounts payable	718
Depreciation	1,543	Decrease in taxes payable	180
Increase in accounts receivable	549	Increase in other liabilities related to operations	738
Increase in inventory	345		

Required:

1. Compute cash flows from operating activities for PepsiCo using the indirect method.
2. Compute the quality of income ratio to one decimal place.
3. What was the main reason that PepsiCo's quality of income ratio did not equal 1.0?

**E12-15 Calculating and Understanding Operating Cash Flows Relating   LO2
to Inventory Purchases (Indirect Method)**

The following information was reported by three companies. When completing the requirements,
assume that any and all purchases on account are for inventory.

	Aztec Corporation	Bikes Unlimited	Campus Cycles
Cost of goods sold	$175	$175	$350
Inventory purchases from suppliers made using cash	200	0	200
Inventory purchases from suppliers made on account	0	200	200
Cash payments to suppliers on account	0	160	160
Beginning inventory	100	100	200
Ending inventory	125	125	250
Beginning accounts payable	0	80	80
Ending accounts payable	0	120	120

Required:

1. What amount did each company deduct on the income statement related to inventory?
2. What total amount did each company pay out in cash during the period related to inventory
   purchased with cash and on account?
3. By what amount do your answers in 1 and 2 differ for each company?
4. By what amount did each company's inventory increase (decrease)? By what amount did
   each company's accounts payable increase (decrease)?
5. Using the indirect method of presentation, what amount(s) must each company add (deduct)
   from net income to convert from accrual to cash basis?
6. Describe any similarities between your answers to requirements 3 and 5. Are these answers
   the same? Why or why not?

E12-16 Reporting Cash Flows from Investing and Financing Activities   LO3, 4

Rowe Furniture Corporation is a Virginia-based manufacturer of furniture. In a recent quarter, it
reported the following activities:

Net income	$ 4,135	Payments to reduce long-term debt	46
Purchase of property, plant, and equipment	871	Sale of investments	134
Borrowings under line of credit (bank)	1,417	Proceeds from sale of property and equipment	6,594
Proceeds from issuance of stock	11	Dividends paid	277
Cash received from customers	29,164	Interest paid	90

Required:

Based on this information, present the cash flows from investing and financing activities sections of the cash flow statement.

LO3, 4, 5   **E12-17 Reporting and Interpreting Cash Flows from Investing and Financing Activities with Discussion of Management Strategy**

Gibraltar Industries, Inc.   Gibraltar Industries, Inc., is a manufacturer of steel products for customers such as Home Depot, Lowe's, Chrysler, Ford, and General Motors. In the year ended December 31, 2008, it reported the following activities:

Net income	$24,068	Proceeds from sale of property, plant, and equipment	28,669
Purchase of property, plant, and equipment	21,595	Decrease in accounts receivable	12,273
Payments on notes payable (bank)	184,937	Proceeds from notes payable (bank)	53,439
Net proceeds from stock issuance	250	Payment of dividends	5,985
Depreciation	33,907	Other financing cash outflows	1,694

Required:

1. Based on this information, present the cash flows from the investing and financing activities sections of the cash flow statement.
2. Referring to your response to requirement 1, comment on whether you think Gibraltar's cash flows are typical of a healthy or struggling company.

LO5   **E12-18 Analyzing and Interpreting the Capital Acquisitions Ratio**

Sportsnet Corporation reported the following data for the three most recent years:

	(in thousands)		
	2010	2009	2008
Cash flows from operating activities	$ 801	$1,480	$619
Cash flows from investing activities	(1,504)	(1,415)	(662)
Cash flows from financing activities	42,960	775	360

Required:

1. Assuming that all investing activities involved acquisition of new plant and equipment, compute the capital acquisitions ratio for the three-year period in total.
2. During the three-year period, what portion of Sportsnet's investing activities was financed from cash flows from operating activities? What portion was financed from external sources or preexisting cash balances during the three-year period?
3. What are two plausible explanations for the dramatic increase in cash flow from financing activities during the period?

LO5   **E12-19 Calculating and Interpreting the Capital Acquisitions Ratio**

Walt Disney Company   The Walt Disney Company reported the following in its 2008 annual report (in millions).

	2008	2007	2006
Net income	$4,427	$4,687	$3,374
Net cash provided by operating activities	5,446	5,398	5,960
Purchase of parks, resorts, and other property	(1,578)	(1,566)	(1,292)

Required:

1. Calculate, to two decimal places, the average capital acquisitions ratio for the period covering 2006–2008.
2. Interpret the results of your calculations in requirement 1. What do they suggest about the company's need for external financing to acquire property and equipment?

E12-20 Calculating and Interpreting the Quality of Income Ratio

Refer to the information about the Walt Disney Company in E12-19.

LO5

Walt Disney Company

Required:

1. Calculate, to one decimal place, the quality of income ratio for each year.
2. Interpret the results of your calculations in requirement 1. Given what you know about the Walt Disney Company from your own personal observations, provide one reason that could explain the sizable difference between net income and net cash provided by operating activities.

E12-21 Comparing the Direct and Indirect Methods

To compare statement of cash flows reporting under the direct and indirect methods, enter check marks to indicate which line items are reported on the statement of cash flows with each method.

LO2, 6

Cash Flows (and Related Changes)	Statement of Cash Flows Method	
	Direct	Indirect
1. Net income		
2. Receipts from customers		
3. Accounts receivable increase or decrease		
4. Payments to suppliers		
5. Inventory increase or decrease		
6. Accounts payable increase or decrease		
7. Payments to employees		
8. Wages payable, increase or decrease		
9. Depreciation expense		
10. Cash flows from operating activities		
11. Cash flows from investing activities		
12. Cash flows from financing activities		
13. Net increase or decrease in cash during the period		

E12-22 Reporting and Interpreting Cash Flows from Operating Activities from an Analyst's Perspective (Direct Method)

Refer to the information for New Vision Company in E12-9.

LO5, 6

Required:

1. Present the operating activities section of the statement of cash flows for New Vision Company using the direct method. Assume that Other Accrued Liabilities relate to Other Expenses on the income statement.
2. Of the potential causes of differences between cash flow from operations and net income, which are the most important to financial analysts?

E12-23 Reporting and Interpreting Cash Flows from Operating Activities from an Analyst's Perspective (Direct Method)

Refer back to the information given for E12-10, plus the following summarized income statement for Pizza International, Inc. (in millions):

LO5, 6

Revenues	$136,500
Cost of Sales	45,500
Gross Profit	91,000
Salary Expense	56,835
Depreciation	33,305
Other Expenses	7,781
Net Loss before Income Taxes	(6,921)
Income Tax Expense	2,561
Net Loss	$ (9,482)

Required:

1. Based on this information, compute cash flow from operating activities using the direct method. Assume that prepaid expenses and accrued liabilities relate to other expenses.

2. What were the major reasons that Pizza International was able to report positive cash flow from operations despite having a loss?

3. Of the potential causes of differences between cash flow from operations and net income, which are the most important to financial analysts?

E12-24 (Supplement A) Determining Cash Flows from the Sale of Property

AMC Entertainment

AMC Entertainment operates 307 movie theaters in the United States, Canada, and Europe. During fiscal 2008, the company sold its Fandango assets for $20,360,000 cash and recorded a gain an disposal of $18,360,000, which was included in the company's net income of $43,445,000.

Required:

1. Show how the disposal would be reported on the statement of cash flows, using the following format (which assumes the indirect method):

(in thousands)	
Cash flows from operating activities	
Net income	$43,445
Gain on sale of property	
Cash flows from investing activities	
Proceeds from disposition of property	

2. Compute the book value of the Fandango assets that were sold.

E12-25 (Supplement A) Determining Cash Flows from the Sale of Equipment

During the period, Teen's Trends sold some excess equipment at a loss. The following information was collected from the company's accounting records:

From the income statement	
Depreciation expense	$ 700
Loss on sale of equipment	4,000
From the balance sheet	
Beginning equipment	12,500
Ending equipment	7,000
Beginning accumulated depreciation	2,000
Ending accumulated depreciation	2,200

No new equipment was bought during the period.

Required:

For the equipment that was sold, determine its original cost, its accumulated depreciation, and the cash received from the sale.

E12-26 (Supplement B) Preparing a Statement of Cash Flows, Indirect Method: Complete Spreadsheet

To prepare a statement of cash flows for Golf Champion Store, you examined the company's accounts, noting the following:

Purchased equipment, $20,000, and issued a promissory note in full payment.
Purchased a long-term investment for cash, $15,000.
Paid cash dividend, $12,000.
Sold equipment for $6,000 cash (cost, $21,000, accumulated depreciation, $15,000).
Issued shares of no-par stock, 500 shares at $12 per share cash.
Net income was $20,200.
Depreciation expense was $3,000.

You also created the following spreadsheet to use when preparing the statement of cash flows.

	Beginning Balances, December 31, 2009	Analysis of Changes Debit	Analysis of Changes Credit	Ending Balances, December 31, 2010
Balance Sheet Items				
Cash	$ 20,500			$ 19,200
Accounts Receivable	22,000			22,000
Merchandise Inventory	68,000			75,000
Investments	0			15,000
Equipment	114,500			113,500
Accumulated Depreciation	32,000			20,000
Accounts Payable	17,000			14,000
Wages Payable	2,500			1,500
Income Taxes Payable	3,000			4,500
Notes Payable	54,000			74,000
Contributed Capital	100,000			106,000
Retained Earnings	16,500			24,700
		Inflows	Outflows	
Statement of Cash Flows				
Cash flows from operating activities				
Cash flows from investing activities				
Cash flows from financing activities				
Net increase (decrease) in cash				
Totals				

Required:

1. Complete the spreadsheet.
2. Prepare the 2010 statement of cash flows using the indirect method.

PROBLEMS–SET A

PA12-1   Determining Cash Flow Statement Effects of Transactions |ACCOUNTING   LO1

Motif Furniture is an Austin-based furniture company. For each of the following first-quarter transactions, indicate whether operating (O), investing (I), or financing activities (F) are affected and whether the effect is a cash inflow (+) or outflow (−), or (NE) if the transaction has no effect on cash.

_____ 1. Bought used equipment for cash.

_____ 2. Paid cash to purchase new equipment.

_____ 3. Declared and paid cash dividends to stockholders.

_____ 4. Collected payments on account from customers.

_____ 5. Recorded an adjusting entry to record accrued salaries expense.

_____ 6. Recorded and paid interest on debt to creditors.

_____ 7. Repaid principal on loan from bank.

_____ 8. Prepaid rent for the following period.

_____ 9. Made payment to suppliers on account.

LO2 **PA12-2 Computing Cash Flows from Operating Activities (Indirect Method)**

The income statement and selected balance sheet information for Direct Products Company for the year ended December 31, 2010, is presented below.

Income Statement	
Sales Revenue	$48,600
Expenses:	
Cost of Goods Sold	21,000
Depreciation Expense	2,000
Salaries Expense	9,000
Rent Expense	4,500
Insurance Expense	1,900
Interest Expense	1,800
Utilities Expense	1,400
Net Income	$ 7,000

Selected Balance Sheet Accounts		
	2010	2009
Accounts Receivable	$560	$580
Merchandise Inventory	990	770
Accounts Payable	440	460
Prepaid Rent	25	20
Prepaid Insurance	25	28
Salaries Payable	100	70
Utilities Payable	20	15

Required:

Prepare the cash flows from operating activities section of the 2010 statement of cash flows using the indirect method.

LO2, 3, 4, 5 **PA12-3 Preparing a Statement of Cash Flows (Indirect Method)**

www.mhhe.com/whitecotton1e

XS Supply Company is developing its annual financial statements at December 31, 2010. The statements are complete except for the statement of cash flows. The completed comparative balance sheets and income statement are summarized:

	2010	2009
Balance Sheet at December 31		
Cash	$ 34,000	$ 29,000
Accounts Receivable	35,000	28,000
Merchandise Inventory	41,000	38,000
Property and Equipment	121,000	100,000
Less: Accumulated Depreciation	(30,000)	(25,000)
	$201,000	$170,000
Accounts Payable	$ 36,000	$ 27,000
Wages Payable	1,200	1,400
Note Payable, Long-Term	38,000	44,000
Contributed Capital	88,600	72,600
Retained Earnings	37,200	25,000
	$201,000	$170,000
Income Statement for 2010		
Sales	$120,000	
Cost of Goods Sold	70,000	
Other Expenses	37,800	
Net Income	$ 12,200	

Additional Data:

a. Bought equipment for cash, $21,000.
b. Paid $6,000 on the long-term note payable.
c. Issued new shares of stock for $16,000 cash.
d. No dividends were declared or paid.
e. Other expenses included depreciation, $5,000; wages, $20,000; taxes, $6,000; other, $6,800.
f. Accounts Payable includes only inventory purchases made on credit. Because there are no liability accounts relating to taxes or other expenses, assume that these expenses were fully paid in cash.

Required:

1. Prepare the statement of cash flows for the year ended December 31, 2010, using the indirect method.
2. Evaluate the statement of cash flows.

PA12-4 Preparing and Interpreting a Statement of Cash Flows   **LO2, 3, 4, 5**
(Indirect Method)

Heads Up Company was started several years ago by two hockey instructors. The company's comparative balance sheets and income statement follow, along with additional information.

	2010	2009
Balance Sheet at December 31		
Cash	$ 6,000	$4,000
Accounts Receivable	1,000	1,750
Equipment	5,500	5,000
Less: Accumulated Depreciation	(1,500)	(1,250)
	$11,000	$9,500
Accounts Payable	$ 500	$1,000
Wages Payable	500	750
Long-Term Bank Loan Payable	1,500	500
Contributed Capital	5,000	5,000
Retained Earnings	3,500	2,250
	$11,000	$9,500
Income Statement for 2010		
Lessons Revenue	$37,500	
Wages Expense	35,000	
Depreciation Expense	250	
Income Tax Expense	1,000	
Net Income	$ 1,250	

Additional Data:

a. Bought new hockey equipment for cash, $500.
b. Borrowed $1,000 cash from the bank during the year.
c. Accounts Payable includes only purchases of services made on credit for operating purposes. Because there are no liability accounts relating to income tax, assume that this expense was fully paid in cash.

Required:

1. Prepare the statement of cash flows for the year ended December 31, 2010, using the indirect method.
2. Use the statement of cash flows to evaluate the company's cash flows.

PA12-5 Computing Cash Flows from Operating Activities (Direct Method)   **LO6**

Refer to the information in PA12-2.

Required:

Prepare the cash flows from operating activities section of the 2010 statement of cash flows using the direct method.

PA12-6 Preparing and Interpreting a Statement of Cash Flows (Direct Method)   **LO3, 4, 5, 6**

Refer to PA12-4.

Required:

Complete requirements 1 and 2 using the direct method.

PA12-7 (Supplement A) Preparing and Interpreting a Statement of Cash Flows
with Loss on Disposal (Indirect Method)

Assume the same facts as PA12-4, except for the income statement and additional data item a. The new income statement is shown on the following page. Instead of item a from PA12-4, assume that the company bought new equipment for $1,500 cash and sold existing equipment for $500 cash. The equipment that was sold had cost $1,000 and had Accumulated Depreciation of $250 at the time of sale.

Income Statement for 2010	
Lessons Revenue	$37,500
Wages Expense	35,000
Depreciation Expense	500
Loss on Disposal of Equipment	250
Income Tax Expense	500
Net Income	$ 1,250

Required:

1. Prepare the statement of cash flows for the year ended December 31, 2010, using the indirect method.

2. Use the statement of cash flows to evaluate the company's cash flows.

PROBLEMS–SET B

LO1

PB12-1 Determining Cash Flow Statement Effects of Transactions

For each of the following transactions, indicate whether operating (O), investing (I), or financing activities (F) are affected and whether the effect is a cash inflow (+) or outflow (−), or (NE) if the transaction has no effect on cash.

_____ 1. Received deposits from customers for products to be delivered the following period.

_____ 2. Principal repayments on loan.

_____ 3. Paid cash to purchase new equipment.

_____ 4. Received proceeds from loan.

_____ 5. Collected payments on account from customers.

_____ 6. Recorded and paid salaries to employees.

_____ 7. Paid cash for building construction.

_____ 8. Recorded and paid interest to debt holders.

LO2

PB12-2 Computing Cash Flows from Operating Activities (Indirect Method)

The income statement and selected balance sheet information for Calendars Incorporated for the year ended December 31, 2010, is presented below.

Income Statement	
Sales Revenue	$78,000
Expenses:	
Cost of Goods Sold	36,000
Depreciation Expense	16,000
Salaries Expense	10,000
Rent Expense	2,500
Insurance Expense	1,300
Interest Expense	1,200
Utilities Expense	1,000
Net Income	$10,000

Selected Balance Sheet Accounts		
	2010	2009
Merchandise Inventory	$ 430	$ 490
Accounts Receivable	1,800	1,500
Accounts Payable	1,200	1,300
Salaries Payable	450	300
Utilities Payable	100	0
Prepaid Rent	50	100
Prepaid Insurance	70	90

Required:

Prepare the cash flows from operating activities section of the 2010 statement of cash flows using the indirect method.

PB12-3 Preparing a Statement of Cash Flows (Indirect Method)   LO2, 3, 4, 5

Audio City, Inc., is developing its annual financial statements at December 31, 2010. The statements are complete except for the statement of cash flows. The completed comparative balance sheets and income statement are summarized below:

	2010	2009
Balance Sheet at December 31		
Cash	$ 63,000	$ 65,000
Accounts Receivable	15,000	20,000
Merchandise Inventory	22,000	20,000
Property and Equipment	210,000	150,000
Less. Accumulated Depreciation	(60,000)	(45,000)
	$250,000	$210,000
Accounts Payable	$ 8,000	$ 19,000
Wages Payable	2,000	1,000
Note Payable, Long-Term	60,000	75,000
Contributed Capital	100,000	70,000
Retained Earnings	80,000	45,000
	$250,000	$210,000
Income Statement for 2010		
Sales	$190,000	
Cost of Goods Sold	90,000	
Other Expenses	60,000	
Net Income	$ 40,000	

Additional Data:

a. Bought equipment for cash, $60,000.
b. Paid $15,000 on the long-term note payable.
c. Issued new shares of stock for $30,000 cash.
d. Dividends of $5,000 were paid in cash.
e. Other expenses included depreciation, $15,000; wages, $20,000; taxes, $25,000.
f. Accounts Payable includes only inventory purchases made on credit. Because a liability relating to taxes does not exist, assume that they were fully paid in cash.

Required:

1. Prepare the statement of cash flows for the year ended December 31, 2010, using the indirect method.
2. Evaluate the statement of cash flows.

PB12-4 Preparing and Interpreting a Statement of Cash Flows (Indirect Method)   LO2, 3, 4, 5

Dive In Company was started several years ago by two diving instructors. The company's comparative balance sheets and income statement are presented below, along with additional information.

	2010	2009
Balance Sheet at December 31		
Cash	$ 3,200	$4,000
Accounts Receivable	1,000	500
Prepaids	100	50
	$ 4,300	$4,550
Wages Payable	$ 350	$1,100
Contributed Capital	1,200	1,000
Retained Earnings	2,750	2,450
	$ 4,300	$4,550
Income Statement for 2010		
Lessons Revenue	$33,950	
Wages Expense	30,000	
Other Operating Expenses	3,650	
Net Income	$ 300	

Additional Data:

a. Prepaid Expenses relate to rent paid in advance.
b. Other Operating Expenses were paid in cash.
c. An owner contributed capital by paying $200 cash in exchange for the company's stock.

Required:

1. Prepare the statement of cash flows for the year ended December 31, 2010, using the indirect method.

2. Use the statement of cash flows to evaluate the company's cash flows.

LO6   **PB12-5 Computing Cash Flows from Operating Activities (Direct Method)**

Refer to the information in PB12-2.

Required:

Prepare the cash flows from operating activities section of the 2010 statement of cash flows using the direct method.

LO3, 4, 5, 6   **PB12-6 Preparing and Interpreting a Statement of Cash Flows (Direct Method)**

Refer to PB12-4.

Required:

Complete requirements 1 and 2 using the direct method.

SKILLS DEVELOPMENT CASES

LO5   **S12-1 Internet-Based Team Research: Examining an Annual Report**

As a team, select an industry to analyze. Using your Web browser, each team member should access the annual report or 10-K for one publicly traded company in the industry, with each member selecting a different company.

Required:

1. On an individual basis, each team member should write a short report that incorporates the following:
    a. Has the company generated positive or negative operating cash flows during the past three years?
    b. Has the company been expanding over the period? If so, what appears to have been the source of financing for this expansion (operating cash flow, additional borrowing, issuance of stock)?
    c. Compute and analyze the capital acquisitions ratio averaged over the past three years.
    d. Compute and analyze the quality of income ratio in each of the past three years.
2. Then, as a team, write a short report comparing and contrasting your companies using these attributes. Discuss any patterns across the companies that you as a team observe. Provide potential explanations for any differences discovered.

LO1, 5   **S12-2 Ethical Decision Making: A Real-Life Example**

Enron

In a February 19, 2004, press release, the Securities and Exchange Commission described a number of fraudulent transactions that Enron executives concocted in an effort to meet the company's financial targets. One particularly well-known scheme is called the "Nigerian barge" transaction. According to court documents, Enron arranged to sell three electricity-generating power barges moored off the coast of Nigeria. The "buyer" was the investment banking firm of Merrill Lynch. Although Enron reported this transaction as a sale in its income statement, it turns out this was no ordinary sale. Merrill Lynch didn't really want the barges and had only agreed to buy them because Enron guaranteed, in a secret side-deal, that it would arrange for the barges to be bought back from Merrill Lynch within six months of the initial transaction. In addition, Enron promised to pay Merrill Lynch a hefty fee for doing the deal. In an interview on National Public Radio on August 17, 2002, Michigan Senator Carl Levin declared, "(t)he case of the Nigerian barge transaction was, by any definition, a loan."

Required:

1. Discuss whether the Nigerian barge transaction should have been considered a loan rather than a sale. As part of your discussion, consider the following questions. Doesn't the Merrill Lynch payment to Enron at the time of the initial transaction automatically make it a sale, not a loan? What aspects of the transaction are similar to a loan? Which aspects suggest revenue has not been earned by Enron?

2. The income statement effect of recording the transaction as a sale rather than a loan is fairly clear: Enron was able to boost its revenues and net income. What is somewhat less obvious, but nearly as important, are the effects on the statement of cash flows. Describe how including the transaction with sales of other Enron products, rather than as a loan, would change the statement of cash flows.

3. How would the difference in the statement of cash flows (described in your response to requirement 2) affect financial statement users?

S12-3 Ethical Decision Making: A Mini-Case

LO1

Assume you serve on the board of a local golf and country club. In preparation for renegotiating the club's bank loans, the president indicates that the club needs to increase its operating cash flows before the end of the current year. With a wink and sly smile, the club's treasurer reassures the president and other board members that he knows a couple of ways to boost the club's operating cash flows. First, he says, the club can sell some of its accounts receivable to a collections company that is willing to pay the club $97,000 up front for the right to collect $100,000 of the overdue accounts. That will immediately boost operating cash flows. Second, he indicates that the club paid about $200,000 last month to relocate the 18th fairway and green closer to the clubhouse. The treasurer indicates that although these costs have been reported as expenses in the club's own monthly financial statements, he feels an argument can be made for reporting them as part of land and land improvements (a long-lived asset) in the year-end financial statements that would be provided to the bank. He explains that, by recording these payments as an addition to a long-lived asset, they will not be shown as a reduction in operating cash flows.

Required:

1. Does the sale of accounts receivable to generate immediate cash harm or mislead anyone? Would you consider it an ethical business activity?

2. What category in the statement of cash flows is used when reporting cash spent on long-lived assets, such as land improvements? What category is used when cash is spent on expenses, such as costs for regular upkeep of the grounds?

3. What facts are relevant to deciding whether the costs of the 18th hole relocation should be reported as an asset or as an expense? Is it appropriate to make this decision based on the impact it could have on operating cash flows?

4. As a member of the board, how would you ensure that an ethical decision is made?

S12-4 Critical Thinking: Interpreting Adjustments Reported on the Statement of Cash Flows from a Management Perspective (Indirect Method)

LO2

QuickServe, a chain of convenience stores, was experiencing some serious cash flow difficulties because of rapid growth. The company did not generate sufficient cash from operating activities to finance its new stores, and creditors were not willing to lend money because the company had not produced any income for the previous three years. The new controller for QuickServe proposed a reduction in the estimated life of store equipment to increase depreciation expense; thus, "we can improve cash flows from operating activities because depreciation expense is added back on the statement of cash flows." Other executives were not sure that this was a good idea because the increase in depreciation would make it more difficult to report positive earnings: "Without income, the bank will never lend us money."

Required:

What action would you recommend for QuickServe? Why?

LO2   **S12-5 Using a Spreadsheet That Calculates Cash Flows from Operating Activities (Indirect Method)**

You've recently been hired by B2B Consultants to provide financial advisory services to small business managers. B2B's clients often need advice on how to improve their operating cash flows and, given your accounting background, you're frequently called upon to show them how operating cash flows would change if they were to speed up their sales of inventory and their collections of accounts receivable or delay their payment of accounts payable. Each time you're asked to show the effects of these business decisions on the cash flows from operating activities, you get the uneasy feeling that you might inadvertently miscalculate their effects. To deal with this once and for all, you e-mail your friend Owen and ask him to prepare a template that automatically calculates the net operating cash flows from a simple comparative balance sheet. You received his reply today.

From:	Owentheaccountant@yahoo.com
To:	Helpme@hotmail.com
Cc:	
Subject:	Excel Help

Hey pal. I like your idea of working smarter, not harder. Too bad it involved me doing the thinking. Anyhow, I've created a spreadsheet file that contains four worksheets. The first two tabs (labeled BS and IS) are the input sheets where you would enter the numbers from each client's comparative balance sheet and income statement. Your clients are small, so this template allows for only the usual accounts. Also, I've assumed that depreciation is the only reason for a change in accumulated depreciation. If your clients' business activities differ from these, you'll need to contact me for more complex templates. The third worksheet calculates the operating cash flows using the indirect method and the fourth does this calculation using the direct method. I'll attach the screenshots of each of the worksheets so you can create your own. To answer "what if" questions, all you'll need to do is change selected amounts in the balance sheet and income statement.

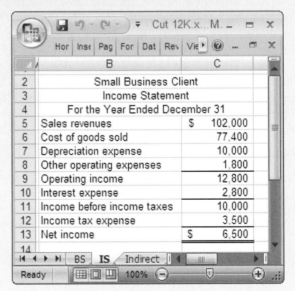

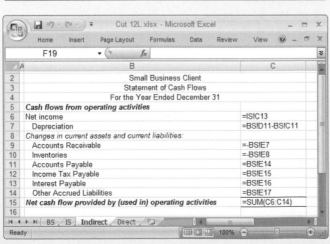

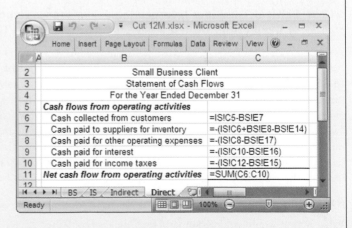

Required:

Copy the account balances from the worksheets for the balance sheet and income statement into a spreadsheet file. Enter formulas into the balance sheet worksheet to compute the change in each account balance, and then enter the formulas for the statement of cash flows (indirect method only) into a third worksheet. From this third worksheet, report the net cash flow from operating activities.

S12-6 Using a Spreadsheet That Calculates Cash Flows from Operating Activities (Direct Method)   LO6

Refer to the information presented in S12-5.

Required:

Complete the same requirement in S12-5 using the direct method.

S12-7 Using a Spreadsheet to Answer "What If" Management Decisions (Indirect or Direct Method)   LO5

Change the amounts for selected balance sheet accounts in the spreadsheets created for either S12-5 or S12-6 to calculate the net cash flows from operating activities if, just before the current year-end, the company's management took the actions listed in the following requirements. Consider each question independently, unless indicated otherwise.

Required:

1. What if the company collected $10,000 of the accounts receivable?
2. What if the company had paid down its interest payable by an extra $2,000?
3. What if the company waited an additional month before paying $6,000 of its accounts payable?
4. What if the company had reported $5,000 more depreciation expense?
5. What if all four of the above events had taken place at the same time?

CHAPTER 13

Measuring and Evaluating Financial Performance

YOUR LEARNING OBJECTIVES

After completing this chapter, you should be able to:

LO1   Describe the purposes and uses of horizontal, vertical, and ratio analyses.

LO2   Use horizontal (trend) analyses to recognize financial changes that unfold over time.

LO3   Use vertical (common size) analyses to understand important relationships within financial statements.

LO4   Calculate financial ratios to assess profitability, liquidity, and solvency.

LO5   Interpret the results of financial analyses.

Lecture Presentation-LP13
www.mhhe.com/whitecotton1e

FOCUS COMPANY: Lowe's

www.lowes.com

Measuring and evaluating financial performance is like judging gymnastics or figure skating at the Olympics. You have to know three things: (1) the general categories to evaluate for each event, (2) the particular elements to consider within each category, and (3) how to measure performance for each element. On the financial side, analysts follow the same process. They evaluate general categories such as profitability, liquidity, and solvency, which are separated into particular elements such as gross profit margin and net profit margin. For each of these elements, analysts measure performance by computing various percentages and ratios, which themselves are based on information reported in the financial statements.

In this chapter, we focus on Lowe's, the second largest home improvement retailer in the world. Lowe's is a giant with nearly 1,650 stores and 230,000 employees. Yet the company's continued success still requires innovations to increase sales in existing markets and to successfully enter new markets. At the same time, Lowe's must control costs while maintaining a high level of customer service in their stores. Finally, Lowe's management must anticipate the actions of its larger rival, The Home Depot, and deal with changes in overall demand for building products over which it has no control.

How do analysts, investors, and creditors assess Lowe's success in meeting these challenges? This is the purpose of financial statement analysis. Our discussion begins with an explanation of how to analyze financial statements to understand the financial results of a company's business activities. We conclude the chapter with a review of the key accounting decisions analysts consider when evaluating financial statements.

Horizontal, vertical, and ratio analyses
• Horizontal (trend) computations
• Vertical (common size) computations
• Ratio computations

Interpreting the results
• Interpreting horizontal and vertical analyses
• Interpreting ratio analyses

Horizontal, Vertical, and Ratio Analyses

Learning Objective 1
Describe the purposes and uses of horizontal, vertical, and ratio analyses.

As you first learned in Chapter 1, the goal of accounting is to provide information that allows decision makers to understand and evaluate the results of business decisions. Creditors use financial statements to assess compliance with loan covenants. Managers analyze financial statements to evaluate past financial performance and make future decisions. And, of course, analysts use financial statements to generate advice for investors and others. You have learned that no single number fully captures the results of all business activities nor does it predict a company's success or failure. Instead, to understand and evaluate the results of business activities, you need to look at a business from many different angles. An understanding of whether a business is successful will emerge only after you have learned to combine all of your evaluations into a complete picture or story that depicts the company's performance. Our goal for this chapter is to demonstrate how you can do this, relying on horizontal, vertical, and ratio analyses to develop the "story" of how well a company has performed.

Most good stories have a plot, which the reader comes to understand as it unfolds over time or as one event relates to another. This is the same way that financial analyses work. **Horizontal (trend) analyses are conducted to help financial statement users recognize important financial changes that unfold over time.** Horizontal analyses compare individual financial statement line items horizontally (from one period to the next), with the general goal of identifying significant sustained changes (trends). These changes are typically described in terms of dollar amounts and year-over-year percentages. For example, trend analyses could be used to determine the dollar amount and percentage by which Cost of Goods Sold increased this year, relative to prior years. **Vertical analyses focus on important relationships between items on the same financial statement.** These items are compared vertically (one account balance versus another) and are typically expressed as percentages to reveal the relative contributions made by each financial statement item. For example, vertical analyses could show that operating expenses consume one quarter of a company's net sales revenue. **Ratio analyses are conducted to understand relationships among various items reported in one or more of the financial statements.** Ratio analyses allow you to evaluate how well a company has performed given the level of other company resources. For example, while vertical analyses can show that Cost of Goods Sold consumes 65 percent of Net Sales and horizontal analyses can show that this percentage has increased over time, ratio analyses can relate these amounts to inventory levels to evaluate inventory management decisions.

Before we show you how to calculate horizontal, vertical, and ratio analyses (in the next section), we must emphasize that **no analysis is complete unless it leads to an interpretation that helps financial statement users understand and evaluate a company's financial results.** Without interpretation, these computations can appear as nothing more than a list of disconnected numbers.

HORIZONTAL (TREND) COMPUTATIONS

Learning Objective 2
Use horizontal (trend) analyses to recognize financial changes that unfold over time.

Horizontal (trend) analyses helps financial statement users to recognize financial changes that unfold over time. This approach compares individual financial statement items from year to year with the general goal of identifying significant sustained changes or trends. For example, trend analysis can be used to determine the dollar and percentage changes in the cost of goods sold this year relative to prior years. Because this type of analysis compares the results on each line of the financial statements across several years, trend analysis is also known as horizontal analysis. Because it compares results over a series of periods, it is sometimes called **time-series analysis.**

Regardless of the name, trend analyses are usually calculated in terms of year-to-year dollar and percentage changes. A year-to-year percentage change expresses the current year's dollar change as a percentage of the prior year's total by using the following calculation:

COACH'S TIP

Horizontal (trend) analyses compare across time, often expressing changes in account balances as a percentage of prior year balances.

$$\text{Year-to-Year Change (\%)} = \frac{\text{Change This Year}}{\text{Prior Year's Total}} \times 100 = \frac{(\text{Current Years Total} - \text{Prior Year's Total})}{\text{Prior Year's Total}} \times 100$$

To demonstrate how to calculate a trend, we analyze Lowe's financial statements. Summaries of Lowe's balance sheets and income statements from two recent years appear in Exhibits 13.1 and 13.2. Dollar and percentage changes from fiscal year 2007 to 2008[1] are shown to the right of the balance sheet and income statement. The dollar changes were calculated by subtracting the fiscal 2007 balances from the fiscal 2008 balances. The percentage changes were calculated by dividing those differences by the fiscal 2007 balances. For example, according to Exhibit 13.1, Cash decreased by $36 ($245 − $281) in 2008 relative to 2007 (all numbers in millions). That dollar amount represented a decrease of 12.8% [($36 ÷ $281) × 100].

In a later section, we will explain and evaluate the underlying causes of significant changes in account balances. But before we leave this topic, we must note that not all large percentage changes will be significant. For example, the 67.1 percent increase in Short-Term Investments is the largest percentage change on the balance sheet (Exhibit 13.1) but the dollar amount is relatively small when compared to other changes, such as the $598 million increase in Inventories. To avoid focusing on unimportant changes, use the percentage changes to identify potentially significant changes but then check the dollar change to make sure that it too is significant.

Video 13.1
www.mhhe.com/whitecotton1e

VERTICAL (COMMON SIZE) COMPUTATIONS

Learning Objective 3
Use vertical (common size) analyses to understand important relationships within financial statements.

A second type of analysis, **vertical (common size) analysis,** focuses on important relationships within financial statements. When a company is growing or shrinking overall, it is difficult to tell from the dollar amounts whether the proportions within each statement category are changing. Common size financial statements provide this information by expressing each financial statement amount as a percentage of another amount on that statement. The usefulness of common size statements is illustrated by the fact that Lowe's presents its balance sheet and income statements in the common size format illustrated in Exhibits 13.3 and 13.4.

In a common size balance sheet, each asset appears as a percent of total assets, and each liability or stockholders' equity item appears as a percent of total liabilities and stockholders' equity. For example, in Exhibit 13.3, which presents Lowe's common size balance sheets, cash was 0.7 percent of total assets [($245 ÷ $32,686) × 100] at the end of fiscal 2008.

COACH'S TIP

Vertical (common size) analyses express each financial statement amount as a percentage of another amount on the same financial statement.

---

[1]Like many retail companies, Lowe's fiscal year ends at the end of January.

EXHIBIT 13.1	Horizontal (Trend) Analysis of Lowe's Summarized Balance Sheets	Lowe's

LOWE'S
Balance Sheets
(in millions)

			Increase (Decrease)	
Year Ended:	January 30, 2009 (Fiscal 2008)	February 1, 2008 (Fiscal 2007)	Amount	Percent*
Assets				
Current Assets				
Cash	$ 245	$ 281	$ (36)	(12.8)%
Short-Term Investments	416	249	167	67.1
Accounts Receivable	—	—	—	0.0
Inventories	8,209	7,611	598	7.9
Other Current Assets	381	545	(164)	(30.1)
Total Current Assets	9,251	8,686	565	6.5
Property and Equipment, Net	22,722	21,361	1,361	6.4
Other Assets	713	822	(109)	(13.3)
Total Assets	$32,686	$30,869	$1,817	5.9
Liabilities and Stockholders' Equity				
Current Liabilities	$ 8,022	$ 7,751	$ 271	3.5
Long-Term Liabilities	6,609	7,020	(411)	(5.9)
Total Liabilities	14,631	14,771	(140)	(0.9)
Stockholders' Equity	18,055	16,098	1,957	12.2
Total Liabilities and Stockholders' Equity	$32,686	$30,869	$1,817	5.9

*Amount of Increase (Decrease) ÷ Fiscal 2007 × 100

EXHIBIT 13.2	Horizontal (Trend) Analysis of Lowe's Summarized Income Statements	Lowe's

LOWE'S
Income Statements
(in millions)

			Increase (Decrease)	
Year Ended:	January 30, 2009 (Fiscal 2008)	February 1, 2008 (Fiscal 2007)	Amount	Percent*
Net Sales Revenue	$48,230	$48,283	$ (53)	(0.1)%
Cost of Sales	31,729	31,556	173	0.5
Gross Profit	16,501	16,727	(226)	(1.4)
Operating and Other Expenses	12,715	12,022	693	5.8
Interest Expense	280	194	86	44.3
Income Tax Expense	1,311	1,702	(391)	(23.0)
Net Income	$ 2,195	$ 2,809	$ (614)	(21.9)
Earnings per Share	$1.51	$1.90	$(0.39)	(20.5)

*Amount of Increase (Decrease) ÷ Fiscal 2007 × 100

EXHIBIT 13.3 | Vertical (Common Size) Analysis of Lowe's Summarized Balance Sheets | Lowe's

LOWE'S
Balance Sheets
(in millions)

	Fiscal 2008 Amount	Percent	Fiscal 2007 Amount	Percent
Assets				
Current Assets				
Cash	$ 245	0.7%	$ 281	0.9%
Short-Term Investments	416	1.3	249	0.8
Inventories	8,209	25.1	7,611	24.6
Other Current Assets	381	1.2	545	1.8
Property and Equipment, Net	22,722	69.5	21,361	69.2
Other Assets	713	2.2	822	2.7
Total Assets	$32,686	100.0%	$30,869	100.0%
Liabilities and Stockholders' Equity				
Current Liabilities	$ 8,022	24.5%	$ 7,751	25.1%
Long-Term Liabilities	6,609	20.3	7,020	22.8
Stockholders' Equity	18,055	55.2	16,098	52.1
Total Liabilities and Stockholders' Equity	$32,686	100.0%	$30,869	100.0%

EXHIBIT 13.4 | Vertical (Common Size) Analysis of Lowe's Summarized Income Statements | Lowe's

LOWE'S
Income Statements
(in millions)

	Fiscal 2008 Amount	Percent	Fiscal 2007 Amount	Percent
Net Sales Revenue	$48,230	100.0%	$48,283	100.0%
Cost of Sales	31,729	65.8	31,556	65.4
Gross Profit	16,501	34.2	16,727	34.6
Operating and Other Expenses	12,715	26.3	12,022	24.9
Interest Expense	280	0.6	194	0.4
Income Tax Expense	1,311	2.7	1,702	3.5
Net Income	$ 2,195	4.6%	$ 2,809	5.8%

The common size income statement reports each income statement item as a percentage of sales. For example, cost of sales was equal to 65.8 percent of net sales revenue in 2008 [($31,729 ÷ $48,230) × 100]. Exhibit 13.4 presents common size income statements for Lowe's for fiscal 2007 and 2008.

RATIO COMPUTATIONS

Ratio analyses help financial statement users to understand relationships among various items reported in the financial statements. This type of analysis compares the amounts for one or more line items to the amounts for other line items in the same year.

Learning Objective 4
Calculate financial ratios to assess profitability, liquidity, and solvency.

Ratio analyses are useful because they consider differences in the size of the amounts being compared, similar to common size statements. In fact, some of the most popular ratios, such as net profit margin and debt to assets ratios, are taken from the common size statements. Ratios allow users to evaluate how well a company has performed given the level of its other resources.

Most analysts classify ratios into three categories:

1. **Profitability** ratios, which relate to the company's performance in the current period—in particular, the company's ability to generate income.
2. **Liquidity** ratios, which relate to the company's short-term survival—in particular, the company's ability to use current assets to repay liabilities as they become due.
3. **Solvency** ratios, which relate to the company's long-run survival—in particular, the company's ability to repay lenders when debt matures and to make the required interest payments prior to the date of maturity.

Exhibit 13.5 organizes several commonly used ratios according to these three categories, and demonstrates their calculations for fiscal 2008 using data from Exhibits 13.1 and 13.2.

COACH'S TIP

Profitability is the extent to which a company generates income. **Liquidity** is the extent to which a company is able to pay its currently maturing obligations. **Solvency** is the ability to survive long enough to repay lenders when debt matures.

 Self-Study Practice

For the year ended February 1, 2009, The Home Depot reported net income of $2.2 billion on sales of $71.3 billion. If the company's cost of sales that year was $47.3 billion, what was the company's gross profit percentage and net profit margin? If sales were $77.3 billion in the prior year, what was the year-over-year percentage decrease in the most recent year?

$$\text{Gross Profit Percentage} = \frac{(\$\quad - \$\quad)\text{ billion}}{\$71.3\text{ billion}} \times 100 =$$

$$\text{Net Profit Margin} = \frac{\$2.2\text{ billion}}{\quad} \times 100 =$$

$$\text{Sales Decrease (Percentage)} = \frac{(\$\quad - \quad)\text{ billion}}{\$\quad\text{ billion}} \times 100 =$$

After you have finished, check your answers with the solutions in the margin.

Solution to Self-Study Practice

Gross Profit Percentage = ($71.3 − $47.3)/$71.3 × 100
= 33.7%

Net Profit Margin = $2.2 / $71.3 × 100 = 3.1%

Sales Decrease (Percentage) = ($71.3 − $77.3)/$77.3 × 100
= 7.8%

Interpreting the Results

INTERPRETING HORIZONTAL AND VERTICAL ANALYSES

Learning Objective 5
Interpret the results of financial analyses.

As noted in the previous section, financial statement analyses are meaningless unless they help users understand and evaluate a company's financial results. When interpreting analyses, your goals should be to understand what each analysis is telling you and then combine your findings into a coherent "story" that explains the results of the company's business activities. We demonstrate how to do this, beginning with interpretations of each set of analyses shown in Exhibits 13.1–13.5 and later concluding with an overall summary of Lowe's results.

Trends Revealed in Horizontal Analyses

Horizontal (trend) analysis of Lowe's balance sheet in Exhibit 13.1 shows that the company grew in fiscal 2008. Overall, total assets increased approximately 5.9 percent. Lowe's explains the major driver of this increase in its Management's Discussion and

EXHIBIT 13.5	Common Ratios Used in Financial Statement Analysis

Profitability Ratios

	Fiscal 2008
(1) Net Profit Margin $= \dfrac{\text{Net Income}}{\text{Net Sales Revenue}} \times 100$	$\dfrac{\$2,195}{\$48,230} \times 100 = 4.6\%$
(2) Gross Profit Percentage $= \dfrac{\text{Net Sales Revenue} - \text{Cost of Goods Sold}}{\text{Net Sales Revenue}} \times 100$	$\dfrac{\$16,501}{\$48,230} \times 100 = 34.2\%$
(3) Asset Turnover $= \dfrac{\text{Net Sales Revenue}}{\text{Average Total Assets}}$	$\dfrac{\$48,230}{(\$32,686 + \$30,869)/2} = 1.52$
(4) Fixed Asset Turnover $= \dfrac{\text{Net Sales Revenue}}{\text{Average Net Fixed Assets}}$	$\dfrac{\$48,230}{(\$22,722 + \$21,361)/2} = 2.19$
(5) Return on Equity (ROE) $= \dfrac{\text{Net Income}}{\text{Average Stockholders' Equity}} \times 100$	$\dfrac{\$2,195}{(\$18,055 + \$16,098)/2} \times 100 = 12.9\%$
(6) Earnings per Share (EPS) $= \dfrac{\text{Net Income*}}{\text{Average Number of Common Shares Outstanding}}$	$\dfrac{\$2,195}{1,454} = \$1.51$
(7) Quality of Income $= \dfrac{\text{Net Cash from Operations}}{\text{Net Income}}$	$\dfrac{\$4,122}{\$2,195} = 1.88$
(8) Price/Earnings $= \dfrac{\text{Stock Price}}{\text{EPS}}$	$\dfrac{\$18.25}{\$1.51} = 12.1$

Liquidity Ratios

	Fiscal 2008
(9) Receivables Turnover $= \dfrac{\text{Net Sales Revenue}}{\text{Average Net Receivables}}$	n/a
Days to Collect $= \dfrac{365}{\text{Receivables Turnover Ratio}}$	n/a
(10) Inventory Turnover $= \dfrac{\text{Cost of Goods Sold}}{\text{Average Inventory}}$	$\dfrac{\$31,729}{(\$8,209 + \$7,611)/2} = 4.0$
Days to Sell $= \dfrac{365}{\text{Inventory Turnover Ratio}}$	$\dfrac{365}{4.0} = 91.3$
(11) Current Ratio $= \dfrac{\text{Current Assets}}{\text{Current Liabilities}}$	$\dfrac{\$9,251}{\$8,022} = 1.15$
(12) Quick Ratio $= \dfrac{\text{Cash} + \text{Short-Term Investments} + \text{Accounts Receivable, Net}}{\text{Current Liabilities}}$	$\dfrac{\$245 + \$416 + \$0}{\$8,022} = 0.08$

Solvency Ratios

	Fiscal 2008
(13) Debt to Assets $= \dfrac{\text{Total Liabilities}}{\text{Total Assets}}$	$\dfrac{\$14,631}{\$32,686} = 0.45$
(14) Times Interest Earned $= \dfrac{\text{Net Income} + \text{Interest Expense} + \text{Income Tax Expense}}{\text{Interest Expense}}$	$\dfrac{\$2,195 + \$280 + \$1,311}{\$280} = 13.5$
(15) Capital Acquisitions $= \dfrac{\text{Net Cash from Operations}}{\text{Cash Paid for PPE}}$	$\dfrac{\$4,122}{\$3,266} = 1.26$

*If a company has preferred stock outstanding, preferred dividends are subtracted from net income in the numerator to assess the earnings for each share of common stock.

Analysis (MD&A) section of the 2008 annual report. In fiscal 2008, Lowe's opened 60 new stores, resulting in significant increases in Inventories (7.9 percent) and Property and Equipment (6.4 percent). To finance this expansion, Lowe's relied on equity rather than debt (Stockholders' Equity increased 12.2 percent while Total Liabilities decreased 0.9 percent).

Horizontal analysis of Lowe's income statement in Exhibit 13.2 indicates that the company faced a challenging economic environment in fiscal 2008. Despite the increase in the number of stores, Net Sales Revenue fell slightly (0.1 percent). Lowe's MD&A explains that the company was forced to cut prices in 2008 to sell its seasonal inventory. Making matters worse, according to the MD&A Lowe's experienced higher fuel costs, which contributed to an increase in its Cost of Sales (0.5 percent). The lower selling prices and higher cost of sales combined to decrease Gross Profit by 1.4 percent. Operating Expenses rose by 5.8 percent, largely as a result of having added the 60 new stores. The overall impact on Lowe's was a reduction in Net Income of $614 million (21.9 percent).

In summary, the story revealed by the trend analysis is that despite its asset growth in 2008, Lowe's was unable to increase profits. The weak economy led the company to cut selling prices and incur greater costs (for goods and operations).

Relationships Noted in Vertical Analyses

Vertical (common size) analysis of Lowe's balance sheet in Exhibit 13.3 highlights key elements of the company. Its most significant assets have always been Inventories and Property and Equipment, but with the additional store openings in 2008, these assets now represent 25.1 and 69.5 percent of Lowe's total assets. As noted in the horizontal analysis, the company's financing strategy shifted somewhat in 2008 from debt to equity. Compared to fiscal 2007, when debt and equity financing were nearly equally balanced (52.1 percent equity), Lowe's has shifted its financing more to equity in fiscal 2008 (55.2 percent).

Vertical analysis of Lowe's income statement in Exhibit 13.4 indicates that Cost of Sales and Operating Expenses are the most important determinants of the company's profitability. Cost of Sales consumed 65.8 percent of Sales in 2008 and Operating Expenses consumed an additional 26.3 percent. Much of the reduction in the company's Net Income (from 5.8 percent of Sales in 2007 to 4.6 in 2008) is explained by these two categories of expenses, as suggested by the horizontal analyses.

These findings from the vertical analyses serve to underscore findings from the horizontal analyses. The emerging story is that Lowe's success depends on its ability to use significant investments in Inventory and Property and Equipment to generate sales. Its expansion efforts in 2008 were not successful because a weak economy hampered sales, higher fuel costs cut into gross profit, and its larger labor force led to rising operating expenses, all of which combined to shrink Lowe's net income.

INTERPRETING RATIO ANALYSES

As shown throughout other chapters in this book, benchmarks help when interpreting a company's ratios. These benchmarks can include the company's prior year results, as well as the results of close competitors or the average for the industry. In a competitive economy, companies strive to outperform one another, so comparisons against other companies can provide clues about who is likely to survive and thrive in the long run. In the following analyses, we compare Lowe's financial ratios to the prior year and in some cases to those for The Home Depot and the home improvement industry as a whole.

Profitability Ratios

The analyses in this section focus on the level of profits the company generated during the period. We will analyze ratios (1) through (8) from Exhibit 13.5. The first two profitability ratios come right from the common size income statement in Exhibit 13.4.

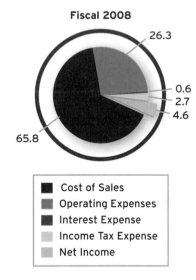

Fiscal 2008

26.3
0.6
2.7
4.6
65.8

■ Cost of Sales
■ Operating Expenses
■ Interest Expense
□ Income Tax Expense
▨ Net Income

COACH'S TIP

Industry averages are reported in the *Annual Statement Studies,* which are published by the Risk Management Association. You can obtain industry averages also from reuters.com/finance or google.com/finance, which were available free of charge at the time this book was written.

(1) Net Profit Margin Net profit margin represents the percentage of sales revenues that ultimately make it into net income, after deducting expenses. Using the equation in Exhibit 13.5, the calculation of Lowe's net profit margins for each of the last two years yields:

Fiscal Year:	2008	2007
Net profit margin $= \dfrac{\text{Net Income}}{\text{Net Sales Revenue}} \times 100$	4.6%	5.8%

As discussed in the previous sections, Lowe's faced a challenging economic environment in 2008. Weak sales and higher product costs and operating expenses hampered the company's attempts to generate net income through store expansion. Lowe's declining net profit margin from 5.8 percent in 2007 to 4.6 percent in 2008 is a downer because, when considered in light of over $48 billion in sales, this drop of 1.2 percent (4.6 − 5.8) equates to a profit decline of about $576 million.

(2) Gross Profit Percentage Our earlier analysis indicated that Lowe's gross profit from 2007 to 2008 decreased in terms of total dollars, but it did not indicate whether that decrease was caused by less total sales or less profit per sale. The gross profit percentage is particularly helpful in this kind of analysis because it indicates how much profit was made, on average, on each dollar of sales after deducting the cost of goods sold. Lowe's gross profit percentage for the last two years was:

Fiscal Year:	2008	2007
Gross Profit Percentage $= \dfrac{\text{Net Sales} - \text{Cost of Goods Sold}}{\text{Net Sales}} \times 100 =$	34.2%	34.6%

This analysis shows that in 2008, after deducting the cost of merchandise sold, 34.2 cents of each sales dollar were left to cover other costs, such as employee wages, advertising, and utilities and to provide profits to the stockholders. The decrease in the gross profit percentage from 2007 to 2008 (34.2% − 34.6%) means that Lowe's made 0.4¢ less gross profit on each dollar of sales in 2008 than in 2007. There are two potential explanations for this decrease: (1) Lowe's charged lower selling prices without experiencing a corresponding decrease in the cost of merchandise and (2) Lowe's obtained merchandise at a higher unit cost. The MD&A section of Lowe's annual report explains that the decrease in gross profit percentage came from both a cut in selling prices and an increase in product costs (primarily higher freight-in).

(3) Asset Turnover The asset turnover ratio indicates the amount of sales revenue generated for each dollar invested in assets during the period. Lowe's ratios for the two years were:

	2008	2007
Asset Turnover $= \dfrac{\text{Net Sales Revenue}}{\text{Average Total Assets}} =$	1.52	1.65

The asset turnover ratio suggests that Lowe's assets did not generate sales as efficiently in 2008 as in the prior year. To understand why, it is helpful to focus on the key assets used to generate sales. For a retailer such as Lowe's, the key asset is store properties, which we can compare to sales using the fixed asset turnover ratio, discussed next.

(4) Fixed Asset Turnover   The fixed asset turnover ratio indicates how much revenue the company generates in sales for each dollar invested in fixed assets, such as store buildings and the property they sit on. Lowe's fixed asset turnover ratios for the two years were:

	2008	2007
$\text{Fixed Asset Turnover} = \dfrac{\text{Net Sales Revenue}}{\text{Average Net Fixed Assets}} =$	2.19	2.39

This analysis shows that Lowe's had $2.19 of sales in 2008 for each dollar invested in fixed assets. Although the decline from 2007 was not good, it is understandable because 2008 was a difficult year for retailers, as consumers struggled to keep their jobs and pay their mortgages, let alone work on major home improvement projects. Lowe's 2008 fixed asset turnover also suffered because the company added stores during the year. Those stores will likely need some time to establish a strong customer base and begin generating sales at full capacity. Moreover, as additional stores are opened, they are likely to be located in areas of greater competition. Still, Lowe's fixed asset turnover ratio is low compared to that of its main competitor, The Home Depot, whose fixed asset turnover ratio was 2.65 in 2008. In terms of using fixed assets to generate sales revenue, The Home Depot has a competitive advantage over Lowe's. In other words, Lowe's is operating less efficiently than its major competitor.

(5) Return on Equity (ROE)   The return on equity ratio compares the amount of net income to average stockholders' equity. Like the interest rate on your bank account, ROE reports the net amount earned during the period as a percentage of each dollar contributed by stockholders and retained in the business. Lowe's ROE ratios for the past two years were:

	2008	2007
$\text{Return on Equity (ROE)} = \dfrac{\text{Net Income}}{\text{Average Stockholders' Equity}} \times 100 =$	12.9%	17.7%

Lowe's ROE decline from 17.7 to 12.9 percent was inevitable, given our previous analyses. Specifically, horizontal analysis indicated that the company had increased its stockholders' equity to finance store expansion. But store expansion failed to increase sales in 2008, as indicated by the asset turnover ratio, and each dollar of sales generated less profit, as indicated by the net profit margin. Taken together, these results imply that net income as a percentage of average stockholders' equity was sure to fall in 2008. And fall it did. The only good news for Lowe's is that its 12.9 percent ROE was marginally better than The Home Depot's fiscal 2008 ROE of 12.7 percent.

(6) Earnings per Share (EPS)   Earnings per share (EPS) indicates the amount of earnings generated for each share of outstanding common stock. Consistent with the decline in ROE, the EPS ratio decreased from $1.90 in 2007 to $1.51 in 2008, as shown below. This represents a decline of $0.39 per share ($1.51 − $1.90).

Fiscal Year	2008	2007
$\text{Earnings per share (EPS)} = \dfrac{\text{Net Income}}{\text{Average Number of Outstanding Common Shares}}$	$1.51	$1.90

(7) Quality of Income The quality of income ratio relates operating cash flows (from the statement of cash flows) to net income, as follows:

Fiscal Year		2008	2007
Quality of Income $= \dfrac{\text{Net Cash from Operations}}{\text{Net Income}}$		1.88	1.55

The ratio of 1.88 in 2008 indicates that Lowe's generated $1.88 of operating cash flow for every dollar of net income. Because this ratio is much greater than 1.0, it is interpreted as "high quality," meaning that operations are producing even more positive results (cash flows from operating activities) than what is suggested by the net income number. Most cash-based businesses, like home improvement stores, have high quality of income ratios because their sales are collected in cash immediately, and they report substantial noncash expenses like depreciation. Consistent with this expectation, we see a high quality of income ratio for The Home Depot (2.45) for fiscal 2008.

(8) Price/Earnings (P/E) Ratio The P/E ratio relates the company's stock price to its EPS, as follows:

Fiscal Year		2008	2007
Price/earnings ratio $= \dfrac{\text{Stock Price}}{\text{EPS}}$		12.1	12.1

Using the market price for Lowe's stock when its 2008 and 2007 earnings were announced, the P/E ratio was 12.1 in both years. This means investors were willing to pay 12.1 times earnings to buy a share of Lowe's stock. The Home Depot's P/E ratio at that time was around 18.5, suggesting that investors were less willing to buy stock in Lowe's than in The Home Depot.

Let's pause to summarize what we've learned so far. In fiscal 2008, Lowe's continued to expand by opening 60 new stores. Unfortunately for Lowe's, this expansion took place at the same time as a general economic crisis. Consumers were faced with rising interest and fuel costs and swelling unemployment rates, so they cut back on unnecessary spending such as major home improvement projects. To combat the fall in demand for its products and services, Lowe's cut prices. At the same time, Lowe's incurred higher product costs, which caused a decline in the company's gross profit. Adding to these problems, Lowe's operating expenses grew in 2008 as a result of the store expansion program. The company's net income fell by 21.9 percent, or $0.39 per share. Investors seemed to anticipate these results because they were just as willing to buy Lowe's stock in 2008 as they were in 2007 (at a price of 12.1 times earnings in each year). The bottom line is that Lowe's fared reasonably well during the 2008 economic crisis, although the company trails its main competitor, The Home Depot, on several key ratios.

Liquidity Ratios

The analyses in this section focus on the company's ability to survive in the short term, by converting assets to cash that can be used to pay current liabilities as they come due. We interpret ratios (9) through (12) from Exhibit 13.5.

(9) Receivables Turnover Most home improvement retailers have low levels of accounts receivable relative to sales revenue because they collect the majority of their sales immediately in cash. Although the formula calls for net **credit** sales in the top of the ratio, companies rarely report their credit sales and cash sales separately. Consequently, financial statement users must use total net sales revenue in the formula, which results in a receivables turnover ratio that is not terribly meaningful for businesses that make few sales on account. The formula is presented in Exhibit 13.5 simply to remind you of how it's calculated.

(10) Inventory Turnover

The inventory turnover ratio indicates how frequently inventory is bought and sold during the year. The measure "days to sell" converts the inventory turnover ratio into the average number of days needed to sell each purchase of inventory.

Fiscal Year		2008	2007
Inventory Turnover $= \dfrac{\text{Cost of Goods Sold}}{\text{Average Inventory}}$		4.0	4.3
Days to Sell $= \dfrac{365}{\text{Inventory Turnover Ratio}}$		91.3	85.3

Consistent with the weaker economy in 2008, Lowe's inventory turned over less frequently. On average, its inventory took an additional 6.0 days to sell (91.3 − 85.3). These results are troubling because almost every retailer's success depends on its ability to offer customers the right product when they need it at a price that beats the competition. Although most retailers experienced a decline in inventory turnover in 2008, Lowe's decline was disappointing because it prevented the company from catching up to The Home Depot (where inventory takes an average of 87 days to sell). The Home Depot enjoys a faster inventory turnover because it carries fewer big-ticket items than Lowe's. According to their 2008 annual reports, the average ticket price was $65.15 at Lowe's and $55.61 at The Home Depot.

Turnover ratios vary significantly from one industry to the next. Companies in the food industry (restaurants and grocery stores) have high inventory turnover ratios because their inventory is subject to spoilage. Companies that sell expensive merchandise (automobiles and high-fashion clothes) have much slower turnover because sales of those items are infrequent, but these companies must carry lots of inventory so that customers have a wide selection to choose from when they do buy.

(11) Current Ratio

The current ratio compares current assets to current liabilities, as follows:

Fiscal Year		2008	2007
Current Ratio $= \dfrac{\text{Current Assets}}{\text{Current Liabilities}}$		1.15	1.12

The current ratio measures the company's ability to pay its current liabilities. Lowe's ratio increased slightly from 2007 to 2008, ending the year with a ratio of 1.15. In this industry, a current ratio greater than 1.0 is deemed acceptable. Most analysts would judge Lowe's ratio to be very strong, especially considering the company's ability to generate cash.

(12) Quick Ratio

The quick ratio compares the sum of cash, short-term investments, and accounts receivable to current liabilities as follows:

Fiscal Year		2008	2007
Quick Ratio $= \dfrac{\text{Cash} + \text{Short-Term Investments} + \text{Accounts Receivable, Net}}{\text{Current Liabilities}}$		0.08	0.07

The quick ratio is a much more stringent test of short-term liquidity than is the current ratio. Lowe's quick ratio increased slightly in 2008, just as its current ratio did. The low quick ratio shown here is typical for industries where most customers buy with cash or credit card. These forms of payment result in very low levels of accounts receivable and the cash received from sales is often used immediately in other business activities. In industries where credit sales are common, the quick ratio may be much higher. For example, the average quick ratio in 2008 for the homebuilding industry was 0.66.

Solvency Ratios

The analyses in this section focus on Lowe's ability to survive over the long term—that is, its ability to repay debt when it matures, pay interest until that time, and finance the replacement and/or expansion of long-term assets. We interpret ratios (13) through (15) from Exhibit 13.5.

(13) Debt to Assets   The debt-to-assets ratio indicates the proportion of total assets that creditors finance. Remember that creditors must be paid regardless of how difficult a year the company may have had. The higher this ratio, the riskier is the company's financing strategy. Lowe's ratio for the two years was:

		2008	2007
$\text{Debt to Assets} = \dfrac{\text{Total Liabilities}}{\text{Total Assets}} =$		0.45	0.48

COACH'S TIP

Instead of the debt-to-assets ratio, analysts might use a debt-to-equity ratio, which gives the same basic information as debt-to-assets. Debt-to-equity typically is calculated as total liabilities ÷ total stockholders' equity. As with debt-to-assets, the higher the debt-to-equity ratio, the more the company relies on debt (rather than equity) financing.

Lowe's ratio of 0.45 in 2008 indicates that creditors contributed 45 percent of the company's financing, implying that stockholders' equity was the company's main source of financing at 55 percent (100 percent − 45 percent). The debt-to-assets ratio decreased slightly from 2007 to 2008, suggesting that Lowe's relies less on creditors and more on stockholders when financing its acquisition of assets. The Home Depot, which had a debt-to-assets ratio of 57 percent in 2008, relies much more on debt financing.

(14) Times Interest Earned   The times interest earned ratio indicates how many times the company's interest expense was covered by its net operating income. This ratio is calculated using accrual-based interest expense and net income before interest and income taxes, as follows:

		2008	2007
$\text{Times Interest Earned} = \dfrac{\text{Net Income} + \text{Interest Expense} + \text{Income Tax Expense}}{\text{Interest Expense}} =$		13.5	24.3

COACH'S TIP

If the company reports a net loss, rather than net income, include the loss as a negative number in the formula. A negative ratio indicates that the operating results (before the costs of financing and taxes) are insufficient to cover the interest costs.

A times interest earned ratio above 1.0 indicates that net operating income (before the costs of financing and taxes) is sufficient to cover the company's interest expense. Lowe's ratio of 13.5 indicates the company is generating more than enough profit to cover its interest expense.

(15) Capital Acquisitions Ratio   The capital acquisitions ratio compares cash flows from operations with cash paid for property and equipment. The ratio for the two recent years follows:

Fiscal Year		2008	2007
$\text{Capital Acquisitions} = \dfrac{\text{Net Cash from Operations}}{\text{Cash Paid for PPE}}$		1.26	1.08

The 1.26 capital acquisitions ratio in 2008 indicates that Lowe's was able to pay for all its store expansion using cash generated from operating activities.

In sum, these solvency ratios suggest that Lowe's is financially well-positioned, even though the economy has sputtered. In fiscal 2008, the company reduced its reliance on debt and was able to comfortably cover the interest expense incurred on that debt. Further, the company was able to expand without taking on more debt because its cash flow from operating activities exceeded the cost of its new property and equipment.

 ## Self-Study Practice

Show the computations for the following two ratios for Lowe's for fiscal 2007. Use the information in Exhibits 13.1 and 13.2.

a. Times interest earned ratio
b. Current ratio

After you have finished, check your answers with the solutions in the margin.

Solution to Self-Study Practice
a. ($2,809 + $194 + $1,702)/$194 = 24.3
b. $8,686 ÷ $7,751 = 1.12

DEMONSTRATION CASE

The following information was taken from The Home Depot's fiscal 2006 annual report.

(in millions of dollars)	Year ended January 28, 2007 (Fiscal 2006)	
Net Sales Revenue	$90,837	
Cost of Goods Sold	61,054	
Net Income	5,761	
	January 28, 2007 (Fiscal 2006)	January 29, 2006 (Fiscal 2005)
Inventory	$12,822	$11,401
Current Assets	18,000	15,269
Property and Equipment, Net	26,605	24,901
Total Assets	52,263	44,405
Current Liabilities	12,931	12,706
Total Liabilities	27,233	17,496

Required:

1. Compute the following ratios for The Home Depot for the year ended January 28, 2007.

   Fixed Asset Turnover
   Return on Equity
   Days to Sell
   Current Ratio
   Debt to Assets

2. Interpret the meaning of the ratios you calculated in requirement 1.

See page 507 for solution.

CHAPTER SUMMARY

LO1   Describe the purposes and uses of horizontal, vertical, and ratio analyses. p. 494

- Horizontal analyses (also called trend analyses) compare financial statement items to comparable amounts in prior periods with the goal of identifying sustained changes, or trends.

- Vertical analyses create common size financial statements that express each line of the income statement (or balance sheet) as a percentage of total sales (or total assets).

- Ratio analyses compare one or more financial statement items to an amount for other items for the same year. Ratios take into account differences in the size of amounts to allow for evaluations of performance given existing levels of other company resources.

Use horizontal (trend) analyses to recognize financial changes that unfold over time. p. 495   LO2

- Trend analysis involves computing the dollar amount by which each account changes from one period to the next and expressing that change as a percentage of the balance for the prior period.

Use vertical (common size) analyses to understand important relationships within financial statements. p. 495   LO3

- The statements tell the reader whether the proportions within each statement category are changing.

Calculate financial ratios to assess profitability, liquidity, and solvency. p. 497   LO4

- Financial ratios are commonly classified with relation to profitability, liquidity, or solvency. Exhibit 13.5 lists common ratios in these three categories and shows how to compute them.

- Profitability ratios focus on measuring the adequacy of a company's income by comparing it to other items reported on the financial statements.

- Liquidity ratios measure a company's ability to meet its current debt obligations.

- Solvency ratios measure a company's ability to meet its long-term debt obligations.

Interpret the results of financial analyses. p. 498   LO5

- Financial analyses are not complete unless they lead to an interpretation that helps financial statement users understand and evaluate a company's financial results.

- An understanding of whether a business is successful emerges only after you have learned to combine analyses into a complete picture or story that depicts the company's performance.

- To assist in developing this picture or story, most analysts compare to benchmarks such as the company's performance in prior years or to competitors' performance in the current year.

SOLUTION TO DEMONSTRATION CASE

1. Calculating ratios:

Fixed Asset Turnover	= Net Sales Revenue/Average Net Fixed Assets
	= $90,837 ÷ [($26,605 + $24,901) ÷ 2]
	= 3.53
Return on Equity	= Net Income/Average Stockholders' Equity
	= $5,761 ÷ [($25,030 + $26,909) ÷ 2]
	= 0.2218, or 22.2%
Days to Sell	= 365 ÷ Inventory Turnover Ratio
	= 365 ÷ (Cost of Goods Sold/Average Inventory)
	= 365 ÷ [$61,054 ÷ [($12,822 + $11,401) ÷ 2]]
	= 72

Current Ratio = Current Assets/Current Liabilities
= $18,000 ÷ $12,931
= 1.39

Debt to Assets = Total Liabilities/Total Assets
= $27,233 ÷ $52,263
= 0.52

2. Interpreting ratios

- The fixed asset turnover ratio of 3.53 means that on average, The Home Depot generated $3.53 of sales for each dollar of fixed assets.

- The return on equity of 22.2 percent means that The Home Depot's net income for the year was 22.2 percent of the amount investors contributed to and left in the company.

- The days to sell ratio of 72 means that on average, 72 days elapsed between the time The Home Depot acquired the inventory and the time the company sold it.

- The current ratio of 1.39 means that at year-end, The Home Depot had $1.39 of current assets for each dollar of current liabilities.

- The debt-to-assets ratio of 0.52 means that The Home Depot relied on short-term and long-term debt to finance 52 percent of its assets, implying that stockholders' equity financed 48 percent (=100 − 52) of its total assets.

KEY TERMS

Horizontal (Trend)
   Analysis p. 495

Vertical (Common Size)
   Analysis p. 495

See complete definitions in glossary at back of text.

QUESTIONS

1. What is the general goal of trend analysis?

2. How is a year-over-year percentage calculated?

3. What is ratio analysis? Why is it useful?

4. What benchmarks are commonly used for interpreting ratios?

5. Into what three categories of performance are most financial ratios reported? To what in particular do each of these categories relate?

6. Why are some analyses called *horizontal* and others called *vertical?*

7. Slow Cellar's current ratio increased from 1.2 to 1.5. What is one favorable interpretation of this change? What is one unfavorable interpretation of this change?

8. From 2009 to 2010, Colossal Company's current ratio increased and its quick ratio decreased. What does this imply about the level of inventory and prepaids?

9. From 2009 to 2010, Shamwow reported that its Net Sales increased from $300,000 to $400,000, and its Gross Profit increased from $90,000 to $130,000. Was the Gross Profit increase caused by (a) an increase in sales volume only, (b) an increase in gross profit per sale only, or (c) a combination of both? Explain your answer.

10. Explain whether the following situations, taken independently, would be favorable or unfavorable: (a) increase in gross profit percentage, (b) decrease in inventory turnover ratio, (c) increase in earnings per share, (d) decrease in days to collect, (e) increase in net profit margin, and (f) decrease in quick ratio.

MULTIPLE CHOICE

Quiz 13
www.mhhe.com/whitecotton1e

1. Which of the following ratios is *not* used to analyze profitability?
   a. Quality of income ratio.
   b. Gross profit percentage.
   c. Current ratio.
   d. Return on equity.

2. Which of the following would *not* directly change the receivables turnover ratio for a company?
   a. Increases in the selling prices of your inventory.
   b. A change in your credit policy.
   c. Increases in the cost you incur to purchase inventory.
   d. All of the above would directly change the receivables turnover ratio.

3. Which of the following ratios is used to analyze liquidity?
   a. Earnings per share.
   b. Debt-to-assets.
   c. Current ratio.
   d. Both *b* and *c*.

4. Analysts use ratios to
   a. Compare different companies in the same industry.
   b. Track a company's performance over time.
   c. Compare a company's performance to industry averages.
   d. All of the above describe ways that analysts use ratios.

5. Which of the following ratios incorporates cash flows from operations?
   a. Inventory turnover.
   b. Earnings per share.
   c. Quality of income.
   d. All of the above.

6. Given the following ratios for four companies, which company is least likely to experience problems paying its current liabilities promptly?

	Current Ratio	Receivable Turnover Ratio
a.	1.2	7.0
b.	1.2	6.0
c.	1.0	6.0
d.	0.5	7.0

7. A decrease in Selling and Administrative Expenses would directly impact what ratio?
   a. Fixed asset turnover ratio.
   b. Times interest earned.
   c. Current ratio.
   d. Gross profit percentage.

8. A bank is least likely to use which of the following ratios when analyzing the likelihood that a borrower will pay interest and principal on its loans?
   a. Current ratio.
   b. Debt-to-assets ratio.
   c. Times interest earned ratio.
   d. Price/Earnings ratio.

> Answers to Multiple-Choice Questions located in back of the text.

MINI EXERCISES

M13-1 Calculations for Horizontal Analyses
LO2

Using the following income statements, perform the calculations needed for horizontal analyses. Round percentages to one decimal place.

LOCKEY FENCING CORPORATION
Income Statements
For the Years Ended December 31

	2010	2009
Net Sales	$100,000	$75,000
Cost of Goods Sold	58,000	45,000
Gross Profit	42,000	30,000
Selling, General, and Administrative Expenses	9,000	4,500
Income from Operations	33,000	25,500
Interest Expense	3,000	3,750
Income before Income Tax	30,000	21,750
Income Tax Expense	9,000	6,525
Net Income	$ 21,000	$15,225

M13-2 Calculations for Vertical Analyses
LO3

Refer to M13-1. Perform the calculations needed for vertical analyses. Round percentages to one decimal place.

M13-3 Interpreting Horizontal Analyses
LO5

Refer to the calculations from M13-1. What are the two most significant year-over-year changes in terms of dollars and in terms of percentages? Give one potential cause of each of these changes.

M13-4 Interpreting Vertical Analyses
LO5

Refer to the calculations from M13-1. Which of the ratios from Exhibit 13.5 have been included in these calculations? Have these two ratios improved or deteriorated in 2010 compared to 2009?

LO4   **M13-5 Inferring Financial Information Using Gross Profit Percentage**

Your campus computer store reported Sales Revenue of $168,000. The company's gross profit percentage was 60.0 percent. What amount of Cost of Goods Sold did the company report?

LO2, 3, 4   **M13-6 Inferring Financial Information Using Gross Profit Percentage and Year-over-Year Comparisons**

A consumer products company reported a 25 percent increase in sales from 2009 to 2010. Sales in 2009 were $200,000. In 2010, the company reported Cost of Goods Sold in the amount of $150,000. What was the gross profit percentage in 2010? Round to one decimal place.

LO4   **M13-7 Computing the Return on Equity Ratio**

Given the following data, compute the 2010 return on equity ratio (expressed as a percentage with one decimal place).

	2010	2009
Net income	$ 1,850,000	$ 1,600,000
Stockholders' equity	10,000,000	13,125,000
Total assets	24,000,000	26,000,000
Interest expense	400,000	300,000

LO4, 5   **M13-8 Analyzing the Inventory Turnover Ratio**

A manufacturer reported an inventory turnover ratio of 8.6 during 2009. During 2010, management introduced a new inventory control system that was expected to reduce average inventory levels by 25 percent without affecting sales volume. Given these circumstances, would you expect the inventory turnover ratio to increase or decrease during 2010? Explain.

LO4   **M13-9 Inferring Financial Information Using the Current Ratio**

Mystic Laboratories reported total assets of $11,200,000 and noncurrent assets of $1,480,000. The company also reported a current ratio of 1.5. What amount of current liabilities did the company report?

LO4   **M13-10 Inferring Financial Information Using the P/E Ratio**

In 2009, Big W Company reported earnings per share of $2.50 when its stock was selling for $50.00. In 2010, its earnings increased by 10 percent. If all other relationships remain constant, what is the price of the stock? Explain.

LO4, 5   **M13-11 Identifying Relevant Ratios**

Identify the ratio that is relevant to answering each of the following questions.

a. How much net income does the company earn from each dollar of sales?
b. Is the company financed primarily by debt or equity?
c. How many dollars of sales were generated for each dollar invested in fixed assets?
d. How many days, on average, does it take the company to collect on credit sales made to customers?
e. How much net income does the company earn for each dollar owners have invested in it?
f. Does the company's net income convert into more or less cash flow from operating activities?
g. Does the company have sufficient assets to convert into cash for paying liabilities as they come due in the upcoming year?

LO5   **M13-12 Interpreting Ratios**

Generally speaking, do the following indicate good or bad news?

a. Increase in times interest earned ratio.
b. Decrease in days to sell.
c. Increase in gross profit percentage.
d. Decrease in EPS.
e. Increase in asset turnover ratio.

EXERCISES

**E13-1 Preparing and Interpreting a Schedule for Horizontal
and Vertical Analyses**

LO2, 3, 5

The average price of a gallon of gas in 2008 jumped $0.45 (16 percent) from $2.81 in 2007 (to
$3.26 in 2008). Let's see whether these changes are reflected in the income statement of Chevron
Corporation for the year ended December 31, 2008 (amounts in billions).

Chevron Corporation

	2008	2007
Total Revenues	$273	$221
Costs of Crude Oil and Products	171	133
Other Operating Costs	59	56
Income before Income Tax Expense	43	32
Income Tax Expense	19	13
Net Income	$ 24	$ 19

Required:

1. Conduct a horizontal analysis by calculating the year-over-year changes in each line item,
    expressed in dollars and in percentages (rounded to one decimal place). How did the change
    in gas prices compare to the changes in Chevron Corp.'s total revenues and costs of crude oil
    and products?

2. Conduct a vertical analysis by expressing each line as a percentage of total revenues (round
    to one decimal place). Excluding income tax and other operating costs, did Chevron earn
    more profit per dollar of revenue in 2008 compared to 2007?

E13-2 Computing and Interpreting Profitability Ratios

LO4, 5

Use the information for Chevron Corporation in E13-1 to complete the following requirements.

Chevron Corporation

Required:

1. Compute the gross profit percentage for each year (one decimal place). Assuming that the
    change for 2007 to 2008 is the beginning of a sustained trend, is Chevron likely to earn more
    or less gross profit from each dollar of sales in 2009?

2. Compute the net profit margin for each year (expressed as a percentage with one decimal
    place). Given your calculations here and in requirement 1, explain whether Chevron did a
    better or worse job of controlling expenses other than the costs of crude oil and products in
    2008 relative to 2007.

3. Chevron reported average net fixed assets of $85 billion in 2008 and $74 billion in 2007.
    Compute the fixed asset turnover ratios for both years (round to two decimal places). Did the
    company better utilize its investment in fixed assets to generate revenues in 2008 or 2007?

4. Chevron reported average stockholders' equity of $82 billion in 2008 and $73 billion in
    2007. Compute the return on equity ratios for both years (expressed as a percentage with one
    decimal place). Did the company generate greater returns for stockholders in 2008 or 2007?

E13-3 Preparing and Interpreting a Schedule for Horizontal and Vertical Analyses

LO2, 3, 5

According to the producer price index database maintained by the Bureau of Labor Statistics, the
average cost of computer equipment fell 20.9 percent between 2007 and 2008. Let's see whether
these changes are reflected in the income statement of Computer Tycoon Inc. for the year ended
December 31, 2008.

	2008	2007
Sales Revenues	$98,913	$121,761
Cost of Goods Sold	59,249	71,583
Gross Profit	39,664	50,178
Selling, General, and Administrative Expenses	36,943	36,934
Interest Expense	565	474
Income before Income Tax Expense	2,156	12,770
Income Tax Expense	1,024	5,540
Net Income	$ 1,132	$ 7,230

Required:

1. Conduct a horizontal analysis by calculating the year-over-year changes in each line item, expressed in dollars and in percentages (rounded to one decimal place). How did the change in computer prices compare to the changes in Computer Tycoon's sales revenues?

2. Conduct a vertical analysis by expressing each line as a percentage of total revenues (round to one decimal place). Excluding income tax, interest, and operating expenses, did Computer Tycoon earn more profit per dollar of sales in 2008 compared to 2007?

LO4, 5   E13-4 Computing Profitability Ratios

Use the information in E13-3 to complete the following requirements.

Required:

1. Compute the gross profit percentage for each year (one decimal place). Assuming that the change for 2007 to 2008 is the beginning of a sustained trend, is Computer Tycoon likely to earn more or less gross profit from each dollar of sales in 2009?

2. Compute the net profit margin for each year (expressed as a percentage with one decimal place). Given your calculations here and in requirement 1, explain whether Computer Tycoon did a better or worse job of controlling operating expenses in 2008 relative to 2007.

3. Computer Tycoon reported average net fixed assets of $54,200 in 2008 and $45,100 in 2007. Compute the fixed asset turnover ratios for both years (round to two decimal places). Did the company better utilize its investment in fixed assets to generate revenues in 2008 or 2007?

4. Computer Tycoon reported average stockholders' equity of $54,000 in 2008 and $40,800 in 2007. Compute the return on equity ratios for both years (expressed as a percentage with one decimal place). Did the company generate greater returns for stockholders in 2008 than in 2007?

LO4, 5   E13-5 Computing a Commonly Used Solvency Ratio

Use the information in E13-3 to complete the following requirement.

Required:

Compute the times interest earned ratios for 2008 and 2007. In your opinion, does Computer Tycoon generate sufficient net income (before taxes and interest) to cover the cost of debt financing?

LO4   E13-6 Matching Each Ratio with Its Computational Formula

Match each ratio or percentage with its formula by entering the appropriate letter for each numbered item.

Ratios or Percentages	Formula
____ 1. Current ratio	A. Net income ÷ Net sales revenue
____ 2. Net profit margin	B. (Net sales revenue − Cost of goods sold) ÷ Net sales revenue
____ 3. Inventory turnover ratio	C. Current assets ÷ Current liabilities
____ 4. Gross profit percentage	D. Cost of goods sold ÷ Average inventory
____ 5. Fixed asset turnover	E. Net credit sales revenue ÷ Average net receivables
____ 6. Capital acquisitions ratio	F. Net cash flows from operating activities ÷ Net income
____ 7. Return on equity	G. Net income ÷ Average number of common shares outstanding
____ 8. Times interest earned	H. Total liabilities ÷ Total assets
____ 9. Debt-to-assets ratio	I. (Net income + Interest expense + Income tax expense) ÷ Interest expense
____ 10. Price/earnings ratio	J. Net cash flows from operating activities ÷ Cash paid for property, plant, and equipment
____ 11. Receivables turnover ratio	K. Current market price per share ÷ Earnings per share
____ 12. Earnings per share	L. Net income ÷ Average total stockholders' equity
____ 13. Quality of income ratio	M. Net sales revenue ÷ Average net fixed assets

E13-7 Computing and Interpreting Selected Liquidity Ratios

Double West Suppliers (DWS) reported sales for the year of $300,000, all on credit. The average gross profit percentage was 40 percent on sales. Account balances follow:

	Beginning	Ending
Accounts receivable (net)	$45,000	$55,000
Inventory	60,000	40,000

Required:

1. Compute the turnover ratios for accounts receivable and inventory (round to one decimal place).
2. By dividing 365 by your ratios from requirement 1, calculate the average days to collect receivables and the average days to sell inventory (round to one decimal place).
3. Explain what each of these ratios and measures mean for DWS.

E13-8 Computing and Interpreting Liquidity Ratios

Cintas Corporation is the largest uniform supplier in North America, providing products and services to approximately 800,000 businesses of all types. Selected information from its 2008 annual report follows. For the 2008 fiscal year, the company reported sales revenue of $2.8 billion and Cost of Goods Sold of $1.6 billion.

Fiscal Year	2008	2007
Balance Sheet (amounts in millions)		
Cash	$ 70	$ 35
Accounts Receivable, less allowance of $15 and $15	430	410
Inventories	240	230
Prepaid Expenses	10	15
Other Current Assets	410	345
Accounts Payable	95	65
Wages Payable	50	60
Income Taxes Payable	10	70
Other Current Liabilities	210	205

Required:

Assuming that all sales are on credit, compute the current ratio (two decimal places), inventory turnover ratio (one decimal place), and accounts receivable turnover ratio (one decimal place) for 2008. Explain what each ratio means.

E13-9 Computing the Accounts Receivable and Inventory Turnover Ratios

Procter & Gamble is a multinational corporation that manufactures and markets many products that you use every day. In 2008, sales for the company were $83,503 (all amounts in millions). The annual report did not report the amount of credit sales, so we will assume that all sales were on credit. The average gross profit percentage was 51.3 percent. Account balances follow:

	Beginning	Ending
Accounts receivable (net)	$6,761	$6,629
Inventory	8,416	6,819

Required:

1. Rounded to one decimal place, compute the turnover ratios for accounts receivable and inventory.
2. By dividing 365 by your ratios from requirement 1, calculate the average days to collect receivables and the average days to sell inventory.
3. Interpret what these ratios and measures mean.

LO4, 5

Dollar General Corporation

E13-10 Inferring Financial Information from Profitability and Liquidity Ratios

Dollar General Corporation operates approximately 8,400 general merchandise stores that feature quality merchandise at low prices to meet the needs of middle-, low-, and fixed-income families in southern, eastern, and midwestern states. For the year ended January 30, 2009, the company reported average inventories of $1,352 (in millions) and an inventory turnover of 5.47. Average total fixed assets were $1,272 (million), and the fixed asset turnover ratio was 8.22.

Required:

1. Calculate Dollar General's gross profit percentage (expressed as a percentage with one decimal place). What does this imply about the amount of gross profit made from each dollar of sales?

   TIP: Work backward from the fixed asset turnover and inventory turnover ratios to compute the amounts needed for the gross profit percentage.

2. Is this an improvement from the gross profit percentage of 28.2 percent earned during the previous year?

LO4, 5

E13-11 Analyzing the Impact of Selected Transactions on the Current Ratio

In its most recent annual report, Appalachian Beverages reported current assets of $54,000 and a current ratio of 1.80. Assume that the following transactions were completed: (1) purchased merchandise for $6,000 on account, and (2) purchased a delivery truck for $10,000, paying $1,000 cash and signing a two-year promissory note for the balance.

Required:

Compute the updated current ratio, rounded to two decimal places, after each transaction.

LO4, 5

E13-12 Analyzing the Impact of Selected Transactions on the Current Ratio

In its most recent annual report, Sunrise Enterprises reported current assets of $1,090,000 and current liabilities of $602,000.

Required:

Determine for each of the following transactions whether the current ratio, and each of its two components, for Sunrise will increase, decrease, or have no change: (1) sold long-term assets for cash, (2) accrued severance pay for terminated employees, (3) wrote down the carrying value of certain inventory items that were deemed to be obsolete, and (4) acquired new inventory by signing an 18-month promissory note (the supplier was not willing to provide normal credit terms).

LO4, 5

The Sports Authority, Inc.

E13-13 Analyzing the Impact of Selected Transactions on the Current Ratio

The Sports Authority, Inc., is the country's largest private full-line sporting goods retailer. Stores are operated under four brand names: Sports Authority, Gart Sports, Oshman's, and Sportmart. Assume one of the Sports Authority stores reported current assets of $88,000 and its current ratio was 1.75. Assume that the following transactions were completed: (1) paid $6,000 on accounts payable, (2) purchased a delivery truck for $10,000 cash, (3) wrote off a bad account receivable for $2,000, and (4) paid previously declared dividends in the amount of $25,000.

Required:

Compute the updated current ratio, rounded to two decimal places, after each transaction.

LO4, 5

E13-14 Analyzing the Impact of Selected Transactions on the Current Ratio

Current assets totaled $500,000, the current ratio was 2.00, and the company uses the perpetual inventory method. Assume that the following transactions were completed: (1) sold $12,000 in merchandise on short-term credit for $15,000, (2) declared but did not pay dividends of $50,000, (3) paid prepaid rent in the amount of $12,000, (4) paid previously declared dividends in the amount of $50,000, (5) collected an account receivable in the amount of $12,000, and (6) reclassified $40,000 of long-term debt as a current liability.

Required:

Compute the updated current ratio, rounded to two decimal places, after each transaction.

PROBLEMS–SET A

PA13-1 Analyzing Financial Statements Using Horizontal Analyses

LO2, 5

The comparative financial statements prepared at December 31, 2010, for Pinnacle Plus showed the following summarized data:

	2010	2009	Increase (Decrease) 2010 over 2009 Amount	Percentage
Income Statement				
Sales Revenue*	$110,000	$ 99,000		
Cost of Goods Sold	52,000	48,000		
Gross Profit	58,000	51,000		
Operating Expenses	36,000	33,000		
Interest Expense	4,000	4,000		
Income before Income Tax Expense	18,000	14,000		
Income Tax Expense (30%)	5,400	4,200		
Net Income	$ 12,600	$ 9,800		
Balance Sheet				
Cash	$ 49,500	$ 18,000		
Accounts Receivable, Net	37,000	32,000		
Inventory	25,000	38,000		
Property and Equipment, Net	95,000	105,000		
Total Assets	$206,500	$193,000		
Accounts Payable	$ 42,000	$ 35,000		
Income Tax Payable	1,000	500		
Note Payable, Long-Term	40,000	40,000		
Total Liabilities	83,000	75,500		
Common Stock (par $10)	90,000	90,000		
Retained Earnings†	33,500	27,500		
Total Liabilities and Stockholders' Equity	$206,500	$193,000		

* One-half of all sales are on credit.

† During 2010, cash dividends amounting to $6,600 were declared and paid.

Required:

1. Complete the two final columns shown beside each item in Pinnacle Plus's comparative financial statements. Round the percentages to one decimal place.
2. Does anything significant jump out at you from the horizontal analyses?

PA13-2 Analyzing Comparative Financial Statements Using Selected Ratios

LO4, 5

Use the data given in PA13-1 for Pinnacle Plus.

Required:

1. Compute the gross profit percentages in 2010 and 2009. Round the percentages to one decimal place. Is the trend going in the right direction?
2. Compute the net profit margin ratios in 2010 and 2009. Round the percentages to one decimal place. Is the trend going in the right direction?
3. Compute the earnings per share for 2010 and 2009. Does the trend look good or bad? Explain.
4. Stockholders' equity totaled $100,000 at the end of 2008. Compute the return on equity (ROE) ratios for 2010 and 2009. Express the ROE as percentages rounded to one decimal place. Is the trend going in the right direction?
5. Net property and equipment totaled $110,000 at the end of 2008. Compute the fixed asset turnover ratios for 2010 and 2009. Round the ratios to two decimal places. Is the trend going in the right direction?
6. Compute the debt-to-assets ratios for 2010 and 2009. Round the ratios to two decimal places. Is debt providing financing for a larger or smaller proportion of the company's asset growth? Explain.

7. Compute the times interest earned ratios for 2010 and 2009. Round the ratios to one decimal place. Do they look good or bad? Explain.

8. After Pinnacle Plus released its 2010 financial statements, the company's stock was trading at $18. After the release of its 2009 financial statements, the company's stock price was $15 per share. Compute the P/E ratios for both years, rounded to one decimal place. Does it appear that investors have become more (or less) optimistic about Pinnacle's future success?

LO3, 5   **PA13-3 Vertical Analysis of a Balance Sheet**

A condensed balance sheet for Simultech Corporation and a partially completed vertical analysis are presented below.

SIMULTECH CORPORATION
Balance Sheet (summarized)
January 31, 2010
(in millions of U.S. dollars)

Cash and Short-Term Investments	$ 433	29%	Current Liabilities	$ 409	27%
Accounts Receivable	294	19	Long-Term Liabilities	495	33
Inventories	206	14	Total Liabilities	904	(b)
Other Current Assets	109	(a)	Contributed Capital	118	(c)
Property and Equipment	27	2	Retained Earnings	492	32
Other Assets	445	29	Total Stockholders' Equity	610	(d)
Total Assets	$1,514	100%	Total Liabilities & Stockholders' Equity	$1,514	100%

Required:

1. Complete the vertical analyses by computing each line item (a)–(d) as a percentage of total assets. Round to the nearest whole percentage.

2. What percentages of Simultech's assets relate to inventories versus property and equipment? What does this tell you about the relative significance of these two assets to Simultech's business?

3. What percentage of Simultech's assets is financed by total stockholder's equity? By total liabilities?

LO3, 5   **PA13-4 Vertical Analysis of an Income Statement**

A condensed income statement for Simultech Corporation and a partially completed vertical analysis are presented below.

SIMULTECH CORPORATION
Income Statement (summarized)
(in millions of U.S. dollars)

	For the Years Ended			
	January 31, 2010		January 31, 2009	
Sales Revenues	$2,062	100%	$2,200	100%
Cost of Goods Sold	1,637	79	1,721	(d)
Selling, General, and Administrative Expenses	333	(a)	346	16
Other Operating Expenses	53	3	12	1
Interest Expense	22	(b)	26	1
Income before Income Tax Expense	17	1	95	(e)
Income Tax Expense	6	0	33	1
Net Income	$ 11	(c)%	$ 62	(f)%

Required:

1. Complete the vertical analysis by computing each line item (a)–(f) as a percentage of sales revenues. Round to the nearest whole percentage.

2. Does Simultech's Cost of Goods Sold for the year ended January 31, 2010, as a percentage of revenues, represent better or worse performance as compared to that for the year ended January 31, 2009?
3. Do the percentages that you calculated in 1 (c) and (f) indicate whether Simultech's net profit margin has changed over the two years?

PA13-5 Interpreting Profitability, Liquidity, Solvency, and P/E Ratios

LO4, 5

Coke and Pepsi are well-known international brands. Coca-Cola sells nearly $32 billion worth of beverages each year while annual sales of Pepsi products exceed $43 billion. Compare the two companies as a potential investment based on the following ratios:

Coca-Cola Company
Pepsico

Ratio	Coca-Cola	PepsiCo
Gross profit percentage	64.3%	53.1%
Net profit margin	17.9%	11.9%
Return on equity	25.9%	35.8%
EPS	$ 2.51	$ 3.26
Receivables turnover ratio	9.6	9.2
Inventory turnover ratio	4.8	8.0
Current ratio	1.12	1.36
Debt-to-assets	0.37	0.45
P/E ratio	20.0	16.4

Required:

1. Which company appears more profitable? Describe the ratio(s) that you used to reach this decision.
2. Which company appears more liquid? Describe the ratio(s) that you used to reach this decision.
3. Which company appears more solvent? Describe the ratio(s) that you used to reach this decision.
4. Are the conclusions from your analyses in requirements 1–3 consistent with the value of the two companies suggested by the P/E ratios of the two companies? If not, offer one explanation for any apparent inconsistency.

PA13-6 Using Ratios to Compare Loan Requests from Two Companies

LO4, 5

The 2010 financial statements for Royale and Cavalier companies are summarized here:

	Royale Company	Cavalier Company
Balance Sheet		
Cash	$ 25,000	$ 45,000
Accounts Receivable, Net	55,000	5,000
Inventory	110,000	25,000
Property and Equipment, Net	550,000	160,000
Other Assets	140,000	57,000
Total Assets	$880,000	$292,000
Current Liabilities	$120,000	$ 15,000
Long-Term Debt	190,000	55,000
Capital Stock (par $20)	480,000	210,000
Additional Paid-in Capital	50,000	4,000
Retained Earnings	40,000	8,000
Total Liabilities and Stockholders' Equity	$880,000	$292,000
Income Statement		
Sales Revenue	$800,000	$280,000
Cost of Goods Sold	(480,000)	(150,000)
Expenses (including interest and income tax)	(240,000)	(95,000)
Net Income	$ 80,000	$ 35,000
Selected Data from 2009 Statements		
Accounts Receivable, Net	$ 47,000	$ 11,000
Long-Term Debt	190,000	55,000
Property and Equipment, Net	550,000	160,000
Inventory	95,000	38,000
Total Stockholders' Equity	570,000	202,000
Other Data		
Per share price at end of 2010	$ 14.00	$ 11.00

These two companies are in the same line of business and the same state but different cities. One-half of Royale's sales and one-quarter of Cavalier's sales are on credit. Each company has been in operation for about 10 years. Both companies received an unqualified audit opinion on the financial statements. Royale Company wants to borrow $75,000 cash, and Cavalier Company is asking for $30,000. The loans will be for a two-year period. Both companies estimate bad debts based on an aging analysis, but Cavalier has estimated slightly higher uncollectible rates than Royale. Neither company issued stock in 2010.

Required:

1. Calculate the ratios in Exhibit 13.5 for which sufficient information is available. Round all calculations to two decimal places.
2. Assume that you work in the loan department of a local bank. You have been asked to analyze the situation and recommend which loan is preferable. Based on the data given, your analysis prepared in requirement 1, and any other information, give your choice and the supporting explanation.

LO5   **PA13-7 Analyzing an Investment by Comparing Selected Ratios**

You have the opportunity to invest $10,000 in one of two companies from a single industry. The only information you have is shown here. The word *high* refers to the top third of the industry; *average* is the middle third; *low* is the bottom third.

Ratio	Company A	Company B
Current	Low	High
Inventory turnover	High	Low
Debt-to-assets	Low	Average
Times interest earned	High	Average
Price/earnings	High	Average

Required:

Which company would you select? Write a brief explanation for your recommendation.

PROBLEMS—SET B

LO2, 4, 5   **PB13-1 Analyzing Financial Statements Using Horizontal and Ratio Analyses**

The comparative financial statements prepared at December 31, 2010, for Tiger Audio showed the following summarized data:

	2010	2009	Increase (Decrease) 2010 over 2009 Amount	Percentage
Income Statement				
Sales Revenue	$222,000	$185,000		
Cost of Goods Sold	127,650	111,000		
Gross Profit	94,350	74,000		
Operating Expenses	39,600	33,730		
Interest Expense	4,000	3,270		
Income before Income Tax Expense	50,750	37,000		
Income Tax Expense (30%)	15,225	11,100		
Net Income	$ 35,525	$ 25,900		
Balance Sheet				
Cash	$ 40,000	$ 38,000		
Accounts Receivable, Net	18,500	16,000		
Inventory	25,000	22,000		
Property and Equipment, Net	127,000	119,000		
Total Assets	$210,500	$195,000		
Accounts Payable	$ 27,000	$ 25,000		
Income Tax Payable	3,000	2,800		
Note Payable, Long-Term	75,500	92,200		
Total Liabilities	105,500	120,000		
Capital Stock (par $1)	25,000	25,000		
Retained Earnings	80,000	50,000		
Total Liabilities and Stockholders' Equity	$210,500	$195,000		

Required:

1. Complete the two final columns shown beside each item in Tiger Audio's comparative financial statements. Round the percentages to one decimal place.

2. Does anything significant jump out at you from the year-over-year analyses?

PB13-2 Analyzing Comparative Financial Statements Using Selected Ratios   LO4, 5

Use the data given in PB13-1 for Tiger Audio.

Required:

1. Compute the gross profit percentages in 2010 and 2009. Is the trend going in the right direction?

2. Compute the net profit margin ratios in 2010 and 2009. Is the trend going in the right direction?

3. Compute the earnings per share for 2010 and 2009. Does the trend look good or bad? Explain.

4. Stockholders' equity totaled $65,000 at the end of 2008. Compute the return on equity ratios for 2010 and 2009. Is the trend going in the right direction?

5. Net property and equipment totaled $115,000 at the end of 2008. Compute the fixed asset turnover ratios for 2010 and 2009. Is the trend going in the right direction?

6. Compute the debt-to-assets ratios for 2010 and 2009. Is debt providing financing for a larger or smaller proportion of the company's asset growth? Explain.

7. Compute the times interest earned ratios for 2010 and 2009. Do they look good or bad? Explain.

8. After Tiger released its 2010 financial statements, the company's stock was trading at $17. After the release of its 2009 financial statements, the company's stock price was $12 per share. Compute the P/E ratios for both years. Does it appear that investors have become more (or less) optimistic about Tiger's future success?

PB13-3 Vertical Analysis of a Balance Sheet   LO3, 5

A condensed balance sheet for Southwest Airlines and a partially completed vertical analysis are presented below.

SOUTHWEST AIRLINES
Balance Sheet (summarized)
December 31, 2008
(in millions of U.S. dollars)

Cash	$ 1,803	13%	Current Liabilities	$ 2,806	(b)%
Accounts Receivable	209	1	Long-Term Liabilities	6,549	45
Inventory of Parts and Supplies	203	1	Total Liabilities	9,355	65
Other Current Assets	678	5	Contributed Capital	1,018	7
Property and Equipment, Net	11,040	(a)	Retained Earnings	3,935	28
Other Assets	375	3	Total Stockholder's Equity	4,953	(c)
Total Assets	$14,308	100%	Total Liabilities & Stockholders' Equity	$14,308	100%

Required:

1. Complete the vertical analysis by computing each line item (a)–(c) as a percentage of total assets. Round to the nearest whole percentage.

2. What percentages of Southwest's assets relate to inventory of parts and supplies versus property and equipment? What does this tell you about the relative significance of these two assets to Southwest's business?

3. What percentage of Southwest's assets is financed by total stockholders' equity? By total liabilities?

PB13-4 Vertical Analysis of an Income Statement   LO3, 5

A condensed income statement for Southwest Airlines and a partially completed vertical analysis are presented below.

SOUTHWEST AIRLINES
Income Statement (summarized)
For the Year Ended December 31
(in millions of U.S. dollars)

	2008		2007	
Sales Revenues	$11,023	100%	$9,861	100%
Salaries, Wages, and Benefits	3,340	30	3,213	(d)
Fuel, Oil, Repairs, and Maintenance	4,434	(a)	3,306	33
Other Operating Expenses	2,800	(b)	2,551	26
Other Expenses (Revenues)	171	2	(267)	(3)
Income before Income Tax Expense	278	3	1,058	(e)
Income Tax Expense	100	1	413	4
Net Income	$ 178	(c)%	$ 645	(f)%

Required:

1. Complete the vertical analysis by computing each line item (a)–(f) as a percentage of sales revenues. Round to the nearest whole percentage.
2. Does the percentage that you calculated in 1(a) suggest that Southwest tried to increase its profit by cutting repairs and maintenance costs in 2008 compared to 2007?
3. Refer to the percentages that you calculated in 1(c) and (f). Is Southwest's net profit margin improving, or declining?

LO4, 5

Mattel, Inc.

PB13-5 Interpreting Profitability, Liquidity, Solvency, and P/E Ratios

Mattel and Hasbro are the two biggest makers of games and toys in the world. Mattel sells nearly $6 billion of products each year while annual sales of Hasbro products exceed $4 billion. Compare the two companies as a potential investment based on the following ratios:

Ratio	Mattel	Hasbro
Gross profit percentage	45.5%	57.7%
Net profit margin	6.5%	7.3%
Return on equity	17.1%	21.8%
EPS	$ 1.05	$ 2.18
Receivables turnover ratio	8.9	10.5
Inventory turnover ratio	6.2	5.7
Current ratio	2.38	2.54
Debt-to-assets	0.31	0.35
P/E ratio	15.9	13.8

Required:

1. Which company appears more profitable? Describe the ratio(s) that you used to reach this decision.
2. Which company appears more liquid? Describe the ratio(s) that you used to reach this decision.
3. Which company appears more solvent? Describe the ratio(s) that you used to reach this decision.
4. Are the conclusions from your analyses in requirements 1–3 consistent with the value of the two companies suggested by the P/E ratios of the two companies? If not, offer one explanation for any apparent inconsistency.

LO4, 5

PB13-6 Using Ratios to Compare Loan Requests from Two Companies

The 2010 financial statements for Thor and Gunnar Companies are summarized here:

	Thor Company	Gunnar Company
Balance Sheet		
Cash	$ 35,000	$ 54,000
Accounts Receivable, Net	77,000	6,000
Inventory	154,000	30,000
Property and Equipment, Net	770,000	192,000
Other Assets	196,000	68,400
Total Assets	$1,232,000	$350,400
Current Liabilities	$ 168,000	$ 18,000
Long-Term Debt (12% interest rate)	266,000	66,000
Capital Stock (par $20)	672,000	252,000
Additional Paid-in Capital	70,000	4,800
Retained Earnings	56,000	9,600
Total Liabilities and Stockholders' Equity	$1,232,000	$350,400
Income Statement		
Sales Revenue	$1,120,000	$336,000
Cost of Goods Sold	(672,000)	(180,000)
Expenses (including interest and income tax)	(336,000)	(114,000)
Net Income	$ 112,000	$ 42,000
Selected Data from 2009 Statements		
Accounts Receivable, Net	$ 65,800	$ 13,200
Inventory	133,000	45,600
Property and Equipment, Net	770,000	192,000
Long-Term Debt (12% interest rate)	266,000	66,000
Total Stockholders' Equity	798,000	266,400
Other Data		
Per share price at end of 2010	$ 13.20	$ 19.60

These two companies are in the same line of business and the same state but in different cities. One-half of Thor's sales and one-quarter of Gunnar's sales are on credit. Each company has been in operation for about 10 years. Both companies received an unqualified audit opinion on the financial statements. Thor Company wants to borrow $105,000, and Gunnar Company is asking for $36,000. The loans will be for a two-year period. Neither company issued stock in 2010.

Required:

1. Calculate the ratios in Exhibit 13.5 for which sufficient information is available. Round all calculations to two decimal places.

2. Assume that you work in the loan department of a local bank. You have been asked to analyze the situation and recommend which loan is preferable. Based on the data given, your analysis prepared in requirement 1, and any other information, give your choice and the supporting explanation.

PB13-7 Analyzing an Investment by Comparing Selected Ratios   L05

You have the opportunity to invest $10,000 in one of two companies from a single industry. The only information you have is shown here. The word *high* refers to the top third of the industry; *average* is the middle third; *low* is the bottom third.

Ratio	Company A	Company B
EPS	High	High
Return on equity	High	Average
Debt-to-assets	High	Low
Current	Low	Average
Price/earnings	Low	High

Required:

Which company would you select? Write a brief explanation for your recommendation.

SKILLS DEVELOPMENT CASES

L05   **S13-1 Evaluating Financial Information**

Lumber Liquidators

Lumber Liquidators, Inc., competes with Lowe's in product lines such as hardwood flooring, moldings, and noise-reducing underlay. The two companies reported the following financial results in fiscal 2008:

	Lumber Liquidators	Lowe's
Gross profit percentage	35.0%	34.2%
Net profit margin	4.7%	4.6%
Return on equity	21.1%	12.9%
Earnings per share	$ 0.83	$ 1.51

Required:

1. Explain how Lumber Liquidators could have a substantially higher gross profit percentage than Lowe's but a nearly identical net profit margin. What does this suggest about the relative ability of the two companies to control operating expenses?

2. Explain how Lumber Liquidators could have a higher return on equity but lower earnings per share. What does this suggest about the companies' relative number of outstanding shares? What other explanations could account for this seemingly contradictory pattern?

L05   **S13-2 Ethical Decision Making: A Real-Life Example**

During its deliberations on the Sarbanes-Oxley Act, the U.S. Senate considered numerous reports evaluating the quality of work done by external auditors. One study by Weiss Ratings, Inc., focused on auditors' ability to predict bankruptcy. The study criticized auditors for failing to identify and report going-concern problems for audit clients that later went bankrupt. Based on a sample of 45 bankrupt companies, the Weiss study concluded that had auditors noted unusual levels for just two of seven typical financial ratios, they would have identified 89 percent of the sample companies that later went bankrupt. A follow-up to the Weiss study found that had the criteria in the Weiss study been applied to a larger sample of nonbankrupt companies, 46.9 percent of nonbankrupt companies would have been predicted to go bankrupt.* In other words, the Weiss criteria would have incorrectly predicted bankruptcy for nearly half of the companies in the follow-up study and would have led the auditors to report that these clients had substantial going-concern problems when, in fact, they did not. Discuss the negative consequences that arise when auditors fail to identify and report going-concern problems. Who is harmed by these failures? Discuss the negative consequences that arise when auditors incorrectly report going-concern problems when they do not exist. Who is harmed by these errors? In your opinion, which of the potential consequences is worse?

L04, 5   **S13-3 Ethical Decision Making: A Mini-Case**

Capital Investments Corporation (CIC) requested a sizable loan from First Federal Bank to acquire a large piece of land for future expansion. CIC reported current assets of $1,900,000 (including $430,000 in cash) and current liabilities of $1,075,000. First Federal denied the loan request for a number of reasons, including the fact that the current ratio was below 2:1. When CIC was informed of the loan denial, the controller of the company immediately paid $420,000 that was owed to several trade creditors. The controller then asked First Federal to reconsider the loan application. Based on these abbreviated facts, would you recommend that First Federal approve the loan request? Why? Are the controller's actions ethical?

L04, 5   **S13-4 Critical Thinking: Analyzing the Impact of Alternative Depreciation Methods on Ratio Analysis**

Speedy Company uses the double-declining-balance method to depreciate its property, plant, and equipment, and Turtle Company uses the straight-line method. The two companies are exactly alike except for the difference in depreciation methods.

---

*Michael D. Akers, Meredith A. Maher, and Don E. Giacomino, "Going-Concern Opinions: Broadening the Expectations Gap," *CPA Journal,* October 2003. Retrieved June 12, 2009 from www.nysscpa.org/cpajournal/2003/1003/features/f103803.htm.

Required:

1. Identify the financial ratios discussed in this chapter that are likely to be affected by the difference in depreciation methods.
2. Which company will report the higher amount for each ratio that you have identified in response to requirement 1? If you cannot be certain, explain why.

S13-5 Using a Spreadsheet to Calculate Financial Statement Ratios

LO2, 3

Enter the account names and dollar amounts from the comparative balance sheets in Exhibit 13.1 into a worksheet in a spreadsheet file. Create a second copy of the worksheet in the same spreadsheet file.

Required:

1. To the right of the comparative numbers in the first worksheet, enter the necessary formulas to compute the amount and percent change as shown in Exhibit 13.1.
2. To the right of each column in the second worksheet, enter the necessary formulas to create common size statements similar to those shown in Exhibit 13.3.

A

Accounting Rate of Return Annual net income as a percentage of the original investment in assets. (290)

Activity Based Costing Method of assigning indirect costs to products or services based on the activities they required. (137)

Activity Based Management All actions that managers take to improve operations or reduce costs based on ABC data. (147)

Activity Cost Driver Measure used to assign cost in an ABC system.

Activity Rate Computed by dividing total activity cost by total activity driver. (142)

Actual Manufacturing Costs Actual amount of indirect manufacturing costs incurred during the period. (48)

Allocation Base Measurable item used to apply indirect overhead costs to products or services. (43)

Annuity Stream of cash flows that occurs uniformly across time. (293)

Appraisal or Inspection Cost Cost incurred to identify defective products before shipping them to customers. (149)

Avoidable Cost Cost that can be avoided by choosing one decision option instead of another. (254)

B

Balanced Scorecard Comprehensive performance measurement system that translates an organization's vision and strategy into a set of operational performance metrics. (417)

Batch-Level Activities Activities performed for a group of units all at once. (139)

Benchmarking Process for comparing a company's practices with those of other firms in an industry or the best performing firms in other industries. (147)

Bottleneck Most constrained resource or the process that limits a system's output. (266)

Break-Even Analysis A form of cost-volume-profit analysis that determines the level of sales needed to break even, or earn zero profits. (216)

Break-Even Point Point at which total revenue equals total cost, resulting in zero profit; the point at which fixed costs exactly equal the contribution margin. (216)

Budget Quantification of the resources and expenditures that will be required during a given period of time to achieve a plan. (8)

Budget Slack Cushion that managers may try to build into their budget by understating expected sales or overstating budgeting expenses so that they are more likely to come in under budget for expenses and over budget for revenues. (327)

Budgeted Balance Sheet Balance sheet created from a combination of the financial budgets; shows expected balance of assets, liabilities, and owners' equity at the end of the budget period. (329)

Budgeted Cost of Goods Sold Budgeted manufacturing cost per unit multiplied by the number of units of expected sales. (330)

Budgeted Gross Margin Budgeted sales less budgeted cost of goods sold. (330)

Budgeted Income Statement Expectation of income after combining all operating budgets. (329)

Budgeted Manufacturing Cost per Unit Combination of all budgeted manufacturing costs. (330)

C

Capacity Measure of the limit placed on specific resources. (255)

Capital Budgeting Decision-making approach aimed at helping managers make decisions about investments in major capital assets. (288)

Cash Budget Financial budget that provides information about budgeted cash receipts and disbursements. (330)

Cash Flows from Financing Activities Cash inflows and outflows related to financing sources external to the company (owners and lenders). (445)

Cash Flows from Investing Activities Cash inflows and outflows related to the purchase or sale of investments and long-lived assets. (444)

Cash Flows from Operating Activities (Cash Flows from Operations) Cash inflows and outflows related to components of net income. (444)

Centralized Organization Organization in which decision-making authority is kept at the top level of the organization. (407)

Common Fixed Cost Cost shared by multiple segments that will be incurred even if a section is eliminated. (262)

Complementary Product Products that are used together such as a printer and ink cartridge. (264)

Compounding Process of interest being earned on top of interest. (292)

Constrained Resource Resource that is unable to meet the demand placed on it. (265)

Contribution Margin Difference between sales revenue and variable costs. (187)

Contribution Margin Income Statement Type of income statement that separates costs into variable or fixed costs; used to address many managerial problems. (186)

Contribution Margin Ratio Contribution margin divided by sales revenue; stated as a percentage of sales. (188)

Control Process of monitoring actual results to see whether the objectives set in the planning state are being made. (7)

Controllability Principle Concept that managers should be held responsible for only those things that they can control. (408)

Conversion Cost Sum of direct labor and manufacturing overhead; total cost incurred to convert direct materials into a finished product. (16)

Cost Value given up in exchange for something else. (12)

Cost Behavior Description of how total costs change when some measure of activity level changes. (175)

Cost Center Responsibility center in which manager has authority and responsibility for cost. (408)

Cost Driver Activity that causes some measure of activity to change; measure used to allocate or assign indirect costs to products. (175)

Cost Object Any item for which one wants to determine cost. (13)

Cost of Capital A rate that reflects the cost of funds used to finance a company's operations. (294)

Cost of Goods Completed Total production cost assigned to goods that were manufactured or completed during an accounting period. (50)

Cost of Goods Manufactured See *cost of goods completed*. (50)

Cost of Goods Sold (COGS) Total manufacturing cost of jobs or units sold during the period. (45)

Cost-Volume-Profit Analysis Analysis that focuses on relationships among product prices, volume and mix of units sold, variable and fixed costs, and profit. (214)

Customer-Level Activities Activities performed for a specific customer. (138)

CVP Graph Graph that is useful for visualizing the relationship among unit sales volume, total revenue, total cost, and profit. (215)

D

Decentralized Organization Organization in which decision-making authority is spread throughout, and managers are responsible for deciding how to manage their particular area of responsibility. (407)

Dependent Variable Variable that depends on the level of X. (179)

Differential Analysis See *Incremental Analysis*. (253)

Differential Cost Cost that differs between decision alternatives. (15)

Direct Cost Costs that can be directly attributed or traced to a specific cost object. (13)

Direct Fixed Cost Fixed cost that can be attributed to a specific business segment. (262)

Directing/Leading One of the key functions of management that involves all of the actions required to put a plan into action. (7)

Direct Labor Cost of labor that can be physically and conveniently traced to the final product. (16)

Direct Labor Budget Budget indicating the amount of direct labor needed to meet expected production. (330)

Direct Labor Efficiency Variance Difference between the actual number of labor hours used and the standard number of labor hours multiplied by the standard labor rate. (369)

Direct Labor Rate Variance Difference between the actual labor rate and the standard labor rate multiplied by the actual number of labor hours used. (369)

Direct Labor Spending Variance Variance that represents the sum of the direct labor rate variance and the direct labor efficiency variances. (370)

Direct Labor Time Ticket Source document used to keep track of direct labor costs in a job order cost system. (42)

Direct Materials Major material inputs that can be physically and conveniently traced to the final product. (16)

Direct Materials Price Variance Difference between the actual price and the standard price paid for direct materials multiplied by the actual quantity of direct materials purchased. (367)

Direct Materials Quantity Variance Difference between the actual quantity and the standard quantity of direct materials used multiplied by the standard price. (367)

Direct Materials Spending Variance Sum of the direct materials price variance and the direct materials quantity variances. (368)

Direct Method Method of presenting the Operating Activities section of the cash flow statement to report the components of cash flows from operating activities as gross receipts and gross payments. (447)

Discounted Cash Flow Method Decision-making approach that incorporates the time value of money. (293)

Discounting Process of calculating the cash-equivalent present value of future payments by removing the interest component that is built into future payments. (293)

Discount Rate Rate used to discount future cash flows to reflect the time value of money. (294)

DuPont Method Formula developed by executives at DuPont in the early 1900s; shows that the return on investment is a function of profit margin and investment turnover. (413)

E

Easily Attainable Standard Standard that can be met with relative ease. (360)

Equivalent Unit Measure used to convert partially complete units into the equivalent of a whole unit. (94)

Ethics Standards of conduct for judging right from wrong, honest from dishonest, and fair from unfair. (9)

Excess Capacity Occurs when a company has more than enough resources to satisfy demand. (255)

External Failure Cost Cost that occurs when a defective product makes its way into the customer's hands. (149)

F

Facility/Companywide Activities Activities performed to benefit the organization as a whole. (138)

Favorable Variance Variance indicating that actual costs were less than budgeted or standard costs. (365)

Financial Accounting Accounting area focused on providing financial information to external users such as investors, creditors, and regulators. (5)

Financial Budget Budget that focuses on the financial resources needed to support operations. (329)

Finished Goods Inventory Cost of all units completed but not sold. (45)

Fixed Cost Cost that remains the same, in total, regardless of activity level. (15)

Fixed Overhead Budget Variance See *fixed overhead spending variance*. (374)

Fixed Overhead Spending Variance Variance that represents the difference in actual and budgeted fixed overhead costs. (374)

Fixed Overhead Volume Variance Variance resulting from the difference

between actual and budgeted production volume. (377)

Flexible Budget Budget showing how budgeted costs and revenues will change for different levels of sales. (362)

Full Absorption Costing Costing method required for external reporting (GAAP) in which all manufacturing costs must be fully assigned to the unit produced. (174)

Full Capacity Occurs when a company is operating its resources to the limit of its capacity. No additional units can be produced or customers served without increasing capacity or incurring opportunity costs. (255)

Future Value Value of cash received in the future. (292)

G

Goal Incongruence Conflict between a manager and the organization that may cause managers to make decisions that are not in the best interest of the overall organization. (417)

General and Administrative Expenses Costs incurred in running the overall organization. (16)

H

High-Low Method Method of analyzing mixed costs using the two most extreme activity levels (X values) to estimate fixed and variable costs. (179)

Horizontal (Trend) Analysis Comparison of individual financial statement items from year to year with the general goal of identifying significant sustained changes or trends. (495)

Hurdle Rate Minimum required rate of return for a project. (294)

I

Ideal Standard Standard that can be achieved only under perfect or ideal conditions. (360)

Idle Capacity See *Excess Capacity*. (255)

Incremental Analysis Decision-making approach that focuses on the differential costs and benefits of alternate decision choices. (253)

Incremental Cost See *Differential Cost*. (254)

Independent Project Project unrelated to others so that investing in it does not preclude or affect the choice about other alternatives. (289)

Independent Variable Variable that causes Y to change. (179)

Indirect Cost Cost that cannot be traced to a specific cost object or are not worth the effort to trace. (13)

Indirect Materials Materials that cannot be directly or conveniently traced to a specific unit and are therefore treated as manufacturing overhead. (45)

Indirect Method Method that starts with net income from the income statement and then adjusts it by removing items that do not involve cash but were included in net income and adding items that involved cash but were not yet included in net income. (447)

Internal Failure Costs Costs from defects caught before shipping the product to the customer. (149)

Internal Rate of Return Discount rate at which the present value of cash inflows exactly equals the cash outflows. (296)

Inventoriable Cost Cost that is counted as inventory on the balance sheet until the product is sold; another term for product cost. (17)

Inventory Budget Budget that shows how much finished goods, work in process, and raw materials inventory are planned at the beginning and end of each budget period. (330)

Investment Center Responsibility center in which manager has authority and responsibility for profit (revenue − cost) and the investment of assets. (408)

Investment Turnover Ratio of sales revenue to the average invested assets. (408)

Irrelevant Cost Cost that will not differ between alternatives. (15)

J

Job Cost Sheet Document used to record all of the costs of producing a particular job or servicing a specific customer. (40)

Job Order Costing Costing system used by companies that make unique products or provide specialty services. (39)

Just-in-Time (JIT) System "Demand-pull" system in which materials are purchased and units manufactured as needed to satisfy demand. (151)

L

Least-Squares Regression Statistical technique for finding the line that minimizes the sum of squared error. (179)

Linearity Assumption Assumption that the relationships between two variables (X and Y) can be approximated by a straight line. (178)

Long-Term Objective Specific goal that management wants to achieve over a long-term horizon, typically 5 to 10 years. (325)

M

Managerial Accounting Accounting area focused on providing information to assist business owner and managers in making business decisions. (5)

Manufacturing Cost Cost incurred to produce a physical product; generally classified as direct materials, direct labor, or manufacturing overhead. (16)

Manufacturing Firm Company that purchases raw materials and uses them to make a finished product to sell to wholesalers, retailers, or customers. (6)

Manufacturing Overhead All costs other than direct material and direct labor that are incurred to manufacture a physical product. (16)

Manufacturing Overhead Budget Budget that indicates overhead costs to be incurred to support budgeted production. (330)

Margin of Safety Difference between actual or budgeted sales and the break-even point. (220)

Marketing or Selling Expenses Costs incurred to sell a product or service to customer. (16)

Master Budget Comprehensive set of budgets that reflects what management expects to achieve in a specific period. (329)

Materials Requisition Form Document used to authorize the issuance of materials into production; details the cost and quantities of all materials needed to complete specific jobs. (41)

Merchandising Company Company that purchases goods (merchandise) from a supplier and sells them to other businesses or consumers. (7)

Minimum Rate of Return Lowest acceptable rate of return. Also called required rate of return or handle rate. (294)

Mixed Costs Costs that have both a fixed component and a variable component; also known as semivariable costs. (177)

Mutually Exclusive Projects Projects that involve a choice among competing alternatives. Managers choose one or the other, but not both. (289)

N

Net Present Value (NPV) Method Method that compares the present value of the future cash flows for a project to the original investment that is required at the start of the project. (294)

Nonmanufacturing Cost Costs associated with running a business or selling a product as opposed to manufacturing a product; generally classified as marketing or selling costs or administrative costs. (16)

Nonvalue-Added Activity Activity that if eliminated would not reduce the value of the product or service to the customer. (148)

Nonvolume-Based Cost Driver Allocation base not directly related to the number of units produced or customers served. (141)

O

Operating Budget Budgets that cover the organization's planned operating activities for a particular period of time. (329)

Opportunity Cost Forgone benefit or lost opportunity in choosing one alternative instead of another. (13)

Organizing Arranging the necessary resources to carry out the plan. (7)

Out-of-Pocket Costs Costs that involve an outlay of cash. (13)

Overapplied Overhead Difference between actual and applied overhead when applied is greater than actual. (5)

P

Parallel Processing Manufacturing approach in which multiple processes occur simultaneously. (90)

Participative Budgeting Method that allows employees throughout the organization to have input into the budget-setting process. (327)

Payback Period Amount of time it takes to generate enough cash for a project to pay for its original investment. (290)

Period Cost Cost that is expensed as soon as it is incurred. (17)

Planning Future-oriented aspect of the management process that involves setting long-term goals and objectives and short-term tactics necessary to achieve those goals. (7)

Practical Capacity An amount less than the theoretical capacity of a resource that allows a certain amount of downtime for preventive maintenance, employee breaks, etc. Often estimated at 80% of theoretical capacity. (378)

Predetermined Overhead Rate Rate estimated before the accounting period begins and used throughout the period to assign overhead costs to products or services. (43)

Preference Decisions Decisions that require managers to choose from among a set of alternative capital investment opportunities. (288)

Present Value Value of future cash flows expressed in today's equivalent dollars. (293)

Prevention Cost Cost incurred to prevent quality problems from occurring. (149)

Prime Cost Sum of direct materials and direct labor; represents the costs that can be directly traced to the end product. (16)

Process Costing Costing system used by companies that make homogeneous products or services. (38)

Product Cost Cost that becomes a part of the product that is being produced. (17)

Production Budget Budget that shows how many units need to be produced each period to meet projected sales. (329)

Production Report Report that summarizes what occurred in the production process during the accounting period. (90)

Product-Level Activities Activities performed to support a specific product line. (138)

Product Life Cycle Product introduction, growth, maturity, and eventual decline. (149)

Profit Center Responsibility center in which manager has authority and responsibility for profit (revenue − cost). (408)

Profit Margin Ratio of operating profit to sales revenue. (413)

Profitability Index Factor used to prioritize capital investments computed as present value of future cash flows divided by the initial investment. (301)

Q

Quality Cost Report Summary of activities and costs incurred to prevent, detect, and correct quality problems. (149)

R

Raw Materials Inventory Cost of all materials purchased from suppliers that have not yet been used in production. (45)

Raw Materials Purchases Budget Budget that indicates the quantity of raw materials that must be purchased to meet production and raw materials inventory needs. (330)

Related-Party Transactions Business transactions between units or divisions of the same company. (419)

Relevant Cost A cost that has the potential to influence a particular decision. (15)

Relevant Range Range of activity over which assumptions about cost behavior are expected to hold true. (175)

Required Rate of Return See *Minimum Rate of Return*. (294)

Residual Income Difference between operating income and minimum profit needed to cover the required rate of return or hurdle rate. (415)

Responsibility Accounting Area of accounting in which managers are given authority and responsibility over a particular area of the organization and are then evaluated based on the results of that area of responsibility. (408)

Responsibility Center Area over which managers are given responsibility for specific operations of an organization. (408)

Return on Investment (ROI) Most common method of evaluating investment center performance; calculated as operating income/invested assets. (412)

Revenue Center Responsibility center in which manager has authority and responsibility for generating revenue. (408)

R-Square Goodness of fit measure that identifies how much of the variability of the Y variable is explained by the X variable. (184)

S

Sales Budget Estimate of the number of units to be sold and the total sales revenue to be generated in each budget period; also called the *Sales Forecast*. (329)

Sales Forecast Number of units expected to be sold each month or quarter of the budget period. Serves as the starting point for all other components of the master budget. (329)

Sarbanes-Oxley (SOX) Act of 2002 Act passed by Congress to restore investor confidence in and improve the quality of financial reporting by publicly traded companies in the United States. (10)

Scattergraph Graph of the relationship between total cost (Y) and activity level (X). (179)

Screening Decisions Decisions made when managers evaluate a proposed capital investment to determine whether it meets some minimum criteria. (288)

Segment Margin Calculated as revenue minus all costs that are directly traceable to a particular business segment. (262)

Segmented Income Statement Income statement that shows the profitability of individual business segments for a particular period of time. (410)

Selling and Administrative Expense Budget Budget of expected cost of selling and administration based on the planned level of sales. (330)

Sensitivity Analysis Process to determine whether changing any underlying assumptions considered in making a decision would affect the decision. (299)

Sequential Processing Manufacturing approach where production stages must occur in sequence. (90)

Service Company Company that provides services to other businesses or consumers. (7)

Short-Term Objective Specific goal that management wants to achieve in the short run; usually no longer than one year. (325)

Simple Rate of Return See *accounting rate of return.* (290)

Spending Variances Variances calculated by comparing actual costs to the flexible budget cost. (364)

Standard Cost Card Form that summarizes what it should cost to make a single unit of product based on expected production and sales for the upcoming period. (361)

Standard Cost System Cost system that records manufacturing costs at standard rather than actual amounts. (360)

Standard Unit Cost Expected cost to produce one unit based on standard prices and quantities. (361)

Static Budget Budget based on a single estimate of sales volume. (362)

Step Costs Costs that are fixed over some range of activity and then

increase in a steplike fashion when a capacity limit is reached; can be treated as either step-variable or step-fixed costs. (177)

Step-Fixed Cost Step cost with relatively wide steps; typically treated as a fixed cost at least within a relevant range. (177)

Step-Variable Cost Step cost fixed over a narrow range of activity; typically treated as a variable cost because multiple steps are encountered across the relevant range. (177)

Strategic Plan Managers' vision of what they want the organization to achieve over a long-term horizon. (325)

Substitute Products Products where one good can be used instead of another. Examples include butter and margarine, or sugar and artificial sweeteners. (264)

Sunk Cost Cost incurred in the past; is not relevant to future decisions. (15)

T

Tactics Specific actions or mechanisms that management uses to achieve objectives. (325)

Target Costing Determining what target cost is required to meet the target price and provide a profit for a company's shareholders. (150)

Target Profit Analysis Type of cost-volume-profit analysis that determines the number of units or sales necessary to earn a target profit. (219)

Time Value of Money Principle that money is more valuable today than in the future. (292)

Top-Down Approach Method in which top management sets a budget and imposes it on lower levels of the organization. (327)

Transfer Price Amount charged when one division sells goods or services to another division of the same company. (419)

U

Unadjusted Rate of Return See *accounting rate of return.* (290)

Underapplied Overhead Difference in actual and applied overhead when applied is less than actual. (51)

Unfavorable Variance Variance indicating that actual costs were more than budgeted or standard costs. (365)

Unit Contribution Margin Difference between sales price and variable cost per unit; indicates how much each additional unit sold will contribute to fixed costs and profit. (187)

Unit-Level Activities Activities performed for each individual unit or customer. (139)

V

Value-Added Activity Activity that enhances the value of the product or service to the customer. (148)

Value Engineering A process for determining how much value consumers receive from a product or service based on its features and functionality. (151)

Variable Costs Cost that changes in total in direct proportion to changes in activity levels. (14)

Variable Costing Costing method used for internal reporting that classifies costs as either variable or fixed. Can be used to analyze many managerial decisions. (189)

Variable Overhead (VOH) Rate Variance Variance driven by the difference in actual and standard variable overhead rates. (372)

Variable Overhead Efficiency Variance Variance driven by the difference in actual amounts and standard amounts of a cost driver (e.g., direct labor hours) multiplied by the standard variable overhead rate. (372)

Variance Difference between actual costs and budgeted or standard costs. (359)

Vertical (Common Size) Analysis Analytic technique that expresses each line of the income statement (or balance sheet) as a percentage of total sales (or total assets). (495)

Visual Fit Method Method of analyzing mixed costs that involves "eyeballing" the data on a scattergraph. (179)

Volume Variance Variance driven by the difference in actual and budgeted sales volume. (364)

Volume-Based Allocation Measures Allocation bases traditionally used to assign indirect costs that are directly related to number of units produced or customers served. (135)

W

Weighted Average Contribution Margin Ratio Average contribution margin ratios of multiple products weighted according to the percentage of total sales revenue. (230)

Weighted Average Unit Contribution Margin Average unit contribution of multiple products weighted according to the percentage of units sold. (227)

Work in Process Inventory Cost of units that have been started in the manufacturing operation but are incomplete at the end of an accounting period. (45)

Chapter 1

PA1-4

(2)

    a. Direct Material = $4,000
    b. Direct Labor = $37,500
    c. Manufacturing Overhead = $11,200
    d. Prime Cost = $41,500
    e. Conversion Cost = $48,700
    f. Total Product Cost = $52,700

Chapter 2

PA2-1

(3) $15,085 overapplied
(5) Net Income = $102,565

PA2-3

(1) $4.00 per machine hour
(3) $16,000
(5) $1,000 underapplied

PA2-5

(1)

    Raw Materials Inventory = $19,000
    Work in Process Inventory = $8,100
    Finished Goods Inventory = $16,700
    Cost of Goods Sold = $50,000
    Manufacturing Overhead = $1,300 overapplied
    Selling and Administrative Expenses = $4,500
    Sales Revenue = $65,000
    Other accounts (Cash, Payables, etc.) = $8,000

(4) $16,300

PA2-6

    Direct Materials Used In Production = $112,000
    Direct Labor = $100,000
    Total Current Manufacturing Costs = $292,000
    Ending Work in Process Inventory = $12,000
    Cost of Goods Manufactured = $290,000
    Ending Finished Goods Inventory = $15,000
    Unadjusted Cost of Goods Sold = $295,000
    Adjusted Cost of Goods Sold = $300,000

PA2-7

(1)

    a. $40.00 per direct labor hour
    b. $640,000
    c. $15,000 Underapplied

(3)

    a. $50 per machine hour
    b. $650,000
    c. $5,000 Underapplied

PA2-8

(1) 150% of Direct labor cost
(3) $2,000 Overapplied
(5) Net Income from Operations = $69,000

Chapter 3

PA3-1

(1)

    a. Ending units = 34,000
    b. Materials = 116,000 e.u.
       Conversion = 99,000 e.u.
    c. Materials = $1.12069
       Conversion = $2.54545
    d. Completed = $300,624
       Ending WIP = $81,376

PA3-2

(1)

    a. Ending units = 34,000
    b. Materials = 76,000 e.u.
       Conversion = 87,000 e.u.
    c. Materials = $1.18421
       Conversion = $1.80460
    d. Started & Completed = $125,530
       Ending WIP = $70,941

PA3-3

(1)

    a. Ending units = 13,000
    c. Materials = $1.93847
       Conversion = $2.82059

PA3-5

(1)

    b. Materials = 121,500 e.u.
       Conversion = 158,180 e.u.
    d. Started & Completed = $448,797
       Ending WIP = $44,453

PA3-6

(1)

    b. Materials = 28,325 e.u.
       Conversion = 25,594 e.u.
    d. Completed = $1,791,637
       Ending WIP = $1,023,963

PA3-7

(1)

    a. Ending units = 10,925
    c. Materials = $66.00000
       Conversion = $29.39333

Chapter 4

PA4-1

(1) Standard Model $68,625
    Deluxe Model $68,625
(3) $73,500
(4) $63,750

PA4-2

(1) Roundabout Model: $67,200
    Sassafras Model $64,000
(3) $73,098.75

PA 4-3
(2) Castle $245.29
    Mansion $344.25
(4) $860 per setup
    $100.00 per inspection
    $20 per machine hour
(6) Castle $216.74
    Mansion $394.20

PA4-4
(1) Sportsman $ 5,590
    Expedition $ 5,590
(3) Sportsman $42.35
    Expedition $52.18
(5) Sportsman $ 4,200
    Expedition $ 6,980
(7) Sportsman $43.50
    Expedition $50.73

Chapter 5

PA5-1
(3) Total Cost = $1,260 + $9.24 (# Bottles)
(6) Total Cost = $2,796 + $7.831 (# Bottles)

PA5-2
(3) Total Cost = $3,703 + $8.15 (# Jerseys)
(4) $7,615
(6) Total Cost = $3,561.25 + $8.66 (# ofJerseys)
(7) $ 8,973.75

PA5-3
(2) January: $5,659.00; $5,639.65
    March: $6,148.00; $6,159.25
    May: $9,489.50; $9,709.85
(4) Feb Income $(1,880.05)
    April Income $1,949.35
    June Income $2,603.15
(5) $3,561.25 per month

PA5-4
(2) For 800 units: $320,000; 61.54%

PA5-5
(2) Absorption Income: $297,250
    Variable Costing Income $215,000

PA5-6
(1) $10.90
(3) $21.48
(5) Difference = $1,327.50

Chapter 6

PA6-1
(4) 588 bikes

PA6-2
(1) 1,200 miles
(3) 3,200 miles
(4) DOL = 5.0

PA6-3
(1) Income $3,760
(3) $16.00 per unit; 53.33%
(5) 2,115 units

PA6-4
(2) For 1,000 units, Income = $200,000
(4) 715 carts
(6) 808 units
(8) 62.632% decrease

PA6-5
(1) $14 per unit; 70%
(4) Margin of Safety = 2,393 units; 29.91%

Chapter 7

PA7-1
(1) Incremental Profit $2,250
(4) $19.00

PA7-3
(1) Increase by $950

PA7-4
(1) Income $12,500 greater if processed further

PA7-5
(2) Product A 50,000 units
    Product B 20,000 units
    Product C 20,000 units
(4) Product C 30,000 units
    Product B 20,000 units
    Product A 40,000 units

Chapter 8

PA8-1
(1) 8.4%
(3) $29,970
(4) $(51,004)

PA8-2
(1) Current Income $1,710,000
(3) 5.77 years
(5) $ 1,166,268

PA8-3
(1) Project 1 = 3.75%
    Project 2 = 35.3%
    Project 3 = 26.7%
(3) Project 1 = $(532,325.00)
    Project 2 = $3,726,704.00
    Project 3 = $2,320,792.50
(4) Project 1 = 0.8935
    Project 2 = 2.0961
    Project 3 = 2.2378

PA8-4
(2) 7.14 years
(4) $8,930

PA8-5
(1) Option 1 = $1,000,000
    Option 2 = $589,086
    Option 3 = $553,065

Chapter 9

PA9-1
(1) May $6,000
(2) April 270 units

(3) June $2,349
(4) 2nd Quarter $5,000
(5) May $685.00
(6) June $5,220
(7) 2nd Quarter $2,520

PA9-2
April $937.50

PA9-3
(1) May $5,820
     2nd Quarter $18,550
(2) April $4,464.30
     June $5,692.70
(3) June 30 balance = $13,074.80

PA9-4
(1) March $108,000
(3) February $16,730
     1st Quarter $49,595

PA9-5
(1) March $74,655
(2) 1st Quarter $73,320

Chapter 10

PA10-1
(1) DM Price Var = $9,000 F
     DM Quantity Var = $24,000 U
(3) VOH Rate Var = $15,000 U
     VOH Efficiency Var = $18,000 F

PA10-2
(2) FOH Volume Var = $25,000 F

PA10-5
(1) DM Price Var = $18,000 U
     DM Quantity Var = $10,000 U
(3) VOH Rate Var = $1,500 F
     VOH Efficiency Var = $2,500 U

PA10-6
(2) FOH Volume Var = $2,500 U

PA10-9
(2) DL Rate Var = $1,275 U
     DL Efficiency Var = $750 F

Chapter 11

PA11-1
(1) Northern Division ROI = 30%
     Southern Division ROI = 33.3%
(2)
     b. Northern Division ROI = 27%
     d. Southern Division ROI = No effect

PA11-2
(3) 6%

PA11-3
(1) ROI Division B = 5%
(2) RI Division C = ($32,150)
(4) 8%
(6) ROI Division A = 8.907%
     RI Division C = $17,850

PA11-4
(1) $54,000
(4) $31.00

PA11-5
(1) $2.40 per lock
(4) $1.80

Chapter 12

PA12-1
(1) Activity ="I", Cash Flow = "−"

PA12-2
Net cash provided by operating activities = $8,813

PA12-3
(1) Net cash provided by operating activities = $16,000

PA12-4
(1) Net cash provided by financing activities = $1,000

PA12-5
Net cash provided by operating activities = $8,813

PA12-6
(1) Net cash used for investing activities = $(500)

PA12-7
Net cash provided by operating activities = $2,000

Chapter 13

PA13-1
(1) Change in cash = $31,500, 175.0% increase

PA13-2
(1) 2010 Gross profit percentage = 52.7%
(6) 2010 Debt-to-assets ratio = 0.40

PA13-3
(3) Simultech's assets are financed more by liabilities (60%)
     than by equity (40%)

PA13-4
(1) (e) 4%

PA13-5
(2) Pepsi appears more liquid

PA13-6
(1) (9) Receivables turnover: Royale = 7.84, Cavalier = 8.75

PA13-7
Company A appears to be a better choice

Solutions to Multiple-Choice Questions

Chapter 1
1. c   2. d   3. b   4. c   5. b   6. c   7. a   8. d   9. b   10. c

Chapter 2
1. b   2. b   3. e   4. b   5. d   6. e   7. a   8. e   9. e   10. f

Chapter 3
1. b   2. d   3. c   4. a   5. d   6. h   7. d   8. a   9. d   10. b

Chapter 4
1. b   2. b   3. d   4. b   5. c   6. d   7. d   8. a   9. b   10. c

Chapter 5
1. d   2. b   3. c   4. a   5. d   6. d   7. d   8. a   9. b   10. c

Chapter 6
1. d   2. b   3. c   4. a   5. d   6. d   7. d   8. a   9. b   10. c

Chapter 7
1. d   2. b   3. d   4. a   5. d   6. c   7. b   8. d   9. a   10. c

Chapter 8
1. b   2. c   3. a   4. c   5. b   6. a   7. a   8. b   9. d   10. a

Chapter 9
1. c   2. d   3. d   4. a   5. c   6. d   7. d   8. b   9. a   10. d

Chapter 10
1. c   2. b   3. a   4. d   5. a   6. a   7. b   8. c   9. d   10. a

Chapter 11
1. b   2. d   3. d   4. a   5. d   6. a   7. d   8. d   9. b   10. d

Chapter 12
1. c   2. d   3. d   4. a   5. a   6. d   7. d   8. a   9. c   10. b

Chapter 13
1. c   2. c   3. c   4. d   5. c   6. a   7. b   8. d

Chapter 1

Opener: © Editorial Image, LLC/Alamy; p. 6 (left): © Andersen Ross/Brand X/ Corbis; p. 6 (right): © Jim Craigmyle/ Corbis; Tombstone logo used courtesy of Tombstone.

Chapter 2

Opener: © Welcome Home/Alamy; Toll Brothers logo used courtesy of Toll Brothers, Inc.

Chapter 3

Opener: © Royalty-Free/Corbis; p. 97: © Goodshoot/PunchStock; CL Mondavi logo used courtesy of CK Mondavi.

Chapter 4

Opener: © izmostock/Alamy; p. 134: © Toshifumi Kitamura/AFP/Getty Images; p. 138 (manufacturing plant): © Francois Lo Presti/AFP/Getty; p. 138 (parts): © Dibyangshu Sarkar/AFP/Getty; p. 138 (testing engine): © Kazuhiro Nogi/AFP/Getty; p. 138 (car body): AP Photo/ James Crisp; p. 138 (assembly line): © Toshifumi Kitamura/AFP/Getty; p. 138 (Avalon): © Stan Honda/AFP/ Getty Images; p. 138 (Camry): © Drive Images/Alamy; p. 138 (Camry Hybrid): © Jim West/Alamy; p. 140 (manufacturing plant): © Francois Lo Presti/AFP/ Getty; p. 140 (parts): © Kazuhiro Nogi/ AFP/Getty; p. 140 (testing engine): AP Photo/ James Crisp; p. 140 (car body): © Toshifumi Kitamura/AFP/Getty; p. 140 (assembly line): © Stan Honda/ AFP/Getty Images; p. 142 (parts): © Dibyangshu Sarkar/AFP/Getty; p. 142 (testing engine): © Kazuhiro Nogi/AFP/ Getty; p. 142 (car body): AP Photo/ James Crisp; p. 142 (assembly line): © Toshifumi Kitamura/AFP/Getty; p. 142 (Avalon): © Stan Honda/AFP/ Getty Images; p. 142 (Camry): © Drive Images/Alamy; p. 142 (Camry Hybrid): © Jim West/Alamy; Toyota logo used courtesy of Toyota Motor Company.

Chapter 5

Opener: AP Photo/Don Ryan; Starbucks logo used courtesy of Starbucks.

Chapter 6

Opener: © Duane Branch/Alamy; p. 221: © paulasfotos/Alamy; Starbucks logo used courtesy of Starbucks; Cereality logo used courtesy of Kahala Corporation.

Chapter 7

Opener: © Felicia Martinez/PhotoEdit; p. 266: © Twilight Images/Alamy;

Chapter 8

Opener: © David McNew/Getty Images;

Chapter 9

Opener: Courtesy of Coldstone Creamery; Cold Stone Creamery logo used courtesy of Kahala Corporation; Black & Decker logo used courtesy of Black & Decker.

Chapter 10

Opener: Courtesy of Coldstone Creamery; p. 368: © Lon C. Diehl/ PhotoEdit; Cold Stone Creamery logo used courtesy of Kahala Corporation.

Chapter 11

Opener: © Bill Aron/PhotoEdit; p. 418: © Andrew H. Walker/Getty; Kraft Foods logo used courtesy of Kraft Foods; Peter Piper Pizza logo used courtesy of Peter Piper Pizza, Inc.

Chapter 12

Opener: © Comstock Images/Alamy; Northwest Airlines logo used courtesy of Northwest Airlines; Brunswick logo used courtesy of Brunswick Corporation; Cybex logo used courtesy of Cybex International; Nike logo used courtesy of Nike; AMC Theaters logo used courtesy of AMC Theaters; Gymboree logo used courtesy of Gymboree; Colgate-Palmolive logo used courtesy of Colgate-Palmolive; Apple logo used courtesy of Apple; Pepsi logo used courtesy of PepsiCo; Gibraltar logo used courtesy of Gibraltar; Disney logo used courtesy of Disney; Home Depot logo used courtesy of Home Depot; Lowe's logo used courtesy of Lowe's.

Chapter 13

Opener: AP Photo/Nell Redmond; Lowe's logo used courtesy of Lowe's; Home Depot logo used courtesy of Home Depot; Chevron logo used courtesy of Chevron; Procter & Gamble logo used courtesy of Procter & Gamble; Dollar General logo used courtesy of Dollar general; Coca-Cola logo used courtesy of Coca-Cola; Pepsi logo used courtesy of PepsiCo; Hasbro logo ©Hasbro, Inc. Used with permission.

Subject Index